Geo-Economics
The New Science

or

The Gospel of Development According to Chairman Mac

by H. McKinley Conway

CONWAY DATA, INC.

40 Technology Park/Atlanta, Suite 200
Norcross, GA 30092-9934 USA
Phone: (404) 446-6996
FAX: (404) 263-8825

Cataloging in Publication Data

Conway, McKinley

GEO-ECONOMICS, THE NEW SCIENCE
The Gospel of Development According to Chairman Mac
Includes index

1. Economic development   2. Industrial Development Research Council
3. World Development Council   4. Transportation, aviation
5. Super projects 6. Futurism

Library of Congress Catalog Card Number: 94-94150

ISBN: 0-910436-33-9

International Standard Book Number: 0-910436-33-9

Printed in the United States of America

To Becky

We men, chauvinists that we are, think we can marry a beautiful young girl, drag her around the world for more than 50 years while subjecting her to all manner of hardships and, then, as our time runs out, square accounts by dedicating to her some obscure book we have written.

However, knowing Becky's almost unlimited capacity for forgiveness, she might just buy it.

Introduction

What does it all mean?

I suspect that most old people, looking back over their careers, ask themselves that question?

Old people also get a lot of questions from friends and associates along the line of "What have you done that you are most proud of?"

This leads to more soul-searching. Have I done anything truly significant? Did I make my part of the world any better? If so, what?

The old person soon discovers that he has no satisfactory answers to these questions. It will remain for others to judge him and evaluate his work after he's gone.

About the only constructive contribution the old person can make to this process is to leave his files in reasonable order and provide some explanatory footnotes.

That's what this book is all about. It is an attempt to identify many different projects on which we have worked, compile some of the more significant findings and put the diverse items together so that a reasonably cohesive picture emerges.

Each chapter consists of three elements. The first element is my current comment on the chapter subject. The second element consists of excerpts from my earlier writing on the subject. The third element is a list of citations of my additional writing on the subject.

If we had enjoyed the luxury of microcomputers and word processors throughout our life, this task would have been a lot easier. Unhappily, we could refer to our disk files for only the past decade. Before that, our sources were bound volumes in the library, microfiche and yellowing pages of old files.

Even though we have always attempted to maintain archives, there are many missing links, and we have certainly overlooked some worthwhile projects.

As this is being published, work is proceeding on the development of the GeoTEAM/Fax system for delivering data files to users. Many of the items uncovered in our archives search will be available from the new service.

In these efforts we must not overlook all of the help we have had from a diligent and loyal staff. Altogether, I'd guess that there have been more than 200 who have contributed directly to building data bases, conducting surveys and otherwise gathering the raw materials we have used.

In particular, we want to acknowledge the important contributions of

Linda Liston, our chief editorial associate for some 25 years. Her name appears as co-author on many significant works.

Also, we cannot overlook the support and help provided by the members of the Industrial Development Research Council. What a privilege it has been to be associated with this magnificant group of people for so many years! The IDRC membership includes the top minds in the development industry. They have constituted a wonderful panel for advice and guidance.

In the preparation of this particular book, Eileen Porter has been indispensable. She helped gather old files, organize them and convert them to usable formats. This was a task running for several months.

The final processing and production was handled by Laura Lyne and Claire Fleisig. They have contributed significantly — bringing order out of the chaos of my notes and comments.

And, finally, my appreciation to Cheri Edmondson for the cover design.

My sincerest thanks to one and all!

—H.M.C.

Outline of Contents

Chapter 1

Chapter 2

Chapter 3

Chapter 4

Chapter 7

Chapter 8

Chapter 9

Chapter 10

1

A New Science is Born

Chapter 1

A. Overview, With Recent Thoughts
Career Decisions!
A Breakthrough? Relating Science and Industry
The SASI, Pioneering Regional Program
Developing Communications
The Community Audit
The Basic Law of Geo-economics
Going Global in the 60s
Keeping Score, New Plants
Geo-economics Defined

B. Excerpts from Selected Works
"Geographical Distribution of Engineering Research and Related
    Industries in the United States," 1948
"Area Development: A Guide for Community Leaders," 1960
Area Development Organizations, 1966
"AID/PEP Program for Mobilizing Private Enterprise and Local
    Initiative in Latin America," 1968
New Industries of the Seventies, 1978
Marketing Industrial Buildings and Sites, 1980
"Geo-Economics, A New Science in the Service of Mankind," 1983
"New Plant Locations," 1987

C. Bibliography

A. Overview, With Recent Thoughts

Career decisions!

Since no university yet awards a degree in geo-economics, how does one get to be a geo-economist? I will quickly admit that my route was circuitous, involving a series of unplanned steps.

I was born in 1920 in a small town in rural Alabama where, at that time, conditions were similar to what we see today in the Third World. There was no electricity, no running water and no pavement.

My Grandad and his sons ran a general store and had several small farms. The main cash crop was cotton. Farmers came to town for supplies via horse and buggy. The economic system was primarily barter.

Once a year, activity reached a peak. That was harvest time — the cotton picking season at the end of the summer. Empty wagons met at dawn in the main street and took pickers out to the farms. This was an opportunity for wives, children, old people and the unemployed to make some money.

Pickers were paid a penny a pound. An average picker could pick over 100 pounds per day, earning a dollar or more. That was big money!

Incidentally, these workers were not blacks, Hispanics or other minorities. In that part of Northwest Alabama there was no history of slavery. The work force was composed entirely of stubbornly independent poor white folks from the foothills of Appalachia.

By the time I was about seven years old, I decided I was ready to go out with the pickers and get some of the easy money. My Grandad, who ran the operations, kept putting me off, telling me I was too little and the work was too hard.

Finally, he got tired of my nagging and let me go. I climbed onto a wagon with the big folks and rode off to a nearby farm just after daybreak. At the farm they gave each of us a big bag, assigned each of us to two rows of cotton, and we began work.

It only took a few minutes to see that we were not all created equal. Some of the veteran pickers looked like machines as they moved along the rows, snatching bolls right and left. Others moved more slowly but methodically. I was soon bringing up the rear.

By mid-morning the sun was bearing down and the insects were attacking. There was a haze of dust and lint in the air. Perspiration blurred my vision. My fingers were sore and my back ached.

And it got worse and worse. By mid afternoon one of the elders — no doubt appointed by my Grandad — looked me over and instructed me to stop picking and go sit under a tree. I sat there, miserable and defeated, until the wagons came for us.

That brought my first career decision. I would not be a professional cotton picker.

By the time I was a teenager my family had moved to Georgia and my Dad was in the cotton ginning business. During the summers I would often go with him to a gin site on a trouble-shooting mission.

I still remember one blazing hot day when we went out to check a malfunction. The gin, like most others, was housed in a sheet metal building, and, unhappily the problem involved a transmission line about three stories above the ground just under the roof.

The temperature under the roof must have been over 120 degrees, the air was full of dirt and lint, and it was very noisy. Working conditions probably would have run contrary to just about every regulation in the latest OSHA book.

That day I decided that fixing cotton gins would not be my life's work.

A few years later, while in my early 20s I came upon yet another career decision. I had graduated from Georgia Tech in aeronautical engineering, been through flight training and was assigned by the Navy to the NACA/NASA Ames Laboratory at Moffett Field, California.

It sounded like a perfect assignment. We were at the leading edge of technology, the astronauts of our time.

At Ames our mission was to test new experimental aircraft in what was the world's newest and largest wind tunnel. Literally, we hoisted the new experimental aircraft into a test chamber where we could reproduce actual flight conditions up to cruising speeds.

The remote control system for the wind tunnel had not been delivered due to some wartime delay or snafu, so we had to sit in the airplanes and "fly" them. That is, we set control positions, engine power levels and things like that.

Picture a huge steel shell, with the sun beating down on the outside, and an aircraft engine (or two) running full power inside. On a summer day, the temperature quickly got up over 100 degrees. Further, the carbon monoxide from the engine exhaust soon contaminated the air, so we had to wear oxygen masks.

I remember sitting there one day in the cockpit of a new Navy fighter, with the airplane shaking, with sweat running down inside the mask and with the noise of the engine blasting back from the steel shell. Because the mask leaked, I had breathed enough monoxide to be nauseated.

Suddenly, it occurred to me that this high-tech job was an awful lot like picking cotton and fixing gins. My career objectives began to come into sharper focus. What I really wanted was to fly airplanes out in the cool clean air and, when not flying, do research at the cutting edge of technology.

When the war ended I returned to Atlanta and, like several million other veterans, began looking for a job that might somehow harmonize with my hopes and aspirations.

Perceiving a need in the Southern region, I set out to launch a small research institute that would sponsor programs and studies beneficial to the region.

A Breakthrough? Relating Science and Industry

The effort was small, but I did publish enough papers to attract some notice. One of them, written in 1947, was "Geographical Distribution of Engineering Research and Related Industries in the United States." We suggested a method in the paper for predicting the relative growth of high-technology industry in various regions of the country.

In that 1947 report we rated the growth potential of regions of the USA as follows:

Southeast	1.39
Northeast	.96
North Central	.98
Plains	1.04
Mountain	no data
Far West	1.26

Up to this time, the Southeast typically brought up the rear in almost every measure of development. Sitting here in 1994 in an air-conditioned office using a word-processing program with an electronic spelling checker and style guide, it is difficult to roll back the clock and remember what it was like in those days.

The South was an impoverished agricultural region. Some three-fourths of all economic activity was directly related to agriculture.

The fastest transportation was by DC-3 between cities lucky enough to have air service. Neither homes nor offices were yet air-conditioned, although some theaters had "ice" systems. There were no TV sets or inter-state highways. Long distance calls were expensive, and telegrams usually meant there was a death in the family. Worst of all, we had no copy machines, recorders or computers.

In that environment came a kid with some fancy theories that said the Southeast could grow faster than any other in developing what would later be called "high tech" industries.

Few people took us seriously, but subsequent years revealed our premise to be surprisingly valid. I don't think it was all luck.

As scientific research, our paper reflected a crude piece of work. There were not enough data to permit precise and sophisticated forecasts. Perhaps the most important thing it accomplished was to assert boldly that there was a direct relation between science, technology and development.

Never forget that science breeds technology which breeds development! We have spent a lifetime observing and documenting that basic relationship we espoused in our 1947 study.

The report did little, however, to raise support or generate revenue for my new research entity. Soon. I had exhausted my meager savings, and we were in eminent danger of starving.

Luckily, our paper caught the eyes of others who liked our thoughts and saw an application to the problems of the South.

The SASI, Pioneering Regional Program

At this psychological moment we encountered a group that was organizing the "Southern Association of Science and Industry (SASI)." This was an effort undertaken by several dozen college presidents, professors, bankers, newspaper editors and business executives who were deeply concerned about the South's low level of development.

The SASI was looking for someone to serve as executive director and organize the new program. Several members of the board thought they ought to employ someone with sales and promotional experience, while others felt that the man ought to come from the scientific community.

The latter sentiment prevailed, and they picked me. At the ripe old age of 29 I became the architect of a pioneering regional development program. It was a new venture unlike any yet undertaken in the development field.

The shift was traumatic. I moved from the research laboratory mindset into the confounding realm of business factors, news media interests and politics. At the time, I did not realize that I had just been assigned to forge a new science that we would someday call geo-economics.

If there was a body of literature I could study, or any contemporary practitioners to consult I didn't know of them. I broke new ground every day, learning from my mistakes.

As some of the old documents cited below will indicate, we spent much time meeting with groups throughout the region doing missionary work. We urged states to set up research units and support research programs. We urged local groups to identify resources.

We began to talk about developing research complexes and research parks. I had seen the beginning of the Stanford Research Park at Palo Alto (the nation's first) and urged sponsors in the south to undertake similar efforts. The first group to plan such a venture was the Research Triangle entity in North Carolina.

I believe our SASI discussions constituted the first deliberate attempt to launch such projects as a strategy for attracting technological enterprises and accelerating the economic development of an area. Several decades later, this thinking had blossomed into the concept of science cities and technopolises around the world.

Developing Communications

Every profession and every industry needs communications media. We set out to fill that need in the new field of planned development.

Our efforts to establish a publication program had begun with a small regional research journal in 1949. Over several years we expanded the scope both geographically and in terms of subject.

In 1954 we launched a national magazine entitled *Industrial Development.* ID was well received and we added the *Site Selection Handbook* edition in 1956. Soon we were able to buy the long-established *Manufacturers Record,* then published in Baltimore. I still remember negotiating that deal in the bar of the old Algonquin Hotel in New York.

In 1956 we merged MR with ID/SSH. With those moves, we had the basis for a successful program that is now in its fourth decade.

Our circulation has grown from 11,000 in the 1950s to 60,000 in the 1990s. Also, our definition of an "industrial facility" has been expanded to include not just manufacturing units but large service facilities and major travel installations.

Perhaps most important, our coverage has expanded globally, with the addition of new editions. In the 1990s we began publishing a Japanese edition with a partner in Tokyo and *Site Selection's* European edition from an office in Amsterdam, with printing in Ireland. Most recently, we have announced that the Japanese edition will give way to a new Pacific Rim edition covering the entire region from eastern Russia to Australia.

Parallel with these efforts we saw a need for training materials to serve the organizations being set up to carry out development programs. The first effort was a loose-leaf manual called "Area Development," issued in 1960. (Some years later a rival company pilfered this name for a magazine.)

During the late 1950s we also began to see the need for a national forum of corporate growth planning executives, and in 1961 we founded the Industrial Development Research Council (IDRC). This is detailed in the next chapter.

The Community Audit

Nothing better illustrates the state of the geo-economic art in the late 1950s than the introduction of the community audit. We had observed that many communities were gearing up to solicit investment, and they were beginning to produce a variety of documents and promotion pieces.

In order to provide some guidance, we promulgated a "community audit" form — a proposed standard for small cities and counties. It was a four-page form which covered such items as

•Location: distance and direction to major cities. Elevation.

•Population: last three Census counts for city, county, metro area; percent minorities.

•Employment: manufacturing, non-manufacturing, unemployed; percent in unions; strikes last five years; Right-to-work law, prevailing wage rates for male, female, skilled, semi-skilled, clerical; estimated cost of fringe benefits.

•Transportation: inter-city bus, passenger rail service, reciprocal switching, distance to main line switching, overnight truck service, flights per day, highways, distance to interstate, water channel depth.

•Taxes: retail sales tax; income tax; unemployment compensation rate; workers compensation rate; corporate franchise tax, machinery, equipment and inventory tax, corporate organization and qualification tax, municipal tax rate; county or township rate; school rate; exemptions; special taxes.

•Government: organization; per capita debt; annexation plans; industrial plant approval process; regulations affecting smoke, odor, noise; fire and police service

•Utilities: water source and capacity, industrial rate, sewage capacity and rate, electric and gas service source and rate, delivered price of fuel oil.

•Community services: hotels, hospitals, cultural attractions, golf courses, sports, news media, laws concerning alcoholic beverages, meeting facilities, libraries.

•Education: enrollment in elementary, junior high and high schools; vocational training; cost of education per pupil; pupil-to-teacher ratio; colleges and universities within a 20-mile radius; research institutes.

•Climate: average and extremes for temperature, monthly precipitation; history of hurricanes, storms.

•Sites and industry: sites on deep water, airport, planned park undeveloped; availability of site data; available vacant buildings; availability of financing; major manufacturers in area; plant openings and closings in the last five years; major construction projects underway.

•Developers affidavit and state or regional organization endorsement.

When the IDRC came into existence in 1961, the community audit effort gained support. A committee of IDRC active members adopted the format, and IDRC promoted it for the next decade.

Over a period of about 10 years we built a file of approximately 1,000 audits from communities throughout the USA. Thousands of copies of the form were also published in Spanish and Portuguese and were used widely in Latin America. Further, the form was distributed to State Department personnel around the world, and they handed it on to the groups in many countries.

Several years after we introduced the form we were amused to read a bulletin from a government official in India commenting on the important new standard they had invented. It was our form down to the last dot.

With the coming of computers, numerous states and large-scale development agencies loaded the audits into their data banks and began serving corporate planners directly. We did not contest that, although we still believe it would be advantageous to maintain a composite file.

The Basic Law of Geo-economics

By 1966 we felt comfortable enough with our experience with both area development and corporate asset management to promulgate what we consider today to be the fundamental law of geo-economics. Set forth in our book (*Area Development Organizations*) was the formula:

$$\mathbf{Dmax = (Emax)(Mmax)(Rmax)}$$

This simply says that maximum development (D) is achieved by multiplying maximum manpower (M) times maximum resources (R) times maximum efficiency (E). This relationship applies to the development of nations, areas or companies.

Everything we do is related. The local development group that rounds up volunteers to help with the program is trying to maximize M. The fundraiser is trying to maximize R. A new data processing system is installed to maximize E.

On the corporate side there are constraints on the amount of M and R that can be invested, so much effort is devoted to maximizing E. Selecting the best possible location is such a strategy.

These early documents preached the doctrine of developing every area (and company) to its full potential. For some areas that might mean developing a large manufacturing complex. For others, it might mean preserving a primeval forest.

There is an important lesson here. The people working quietly in the development organizations and the industries they serve are the real source of enhancements in our quality of life. They are the producers.

Don't be confused by politicians who promise great improvements in quality of life. They may take something from one segment of society and give it to another, but they don't produce anything!

We also taught that the essence of organization management is that the staff stays in the background while the volunteers occupy the stage. It's amazing how much you can accomplish if you don't worry about who gets the credit.

Even so, I will be the first to admit that I personally benefited from the success of the southern regional program and the new national forum and publications.

Increasingly, I was invited to speak to groups around the nation and new opportunities opened for my small consulting practice. I advised many states — both in the South and elsewhere — on their development programs.

Going Global in the 60s

The most interesting opportunity came in the early 1960s when President Kennedy launched the Alliance for Progress program for Latin America. To administer the program he chose Teodoro Moscoso, manager of the very successful "Fomento" plan in Puerto Rico.

I had known Ted for some time, having visited with him in San Juan. Still, I was surprised when he called one day and asked me to meet him in Washington. He said it was urgent, so I went.

Ted wasted no time. He wanted me to be Deputy Administrator. It was a top Washington job, with a State Department office, chauffeur, diplomatic flag, and all the trimmings. In particular, he wanted me to direct the part of the program aimed at promoting private enterprise.

I thought about it overnight and said no. I told Ted I simply did not think I could run a private enterprise program effectively in the Washington environment.

A couple of months later Ted called and said, "Okay, have it your way — we'll contract with you to run the program from Atlanta."

And so we did, as reported in "The AID/PEP Program."

Much of the AID/PEP effort was spent teaching development groups how to promote their areas to outside investors. This was also a need in the USA, leading to the book *Marketing Industrial Buildings and Sites* in 1980.

Keeping Score, New Plants

Among other efforts, we launched a continuing campaign to encourage large-scale development groups to keep an accurate tally of new facilities located in their service areas. Many groups, including state development agencies, were not measuring their own performance — it was like playing a ball game and not keeping score.

Over the years, we became the unofficial scorekeeper for the development industry. While there were government reports on economic growth, ours was the only tally of actual units. In effect, the government measured forests, while we counted trees.

By 1987 we were able to publish a summary report and a monograph on "New Plant Locations." It gives some insight into the problems of measuring results and who was winning the game.

Although we devoted much effort to this kind of data-gathering and score-keeping, we fell far short of amassing the kind of numerical data-base needed to flesh out the basic laws of geo-economics. That is one of the frustrations of my career.

For example, in the 1980s we proposed that development agencies around the world collaborate in the observance of an International Geo-Economic Year (IGY). We hoped that through the efforts of many professionals in many nations we could begin the establishment of a global data base that would be of benefit to all.

Unfortunately, our proposal brought a woeful response. Most nations confessed that they had not been compiling significant data. I'm certain that the next generation will do better.

Geo-economics Defined

Step-by-step, the art or science in which we were engaged began to take shape. By 1983, we were emboldened to publish *Geo-Economics — A New Science In The Service of Mankind.*

This was not followed by fireworks in the sky or a Nobel prize, but it did bring some nods of approval. We were encouraged to continue. Today, when we survey the geo-economic scene, we can, however, see some progress. Where there was once just a handful of practitioners, today there are thousands. And, they are the leaders of substantial organizations and firms. There are growing research and education programs. We have a library full of publications and a telecommunications network that runs 24 hours a day. We conduct seminars around the world.

Our conclusion is that geo-economics is now an established scientific entity with a very bright future. We're proud!

B. Excerpts from Selected Works

1948 Excerpt	"Geographical Distribution of Engineering Research and Related Industries in the United States." Southeastern Research Institute. 1948. 74 pp. Reprinted 1987 as IDRC research study number 37.

It is often charged that a few northern states maintain the remainder of the states as virtual economic colonies by controlling key industries. Our purpose here is to examine this charge from the viewpoint of its relation to scientific research activity.

In order to check the theories set forth, the distribution of specific activities will be examined. These include:

1. Research input indicators
    a. Number of industrial research laboratories in operation
    b. Number of universities conducting research work

2. Research output indicators
    a. Authors of technical books
    b. Engineers recognized in *Who's Who*

It should be noted that the list of selected industries does not include enterprises that are limited by nature to specific regions, such as mining, forestry and petroleum recovery. Those selected are "mobile" industries, which presumably might be located in any area.

In case of each activity, a large number of units have been tabulated, so that the reliability of results is increased. In the case of research laboratories, the total number tabulated amounted to some 3,800. The number of engineers counted to obtain the *Who's Who* breakdown totaled more than 20,000.

The manufacturing Activity Factors are based on the distribution of approximately 100 plants in each field.

It is doubtful whether the average citizen realizes how greatly the nation's scientific industries are concentrated. The Northeastern and North Central states hold almost 90 percent of the selected mobile industries, as shown below:

Concentration of Selected Mobile Industries
in Northeast and North Central States

Industry	Percent
Air-conditioning	86.1
Aircraft and accessories	48.8
Automotive vehicles/accessories	95.2
Ceramic products	91.0
Chemical processing	95.3
Electrical devices	94.6
Internal combustion engines	83.4
Scientific instruments	97.0
Plastic products	97.9
Radio components	98.3
Textile processing	93.2
Average Mobile Industries	**89.2**

We have defined an "activity factor" as the ratio of share of total U.S. activity in a field to share of total U.S. population

The average activity factors for the mobile industries are particularly expressive of the concentration of scientific activities:

	Research	Manufacturing
Southeast	.32	.23
Northeast	1.73	1.81
North central	1.55	1.58
Plains	.25	.24
Mountain	—	—
Far West	.77	.61

The data provide conclusive proof that a small northern region dominates the industrial activity of the entire nation. This concentration of enterprise may be traced to two causes:

1. The system of absentee ownership established decades ago
2. Greater attention to scientific research in northern areas

The first cause, absentee ownership, has been the subject of inspired editorials and fiery orations since Reconstruction days. Following the War Between the States, northern financiers gained control of southern industries and subsequently were able to extend their control west of the Alleghenies to the Pacific.

By gaining control of complete industries, they were able to limit outlying states to the production of raw materials, while reserving the lucrative finishing operations for the chosen industrial states. There is adequate proof that this system has been used, especially in the older industries, such as textiles, for vicious exploitation of the "colonial" states. Many laws have helped perpetuate this system, and politicians in lagging areas are quick to trace all maldistribution of industry to such political conditions. It is easy to blame others for our own shortcomings, and it is encouraging to believe that all troubles can be eradicated quickly and easily by remedial legislation. But the hard facts will not support this viewpoint.

What of the new industries, such as plastics and radio? Certainly the nineteenth century carpet-baggers cannot be blamed for concentration of these industries in the North. New industries, and this includes almost all the mobile industries, are born and bred of scientific research. If these new industries are located in one region, the only logical conclusion is that this region has surpassed all others in the extent and success of research efforts.

This carries us back to the original assumptions concerning the relation of research and industry, which now can be checked against actual data.

From the evidence presented, it can be concluded that a region must be active in scientific research in order to enjoy corresponding industrial activity. There is reason to believe that if every section of the nation conducted an equal amount of research, industrial activity would tend to be equally distributed. Inequalities in research effort furnish an explanation for nonuniform disposition of industries.

If this idea is pursued, it may now be possible to find a basis for predicting future geographic distribution of activities. At least, it should be possible to determine whether industrial activity centers are likely to shift, and, if so, in which direction they will move.

The basis of prediction of future industrial trends lies in the relation of industry to research. In this connection, it must be recognized that there is an important time lag between the inception of an idea and the application of the idea in industry. This time lag may in some cases be very brief, or it may be a matter of years. Television has been the subject of research almost as long as radio, but it has taken much longer to develop industrially.

The existence of this time lag means that today's distribution of industry results from yesterday's distribution of research. Similarly, today's distribution of research provides the key to tomorrow's distribution of industry. This leads to the theory that the ratio of research to industrial activity in various regions constitutes an indicator of future trends.

Let this ratio be called the "Growth Potential," defined as:

$$\text{Growth Potential} = \frac{\text{Present research activity factor}}{\text{Present industry activity factor}}$$

The Growth Potentials for the 11 selected industries combined are:

Section	Growth Potential
Southeast	1.39
Northeast	.96
North Central	.98
Plains	1.04
Mountain	—
Far West	1.26

Now, according to our theory, when the regional Growth Potential is 1.0, the mobile industries are stabilized in the region considered. A region having a Growth Potential of 1.0 would be expected to hold in the future about the same share of the nation's total mobile industries as it now holds. If the region has a ratio less than 1.0, it is expected that the region will lose industry percentage-wise. But a ratio greater than 1.0 indicates a tendency to gain a greater share of industry in the future.

The Growth Potential acts, therefore, as a barometer of industrial winds. According to our theory, industrial activity will move from regions having ratios less than 1.0 into regions having ratios greater than 1.0.

It is shown that for the selected mobile industries the Southeastern states have the highest Growth potential. It is to be expected that the Southeast will gain these new industries at a faster rate than any other section.

The Growth Potential for the Northeastern states is slightly below 1.0, and it is indicated that this section in the future may hold a slightly smaller percentage of the nation's total mobile industry. The situation in the North Central states is similar, although there appears less tendency for these states to lose industry in the future.

The Plains states, with a Growth Potential slightly greater than 1.0, appear to be in position to gain a slightly larger share of industry. The industrial activity of the Mountain states is negligible at present, but this region stands to gain from any general decentralization of effort.

The Far Western states, with a Growth Potential of well over 1.0, may expect in the future to obtain a considerably larger share of the nation's industry than they now hold.

It is not yet possible to predict the length of time required for research to cause changes in industrial activity. Data on industrial activity have been collected for many decades, but data on research activity are available only for a few years. It probably will be necessary to collect information on research activity for two or three more generations before the time lag between research discovery and industrial exploitation can be determined with any degree of accuracy.

Statistics have shown that business activity follows cyclical patterns, rising to heights and dropping to lows with regularity. When data have been collected for a long enough period, it is likely that research activity will be observed to behave in a similar manner. In fact, it may be found that fluctuations in research activity will provide advance indication of business trends. This is but one of many questions concerning the relation of research and industry that must be left for future study to answer.

The foregoing discussions brought out that certain regions of the nation lead and others lag in the support of engineering research activity. It has been shown that the distribution of industrial activity coincides with the distribution of research activity, confirming the theoretical relation of research and industry.

The objective of the discussions that follow is to outline steps by that research may be stimulated and expanded in any region, thereby enabling that section to obtain a greater share of the nation's industries. While this study was prompted by a desire to increase the scientific effort in the Southeast, it is believed that the policies that will be promulgated would prove worthwhile in any region.

Improvement of Educational Facilities

The first step necessary in the development of scientific enterprise is the education of the people, including not only the scientists who conduct research work, but also the citizens who directly or indirectly provide financial support for research activity.

Every citizen has a stake in scientific research: taxpayers support government research, and consumers support industrial research. It is important that every citizen receive widespread knowledge of scientific subjects by means of both formal schooling and the informal training received from reading newspapers, listening to the radio and by other means.

The need for facilities for advanced study and research requires no further discussion — it is significant that no outstanding scientific institution in the nation lacks such facilities.

The accumulated support of every segment of society is required for the most successful exploitation of research potential. To achieve this wide support, the public in general and government and business in particular must be made to feel the vital necessity for widespread research activity. This requires the utilization in a skillful manner of the newspaper, radio and other means of dispensing information.

Experience has shown that most scientists are poor propagandists. They are handicapped by traditional modesty and inability to look at their work from the layman's viewpoint. Also, they lack a "nose for news." On the other hand, the average reporter is not equipped to do justice to scientific subjects, for he cannot sort the rotten apples from the research barrel.

The conclusions drawn from this study may be summarized briefly as follows:

1. Research must precede industry.
2. The extent of research effort determines the possible scale of industrial success.
3. The Northeastern and North Central states at present dominate the mobile industries of the nation because these states lead in scientific research activity.
4. It is indicated that activity in the mobile industries will be increased substantially in the Southeastern and Far Western areas in the immediate future, due to increasing research activity in these regions.
5. The development of industry in lagging areas can be accelerated by adoption of a plan that includes these features:
   a. Improvement of educational facilities (staffs and equipment), particularly at the post-graduate level.
   b. Stimulation of research support among citizens, especially business and government leaders, by use of news channels.
   c. Establishment of new research units, including small privately financed units as well as larger units supported by industrial and philanthropic organizations.
   d. Obtaining more uniform distribution of federal research support.
   e. Selection of research programs which yield greatest results with least input.

1960
Excerpt

Area Development: A Guide For Community Leaders. 1960. 8 1/2x11 loose-leaf binder, 2 vol. With Frank Stedman. Vol. I. Understanding Growth Process, Organizing for Area Development, Area and Community Analysis, Planning and Zoning, Financing, Buildings, Selling, Future Trends, 278pp. Vol. II. Bibliography, 142 pp.

Optimism is essential! There have always been plenty of seemingly well-informed people who had no faith in the future. For example:

"All is darkness and despair. As a nation, we are at the bottom of the hill." *Detroit Free Press,* 1837.

"Nothing in this country is safe, solvent or reliable." *Philadelphia Gazette,* 1857.

"Collapse is a grim reality. The days of the Republic are numbered." *New York World,* 1873.

"On every hand, there is depression, wreck and ruin. We can't go much farther." (New Orleans *Picayune,* 1893.

"The old ship of state is sinking. Even Morgan is using the subway." *Wall Street Journal,* 1907.

Importance of Community Evaluation

The casual highway traveler, may, in the course of an afternoon, drive through several dozen communities which, on the surface, seem almost identical. All have welcome signs at the city limits and announcements of meetings of Rotary and Kiwanis. But the expansion planner who digs beneath the surface soon finds that there can be a world of difference between communities only a few miles apart.

One national firm recently made a site survey in which some really astounding figures were compiled. This firm discovered that, between best and worst communities, there could be, for example, a four-and-one-half year differential in median school years completed. Between two locations, there was a 700 percent difference in the number of engineers and scientists per 1,000 population.

Comparing the worst and best possible locations, this firm found a 45 to 1 ratio in mental rejects by Selective Service. It found differences in average hourly wages in manufacturing of as much as 77 cents per hour. It found crime rates in one spot 40 times as high as in another.

Going further, the company found per capita debt of $350 in one location and less than $1 in another. It found that the percentage of non-farm workers organized by unions was six times as great in one spot as in another, and that work stoppages for non-farm employees were 12 times as great in one location as in another.

Continuing, the survey showed that the percentage of persons of voting age who voted in the last presidential election ranged from 22.1 percent in one area to 77.3 percent in another. It found that the accidental death rate was four times as great in some spots as in others and that community chest contributions per capita were 12 times as great in some areas as in others.

Significantly, every one of these factors represents an intangible which might not be seen in a casual glance at the community.

If site-seeking firms are so careful in appraising communities, it is axiomatic that those communities that want to attract industry must be equally thoughtful. In fact, it is imperative for the community leaders to make their appraisal long before a site-seeking firm comes to town so that the community will be aware of its deficiencies and will have programs designed to remedy them.

The Registered Community Audit

Over the past 10 to 15 years, hundreds upon hundreds of communities have prepared various types of surveys, appraisals and audits of their plant location attractions and the competitive factors that apply to them. This material, in the form of pamphlets, leaflets, brochures and reports of all sizes and descriptions, has been sent to major growth firms to try to attract their attention.

It is not difficult to imagine the problem that this has created for those individuals in industry who must appraise a number of different communities in different states. They have been confronted with literature that is not in any standard form and which presents information that is in no way directly comparable.

Recognizing this problem, in 1958 we put together a new "short form" designed to serve as a national standard. This form seeks to present the essential basic facts on a community in a very convenient and concise form so that a site-seeking company can easily make valid comparisons.

Ideal Location, USA

During recent years, our staff has worked with a great many firms in gathering location data. Based on specifications submitted, and on final location decisions made, there emerges a picture of the community which the average firm considers ideal. Here's an outline:

"Ideal Location, USA" is a small city with a steadily growing population. (About two-thirds of all significant new plants are being placed in communities of less than 100,000 population, or in "satellite" communities close to major cities.)

The ideal community has an honest government that delivers maximum service to the people for each tax dollar. Ideal has a professional city or county manager who reports to a council or board which includes responsible local business and civic leaders. There is an active two-party system and a high percentage of the voters cast ballots in every election.

Ideal has a comprehensive planning and zoning program carried out with professional advice and assistance. Residential areas are protected from industrial growth, and industrial areas are protected from residential encroachment. There is a long-range plan for providing major thoroughfares as required by increasing traffic.

Community leaders in Ideal have dealt effectively with the parking problem. There are ample spaces in the downtown area, and off-street parking is required for all new projects throughout the area.

Construction of school facilities in Ideal is keeping pace with rising enrollment, so there are no double sessions or overcrowded classrooms. Curriculi are revised and improved periodically to reflect changing needs. There are strong science programs in the high schools.

Ideal has an effective law enforcement program, as indicated by a crime rate substantially below the national average. Similarly, good insurance ratings indicate that the fire department is efficient.

During the past summer there have been no water shortages in Ideal and no limitations on the use of water for washing cars or watering lawns. The pumping capacity of the municipal system is greater than the peak demand and plans have already been made to expand the system to keep ahead of increasing use. The same can be said for the sewer system and the sewage treatment plant.

Ideal can offer the new resident excellent medical facilities. The ratio of hospital beds per 1,000 population is well above the national average, as is the ratio of doctors per population unit. There are churches for the major faiths, and local membership is high.

Evidence of local interest in cultural pursuits may be seen in the Ideal museum — not a musty vault but an active community center with art classes for youngsters and adults alike.

Keen civic awareness is further evidenced in Ideal by the existence of an alert newspaper and a busy radio station. Television reception in the area is good.

When you visit Ideal you can choose between a new motel on the outskirts or the new wing of the hotel downtown. You'll find good food and good service, at reasonable cost.

For a city of its size, Ideal has fine transportation service. It's on a major rail line and has feeder airline service connecting with larger systems. Major market centers can be reached overnight through several trucking lines. There's a convenient airstrip, with hard-surface runways, lights and radio facilities for private and company aircraft.

Ideal is also fortunate in being located on a navigable waterway, which affords inexpensive transport for bulk materials. Most important, Ideal is on a branch of the new federal interstate highway system.

The firm locating a plant in Ideal will have no difficulty finding adequate labor. A labor force survey conducted just this year shows a substantial number of workers in the area who would be attracted to a new plant. This does not mean that there are large numbers unemployed but that such trends as farm mechanization are resulting in an increased pool of available labor.

Further, the new employer is happy to note good relations between labor and the industries already located in the area. There hasn't been a major strike in five years. Moreover, Ideal is in a state with a Right To Work Law and intends to keep it. Union racketeering is dealt with quickly and effectively.

The cost of producing goods in Ideal is below the national average, not because of low wage rates but because of high efficiency and productivity inherent in the character of the labor force.

Ideal is geared to handle industries of the space age, and has a special interest in technological activities. There's a vocational training program for developing new skills. More important, there's a top-flight engineering college nearby which each year graduates a new crop of young scientists. There is a graduate school where advanced degrees are awarded in chemistry, physics and mathematics.

The distribution of the tax burden between industries, individuals and other interests is considered to be fair and reasonable in Ideal. The per capita debt is low. There are no "giveaways" or tax exemptions for new industry, but government officials are noted for the fine cooperation they give in extending utilities and providing other assistance for new plants.

The city fathers have seen to it that there are plenty of good sites at reasonable cost available in Ideal. Good tracts along rail lines and major highways have been reserved by zoning or by direct acquisition. There's plenty of information available in the form of aerial photos, topographic maps and engineering studies.

There are alert groups in Ideal ready to assist in financing a new plant.

There's a substantial fund in the local development corporation ready to be used to help a worthwhile enterprise get started in the community.

Ideal is fortunate in that its well-balanced economy includes such major sources of revenue as farm products, forest products, mining and a variety of manufacturing. No one operation dominates the economy.

One of the outstanding factors in Ideal's favor is the wealth of recreational opportunities. The climate favors outdoor activities and there are wide opportunities for swimming, fishing, hunting and other sports. Tourism is, in fact, a substantial business in the area.

There's a strong chamber of commerce, well-financed, and well-staffed. The business firm looking for a site can be assured of prompt, professional assistance. Where desired, the plant location experts in Ideal can handle a project in complete secrecy, to protect the new industry's interests right up to the moment that public announcement is made.

In short, Ideal is a healthy community in every respect. It's a city without urban congestion, growing with a minimum of growing pains. It's prosperous now, and it's going to be even more prosperous in the years ahead. Its citizens take pride in its accomplishments and share a determination to make Ideal even more ideal in the future.

1966
Excerpt

Area Development Organizations. Principles of organizing for development. The pyramid concept. Secret of U.S. progress. Organizations above the state level. State development organizations. Local development organizations. Rural community improvement organizations. Supporting organizations. 1966. 331 pp. Includes geographical index of several thousand U.S. organizations.

Development today is an art rather than a precise science. However, progress is being made in establishing basic principles upon which to build. It is possible to postulate several fundamental concepts which, like the law of gravity, are not repealed when the developer crosses geographic and political boundaries. These concepts, we believe, are universally applicable and should be fully appreciated by every practitioner of the development art. They include:

The equation for maximum area development

Dmax = EMR

where

D max is the maximum degree of development possible for any area.

E is the efficiency of the development process.

M is the manpower applied.

R is the resource invested.

This relationship indicates what is necessary to achieve maximum results in any area (a nation, a state or province, or a smaller subdivision). It shows that there must be brought into play the maximum amount of manpower, utilizing the greatest possible magnitude of resources in the most efficient manner possible.

If we look at the development of an area, the efficiency factor, **E**, is the composite efficiency of the complete work of development programs and activities in the area. The manpower factor, **M**, is the total effort of all workers, professional and non-professional, paid and voluntary, in all development groups in the area. And the resource factor, **R**, is the total value of resources invested in all development programs in the area.

It is evident, therefore, that executives concerned with the overall development of an area must have three basic objectives:

1.To mobilize a maximum number of workers to participate in the development activities. If the area to be developed is a small community, this means that the goal must be to involve every effective citizen of the community in the development effort. If the area to be developed is a large one, it means that there must be established many organizations through which to mobilize many people.

2.To funnel into the development programs of the area a maximum of resources. This includes both money and materials.

3.To achieve a maximum degree of efficiency by intelligent management, shrewd determination of goals, effective use of people, the avoidance of duplication and the coordination of diverse activities.

It is easy to find development programs that are falling short of their objectives through failure to apply this equation for maximum result. A common mistake is to attempt to do the job with too few organizations and people. In such cases, even if the program should achieve an efficiency of 100 percent, it would still fall short of its goals.

There are other examples of programs in which there is a high degree of efficiency and a large number of workers, but goals cannot be reached because of a lack of money. Most development program directors who fail are prone to give this as the reason.

The third type of failure is the abundantly staffed and well-financed program that is grossly inefficient, wasting people and funds. There are some glaring examples to be found.

Certainly, the development process is still so inexact we would not attempt to assign numbers to the factors in the equation for maximum result and compute the precise effect of, say, a 10 percent increase in budget or a particular change in manpower. At this time we only presume to suggest that broad relationships do exist and that general effects can be anticipated.

The Relationship Between Internal and External Effort

The second basic concept we should understand is the interrelationship between development factors in different areas. Theoretically, an area development program undertaken anywhere in the world is subject to the influence of every other program. In practical terms, virtually every area program is, indeed, affected by factors external to the area. Hence, the equation:

$$EMR = (EMR) + (EMR)$$

This simply says: The total potential development of an area is the sum of the development that can be achieved from within and that which can be achieved using manpower and resources from outside the area. This relationship applies to small communities and nations alike.

In the small community, the equation recognizes that the community can achieve only so much with the manpower and resources it contains. By going outside the community to more affluent communities ties, it may obtain, for example, money with which to achieve a more rapid rate of development.

The same thinking, of course, applies to nations. The underdeveloped nations can accelerate their growth by adding to their own EMR the EMR they can attract from developed nations. This is the basis for what we have called the grand strategy of world development:

$$Dw = Ew \, (MuRu + MdRd)$$

where:

Dw is the maximum development for the world. Ew is the composite efficiency of all development programs. **MuRu** is the manpower and resources of the underdeveloped nations. **MdRd** is the manpower and resources of the developed nations.

This relationship merely says that the area that brings about a suitable combination of outside and inside interests can achieve a rate of progress greater than would be possible by relying wholly on either interest alone. This is a principle every development official should appreciate and follow.

Elements Contributing to Maximum Efficiency

From the foregoing, it is apparent that the efficiency of the development process is of vital importance in any area program, whether it be abundantly or inadequately staffed or richly or poorly supported. Getting maximum results from what is available requires maximum efficiency.

What elements determine E? We are not yet prepared to answer this in mathematical terms; but we can, with considerable confidence, list the factors that are controlling. We assert that achievement of maximum efficiency in any area depends fundamentally on five major factors that are encountered in sequence as a program is undertaken:

1. *Selection of leaders*. It is necessary in setting up any area development program to select as the leaders of the effort those individuals in the area who are most capable of getting things done. This capability may be a matter of personal talent, education, wealth, political influence, technical skill, or a combination of these factors.

If the program is being organized in a remote and primitive village, the leaders could conceivably include the village chieftain, the village strong man, the village witch doctor, the man who owns the greatest number of elephant tusks, and the best swimmer. More often, the area leaders include leading businessmen, prominent citizens and key government officials.

2. *Getting organized*. Having identified the leaders in the area, the second step is to bring them together in an organization. In the remote village, this may simply involve getting the men together around a campfire to agree upon a spokesman. In a more sophisticated area, it may mean drafting a charter and recording a set of bylaws under which a formal organization will function. In any event, the leaders of the area are put into an effective team which henceforth guides and governs the development.

3. *Appraising needs and opportunities*. After the team is organized, its first mission is to take a critical look at the area and to determine the needs and opportunities for development. This appraisal should be objective and comprehensive, normally resulting in a very formidable list of projects.

In the small village, it may include a footbridge across the nearby stream, a new well or an outboard motor for the village canoe. In a developed area, the list might include slum clearance, traffic engineering, industrial zoning or a host of other needs. Opportunities may exist in tourism, industry, foreign trade and in a variety of other fields.

4. *Setting priorities.* Any good survey of area needs and opportunities will inevitably produce a list of projects so extensive that the area organization cannot hope to undertake all items simultaneously and achieve all goals at once. Thus, it is necessary to study the alternatives and establish a set of priorities.

5. *Acting and following up.* Having set priorities, the area program is put into action and is checked continuously. Successful effort is applauded and weak activities are strengthened.

These five steps are essential parts of any effort that enjoys maximum effectiveness. A program will not reach full potential if any one of the steps is omitted. Moreover, there must be a periodic re-evaluation at each factor, including leadership, organization and program; and changes must be made as dictated by experience.

Unhappily, a great many programs to be found in various parts of the world are failing to reach full potential because these fundamental laws of development are being ignored. Many programs fail to involve the real leaders in the area they seek to promote.

Many more programs have been launched without suitable study of objectives. Others have permitted special interests rather than the area's true needs to dictate priorities. And, all too often, area programs that are well planned and organized fail miserably due to lack of vigorous action and follow-up.

Therefore:

$$E = (MR)CORR/(MR)TOT$$

where

E is the composite efficiency of the area program, **(MR)CORR** is the manpower and resource used correctly, and **(MR)TOT** is the total manpower and resource used.

Since the science of development is still in its infancy, it is probably safe to say that no area program has yet achieved such a high order of efficiency that a substantial improvement is no longer possible.

The Pyramid Concept

The pyramids of Egypt were rightfully heralded as wonders of an early civilization. They served well as guardians of historical lore, treasure and noble bones. Today, we are building other pyramids which may well merit even greater acclaim as wonders of this age. For these are the program and organization pyramids through which we can promote the maximum development of areas at all levels. Through ages to come, these pyramids will profoundly benefit all mankind.

The pyramid of development programs and organizations for a nation fully organized from the smallest rural settlements to the national level includes: a national effort; programs for each major region; within each region programs for each state, province or district; in each state programs for every major city or metropolitan area; around each city programs for the smaller towns and communities; and in the countryside there are programs in every rural community.

In picturing the pyramid, it is important to note a distinction between programs and organizations. There is, hopefully, just one program at each level of the pyramid. But there may be several organizations functioning at each level. Their composite efforts constitute the program for that level.

It is also vital to note that all organizations in the pyramid chart are joined by dashed lines. There is no "chain of command." The directors of the national program do not impose their orders on those in the lower echelons. Cooperation and coordination is on a voluntary basis.

Ideally, each organization knows its proper role and its relationship to each of the other organizations in the pyramid. In order to make this free system work, it is necessary to have good communication and understanding throughout the pyramid.

There must be an effective exchange of ideas among all levels. It is not enough for program directives to flow downward through the pyramid from the top. The system must also permit and encourage the flow of ideas from the lowest level upward and laterally throughout the entire structure.

The national program thus represents the composite thinking of all elements in the pyramid. Similarly, a state program should reflect the composite thinking of the city, community and rural programs within its boundaries. Every element of the pyramid is essential — none is more important than another. No area can achieve maximum development until it establishes a complete pyramid of fully effective units.

We include in the primary organization pyramid only those organizations that have as their main function the development of an area. These include groups variously labeled as "area development," "industrial development," and "economic development" agencies.

We will not attempt to draw a distinction between "area," "industrial," and "economic" development units. Around the world these terms are com-

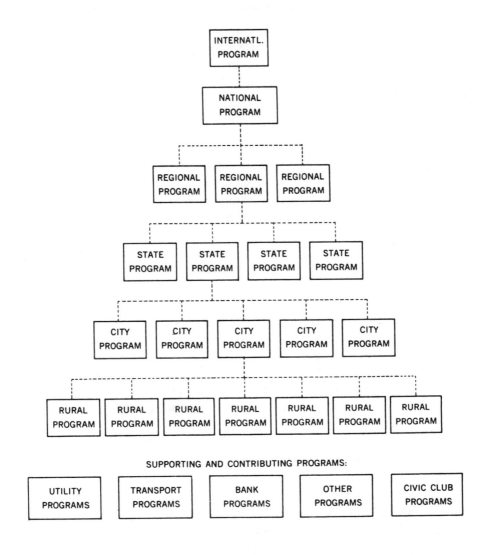

The pyramid concept. This is the organization plan introduced in the late 1950s. Each unit is independent. Pyramids are best built from the bottom up.

ing to mean about the same thing, with "industrial" and "economic" units broadening their concepts to encompass the total development of their service areas.

Few industrial development organizations today limit their efforts to expansion of manufacturing activity. Instead, the alert groups define "industry" as anything that produces revenue; and attention is given to promoting expansion of distribution activities, tourism, agriculture, mining, and services, as well as manufacturing.

Another group of organizations exists primarily to serve non-development needs but has units or departments devoted to development activities. Units of this type are classified as supporting organizations. Still another group of organizations has no development departments but occasionally undertakes a development activity. Units of this type are designated as organizations.

The complete pyramid for a large area is big and complex. It is often unwieldy. Building the pyramid — as the Egyptians found — can be frustratingly slow. But it is axiomatic that no area can achieve fullest development until it has a complete pyramid of effective programs and organizations. That is the challenge!

The Secret of U.S. Progress

Students of economic development have long debated the reasons for the high level of development in the United States as compared with most of the other nations of the world. Some analysts credit the nation's progress to strategic location, others to natural resources, and still others to political stability.

Undoubtedly, all of these factors have exerted an important influence on the development process. Scholars are correct in attaching importance to them. However, we believe very few researchers have given due credit to organization as the secret of U.S. progress in development.

We believe that the pyramid of programs and organizations that propels U.S. development is a "secret weapon" of great importance. No nation has been so well-organized —from the smallest rural community to the national capital — with a network of organizations that places heavy reliance on private enterprise and local initiative.

Some will argue this is a "chicken-and-egg" situation — that a nation which is wealthy can afford many programs and organizations. To some extent, this is true. But close study reveals that organized development efforts have run parallel with the entire development history of the United States.

The propensity of Americans for organizing locally to meet common needs was recognized in the very early days of the nation. For example, Alexis de Tocqueville (1805-1859), French Minister of Foreign Affairs, included in his *Democracy in America* (Saunders and Otley. London, 1838) this illuminating comment:

"These Americans are the most peculiar people in the world. You'll not believe it when I tell you how they behave. In a local community in their country, a citizen may conceive of some need which is not being met. What does he do? He goes across the street and discusses it with his neighbor. Then what happens? A committee comes into existence, and then the committee begins functioning on behalf of that need; and you won't believe this, but it's true. All of this is done without reference to any bureaucrat. All of this is done by the private citizens on their own initiative."

The construction of the U.S. pyramid has continued quietly but effectively down to the present, and today the U.S. has a mammoth composite program being carried forward by many thousands of organizations. These include several agencies working at the international and national level; some 10 significant regional groupings; a program for each of the 50 states; approximately 200 major metropolitan area programs; several thousand local programs; and rural and supporting bodies.

Our estimate is that more than 15,000 organizations are directly involved.

Perhaps the most significant aspect of this U.S. pyramid is that the local units dominate the scene. They conduct the bulk of the program activity and, in the aggregate, involve the greatest proportion of people and resources.

Another key point is that the U.S. pyramid functions without any central authority. The units that function at various levels in the pyramid are autonomous. Coordination is achieved by communication and persuasion. Competition between units is fierce.

What motivates U.S citizens to unite in organizations to under-take development programs? Each citizen is probably influenced by a slightly different combination of factors, but principal considerations often include:

1. *Creation of job opportunities*. Most U.S. area development programs are job-oriented, especially in rural sections. Parents are anxious to generate opportunities for their children near home so that the young people will not have to move to another region to find employment. Citizens of all ages want better jobs for greater personal purchasing power and security. Unemployment breeds political discontent and puts pressure on government leaders to expedite development efforts.

2. *Expansion of tax base*. In recent years many development efforts have been stimulated by the need for additional tax revenue to pay for gov-

ernmental services and social benefits. Individual home owners, as well as other interests in an area, may see the need for attracting new investment to the tax burden.

3. *Indirectly stimulating private business.* Many business firms that support development efforts do so in the realization that expansion of industrial activity will produce expansion of the local economy and open new opportunities for them. Hence, hotel owners support tourism efforts; railroads actively promote industries that have heavy freight movements; and utility firms encourage development that will mean greater utilization of energy.

It should be emphasized that a common denominator among successful development efforts is the willingness of the citizens and business firms of the area to place the public interest before any personal or private interest. Public-spirited individuals and business firms thus provide most of the funds used by local development organizations in the United States.

Development executives from other nations who visit the United States are almost always astonished to discover that in this country the main development effort is carried forward by state and local organizations. Until very recently the national government had no area development functions of consequence. The U.S. pyramid of development programs and organizations has, for the most part, grown from the base upwards, rather than from the top down.

Building Pyramids Around the World

Active and effective development organizations led by professionals of high caliber are by no means found only in the United States. While the U.S. is organized in greater depth, there are fine examples to be found elsewhere. Many nations have begun to devote substantial efforts toward filling out their pyramids of development organizations and programs.

If there is any important difference between the U.S. pyramid and those of other nations, it may be that the U.S. generally places heavier emphasis on private enterprise and local initiative. Another way of saying this is that in other countries development organizations more frequently are publicly funded and centered in the national capital. The role of small, privately sponsored bodies in outlying areas is correspondingly less important.

Recognizing that a wealth of practical experience is to be found in the U.S. pyramid and others in developed nations, it is natural that those concerned with the developing nations would seek to utilize this asset. A great deal of random activity has been devoted to transferring specific experience from one agency in one nation to another agency in another country.

(Editor's note: Perhaps the first plan for systematically attempting large-scale transfer is our AID/PEP program discussed below.)

1968 Excerpt	The AID/PEP Program for Mobilizing Private Enterprise and Local Initiative in Latin America. Short-term orientation tours. Interamerican development seminars. Working materials. Investment promotion reports. U.S. development specialists. Interns. (Summary Report). Dec. 1968. 138 pp. illus. Appendix. Sponsored by the Agency for International Development.

In the summer of 1960 we made a survey trip around Latin America at company expense to gather information on the status of development programs. We visited some 12 nations, talking with Latin leaders of both public and private sector organizations, as well as with officials of various offices of the U.S. Agency of International Development.

Brief discussions were sufficient to reveal that the available reservoir of experience with successful development programs in the U. S. was not being utilized generally in the establishment and refinement of new programs in Latin America.

At the conclusion of this trip, we began urging AID officials in Washington to set up a program for systematic transfer of technology between successful area development organizations in the U.S. and the less-experienced units in Latin America. By 1962 this idea gained some acceptance and in 1963 a series of pilot projects was authorized. The first pilot efforts were conducted in El Salvador, Colombia and Costa Rica in 1963 and 1964. These projects were favorably received, and in 1964 AID decided to establish the program on a regional basis.

After some six months of planning, and following a competition involving 18 firms, a contract was awarded to Conway Research, Inc., on October 9, 1964. The effort which had been identified informally as "AID/PEP" became official and was expanded to include additional program elements. The contract specifically called upon Conway to undertake a program of institutional development defined as follows:

"The purpose of this contract is to encourage and promote the development of the private enterprise system in Latin America by providing training and indoctrination for selected individuals from the public and private sectors of the less developed countries of Latin America in the self-help activities required to realize the industrial potential of their respective areas.

It is anticipated that such training and indoctrination will hasten the industrial development process within these countries by encouraging the creation of multi-level general and specific purpose development institutions."

This regional program was renewed annually in 1965, 1966, and 1967, and the termination date was extended to December 31, 1968. This report, therefore, summarizes activities which extended over a period of about five years.

The Job Challenge in Latin America

There are many ways to describe the development challenge in Latin America. One specific and convenient approach is to discuss the problems in terms of jobs. This is seldom done in Latin America, due perhaps to the inadequacy of statistical data on population, labor force, unemployment, underemployment and growth rates.

However, crude estimates may serve to illustrate the magnitude of the industrial development effort required in the region. The population of Latin America has long since passed the 200 million mark, and may now be estimated at more than 240 million. The growth rate is about three percent per year — one of the world's highest.

It has been proposed that Latin America set as a goal the creation of some two million new jobs per year. While statistics are vague, it is possible that even this massive injection of new jobs into the economy of the region would only permit maintaining the status quo. Sidestepping precise statistical surveys, it is useful to speculate on just what the addition of two million new jobs involves.

For all of Latin America, it is estimated that 500,000 new jobs must be created in industry each year. If 75 percent of these are created by the expansion of existing industries and 25 percent must come from new ventures, this means that new plants must be built to provide jobs for 125,000 workers.

Assuming further that the typical new plant will employ 50 workers, we find a requirement of 2,500 new units per year, or 10 for each working day of the year!

Each new plant requires many things. One of the universal requirements is money. In the U.S. it is known that the average new job in industry requires an investment of some $15,000. (This ranges from as low as $1,000 per job in a simple sewing operation to well over $100,000 per job in a steel mill or petroleum refinery.)

In Latin America it is estimated that the average new industrial job requires an investment of at least $6,000. Hence, creating 500,000 new jobs per year requires an overall investment of at least $3 billion. Generating other necessary jobs in agriculture, services and related activities will require additional billions — far more than can be supplied by all the governments of the hemisphere, and the goals grow larger every year!

This leads to recognition of the first basic concept of AID/PEP — that the development goals of Latin America cannot be met except through the promotion of private investment on a very large scale.

The Necessity of Organizing for Development

Having recognized the magnitude of the goals to be achieved, it is then necessary to accept the fact that they can be attained only by mobilizing private enterprise and local initiative at many levels, especially subnational. If 3,000 new industrial plants are to be built each year, it is evident that at least 3,000 industrial sites must be ready, and 3,000 industrial buildings must be erected. In fact, it will be necessary to make many other preparations.

In the United States, a pyramid structure of some 15,000 development organizations has emerged to meet such needs. Since the number of similar organizations presently active in Latin America is less than 600, it is evident

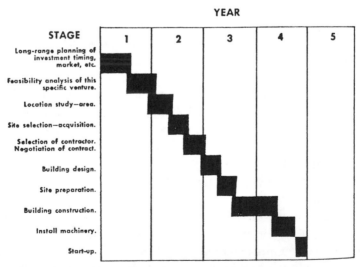

Rationale for speculative buildings. This was one of the training aids we used in Latin America in the 1960s. Having industrial buildings ready for occupancy was a key factor — typically saving more than 2 years in getting started. In Puerto Rico more than 1000 speculative factories were built.

that many additional organizations must be brought into operation if the job is to be done. In short, Latin America must build its own pyramid of effective area development organizations.

The Role of AID/PEP

Having accepted the fact that widespread institutional development is necessary to get the job done in Latin America, it may then be suggested that this process of institutional development can be accelerated by using the reservoir of experience in the U.S. structure. The AID/PEP program, then, is nothing more than a mechanism for expediting the flow of technical assistance from the existing U.S. pyramid of 15,000 organizations to the emerging Latin pyramid of 500 to 600 organizations.

From the outset, AID/PEP was envisioned as a device whereby AID, with a small investment in central staff and headquarters operations, might generate a large-scale transfer between U.S. and Latin groups. Hopefully, hundreds of successful U.S. organizations would share their experience with scores of new organizations in Latin America. The program was premised on this expectation of obtaining a large amount of "leverage" in every element.

Short-term Orientation Tours

One of the first and most vital elements of the AID/PEP program was the Short-Term Orientation tour. Typically, this involved the selection of a small group of leaders from a country or area and bringing them to the U.S. for exposure to certain types of development activities. In the early days of the effort, many groups were brought in for a "Stage I Motivation," simply to convince a panel of public and private officials that they should undertake to build a pyramid structure for the mobilization of private enterprise and local initiative in their area.

A typical schedule involved two to three weeks, with travel to several states. Each program was planned to give exposure to organizations at various levels of state development agencies, metropolitan organizations, county and local groups. Generally, large cities were avoided and there were numerous visits to small, rural communities. Less-developed areas of the U.S. were frequently chosen, and to some extent ecology of the area visited was matched with that of the visitor's own country or area.

Interamerican Development Seminars

Very early in the AID/PEP effort it was confirmed that lack of adequate professional communication among the development executives of the region was a serious problem. Groups struggling to establish programs in one country were unaware of efforts in adjoining countries where similar problems had been met. There was only haphazard exchange of experience and little opportunity for personnel to gain inspiration and enthusiasm from one another. Further, there was no forum before which new concepts could be proposed or success stories told.

As a partial solution to this problem, the first Interamerican Development Seminar was held in Caracas in 1965. It attracted some 150 executives of development organizations from 17 countries. There were sessions devoted to such topics as "organizing for development," "the role of private enterprise," "research and promotion," and "meeting the competition." Most important, working-level executives from national, regional, departmental and local groups — some of them newly formed under AID/PEP impetus — gave progress reports on their concrete achievements.

The second annual session was held in Panama in 1966 and the third in Arequipa, Peru, in 1967. Altogether, the three seminars attracted a total of 564 participants, from 21 nations.

Investment Promotion Reports

A typical project involved, first, gathering information on investment factors in a given area; second, presentation of the facts in an attractive format; next, distribution of the reports to an audience of prospective investors; and, finally, follow-up which, hopefully, led to direct negotiation and actual investment.

One series of promotion reports dealt with specific countries or geographic sections. Subjects covered in this manner included: El Salvador, Costa Rica, Colombia, Nicaragua, Guatemala, Central America, Honduras, Peru, Panama, Northeast Brazil, Ecuador, Southern Peru, Paraguay and Brazil.

U.S. Development Specialists

In all, 20 U.S. development executives contributed their services in 14 countries. Those who served included several heads of state development organizations and specialists in a variety of fields, including tourism, community development, industrial park planning and investment promotion.

Positive Results of the AID/PEP Program

The specific purpose was to motivate, indoctrinate and train Latin executives for carrying forward successful area development activities. At the outset, there were many doubts regarding the program. Both high-ranking U.S. officials and key Latin officials wondered whether outsiders (*gringos*) could actually motivate Latins to adopt new approaches, form new organizations and undertake new projects.

There was doubt regarding the willingness of central government agencies to support grass-roots efforts and decentralization. There were doubts regarding genuine collaboration between the public and private sector.

There were doubts as to the availability of sufficient leadership for new units in remote areas. There were doubts regarding the extent of local initiative and the willingness of private businessmen to invest their energy and money in new ventures for the common good.

To what extent has AID/PEP resolved these questions? Has AID/PEP demonstrated that rapid progress in institutional development can be achieved in Latin America despite the problems which exist? No attempt will be made to give a detailed report on each country and each area served; however, by 1965 it was possible to tally these results. There were:

1. More than 20 new organizations at the department (state) level.

2. At least 50, and perhaps a great many more, new units at the local community level.

3. More than 100 significant new projects undertaken by the above units to establish specific industries and generate employment.

4. Many new plants already in operation, others financed and in development stages.

The inevitable conclusion, however, is that within the short space of five years AID/PEP has sparked a major new thrust in Colombia, and the results will become more impressive with each passing year.

1978
Excerpt

New Industries Of The Seventies. 1978. 302 pp. With Linda L. Liston.

Executives whose responsibility it is to keep abreast of new industrial growth may obtain an overview of activity by scanning the statistical summaries produced by the U.S. Departments of Commerce and Labor, the Federal Reserve or other entities. Best-known, perhaps, is the periodic report on expenditures for new plants and equipment.

New plant and equipment (NPE) totals have been issued rather consistently for three decades, and they provide an historic basis for comparison, as well as a point of departure for various current analyses. A glance at the chart reveals several useful facts:

First, the curve of NPE outlays is remarkably smooth. It does not show the great fluctuations found in historic plots of stockmarket indices, housing starts or most other business barometers. Second, the volume has been at a very impressive level — rising from about $80 billion per year in 1970

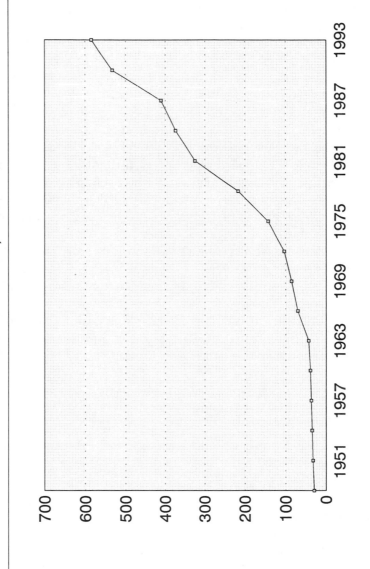

New Plant & Equipment Expenditures

in the United States, 1948-1993

(billions of current dollars)

Spending for new plants. Contrary to impressions given in the mass media, investment in big new industrial facilities is relatively steady. Substantial spending continues through recessions, wars, and other events.

to more than $150 billion expected in 1978.

Experience suggests that NPE expenditures may be more stable because they are inherently more long-term in nature than such categories as consumer spending. Long-range corporate planning and capital budget programming executives must of necessity think five years or more ahead, and for many facilities the time required from project approval to start-up is three or more years.

This means that brief recessions may have little effect on plans for construction of major new plants. However, corporations may well delay purchase of new equipment for existing plants or other small or short-term projects. On the other hand, during a period of reduced interest rates, many firms may rush to make loan commitments for new projects.

For those who need to know how many new plants are being built, the fact that there was a total investment of more than $150 billion in NPE in one year is not enough. For executives with market research or area research functions, this is merely a tantalizing morsel of information. Quick arithmetic reveals that if the $150 billion investment went into new plants each costing $1 million, there would be 150,000 important new facilities located!

It is estimated that the actual number of significant new projects each year is about 3,000. This estimate suggests that if the new projects were evenly divided among the 50 states, each would receive fewer than 60 new projects per year. Of course, the distribution is not even, with some states getting more than 100 substantial new facilities each year and others fewer than 20.

An effort to establish a regular reporting system for new plants on a state-by-state basis was begun by the senior author about 1950 as a part of the program of the Southern Assn. of Science and Industry (SASI).

So much for history! During the past two decades, we have sought to produce annual tallies of new plants, new expansion projects and total capital investment in cooperation with development agencies in all of the states, Puerto Rico and Canada.

Originally, we promulgated criteria for reporting and asked each state to supply data. However, a number of states chose different criteria, the most common variation being the size of units included in their survey.

Further, some states evidently deemed the tallying of new development to be an important aspect of their programs, but others neglected the function. There was a tendency for states which were doing well to furnish reports and for those which were faring badly not to report.

The result is that state statistics on actual new plant activity are very spotty. Fewer than half of the states reported consistently and completely during the past decade. While this spotty data is interesting and useful from several viewpoints, readers are cautioned not to attempt to use the data in statistical analyses without a good understanding of their limitations.

It is probably safe to say that no two states report new activity in exactly the same way. Hence, it is hazardous to make a direct comparison between two states on the basis of these numbers. One state may be reporting apples while the other is counting oranges.

Most of the content of this study is based on compilation and analysis of projects reported to *Industrial Development* magazine during the period January 1970, through December 1977. Over the years, the staff of ID and its research adjunct, *Site Selection Handbook*, developed a variety of sources for new plant information, including periodic reports from area development agencies, questionnaires, press releases, newspaper clippings, telephone inquiries and field work.

Despite this effort, readers are cautioned that many reports may be inaccurate or incomplete. Some projects may have been canceled after being announced or abandoned after being started. Others may have been relocated!

Readers are cautioned that there are no commonly accepted definitions of "new industries" or "new plants." Purists will argue that an "industry" is a category of industrial activity, as might be described by a two-digit SIC number. This term usually is employed to refer to groups of plants.

The better term for describing an individual industrial facility is "plant," and the new plant reports are designed primarily to tally individual units. However, there is still a problem of terminology. Some purists may argue that the term "plant" refers only to a manufacturing unit. We do not agree. We use "plant" in a more general sense to refer to various corporate facilities.

More than 10,000 projects reported in *Industrial Development* during 1970-77 have been examined individually and cross-referenced to eliminate duplicates, as well as to identify those projects that may have been reported at more than one stage of development.

To study in detail such facets as site/building ratio, space allocation per worker, and investment per worker or investment per square foot, the sample was further refined to include only reports that were essentially complete and consistent. This gave a sample of about 1,000 projects for these analyses.

A major consideration in site selection is the size of the site required. Both site size and building size are a key factor in determining project cost.

The ratios of gross building square footage to number of employees were computed to give an approximate indication of space allocation per worker.

The composite figure for the U.S., about 600 sq. ft. per worker, checks nicely with the result given in the more comprehensive analysis of some 50 manufacturing projects reported recently by the Industrial Development Research Council in its research study, "A Composite Case History of New Facility Location."

While the spotty data make geographic analysis perilous, it seems evident that the larger site-to-building ratios are found in the South Atlantic, West South Central and Mountain states. Smaller site ratios are seen in New England, the Middle Atlantic and Pacific regions.

Land costs are undoubtedly a factor. Also, the types of industries must be considered. The petrochemical and minerals processing units in the South and West require large sites.

Perhaps the most interesting observation is that industry generally appears to be buying with expansion in mind. A ratio of 9.7 to one obviously permits considerable addition on the same site, except for sites with very unusual terrain.

How much does a job cost? This is a question of much interest both to private sector executives who build the job-producing facilities and to public officials who seek to promote job-creating investments.

Analysis of the new plant data gives a very crude picture of job-creation costs — insofar as direct investment is concerned. For the plants reported during 1970-77, the mean was $16,566 invested for each new worker (figures adjusted to 1977 dollars).

The data suggest strongly that a higher-than-average investment per worker is characteristic of the new plants being located in the South Atlantic and, especially, the East South Central regions. Lower-than-average investments appear to be typical of the New England, Mountain and Pacific regions. While lack of uniformity in the raw data negates any precise comparison, an apparent ratio of nearly three to one between the East South Central region and New England is difficult to ignore.

At the least, the data seem to confirm the passing of the traditional location pattern of the years following World War II — when the textile industries of New England expanded south to use low-cost labor in facilities that involved a lower-than-average investment per worker. Development observers have long been aware that the facilities seeking low-cost labor have been going farther south, first to Puerto Rico, and, more recently, into twin plants in Mexico and elsewhere.

Hence, the data for the decade of the Seventies indicate that the low-investment industries are no longer the dominant factor in the South. There is substantial evidence in the South of the impact of such high-investment industries as petroleum refining, petrochemical and high-technology manu-facturing.

1980
Excerpt

Marketing Industrial Buildings and Sites. Introduction: promotion is not a dirty word! The sellers: promotion and marketing organizations. The customers: target industry groups, companies, executives. Elements of a marketing plan. Media advertising. Special publications. Selling a specific building or site. Marketing professional services. Outlook for the future. 1980. 358 pp. Hard Cover.

Promotion Is Not a Dirty Word!

We believe fervently that those active in promotion, selling and marketing are engaged in an important and honorable profession. Marketing in a highly competitive environment is a cornerstone of the American enterprise system.

While marketing science is not yet as exact as mathematics or as socially acceptable as medicine, it is a science for which no apology is needed. The effective application of sound marketing technology has contributed

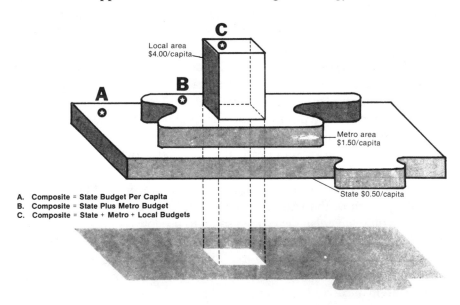

A. Composite = State Budget Per Capita
B. Composite = State Plus Metro Budget
C. Composite = State + Metro + Local Budgets

Local area $4.00/capita

Metro area $1.50/capita

State $0.50/capita

Development program overlay. This sketch shows the competitive advantage held by local area development units which are located in the service area of active regional and state units.

greatly to the public good. Direct benefits include wider distribution of goods and services, reduced prices and improved quality.

More germane to this study, sound marketing has contributed much to the effectiveness of economic development programs. Competition in the market place has produced a wealth of incentive packages, a great inventory of prepared sites and facilities and a broad spectrum of supporting services. Around the world, strategists in poorer nations seek to emulate this American promotion and entrepreneurial talent.

The experience of the past 25 years demonstrates that marketing is an essential component of any well-conceived program. Further, we believe there is a relationship between the effect of the marketing effort and its cost.

This relationship suggests strongly that any program receives significant benefits from moderate expenditures (A). Also, it is suggested that for every program there may be a point beyond which increased effect may be achieved only at prohibitive cost (B). Designing and implementing programs to exploit realm A to the fullest without getting into realm B is really what economic development marketing is all about.

Target Industry Groups, Companies and Executives

The ultimate customer for a site or building is typically a corporate executive who represents a company that falls within a certain industry group. All three — the executive, the company and the industry group — are targets the successful marketer must identify.

For a full-scale area marketing program, the target identification process is expensive, complex and time-consuming. The scope of the problem is best understood by looking at each of the three more-or-less distinct entities to be identified.

Target industry groups: In this category, we will list factors which do not pertain so much to a particular company as to an industry category, such as a four-digit SIC class, or to a type of facility. These entities may tend to have certain common features no matter what firms or planning personnel are involved.

First, there may be distinctions related to the kind of facility. Some of the possibilities include:

1. Offices: HQ, regional or local.
2. Manufacturing plants: multi-purpose, process, national product line, regional product line, national mixed lines or regional mixed lines.
3. Distribution facilities: national, regional or local.
4. Other: R&D, maintenance, service, combinations.

Some business and industry groups tend to invest more heavily in office facilities (insurance, for example), while others have a greater need for warehousing or manufacturing space. Obviously, the location requirements vary greatly.

The astute marketer will thus be persuaded to tailor his efforts to the type of facility he seeks to attract. If the area he is promoting has obvious potential for, say, warehousing but not for office facilities, he will plan accordingly. His first group sort, therefore, may be on the basis of the facility profile.

Another approach some marketers use to exploit inherent group characteristics is a geographic/age sort — selecting industries, such as leather, textiles or some other industry groups, which were historically centered in older industrial areas of the Northeast. This strategy is based on the assumption that many such firms occupy obsolete facilities on small urban sites offering no room for expansion.

One of the most common techniques for selecting target industry groups is the look for four-digit groups having a growth rate substantially higher than average.

These statistical methods for identifying growth categories are useful, but they are by no means the ultimate answer. Some of the pitfalls are obvious. Industry groups tend to grow in surges or cycles, not along smooth linear courses. A group with a low growth rate for several years may be on the verge of a period of rapid growth.

The possibility of designing a reliable method for identifying prospects by matching an area's assets with an industry's needs has tantalized marketers from the earliest days of organized area promotion. On the surface, the concept appears to be as good as apple pie, motherhood and Old Glory.

Even those totally lacking in area marketing experience can easily see that some industry groups obviously fit certain locales. Pulp and paper mills go to river sites in pulpwood-producing areas. Potential sites are so well-defined that two competitive secret location studies may recommend the same piece of ground.

These spectacularly obvious match-ups are the exception, however. For most industry groups, many locations are possible. Hundreds of areas have potential for a large variety of industry groups. Systematic approaches to area/industry matching can thus become very complicated.

Two of the approaches that have been used most often by area researchers and marketers are input/output analysis and profile-matching. In the former, the study area boundaries are defined and data are collected to describe all economic activity in terms of what comes in and what goes out. The object is to identify supply-and-demand gaps which may be filled by new local activity. The technique encounters myriad practical problems, such as lack of sufficient valid data and the unmeasured influence of other spheres of economic activity on the local sphere.

Profile-matching involves the establishment of a set of location criteria for an industry group — a perilous task — and matching this against an inventory of area assets.

Profile-matching has been used for various geographic areas. This approach may also be used in attempting to identify industry groups more prone to elect certain types of sites, such as waterfront, urban renewal or airport.

The prime reason for disillusionment with this method is the fact that many of the desirability criteria are based on erroneous thinking. For example, many areas announce that they are limiting their search to "clean" industries.

This may have made sense in 1960, but it accomplishes little today for the simple reason that "unclean" plants cannot be built legally in any state. Federal EPA regulations are all-pervasive. For new plants, therefore, the dirty smokestack is a myth.

The most wearisome phrase of all — one that is heard in hundreds of communities — is, "We want industries like electronics." Those who utter this phrase have a mental image of a small plant producing very expensive little black boxes so quietly the neighbors don't know the plant is there.

They have never seen such a company after 10 years of frantic growth, sprawling over the community in multi-plant facilities, with traffic jams on all sides and toxic wastes streaming into the collector system.

Some rather elaborate matching programs have been undertaken using EDP systems. Clearly, matching procedures, no matter how elaborate, have serious limitations.

What appears to be a good economic fit to an area marketer may not come close to fitting the strategy of the target industry. The marketer may be unaware of changes in industry strategy such as:

1. Launching of new product lines. Each new product line raises the possibility of a new mix of location factors.
2. Shifting transport modes. Significant changes in transportation policy may change the geography of the industry.
3. Introduction of new production method. Such changes, prompted by energy costs or other factors, may change location factors for new facilities.
4. Shifting raw material base. The resource picture changes constantly, with attendant site ramifications.

Dependence on SIC group analyses is perilous in many other ways. Studies made by IDRC have revealed substantial differences in location criteria for facilities within the same SIC category. Clearly, two plants may produce similar products while using substantially different methods and having different site needs.

The marketer must not forget, moreover, that the SIC system applies to establishments, rather than to companies or business enterprises.

To summarize, the marketer should think of industry group selection and matching as a theoretical process that establishes a useful background for the more important screening of specific companies and executives.

Target companies: While one may gain some insight into location decisions by scanning entire industry groups, many factors vary according to the nature of the company itself. Whereas industry statistics may have been very helpful in selecting target industry groups, they may be downright dangerous in choosing companies. Marketers who ignore specific company traits may overlook a large part of their market.

First, the size of the firm is extremely important. Few companies in the small employment bracket are good prospects for buying substantial sites and buildings. Industrial production is concentrated in large firms to a degree far greater than most executives realize.

There are several hundred thousand manufacturing firms in the United

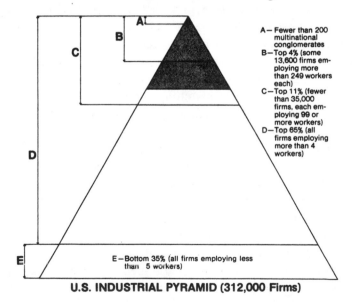

A— Fewer than 200 multinational conglomerates
B—Top 4% (some 13,600 firms employing more than 249 workers each)
C—Top 11% (fewer than 35,000 firms, each employing 99 or more workers)
D—Top 65% (all firms employing more than 4 workers)

E—Bottom 35% (all firms employing less than 5 workers)

U.S. INDUSTRIAL PYRAMID (312,000 Firms)

▨ BASIC GROWTH GROUP

Industry concentration. In the 1950s we noted the extreme concentration of industrial activity. The 1972 Census of Manufacturing gave these numbers, meaning that we could reach most of the significant firms with a publication having a circulation of only a few thousand copies.

NO. OF EMPLOYEES	NO. OF FIRMS	% TOTAL	MILLION $ CAP. EXP.
2500 +	582	0.2	4,840.9
1000-2449	1,527	0.5	3,553.2
500-999	3,483	1.1	3,102.5
250-499	8,031	2.6	3,449.9
100-249	20,807	6.7	3,854.1
50-99	25,628	8.2	2,027.9
20-49	49,892	15.9	1,837.4
10-19	43,736	14.0	657.9
5-9	46,696	14.9	382.8
1-4	112,289	34.8	371.4
TOTAL	312,671	100.0	24,077.7

The latest Census of Manufacturing (1972 General Summary, *dated November 1975) reveals the high degree of concentration in U.S. manufacturing activities.*

States. Census of Manufacturing data show that fewer than 35,000 firms (those employing more than 99 workers each) make up about 11 percent of all manufacturing companies and account for 78 percent of capital expenditures.

Approximately 13,600 firms (those employing more than 249 workers each) make up about four percent of all manufacturing firms and account for 62 percent of capital expenditures.

This "mighty four percent" was shown in the Census of Manufacturers to employ 58 percent of all production workers, to account for 64 percent of value added, to represent 66 percent of capital investment and to use 79 percent of the electric power consumed by industry. The change over the past two decades was only a few percentage points, and it is likely that any change in the future will be small: The concentration will continue.

A similar situation is found among service firms. According to the Census of Selected Service Industries, there were 1.5 million establishments in the United States. However, only 85,000 were multi-unit operations, and just 13,000 had sales over $1 million. This suggests that substantially fewer than one percent of service establishments would constitute significant prospects for expansion.

It is estimated that fewer than 50 firms account for 99 percent of petroleum production; fewer than 150 firms account for 90 percent of chemical sales; and fewer than 160 firms account for 96 percent of transportation equipment.

(While most area/site marketers must face the reality that the great majority of their prospects will be found among large multi-plant operators, marketers should not automatically rule out all other possibilities. For marketers in certain locations it may be worthwhile to direct some attention to small firms, especially those in high-technology categories.

Among the small, high-technology units, growth cycles come and go swiftly, so the marketer must realize that he is shooting at an elusive, fast-moving target. For those rare marketing units that possess strong scientific capabilities, this may constitute, however, a fertile field for future development.)

It is not enough to identify target companies. It is also necessary to identify target projects. A key question at the outset is, "How many projects do the target firms launch each year?"

Again, the statistics lead the casual reader to believe that the market is much bigger than it actually is. During the past several decades annual expenditures for new plants and equipment in the U.S. have grown steadily from less than $20 billion to more than $150 billion.

Theoretically, this is equivalent to 150,000 new projects, each valued at $1 million. However, much of this investment will go into equipment and expansion of existing facilities, and, of course, many new facilities cost far more than $1 million.

The result is that the actual number of significant new projects in the USA each year is estimated to be fewer than 3,000, according to the editorial staffs of *Industrial Development* and *Site Selection Handbook*, which have operated a new plant reporting service for some 20 years.

This estimate suggests that if the new projects were evenly divided among the 50 states, each would receive fewer than 60 new projects per year. Of course, the distribution is not even, with some states getting more than 100 substantial new facilities each year and others fewer than 20.

A look at the chart of capital expenditures for the past two decades makes it apparent that annual dips and spurts are relatively small compared to the total outlay. Capital spending does not reflect boom or bust years with a drastic fluctuation of, say 50 percent. An annual change of more than 10 to 15 percent is unusual.

One should keep this firmly in mind when reading "scare" headlines in the financial press. The banner headline that screams, "New Plants Drop by One-Third," probably means, upon close examination, that the increase for the second quarter of this year, for example, is one-third less than the increase for the same quarter last year. The change in total spending is probably a few percentage points at most.

Despite many differences between companies in their policies and strategies, almost all have one element in common: Before a commitment is made for a large new investment, a comprehensive cost analysis is made. The objective of this study is to estimate the total annual operating cost of the proposed new facility at the various locations proposed.

The analysis should include every major cost item: wages, transportation, materials, services, amortization, utilities, taxes and others. Many facility planners reduce these, for purposes of comparison, to annual cost per unit or pound of product or for each proposed location. These costs should be estimated not only for the current year but also for future years.

The use of the cost analysis is misunderstood by many area executives. Some assume, erroneously, that companies automatically select locations that promise lowest costs.

The real purpose of the cost analysis is to inform top management of the relative importance of the cost factor at various locations as measured against other considerations. If a cost analysis shows a substantial advantage for a particular location, management will probably choose that site. However, if the analysis suggest that costs at several locations are similar — the differences being within the range of error in the analysis — management is then free to make the location decision on the basis of other factors, such as quality of life or even personal preferences of key executives.

The marketer should thus be aware that each new company facility will have a characteristic cost profile which will be a major factor in determining its location. An IDRC survey of new projects located during 1977 gave a composite profile. The reader is warned that the numbers given are the averages for a number of projects.

Most significant, the actual costs for the projects investigated were highly variable. For the manufacturing plant projects, variations were as follows:

Cost Item	Range (% of total costs)
Wages and salaries	3 to 85
Transportation	1 to 32
Utilities	1 to 18
Amortization	1 to 33
Taxes	1 to 20

For warehouses, wages and salaries ranged from 23 to 50 percent of total costs, and transportation was from 20 to 67 percent of the total. For office projects, wages and salaries were 40 to 89 percent of total. There were large differences between the cost profiles of projects in the same SIC category!

These figures suggest the hazard of attempting to identify target firms on the basis of average requirements for groups. Even when dealing with similar types of facilities, cost data may lead to a variety of location decisions.

In the identification of target groups and in obtaining a beginning list of companies, the marketer may have been able to employ EDP systems and sophisticated procedures. Beyond this point, however, target company selection becomes more of a detective game.

Veteran area marketers have many prospecting techniques. Some concentrate on publicly held companies registered with the SEC, since they know that SEC regulations require the companies to disclose significant financial plans. SEC-registered firms must file annual reports, including a "Section 10-K" form; and the SEC issues a list each year of the firms classified alphabetically and by industry groups.

Annual reports to shareholders often provide data on capital expenditure plans, and sometimes refer to plans to expand into a particular market. An area marketer interested in a particular firm can look at annual reports for five to 10 years, keep a tally of capital outlays, subtract outlays for modernizing machinery, and come up with a typical budget. Then, whenever a new report shows an abnormal capital budget, he can be alert to an opportunity.

Other area executives scan newspapers for reports of fires and disasters that might set up a need for replacing a plant. Insurance underwriters may also have access to useful data.

The typical marketer may, over a period of time, collect a substantial number of good company names using these various targeting methods. However, most will be names of firms he suspects might be interested at some time in the future rather than those he knows are interested now.

Thus, he will undertake a program of direct mail promotion and media advertising in order to pull inquiries which will confirm the names of those currently interested.

Target Executives: Site negotiations are not conducted with industry groups nor even with companies. Before a sale can be made, the marketer must almost always come face-to-face with a person. This individual who is engaged in corporate facility planning may fall into one of several classes:

1. He may be one of the elite — a full-time professional facility planner for one of the nation's top 3,000 firms. He and his kind account for about one-half (a crude estimate) of all major site investigations.

2. He may be a part-time facility planner for a medium-to-large compa-

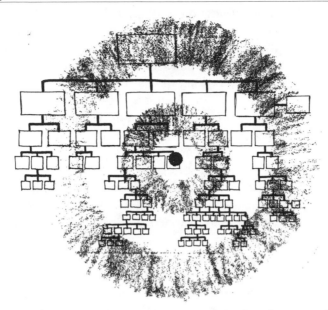

Finding the target executive. Where is the corporate facility planner in this compa-ny? We have identified thousands in the USA where organization structure is more open. Progress is being made in finding the key people in European and Pacific Rim firms.

ny. Normally, he has other duties; but when the firm decides to build a new plant, he will be detailed to handle the plans. He may have never conducted the same kind of site search before. His type accounts for another one-third (a cruder estimate) of the significant new units located.

3. He is a top executive of a small-to-medium-sized company, who is handling the new project while, at the same time, carrying his usual respon-sibilities. In all probability, he has never handled any kind of new facility planning project. He and his kind account for another 20 to 25 percent (another guess) of the market, leaving less than five percent to "others."

Area marketing executives soon learn that each of these groups of executives requires different handling. Those in the latter group are highly unpredictable, for example. Many are entrepreneurs whose style and per-sonality are interwoven with company policy.

In dealing with this group, basic selling skills may weigh as heavily as economic development strategy and techniques. Psychology may loom larg-er than data print-outs.

With the first group, the professional facility planners, it is, however, a different world. Facts, economic planning and corporate strategy count heavily. These executives are more predictable. Thus, it is imperative that the marketer understand how the professional works and what motivates him. A study of this target executive is important not only because he represents a sizable part of the market today, but also because the trend throughout industry is toward greater reliance on such professionals. Thus, the marketer who is unable or unwilling to deal with the professionals on their terms appears to face a rather bleak future.

For those who wish to study corporate facility planners and their habits, there are special opportunities. Unlike the situation that existed in the 1950s, today there is a growing body of literature on the subject, plus significant seminars and other learning opportunities.

This change is due in part to the establishment of the Industrial Development Research Council, established in 1961 as a non-profit national association of professional facility planners and real estate specialists serving major industrial firms.

Elements of a Marketing Plan

For a typical area development organization, the marketing of industrial buildings and sites is the end result of a series of interrelated marketing activities. In most cases, there is research, mapping, literature production, media advertising, direct mail and press relations, as well as telephoning, travel, site inspections and negotiations. These vary in scope and sophistication with the aims and resources of the organization.

Media Advertising: The success or failure of a media advertising program is often determined before the first ad is run. A program based on a negative attitude, unrealistic goals or unsuitable objectives may never have a chance.

First, it is essential that the area marketing executive have an appreciation for the real value of media advertising. It is astonishingly true that a substantial percentage of otherwise well-educated and pragmatic businessmen can wake up to a widely advertised brand of clock radio, shave with a widely advertised razor, brush their teeth with a widely advertised toothpaste, eat a widely advertised cereal, drive a widely advertised car to the office and proclaim that advertising is not important!

The "professional" area marketer who rather smugly asserts that he saves money by not advertising is in much the same position as a charter flight operator who doesn't spend money for aircraft maintenance. While all appears to be going well, he may be heading for a crash.

Equally troubled is the marketing executive who thinks advertising can cure a sick development effort, or work miracles. The safe approach is to define communications goals in terms of certain messages to be conveyed to certain target groups. Advertising can do that and is accountable for such

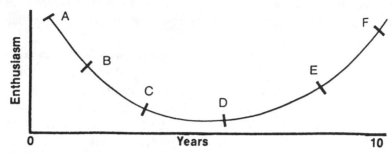

A. Initial expectations high—(probably too high)
B. Money has been spent, no results, enthusiasm wanes.
C. More money spent, time lost, no results, morale low.
D. Even more spent, years gone by, results don't justify, lowest point.
E. Results begin to show, some restoration of morale.
F. Project begins to pay off, morale is high. (Those who were most critical of management during C and D phases now make speeches in which they say, "I've believed in this project from the start.")

Enthusiasm cycle for program. Everyone in the development industry becomes familiar with this cycle. We used the chart to urge sponsors to continue to support programs during the difficult early years.

efforts.

A common pitfall is to establish media advertising goals in terms of overall program objectives, such as new plants, jobs, tax base and investment. While advertising can help mightily in achieving these goals, the total effort may fail due to poor follow-up, unskilled negotiation or a host of other factors unrelated to advertising. Sound program evaluation thus becomes impossible.

Importance of Continuity: Ask a veteran industrial site marketer to name the most important single factor in the success of advertising campaigns, and he will very probably say continuity of effort. Conversely, one of the most common causes of failure is inconsistent and intermittent effort.

The overwhelming logic of this is seen in any analysis of the time span involved in the planning, feasibility analysis and location of major new corporate facilities. Typical projects are in the "gestation" stage for several years, and many projects require lead times of five to ten years.

Hence, shrewd marketers seek to remind the industrial facility planner of their interest throughout the planning period. Further, they know that large multi-plant operators, who constitute the majority of prospects, usually have several large projects in various planning stages at any one point in time.

The marketer who builds a modest but distinct identification and maintains it constantly is usually more successful than the promoter who produces a splashy effort and then fades out of the picture for a long period.

Easier said than done! Many area/site marketers believe in continuity, but few achieve it. In order to obtain numerical data on this, a survey was made of the continuity achieved by advertisers in the *Site Selection Handbook*'s annual "Geo-Economic Index" for a 20-year period.

In the survey, a total of more than 900 advertiser campaigns were scrutinized for continuity. For this large sample composed of all types of firms and organizations, it was found that

- three percent achieved 10 or more years of consecutive insertions;
- 12 percent recorded five to nine years consecutively;
- 14 percent ran three or four years consecutively;
- 17 percent had two consecutive years.

This means that about half of all advertisers ran only one year before interruption! While most returned in subsequent years, their pattern continued to be intermittent.

There are more than 10,000 business periodicals published in the United States. Fewer than 200 are covered by the *Business Periodical Index*, the standard indexing service used by major libraries. Of those publications most likely to report site data, only half a dozen are covered. The information explosion of recent years has placed a tremendous burden on librarians, and they don't have the staff to catalog and index other publications.

A recent list of publications covered by the *Business Periodical Index* included:

Business Week
Forbes
Fortune
Harvard Business Review
Nation's Business
Site Selection and Industrial Development

Not included were:
American Industrial Properties Report
Area Development
Plant Location
Plants, Sites and Parks

We will mention a few factors that relate specifically to ads run by area marketers. We will argue that whether the goal is to sell a building, a site or an area, the essential element is location. Thus, the ad should always specify the location involved.

A common error is to assume that everyone knows where Columbus is. Even in the case of a town whose name is not duplicated elsewhere, the name of the town may not describe the location enough. When in doubt, the marketer should include a map. Our feeling is that 90 percent of all ads for local areas, sites and buildings should include maps. In many cases, these need to be only a postage-stamp-sized inset.

A second point about which we are almost fanatic is that ads that seek to draw response should include a clearly legible "identification block" that contains:

1. The name of the organization or agency
2. The name of the person to contact and his/her title
3. Postal address and street address
4. Telephone number, with area code

This identification block is not the place to get cute with confusing graphics or extraneous messages. By the time the reader gets to this point, the copy writers and graphic designers have already achieved their purpose!

Inquiry response and follow up: Handling the many questions that arise relative to inquiry response challenges the professional competence and composure of the development executive. Experienced professionals know that inquiries generated by specific advertising programs are usually important but seldom all-important. They have learned to relate advertising to other functions, to recognize their competitive position, and otherwise to make intelligent evaluations.

However, most professional development executives must report to a board of directors or governing body made up of non-professionals and/or political appointees who lack experience or insight relative to advertising for development. Worse, some board members may have experience with consumer advertising and attempt to apply it to the development program.

The result is that completely unrealistic expectations are raised. Those who control the purse strings may, despite admonitions from the professional staff, anticipate that relatively modest advertising outlays will produce large and immediate returns.

The board member who operates a retail business knows that he can run an ad on Thursday and see the response in his store on Saturday. It is hard for him to understand that one cannot always run a site ad this week and spend next week showing the property to the qualified prospects who respond.

The distinct and often extremely frustrating aspects of the site market are difficult to explain, even to sophisticated managers. For example, an executive with jurisdiction over several programs, such as tourism, conventions and industrial development, cannot help wondering why the travel ads are bringing bushels of replies while the industry ads pull only a trickle.

Having put inquiry response in perspective, we cannot, however, overlook the fact that in most programs inquiries are important. How, then, can an advertising effort be geared to produce more direct response?

First, the advertiser should look to the things that make any ad effective, including the size and use of color. Beyond these basic considerations, we believe there are certain specific things that produce better response from facility planners, as outlined here:

1. Offer a useful research report.
2. Offer a site map or guide.
3. Offer a specific professional service of value.
4. Stress that service is offered without obligation.
5. Mention the offer in the ad headline.
6. Include a specific description of what is offered.
7. how a photo or sketch of what is offered.
8. Include a testimonial from a corporate executive.
9. Provide a telephone number.
10. Provide a coupon.

It is astonishing to find that so few of the advertisers who say that inquiries are important to them use these basic approaches to generating direct response.

What Is The Future Of Area/Site Marketing?

Whatever the problems, the inescapable fact is that there is a huge economic development job waiting to be done.

The burgeoning billions of human beings populating the earth must, at the least, be fed and clothed. And few will settle for just that. The magnitude of this supply task demands a continuation of the development of large-scale projects.

Thus, we have in the future great needs. Throughout recorded history, great needs have meant great opportunities. And great opportunities breed great competition. We must expect, therefore, that the future will see the most intensive competition for economic development ever conceived — competition involving more than 100 nations, every state and province, every city and community. It will surely be a case of survival of the fittest as measured by development capability.

Let no one suggest that marketing will not be a major factor! Even the communist nations are moving toward large marketing programs to compete in the global battle for economic position. There appears absolutely no reason to anticipate that competition — hence marketing — will diminish in any major market, be it international, national or regional.

Ladies and gentlemen, sharpen your pencils!

1983 Excerpt	"Geo-Economics: A New Science in the Service Of Mankind." A study for the Industrial Development Research Council. The new geo-economic discipline is directly responsible for significant achievements in the planning and implementation of a large number of projects which have created jobs and other benefits for societies around the world. Yet the new technical capability is little known or appreciated outside the circle of those who practice it. May 1983. 45pp. IDRC Research Report #31.

A definition: *Geo-Economics is the science of integrating investment strategies with the resources and objectives of specific geographic entities to achieve appropriate economic development and, thus, a better quality of life.*

The two main elements of Geo-Economics are:
1. Corporate facility planning, location analysis and site selection aimed at finding optimum locations for new investments; and
2. Area planning, promotion and development aimed at attracting investment and creating jobs.

Hidden Factor in Economic Growth?

Economic growth is a high priority goal of most of the world's nations. It is the continuing objective of successful businesses and industries. Most of the world's citizens depend on it for their job security, income growth and future social benefits.

Even so, as recently as the middle of this century the economic development of geographic areas, states and nations was an unsystematic, non-scientific process characterized by a high failure rate and a low return on investment. During the last several decades, however, there has emerged a new science of geo-economic development which has led to improvement of area strategies, a higher success rate for new ventures and greater returns for both public and private sectors.

The new geo-economic discipline is directly responsible for significant achievements in the planning and implementation of a large number of projects which have created jobs and other benefits for societies around the world. The new literature of geo-economics, which documents these strides, is now on record in official libraries of many nations.

Yet the new technical capability is little known or appreciated outside the circle of those who practice it. There is virtually no reference to the discipline in the mainstream of economic or scientific literature. A scan of some of the more prominent contributions of scholars, ranging from Friedman, Tobin and Galbraith to Smith and Keynes, suggests the possibility of general approval of a geo-economic concept but affords little specific confirmation.

This is interesting, but not particularly significant, since those who work in the field and those who travel in academic circles often are not in communication. Further, those working in long-established fields may quite naturally view those working in new and unproven areas with apathy or skepticism.

As a matter of fact, some may challenge the assertion that the art of area economic development and industrial growth stimulation has progressed to the point that we may properly recognize it as a new branch of science. It is true that, to date, there have been few, if any, discoveries that could be described as spectacular. Evolution, not revolution, has been the pattern.

We believe it is clear, however, that a considerable number of significant findings have been recorded. To an impressive degree, area economic development and corporate growth management have been systematized. We hope that those who take the time to familiarize themselves with the scope and diversity of work already done will concur that something new has been added to the spectrum of sciences serving mankind.

Typical studies produced by classical economists attribute real growth to such traditional factors as economies of scale, greater capital investment per worker, improved productivity and advances in technology. We do not challenge the significance of these factors; however, we submit that new "hidden" geo-economic factors may have contributed much to real growth in the past quarter century.

One of the new factors is the geographic competition for new investment led by local, state and national development organizations. Such programs, which were virtually nonexistent a few decades ago, have greatly improved the process by which new industrial facilities are developed, leading to substantial improvements in productivity. While there was, no doubt, a degree of competition in the past, the extent and quality of competition has been vastly improved.

Today, there is, within most states, organized competition among cities, counties and local areas. Within the U.S. and many other large nations, there is also intense competition among states or provinces. Globally, there is additional competition among nations.

(It is interesting to note that widespread competition at the local and state levels is found only in the free nations. This is an important advantage enjoyed by the West in competition with Socialist nations of the Soviet bloc, where central planning substitutes for competition in determining internal area growth patterns.)

Another geo-economic factor generally overlooked is the development within major corporations of new professional skills for planning and locating new facilities. These programs, which have advanced on a broad front during the past 20 years, have produced substantial improvements in such functions as selection of sites and solutions to environmental problems. Important results have been recorded in reduced costs or improved efficiencies in gathering raw materials, transporting goods, recruiting labor force and controlling energy costs.

When the contribution to productivity of organized area competition is added to that of improved corporate planning, the total result is certainly substantial. In fact, these "unrecognized" factors may be as important as any industrial advance of recent times.

1987
Excerpt

"New Plant Locations." A review and forecast. Monograph. 1987. 10 pp.

New corporate facilities bring to the chosen site area new investment, new jobs and new economic opportunities. While some residents may perceive negative aspects, the area usually enjoys improved community services and other significant benefits.

Thus, the announcement of a new facility is usually big news in the immediate area of the plant site. And, in some cases, the news may be significant, nationally or internationally.

For those in the development business, reports of new plant locations are particularly important — they constitute a scoreboard for the contestants in a high-stakes race.

To satisfy such interests, Conway Data began developing a new plant reporting service more than 25 years ago. The system has grown and now involves some 500+ volunteers working in state and metro development organizations and development departments of railroads, utilities and banks throughout the country.

Reports from these volunteers, plus data from many other sources, flow to our Atlanta headquarters where each report is entered in our data base. Duplications are eliminated, and entries are conformed to uniform criteria.

Every other month a list of entries is published in computer print-out format. Once a year the entries are tallied, and a summary is published in our *Site Selection Handbook.*

A word of warning! Before any numbers are presented, we must caution readers to be careful in seeking to draw sweeping conclusions from new plant reports. It is easy to interpret data and attach undue significance to selected items.

Part of the problem lies in imperfections in the reporting system, and part is due to the sporadic and inconsistent pattern of location decisions.

As to the system, we report new facilities as soon as we first hear about them. Some are picked up when a corporate decision is made to build, others are caught when ground is broken, and some are entered when operations start. Since some large projects have a "gestation" period of several years, this contributes to an inconsistency in reporting.

Also, we depend on tallies made by many diverse groups, some of which report monthly, some quarterly and others that report at random intervals. Further, there are inconsistencies in criteria, despite years of effort to obtain uniformity.

Finally, there may be a psychological problem. It is suspected that states and areas that do not fare well in a certain time period may be less energetic in reporting than those that have high numbers to display.

For these reasons, it is usually meaningless to look at new plant reports for any brief period and attempt to draw comparisons among states and areas. Even a 12-month summary may be misleading.

That is why we have prepared this three-year tally. Over a period of several years many of the reporting inconsistencies tend to balance out, and the results have more significance.

C. Bibliography

The following are citations of McKinley Conway's writings on this chapter's subject. As this book goes to press work is underway to make many of these items available to researchers. To check status, look for a file on GeoTEAM/IDRCNET or telephone GeoTEAM/Fax at (404) 453-4200 for a free catalog.

1. "Geographical Distribution of Engineering Research and Related Industries in the United States." Southeastern Research Institute. 1948. 74 pp. Reprinted 1987 as IDRC research study number 37.
2. "Directory of Engineering Data Sources." Southeastern Research Institute, 1948, 64 pp. 22 cm. A guide to American literature in engineering and related sciences.
3. "Industrial Research in Georgia." Southern Assn. of Science and Industry, Atlanta, Sept. 15, 1949. 9 pp.
4. "Survey of Southern Organizations." Southern Assn. of Science and Industry, Atlanta, April 24, 1950, 13 pp.
5. "Science and Insurance," *The Insurance Index*, Dunne Publications, Louisville, Ky., 1951.
6. "Research, The South's New Resource." Georgia Engineering Society. Atlanta, Jan. 29, 1951.
7. "Directory of Southern Research Services and Facilities," *Journal of Southern Research*, Atlanta. Jan.-Feb., 1951. pp. 7-14.
8. "The Banker and the Scientist," *Southern Banker*, McFadden Publications, Atlanta, Aug. 1951, pp. 22-23.
9. "The Secret of Southern Progress," *Journal of Southern Research*, Sept.-Oct., 1951, pp. 11-16.
10. "Super Weapons in the Land of Cotton," *Think*, International Business Machines, New York, Oct. 1951.
11. "Are Science and Socialism Inseparable?" *Journal of Southern Research*, Atlanta. Nov.-Dec., 1951, pp. 11-12.
12. "Dynamic New Forces Mold South's Future," *Southern Industrial Directory*, 1952. 60 pp.
13. "The Use of Research in Industrial Development," annual Southern industrial Development Conference. Charlotte, N.C., Oct. 27, 1952.
14. "Automatic Processes for Southern Industry," *Journal of Southern Research*, Atlanta. Sept.-Oct. 1952. pp. 22-24.
15. "The Value of Research in Industrial Development," *Journal of Southern Research*, Atlanta. Nov.-Dec. 1952, pp. 29-31.
16. "Ten Point Program for South," *Southern Industrial Directory*, Atlanta. 1953. 80 pp.
17. "Modern Research Progress in the South." (Presented before Food and Drug Law Forum, Emory University, in cooperation with the Food Law Institute, Atlanta, May 7, 1953) *The Food, Drug, Cosmetic Law Journal*, Commerce Clearing House, Chicago, July 1953. pp. 445-451.
18. "Amazing Expansion of Industry," *Editor and Publisher*, Oct. 31, 1953. pp. 174-176, 188.
19. "To Grow or Not to Grow." Industrial Development Symposium. Indiana State Commercial Executives Assn., Michigan City, Ind. May 24, 1954.
20. "Regionalism and Regional Development," *Southern Chemical Industry*, Atlanta. May-June 1954. p. 6.
21. "Paint Industry Survey," (index of manufacturers of paint and allied products), *Southern Chemical Industry*, Sept.-Oct 1954. pp. 7-21.
22. "Opportunities for Small Manufacturers," Southern Farm Equipment Manufacturers Assn., Atlanta. Oct. 1, 1954.
23. "The Value of Libraries in Industrial Research," Southeastern Library Assn. 16th biennial conference. Atlanta, Oct. 1, 1954.
24. "Area Development Activities Across the U.S.," Western Area Development Conference, San Francisco, Stanford Research Institute. Nov. 17, 1954.
25. "Area Development Activities Across the U.S.," Long Beach Chamber of Commerce, Long Beach, Calif., Nov. 22, 1954.
26. "Chemical Industry Survey — Soap and Allied Products," *Southern Chemical Industry*, Nov.-Dec. 1954. pp. 7-16.
27. "Glass-making Industry in the South," *Southern Chemical Industry*, March-April, 1955. pp. 7-10.
28. "Industrial Progress Creates New Opportunities for the Legal Profession," Southeastern Law Review Conference, Emory University, Atlanta. April 29, 1955.
29. "Nationwide Competition in *Industrial Development*." Proceedings of Western Area Development Conference, Sept. 8-9, 1955, Portland, Ore., conducted by Stanford Research Institute, Menlo Park, Calif. pp. 19-27.
30. "Public Relations Program for the South," (remarks on receiving Advertising Federation

of America award for regional program) Birmingham, Ala., Sept. 13, 1955.

31. "How to Pick Growth Firms," *Industrial Development.* Sept.-Oct., 1955. pp. 7-10.

32. "The Research Approach to Promotion and Advertising." Southern Industrial Development Council, Jacksonville, Fla., Oct. 31, 1955.

33. "Ten Reasons for Southern Economic Progress," *Manufacturers Record.* (Blue Book Supplement). Atlanta, 1956. pp. 9-14.

34. "The Atom - Multi-billion Southern Industry," *Manufacturers Record,* Jan. 1956. pp. 11-18.

35. "Building Blocks for Better Community Development," Great Lakes States Industrial Development Council, Madison, Wis., Jan. 6, 1956.

36. "Solar Energy Research Opens New Opportunities for South," *Manufacturers Record,* Atlanta. Feb. 1956. pp. 20-22.

37. "Agriculture and Industry: Partners in Southern progress," 53rd annual meeting, Assn. of Southern Agricultural Workers, Atlanta, Feb. 6, 1956.

38. "South Gains in Electronics," *Manufacturers Record,* April, 1956. pp. 9-13.

39. "Aircraft and Missile Industry (in South)," *Manufacturers Record,* July, 1956. pp. 8-17.

40. "Selecting, Contacting and Selling Industrial Prospects," Conference on Industrial Development, Midwest Research Institute, Kansas City, Mo., Sept. 7, 1956.

41. "Optimism is Essential," Oklahoma Development Council, Tulsa, Nov. 14, 1956.

42. "Advertising and Direct Mail in Industrial Development," Southern Assn. of State Planning and Development Agencies. Oklahoma City, Okla., Nov. 15, 1956.

43. "Selecting, Contacting and Selling Industrial Prospects," Iowa Industrial Development Clinic, Iowa Development Commission. Des Moines, Iowa. Jan. 24, 1957.

44. "Increased Responsibility of the Chamber of Commerce in Industrial Development," American Chamber of Commerce Executives, annual conference, Boston, Oct. 23, 1956. *Journal of American Chamber of Commerce Executives,* Washington, D.C., Jan. 1957, pp. 23-24.

45. "Selecting, Contacting and Selling Industrial Prospects," Louisiana Industrial Development Conference, Shreveport, La., Feb. 7, 1957.

46. "The Phenomenon of Growth," Southern Industrial Editors Assn., Atlanta, Mar. 26, 1957.

47. "New Horizons for the Industrial Development Profession," American Industrial Development Council, 32nd annual meeting, Chicago, April 1, 1957.

48. "Nationwide Competition between Communities," How to Get Ready for Industry Conference, General Extension Division of Florida, Avon Park. April 24, 1957.

49. "The Intense Competition in Industrial Development," First Pennsylvania Industrial Development Clinic, Harrisburg, Pa., May 16, 1957.

50. "Competition in Industrial Development," South Texas Industrial Development Conference, San Antonio, Texas, June 17, 1957.

51. "Competition in Industrial Development," Arizona Development Luncheon, Phoenix, June 18, 1957.

52. "Cooperation between Public and Private Development Agencies," Proceedings of the Southern Assn. of State Planning and Development Agencies Point Clear Conference, Oct. 10, 1957.

53. *Gold Mine on Main Street,* documentary film script. 16mm, full-color, 25-min. Industrial Sound Films, Atlanta, 1958.

54. "Optimism Can Be Justified," *Southern Advertising and Publishing,* Atlanta, April, 1958.

55. Introduction and premiere of film, *Gold Mine on Main Street,* American Industrial Development Council, April 14, 1958, Atlanta.

56. "Improving the Effectiveness of Development Programs," Annual Meeting of American Railway Development Assn., Cincinnati, Ohio. April 28, 1958.

57. "On the Brighter Side," (economic outlook), *The Editors Forum,* Georgia Press Assn., May, 1958, pp. 4-S.

58. "The 'Forward Look' in Industrial Development," address before the New England Council annual industrial development dinner, Springfield, Mass., May 21, 1958.

59. "Increasing the Effectiveness of Industrial Development Activities," American Management Assn. Seminar, Colgate University, Hamilton, N.Y., Aug. 4-8, 1958.

60. "Industrial Progress in the South," a report to the Southern Governors Conference, from the Committee on *Industrial Development.* Lexington, Ky., Sept. 24, 1958. 16 pp.

61. "The South Reports to the Nation," *Industrial Development,* (Blue Book edition) 1959.

pp. 6-9.
62. "Industrial Land Prices" (a national survey), *Industrial Development,* Atlanta, Jan. 1959. pp. 11-14.
63. "Key Location Factors for Washington," Washington D.C. Board of Trade. Feb. 9, 1959.
64. "The Registered Community Audit," *Industrial Development,* April 1959. pp. 6-9. (A proposed uniform format for analyzing community economic potential.)
65. "The South's Competitive Position," report to the Southern Governors Conference, presented by the Committee on Industrial Development, Asheville, N.C. Oct. 13, 1959. 16 pp.
66. "Prospects, Advertising" (marketing electric utility services), Edison Electric Institute, Sixth Annual Area Development Workshop, Phoenix, Ariz. Oct. 21, 1959.
67. "The State of Hawaii" (economic potential of statehood), *Industrial Development,* Dec. 1959. pp. 17-32.
68. *Area Development: A Guide For Community Leaders.* 1960. 2 vols. With Frank Stedman. Vol. I. Understanding the Growth Process, Organizing for Area Development, Area and Community Analysis, Planning and Zoning, Financing, Buildings, Selling, Future Trends. 278 pp. Vol. II. Bibliography. 142 pp.
69. "Washington's Future in Industrial Development," The Governor's Industrial Development Banquet. Seattle. Mar. 9, 1960.
70. "National Roundup of Industrial Development Activity," American Industrial Development Council, 35th annual conference, Atlantic City, N.J. March 29, 1960.
71. "The Factors for Expansion Planning," *Industrial Development, Site Selection Handbook* supplement. Oct. 1960. pp. 64-76.
72. "What's Wrong with Industrial Development in the South?" Southern Industrial Development Council, Little Rock, Ark., Oct. 24, 1960.
73. "Development Trends Here and Abroad," Missouri Industrial Development Conference, Missouri Resources and Development Commission, Jefferson City. Oct. 31, 1960.
74. "Reference Value — Success Factor in Development Advertising," *Industrial Development,* Atlanta. May, 1961. pp. 63-79. Includes bibliography.
75. "Success Factors in Industrial Development Advertising," Assn. of Railroad Advertising Managers, New Orleans, May 9, 1961.
76. "North Dakota: Surprising Growth and Potential," *Industrial Development.* Atlanta. Sept. 1961. pp. 17-48.
77. "New Techniques of Regional Industrial Advertising," Southern Assn. of State Planning and Development Agencies annual meeting, Oct. 11, 1961, Atlanta.
78. "The Pressure Is on (competition for new industry)," Georgia State Chamber of Commerce, luncheon address. Atlanta, Dec. 13, 1961.
79. "The Space Age Moves South," *Industrial Development* (54th annual "Blue Book of Southern Progress" edition). 1962. pp. 4-13.
80. "Getting the Most from Your Promotion Budget," ("Advertising Research Newsletter," 1956) *Area Digest.* Fall 1962. pp. 40-43.
81. "R&D Expansion Creates New Image for Long Island," Industrial Development. Nov. 1962. pp. 57-72.
82. "The Development Decade," Business Lecture Series, Georgia State College, Atlanta, Nov. 29, 1962.
83. "State and Provincial Development Agencies" (2nd annual study), *Industrial Development.* Feb. 1963. pp 6-16. Includes directory. See also Aug. 1961.
84. What Research Can Do for Overall Community Development, annual management conference, American Chamber of Commerce Executives, Atlanta, Oct. 29, 1963.
85. "Preparing Your Community for Industrial Development," 1964-68. (Series of monographs prepared for Agency for International Development). In Spanish and Portuguese:
    1. "What Development Means to Your Community." 16 pp.
    2. "Sites and Buildings." 16 pp.
    3. "Local Industrial Development Corporations." 16 pp.
    4. "The War against Time." 16 pp.
    5. "Filling the Prospect Gap." 16 pp.
    6. "Improving the Business Climate." 16 pp.
86. "Progress Report on the AID/PEP Program." (Private enterprise promotion in Latin America). 1965. 68 pp. (Project for Agency for International Development).
87. *Fomento! Organizing for Progress,* Film script for 16mm full color and sound. 28 mins.

English, Spanish, Portuguese. 1965. (Sponsored by Agency for International Development).

88. "Project LAND: Locations in Appalachia for New Development." Feb. 1965. 30 pp.

89. "Area and Industrial Development (El Desarrollo Regional e Industrial), Proceedings of the First Interamerican Seminar on the Organization and Promotion of Private Enterprise," June 15-18, 1965. Caracas, Venezuela. Published in Spanish. 124 pp. Project for Agency for International Development.

90. *Area Development Organizations.* Principles of organizing for development. The pyramid concept. Secret of U.S. progress. Organizations above the state level. State development organizations. Local development organizations. Rural community improvement organizations. Supporting organizations. 1966. 331 pp. includes geographical index of several thousand U.S. organizations.

91. "Organizing for Development: the Pyramid Concept." 1967. 24 pp. illus. (Issued also in Spanish and Portuguese). Sponsored by Agency for International Development.

92. "Community Audit and Area Data Outline," 1967. 32 pp. (Issued in English and Spanish.) Sponsored by Agency for International Development.

93. "Does Development Effort Pay?" Report shows $65 to $1 return. One of the things we like best about the Puerto Rican program is that officials have been alert enough to keep a running tally on the amount of money invested in the development effort and the benefits enjoyed. *Industrial Development.* March-April 1967. p. 1.

94. "State Science Programs," Joint Army-Navy Research Reserve Seminar, Lockheed-Georgia Research Laboratory, April 15, 1967.

95. "Role of Science in the Economic Development of Georgia," annual banquet, Georgia Academy of Science. Stone Mountain, Ga., April 28, 1967.

96. "A Research Program for Industry," Industrial Development Research Council. Washington, D.C., May 19, 1967.

97. "The Management of and Response to Urbanization in the South: Industrial Viewpoint," Southern Regional Conference on Urbanization, University of Georgia and North Carolina State University, Atlanta, May 31, 1967.

98. "The Most Underrated Generation in American History," (commencement address) Dekalb College, Decatur, Ga., June 3, 1967.

99. "The War against Time: Improving the Time Cycle in Development," Interamerican development seminar, Arequipa, Peru, July 12, 1967. Agency for International Development.

100. *Study of the Potential Traffic for the Proposed Chattahoochee River Navigation Channel to Atlanta,* Sept. 1967. 140 pp. plus appendix.

101. "AID at the Crossroads!" June 1968. 56 pp. illus.

102. "A Feasibility Study for a Regional Slaughterhouse in Carazo, Nicaragua." For Agency for International Development. Feb. 1968. 53 pp. illus.

103. "Travel Investment, a New Guide to Investment Opportunities in Resort, Recreation and Hospitality Facilities," Nov. 1968, pp. 2-3 (foreword to new reference publication), 128 pp.

104. "Travel Investment Study for the Economic Development Council of Northeast Pennsylvania", Dec. 1968. 30 pp.

105. "The AID/PEP Program for Mobilizing Private Enterprise and Local Initiative in Latin America." A. Short-term orientation tours. B. Interamerican development seminars. C. Working materials. D. Investment promotion reports. E. U.S. development specialists. F. Interns. (Summary Report).Dec. 1968.138 pp. illus. Appendix. Sponsored by the Agency for International Development.

106. "Mobilizing Private Enterprise and Local Initiative in Latin America: the AID/PEP Program," Dec. 1968. 22 pp.

107. *Travel Investment Opportunity: "Otocsin" Proposed Resort Complex, Clearfield County, Pa.* For Commonwealth of Pennsylvania. March 1969, 91 pp. illus.

108. *Travel Investment Study: Moraine Reservoir, Butler County, Pa., and Shenango Reservoir, Mercer County, Pa.* For Commonwealth of Pennsylvania. April 1969, 73 pp. illus.

109. *Travel Investment Opportunity: Prince Gallitzen State Park, Cambria County, Pa.* For Commonwealth of Pennsylvania. April 1969. 83 pp. illus.

110. *Travel Investment Study: Black Moshannon State Park and Blanchard Reservoir, Centre County, Pa.* For Commonwealth of Pennsylvania. May 1969. 51 pp. illus.

111. *Travel Investment Study: Kinzua Dam — Allegheny National Forest, Warren and Forest Counties, Pa.* For Commonwealth of Pennsylvania. June 1969. 51 pp.

112. *Travel Investment Study: Ohiopyle-Great Meadows, Fayette County, Pa.* For Commonwealth of Pennsylvania. June 1969. 40 pp.

113. *Summary of Investor Reaction to Pennsylvania's Travel Investment Opportunities.* For Commonwealth of Pennsylvania. Oct. 15, 1969. 153 pp.

114. "New Trends in Travel Investment," *Texas Realtor,* June 1970. Ten reasons large diversified firms go into real estate investments.

115. *A Management Concept for the Lake Lanier Islands.* A guide to investor/concessionaire arrangements and operating policies. 1970. 100 pp.

116. *Survey of Community Audit Programs.* A study for the Industrial Development Research Council. May 1971.

117. "The War against the Clock." Everyone in the development field today is engaged in an uphill struggle against the most relentless enemy of all — time. Never in the history of the profession have there been so many time-consuming pre-development activities. And never has the monetary cost of time been so great. *Site Selection.* 1974. p. 242.

118. "True Professionals Give Due Credit." The magazine (not named) would have its readers believe that it was the pioneer in development of a comprehensive plant location checklist or community audit. The comprehensive checklist was published here in ID in our October 1957 issue nearly 10 years before our rival. *Industrial Development.* Jan 1975. p 2.

119. *New Industries of the Seventies.* 1978. 302 pp. With Linda L. Liston.

120. *Marketing Industrial Buildings and Sites.* Introduction: promotion is not a dirty word! The sellers: promotion and marketing organizations. The customers: target industry groups, companies, executives. Elements of a marketing plan. Media advertising. Special publications. Selling a specific building or site. Marketing professional services. Outlook for the future. 1980. 358 pp. Hard cover.

121. *Geo-Economics: A New Science in the Service of Mankind.* A study for the Industrial Development Research Council. The new geo-economic discipline is directly responsible for significant achievements in the planning and implementation of a large number of projects which have created jobs and other benefits for societies around the world. Yet the new technical capability is little known or appreciated outside the circle of those who practice it. May 1983. 45 pp.

122. "Geo-Economics: A New Science in the Service of Mankind." Monograph. 5pp. Excerpted from IDRC Research Report No. 31.

123. "The Geo-Economists: A New Profession for the Market of Jobs," *The Futurist.* World Future Society. April 1984. pp. 58-59.

124. "Geo-Economics: The Emerging Science." The first of a series which outlines the origin, present scope, and future of a new science which is significant for all professionals involved in the facility planning profession. *Industrial Development.* Sept.-Oct. 1984. pp. 4-7.

125. "Geo-Economics and Corporate Asset Management." A summary of the early efforts to develop the subscience of corporate growth planning and real property management. *Industrial Development.* Nov.-Dec. 1984. pp. 14-19.

126. "New Plant Locations." A review and forecast. Monograph. 1987. 10 pp.

127. "Geo-economics Today and Tomorrow." Quantification of the key variables in the science of geo-economics is of paramount importance to efficient industrial development. A great deal of work remains. Building data bases and improving our research methods are high priorities. Paper for IDRC Orlando conference. *Industrial Development.* March-April 1987. pp. 304-306.

128. "The New Basic Industries — Have You Revised Your Strategy?" A recent IDRC seminar discussed the concept that knowledge is now the world currency, and the top facility location factor is where the brains are. To this we add that factories that produce ideas and data are the new basic industries. *Site Selection.* April 1987. p. 252.

129. "Privatization — Be Sure to Read the Instructions!" The tried and true American private enterprise system that we couldn't give away 25 years ago has a new name: "privatization." And, it's suddenly the straw at which many a floundering socialist bureaucrat from darkest Africa to main street USA is grasping. Even Soviet planners are succumbing to the charm of the "new" concept. *Site Selection.* Oct.1987. p. 956.

130. "Changes in the South." When I was a student at Georgia Tech during the late 1930s Gwinnett County was a place out in the country where people grew cotton. Now my neighbors create satellite equipment and other sophisticated systems for customers around the world. *Gwinnett Daily News.* June 15, 1988.

131. "Geo-Economics: A New Science in the Service of Mankind." Definition: geo-economics is the science of integrating investment strategies with the resources and objectives of specific geographic entities to achieve appropriate economic development and, thus, a better quality of life. Pamphlet. 1988.

132. "Three Strong Forces Allied for the Advancement of the Vital New Science of Geo-economics." Pamphlet. 1988.

133. "Are Latin American Investment Programs Forever Comatose?" During the past 20 years, while many nations sharpened their skills at attracting outside investment, the nations of Latin America have become less effective. Many have virtually dropped out of competition — abandoning programs that were once very promising. *Site Selection.* Dec. 1989. p. 1464.

134. "Area Development Executives and Global Super Projects." Those who provide the leadership for economic development programs around the world are very special. They are creative people who necessarily and routinely make bold development plans. They are not afraid to dream. Pamphlet for World Development Council. 1991.

135. "Engineers, Builders and Global Super Projects." A conservative estimate indicates that the world will add one billion more people by the year 2000. What a monumental challenge for the construction industry! The world must have new productive facilities built on a scale to match its needs. Pamphlet for the World Development Council. 1991.

136. Paper for Maryland Industrial Development Association special publication.

2
Forum Building.
Birth of the IDRC

Chapter 2

A. Recent Comments

Managing a Business
Understanding Corporate Differences
Location Factors Checklist
Code of Ethics
Research Program
Launching Automated Systems
A Strong Organization
Where Now?

B. Excerpts

The IDRC is Launched. *Industrial Development,* August 1961
The IDRC Code of Ethics, 1981
"Weighing Development Factors for the High-Tech Age," *Site Selection*, April 1986
Terror, *Site Selection*, August 1986
Editorials:
* "Are you Building Your Own Personal Data Base?" *Gwinnett Daily News*, June 1988
* "Where Will You Land After the Merger?" *Site Selection*, December 1988
* "Why Joe Lost His Job." *Site Selection*, April 1988
* "Are you a Take-Over Target?" *Site Selection*, February 1989
* "Show us your Company Map!" *Site Selection*, October 1990
* "Had your Annual Check-up?" *Site Selection*, December 1990
* "Are You Preparing for Global Operations?" *Site Selection*, April 1991
* "Don't be Misled about Real Estate Future." *Site Selection*, August 1991
* "Are You Waging Guerrilla Warfare?" *Site Selection*, October 1991
* "Do you have a Strategic Plan?" *Site Selection*, June 1992
* "How Safe Are Your Facilities?" *Site Selection*, December 1992
* "CEOs Come In All Shapes." *Site Selection*, June 1993
* "This is a Test! In Asset Management." *Site Selection*, August 1993

C. Bibliography

A. Recent comments

The scene one wintry morning was the old Roosevelt Hotel in New York. There was a conference room which could be entered only via a small antechamber. The participants came into the first room, had their credentials checked and then were admitted to the inner sanctum.

There were no identification badges and no list of attendees. Several of the participants revealed their identity only to me — the one staff member handling the meeting. After a few minutes there were some 10 or 12 men scated around the table, staring at one another suspiciously.

The discussion began slowly but picked up. After several hours most, but not all, of the attendees had joined in. When it broke up, the consensus was that it was a good meeting. However, there were no media reports, nor were any proceedings or minutes published. No names were kept.

Was it a CIA session, or perhaps a group of conspirators from the Middle East? No, it was a group plotting to organize an association to be called the Industrial Development Research Council.

When I relate this history to people today, they find it difficult to believe that we operated under such a cloak of secrecy. Let me assure you, however, that it is true.

At that point in time most major industrial firms carried out expansion plans as if they were planning the Normandy invasion. It was assumed that secrecy was absolutely essential — a leak might lead to catastrophic failure.

I still remember one man who represented a firm in the top 10 on the *Fortune* 500 list who boasted that he could go into a community, do a survey and select a site without anyone in the community knowing he had been there. He got location data not from the economic development offices but from taxi drivers and waitresses.

Why such an absurd approach? First, there was fear of what competitors would do. Then there was concern that if an area knew a new plant was coming, land prices would shoot up. And, the nosy news media people would be a nuisance.

Of course, all of those fears were real then and they remain so today. We recognize the need for protecting the confidentiality of corporate facility plans as related to a specific project.

(In later years, we came to be a key element in a corporate grapevine.

Members learned that they could call and ask for a particular item of information or an opinion about a location without risk of a leak.

We knew how important this confidentiality was and we were very careful to avoid leaks. All calls of this nature came to me personally. While I might use other staff members to gather information, I was the only one who knew what or who it was for.

We operated this way for about 25 years and, to my knowledge, never had a project leaked.)

What that handful of executives meeting at the Roosevelt believed was that responsible executives could come together and discuss matters of mutual interest without compromising company plans. In fact, it was argued that such a forum could be beneficial both to the executives and to their companies.

That's what we knew and what led to that organizing session.

During the 1950s we had attended many meetings of area development executives. There were state and regional groups and, at the national level, there was the American Industrial Development Council (now AEDC).

We had watched these groups grow in usefulness. They served the area development service providers well. Yet, there was a basic frustration. These groups met and talked about the corporate facility planners, but these much-sought-after executives were not present.

It was somewhat like anti-submarine warfare. The area people knew there were targets out there but they couldn't see them and, hence, they didn't know much about them.

The idea of correcting this situation came to me in the mid-1950s and became more focused late in the decade. During those years I identified several key industry executives, persuaded them to help, and set up the New York meeting.

My motivation was to have access to expert thinking in planning the content of our publications. It was a good trade-off, with everybody winning.

By 1961 we were ready. The first official meeting of IDRC was scheduled for the Roosevelt on October 24. The January 1962 issue of *Industrial Development* carried a summary report, with names of the key people.

I wish every current member of IDRC could have attended that first meeting. They would have seen that IDRC was founded by far-sighted people who laid a very solid intellectual foundation for the association.

Did we have visions of a very large organization having a thousand or more members and an annual budget of several million dollars? No, no and no.

We were thinking in terms of a small, close-knit group that would have significant influence through the power of good thinking. We were long on quality but very short on quantity.

Without really being aware of it, we set the strategy that was to serve IDRC well for coming decades. We started with outstanding people and they attracted other good people. Those good people brought others, and so it grew.

But there were plenty of potholes. During the first several years we had one group of members who still wanted secret sessions and another who contended that we could never develop a respected professional organization unless we had open sessions and placed our findings on record.

Finally, there was a showdown, and the secrecy group dropped out of IDRC. For some years they continued to hold secret sessions. The last time I heard of them, they numbered fewer than 10.

The remaining members of IDRC then adopted operating practices more typical of successful scientific and professional societies, and the organization thrived. New members soon replaced those who had left.

Another crucial issue was the admission of area development executives as associate members. There was a fight, but the broader viewpoint prevailed.

Thus, about 10 years after we started, we had a true forum of those most vitally interested in the practical application of what we now call the science of geo-economics. From that point forward progress became easier. We had some goals in sight.

The primary goal was to improve the quality of our meetings. We wanted to hold outstanding professional seminars, not conventions. We recognized that meetings served important networking needs, but we wanted every seminar to be a good learning experience for all of us.

It was interesting to mesh my thinking with that of the active members. I was CEO of a small business, meeting a payroll, coping with government bureaucracy, taking risks and living within a very tight budget.

I found myself dealing with able executives who were working at the middle level in very large companies. While their firms had vast resources, the executives themselves were on tight reins. They had less freedom to venture than I did, and their entrepreneurial instincts were often smothered.

I had more in common with the bosses to whom our members reported than with them. This was both an advantage and a disadvantage.

Many a board meeting brought out these frustrations. Few members had any experience dealing with such matters as news media relations or managing research programs. I was a decade or so ahead of them in going global. These differences led to a lot of compromises which I suppose were of benefit to all.

In any event, we devoted much effort to giving our rank-and-file members encouragement and support as they slaved away in the corporate trenches. Some hint of the range of issues can be gleaned from a list of our editorials excerpted below.

Managing a Business

While seeking to assist our IDRC members with their business management responsibilities, we have been equally busy coping with our own. While dealing with the techniques and strategies of managing the assets of very large firms, we have developed our own set of policies for running a small enterprise in a highly competitive environment.

First, we have never set size as a goal. We have taken pride in achieving objectives with a small number of people operating on a small budget. Starting with one employee 40 years ago, the company has grown slowly but steadily to 50 staff members today.

We have been extremely conservative in our financial management. We have resisted the siren song of leverage and public stock offerings. We have no debt and have not had any for many years.

Our basic corporate guide has been the golden rule. That applies to management-employee relations, customer relations and intra-staff relations. We defy any management guru to come up with a better or more simple formula.

As far as our staff is concerned, we have no secrets. We try very hard to keep everyone informed about everything we're doing or thinking of doing. This is not easy for a company of our type. We don't have any assembly-line operations with a number of people doing the same thing. Virtually every staff member is doing something different, and each one is a decision-maker.

We look at performance, not at the color of one's skin. We have no dress code. We encourage family participation — key staff members frequently take spouses with them to business conferences.

We were one of the first firms in our area to promote female executives to management positions. At last count we had five women on our nine-member board of directors.

I'm not sure it is correct to claim that we have no secretaries. Perhaps it is more accurate to say that we are all secretaries. Every staff member has a computer work station, and we write our own memos. No supervisor asks anyone to do something he or she has not done or would not do.

Every Monday morning we have a general staff meeting. There is always time allotted for anyone who wishes to sound off on anything he or she wishes.

Most important, we have never missed a payroll. Sometimes I had to take the money from my own pocket and postpone my own paycheck, but no staff member had to wait.

We are organized and prepared to deal with change. We believe we can respond to the rapid changes in our world much faster than big, ponderous corporations.

I suspect that there are a great many small enterprises run in somewhat the same way. That is why small businesses have provided most of the new job opportunities in the USA in recent years.

Moreover, a lot of the restructuring and downsizing in big firms is aimed at creating the kind of environment we have.

Understanding Corporate Differences

When I first organized the IDRC it bothered me that every company had different policies and plans for handling real estate. I thought that after the IDRC brought the managers together for a few years they would come up with a sort of standard organization plan.

I could not have been more wrong. Over the years I began to understand that there were many sound reasons why different companies followed different approaches.

For example, publicly owned firms made decisions that would never be made by a closely held firm. Faced with a bad quarter and prospect for skipping a dividend, they might sell a real estate asset below market. The closely held firm would, of course, wait until it could sell the asset advantageously.

Other differences were revealed as we compared centralized firms and those which were decentralized. One IDRC member firm had 300 people in the real estate department. Another of similar size had one man and secretary at headquarters.

Other differences stemmed from accounting practices. Some firms created separate real estate profit centers. Others treated their real estate departments as consulting units which billed company operating units for their services.

The company's product mix was another factor. Real estate management was different for a firm selling widgets with a life cycle of a few years — compared with firms operating steel mills or petroleum refineries.

We also saw differences in real estate planning between firms whose facilities were market-oriented and those that were resource or labor oriented. Others had fixed geographic ties.

And so it went. We found differences due to such factors as company politics, power structure, risks, takeover posture and the personality and talent of the asset manager. Now we know they will never follow a standard model.

Location Factors Checklist

If there is any topic that has been common to geo-economic studies down through the years, it is facility planning location factors. That was a lively issue in 1960, and today it is very much alive.

I remember that back in the 1950s I compiled a list of 100 plant location factors. It was much in demand, and we reproduced the list many times.

The list grew and grew until we counted some 700 items that might be considered as affecting a location decision. That's where we were when we published our 1979 edition of "New Project File and Site Selection Checklist." This was a file in a loose-leaf binder organized so that the user could make up a customized checklist for a particular project.

After that, the file grew to more than 2,000 factors and sub-factors and sub-sub-factors and became too unwieldly to handle via the binder. We then produced a software program that solved the problem for a while.

But the complexity continues to increase. For example, our early checklists never mentioned terrorism. Now it's a major consideration in global planning. Also, quality-of-life factors have steadily risen in importance. We also have new factors related to high-tech industries.

I don't know what the next new factor will be, but I'm sure life for the facility planner will keep getting more complicated. And the only way we will be able to cope is via automation.

Code of Ethics

From the outset, IDRC brought together the top executives in the field — people who wanted to develop an outstanding professional organization. During the 1970s there was discussion of the desirability of having a code of ethics. After listening to several debates, I drafted a code that was accepted.

I have been unable to locate records showing the exact date the code was adopted. It appears in our bound volumes for 1981, but I believe it was in effect for several years before that. The important thing is that, since adoption, the acceptance of the code has been a prerequisite for membership.

In my opinion, this one act lifted IDRC above many other organizations. Today, members are staunch supporters of the concept that in IDRC we expect standards above and beyond those required by law.

Research Program

From the outset, we wanted IDRC to be a vehicle for doing or fostering significant research. That's why we put "research" in the name!

For many years, the research program was a goal but not a reality. The first projects, such as a glossary of terminology issued in 1968, consisted of efforts contributed by volunteers.

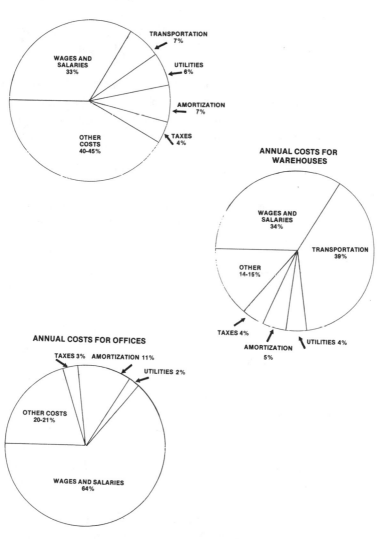

ANNUAL COSTS FOR
MANUFACTURING FACILITIES

TRANSPORTATION
7%

WAGES AND
SALARIES
33%

UTILITIES
6%

AMORTIZATION
7%

OTHER
COSTS
40-45%

TAXES
4%

ANNUAL COSTS FOR
WAREHOUSES

WAGES AND
SALARIES
34%

TRANSPORTATION
39%

OTHER
14-15%

TAXES 4%

AMORTIZATION
5%

UTILITIES 4%

ANNUAL COSTS FOR OFFICES

TAXES 3%   AMORTIZATION 11%

UTILITIES 2%

OTHER COSTS
20-21%

WAGES AND SALARIES
64%

Cost profiles for new facilities. These numbers, reported in one survey of IDRC members, show the distinctly different patterns for office, manufacturing, and distribution facilities.

Later, when we could afford some very limited staff work, we began to conduct surveys among the membership. These studies gave our members support along their career paths and, at the same time, were beneficial to their companies and to the business community.

At last count, there were more than 40 reports in the series, most of them done with virtually no funding. We got a lot for our money! Many of these reports were very useful.

For example, in 1978 we reported, "A Composite Case History of New Facility Location," which showed how site needs of facilities thought to be of the same type might differ. This was all part of the process of refining the thinking of members and increasing the level of sophistication in the facility planning profession.

In 1983 we established the Industrial Development Research Foundation (IDRF). To launch the program, I made an initial challenge gift of 20 percent of the shares in my company. It was a bold and risky move, and for some years there was good reason to question the prudence of the decision.

Unhappily, a fund-raising drive failed to produce enough corporate contributions to match our gift. There were several more years of struggle. Then, in the early 1990s interest was rekindled. The industry-wide recession and restructuring of major firms left many members wondering about their future.

In that atmosphere we promulgated the "Corporate Real Estate 2000" research program. This time, we had a guiding panel made up of some of IDRC's top thinkers, plus consulting support from a group at MIT. As this is written, the new program is attracting support and we fervently hope that IDRF is at last at the take-off stage. Perhaps our dream will come true!

Launching Automated Systems

During the 1960s and 1970s a few corporate facility executives had access to mainframes for running spread sheets and other programs. However, the revolution in data handling did not arrive for most executives in the development field until the microcomputers were introduced in the early 1980s.

I started watching the micros in the late 70s via a subscription to *Byte*, then a skinny magazine struggling to gain a toe-hold. We were then at the hobby stage.

A bit later I bought one of the first Radio Shack computers and began playing with possible applications. These were very limited — that revolutionary machine had a capacity of 32K.

We soon discovered the wonders of word processing and started to improve office systems. I began planning a system for delivering information to members. Using a Radio Shack color computer, I wrote a primitive Basic program to run a demo at the 1982 IDRC meeting at Newport Beach.

We had zero experience with networks, and there wasn't much help around at that time. After a struggle, we developed software with which we successfully transmitted information from our office to my home several miles away. With our crude interfaces, we were then able to connect with existing systems (Telenet, etc.) for service throughout the USA.

We announced SiteNet, the first on-line service in the development field, in mid-1982. Theoretically, we had links to services around the world. However, those who attempted to connect with SiteNet from various nations reported little success.

Thus, I began carrying a portable computer with me on overseas trips. At each stop I would attempt to log on to our SiteNet via protocols which were said to exist.

There were many problems. We discovered that in many nations the government postal and telegraph agencies, which had jurisdiction over data networks, had not actually implemented the services they claimed to be operating.

In Rome we sat in the office of the manager of Italcable, plugged in our portable and demonstrated to him that his announced service was not running. In Vienna, we tried to log on from the headquarters of the United Nations Industrial Development Organization (UNIDO) and showed that their telephone system was inadequate.

We went through this drill in Frankfurt, Oslo, Johannesburg, and elsewhere in Latin America and the Caribbean. In the offices of Cable and Wireless in Hong Kong we encountered an executive who was determined to make the system work. Failing to get a connection via the Pacific route, he patched up a surface-satellite-cable link via Europe.

To check the Pacific link, we stopped at Palau in the Caroline Islands where a major Comsat antenna is located. We found the antenna on a remote hillside and dropped in on the operator in a small concrete structure at the base of the antenna. I think we were his first visitor.

We recite these trials and tribulations to indicate that it was not easy getting started. Yet, we had seen enough evidence of progress to realize that a revolution was coming.

At that point we urged IDRC leaders to set up a "World Site Scan Laboratory" and undertake to develop — over a period of years — an ultrasophisticated information system. We set as the ultimate goal the assembly of all useful information available from our associates and service providers, cataloging it, and delivering it to the desks of our members anywhere in the world. This would include text, graphics and video.

This, of course, was a monumental task and at that time was far beyond our capabilities. We proposed to crawl, then walk, then run with it.

To stimulate efforts, we put up a sign on the first floor of the IDRC headquarters building proclaiming an area as the "World Site Scan Laboratory." Actually, the room contained area files compiled over the years by the editorial staff of Conway Data.

The major funding we hoped for to carry on the effort has yet to come, so the laboratory remains more a dream than a reality.

However, more pedestrian efforts have resulted in steady improvement of the digital data networks. Conway Data has invested heavily in the development of new software and has renamed the system "GEOTEAM" (Geographic and Technical Expertise for Asset Managers).

This has made it possible to upgrade the IDRC private service and to provide connections with other services, such as EuroSite.

The latest report is that GEOTEAM can now be accessed in more than 40 nations. A member in Hong Kong, for example, can use his desktop computer to enter our files in Atlanta and get data on the availability of industrial buildings in, say, Barcelona.

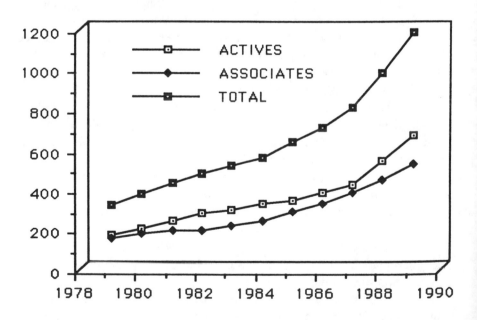

The growth of IDRC membership was fairly steady until the 1980s, when there was a rapid rise. Surprisingly, growth continued through the great real estate recession of 1990-92.

Most important, a new GeoTEAM/Fax service offers same-hour delivery of printed copies of many key files. We expect this service to grow very rapidly.

A Strong Organization

The steady growth of IDRC membership suggests that members applaud the new services. We must be doing something right!

By late 1993, we passed the 1,000 mark in active (corporate) members. And what a fantastic group it is!

The average member company has 42,000 employees, assets of $6.1 billion, annual sales of $6.8 billion. These numbers are all higher than the average of the *Fortune* 500.

The typical IDRC firm owns 191 facilities and leases 296 others. More than 80 percent operate outside the USA.

Not to be overlooked are the Associate members, now numbering more than 800. They represent the cream of the area development and service provider segment.

Where Now?

I am very proud of IDRC and what has been accomplished. However, I assure the young members of the staff that the greatest days of the organization are yet to come.

IDRC is now poised for leadership among all of the elements of the development "industry." Rather than compete, the organization is strong enough to serve as the mechanism for bringing groups together in a new and highly effective federation.

This does not necessarily mean the merger of any groups. What it means is collaboration, the avoidance of duplication and the increase of effectiveness. Within the USA there are at least 10 groups that could collaborate more effectively.

On the world scene, there are other significant opportunities. IDRC should be a part of a global entity that brings in top-level corporate strategists and those who are sponsoring the largest and most important projects in the world.

Recognizing this area of opportunity, I took the lead several years ago in launching the World Development Council. It fills a need and it opens opportunities. Nothing would please me more than to see IDRC and WDC form a close and permanent affiliation.

With these things on the horizon, the future is truly exciting!

B. Excerpts

1961 Excerpt	"The Industrial Development Research Council Is Launched," *Industrial Development*, Atlanta, Jan. 1962. pp. 4-11. Outline of objectives of the Industrial Development Research Council, first annual conference, New York, Oct. 24, 1961.

1. To establish communication between executives with a common interest in the professional planning of industrial growth.

It is obvious from the interest already shown in IDRC that there are a substantial number of executives who share important professional interests. Within the past six months, our small screening effort has produced the names of more than 400 men who could qualify for membership at once. Without doubt, there are a great many more executives in a variety of organizations who have not yet been identified as professional expansion planners who could and should become interested in IDRC.

We estimate that there are some 50 very large firms which maintain specialized industrial development teams on a full-time basis. These companies, such as, GE, Ford, GM, IBM, and DuPont, have up to 15 specialists each, giving a total of several hundred potential members in these firms alone.

There is a second group of some 500 large and middle-size firms with one or more industrial development professionals. The potential membership today among this group is 500 to 1,000. Finally, there are a great many smaller firms wherein the chief executive is sufficiently interested in expansion planning to justify participation in IDRC. Hence, the total membership potential today is well over 1,000. Within five years, the potential may be several times that figure.

2. To advance industrial growth planning as an art and science.

Certainly, one of our most worthwhile objectives is to advance the state of our art. Just a few short years ago there was almost no literature available in this field, little research was underway, and few recognized this as an area for professional effort. Today we can see much evidence of progress, but we can surely agree that the profession is in its infancy. The planning of industrial growth today is definitely an art which many recognize, but few would suggest that it is an exact science.

Theoretically, it should be possible to make precise numerical comparisons to indicate the relative feasibility of several proposed ventures and to choose the one location best suited for successful operation. But in actual fact, even the most expert of those in this group must frequently resort to educated guessing.

There has been a wide gap in communications between those in academic institutions who are conversant with location theory and those in industry who are responsible for practical applications. There is every reason to believe that bringing these two groups together, as we will do tomorrow morning, will be rewarding for both the theorists and the empiricists.

It is not unreasonable to expect that this can eventually lead to the introduction in several institutions of academic programs designed specifically to produce graduates who would work in industrial development offices. There are several of us here today who would jump at the chance to employ such men.

Further, the IDRC may be able to exert its influence toward having one or more research institutes undertake special studies which would contribute to the advancement of the science. I'm sure we could draw up a list of areas in which research is badly needed.

3. To serve as industry's voice in this special field.

We live in a complex society which involves many competitive interests. In the realm of growth planning a great variety of factors come into play. Let's look, for example, at the principles of industrial zoning, which are of interest to government officials, utilities, transportation services, residential developers, and, of course, to industrial firms.

4. To improve the planning programs of members in their own firms.

Every firm which sends a staff member to participate in IDRC should reasonably expect to derive benefits of tangible value. There is the obvious opportunity to exchange ideas regarding practices and techniques which is inherent in every professional organization.

There may be a handful of very large firms which have planning staffs large enough to remain abreast of developments in every field related to their growth planning programs, but such situations are rare. Most IDRC members can and will learn something new at every meeting. The deliberate mixing of long range planners, facility planners, site selectors, and real estate managers — all having somewhat different viewpoints — with their contemporaries from companies of varying sizes and in different industries is bound to be beneficial for all.

Only by such a pooling of effort can we hope to keep abreast of the explosive growth of development activities. Within a few short years we have had to adjust from sectional and regional planning to programming on a global scale. There are men in this room who have engaged in feasibility studies and location surveys in half a dozen nations in Europe, Asia and Latin America in the past two years.

Because of such trends we selected as speakers for our luncheon sessions men who are active on a worldwide basis. Dr. Lurie, whom you will hear at noon today, is head of the development program of the United Nations; and Mr. Blau, whom you will hear tomorrow, is a key figure in the new international program of the U.S. Department of Commerce.

I am certain that the opportunity to engage in such broadening discussions will be of direct benefit to the companies whose executives are represented in the IDRC.

5. To aid IDRC members in their personal advancement.

Even in companies which have set up industrial development groups, there is a general lack of appreciation of the importance of this professional function. We are just beginning to witness a change in attitude which promotes growth planning from the status of a necessary evil to that of a vital corporate operation.

Except for the attention showered on him by the chambers of commerce and other promotional agencies seeking to influence his site preference, the industrial growth planner has generally gone unnoticed and unheralded. This oversight is likely to be more pronounced where each function — long-range planning, facility planning, site selection and real estate management — is separate.

Because there has been no professional forum, little effort has been made to study the role of the expansion planner in the company, his job description, supporting personnel and services and his compensation. There have been some classic examples of penny-wise, pound-foolish companies sending an ill-supported planner out to conduct a survey on which to base a decision affecting the firm's competitive existence.

There is every reason to believe, therefore, that activities of the IDRC can result in better recognition and support for the individual who chooses to make this his career.

There is also the distinct possibility that we will see the emergence of a new pattern in which industrial development specialists can move into top management positions much more rapidly. Few positions provide better training for company-wide management positions. It is a fact that in many companies today the two men most concerned with growth planning are the chief planning executive and the company president.

6. To guide chambers of commerce and promotion groups.

The new 1962 edition of our annual *Site Selection Handbook*, a copy of which has been handed to you, lists more than 10,000 organizations of various types which would like to assist you in expanding your facilities in various areas. No doubt you have been contacted by many of them.

This area development activity has become a big business. The number of full-time personnel runs into thousands, and annual budgets total many millions of dollars. Some 10 percent of the active groups have good professional direction and can render a variety of expert services.

But throughout the area development field, there is a great need for leadership and guidance from industry. Many well-meaning agencies are conducting programs that do not attract industry and that simply waste money and effort. Others are only moderately effective.

There is a tremendous opportunity to direct this effort into more useful channels. I am certain that the great majority of the alert local agencies would be delighted to have the guidance of a group of professional planners.

7. To render a broad public service.

Finally, the most important objective of IDRC should, in my opinion, be the development of stronger communities and a more secure free world. It is obvious that sound planning of the industrial base will improve our community structure. And whatever we do to make our industrial system more efficient — through sound appraisal of ventures and intelligent location and management — improves our competitive position in the cold war.

These are some of the objectives which can be set forth at this stage in IDRC's evolution. Others will come as the future unfolds. As we set up our formal program I believe the one most important requirement is flexibility. We must be prepared to accept changes, for we will know a lot more tomorrow than we do today.

1981 Excerpt   The IDRC Code of Ethics. 1981.

Basic Commitment of All Members — It will be presumed that, by accepting membership in the Council, all participants subscribe to the Code of Ethics.

Standards above the Law — A fundamental premise is that, to justify their status as professionals, members seek to establish and maintain standards of conduct above that required by law.

Honesty in Dealing — It is an inherent duty for members to be honest and straightforward in all agreements, transactions, promises of services and delivery of services.

Integrity of Information — In preparing, presenting, publishing and exchanging information and data, members are pledged to strive for integrity; if presented as fact, information should be accurate; if estimates or guesses are involved, they should be so labeled; if information from other sources is used, the sources should be identified; vital facts should not be deliberately withheld, since errors of omission are as wrong as errors of commission.

Confidentiality — When a member requests information, advice or service regarding a project he states to be in a confidential stage, it will be the responsibility of any member contacted to maintain the confidentiality of the project until released from the obligation by the maker of the request.

Environmental Sensitivity — Members should seek to harmonize new facilities with the natural environment, with appropriate attention to protection of endangered species, maintenance of aesthetic values and conservation of natural resources.

Social and Civic Responsibility — Members should recognize as legitimate concerns the creation of jobs, the economic development of areas, the achievement of civic goals and the coordination of development projects with the needs of modern society.

Freedom of Information — To the maximum extent permitted by corporate policies, members recognize an obligation to report new findings, contribute to the science of corporate facility planning and real property management and exchange information with fellow professionals.

Support Common Programs — It is the responsibility of members to give to, not just take from, the Council, with regard to such activities as: assisting and advising young professional aspirants; promoting education and training; supporting research and innovation; participating in seminars; responding to surveys; promulgating IDRC standards; and updating their own knowledge.

Avoidance of Libel or Slander — Members are pledged not to make slanderous or libelous comments about colleagues or competitors, but rather to consult or compete on the basis of facts and figures professionally presented.

Gifts or Bribes — Members are constrained to represent the best interests of their employers and never to accept gifts or compensation, amounting to bribes, to influence decisions; conversely, not to offer such inducements to others.

Conflict of Interest — Members have a duty to avoid conflict-of-interest situations. Where a member is placed in a position of potential conflict, he has an obligation to advise the other party that a potential conflict exists.

Personal Conduct — Members are obligated to conduct themselves in a reasonable, courteous and considerate manner in their contacts with others.

1986
Excerpt

"Weighing Development Factors for the High-tech Age." If you are responsible for plotting the development strategy for a major corporation or organization, you will want to study this review of factors which have played a dominant role during the past 30 years. The compilation is based on a scan of our bound volumes, staff research and opinions of several hundred readers working in a wide variety of development positions. *Site Selection*. April 1986. pp. 280-288. (Summarized in the monograph "A Technology Review and Forecast for Development Strategists.")

This publication was launched 30 years ago — at about the same time that jet aircraft were being readied for commercial service. During the subsequent three decades the big jets have made a huge difference in our lives.

Yet, the commercial jets are only one of many revolutionary developments which have occurred. In fact, we believe the 1956-86 era has been a time of greater technical, social and political change than any other 30 years in our history.

A quick scan of the bound volumes in our library reveals a panorama of innovations ranging from nuclear energy, microchips, satellites, space travel and organ transplants to air-conditioning, fast food franchises, civil rights, condos and supersonic transports.

Which strategies and concepts are most significant? What can we learn from this experience that will help us plan more intelligently for the future? What does it all mean?

Awed by the scope of these questions, we hastily began a look for help. First, we prepared an outline of typical questions and mailed it to several thousand readers. Hundreds of you who are reading this now took the time to respond with your evaluations.

Then, we put all the ideas in a data file and arranged and rearranged them, adding and deleting.

The result is the following list of geo-economic superlatives for the period 1956-1985 — the first 30 years of publication of *Site Selection Handbook*.

1. Developments in Transportation

Highly Significant
- The construction of the interstate highway system, beginning in the mid '50s under the Eisenhower administration.
- The introduction of jet aircraft on scheduled air routes, about 1960.

Significant
- Worldwide shift to containerization and intermodal shipping.
- Development of "super" airports, such as DFW and ATL.
- Advent of alternate private postal service, such as UPS, and priority mail service, such as Federal Express.
- High-speed trains in France and Japan.
- The supersonic transport (SST) Concorde, 1976.

Deserving Mention
- Opening of St. Lawrence Seaway, 1959.
- Deregulation of air, rail, truck transport, 1980s.
- Development of compact, energy-efficient autos, 1970s.
- Electronic transmission of information in lieu of mail.
- Growth of smaller rural airports.
- The space shuttle, leading to Trans-Atmospheric Vehicles.
- Railroad mergers.
- Super-tankers for oil.
- Shift of emphasis to trucks as major freight carriers.
- High-speed commuter rail lines for urban mass transit.
- Development of inland waterways, such as the Tennessee-Tombigbee.
- Coal slurry lines.

2. Significant State Legislation

Highly Significant
- Right-to-work legislation, numerous states.
- Mississippi act (enacted 1930s, implemented 1950s) setting up bond financing for industry, later adopted by most states.
- Georgia act setting up state science and technology program, 1963-1964, followed by many.
- South Carolina act setting up special technical training and vocational schools for industrial workers, 1960s. Copied by many states.

Significant
- Acts to strengthen state economic development agencies, many states.
- Clarification and improvement of environmental laws, setting up one-stop permitting, many states.
- Reduction/elimination of state inventory taxes, "freeport" legislation, many states.
- California's Proposition 13, other tax abatement programs.

Deserving Mention
- Acts setting up incentives for pollution abatement, many states.
- Acts to create Foreign Trade Zones, where value may be added to goods without payment of import duty until and unless goods enter the USA.
- South Dakota Act inviting national banks to operate credit card centers in the state.
- Nevada act legalizing gambling, leading to development of Las Vegas, other areas.
- Enterprise zone legislation, New Jersey, Louisiana and many other states.
- Ohio act setting up state program for developing airports for small cities. 1960s.
- Pennsylvania act setting up industrial development authority funded by general funds, 1956.
- New England Reciprocal Banking Agreement.
- Removal of unitary tax, Oregon, Colorado and other states.
- California's re-establishment of dominant Dept. of Commerce in 1983-84.
- Acts setting up state lotteries, several states.
- Tax Increment Financing Act, Minnesota, Michigan and elsewhere.

3. Job Creation, Labor Force Utilization Programs

Highly Significant
- Puerto Rico's "Fomento" or "bootstrap" program, 1960s.
- Mexico's "Maquiladora" or twin-plant program, 1970s.
- New development programs in areas of abundant labor — Ireland, Scotland, Hong Kong, Malaysia, Korea, Singapore, recent years.
- China's new economic zones, such as Shenzhen, 1980s.

Significant

- Joint ventures of U.S./foreign manufacturers in U.S. plants.
- Incubator centers for high-tech ventures, 1980s.
- Community college development, Carolinas and elsewhere.

Deserving Mention

- General education advances, many states.
- Vo-Tech training systems, numerous states.
- Job Training Partnership Act (JTPA), replacing CETA, recent years.
- Restructuring of Chrysler via federal loan.
- Title III Dislocated Workers Program.
- Training assistance programs to aid in new plant setup.
- Reagan Caribbean Basin Initiative.
- Job sharing in Arizona.

4. Urban Planning and Zoning

Highly Significant

- Advocacy of performance standards, National Industrial Zoning Committee, 1950s and 1960s.
- Development of research park concept, Stanford Research Park, followed by Research Triangle Park and others.
- Development of industrial and business parks to very high standards, protected by private covenants.
- Emergence of computerized geographic information systems.
- Recognition of the metro loop highway as a new axis for development.

Significant

- Metro/regional planning for rapid transit, BART, MARTA, others.
- Concept of covered regional shopping mall.
- Private planning and development of large mixed-use, mini-cities and new towns, such as Irvine, Calif., Las Colinas, Texas and Columbia, Md.

Deserving Mention

- Comprehensive city planning ideas advocated by Bartholomew and others, 1940s through 1960s.
- Mandates for community comprehensive planning as a prerequisite for federal funding —U.S. Housing Acts of 1950's.
- Advocacy of business park concept via films, surveys and studies,

1950s and 1960s. *Industrial Development* magazine.
- Flood control and drainage planning in small cities.
- Increased emphasis on economic base in comprehensive planning.
- Concept that quality environments pay for themselves in worker productivity.
- Offshore marine zoning plans, such as that to protect Australia's Great Barrier Reef.
- McHartle model of planning based on geophysical structure.
- Concept of the "airport city," uni-modal transportation systems, and fly-in developments.
- Hawaii Land Use Controls, 1980s.
- Transfer of development rights strategy.

5. Development Decisions by Political Leaders

Highly Significant
- Decisions to open China, set up enterprise zones, settle Hong Kong status.
- Decision of Europe's leaders to create common market (EEC).
- U.S. commitment to earth applications of space technology.
- Decision of Japanese MITI agency to adopt a strategy for selectively investing in and promoting certain high-tech industries.

Significant
- Decision to move the capital of Brazil from Rio to Brasilia.
- President Nasser's decision to proceed with construction of Aswan Dam with Soviet help.
- Decision of U.S. officials to permit construction of the Alaska pipeline.

Deserving Mention
- Central Arizona Project, other long-range water projects.
- Investment credits for rehabilitating older buildings in urban areas, downtown revitalization decisions.
- President Roosevelt's creation of Manhattan project, 1940s, subsequent nuclear programs.
- Urban renewal, UDAGs, other federal/state planning programs.
- Reagan's initiative to rebuild U.S. defenses.
- "Unigov" in Indianapolis by then mayor Richard Lugar.
- Tax changes encouraging R&D limited partnerships.
- Michigan Gov. Blanchard's creation of a strategic fund.

- Favorable tax treatment for real estate development.
- Concept of air rights.

6. Decisions Leading to Failures and Disappointments

Highly Significant
- Lack of concern of U.S. leaders for balanced national budget, leading to long-term burden and deterrent to growth.
- OPEC policies fueling global inflation and recession, harming developing nations, causing dislocations in many industries.
- Imprudence of international bankers in making excessively risky loans to developing nations.
- Assumptions, for budget-planning purposes, by many developing nations that oil prices would remain high.

Significant
- Policy of the United Nations of encouraging the formation of many new African nations unable to govern or sustain themselves.
- Decision of Castro to put Cuba in the Soviet bloc, denying his people the opportunity to participate in important regional economic development opportunities in fields of tourism and agribusiness
- Quebec's detour into separatism and dual language programs, which caused great economic losses.
- Nationalization of industry in England by the Labour government.
- Mao's "Great Leap Forward" and Chinese cultural revolution.
- Russia's closed-door policy limiting communication with industrialized nations.

Deserving Mention
- UK financing of the DeLorean auto plant.
- The Antarctic policy of the U.S. and other nations, placing vast regions under bureaucratic control.
- Internal conflicts leading to the collapse of the Central American Common Market.
- UN's Law-of-the-Sea giving rewards not related to performance.
- The Comprehensive Employment Training Act (CETA).
- The U.S. farm policy and its misplaced incentives.
- President Carter's grain embargo and boycott of Moscow Olympic games.
- U.S. relinquishment of Panama Canal to an unstable Panama government.

- Welfare programs which reduce work incentives.
- Inadequate recognition of Central and South America by consecutive U.S. administrations.
- The decline of public education in U.S. during the integration process.
- The "snail darter," "dusky seaside sparrow" and similar extremist environmental confrontations.
- U.S.'s failure to meet foreign competition, especially from the Far East.
- The Great Society, which took away incentive for people to do things for themselves.
- Enactment of tax on employees, Chicago and elsewhere.

7. New Technology

Highly Significant
- Global satellite communications, Telstar (1962), and subsequent enhancements.
- The microchip, (1971), microcomputers, microelectronics.
- Space flight — Sputnik (1957), NASA moon landing (1969), shuttle missions, and concept of Trans Atmospheric Vehicle (TAV).
- Network television.
- Inexpensive air-conditioning for homes and offices.

Significant
- Commercial applications of nuclear energy.
- Automation, robotics.
- Office copying machines.
- New ceramic, plastic, composite materials.

Deserving Mention
- Extension of dependable electric power service almost everywhere at reasonable cost.
- Elevators and other construction techniques permitting high-rise buildings.
- Productivity improvements throughout industry.
- Tilt-up and pre-cast construction methods.
- "Unit" crane for high-rise construction.
- Waste treatment disposal technologies.

8. Social Changes

Highly Significant

- One man, one vote doctrine; equal opportunity employment, other civil rights changes.
- Growth of the environmental movement.
- Nuclear war threat.
- Open heart surgery, organ transplant techniques.

Significant

- Fast food enterprises, "eating out" habit.
- DNA discovery and beginning of genetic engineering.
- Growth of single households.
- Two-wage-earner, two-career families.
- Women/mothers entering work force.
- Declining influence of unions, growth of merit shop contractors.
- Condo form of ownership.
- Increasing mobility of workforce.
- Population shifts from inner cities to suburbs.
- Shifts from North and East to South and West.

Deserving Mention

- Increasing welfare costs.
- Socio-economic mobility.
- Sexual freedom.
- Changing concern for established moral, social, ethical and spiritual values.
- Freedom from large families, birth control.
- Increased land costs.
- Emergence of more independent, individualistic attitude of society
- Larger proportion of population receiving advanced education.
- Access by all people to education in developed countries.
- Availability of credit.
- Greater mobility of American public.
- Increased awareness of entrepreneurial lifestyle.
- Career priority over location of all family units in a centered locality.
- Realization women have a place in career world, increased influence, women's lib.
- Urban lifestyle preference by managers and professionals.
- Integration of blacks, Asians and Hispanics into economy.
- Conversion of Sunbelt states from agriculture to industry economy.

- Salk vaccine and other effective immunization programs.

9. Advancement of the Geo-economics Profession

Highly Significant

- Founding of the Industrial Development Research Council, 1961, as a forum for facility planning executives.
- Development of professional associations for area development executives, such as AEDC, NAIOP, SIDC, NASDA and CUED.
- Founding of first journal, *Industrial Development*, in 1954, and first reference publication, *Site Selection Handbook*, 1956, to serve geo-economic professionals.

Significant

- Expansion and professionalization of economic development functions in most states.
- Introduction of the first standard format for geo-economic data entry, the Community Audit, 1950s.
- The corporate surplus property index introduced by IDRC, 1970s.
- The IDRC research study series beginning 1960s.
- The IDRC code of professional ethics, adopted 1970s.
- Launching of first telecommunications networks, SiteNet and IDRC-NET, 1980s.
- Production of first GEO-ECON software, 1980s.

Deserving Mention

- Creation of an input-output econometric model for geo-economic impact studies.
- Establishment of short-courses and institutes at the University of Oklahoma and elsewhere.
- Introduction of textbooks and reference books written specifically for development executives.
- Increasing recognition by employers of the need for professional training and experience.
- Proliferation of development-oriented publications.
- The annual survey "The 50 Legislative Climates" begun in *Industrial Development/Site Selection Handbook*, 1960s.
- The new plant reporting service established by *Industrial Development/Site Selection Handbook*, 1950s.
- The annual directory of prepared sites, office and industrial parks, begun by *Industrial Development/Site Selection Handbook*, 1950s.

- Production of films "Gold Mine on Main Street," "Blueprint for Progress," about 1960.

10. Innovative Forms of Development

Highly Significant
- Incubator facilities and programs for new, small and/or high-tech ventures.
- The Decoplex, or resource recovery industrial complex, which converts wastes into energy and by-products.
- The space shuttle with bay for carrying out small-scale industrial operations in space.
- The intelligent building with shared computer and telecommunications facilities.
- Drilling rigs for offshore and deep exploration for oil.

Significant
- Floating plants built in one location and floated to sites around the world.
- The fly-in industrial park or community, permitting aircraft to park at door.
- Co-generation of electric power.
- Recycling of surplus facilities for innovative uses — industrial, commercial and residential.
- Condo plants/offices.

Deserving Mention
- Workers equity form of ownership/management to save companies.
- The "appropriate technology" movement.
- Concept of business park for multi-tenant buildings.
- Alternate forms of financing (ventures, insurance, etc.).
- Mergers and acquisitions to meet facility needs.
- Outsourcing of manufacturing jobs, e.g. maintenance, security.
- Payment in lieu of tax programs.

1986
Excerpt

Recent events reveal all too starkly the clouds that hang over development programs in many parts of the world. Business travelers, investors and facility planners must be concerned not only with traditional war risk and political risk, but also with the added risk of bombings, assassinations, hijackings and taking of hostages carried out by international terrorist groups. *Site Selection.* August 1986. pp. 952-956.

There have always been special risks involved in implementing development projects in faraway places. The Phoenicians who set up trade facilities across the Mediterranean centuries ago must certainly have known about war risk. For the British administrators who launched the East India Company and other bold ventures around the world generations ago, political risk could not have been an unfamiliar hazard.

The taking of hostages was widely practiced in medieval times. Assassinations made good copy for Shakespeare. Neither is terrorism a new factor today.

Yet, the threat of terrorism has become the top "new" issue before the world community. This may be explained by the fact that the world has inherited all of the old reasons and methods for such acts, then added a rather exotic set of new factors:

- Today we have satellite TV communications systems which provide terrorists with a wonderful global stage on which to play.
- We have a global jet transportation system that gives terrorists unprecedented mobility for setting up their media events.
- Rising expectations have made many segments of society less tolerant of shortages of food, shelter, clothing and basic social services.
- Population pressures and urban stresses provide new spawning grounds for reaction and rebellion.
- The swift changes brought by high technology offend many who are left behind.
- Religious fanatics — always one of the major sources of problems — have more freedom to foment unrest.

Put it all together and the world has a great and growing dilemma. How is it possible to tighten security while promoting more open societies? Further, how can we promote the constructive economic development so desperately needed while operating in a destructive environment?

For the investor and facility planner, the first and most obvious effect

93

of all this is to limit options. Because of terrorism risks, there are substantially fewer nations and fewer locations in the world where it is prudent to invest.

Add to this a list of nations that have such inept or corrupt governments they cannot or will not preserve law and order. Finally, we are left with an astonishing fact: Of the more than 200 nations recognized by the United Nations, fewer than 50 are currently secure and stable enough to receive serious and consistent consideration as investment locations by free-enterprise ventures.

This is a tragic situation for the 150 or more "lost" nations, for their people, and for the world business community. Nobody wins except the anarchists.

Personal Experiences Confirm Risk

In our years of bouncing around the world to study development processes, we have had many opportunities to see the deadly effect of unrest, violence and terrorism on development programs and projects.

A number of years ago, for example, your author was a member of a five-man U.S. development mission to Southeast Asia. On that project we spent a couple of months in Burma, traveling from the foothills of the Himalayas to the Irrawaddy Delta. We visited with a wide range of ethnic and tribal groups — Burmese, Chinese, Shans, Indians, Sikhs, Kachins, Karens, not to mention some who turned out to be opium warlords.

As we examined industry after industry, it became clear why the economy of Burma and Southeast Asia was dragging. The tin industry was stalled because bandits were blowing up equipment at remote sites. The rubber industry was stagnant because plantation owners were being kidnapped and held for ransom. The teak industry was in disarray because, as logs were floated downriver to port, guerrillas stopped them every 50 miles or so and collected a toll.

The government controlled the cities, but the countryside belonged to the *dacoits*. Travel was risky. We were dropped off at such spots as Tanggyi and Myitkyina in battle-worn DC-3s. (We were somewhat disconcerted at the first drop to learn that the airplanes and crews were returning to Rangoon for the night to avoid being destroyed by guerillas.)

We recall one trip made by motor convoy out of Moulmein, not too far from the site of the famed bridge over the River Kwai. We had an armed guard fore and aft and each time we rounded a curve we wondered if we would be greeted by a log across the road and a hail of bullets from the bush.

There was another memorable trip made from Bassein in a small riverboat running at night without lights. Another night, we were invited to meet with a rebel group which sent a Jeep into Rangoon for us and drove us via a circuitous route to a jungle camp.

Climax of the project occurred one night when the mission team was invited to have dinner with some army brass. Burmese dinners tend to be long, with many ambiguous soup courses, but this one was extra long. At last, one of the officers rose and announced that the army had just overthrown the government with which we had been negotiating for weeks.

The dinner had been for the purpose of getting us out of the way. We were taken to a hotel where we stayed, surrounded by troops, until permitted to leave the country. We fared much better than the prime minister and his cabinet, who, 20 years later, were still incarcerated.

Worse, the Burmese economy is still in gridlock. Our report on the ill-fated mission (June 1962 issue of *Industrial Development*) pointed out that Burma had up to that time been unable to equal its pre-WWII production levels (when under British rule).

Since the 1962 coup the situation has gotten steadily worse. A nation which once had a large rice surplus now imports food. There are shortages of every type of equipment and manufactured goods. The *dacoits* are still active in the hinterland.

Thus, we learned early in our career that successful development programs cannot be carried out in areas where security and stability do not prevail. In subsequent years we have seen many other sad examples.

During the 1960s we spent a lot of time working in Central America. We helped set up development programs in El Salvador, Costa Rica, Nicaragua, Honduras, Panama and Guatemala under the auspices of the Agency for International Development.

Today, those programs are in shambles, thanks to the Marxist revolution in Nicaragua. The much-heralded Central American common market is no more. Even neighboring countries are threatened and economically hamstrung. Once we flew our own airplane freely throughout the region. This year, we were unable to insure our airplane for one quick flight to Belize.

Another of our favorite regions, the Caribbean, has also been torn apart. In the past couple of decades we had to cancel one project because of a revolution in the Dominican Republic; we have tip-toed in and out of Haiti for 20 years; and we have had to fly over and around Cuba many times.

Even where positive programs are being implemented, as in Jamaica and Granada, it will take a long time to restore investor confidence and rebuild. (At least we had the satisfaction of taking aerial photos of the airstrip at Granada right after it was recaptured.)

Elsewhere in the hemisphere, we have managed to dodge guerrilla actions in Colombia, survive an attempted coup in Venezuela and make a peaceful visit to Asuncion, where Somoza was shot. Once we traveled the length of the Amazon from the headwaters in Peru to Manaus and Belem in Brazil, not once encountering hostile political activists. The Indians were friendly, although we had our doubts about the snakes.

The Middle East is, of course, noted for lack of security. In Beirut we visited a prominent bank which had become a small fort. Barbed concertina wire surrounded the building and guards with automatic weapons patrolled the corridors. The official we visited had prudently rearranged his office to put file cabinets over the windows and hide his desk in a corner where a sniper could not pick him off. In Kuwait we had a hotel room across the street from the U.S. embassy compound which was bombed by a PLO group.

A couple of years ago we flew from Beijing to Hong Kong, planning to stop in Manila en route home. At departure, however, news came of the Aquino assassination at the Manila airport and Manila flights were canceled. We took an alternate flight by way of Seoul. That put us on an eastbound KAL 747 at the time the westbound flight 007 was shot down by the Soviets.

On other business trips we have visited the part of Cairo burned in recent riots, as well as the Soweto township in South Africa where there have been repeated incidents. About three years ago we got out of Nairobi a few hours before several hundred people were killed in the downtown area and at the airport in a coup attempt.

Despite these accounts, spectacular near misses are not the main effect of terrorism we have experienced. The most common effect has been to expose us to countless delays, inconvenience, red tape and frustrations.

Almost everyone is familiar with airport security measures. Tokyo's Narita airport has the heaviest protection we've seen; Frankfurt searches are most enthusiastic; the Australians are least concerned.

Our most memorable search came at midnight on the Trans-Siberian Express as we crossed the Siberia-Mongolia border. We were sound asleep, feeling secure in a locked compartment, when a Russian officer burst in, demanding to see our papers. We learned that the doors could be opened from the outside, and apparently it was standard procedure to surprise the occupants.

Recently in Paris we ate at a left-bank Tunisian restaurant which was subsequently bombed by terrorists. Leaving the city, we saw a scene of destruction left after a riot at the famed Tuilleres on the previous evening.

But it would be a mistake to conclude from this brief recollection that incidents occur only in remote foreign places.

We have been on a hijacked plane only once. That was a Continental flight out of Los Angeles. *(see next chapter)*

Psychological Damage Costs Most

To those who don't travel, it might seem that we lead a James Bond life, dodging bullets on every project. We suspect, however, that if the truth were known, the greatest real danger we face is in riding airport taxis at home.

Whatever the real danger, it is the imagined or psychological hazards that are usually most damaging to business ventures and investments. The tourism industry is the early barometer — the effect of a single terrorist act can often be seen in airline reservations and hotel bookings a few hours later. The more subtle impacts of terrorist acts are found in investment decisions that surface later. For example, the recent skirmish with Libya may not have had a large effect on the total amount of U.S. investment in Europe. However, the action of Ms. Thatcher in permitting U.S. aircraft to use bases in the UK may bring a larger share to the UK. Similarly, at least one investor has already told us of a major plant which will not be located in France because of the French refusal to let U.S. aircraft fly over.

Tomorrow — the Spectre

If the trend toward increasing international terrorism continues for another decade, it may be difficult to find any sites in the world where it is safe to live or invest. We are faced with the prospect that such nations as Libya, Iraq and Iran — and, hence, terrorists — will have nuclear weapons. And some of the new weapons are so compact they can be carried in suitcases.

There seems no reason to doubt that such weapons could be smuggled across the U.S. border — uncounted throngs of illegal immigrants do that every night. Urban centers might be the first targets — with the aim of hitting as many people as possible. No city would be safe.

Later, improved techniques will make it possible to zero in on choice targets such as dams, power plants, airports or the White House.

It will take only one such attack to spur a dramatic increase in interest in dispersal planning, evacuation planning, survival planning, records storage, disaster recovery and other topics now neglected!

1988
Excerpt

Editorial: "Are You Building Your Own Personal Data Base?" *Site Selection.* June 1988. p. 580.

The most important data base you will ever have to consult is the one between your ears. Just about everything to which you aspire depends on it. Are you giving it the attention it deserves?

Most of us have no choice but to begin building a personal data base. We are required to go to elementary school and learn the three R's. By the time we reach college we are permitted to select a few options.

Those who choose well and build studiously may store enough data before graduation to carry them for quite a while. Some are naive enough to think their need for data base building ends when they get that diploma.

Out of school, we cannot only choose what to add to our data base, we can decide whether to add *anything*. We are on our own.

Watching the swift flow of world events and the explosive growth of technology, most of us know we have a problem. Those who do not devote a major effort to renewing and developing their personal data bases may soon find themselves left behind.

We live and work in an information age. We are surrounded and some-times overwhelmed by a wealth of information unparalleled in history. Yet, that rich store of data will not find its way into the space between our ears unless we work at it.

Living in an information age does not guarantee that anyone is well informed. In fact, we will argue that none are more ignorant than those who live in the midst of abundant data and fail to use it.

Why this harangue? We are compelled to speak bluntly because we have solid evidence that many of those among us who consider themselves professionals are simply not doing their homework today.

All too often, we see decision-makers shooting from the hip. There are too many executives who don't want to be confused by the facts.

There is a lack of respect for information and a lack of respect for those who can furnish it. Every day we observe bits and pieces of evidence which confirm these serious charges.

Where do you stand? Are you committing time to scan, read and save information essential to you? Here are a few checkpoints:

- Do you read/scan a daily newspaper? You need more than the 6 o'clock TV news or a radio broadcast enroute to work!
- Do you read/scan a weekly newsmagazine?
- Do you read/scan *all* of the key technical and professional publications in your field?
- Do you read/scan at least one global publication issued outside the USA?
- Do you read/scan several serious books per year?
- Is your read/scan mix selected to provide global, national and local

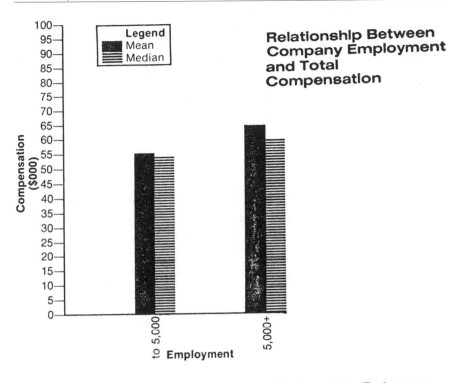

Relationship Between Company Employment and Total Compensation

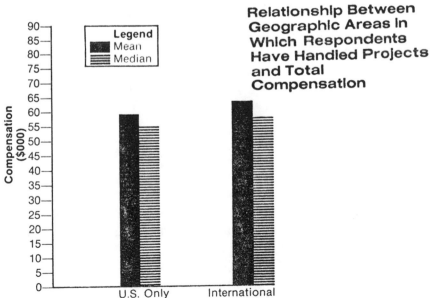

Relationship Between Geographic Areas In Which Respondents Have Handled Projects and Total Compensation

Factors in executive compensation. Several surveys of IDRC members have given information on career opportunities, such as compensation and duties.

views, as well as advances in technology?

If you check positively on these points you can be pleased with your personal data base, right?

Wrong. What you have so far is a raw data base which enables you to carry on luncheon conversations without embarrassment. As far as your profession is concerned, you have just begun. Another set of questions must now be answered:

From among all of the facts that you have, can you select pertinent items of data and access them? Can you bring some order out of the confusion of information?

As proof, have you recently written a paper on *any* subject?

Can you document your sources? Can you record your conclusions? Most important, can you create new and original data via your own analyses?

Can you develop matrices of information — chronological, geographic or other? And, here's a good test: Do you enjoy this process and gain a sense of exhilaration from watching your personal data base grow in sophistication?

Another way to measure the seriousness of your commitment is to check your use of tools to extend your data base: Do you maintain any files on a personal computer? Do you ever access a data network? Do you ever visit a library? Do you ever consult a bibliography?

Wl:y not?

The stock answer is not enough time. Others foolishly believe that they can delegate this responsibility. (At least this helps someone else develop his or her personal data base.)

One response which intrigues us is, "I'm not a professor!". That may sum it up. In this information age, we've all got to be professors in our own backyards.

1988
Excerpt

Editorial: "Where Will You Land After the Merger? The time to make your job secure is before the blood-letting starts. And one of the very best strategies is to develop an automated property inventory with which you are thoroughly familiar. Learn from the sad experience of the veteran real estate manager who was not prepared." *Site Selection.* Dec. 1988.

This is a case history — or horror story — of a recent merger of two large corporations, both of which had active real estate departments.

At a critical stage in the negotiations the representatives of the two firms met to go over the real property assets. Since both firms were large and diversified, the assets of each company were expected to include many owned properties as well as leaseholds, joint ventures, and other interests. Each was to come to the meeting prepared to catalog and compare assets.

The real estate manager for Company A showed up with a large print-out which listed every property with a detailed description, current use and estimated market value. He also brought along a laptop computer with a summary of the properties stored on its hard disk. He was prepared to do quick what-if analyses on the spot.

Company B was represented by a veteran real estate manager who pulled a yellowing file folder from his briefcase. In it he had a list of operating divisions and unit managers scattered throughout the company's empire. He explained that he had no master inventory but could call any of his units to find out what they had.

One afternoon of futility was all it took to prove that this negotiating approach would not work. Every time there was a question about a property, Company B had trouble responding. Data for various properties was not in uniform format, or it was inconsistent, or it was old, or the contact was not in his office.

Finally, it was decided to suspend the negotiations until a crash effort was made to assemble an overall inventory of the more important properties of Company B. Some weeks later that was done, a deal was struck, and the two firms became one.

It requires no crystal ball to guess which real estate manager was fired and which one took over the combined operation. There is nothing like a merger negotiation to find out in a hurry who has been doing a good job of managing real estate assets.

There are many things for which a corporate real estate manager can be excused. But one thing that is an absolute must is an automated property inventory. The absence of such a system tells you a lot about the executive, his supervisors and the company itself.

It is a simple fact that you cannot do an intelligent job of managing assets unless you know what you have. It is truly amazing that today there are many firms high up on the *Fortune* 500 list which have not yet invested the small amount of money necessary to develop an automated inventory of the hundreds of millions of dollars worth of assets they have.

We hear many reports of substantial properties being discovered by outsiders. A company lacking a current inventory of its holdings may be sitting on a piece of unused or under utilized property which another firm sees as a multi-million dollar development opportunity.

In some cases, the real estate executives who see the need for an asset monitoring system are thwarted by lack of support by top management.

101

They are not even authorized to collect data from the various company units. If they send out queries on their own, there is little or no response.

In other cases, support is so vague or weak that results are unsatisfactory. Company units respond slowly and fail to conform to uniform formats, making the inventory difficult to use and of questionable validity at any point in time.

Some will say it's a mundane subject which we should expect to generate little excitement. Yet, surveys show that for most major corporations real estate represents 20 to 40 percent of all assets.

In fact, this may be an area in which corporations still have an opportunity to gain big competitive advantages. That ought to excite someone in the board room!

1988
Excerpt

Editorial: "Why Joe Lost His Job. It's a jungle out there. We all know that. Nothing is absolutely guaranteed. Even the biggest companies fall flat. And a great many are trimming management costs, especially in staff areas. Even so, Joe might have survived the cuts. *Site Selection.*" April 1988. p. 276.

Here's a sad report on a corporate real estate executive who was well-known in the profession, popular with his associates and who had a wealth of experience. Several weeks ago he was unceremoniously canned.

What happened? Why was Joe selected for termination while others less known were kept? We don't know all the facts, but we can surmise that the problem has been building for some time.

We first met Joe many years ago at a professional seminar and have seen him at many such affairs over the years. Although he was not a big drinker or one to skip the work sessions to play golf, we would classify Joe as one who attended to make contacts rather than to gather new technical knowledge.

Joe had a considerable amount of ability and rose to a rather responsible position while he was relatively young. One might have predicted that he would go far in the business world.

However, Joe evidently settled down into a niche. We didn't monitor him specifically, but we just remember that he kept coming to the meetings. Looking back, we now guess that over the decade that we knew him he did not get 10 years of fresh experience. Instead, he got the same one year of experience 10 times over.

While Joe was considered a good member, with a steady attendance record, he never volunteered to present papers at workshops nor to contribute to research studies. We assumed he was just too busy.

If we had been more alert, we would have noticed sooner that Joe was not building any systems. Everything he had saved from his years of experience was limited to what he had in his head. He had built no files, nor set up any systems, nor trained any subordinates. He may have thought that this strategy would make him irreplaceable.

It was only in recent years when the microcomputer automation movement struck our profession that we began to realize just how far out of it that Joe was. We talked with him several times about possible applications in his department but could never seem to get his attention.

We now can see how well Joe fit the profile of computer-illiterate executives described by Dr. Byrne at the IDRC World Congress in San Antonio. Joe was one of those who thought it would never be necessary for him to get personally involved, that he could always delegate that "technical stuff" to a staff member.

He put off "getting involved" with new data systems for so long that he painted himself into a corner. He reached a point that it would be too embarrassing to admit that he knew almost nothing about the systems many of his contemporaries were using.

For the past couple of years he handled this problem by trying to ignore it. He developed such a monumental psychological block that he couldn't face up to buying a desktop computer and making dumb mistakes while learning to use it. Having failed to do this, he couldn't discuss systems intelligently with staff members who might be able to support him.

That was the situation when the new management starting cutting staff. First, there was an overall resource allocation study. That was followed by a review panel which interviewed all key personnel. From what we heard, it was a reasonably objective process.

The review panel was surely looking for duplication and obvious inefficiencies. But it was also looking for sensitive activities which should *not* be cut. These included functions which could contribute to greater productivity and efficiency in the future.

It was the latter test which Joe flunked. The reviewers discovered that Joe's function was organized in 1987 about the same way it was the day Joe started. He had an office full of yellowing documents filled with facts he could neither retrieve nor analyze. The review panelists were appalled.

So Joe is looking for a job, and it's not going to be easy. He has few skills to offer in a fast-moving automated business world.

Had Joe installed systems just a few years ago, he would have been one of those that the company could not afford to fire. He would be too important in the future scheme of things.

103

Why do we add to Joe's discomfort by regurgitating this sad story? We are doing it because Joe is not alone. A survey we just finished suggests at least 25 percent of corporate real estate managers are just as unprepared and, hence, just as vulnerable as Joe.

The moral here is all too obvious. This is the Information Age. Competition is fierce. Without automated systems, we perish.

1989 Excerpt	"Editorial: CEO Confidential: Does Your Real Estate Setup Make Your Company a Takeover Target? Experts in the takeover game have discovered that the real estate department is the Achilles heel of many large corporations. Unmanaged or under-managed properties have become a major lure. It proves once more that what you don't know can hurt you in a big way." *Site Selection.* Feb. 1989. p. 4.

It was quite a shock to officers of XYZ Corporation when the ABC Company launched its hostile takeover raid. XYZ was not on anybody's list of prime takeover targets — the company did not have a spectacular growth record, it wasn't a leader in its market, and there wasn't a lot of cash.

As a matter of fact, XYZ was almost never in the news. It was one of those companies getting along pretty well in a long-established line. The attitude on Wall Street was "let sleeping dogs lie".

But ABC knew something the others didn't. XYZ was sitting on a batch of real estate properties which were worth a whole lot more than indicated on the XYZ books, and, more important, a lot more than the officers of the firm realized.

How could this happen? That's what everybody at XYZ asked when news of the takeover broke. Then everybody started pointing fingers at each other.

XYZ was one of those decentralized organizations with somewhat vague delineations of authority and responsibility between HQ staff and the officers of the operating units. There was a small real estate department at HQ, and there were real estate "managers" in each of the divisions.

The people at HQ saw their role as consultants and coordinators. They kept in touch with the divisions but, lacking authority, made no attempt to direct their efforts.

The people in the divisions saw their role as dealing with day-to-day activities ranging from renewing leases to fixing leaking roofs. They were timid about getting into overall strategy or long-term planning, which they regarded as the role of the folks at HQ.

The picture was further complicated by the occasional pronouncements of corporate officers that, "We're not in the real estate business." They made it clear that in their way of thinking real estate "is just another tool." Entrepreneurial thinking was not encouraged.

These are some of the excuses given for the glaring fact that XYZ did not have an automated inventory of its properties, nor was there a periodic review of their utilization. No one at HQ had a clear picture of what they owned or what its current market value or future potential might be.

ABC had, by accident, run across one property owned by XYZ which was conspicuously under-utilized. Then they found another and, like a shark getting a taste of blood, put someone to work studying XYZ's holdings — all in strict confidence.

The report revealed a prime takeover situation. ABC could grab XYZ and sell its properties for enough to recover its outlay. The rest was gravy.

We have, of course, used fake names and the scenario is doctored. But the case is real enough and, unhappily, it is by no means rare. If you don't have an automated system up and running, sit down today and write your boss a memo. Maybe you'll be one of the survivors.

1990
Excerpt

"Editorial: CEO Confidential: Show Us a Copy of Your Company Map! We're not looking for anything in particular — we just want to know if you have one. Here's why." *Site Selection,* Oct. 1990. p. 1040.

In recent weeks we have scanned the annual reports of some 200 of the world's largest firms. Most of the documents are slick brochures using color, expensive paper stock and special chart graphics to make an impression.

Unfortunately, it appears that many of the authors did not pass Journalism 101. That's the basic course that teaches young reporters to give first priority to answering the "W" questions: who, what, where, when and why.

The corporate reports are woefully weak in answering the "where" question. Some of them have sketchy maps showing where large facilities are located, and many include small-print lists of facility locations. But almost none contain really informative maps showing at a glance the company's actual geography.

In these days of globalization, we think this oversight needs attention at the top level of management. We strongly suspect that many large firms do not have a very good idea of what they own and where it is.

Further, we know for a fact that many major corporations do not have an up-to-date automated property inventory system with a comprehensive data base of all owned and leased properties plus software, for quickly and easily printing out maps of facility locations.

Conduct a test to see if we're right! Call your real estate department and ask for a company map showing offices, manufacturing plants, distribution units, R&D centers and other significant facilities.

If your asset manager is on the ball, you will have a map on your desk within the hour. It will be a fresh printout giving accurate, current information. If you have to wait a day until a map is hastily prepared, and if it consists of symbols glued onto a Rand McNally road map, you know your system is not automated.

If it takes a week or so to get a map, you know you are in deeper trouble. It probably means that a property inventory had to be hastily assembled before a map could be produced. And, you'd better not put a lot of faith in that map.

Before you fire the real estate manager, check the situation. Maybe he's been asking for funds for years to install an automated system and nobody was listening. Maybe yours is a decentralized operation and your diverse units are not cooperating in furnishing data to the HQ office.

You're the boss. You can fix these problems in a hurry.

Why is this important? First, your company map presents your corporate strategy. It shows shareholders and customers how your resources are deployed to meet future needs and opportunities in various geographic regions.

Also, a current map at your elbow makes it easy for you to check the impact of fast-moving events on your operations. What company units are in the path of the hurricane reported on the morning news? What overseas operations will be affected by the coup which toppled a government? How will the marketing program be affected by the new plant in your field just announced by the Japanese?

At the least, your ability to get a company map in a hurry gives you a check on one important facet of your asset management process. And, if yours is a typical large industrial firm, your real property constitutes a substantial percentage of the company's total assets.

Keep those assets in mind! Insist on better corporate maps!

1990
Excerpt
     "Editorial: Had Your Annual Checkup? No, not the one at the Mayo clinic. We're talking about the in-house review of your company's real property assets." *Site Selection,* Dec. 1990. p. 1288.

You don't remember? It's the big fat report that tells you what you own, how you're using it, and what shape it's in. It is a report so useful that you probably have it on the shelf there back of your desk.

What? You actually don't have such a report? When you want information about a property you ask for it? Otherwise, you don't want to be bothered?

Wow! We've got to admire your guts. You're one of the disappearing breed of guys who flies by the seat of your pants. No fancy instruments for you!

We concede that yours is the easy way to manage — until some wiseacre on the Executive Committee starts asking questions. And it can really get sticky if he knows something about corporate real estate management.

Maybe you'd better start buckling up your parachute!

It won't take a critic long to convince your Executive Committee that in the business world of the 1990s it's a cardinal sin not to know exactly what you own, how efficiently the property is being used and the current condition and market potential of each item.

There are plenty of horror stories about what can happen in the absence of such information. Look at the case of the ABC Corporation (all names changed to protect the guilty):

The old manufacturing plant in the Sleepy Division was 80 years old. The building and the business had been going downhill for decades. However, the old plant was still cranking out horseshoes and, if you ignore modern accounting practices, it was making a small profit.

Thus, when the XYZ Corporation made an offer for the Sleepy Division, the incredulous CEO at ABC struck a quick deal. If XYZ thinks there is money in horseshoes, let them dream!

But XYZ promptly shut down the old plant and sold the site to a developer who will build a hotel and high-rise office complex. XYZ made millions because they knew the value of the site, now in the middle of the city.

The CEO of ABC has egg all over his face. Irate shareholders want to know why ABC didn't enjoy the windfall. Moreover, they want to know about other company properties — are there more sleepers out there?

At ABC there is now frenzied activity to assemble a current inventory of all properties and to evaluate them. Funds have been allocated to the real estate department to make an annual survey and report to management. Finally, they're putting in an automated system.

And, the CEO has decided that a periodic checkup is decidedly less painful than the surgery suggested by that shareholder with the twisted sense of humor.

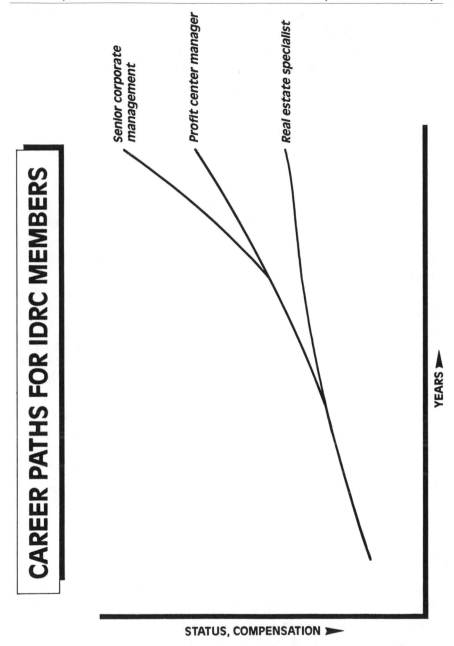

Career paths for IDRC members. In the early days of IDRC most members could expect to spend their careers in routine real estate work. However, as skills increased, new opportunities occurred. Today, many members look forward to roles in senior corporate management.

1991
Excerpt

"Editorial: CEO Confidential: Are You Preparing Your Asset Managers for Global Operations? A memo from your real estate department." *Site Selection.* April 1991. pp. 248.

A memo from your real estate department floats up through the echelons and arrives on the desk of your CFO. Some poor misguided real estate soul has had the temerity to ask for money to attend a meeting in Singapore.

Your company isn't looking at sites anywhere in that part of the world, so the CFO quickly says forget it. Moreover, he makes a mental note to check the travel budget of that real estate fellow more closely — is he prone to plan ventures as far-out as the Singapore junket?

Ho-hum, you say, the CFO is doing his job and all is well.

Or is it? Your last annual report carried a special page on your company's plans to expand around the world. The report carried your signature and was accompanied by a big color photo of you looking at a globe.

We know that page was put in primarily to make the shareholders happy. Everywhere they look they see reports that savvy firms are "going global." They feel better knowing that you are keeping up with the smart crowd.

We also know you have good intentions. Your global plans go well beyond the high-flying phrases in your annual report. You have had your market research people looking at a bunch of countries in Europe and along the Pacific Rim. You've already set up joint ventures in a couple of places.

You've planted some seeds and you hope to see rapid growth. Within a few years you could have as many successful operations overseas as you have at home — provided, of course, that you have a competent global team of middle-level managers.

Our point — at which we have finally arrived — is that going global is not just for the brass. You're not going to make it around the world if the only experienced international executives are those you see around the board room.

And, don't think you can just hire some of those types when you need them. Even if you could find them they wouldn't know your business.

If you're serious about going global you've got to prepare your executives up and down the line. And, from where we sit, it appears that one of the most crucial needs is for competent real property asset managers with global experience.

We're talking about fellows who not only can read 24-hour clocks, use metric measures and tell what time it is in Tokyo but also know how big a 10-rai site is in Bangkok, how brokers work in Amsterdam and where to go for appraisals in Melbourne.

Happily, there is a practical solution to your problem. During the past few years the Industrial Development Research Council has set up global programs at which your people can meet veteran global executives who know how to do business around the world.

All you need to do is approve a small international travel budget so that your people can attend these meetings and get ready for your big expansion program.

Do yourself a favor. Pass the word to your CFO — it's OK for the real estate fellow to go to Singapore.

1991
Excerpt

"Editorial: CEO Confidential: Don't Be Misled! One of the alleged experts in the development field recently made a speech about the end of the golden age of real estate. The implication was that all of the really exciting projects are behind us, and we can look forward only to years of stultifying no-growth." *Site Selection,* August 1991. pp. 708.

For our speechmaking friend, maybe the end is near. There may not be anything out there for him. Those who see real estate only in terms of local deals for spec warehouses or short-term office leases have been hurting for some time, and there's not much relief in sight.

But wait! Is that also the corporate outlook? Should CFOs and others who supervise real estate departments perceive the same gloomy future?

Unhappily, some CFOs, faced with recession economics, have concluded that there's not much work for the real estate department. Hence, many units are being trimmed and some have been eliminated.

This may make some sense for the very short term, but it ignores the company's future. It sounds like the deadly malaise of the salesman who doesn't believe in the company product or the researcher who thinks all the good ideas have been taken.

Here is a situation custom-made for CEO leadership!

You have the big picture. From your vantage point, you can see farther. You can open the eyes of your people to what the future holds. You can show them another world out there that is full of excitement and opportunity for individual practitioners and corporate investors alike.

Europe is bursting with activity and anticipation. The Chunnel, nearing completion, is going to have an enormous impact on areas of the UK and Northern France. Disneyworld Europe is opening and the area East of Paris will never be the same again. Barcelona is about to host the Olympics, having made huge investments in new rail, highway and drainage infrastructure.

Throughout the Pacific Rim there are big new projects. Hong Kong and Osaka have new airports under development. Seoul is about to build a second airport. Singapore is expanding industrial areas into adjacent parts of Indonesia and Malaysia.

Japan is planning a global infrastructure program which involves a Gibraltar crossing, a canal across the Thai Kra peninsula, a North Africa desert reclamation project and flood control for Bangladesh. All of the projects bring great new opportunities.

And in North America, we have a host of new ventures looming. There are big ocean water desalting plants in California; new interstate highway segments; the super collider in Texas; and a long list of new bridges, tunnels, waterways, and pipelines — all of which will have an impact on somebody's real estate.

And, don't forget the new free trade agreement with Mexico. That alone deserves a major study by your people.

And, we haven't mentioned the more than 4,000 big new industrial plants which will be built in the next 12 months. Every one of them is like an economic bomb, which will set off waves of opportunity around the impact site.

It all adds up to the fact that we have more big new projects in the mill than ever before. Further, the early 21st Century promises to be an era of unprecedented large-scale construction— so much so that a global conference has been scheduled for next year to begin discussing priorities.

Thus, if there's a lull in your normal real estate operations, this may be a great time to upgrade the global expertise of your personnel. Send them to the global hot spots to make contacts and discover opportunities. Build a worldwide data base for your future operations.

In short, base your corporate planning on the expectation that the real golden age of real estate development is just a few years down the road. Now is the time to get ready!

1991
Excerpt

"Editorial: CEO Confidential: Are You Waging Guerrilla Warfare Against the Problems of Planning, Locating and Building a New Plant? Does each new project provide a lesson in crisis management? Are your staff departments and operating units stepping on each others toes? Have you considered setting up a new project team?" *Site Selection,* Oct. 1991. pp. 924.

We hear a lot of horror stories about important new facility projects being handled by major corporations in an uncoordinated way, often causing the projects to run over budget and behind schedule. And, the sad thing is that in many cases the problems could have been easily avoided by one stroke of the pen on a memo from the CEO.

Here's a case in point. The vice president in charge of the ABC division of Company XYZ holds a sales meeting and, to his delight, finds that sales of a new product are running far ahead of projections. It is clear that expanded manufacturing capacity will be needed.

Further, the new product is in a field of fierce competition. Any delay in meeting demand will open the door for competitors. Something has to be done in a hurry.

The VP writes a memo to HQ stating the case for the new facility and asks for quick action. Knowing, however, that such requests usually move through HQ like molasses on a cold day, the VP decides to save some time by making a preliminary site search himself.

This is where all the corporate alarm bells and sirens should have gone off, but they didn't. In all good faith, the VP contacted a friend who also happened to be a broker, and the two spent a day driving around looking at properties.

A few days later HQ took quick action on the VP's request and sent a veteran member of the corporate real estate staff out to take over the new project location process. He quickly made a good deal for the company.

Happy ending? Not quite.

The VP's broker friend, who was not involved in the deal, sued. He argued, successfully, that the VP's action in allowing him to show sites cemented a broker relationship even though no papers were signed. The company lost time and money because the VP didn't know what he was getting into.

And this is but one of a thousand pitfalls out there waiting for the unwary. That's why an increasing number of firms set up new project teams which include the company's most experienced people in such fields as environmental planning, legal, engineering, real estate, personnel, shipping and community affairs.

Moreover, alert firms do not wait for a new project to get underway before such a team is set up. The team is organized as a standing committee, ready to go into action at the first hint of a new facility project.

This is important. Even though it may be five years before you need a new facility it would be good management to brief the team on the approximate criteria now. In facility planning and site selection, lead time is priceless.

That's where you come in. A new project team can't organize itself. They need a memo from you!

1992
Excerpt

"Editorial: CEO Confidential: If your company is typical, more than one-fourth of your assets are represented by your real estate. Do you have a strategic plan for these important assets? Do you have a career plan for the executives responsible?" *Site Selection,* June 1992. pp. 510.

Somewhere down there in the bowels of your vast far-flung corporate empire there is a poor wretch who has the responsibility for handling your real estate function in these tumultuous times. If he is normal, he is wondering what lies ahead in his career.

Many corporate real estate people are worried because their CEOs seem to be confused about future real estate operations. If the boss isn't sure where he wants the real estate function to go, it's easy to understand why the poor fellow downstairs is concerned.

This is bad for the company, the CEO and the real estate executive. Everybody needs a sense of direction.

Maybe we can help. Take a quick look at the accompanying chart.

The old concept was that the corporate real estate manager was a technical specialist who handled — more or less blindly — the leases, options and other transactions requested by various operating units. He followed career path "RE."

About 15 or 20 years ago new thinking began to emerge. In many companies the real estate manager became an asset manager who had a broader responsibility. He conducted a periodic review of all properties, recommending acquisitions, disposals and creative uses. His work was integrated with the corporate plan. He followed career path "AM."

Now we see yet another innovative trend. The asset manager, like the company, is going global. He is being developed as a special breed of executive who is familiar with global development projects, new transport facilities, new communications channels and areas of new opportunities. He is a global strategist who is a vital member of the corporation's strategic planning team. He is following career path "GS."

Our question, sir, is simple. Do you have your corporate real estate executives pointed in the right direction?

If you want your real estate people to develop as future asset managers and global strategists so that they can handle the greater responsibilities demanded by worldwide competition, let them know! They'll sleep a lot better and do a better job!

| **1992** Excerpt | "Editorial: It's 11:00 a.m. Do You Know How Safe Your Facilities Are? When was the last time you sat down with your facilities managers and reviewed company thinking regarding disaster risk and recovery?" *Site Selection*, Dec. 1992. pp. 1090. |

One of the easiest things for a busy manager to do is put off planning for disasters. After all, earthquakes, volcanic eruptions and hurricanes don't happen very often, and they seldom hit anywhere your company has major interests. Right?

Wrong!!!

Big disasters occur almost every day somewhere around the world. And with your company fast becoming global, you are constantly assuming new risks, some of them big.

All right, so you know that. And you took care of the problem several months ago by advising your insurance manager to "be sure we're covered against all those things." That's the way a lot of CEOs think. It's just an insurance matter.

Today, thousands of homeowners, business operators and investors in south Florida have discovered that Hurricane Andrew was much, much more than an insurance matter. With claims settlement checks in hand, they face some very difficult years of trying to put their lives back together. Many will never recover.

For most Andrew victims this is a time for agonizing reappraisal of earlier planning and management decisions. It's easy now to see that a little bit of forward thinking could have paid huge dividends.

For the typical corporation this forward thinking begins with global strategy. How many eggs to put in one basket? Where? Which of your facilities around the world are in active seismic zones? Which ones are exposed to tidal waves?

Besides natural disasters, has the company reviewed potential man-made disaster risks for each site? Do you know the proximity to nuclear power plants, military weapons depots and large chemical process installations?

Most importantly, do you have recovery plans ready? If plant X is knocked out, where and how will you resume operations? How long will it take?

Finally, has your disaster response plan been updated during the past year? If there could be a Hurricane Andrew in your future now is the time to think about it.

1993
Excerpt

"Editorial: CEOs come in all shapes, sizes and persuasions. Some were born with the proverbial silver spoon but most come from more humble beginnings — they earn their way to the top. Perhaps the common denominator is ability to recognize an opportunity and make the most of it." *Site Selection,* June 1993.

We were set to thinking about career paths during a recent reunion of the Georgia Senate "class of 1963." That was a pioneering legislative body — first to be reapportioned according to the one-man, one-vote concept.

There were 54 of us, representing a healthy mix of occupations and situations. There was, for example, J.B. Fuqua, who ran a TV station in Augusta; Zell Miller, a school teacher from Dahlonega; and Jimmy Carter, a peanut farmer from Plains.

Most of us were college graduates. Few had any previous political experience.

If a survey had been taken at that time to ask, "Will one of these men become President of the United States?", the answer would have been a resounding, unanimous "no."

If the question had been, "Which of these men is most likely to become President of the United States?", at least a dozen names might have been mentioned, with none having a big bloc of votes.

To my knowledge, only one person had any inkling of what was to happen. One day soon after we were sworn in, my daughter Linda, then about 16, was serving as a page.

The first chore I gave Linda was to deliver an envelope which had been put on my desk by mistake. I was elected from Senate district 41. Someone had transposed the numbers and given me an envelope meant for the senator from district 14.

I handed the envelope to Linda and asked her to take it across the senate chamber and hand it to the fellow from Plains, who represented the 14th.

When Linda came back, she said a strange thing: "That man reminds me somehow of John F. Kennedy — maybe someday he will be President." I quickly admonished her that if she understood politics she would know that the fellow from Plains could never be elected President.

Linda hasn't let me forget that. And, at the recent reunion, the senator from the 14th admitted Linda had more foresight than he did.

But Linda missed a few bets. If she had looked around the chamber more closely she might have seen in Zell the future governor, and she might have tagged J.B. as future head of a global conglomerate.

In 1963, most of us had the same opportunities. Some failed to recognize the possibilities ahead. Some saw the opportunities but declined to take the risks involved. A few saw the opportunities, took the chances, but failed to reach the top for lack of effort.

The CEO from the 14th district taught all CEO aspirants a valuable lesson: Look for the opportunity, risk the venture and then put every ounce of your energy into it.

1993
Excerpt

"Editorial: CEO Confidential: This Is a Test! What is the name of your company's top expert in managing real property assets? When is the last time you talked to him? Do you know his needs and support him? More important, does he know your needs and support you?" *Site Selection,* Aug. 1993. p. 874. (Based on presentation made to first IDRC Management Team Seminar Aug. 16, 1988.)

Wasted millions and opportunities lost forever! Unhappily, that's the story for a lot of corporate asset management programs.

It is a long-reported fact that the typical corporation has about 25 percent of its assets invested in real estate. It is also a sad fact that most corporate managers devote less attention to these properties than to any other major group of assets.

How about a quick review of where your program stands. Which of these descriptions fit?

- *Primitive stage.* (This describes the status of thousands of firms.) Your asset manager is not identified or recognized as such. He is lost on the company organization chart.
  He operates in a vacuum with no access to your strategic thinking.

He is not a part of your management team.

All of his functions are in reaction to instructions or requests from others.

His thinking is short-term.

- *The emerging stage.* (Several hundred companies have reached this level.)

  Your asset manager has your authority to gather information from all units, to consolidate reports and to make analyses.

  He has his own automated departmental systems for compiling, organizing and presenting a wealth of data.

  He can quickly produce accurate status reports on all owned or leased property.

  In special situations, such as acquisition/merger talks, he can provide sound data to support your negotiations.

- *The sophisticated stage.* (A few dozen companies fall into this category.)

  Your asset manager is a member of your management team.

  He helps develop and implement corporate strategy.

  The planning objectives of the real estate department are part of the corporate plan, and the corporate planning objectives are integrated in the department plan.

  Your asset manager monitors the impact on the corporation's assets of technological change, social change and political trends.

  He thinks like an entrepreneur and innovator.

Are you satisfied with your status? If you're not quite pleased with your company's posture do you want to fix it? Good — that's half the battle! If you earned that top management job, you know what to do now.

C. Bibliography

Following are citations of McKinley Conway's writings on the subject of this chapter. As this book goes to press, work is underway to make many of these items available to researchers. To check status, look for a file on GeoTEAM/IDRCNET or telephone GeoTEAM/Fax at (404) 453-4200 for a free catalog.

137. "What Specific Characteristics Industry Looks for in a Community: A Guide for Industrial Development," Chicago and Northwestern Railway, Chicago, 1958. (Proceedings of Conference on Industrial Development for Wisconsin). Milwaukee, Wis., March 20, 1958.
138. "What Industry Seeks When Locating Plants," Georgia State Chamber of Commerce, Atlanta, April 11, 1958.
139. "Seven Hundred Plant Location Factors," *Industrial Development, Site Selection Handbook* Supplement. Oct. 1958. pp. 17-24.

140. "Plant Location Guide," *Industrial Development, Site Selection Handbook* (supplement). 1959. pp. 16-32.

141. "Realistic Criteria for Plant and Facilities Location Seminar," American Management Assn., New York, Feb. 18, 1959.

142. "Ideal location, U.S.A." (criteria for a hypothetical community most appealing to industry site seekers), Annual Conference, Mississippi Assn. of Chamber of Commerce Executives, Natchez, Aug. 21, 1959.

143. "Company Organization for Expansion Planning," *Industrial Development,* May 1959, pp. 6-9.

144. "Site Selection: (10 Key Steps)," *Industrial Development, Site Selection Handbook* (supplement), Oct. 1961, pp.4-5.

145. "The Industrial Development Research Council Is Launched," *Industrial Development,* Jan. 1962. pp. 4-11. Outline of objectives of the Industrial Development Research Council, First Annual Conference, New York, Oct. 24, 1961.

146. "What the Manufacturer Expects of the Industrial Development Man," Northeastern Industrial Development Assn., New York. Oct. 4, 1966.

147. "Is Your Company Flying Blind?" It is truly astonishing that only a handful of manufacturing firms have put their growth planning on a professional basis. It is probably safe to say that more than 90 percent of U.S. companies have no professional or systematic approach to planning their future growth. *Industrial Development,* Feb. 1967. p 4.

148. *Corporate Facility Planning Survey.* A study for the Industrial Development Research Council. 36 pp. April 1970. IDRC #5.

149. *IDRC Skill Inventory.* A survey for the Industrial Development Research Council. A compilation of member skills. Types of projects handled, geographic areas covered. 81 pp. Nov. 1970. IDRC #6.

150. *Surplus Property Index.* A study for the Industrial Development Research Council. Nov. 1971. IDRC #8.

151. *Survey of the Availability of Electric and Gas Service for New Development Projects.* Response to concerns about an energy shortage. A study for the Industrial Development Research Council. Nov. 1972. IDRC #9.

152. *Code of Ethics for the Industrial Development Research Council.* Basic premise: to justify their status as professionals, members must seek to establish and maintain standards of conduct above that required by law. Covers honesty in dealing, integrity of information, confidentiality, environmental sensitivity, social and civic responsibility, freedom of information, support for common programs, avoidance of libel or slander, gifts or bribes, conflict of interest, and personal conduct. Pamphlet. Undated.

153. *Survey of Sales and Lease Prices for Industrial Land, Buildings and Office Buildings.* Sept. 1973. IDRC #10.

154. *Survey of Salaries and Job Responsibilities.* A study for the Industrial Development Research Council. 1974. IDRC #12.

155. *IDRC Skill Inventory.* Study for the Industrial Development Research Council. Jan. 1974. IDRC #11.

156. *IDRC Skill Inventory.* A study for the Industrial Development Research Council. Jan. 1976. IDRC #14.

157. *The IDRC Seminar Series.* Establishing a professional Forum for industrial planning objectives. A study for the Industrial Development Research Council. Not many years ago industry planners worked in secrecy. There was no systematic sharing of information. This report describes the progress which has been made in creating a much-needed forum. Includes program for IDRC's first annual meeting in 1961. May 1977. 151 pp. IDRC #16.

158. *The Industrial Facility Planner's View of Special Incentives.* A study for the Industrial Development Research Council. Conducted at a time when there was considerable debate about the propriety of incentives, this survey reveals diversity of thinking among IDRC members. 36 pp. plus Appendix. May 1977. IDRC #17.

159. *New Industries of the Seventies.* Federal statistics. State summaries. *Industrial Development* magazine reports. Trends in HQ relocations. Geographic index of new plants. 302 pp. 1978.

160. *A Composite Case History of New Facility Location.* A study for the Industrial Development Research Council. Project profile. Financing. Site characteristics. Utility services. Environmental planning. Personnel requirements. Strategies considered. International projects.

Techniques used in site decision. Final cost analysis. Lessons applicable to future projects. May 1978. IDRC #19. With Linda L. Liston.

161. *New Project File and Site Selection Checklist.* Corporate strategy. Company organization for expansion planning. Criteria for site and facility. An index of hundreds of location factors from which the user can prepare a custom checklist for a particular project. 1979. Binder.

162. *Corporate Record Systems For Facility Planning and Management.* A study for the Industrial Development Research Council. Includes 160 forms used By companies to assist them in maintaining property records. These include forms related to property acquisition, construction and start-up, inventory, operating expenses, maintenance and surplus property. Jan. 1979. 429 pp. IDRC #20. With Linda L. Liston.

163. *Improving Career Skills: Professional Training Programs in the Field of Facility Planning and Real Estate Management.* Rankings of subjects of interest. Programs members have attended. Justifying education and training programs. Future personnel requirements. A study for the Industrial Development Research Council. Nov. 1979. 350 pp. IDRC #21. With Linda L. Liston.

164. *Career Paths.* A study for the Industrial Development Research Council. This is undoubtedly the most detailed study of member interests, expertise and aspirations ever conducted by the Council. It reflects the "state-of-the-art" of corporate growth planning. Sept 1980. 140pp. IDRC #23.

165. *IDRC Code of Ethics.* 1981.

166. *Real Estate Profit Centers.* A study tor the Industrial Development Research Council. Some manufacturing companies have had real estate profit centers for decades. While the idea, thus, is not new, there has been in recent years a fresh and growing interest in such profit centers, their purpose, their operating principles and their performance. March 1981. 23 pp. plus appendix. With Linda L. Liston and James D. Mathis. IDRC #24.

167. *Corporate Facility Planning.* A compilation of more than 100 papers of interest to those involved in corporate real estate. Asset management and strategy. Property administration. Location analysis and site selection. Design and construction. 1981.442 pp. Hard cover. With Linda L. Liston.

168. *Survey of Consultants.* A study for the Industrial Development Research Council. Experience of IDRC members in using consultants. Types of consultants used. Evaluation of consultant performance. Roster of consultants. Oct. 1981. 188 pp. IDRC #26.

169. *Developing the IDRC Computer Network.* New revolution in computer applications. Computer utilization by IDRC members. Launching network services for members. Implications of emerging network system. Index of on-line information sources. Glossary of EDP terminology. May 1982. 90 pp. IDRC #29.

170. *Survey of Compensation and Career Paths.* A study for the Industrial Development Research Council. It is intended that this report assist members in achieving their own personal goals... and that the report will be useful to companies in making their real estate and facility planning functions more effective. 1983. 76 pp. IDRC #30.

171. *Survey of the Industrial Facility Planner's View of Special Incentives: an Update.* Study for the Industrial Development Research Council. March 1984. IDRC #32.

172. "IDRC Set to Assume Greater Role in Geo-Economic Research." The executive director of IDRC explores the potential for a massive new geo-economic research program. *Industrial Development,* Jan.-Feb. 1985. pp. 74-75.

173. "The Megatech Industries: What Determines Their Location?" What are the essential components of a Silicon Valley or a Route 128 complex? Do the location factors for R&D activities cover the production of CPUs, peripherals and software? Is the mix changing? *Site Selection,* June 1985. pp. 626-635.

174. "Thanks for Helping Us Pick the Superlatives!" *Site Selection* begins its 31st year. During this action-packed 30-year period corporate executives have planned and built more than 100,000 new plants. Area developers have launched several thousand office and industrial parks. *Site Selection,* Feb. 1986. p. 4.

175. "Weighing Development Factors for the High-Tech Age."

176. If you are responsible for plotting the development strategy for a major corporation or organization, you will want to study this review of factors which have played a dominant role during the past 30 years. The compilation is based on a scan of our bound volumes, staff research and opinions of several hundred readers working in a wide variety of development

positions. *Site Selection,* April 1986. pp. 280-288. (Summarized in the monograph, "A Technology Review and Forecast for Development Strategists.")

177. "Good Life Index — Now It's Here to Stay!" Early checklists of facility location factors listed quality of life items at the bottom, among incidentals. Today, for many facilities, QOL evaluations determine location decisions. *Site Selection,* Aug. 1986. p.772.

178. "Terrorism: Growing Factor in Location Decisions." Recent events reveal all too starkly the clouds which hang over development programs in many parts of the world. Business travelers, investors and facility planners must be concerned not only with traditional war risk and political risk, but also with the added risk of bombings, assassinations, hijackings and taking of hostages carried out by international terrorist groups. *Site Selection,* Aug. 1986. pp. 952-956.

179. "Crisis in Corporate Facility Planning!" One of the most critical issues facing corporate management today is the necessity for providing flexibility in future facility plans. Firms which ignore this warning may find themselves unable to compete and survive in the years just ahead. *Site Selection,* Dec. 1986. p. 1256.

180. *Facility Planning Technology.* A selection of over 200 articles contributed by what resembles a "who's who" of the corporate real estate and industrial development profession. Corporate asset management and strategy. Property administration. Location analysis and site selection. Design and construction. The automated office. 935 pp. Hard cover. With Linda L. Liston. 1987.

181. *Status of the Corporate Facility Planner: a Progress Report.* Research study for the Industrial Development Research Council. March 1987. IDRC #36.

182. "New Plant Locations — a Review and Forecast." New corporate facilities bring to the chosen area new investment, new jobs and new economic opportunities. While some residents may perceive negative aspects, the area usually enjoys improved community services and other significant benefits. A summary of new plant announcements by state. Monograph. 1988.

183. "Club Med Shifts Strategy." While continuing to develop new sites around the world, the French-based resort chain seeks to broaden its market appeal to "every interest and every age group". *Site Selection,* Feb. 1988. pp. 18-19.

184. "Why Joe Lost His Job." It's a jungle out there. We all know that. Nothing is absolutely guaranteed. Even the biggest companies fall flat. And a great many are trimming management costs, especially in staff areas. Even so, Joe might have survived the cuts. *Site Selection,* April 1988. p. 276.

185. "Are You Building Your Own Personal Data Base?" The most important data base you will ever have to consult is the one between your ears. Just about everything to which you aspire depends on it. Are you giving it the attention it deserves? *Gwinnett Daily News,* Dec. 21, 1988.

186. "Where Will You Land after the Merger?" The time to make your job secure is before the blood-letting starts. And one of the very best strategies is to develop an automated property inventory with which you are thoroughly familiar. Learn from the sad experience of the veteran real estate manager who was not prepared. *Site Selection,* Dec. 1988.

187. "Site Planners Take Note!" With the highways and major airports facing gridlock, why not locate your corporate facilities at an uncongested airport with your company plane parked at your door? *Site Selection,* April 1989. p. 276.

188. "Does Your Real Estate Setup Make Your Company a Takeover Target?" Experts in the takeover game have discovered that the real estate department is the Achilles heel of many large corporations. Unmanaged or under-managed properties have become a major lure. It proves once more that what you don't know can hurt you in a big way. *Site Selection,* Feb. 1989. p. 4.

189. "This Is a Test!" Show us a copy of your company map! We're not looking for anything in particular — we just want to know if you have one. Here's why. *Site Selection,* Oct. 1990. p. 1040.

190. "Had Your Annual Checkup?" No, not the one at the Mayo Clinic. We're talking about the in-house review of your company's real property assets. *Site Selection,* Dec. 1990. p. 1288.

191. There's a siren song being wafted on the breezes out there. It is beguiling, and some CEOs are intrigued. The alluring refrain suggests that you can farm out your corporate real estate function to a consultant, eliminate the real estate staff, save a lot of and perform just

as well. *Site Selection,* Aug. 1990. p. 800.

192. "Global Competition for Jobs." Let it be known that your company plans to make an investment in a new manufacturing plant and the world will beat a path to your door. Article for *Atlanta Journal.*

193. "Are You Preparing Your Asset Managers for Global Operations?" A memo from your real estate department. *Site Selection,* April 1991. pp. 248.

194. In the process of gathering information for you, we deal with a lot of corporate PR executives. Some of them are great, but some, we regret to say, look like bums to us. *Site Selection,* June 1991. pp. 564.

195. "Don't Be Misled!" One of the alleged experts in the development field recently made a speech about "the end of the golden age of real estate". The implication was that all of the really exciting projects are behind us and we can look forward only to years of stultifying no-growth. *Site Selection,* Aug. 1991. pp. 708.

196. "Are You Waging Guerrilla Warfare against the Problems of Planning, Locating and Building a New Plant?" Does each new project provide a lesson in crisis management? Are your staff departments and operating units stepping on each others toes? Have you considered setting up a new project team? *Site Selection,* Oct. 1991. pp. 924.

197. "Global Corporations and Global Super Projects." Never before have the productive forces of the world faced such great opportunities and enormous responsibilities. We have the awesome task of meeting global needs for food, shelter, clothing and essential services in a time of mushrooming population growth and explosive pressures of rising expectations. Pamphlet for World Development Council. 1991.

198. Here's how you can exert a powerful influence in the congressional Election next November. You can help keep the good guys in while throwing the rascals out! *Site Selection,* Feb. 1992, pp. 6.

199. "Do the Japanese Really Want You?" Amid the confusion of high-level political blasts and the continuous sniping of opposing business leaders, what is the hard evidence that Japan sincerely wants your new plant? *Site Selection,* April 1992, pp. 250.

200. If your Company is typical, more than one-fourth of your assets are represented by your real estate. Do you have a strategic plan for these important assets? Do you have a career plan for the executives responsible? *Site Selection,* June 1992. pp. 510.

201. "Where Do You Fit in the Washington Mess?" The truth is revealed: Congress doesn't really care what the people think. Special interests are running the system. Are you part of the problem? *Site Selection,* Aug. 1992. pp. 622.

202. "Acres of Diamonds in Our Front Yard?" The death of development pioneer Ted Moscoso reminds us of what can be achieved in Latin America. Now its time for us to implement his vision through the region. *Site Selection,* Oct. 1992. pp. 854.

203. "It's Eleven A.M. Do You Know How Safe Your Facilities Are?" When was the last time you sat down with your facilities managers and reviewed company thinking regarding disaster risk and recovery? *Site Selection,* Dec. 1992. pp. 1090.

203. "Airport Cities: They Could Change Your Company's Future." Can you walk out of your office door, jump into the company airplane, and fly direct to any of your plant sites — all located on airports with taxiways leading to their main entrances — thus completely avoiding the time, expense and frustration of ground transportation? *Site Selection,* Feb. 1993, pp. 6.

204. A special message for the CEO who now lives at 1600 Pennsylvania Avenue. *Site Selection,* April 1993. pp. 242.

205. "CEOs Come in All Shapes, Sizes and Persuasions." Some were born with the proverbial silver spoon, but most come from more humble beginnings — they earn their way to the top. Perhaps the common denominator is ability to recognize an opportunity and make the most of it. *Site Selection,* June 1993

206. "This Is a Test!" What is the name of your company's top expert in managing real property assets? When is the last time you talked to him? Do you know his needs and support him? More important, does he know your needs and support you? *Site Selection,* Aug. 1993. (Based on presentation made to first IDRC Management Team Seminar, Aug. 16, 1988.)

3

Transportation, Aviation, Airports

Chapter 3

A. Recent Comments

Getting serious about airplanes
NACA (NASA) in the old days
What did you do in the war, Daddy?
Principles of High-Speed Flight
Caribbean, Amazon, Arctic, Other
Concept of fly-in and the airport city

B. Excerpts

Site World. Riding with the airlines, 1991
Airport Cities 21, 1993
Airport cities.
New travel patterns.
Safe skies.

C. Bibliography

A. Recent Comments

Let's start with the understanding that the greatest new influence in economic development in the 20th Century has been the airplane. Let's understand, too, that further innovations in air transport will be a very important factor in the decades just ahead.

We submit that is justification enough for devoting a chapter of this book to airplanes, airports and air-transport-related opportunities.

I will not claim to be objective about airplanes. My warp began when, at the age of seven, I sat with my parents listening to a scratchy radio report of Lindbergh's arrival in Paris. The world's excitement was contagious.

Soon, I had my first model airplane — probably as much a toy for my Dad as for me at that time. We flew it until it finally succumbed to repeated crash landings.

But I was hooked, and I built model airplanes with increasing fervor through my early teens. I didn't have enough patience to build fine scale models for display — but I built flying models in profusion and sometimes produced one good enough to enter in competition.

I remember winning a contest in Montgomery, Alabama, with a flying model of the Curtiss Robin, a high-wing monoplane popular in the 1930s. The prize was a 30-minute ride in a Fairchild 22. I took the ride and then went home to report, suspecting that if I asked permission first, the answer would be negative.

That was my fourth ride. My first was in a World War I Jenny. My Dad paid a barnstormer who had landed in a cornfield $5 to make one circuit around the field. I sat in Dad's lap. The second ride was in an open-cockpit Waco biplane hired by a newspaper in Birmingham to make photos of tornado damage. The third was in a Ford Trimotor at an airshow in Montgomery. I still have vivid memories of all of them.

My greatest thrill with model airplanes came in the Junior Birdmen of America Southeastern competition held in Atlanta about 1935. I won a medal in the hand-launched glider event with a flight of 68 seconds. In this competition you throw the glider as high as you can, trying to place it in a spiral orbit from which it will be lifted by thermal currents.

It's not easy. Try it! With a well-designed glider and a good throw you will usually achieve a flight of about 20 seconds.

Getting Serious About Airplanes

In the fall of 1936, at age 15, I entered Georgia Tech as a candidate for a degree in Aeronautical Engineering. I wanted to be an airplane designer — like Wright, Curtiss, Douglas, Boeing, Cessna, Piper, Ryan and all the others.

It didn't take long to discover that studying calculus and thermodynamics was not as much fun as building models. Another frustration was that I wanted to learn to fly and there seemed to be no early prospect for that. The cost was out of reach.

A glimmer of hope appeared when the makers of Wings cigarettes announced a slogan contest with a brand new Piper Cub as first prize — a $1,000 value! I wrote a slogan every week on "why I like Wings," but never got as much as an honorable mention. Maybe the fact that I didn't smoke was a factor.

Then, lightning struck. In my senior year at Tech the federal government — concerned by the spreading war in Europe and our lack of pilots — launched the Civilian Pilot Training Program (CPTP).

Under the plan, senior students in selected universities in each part of the country were invited to volunteer for primary flight training at government expense. Free!

I applied at once and was selected as one of a Georgia Tech class of 40 hopefuls. We were trained by Southern Airways at Atlanta's Candler Field (now Hartsfield International) in the summer of 1940.

It was wonderful. I enjoyed every minute, and at age 19 had my license. Soon, I joined a new organization called the Aircraft Owners and Pilots Association (AOPA). I was member number 8833. Today the new members get numbers in the vicinity of 1,300,000.

But the Tech aeronautical degree program was not so easy — it took five grueling years. In those days we had to get a four-year degree in general engineering and then go for a fifth year in aeronautical sciences. Among other things, we had to take every graduate math course in the curriculum. In 1941 five of us got diplomas.

NACA (NASA) in the Old Days

As I neared graduation, the most sought-after jobs were the few that were offered by the National Advisory Committee for Aeronautics. The NACA began as a committee during World War I and had by 1941 become a highly respected research agency employing several thousand scientists and supporting personnel.

(Many people today are not aware that NASA's roots go back so far. The name was changed from NACA to NASA in the 1950s.)

It was a great thrill to get the telegram from NACA/NASA advising that I had been selected to fill a slot as junior aeronautical engineer at the Langley lab in Virginia. The pay was a handsome $2000 per year.

While I was initially assigned to duties in the laboratory director's office I quickly expressed an interest in joining chief test pilot Mel Gough's small crew. As further evidence of my burning urge to fly, I chipped in with a dozen other staff members to buy an airplane. The deal was $100 each for a share in a used Fairchild 22 high-wing monoplane.

The Pearl Harbor attack December 7, 1941, wiped out the airplane purchase — all civilian aircraft were grounded — and a transfer to NACA/NASA Washington HQ doused my test pilot aspirations. In those days you went where they wanted you to go and liked it.

Actually, the HQ assignment was a fantastic opportunity. I was given an opportunity to meet many people whose names are legendary. For example:

I knew Orville Wright. Yes, the real one.

At that time Dr. Wright was in his eighties and served as honorary chairman of NACA/NASA. Several times a year he came to the office for meetings of our steering committee. I remember that his chair had a brass plate on the back identifying it as his. Nobody else had a brass plate.

When Dr. Wright was in town, our director, Dr. George Lewis, saw to it that our distinguished visitor was taken care of. One of our senior staff people, Charles Helms, usually served as his escort/chauffeur.

I remember one special occasion which gives some insight into the kind of man Wright was. The NACA/NASA board meeting had been scheduled on the same day as the annual Wright Brothers lecture sponsored by the Institute of Aeronautical Sciences.

Late in the afternoon, the board meeting ended and several of us started to the lecture, which was being held in the U.S. Chamber of Commerce auditorium near the White House. I found myself in the car with Helms, Dr. Wright, and another staff member, I think Russ Robinson.

We arrived a few minutes late, found the room almost full, and, following Dr. Wright, took seats in the back row. We chatted and waited, chatted and waited, for about 10 minutes. Then the moderator walked up to the podium and said, "Ladies and gentlemen we have delayed start of the lecture for a few minutes, hoping that Dr. Wright might attend and that we could recognize him."

We flagged the moderator and Dr. Wright was escorted to the front for a standing ovation. Later, after getting to know more about him, I realized that he would have preferred to sit quietly in the back.

What does the Wright incident have to do with this report? That long-ago afternoon is mentioned because Orville Wright, whom I scarcely knew, had a profound influence on my life. He helped make this book possible, for he and his contemporaries, in giving us aviation, shaped the lives of all who sought to cover the world of the 20th Century.

The airplane became a tremendous tool for exploring remote areas, meeting people and understanding the world's problems and opportunities. It enabled an ordinary person like me to see in one lifetime what previously could be covered only by teams of explorers working for generations.

Another noteworthy visitor to the NACA/NASA office was Howard Hughes, then a dashing young man. What I remember most is that he would arrive for a meeting in a taxi and instruct the cabbie to sit there in our driveway on Dupont Circle with the meter running until he was ready to go, even if that was several hours later. I had never before witnessed such extravagance.

In those days NACA/NASA research programs were guided by a system of committees and subcommittees made up of the top scientists in the country in each field. Each committee had a staff secretary assigned from among the six engineers then serving on the small NACA/NASA Washington HQ staff.

Naturally, the senior engineers drew the more prestigious committees. As the junior member of the team, I drew some obscure assignments. For example, I was secretary of the Subcommittee on Lubrication, Friction and Wear. We spent a lot of time worrying about piston rings.

However, there were compensations. I attended the sessions of the fuels and lubricants committee which included Jimmy Doolittle, then representing an oil company. I already regarded him as a hero before he quietly dropped off the committee and turned up a few months later leading the raid on Tokyo.

Also, there was an obscure committee on gas turbines. At that time our interest was in using turbo-superchargers to give our airplanes better performance at high altitudes. Later, this was the group that steered pioneering work on jet propulsion systems.

I remember, too, attending sessions of a committee concerned with rotating wing aircraft. One day Igor Sikorsky came down from Connecticut to describe his experimental machine. The main thing I remember is that he had a hard time pronouncing "helicopter" with his Russian accent. It came out "heel—ee-copiter."

Boot Camp to Shore Patrol

Remember that this was wartime and the young engineers on the NACA/NASA HQ staff were still civilians when many others our age were in uniform. We became increasingly unhappy about the situation.

At the start of the war, the NACA/NASA scientific personnel of draft age had been "frozen" in their positions and made unavailable for military service pending action by the Army-Navy Aeronautical Board. That was a high-level board somewhat like the Joint Chiefs of Staff today.

Finally, after a delay of nearly two years, they acted. Some of us were assigned to a naval aviation unit and some to an Army aviation unit, and these units were in turn reassigned to NACA/NASA duties. In short, we put on uniforms but they kept us working on confidential wartime aircraft projects.

Within a few weeks, I went to California, where I enjoyed the classical pleasures of boot camp as an Apprentice Seaman before receiving a commission as Ensign, USNR, assigned to the Ames Aeronautical Detachment, NAS Moffett Field.

What Did You Do in the War, Daddy?

I was in naval aviation. "Oh, you flew fighters off of a carrier?" Well, not exactly. Actually, I helped test experimental airplanes in a wind tunnel at the NACA/NASA Ames Laboratory. It was the biggest wind tunnel in the world — big enough to test real airplanes, not small scale models.

It was a great experience. Manufacturers brought in their super-secret experimental aircraft, and we tested them for performance. The situation in the control room of the big wind tunnel was somewhat like that depicted at the Houston Space Flight Center during a launch. You felt very special being a part of it.

This is not to say that it was glamorous duty. Because of the wartime urgency, we scheduled the wind tunnel 24 hours a day, seven days a week. I was one of three project engineers who managed test projects in sequence. This meant that at any time one engineer's group was testing an airplane in the tunnel, another group was getting an airplane ready to test, and the third group was writing up reports.

The NACA/NASA full-scale wind tunnel covered an area bigger than a football field and was more than 12 stories high. It was actually a huge duct, varying in size, which ran in a complete loop. At one point, the test section could accommodate a fighter type airplane with a wing span of up to 80 feet.

The tunnel was designed to test airplanes by remote control from a booth under the test section. No one would be in the airplane because during tests the running of the airplane's engines polluted the air with carbon monoxide. Also, it was very hot inside the tunnel during the summer, with temperatures well over 100 degrees.

Unhappily, the remote control system was behind schedule, and we had to put the tunnel in service in 1944 without it. Someone had to sit in the cockpit and change engine or control settings during test runs.

Flying experimental airplanes in the tunnel was the closest I got to being a test pilot. We didn't go anywhere; we added nothing to our log books; but it was a memorable experience.

You climbed an extension ladder to get from the steel deck of the tunnel test section up to the airplane, pulled yourself in and closed the canopy. Meanwhile, the crew removed the ladder from the test section and pressed the switch to drive the hydraulic pumps that closed the huge test section door. There was much grinding and clanking as the 50-ton door swung shut. Wham! When that big door closed, you knew you were on your own. In case of fire or structural failure, you couldn't get out. The crew outside could watch you through portholes but couldn't help.

The biggest hazards, however, were less dramatic. We wore oxygen masks and, after a couple of hours of a test run, sweat ran down inside the masks. We itched, and we were deafened by the roar of the airplane's engine confined inside the steel shell.

Near the end of the war I remember running tests on the Grumman F7F, a twin-engine fighter. The noise was unbelievable — a very physical thing.

Watching the Wing Stall

I particularly enjoyed running low speed stall tests on several different airplanes. To prepare an airplane for these tests, we painted the wings white. Then we cut pieces of black yarn several inches long and glued one end to the wing — scattering the tufts over the whole surface.

Powering the wind in the tunnel up to the airplane's cruising speed, we could sit in the cockpit and note that all of the tufts were lying flat along the wing surface. Then, shifting to low speed and high angle of attack, we could see some of the tufts begin to wiggle. As we went to higher angles the unstable airflow spread over more of the surface until a complete stall occurred, and the tufts all over the wing were fluttering at random.

That was an invaluable experience. Most pilots learn to feel the onset of stall, but I could actually see it. Throughout the rest of my flying career, that picture flashed through my mind as I neared stalling speed in any airplane.

A Dose of Carbon Monoxide Poisoning

One persistent problem we had was carbon monoxide poisoning. During test runs, polluted air would leak around our oxygen masks, and by the time we became aware of it, it was too late to avoid some sickness. I remember that someone asked the flight surgeon about it and he said, "Be more careful."

Then, a year or so later, the flight surgeon casually commented that he had studied the problem a bit more and found that repeated exposure to carbon monoxide might cause insanity. I'm not sure that is true; however, if my family ever needs to get me committed to a Veteran's hospital, they may have a case.

Fire in the Tunnel!

As I have watched the problems with the space shuttle program recently, I have been reminded of many of the problems we had. Thank God we didn't have to explain ours to the news media! Let me give you an example:

Toward the end of the war I drew my most exciting assignment — project engineer for tests of the Ryan FR-1 "Fireball." To be deployed as a carrier-based fighter, this was the Navy's first jet-propelled airplane.

Well, it was the first to have a turbojet engine. There were actually two engines: a conventional reciprocating radial engine in the nose and the new jet engine in the aft fuselage with a tail cone nozzle. This design reflected the lack of confidence in the new turbine engine.

And that lack of confidence was well-justified. The new GE I-16 engine was still very much in the experimental stage. After every run or flight we had to climb inside and check the turbine blades for stretching. After 50 hours of operation the engine required substantial overhaul.

We had some special problems testing this airplane, one of which was the fuel system. Because there was no escape from the tunnel during testing, we didn't like to operate airplanes with full fuel tanks. Instead, we installed auxiliary tanks outside the tunnel and pumped fuel to the airplane. That way, if we had a fire, there wouldn't be so much fuel in the tunnel to fry the pilot.

For the "Fireball" we installed two external tanks, one for high-octane gasoline and the other for kerosene jet fuel. Pipes ran through a jury-rigged control panel to the airplane in the test section.

I will never forget the day when, with the tunnel started and the airspeed up to somewhere between 100 and 150 miles per hour, we got the fuel valves switched. This pumped kerosene to the reciprocating engine in the nose and gasoline to the jet engine in the tail.

The nose engine began belching black smoke and bucking like a bronco, shedding pieces of cowling, while the jet engine blew a plume of red flame back along the tunnel and through the huge turning vanes. It was spectacular.

In fact, it was so spectacular that everybody reacted instantly to shut things down. Damage was confined largely to our egos.

Think what the media could have done with that!

Principles of High-Speed Flight
After the War — New Horizons

Shortly after I left NACA/NASA I decided to put what I had learned into a text, *Principles of High-Speed Flight.* That was in 1947.

This ragged book, produced via mimeograph, reflected the most advanced thinking regarding future aircraft design. It covered jet propulsion, then in its infancy, and supersonic flight, yet to be achieved.

The book was given an excellent review by the Institute of Aeronautical Sciences and was adopted as a text by several dozen universities. It served for some years until better material was prepared.

Unhappily, that book was about as close to an airplane as I could get for some time. In the years immediately after WWII, I was much too poor to own an airplane or even to rent one. My wife Becky and I were busy building a house in Atlanta, starting a family and launching a business. Finally, in the 1950s there was enough money for a down payment on a used Cessna 170.

That was the beginning of a lifetime of exploration and appreciation of this earth on which we live. Now, after more than 50 years of flying, the lure is still there.

Flying your own airplane is addictive. Once you have enjoyed that degree of freedom, you'll never be content without it.

Having an airplane teaches a lot. You soon realize that you enjoy a privilege shared by only a very small percentage of the world's people. You have a vantage point from which to see the world as few see it.

Yes, there is a risk. I thought long and hard about involving my family in exploration flights to remote regions. It is one thing to risk your own life in pursuit of knowledge related to your career objectives, but quite another to expose your family to extraordinary risks.

For example, there was the 1965 flight across the Amazon Basin, some 3,000 miles over trackless jungle with no radio aids and no search-and-rescue coverage. After a lot of soul-searching, we made it a family project, and it turned out to be one of the greatest and most profound experiences in the lives of all of us.

I suppose the obvious conclusion is that the risk is worth taking if all goes well. If we had been lost in the jungle it would not have looked like a good plan.

Flying your own airplane not only provides mobility but also forces you to learn some basic geo-economics. Wherever you go, you learn the elevations of the mountains, the routes of the rivers, the contours of the coastlines and the location of the cities.

Flying also requires study of weather patterns around the world. You learn to scan the maps, make your own forecast, deal with ice, read the radar screens and interpret the stormscope displays.

On the ground, you learn something about a country every time you make a fuel stop. You meet people under everyday working conditions as you clear your airplane, passengers and cargo through customs and immigration, file a new flight plan, get a weather briefing and attend to fueling and other ramp services.

And you discover the value of language skills. Although I studied Spanish in school, it meant little to me until I started flying into Latin America. Thirty years ago you could not count on finding English-speaking personnel manning airport control towers or air traffic control centers as you can today.

My log book now shows close to 7,000 hours. That's nowhere near the totals of veteran air carrier pilots, but a close examination of my log will show an impressive variety.

We've flown the Arctic, including Alaska, Canada, Greenland and Iceland. We have a lot of tropical experience, covering the Amazon Basin, Central America, the Yucatan and several dozen islands of the Bahamas and Caribbean.

We've mingled with the big jets at busy international airports, such as London's Gatwick, Washington's Dulles, Amsterdam's Schiphol, San Francisco, Dallas/Fort Worth, Miami, Los Angeles and Seattle/Tacoma.

In addition, we've been into many remote unpaved strips where the air carriers can't take you. The roughest were in Baja California where we had access to a wonderful world of private beaches, awesome deserts and protected solitude.

We've dealt with just about every kind of weather, from white-out conditions over the Greenland ice cap, to the towering thunderstorms of the inter-tropical convergence zone along the northern shores of South America.

We've skirted the fringes of hurricanes around Florida and dodged tornadoes across the Great Plains. There were also sand storms in West Texas and blizzards from the Sierras to the Adirondacks.

All of this travel was done in small airplanes on our own. There was no company dispatcher or weather advisor. The ground crew was whomever we met at the next stop.

What was it like? Here is a random collection of memories and impressions:

Radios Not to Be Trusted

Today, the electronic aids are so reliable that navigating precisely from point A to point B is easy and routine. In the days before we had good radios, however, it was work. And, there was a lot of tension because we often had no checkpoints in sight.

During the early years in the venerable Cessna 170, the most noteworthy aspect was the lack of dependable communication and navigation equipment. If you could succeed in tuning the radio to a specified frequency, the best you could hope for was a weak, scratchy signal.

For navigation, we had a radio direction finder with a rotating loop antenna. Sometimes, if the weather were good, it would pick up a station. You had to figure out whether the needle was pointing to or away from the station.

The early airways were defined by radio beams consisting of audible Morse code "A" and "N" signals on either side of the course. If you heard a steady tone, you were in the zone where the two signals overlapped and, thus, on course.

Sounds simple, and it was usually better than nothing. However, the system required wearing a headset all the time and listening for the signal against a background of static which often blocked out the signal completely. A few hours of that made a padded cell sound appealing.

Good pilots would never admit to being lost. However, when pressed for a position report by a ground controller, they would sometimes say they were "unsure of exact position."

At night we depended on city lights and the flashes of airway beacons. The beacons were placed 50 to 75 miles apart, and in a stiff crosswind it was a challenge to fly from one to the other. If there were clouds, we had to stay below and take a beating in rough air in order to see the beacons.

We spent a lot of time with cockpit lights dimmed out, peering through the gloom ahead and hoping the faint glow in the sky would grow into a beacon or cluster of lights we could identify.

There were a lot of places in the country where lights on the ground were scarce. The stretch I remember as blackest was the direct route from Reno to Salt Lake City. It was rugged terrain, and on a moonless night it was pitch black. It was easy to imagine that an undefined mountain peak lay dead ahead at the same altitude.

A Handful of Mayonnaise

We have enough memories of early flying to fill a six-foot bookshelf. Some are profound and some are frivolous. For example:

One dark, cold winter night, I was flying the Cessna 170 from Atlanta

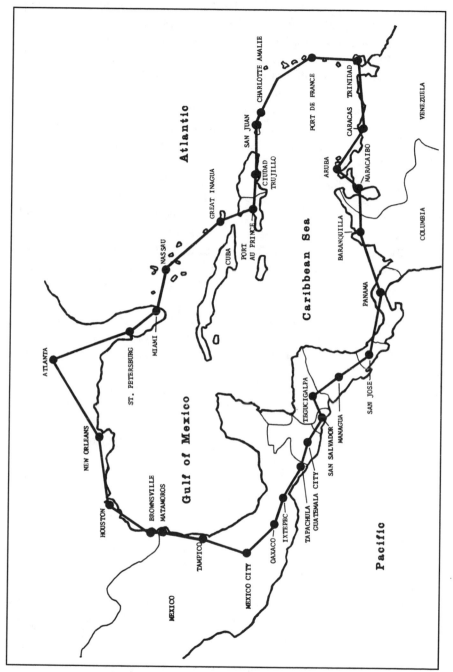

Exploring the Caribbean. This is the route first flown by the author in 1960 in a single-engine Cessna 182. Pan American Airways provided search-and-rescue cover.

135

to Dallas. While stopping for fuel in Meridian, I bought a sandwich in a bag, and soon after take-off and climb to altitude, I decided to eat.

The 170 had no autopilot, so I held the yoke with my left hand and reached blindly into the bag in the backseat with my right to get the sandwich. My aim wasn't good and my hand slipped inside the sandwich, collecting a thick layer of mayonnaise on both sides.

I flew the next hundred miles smearing maps and radio controls until I could lick the mayo off my hand. It wasn't life-and-death, but it was so ridiculous I have remembered it for more than 30 years. In flying there are a lot of little things like that.

Despite its limitations, the 170 took our family to New York, California and Florida. By 1960 we were able to trade it for a Cessna 182, a much more useful airplane. The 182 was a bit faster, could carry more load, and its tricycle landing gear made it safer in crosswinds.

In the summer of 1960 we took off for an historic (for us, at least) circle-the-Caribbean expedition *(see map)*. It was a bold project to prove the feasibility of using a small airplane to explore economic development potential of a region.

In one month, we visited several island nations in the Caribbean, several South America nations, Panama and other Central American countries and Mexico. We met with development officials at each stop, gathered economic research materials and took hundreds of photos.

That one trip told us more about the region than we could have learned in a year of office research. It was an eye-opener both for us and for the development officials with whom we met. It laid the foundation for a series of development studies and projects that were subsequently documented in key development journals.

Caribbean, Amazon, Arctic, Other
An Island is Born

Looking back, we realize how fortunate we have been to have repeated opportunities to visit areas via small aircraft. We have seen the launching of new towns, industrial parks and many other developments and then watched them grow year after year.

That also applies to some natural phenomena. For example, on that first Caribbean trip more than 30 years ago, we had a checkpoint called Hog Sty Reef located about midway between Acklins Island and Great Inagua Island, in the lower Bahamas.

At that time, the reef was mostly underwater and hard to find. From directly overhead on a clear day you could see the circular outline of growing coral, with one small sand spit rising out of the water at low tide. On subsequent flights years later, we began to see more sand, then a palm tree.

Recently, we noted what looked to be a nice, though small, beach and a cluster of palms. Further, the chart showed Hog Sty Cay, a designation indicating that it is now above water even at high tide. We have no doubt that, as the coral grows, there will emerge a series of beaches around a beautiful lagoon, and someone will want to build a hotel there.

Amazon Basin Scan

After a few years the Cessna 182 gave way to an Aero Commander 560A that offered additional possibilities. It was a comfortable twin-engined airplane with good range and instrument flying capabilities. It could carry seven people with no baggage or four people with a lot of baggage.

By 1965 we had laid plans to use the airplane for an expedition across the Amazon Basin *(see map)*. Our motivation was to answer questions raised during several years of work in South America.

Our company, with the support of the Agency for International Development, had been involved in setting up development programs in Brazil, Colombia, Ecuador, Venezuela and Peru. In many meetings with local officials we had found that little attention was being given to the Amazon Basin. When we asked questions about the area, we were given a variety of explanations.

Some said it was too hot to live there. Others said it was too dangerous, citing such hazards as savage Indians, big snakes, wild animals and mysterious diseases. Still others said locating anything along the river was impractical because it flooded every year, taking everything in its path.

Upon inquiry, we discovered that most of those who gave us these warnings had never been into the basin. So, we decided to go and find out what it was like.

Reports on the expedition have been published elsewhere, so we will not repeat them here. We'll just say that almost everything we had been told turned out to be wrong.

It was hot along the route, but no worse than the Gulf Coast of the USA. The Indians were so friendly that our biggest worry after landing at a strip was to get the propellers stopped before the Indians crowded around the airplane. Along much of the river there were high banks, well above flood level.

What we saw over a distance of some 3,000 miles was an ocean of green rainforest. In the upper basin there were stretches of hundreds of miles with virtually no evidence of mankind.

As we neared Manaus we began to see a few clearings. Farther downstream there was some clearing around Santerem and more activity near

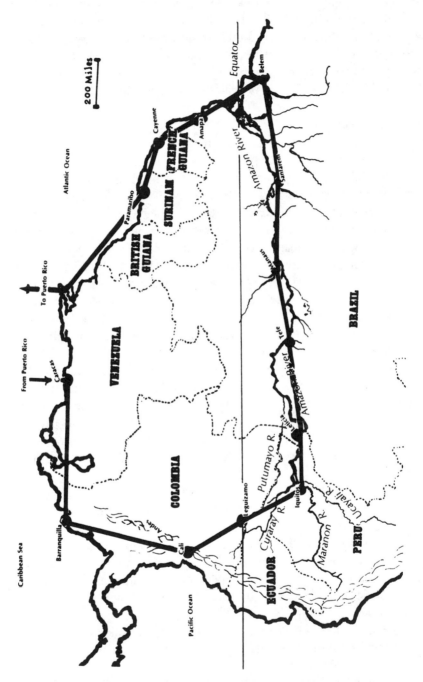

Exploring the Amazon basin. This is the route flown by the author in 1965 in an Aero Commander 560A. There were no radio facilities across the region.

Belem. (The much-discussed destruction of the rainforest was beginning to occur on the southern edge of the basin, far south of our route.)

Our report on the expedition called attention to the basin's resources and asked about its future. We like to think that we prompted local governments to start giving serious attention to the region's future.

Single Versus Multi-engine

Ask non-pilots what kind of small airplane they prefer to ride in, and almost all will say they like twin-engine aircraft "because they are safer." They have been led to believe that at any time an engine fails, the twin can continue the trip on the other engine.

Pilots know better. They are well-aware of many fatal accidents involving twin-engine aircraft that resulted when one engine failed. It is true that the twin can proceed on one engine *if the pilot does exactly the right thing immediately.*

We won't bother with details here, but let's just say we think the safety difference is a small one. About two-thirds of our flying has been in single-engine craft, which we have flown day and night, good weather and bad, over land and over water.

In general, we have bought twin-engined airplanes when our business involved carrying customers in our airplane. Mostly non-pilots, they are happier with two engines. Psychology triumphs over economics.

When buying an airplane to be used primarily for my own transportation, including staff and family, I have opted for a single engine. This is a decision influenced by two factors: economics and conservation.

We see a lot of companies take an ego trip when buying aircraft. They buy jets when a good turbine twin would be more logical, and they buy "cabin cruisers" when they ought to buy single-engine utility craft.

Our small company owned a single-engine Cessna 210 for several years and followed that with a Beech Baron twin. As our business spread geographically from the southeastern states to the USA to North America to global, we reached a point at which we had to have jet transportation.

We could not afford a corporate jet, first, because of the capital cost, and second, because of the inefficient use we would have for it. Our staff travel consists mainly of individual missions rather than groups. Our jet would fly with most seats empty.

Thus, we sold the company Baron and committed our staff (including me) to covering the world via the air carriers. I bought a single-engine Mooney for travel to remote locations, for taking photos, and for special projects.

Arctic Region Scan — to Europe via Mooney

For those not familiar with airplanes, the Mooney is a small craft about the size of a Fiat with wings. It is powered by a four-cylinder, 200 horsepower engine, has four seats, and no de-icing equipment. The normal range is about 900 miles.

It is not the airplane of first choice for flying the Arctic route from North America to Europe. However, if you take out the two back seats and install an auxiliary fuel tank (actually a 55-gallon drum) you can extend the range enough to fly from Northern Canada to Greenland to Iceland to Scotland.

That is what we did, and in 1980 we set out with daughter Laura, life raft and emergency gear. There was an obligatory stop at Moncton, New Brunswick, for inspection and interview by Canadian search-and-rescue officials before we could get a permit to depart Canada on the overseas leg. They had grown weary of trying to rescue pilots who attempted the treacherous crossing without proper equipment, training or planning.

We soon developed a keen appreciation for the hazards they described. Although we made the trip in mid-summer, we encountered icing almost every day. First, we picked up a moderate load of ice over the Davis Strait before letting down to land at Sondrestromfiord on the west coast of Greenland.

Crossing the Greenland ice cap proved to be the biggest challenge. The ice cap is several hundred miles across and rises from an elevation of about 7,000 feet at the edges to about 9,000 feet near the middle.

On our first attempt at crossing, the remote compass system froze and we returned to Sondrestromfiord. The second day we got out about 100 miles before encountering clouds that extended down to within about 1000 feet of the surface. We were flying in a slot between the white ice below and the white cloud base above.

As we proceeded eastbound our slot got thinner, and it became obvious we could not clear the ridge that runs north-south across Greenland. Putting on our oxygen masks, we elected to try to climb on top of the clouds. At about 16,000 feet the clouds were still thick and we were picking up ice. Back to Sondrestromfiord!

On the third day we made it across Greenland to Iceland, and the next morning we took off for Prestwick, some 800 miles east. About half way, in instrument conditions, the drive shaft on our suction pump sheared off, leaving us without our gyro.

With the aid of Shanwick Approach, we made the approach under a low ceiling. The weather continued to be bad every day as we slogged our way to London Gatwick and Amsterdam Schiphol. At Brussels, we turned

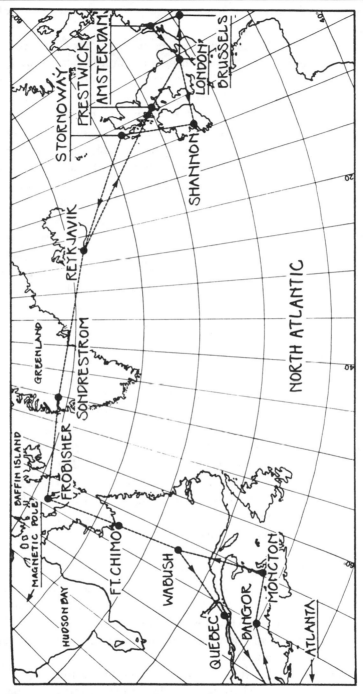

Exploring the Arctic. This is the route — to Europe and back — flown by the author in 1980 in a single-engine Mooney M20.

around and returned via Shannon, Stornoway, Rekjavik, Greenland, and Canada.

The expedition took about a month. At times it was very grim. We learned things about ourselves during those times when we were over uninhabited tundra or ice-choked waters. There were no navaids or communications stations, and we were completely on our own. For a few fleeting moments we understood some of the feelings Lindbergh must have had.

What we learned was invaluable in understanding the Arctic region and its future. You can fly across every day on a big comfortable jet at 35,000 feet and have no concept of what the region is really like. There is no substitute for skimming along a few hundred feet above the awesome icecap with its miles of fissures that could swallow Manhattan Island.

The flights across Canada to the northern edge of Quebec, the Ungava Peninsula and Frobisher Bay remind that Canada is a huge nation, largely unpopulated. We gained respect for the Inuits who have long since learned to deal with the harsh terrain and long winters. And we saw a region rich in resources that will be important to the world in the decades just ahead.

We're glad we did it. And, with GPS and LORAN, which we did not have in 1980, we might be tempted to do it again.

Welcome to Oaxaca

During our first flights into Mexico more than 30 years ago, it was our practice, as we approached an airport for landing, to call the control tower first in English and then, if there were no response, to repeat the call in our primitive Spanish. The first call might be at 25 miles out, and we might repeat the process several times before arriving in the pattern.

One day we arrived at Oaxaca, down in the southern part of Mexico, in just that fashion. Having received no response to any of our calls, we landed and taxied up to the small airport building. Just as we were about to cut the switches and get out, there came a response in halting English: "Aero Commander N6741B, you are cleared to land."

Weather Report at Ixtepec

One hot day I departed Tapachula on the Mexico-Guatemala border, planning to follow the coastline Northwest to Acapulco. After an hour or so a line of dark towering cumulus could be seen ahead, so I decided to stop at the nearest airport shown on my chart, Ixtepec, get some gas and ask about the weather ahead.

We landed, taxied to a little shack alongside the strip, shut off the engine and got out. There was an almost dead silence. All that could be heard was the ticking noises made by the engine as it cooled, plus the crow of a rooster over an adjacent hill.

After a while a solitary figure could be seen trudging along the dirt road coming to the airport. He turned out to be a cheerful fellow anxious to help, but his English was almost as bad as my Spanish.

He did, however, undertake to provide gas. He rummaged around and, after a while, found a ladder. A further search produced a funnel, and, still later, he turned up a dirty chamois cloth to use as a filter.

The next procedure involved rolling a 55-gallon drum onto the ramp from a nearby stockade, looking for a wrench, finding it and opening the drum. Then an old hand-cranked pump was inserted into the drum. More time went into getting the pump primed, but finally he began the laborious process of hand-pumping the fuel up over the wing into the tanks.

During this process, my family had dug into our emergency supplies for a lunch of peanut butter crackers — while standing under the wing to avoid the fierce noonday sun. A crowd of local citizens had arrived from the nearby village to watch the whole fascinating affair.

After fueling, the process of stowing away the drum, pump and ladder, computing the number of liters delivered, and counting out the cash payment took, I would guess, another hour. At long last I was ready to check the weather and take off.

Having spotted a telephone in the shack, I asked the attendant in my best Spanish if he could call for weather information. He said no. Then, I suggested, that — at my expense — he call the Mexico City airport office of Mexicana, the Mexican airline, and ask them for weather en route to Acapulco. I knew Mexicana flew that route.

It took several iterations of this strategy before he understood exactly what I wanted him to do. Evidently the cost and complexity of the plan was overwhelming. At last he shrugged his shoulders and said, "But, Senor, when you get to Acapulco you will *see* what the weather is like."

Fuel Stop at Zihuatanejo

Another year, another trip: I had filed out of Mexico City for Mazatlan. It was mid-winter, and a major weather system was moving across central Mexico. After considerable zigging and zagging to avoid fast-moving storm cells, I decided to land at an intermediate airport, refuel, wait awhile and then proceed.

The nearest airport that, according to my chart, had fuel, was Zihuatanejo, more than a hundred miles behind. Having found the chart information not too reliable, I called Zihuatanejo by radio and asked if they had fuel. The answer was, "Si, Señor," so we turned back.

Landing at the old Zihuatanejo airstrip was an experience in its own right. You flew along the coast at about 1,000 feet, until you found a gap in the hills. Turning into the gap you lowered your gear and got ready. Popping out on the other side of the gap, you made a quick left turn and there the strip was, right ahead, guarded by a power line stretching across the approach end.

We landed, using full brakes on the short strip and taxied to the gas pump, finding several airplanes ahead of us. We soon learned that the back-up was not the result of heavy traffic. The power in the area was off, the electric pump was inoperative, and fuel could not be delivered. It had been that way all afternoon.

Yes, Zihuatanejo had fuel. No, they could not deliver it. I had asked the wrong question.

Go with God

Still another trip, I was departing Mexico City under low visibility conditions, headed south to Puerto Escondido. This required an instrument departure via a rather complicated routing that would take me around the higher mountains through a pass to lower terrain.

At that time the aeronautical radio check points in that part of Mexico were given the names of the nearest town. Almost all were villages with — to a gringo — unpronounceable, unspellable Indian names.

As per routine procedure, I taxied out to the end of the runway, where the Mexico City controller gave me my clearance. It went something like this: "After takeoff fly directly to the Chimalhuacan beacon, turn right to 175 degrees to Netzahualcoyoti intersection, proceed over Ztapalapa at 10,000 feet, then 230 degrees to Tlanguistengo, then flight plan route."

I tried valiantly to copy the clearance and read it back, but mangled it. The controller tried again. I tried again. Then we both tried again. Finally, the controller said, "You are cleared. Vaya con Dios."

Don't Shoot!

Recently a measure was introduced in the U.S. Congress to authorize the shooting down of aircraft suspected of smuggling drugs into the country. While aimed at a good objective, the act was immediately opposed by aircraft owners and pilots.

Only those who have had extensive experience flying in and out of Latin America can realize how difficult it is for a pilot — with all of the best intentions — to properly notify U.S. authorities as he approaches the border.

We still have a vivid memory of an incident that occurred many years ago — during a period when relations with Cuba were particularly tense.

We had filed out of Cozumel for Key West, and about a hundred miles southwest of Key West a Navy jet fighter pulled alongside. He was so close we could read all his markings and vice versa. He was tapping his microphone, indicating he wanted to talk.

We went to the common emergency frequency (121.5), and he asked who we were and where we were going. We told him we were enroute to Key West as per flight plan. He said they had no plan on us and, when we showed up on radar he was scrambled to intercept us.

On the ground at Key West we explained the whole thing again. Happily, we had a copy of the Mexican flight plan. After awhile, Key West was able to get Cozumel on the radio and confirm. Cozumel had just been slow in filing our plan. Mañana!

On another trip we filed from Tampico to Matamoros, intending to close our plan in Mexico, then telephone Brownsville just across the border and tell them we were coming. That is the easiest way to minimize confusion.

Unhappily, by the time we arrived over Matamoros a fast-developing weather system had closed both the Matamoros and Brownsville airports. I called the controller on the U.S. side and told him I would proceed north, looking for an open airport. He said that was illegal and couldn't be approved.

Having no choice, I continued past Corpus Christi, advising radar controllers who I was and what I was doing, and finally was able to land at San Antonio. The customs and immigration people there checked my story and said, "Welcome home."

On these and other occasions we have crossed the border under less than ideal circumstances. I'm glad, therefore, that Congress killed that bill that would have encouraged some trigger-happy fighter pilot to shoot.

Not All Airstrips Are Created Equal

In order to get into remote areas it is sometimes necessary to land on unpaved airstrips. Many times we have arrived over such landing spots where there was no radio communication, and the latest data on the airstrip may have come from a chart five or 10 years old.

What you do is make a low pass over the strip, looking for ditches, cows, obstructions and unsurfaced areas. It is very difficult, however, to judge the roughness of unpaved surfaces or the depth of grass.

To complicate matters, many crude strips are not level and may be subject to fierce and unpredictable crosswinds. As you flare out for landing, they get your full attention.

The strips of Baja California on the Pacific side of Mexico are particularly notorious. Flying a Beech Baron I have had several interesting "arrivals" on short strips. These involved dropping onto the approach end, bouncing along and trying to dodge bigger rocks and skidding to a stop at the end in a cloud of dust.

Once, we arrived at a strip on the Sea of Cortez near La Paz just as it was getting dark. As we touched down our landing lights picked up some white objects moving across the strip in front of us. Rolling out, we found that the objects were white spots on black cows ambling across the runway.

Going into Puerto Escondido before the new airport was built there, we landed on a dirt strip that looked all right when we dragged over it. What we didn't see, however, was a shallow swale in the middle of the strip that we straddled with our landing gear. To our surprise, the depression got deeper as we rolled down the strip, and we came to a stop sitting astride a ditch.

Even when the chart says the runway ahead is paved, you learn to be wary. Going into Iquitos, Peru, on a rainy day, we were just touching down when we discovered that some small piles of rock had been placed at intervals along the runway. Evidently part of a repair plan, the piles extended from the runway edge to about the middle and alternated every few hundred feet between the left side and right side.

We skidded around on the wet runway, zigging and zagging around the rock piles. And about half way along the runway a pack of stray dogs ran across in front of us. It must have been a routine landing, since the airport personnel had no comment.

Surrounded by Flames

One of the things pilots fear most is an airplane fire. Even a wisp of smoke in the cockpit commands rapt attention.

My worst fire scare — so far — occurred during a fuel stop on a remote island in the Bahamas. I taxied my twin-engine Aero Commander to the gas pump, asked the attendant to top both tanks and walked away to the rest room. A few minutes later I came back, paid the gas bill and got in the airplane to move it to an overnight parking spot.

What I did not know was that the attendant had overfilled one of the wing tanks, and a considerable amount of gas had run along the wing and over the engine cowling. As soon as I cranked the engine, flames appeared everywhere.

My family stood watching in horror as it appeared the fire would get to the fuel tanks and I would disappear in a spectacular explosion.

Inside the cockpit, I realized I could not open the cabin door under the wing without having the burning fuel fall on me, so I revved up the active engine to full power. Happily, the prop stream blew the flames away from the airplane and evaporated whatever fuel remained on the surfaces. The fire was out so quickly the only damage to the airplane was some scorched paint.

All of this took place within a few seconds, but it left a permanent impression on me. After that experience I started checking for spills after every fueling operation.

Mud on the Windshield

At 13,000 feet you don't expect to see mud on your windshield. It is particularly disconcerting when you are beginning an instrument approach to a strange airport in a foreign country.

On a morning in the midst of the rainy season we had departed Guatemala City on a flight plan to San Jose, Costa Rica, where the airport is cradled among several mountains. The old approach involved flying overhead until intercepting a beacon, then spiraling down through the clouds. Breaking out of the clouds, one spotted the runway and circled for landing.

As we came up on the beacon, we started getting the mud on the windshield, and it persisted for awhile as we spiraled down. That served to heighten the tension as we dropped to about 4,000 feet — some 1,000 feet above the ground level, before breaking out of the clouds.

The ramp attendant quickly explained the mud aloft. "One of our volcanoes is active today," he said, indicating that the situation was not unusual. That was before we learned — from air carrier incidents several years later in Indonesia and Alaska — that one can experience total engine failure when flying through the plume of a volcano.

Kamikaze Volunteer

Sometimes when exploring development situations in various nations I have invited local officials to fly with me. In many nations then (30 years ago) officials did not have access to airplanes as they have today.

Thus, I took off one day to scan a remote province with a cabinet minister in the seat beside me and several of his aides in the back. Reaching the area of interest, we found our checkpoint, a winding river bounded by heavy tropical vegetation.

My guest, in the co-pilot's seat, was elated. "This is where I was born," he said. "I used to hunt turtles here — let me show you." I eased down to just above treetop level to give him a better look when, without warning, he grabbed the wheel and began steering the airplane along the winding stream *below* treetop level.

I recovered control before we snagged a wing on a tree and, trying to be casual, said, "I didn't know you were a pilot." His reply, "I'm not, but I've always wanted to be," led to a lifelong pledge to ask that question before taking off with strange people in the right seat.

Bug Attack

Once, while looking at a site in northern Canada on a bright summer day, I ran into a small cloud that disappeared as quickly as it had come. At the next stop I found that the leading edges of my white airplane were black.

We had smashed a few million mosquitos and black flies, and it took a steam cleaning to restore the airplane. I had learned why some people call small airplanes bug smashers.

Over the Andes without Oxygen

Those who ride in the big airplanes with pressurized cabins can forget about oxygen problems, unless there is a malfunction — and then the little mask drops down, and the problem is solved. In small airplanes, we must carry oxygen bottles if we plan to do much flying above 10,000 to 12,000 feet.

Thus, we had our oxygen bottle charged to capacity before leaving Atlanta on a trip to South America. We planned to cross the Andes through a 16,000-foot pass in southern Colombia near Popoyan.

All went well as we approached the pass, climbing from the 3,000-foot level of the Cauca valley to an intended level of 17,000. We handed out the oxygen masks and got ready to penetrate the pass, which was filled with clouds. We planned to line up with two peaks on either side, hold a heading through the pass and let down on the other side. The critical part of the passage would take only half an hour.

Shortly before we got to the planned altitude, we discovered a real problem. Evidently there was a leak in our oxygen system, and somewhere between Atlanta and Cali our bottle had lost its charge.

Fortunately, I had some experience flying at altitudes without oxygen. I was confident that I could remain coherent for the half hour required to get through the pass. (One check you can make is to look at your fingernails. When they start turning blue, you know you are in immediate need of oxygen.)

I will never forget the few minutes it took to go through that pass. The weather was bad — rain and turbulence — and we had no radio communication or navigation aids. It was strictly a matter of holding a compass course and counting the minutes. Finally, my watch said we had made it and we began circling down through the clouds, hoping not to hit a rocky mountainside. When we broke out over the Amazon jungle, I indulged in a big sigh of relief.

But a couple of family members in the back seats had been made so drowsy by the lack of oxygen that they were perfectly relaxed about the whole experience — they were sound asleep.

Select the Right Tubing!

As yet, no small airplanes have sufficient range to fly the oceans in their normal configuration. For ferry flights the practice is to remove cabin seats and install additional fuel tanks. Several years ago, when I decided to fly the North Atlantic in a small single-engine Mooney, I had the two back seats taken out and put in a fuel drum. For the ferry flight a makeshift fuel transfer system was rigged, using clear plastic tubing to connect the temporary tanks to the airplane system. A valve was located within reach so that I could select the auxiliary tank or either wing tank.

The procedure crossing the Atlantic was to take off while drawing fuel from one of the regular wing tanks, then at cruising altitude to switch to the drum. This switching procedure commanded the rapt attention of the crew — myself and daughter Laura.

When the valve was switched to the temporary tank, one could see a train of air bubbles moving through the tubing toward the engine. Then, as the bubbles got to the engine, the fuel pressure would start dropping. Just at the moment when you knew the engine was going to quit, there would be a surge of power confirming that all the bubbles were gone and the flow was again normal.

While this procedure was tested over the mainland before the trip and deemed to be safe, the actual transfers over a remote stretch of the icy waters between Greenland and Iceland were made with somewhat less confidence.

We discussed this one day with two Australian pilots who had come to the Mooney factory in Texas to pick up new airplanes for delivery to Sydney. We wondered what it must be like to watch those air bubbles flow to the engine while out over the trackless Pacific a thousand miles from the nearest search-and-rescue unit.

To our surprise, the Aussies said they were no longer bothered by the bubbles. We surmised that they had a more complex fuel system that kept pressure on the lines. "No," they said, "we changed to opaque tubing."

Flying Tarzoo Home

During a stop at Leticia, Colombia, in the upper Amazon Basin, the well-known zoo supplier Mike Tsilickis gave my daughter Laura a pygmy marmoset, which she promptly named Tarzoo. Tarzoo was fitted with a small wicker cage that fit neatly between the pilot and co-pilot seats of our Aero Commander.

During the trip down the Amazon to Manaus and Belem it appeared that Tarzoo was a bit apprehensive. But during the northward legs to Para- maribo and Trinidad he seemed to relax and keep a close eye on the instru- ment panel.

By the time we got to Puerto Rico, I was sure he had learned to com- prehend what some of the instruments were saying. When we would drift a few degrees off course and a needle would deflect, Laura reports that he would turn toward me and give me a hard look.

Tarzoo captivated the customs and immigration people at West Palm Beach, and we were able to get him to Atlanta where he became a member of the family. I have often wondered what kind of report he would send back to his fellow marmosets in Leticia. Perhaps he would say: "These large primates, stupid as they are, seem to be trainable — perhaps we can teach them to protect the rainforest and grow bigger and better bananas."

Vienna Sausage Spray

You learn to be careful with sealed containers in unpressurized air- planes. A thermos of hot coffee sealed tight at sea level becomes a hazard at 10,000 feet — spraying hot coffee if opened suddenly.

Things you don't regard as liquid can also be a surprise. One day a family member who shall remain anonymous opened a can of Vienna sausage at altitude, and the juice sprayed all over the instrument panel and interior of our Cessna. A good paint spray rig could not have distributed that small amount of juice so well.

Weather Briefings

Before every flight we try to get a weather briefing from the best avail- able source. In the USA, that usually means a phone call to an FAA flight ser- vice station. Outside the USA, the service may range from a visit to the "met" office on the airport, to looking at a map on the TV news.

We have spent a total of many days listening to briefings from hun- dreds of different experts. Most were helpful. Some may have saved our life.

But meteorology is still a very inexact science. None are more painfully aware of that than the professionals working in the met offices amid their radar scans, high altitude wind data, station reports and teletype machines. They may be able to predict the movement of a big frontal system for days ahead, yet cannot tell you if there will be rain overhead within the next hour.

Some long-forgotten pilot-businessman once said that if all of the meteorologists in the world could swap jobs with all of the economists, no one would know the difference.

We remember a forecaster in Chicago who advised us, "There's a static front moving across the Midwest." He could have swapped jobs with a State Department official we heard tell an economic development group in Rio that the situation in Uruguay was "in unstable equilibrium."

The pilot listens to all this and then makes his own forecast. We wouldn't have it any other way.

Controllers

Another oft-maligned but able group is the air traffic controllers. They work as a team with pilots to make a complicated system function very efficiently most of the time.

It is when the traffic is heavy and diverse that they earn their keep. For example, we remember getting a clearance somewhat like this going into Teterboro:

"Cleared for ILS runway 6, circle to land runway 1 — disregard skywriting aircraft overhead — look for aircraft towing banner over stadium — blimp mooring right of runway — helicopter maneuvering over infield — Learjet closing at your 6 o'clock."

A routine Sunday afternoon in New York!

Success in Mexico

One wintry day while northbound from Guadalajara we encountered a line of unpredicted weather and had to divert to an alternate destination. When we called the nearest radio facility we found a controller who did not speak English.

As we bounced along, in instrument conditions and with weather worsening, we attempted to refile in our very limited Spanish. Finally, without knowing whether he had received or confirmed our change, we proceeded to the alternate.

On arrival, we were delighted to discover that the controller had indeed gotten the message, approved the rerouting, and all was well. This may not have been our finest moment as a pilot, but it ranks high in language improvisation.

Communication Etiquette

In more than 50 years of flying we can recall only a few instances in which a controller lost his cool and chewed out a pilot on the air. Veteran controllers know that pilots may be under stress in some situations, and the last thing the pilot needs is an untimely lecture by some officious fellow sitting safely on the ground.

One instance I do remember occurred over the Delmarva peninsula one afternoon when traffic was heavy and the thunderstorms were numerous. An airline pilot was detouring around a particularly active cell and obviously causing some problems for the controller in that sector.

The controller, probably new, proceeded to advise the pilot that his maneuvers were causing some inconvenience. The pilot's response was a classic: "I thought you were down there so I could be up here."

One Less Lake

Pilots avoid thunderstorms religiously. Tornadoes, which often are spawned out of lines of thunderstorms, are even more to be feared.

Pilots routinely circle around active thunderstorms, remaining far enough away for safety but close enough to watch the lightning strikes and heavy downpours. In some parts of the country, such as central Florida, that is a way of life.

During these evasive maneuvers, a pilot may have a grandstand seat for a funnel cloud or waterspout. He may see a tornado develop, touch down, scatter trees and buildings then move on.

We had such a view one afternoon over central Kansas. Flying parallel to a line of thunderstorms, we saw a funnel develop under a particularly black cloud, touch down and begin moving across what was, fortunately, open country. With fascination we watched the funnel approach a small lake, slurp it up completely and move on. In the space of just a few seconds, that lake just disappeared.

Unidentified Flying What?

We have probably been asked about a thousand times, "Do you believe in UFOs?" The question usually comes at a cocktail party or reception from some nice non-flying person.

We find it difficult to answer the question without being misunderstood, because so many of the questioners assume that an unidentified flying object is an alien visitor.

We do not believe that any of the reports we have ever heard constitute any evidence whatsoever of visitors from outer space. We feel certain that if any beings traveled light years through space to get here, they would let us know.

On the other hand, we know that there are many authentic reports of flying objects or things that no one can identify. These result from a wide variety of events and phenomena, such as meteor showers, comets, the interplay of lights and clouds, airplanes not on flight plans, research activities and countless other factors.

There have been so many spurious reports of UFO sightings from crackpots seeking publicity that many pilots are hesitant to report real sightings. Here's an example:

One winter night we were cruising at about 8,000 feet between Richmond and Washington when a bright light moved across our path at a very high rate and disappeared in the east. We knew at once that it was not an airplane and sat wondering what it could be.

A moment later, an Eastern pilot above us called the controller and said, "You may wonder about us, but we've got to tell you we've just seen something flash across in front of us at about the same altitude — too fast to be an airplane."

Rather sheepishly, we picked up the mike and told the controller we too had seen whatever it was. The Eastern skipper then said, "Thank You," and we both felt better.

A Busy Passenger Is a Good Passenger

When you fly for decades you learn a lot about passengers, nerves, air sickness and related phenomena. For example, you soon discover that negative response is mostly a mental thing and has little to do with how rough the air is.

Also, you learn that the best way to put someone at ease is to keep him occupied. You don't let an inexperienced passenger sit alone in a back seat and think about all of the bad things that might happen.

One strategy is to put the nervous passenger in the right seat and ask him or her to file a few charts. If they can focus on that for half an hour, they're over the initial tension. Not many people can stay scared for hours at a time.

From the Mouths of Babes

We were on a flight along the northern coast of South America between Cartagena, Colombia, and Panama. Passing the Gulf of Turbo, we were plowing through heavy rain squalls in a single-engine Cessna.

It was many years ago when we had no stormscope and there was no ground radar. For some minutes we had been trying unsuccessfully to make radio contact with a ground station, when a small voice in the back seat said, "Daddy, is this what they call togetherness?"

On another day, circa 1950s, our daughter Laura had invited a friend to go with us to Raleigh. For the friend, it was the first airplane ride of any kind, and there were many questions. As we parked at RDU next to a DC-3, we heard Laura explain, "It's like a bus for people who don't have airplanes."

Years later, we had as a guest celebrity passenger for a trip to the West Coast, our granddaughter Piper, who was then five years old. Piper held up well during the early part of the trip. There were frequent stops, and we managed to visit a dude ranch and other attractions.

However, after the long stretch across the Sonora Desert and the swing up California's central valley to San Jose, we overheard an objective appraisal from the by-now sophisticated passenger. It was, "the pits of boring," she said.

Captain Laura

Our daughter Laura inherited our fascination with airplanes and at an early age claimed the right front seat of the family airplane. By age eight she had learned to fly straight and level on instruments and at 16 was ready for her license.

The summer of her 18th year Laura backed me into a corner and extracted an agreement. She would be my pilot that summer. She would check weather, do flight plans, prep the airplane, handle all the flying — leaving me free to concentrate on business. The deal was that I would offer no unsolicited advice whatever.

Since one cannot really reason with persuasive daughters, my only choice was to agree.

One bright morning we took off in our Cessna 210 for several business appointments in the Northeast. Somewhere over the mountains past Roanoke the engine suddenly got rough.

Laura checked the panel, fuel tank selection, boost, etc., and then said she would like to ask a "hypothetical question." I said, "sure," and she asked, "Under these circumstances would you switch the mags?" and I said, "yes."

It took only a few seconds to confirm that the engine would run all right on one mag but not at all on the other. Whereupon Laura had another "hypothetical question" "Under these circumstances, would you go back to Roanoke?" I said, "yes," and we did.

Several hours later we had a new mag installed, and we were off again. About 10 miles north of Lynchburg oil began spreading from under the cowling up and over the windshield. There was another "hypothetical question," and we turned back to Lynchburg. By the time we turned final, the windshield was covered, and Laura was having to look out of the side windows.

In installing the mag back at Roanoke someone had overtorqued a bolt, causing the oil leak. Several hours later repairs were made, the windshield was cleaned, and we were able to push on to Philadelphia International for a night arrival in marginal weather.

The next day we had an electrical failure, and on the way home the following day the suction pump drive shaft sheared. Although there was no discussion of it, my guess was that Laura did not consider me to be excess baggage on that trip.

Laura was a veteran in handling emergencies, thus, when a few months later the 210 gear jammed with one main wheel down and the other dangling at about 45 degrees. There was no one to answer hypothetical questions, but she made a great emergency landing, cutting switches, leveling the prop, easing the airplane onto the runway, holding the wingtip off and minimizing damage.

Altogether, Laura has had an extraordinary number and variety of experiences in a relatively small number of flying hours. She has flown in the right seat with me across the Amazon Basin, to remote areas in Alaska and Canada, through the islands of the Caribbean and across the North Atlantic.

In every pilot's career there is probably a moment when he moves from the status of a student or apprentice to the confidence level of the pilot-in-command. I know exactly when this happened for Laura.

One day we were headed for the islands for a quick holiday. I had the flu and Laura, then in her teens, was doing the flying. We filed out of somewhere in Florida for a stop at Georgetown in the Bahamas. Georgetown is a convenient stop where fuel service is quick and the customs officials are friendly.

As we parked on the ramp, the customs officer walked out to the airplane on the driver's side and greeted Laura as she stepped out. Noting that she must be the pilot, the officer said, "Good morning, Captain. Would you please come into the office and sign some papers."

At the word "Captain," I saw Laura do a double take, but she quickly recovered and marched proudly in to do the paperwork. I knew she would never again be content to be a co-pilot for someone.

Flashbacks — Highs and Lows

• When grandson Adam was 10, we took him on a trip to Alaska. Along the scenic Edmonton-Watson Lake-Whitehorse route he had about 3,000 miles of questions. However, he turned out to be an excellent and reliable airplane spotter, keeping his cool when we went into busy Fairbanks with its seaplane lane between the parallel runways.

• It was the morning after a frontal system brought snow and ice across Western Pennsylvania. We had filed to a small city (which shall remain nameless) after being advised that the frozen precip on the runway had been covered with cinders to make it usable.

Flying our Baron, we touched down near the approach end, expecting to turn off at the intersection about halfway down the 5,000-foot strip. When we applied the brakes, nothing much happened. We kept pumping the brakes as the end of the runway approached. Less than 100 feet from the end, we ground to a stop with a pile of cinders in front of each wheel.

•Approaching a remote town in Kenya while on a commercial flight, we found some elephants moving slowly across the short grass strip. In East Africa, elephants have the right of way. We circled until they decided to leave.

•Among the world's most beautiful natural scenes are the shallow waters in and around the lagoons and islets of Australia's Great Barrier Reef, the Exuma cays of the Bahamas and along the offshore reefs of Honduras. No artist could portray the blends of blue, green and turquoise.

•On many Cessnas the cabin ventilation system is very simple — an airscoop near the wing root channels outside air directly to a vent near the pilot's ear. We were reminded of how efficient the system is while making an approach to Boston Logan one winter day.

We had opened the vent briefly while letting down from an intersection just offshore. As we turned on the localizer, we encountered, without warning, an area of ice pellets. Within seconds we had a lap full of ice. And the tower probably wondered why we spluttered.

•During a shopping expedition in New York, Becky bought a large glass ball (about 18 inches in diameter) of the type the Japanese attach to fishing nets. Fearing that it would explode when we climbed to altitude, I took the ball into the hangar at Teterboro and asked a mechanic to drill a hole in it.

An hour and several broken bits later we had not made a dent in the ball. The Japanese made hard glass. The solution was to wrap our coats around the ball, put it behind the back seats and fly to Atlanta at 1,000 feet. For the last decade or so, the ball has gathered dust in a corner of our basement.

•Many years ago we were doing an economic survey involving Staten Island at the time the Verrazano bridge opened. We flew in to the then Staten Island airport, a grass strip, and began taxiing toward a small building, which we assumed to be the FBO.

Suddenly, a white object flew past our wingtip, then another. We identified the object as a golf ball. It seems that the strip doubled as a golf driving range. The golfers were supposed to stop hitting when an airplane was on the strip.

•We have a file of several thousand photos made from airplanes, taken in connection with our economic development work. Some are excellent and indispensable. There are others we can't even identify.

One important factor is always having a camera loaded and ready whenever and wherever you fly.

Thus, we happened to be in the Eastern Caribbean when President Reagan sent the U.S. task force to take the Cuban-built airstrip at Grenada. We were able to swing by and get some good photos, showing status of construction at the facility.

A few hours before Mount St.Helens erupted, we happened to be going by and got some close-up shots of the big bulge that blew. We furnished prints to the Coast and Geodetic people and they gave us some great after shots.

• They say that flying is hundreds of hours of sheer boredom punctuated by occasional moments of utter panic. A few of the panicky seconds we can recall included an electrical failure off the coast of Jamaica, an exhaust stack that fell off during rollout at Prestwick, a hatch cover that blew off one stormy night over South Georgia, a gear switch failure at Calgary, a door opening over Cuba, and an engine failure that occurred just after takeoff in a Commander (a curious passenger flipped an overhead fuel switch).

• Some airports are easy to remember. There's Juneau with the glacier nearby, and South Lake Tahoe with a mountain inside the pattern. And you can't forget the take-off at Aspen in an unsupercharged airplane — you stagger off the strip, which is situated 9,000 feet above sea level, and drop down a valley to gain speed.

• There are certain good sights that bring a pilot's blood pressure back down to the normal range. In the early days of dead reckoning without radio, it was the identification of a sure-fire checkpoint, such as a prominent water tank or railroad crossing.

At night, when the weather is deteriorating, a glimpse of strobes and runway lights can be mighty comforting. And, on the long overwater flights, there is the exhilaration of finding an island or shore line.

Flying the World with the Big Boys

By now, we hope we have convinced you that small airplanes can provide unique opportunities for exploring the world. There are also, however, things they cannot do for you. They can't whisk you around from continent to continent in a hurry.

Thus, we have relied primarily on the airlines for global travel. We gave a summary of this experience in our book *Site World* in 1991.

Concept of the Airport City

Our records reveal that we have flown into more than 700 different airports around the world. That's enough to form some rather strong feelings about these transport centers and how they serve the flying public.

Our conclusion, reached long ago, is that there is a great deal of room for improvement. Our ideas are set forth in several books, starting with the original *Airport City* book in 1978 and extending through the latest, *Airport Cities 21,* which is excerpted later in this chapter.

B. Excerpts

1991 Excerpt	"Riding with the airlines. Let's get this straight for the record! I have always preferred to fly myself from point A to point B. However, this does not reflect in any way on the airlines or, more particularly, on their crews." *Site World,* 1991.

I suspect that the people who fly the big airplanes for the major air carriers are the most proficient pilots in the world. Without hesitation, I ride with them to any destination on their route systems.

To me it seems pointless to try to draw comparisons between pilots in different roles. The airline people certainly are more familiar with their routes, some of which they have flown every week for years. Yet, this overkill in route familiarity may induce complacency.

By contrast, some private pilots fly different routes to different destinations on almost every trip. I am one of those, and I know that this heightens my alertness.

There are a lot of other offsets. The air carriers fly above much of the weather, but they have to worry about cabin pressurization, drunk passengers and tight schedules. Those of us who fly our own small aircraft cruise at low altitudes, often in the thick of weather without radar. But we can cancel a flight instantly without having to explain or apologize.

While we private pilots envy the air carrier crews their food service and toilets, we are spared the necessity of being nice to nit-picking passengers. Nor do our reputations, after decades of flying, depend on whether or not we bounced on the last landing.

So, let's face up to the fact that there are good, better and not-so-good pilots in each category: airline, military and private aviation. The competent veterans respect one another no matter what their missions.

What Is an Airport?

You hear a lot of non-pilots say they like this airport and hate that one. They are really talking about the terminal buildings, not the airports.

Ask pilots about airports and they will say they hate this one and like that one, but they are talking about the approaches and the runways. An airport may have a slick modern terminal, but if there are mountains in the approach zone, and the runway is short, the pilots are not going to give it high marks.

They Doth Complain Too Much

During most of my flying career I have subsisted on stale peanut butter crackers while grinding along at DC-3 speeds in a cabin offering minimal elbow room. Hence, I am not overly impressed by the complaints that flow so easily from "sophisticated" passengers.

When I hear some of them complaining bitterly about the salad dressing on their luncheon tray, I wish the attendant would dump a gallon or so of it in their laps. Considering all of the problems that must be overcome, the service on air carrier flights today is wonderful.

In order to appreciate the job most of them do, you need to ride with carriers that have, to put it politely, somewhat unusual concepts of service.

To Siberia with Aeroflot

Some years before the current thaw in relations between the USA and the former USSR, I rode from Moscow several thousand miles across Siberia to Novosibirsk and Irkutsk with Aeroflot. The service was a notch below that encountered on Aeroflot in Europe (which itself was sub-standard).

The seat density was the worst I have ever found on any airplane. I could not sit with my knees straight ahead. I had to sit at an angle, and when cramps forced a move, struggle to an almost-erect position, shift my knees to the other side, and settle back into a crab-like posture.

When an unsmiling attendant brought food, the tray could just barely be wedged in between my chest and the seat ahead. I sat there wondering how a big man (I am only six feet, 165 pounds) could manage it.

And, my impression was that I was treated as well as the Russian passengers, and maybe better.

There was a stop in the middle of the night at Novosibirsk where we discovered a small terminal building crammed with Russian passengers waiting for flights. They had apparently been waiting a long time, and entire families were sleeping on the floor. It looked like photos of the Jonestown mass suicide.

We non-Soviets, numbering about a dozen, were taken upstairs to a room that had some hard benches. A guard was posted, and we sat there for about six hours. There were no explanations or status reports. Finally, at dawn, we took off, having never been told why we were delayed.

I don't think any Aeroflot personnel intended any offense toward us, nor do I think they felt that an apology or explanation was in order. Passengers were like cargo. That's just the way it was.

Military Operations with UBA

In the early 1960s several of us on a U.S. mission rode throughout Burma with UBA (Union of Burma Airways). They flew tired DC-3s left over from flying the hump in the China-Burma-India theatre during WWII. All flights originated at Rangoon in the morning and returned there in the evening — to avoid having the aircraft blown up by guerrillas at way stations. We traveled from Myitkyina in the foothills of the Himalayas to Bassein down in the Irrawaddy Delta.

I remember once sitting around a grass strip in the Shan state waiting for an airplane that was very late.

The airport services and facilities consisted of an outdoor toilet and a couple of military guards. One of the guards amused himself by sticking his finger inside the trigger guard of his automatic weapon and twirling it like a baton. I kept wondering if he had the safety on.

When the old Dakota finally arrived it carried a contingent of military personnel who had been in some sort of skirmish. We were told nothing about the operation. All I know is that I sat next to a wounded man, unable to speak enough of his language to express any sympathy.

I wonder if UBA operations are very much different today.

Across the Pacific with Air Nauru

Nauru is one of the richest nations in the world, ranking up there with Kuwait and Brunei in per capita income. The latter two are postage-stamp size nations sitting on pools of oil.

Nauru's wealth is bird droppings. For untold centuries great flocks of migratory birds stopped and dumped on Nauru, which is a dot on the map in the central Pacific. Ultimately, the Nauruans discovered they had a large reservoir of the highest-concentrate phosphate fertilizer in the world. In recent times, they have been selling off their island a boatload at a time and getting rich in the process.

The newly rich Nauruans wanted to go shopping, and they had no transportation, so they established their own airline, Air Nauru. And they went first class, buying Boeing jets and hiring Australian flight crews.

I came upon this story while visiting Saipan in the Northern Mariana Islands in the early 1980s. There, on that remote island, stood a bright new, empty, high-rise office building. I was told it was part of a Nauru investment program.

Later, I encountered other Nauru projects from Hawaii to Australia. Wanting to know more, I decided to visit the island, which was served only by Air Nauru.

That's when problems started for my travel agent. Air Nauru wasn't listed in the usual airline guides. Inquiries finally produced a phone number in Honolulu. That phone had an answering machine with a message to call back Monday.

At last, my agent was able to contact someone at Air Nauru to make my reservations. She confirmed that there was a regular weekly flight, but Air Nauru said they couldn't take me in January.

"Oh, you're booked solid," my rep said. "No, the airplane is in the shop," said Air Nauru, suggesting we call back in a few weeks. We did, and our seats were confirmed. Air Nauru added, "We have no desk at Honolulu airport, so tell your client we will meet him at the Western ramp at 7:00 am."

It all sounded pretty shaky, so we were pleasantly surprised on the assigned date to be greeted by name in the airport concourse. Any air carrier that can identify and greet individual passengers even before they check in is sharp, we thought.

That was only the beginning of the special personal attention we enjoyed. There was a crew of eight assigned to deal with the passenger list of five — that's right, five passengers. Besides Becky and I, there were an English school teacher and two Samoans.

We flew across the Pacific in the big Boeing with a sea of empty seats behind us.

There was a super breakfast, anchored by eggs Benedict, and an equally nice luncheon. discovering that I was a pilot, the Captain invited me to visit up front. As we passed Johnston Island, he maneuvered until I got a good photo.

The crew skillfully put the jet down on Nauru's short runway, which extended from coast to coast on the small island. There was a neat little terminal building. Alongside, two more Boeings sat on a crushed coral ramp with their tails poked into a grove of palm trees.

We were intrigued. "How can they make a go of an operation like this," we asked ourselves. We have been around airplanes long enough to have some ideas about operating costs and break-even load factors.

Inquiries revealed that the passenger volume we had seen was not unusual. An architect from New Zealand said he had been the only passenger on some flights. Also, we were told that top Nauru officials sometimes canceled regular flights and used the airplanes for shopping trips to Hong Kong.

Our amazement was increased when, riding another empty Air Nauru flight to Guam one morning, we learned that there was another Air Nauru flight, equally empty, on the same route the same morning. We thought the dispatcher must be trying for a place in the Guinness *Book of World Records*.

It was not surprising, then, to hear that Air Nauru had piled up a huge deficit. Recently, news came that operations had been suspended. What a shame! It was nice having our own Boeing.

An Unplanned Ride to the Chaco

It was a long time ago. Avianca, the Colombian airline, was using DC-3s on their internal routes. Although everybody seemed to be trying, service was a bit on the ragged side.

I had gone down to Medellin from Bogota one morning for a meeting and about mid-afternoon returned to the Medellin airport for the return flight.

Stand by for a series of alibis: The PA system in the small terminal building was lousy, all announcements were in rapid-fire Spanish, and there was no formal check-in with boarding passes, etc., as we have today.

I heard an announcement, saw a DC-3 at the gate, went up the airplane steps and asked the stewardess, "¿Este es el aeroplano para Bogota?" She said, "Si," smiled sweetly, took my ticket, and I got on.

After take-off the airplane swung toward the west — opposite to the heading for Bogota. I thought we must be dodging around some thunderstorms building in the area. But we continued westbound and the mountainous terrain soon began sloping away. We were not going to Bogota.

I stopped the stewardess in the aisle, and this time I said, "¿Este no es el aeroplano para Bogota?" She gave me a curious look, said, "Si," and continued down the aisle. I could find no one who spoke English, but with my limited Spanish I confirmed with several passengers that they were going to a strip down in the Chaco jungle. And so was I.

After we had landed on a grass strip and workers were unloading cargo, I was able to tell the pilot about my problem. We both laughed and he gave me the good news that his schedule called for a quick return to Medellin. Further, he invited me to ride in the jump seat on the return leg.

It was a valuable lesson. I learned that in a foreign situation *never* make an inquiry that can be answered by a smile, a nod, or a "yes." Most of the people you meet are nice people trying to be helpful, and they sincerely want to smile, nod and say "yes."

You don't ask if this is the airplane going to Point A. You ask, "Where is this airplane going?" Remember that.

The Aussie Closed-Door Policy

Ansett is a fine Australian airline that made its early reputation serving remote stations scattered over the vast expanse of the Australian continent. Their crews are competent but relaxed.

Early one morning we boarded a twin-propeller F-27 at Darwin on the north coast for a flight to Cairns on the east coast near the Great Barrier Reef. I remember that the pilots wore shorts and sneakers and the comely flight attendants wore summer dresses or sun suits.

There was no need for spit and polish. We were in the tropics and there were no big cities on the route. The only stop listed was at Gove, an outpost on the north coast not far from Papua New Guinea.

Gove, we learned, merited air service because of a large alumina mine that had a substantial movement of personnel and supplies. Evidently, the all-male work force signs on for a long season during which there are no females to be seen.

This explained the strange procedure during our stop. We sat with the door closed while the airplane was fueled. Then, as we were about to taxi out, the door was opened and a couple of passengers boarded. The door was quickly slammed, followed by a loud thumping on the door, which was ignored. The engines were started, and we were on our way.

It seems that the flight attendants — typically pretty girls — had had so many bad trips with amorous Gove passengers that they had demanded and received from management the right to look over the boarding passengers and decide whether or not to open the door.

I can only suppose that much practice enabled the girls to make their evaluations in the few seconds it took for the would-be passengers to walk across the ramp. Compare that with the shrinks who need a dozen half-hour sessions to size up a client!

Lost among the Chinese

There used to be an immigration law that required Chinese residents of Manila to go back to China once a year. Toward the end of the Chinese year, in February, special excursion flights were put on by Cathay Pacific to handle the crush of passengers.

I didn't know about this in Atlanta when my space was booked. All I know is that one day I got on an airplane in Manila and, after everybody was seated, I began to notice something strange. This sense of disquiet was increased when the preflight announcements were made only in Chinese, and the attendant came down the aisle handing out newspapers in Chinese script.

After take-off, I started looking around systematically. Yep, I was alone among a sea of Chinese of all ages and descriptions. Soon the attendant brought a rather strange luncheon. I was not asked whether I wanted the chopsticks or the tea. That's what we all got.

When we arrived at Kai Tak and walked into the terminal there was a mob scene. We were surrounded by a throng of at least a thousand relatives pressing in to greet us. I was in the middle. It was my first visit to China, and while I had heard about the population density I was not prepared for the reality of it.

What Do Arab Robes Conceal?

It was during the early days of fighting in Beirut and a period of typical tension in the Middle East. Americans traveling without escort found it prudent to make no waves. And, there was a tendency to see something sinister lurking behind every veil and robe.

Thus brainwashed, we boarded a Kuwait Airlines flight in Kuwait City for a trip across Saudi Arabia to Cairo. The airplane was loaded with Arabs in their great flowing robes, headdresses, and, for the women, veils. It was footage for a travel film.

Across the aisle were two large, swarthy men with heavy beards. Something about them suggested that they might be officials, perhaps security agents. Knowing how strict some of the Moslems are in their adherence to the teachings of the Koran, we wondered if we had done something to elicit surveillance.

After we took off and reached cruising altitude, the men across the aisle seemed to be casting furtive glances in our direction. Tension mounted until, in one swift motion, one of the men reached under his robe and handed the other a dark object, which he quickly hid under his robe.

Was it a gun or a grenade? No, in the fraction of a second that the object was bared we got a precise fix on it. It was a bottle of Jack Daniels, a rare prize in the dry communities of the Middle East.

No Loitering!

A well-known travel magazine recently carried a feature by a so-called expert on how to minimize your vulnerability to terrorist attacks while traveling abroad. One of the jewels of advice was, "Don't loiter around airports."

We can only assume that the author has never been anywhere. The fact is that if you travel very much you spend a substantial part of your life "loitering around airports."

I can recall some king-sized loitering episodes of six to eight hours in such diverse locations as Guam, where they closed the airport shops and turned down the lights as our airplane load of people arrived; Darwin, where we tried to sleep on hard benches next to the bar populated by several drunks who sang all night; and Novosibirsk, where the only rest room had just been repainted and everything was wet, including the toilet seats.

Our personal record for length-of-loiter was 12 hours at Bangkok, where we were marooned when our 747 lost an engine, and we had to go back and wait for another flight.

According to the same expert, the worst place to loiter was the Athens airport. We might agree on that.

There have been several terrorist incidents in Greece, including a deadly attack at the Athens airport. Several summers ago, American tourists were staying away and the tourism business was hurting badly. Action was demanded.

The Greek officialdom responded by putting in special security procedures at the airport. We arrived just in time to participate: An extra baggage search was set up on tables at the terminal entrance, and lines of waiting passengers backed up through the terminal doors and onto the sidewalk.

This made it much easier for terrorists. All they had to do was drive by and toss a grenade into the waiting group. Amazing!

I guess we loitered there for an hour before the line moved inside.

Good, Better, Best

We think most air carriers do a good job. But some do better.

We have always been most comfortable with Delta, probably because we have grown up with them. We learned to fly with some of their senior pilots. They don't come any finer than Captain Mac Long, recently retired. Besides, they speak our language.

We'd give a high mark to United on the Hawaii run. The first time we rode with them in a DC-6 the trip took 14 grueling hours from San Francisco.

We've also enjoyed Air Micronesia (Continental) from Honolulu to Johnston Island, Majuro, Kwajalein, Ponape, Truk, Guam, Yap and Palau. This is a global milk run, with barefoot natives mingling with the jet set.

Everybody's favorite is Singapore Air. They set a standard of service others can't match. It starts with the check-in people and extends throughout the organization. The key is the cabin crews of charming young oriental girls who remember every passenger's name.

Without trying, we seem to have a collection of the kits handed out by the intercontinental airlines on the long overnight legs. We have slippers from South African Air, JAL toothpaste and SAS combs. We have enough of the padded Delta pouches to use them for clubhead covers on several sets of golf clubs.

Those Helpful Airport Signs

The last time we were at Narita, Tokyo's main airport, we saw a sign at the immigration desk that warned, "Once you pass here, you cannot return to ticket area. Take care of foreign exchange and other needs before proceeding."

We did as directed. Proceeding another 50 feet we encountered another sign that said, "Airport departure tax 2,500 yen." We had just converted all of our yen.

A Hijacking for Breakfast

We were on the way home from Australia and had a change of planes in Los Angeles. Thus, early one morning we settled down on a Continental Boeing for an eastbound flight. When the flight attendant began making the cabin announcement, I noticed that she seemed out of breath. I said to Becky, "That girl must have run all the way to the airport."

We later learned that Continental had an emergency plan — if a hijacking were underway the cabin announcement would contain a certain phrase that sounded innocuous but which would tip off all crew members. The warning phrase that morning was, "All of your crew members are based in Long Beach."

Given that warning, the rule required the pilots to close the door to their compartment, tie a rope to a bulkhead and lower themselves through a window to the ground, leaving the aircraft without pilots.

Other crew members pulled curtains across the cabin and began quietly getting passengers out through the rear exit. Soon the hijacker, a disgruntled airline employee with a gun, was left with one flight attendant and 11 passengers. The airplane was towed to a remote part of the airport, and after about 12 hours of confrontation the hijacker gave up.

Only a few months before, a gunman killed both pilots on a flight over California, and all on board died in the crash. The cool performance of the Continental crew may have saved us from a similar fate.

Charters to Special Places

When we travel to the other side of the world, we ride an air carrier jet. On arrival in a distant country, sometimes we find ourselves needing a small airplane to get to a remote site. Then we use a charter.

Frankly, we don't have as much confidence in charter operations. They don't have as much invested as do the airlines. Hence, we approach them cautiously.

We look at the weather, the route and the airplane. Then we ask to sit in the co-pilot's seat. No offense to the pilot, but we like to see him run through his checklist.

Thus assured, we have had some very interesting flights to places we could not otherwise have seen. We recall chartering a Cessna at Cairns, Queensland, for a flight along a stretch of the Great Barrier Reef. It was a magnificent sight.

On another day, we chartered a Piper Cherokee in Nairobi to fly to a grass strip on the Indian Ocean coast near the island of Lamu. When we arrived over the strip it was necessary to circle to encourage a herd of elephants to move out of the way. Prior to that, the most exotic runway obstacle we had encountered was a pair of antelopes at Rawlins, Wyoming.

Better Not Ask

Johnston Island in the Pacific is a lonely outpost. For a long while it was off limits to civilian craft and most others. There were few complaints for it is no garden spot. The runway reaches from one side of the small atoll to the other, leaving very little room for airport facilities, let alone a resort complex.

While refueling there one day, we discovered another reason it does not draw crowds of tourists: We casually inquired about a row of drab warehouses on the other side of the runway. "Oh, that's where the U.S. stores nerve gas," the attendant explained.

Airport Names

Most international airports are named for leading citizens, such as Charles de Gaulle, JFK or Leonardo da Vinci. Heathrow sounds properly British. But the one we like best is Dum Dum, at Calcutta.

1993
Excerpt

Airport Cities 21. The new global transport centers of the 21st Century. A study prepared for the World Development Council. 113 pp. 1993. *Airport City*, first edition 1977. Comment received from Laurene Kliegl, Executive Secretary, British Columbia Aviation Council: "Our copy has been referred to so many times over the past eight years that it is now falling apart." *The Airport City.* Second edition. Development concepts for the 21st Century. Introduction: unimodal to multimodal. Intermodal and transmodal systems. Market factors for airport projects. Design factors for airport projects. Office and industrial parks. Cargo and distribution facilities. Travel facilities, resorts, attractions. Planned airport communities. Jetport cities and metro complexes. A glimpse of Century 21. 1980. 283 pp. World Future Society review: "timely, imaginative and readable."

Despite revolutionary changes in transport vehicles, the basic desire of the traveler has remained the same for centuries. The transportation customer wants to go from Point A to Point B with a minimum of time, cost, stress and discomfort.

The history of development appears to fall into four major stages, each of which has been dominated by a mode of mechanized transportation. While these periods differ, it may be helpful to look briefly at some of the common denominators.

The four periods of interest include the early centuries of reliance on water transportation; the subsequent age of emerging rail transportation; the more recent decades of automobile use; and the current era dominated by air transportation.

During the period when water transportation was the dominant mode, new communities and cities grew up where there were natural harbors along the ocean shores and at the confluence of principal rivers. The main routes were served by sailing vessels, and the "feeder lines" were canoes and rowboats.

Many of the major world cities of today owe their existence to the early influence of water transportation. These range from Amsterdam and London to New York and Philadelphia. Call them "boat cities."

Examination of the first recorded plats of such cities reveals that the waterfront was the center of activity. Wherever it was possible to moor a boat entrepreneurs built facilities to cater to the traveler and shipper.

These included the inns, the taverns and the many other service establishments clustered within walking distance of the wharf. This also happened to be the most expensive real estate in town because of its proximity to transportation.

As this age of development proceeded, the waterfront areas expanded, and warehouses and other facilities were developed to serve the growing fleet of water transport units.These, in turn, grew from the small sailing sloops to the great steam-powered vessels.

Throughout this period, the basic orientation of development was toward the point at which the passengers and cargos arrived and departed.

Another similar era of development occurred with the coming of the railroads. New communities burst into life at the new railheads and at the intersections of major rail lines. Atlanta, Dallas and Denver are examples. They were "rail cities."

At these new rail locations there was the same pattern of developing the service facilities within walking distance of the railroad station. A study of the plans for these early communities reveals that there was usually a railroad hotel, a restaurant, a barbershop and a saloon near the station.

Again, as the rail services grew, the rail yards became the center of the city, with the warehouses, distribution facilities and industries locating on adjacent sites.

Still another wave of new development occurred with the arrival of the automobile. The automobile stretched things out and spread development to a much greater degree than had the water and rail modes because of the ubiquitous nature of the automobile itself.

However, the basic desire of the passenger to step from the vehicle directly into a center of activity has been evidenced by the proliferation of drive-in facilities and the emergence of shopping centers, office parks, motels and other automobile-oriented facilities.

Nothing more dramatically revealed the impact of the automobile than the construction of the USA's interstate highway system during 1950-1990. In effect, this was the largest community development and industry relocation project in the history of the United States. Scores of "auto cities" emerged.

It is interesting to observe that while Congress refused for years to approve a program of creating new towns, the interstate highway program did that in virtually every state.

The automobile/truck has been immensely popular because it has provided a "through" system. This is the principle of carrying the passenger or the cargo from origin to destination via a system that involves no changes of vehicle, no transfers, no handling and an absolute minimum of time and cost. This ideal system means for the passenger minimum frustration, inconvenience and discomfort. For cargo, it means minimum risk of damage, pilferage and loss.

The fourth great wave of transportation-oriented change in development patterns — brought about by the emergence of air transportation — is, of course, well underway.

While the auto/truck has proven to be the ideal system for short distances and for uncongested areas, the airplane has proven to be better for great distances. It also offers advantages for some short routes, because it can span water or rise above the growing gridlock on the surface.

The airplane is already the dominant mode of transportation for a great many people and businesses. Again, new patterns are unfolding as attempts are made to locate new activity centers near runways. Just as the "drive-in" feature was attractive to automobile users, the new "fly-in" concept lures air travelers.

In fact, there may be even more demand to provide time-saving arrangements for the air traveler because he is committed to a faster mode of transportation and is even less patient with delays and cumbersome procedures.

We called attention to these changing patterns in the first edition of *Airport City* published in 1977, and in the second edition, issued in 1980. This presentation constitutes another look at these rapidly unfolding developments.

What does it all mean?

The customer rules!

In a world now almost completely committed to market-oriented economies it is safe to say that the customer has taken charge! What the customer wants he will get! And this applies to all of the passengers who are the customers of the air transport system.

It will no longer be acceptable to herd passengers like cattle. Nor will it be enough to give the passenger a seat and forget him. He will have to have a telephone, fax, TV and other conveniences at his seat, plus genuinely personal service.

The message for government officials, planners, designers, engineers, builders, investors and managers is loud and clear. Development teams must provide far better ways to move a passenger and his suitcase around the world.

Those areas in which better systems are provided will flourish. Others will be left behind.

Unplanned Airport Cities

Visit any large and long-established jetport such as Los Angeles International, London Heathrow or Paris Orly and you'll find a substantial airport city that has sprung up since the airport was built. Across the fence from the runways are the motels, office parks, industrial and distribution plants and myriad service units attracted to the air transportation center.

Almost without exception these old airport cities are a civic mess. They are characterized by functional inefficiency and aesthetic chaos. Everyone pays in confusion, noise, ugliness and congestion.

At many airports these problems have reached crisis proportions. There is an urgent need to look at the planning and development process, not just for airports, but for the areas that surround them.

A number of causes can be found for this problem. A major factor was the thinking that went into the airport site selection and site planning at the outset.

Unhappily, most of today's busiest airports were planned at a time when the concept of the airport city had not emerged. Airports were separate things placed well away from the city to "avoid problems." Frequently, the site was the cheapest tract available; that which needed the least grading; or perhaps a plot donated by a civic-minded citizen.

There is an abundance of experience now available that demonstrates that development clusters quickly around big, busy airports even if they are built at some distance from the central business district in relatively undeveloped areas.

In short, it is impossible for the big airport to escape from the city. "Before and after" photos of almost any large airport show that growth of all types, including single-family residential, will move right up to the airport fence and occupy any space not controlled by the airport.

Some cities, like Chicago, have seen this happen repeatedly. The Midway Airport was boxed in by development, so a larger tract was bought and a new airport, O'Hare, was built in a suburban location. Now O'Hare is boxed in. Another suburban site for a third airport has been chosen.

Building airports with incompatible neighbors is a problem anywhere. In Japan, a new second airport for Tokyo was built on a 23,000-acre site 40 miles from Tokyo at Narita. Opposition of neighboring farmers was so great that the opening of the airport was delayed for years, and it is still closed from midnight to 6:00 a.m.

Unplanned airport cities have obvious problems around their peripheries. And, if we look more closely, there are many more inside the airport city. The typical large airport is a sprawling complex occupying several thousand acres. (Bear in mind that the Principality of Monaco, albeit a small nation, occupies less than 1,000 acres.)

Thousands of people work at the airport; their commuting to work plus passenger traffic comprises one of the biggest ground movements in the metro area. The airport manager is now "mayor," with a large and diverse constituency.

The hard-pressed airport management, originally set up to deal with support for flight operations, now must operate such typical city services as fire protection, emergency medical, police and security services, and, in many cases, a water system, sewage treatment system and communications system.

At the same time, the administration must deal with concessions, ground transport and maintenance of buildings and grounds, all for a "city" having a daily population of tens of thousands.

Concept of the True Airport City

If airports cities are going to develop anyway, why not plan them? Why not stop ignoring their inevitable growth and start taking advantage of all the opportunities that are inherent in planning new, highly functional entities?

By "true" airport city, we mean a complex that stands alone — not an appendage of another. We mean a project planned from the outset to maximize use of the air transport mode and to integrate it efficiently into the systems of the area it serves.

As will be discussed later, not all new airport cities will be built around huge jetports. They will come in all sizes and will serve a variety of needs.

The New Global System

There is no world government planning board to decide what kind of new airport cities to build or where to put them. These decisions will be made on the basis of market factors in the highly competitive world business arena.

The global air system will be the composite of units built in many jurisdictions under a variety of circumstances. The system will change constantly as new facilities and new aircraft come into operation.

In this new global competition there will be winners and losers. Many airports that occupy strategic positions today will be skipped over in the future. That is what happened to Shannon, Ireland — once one of the world's key airports — when the long-range jets were put into service on the North Atlantic route.

There are many things we don't know about the new system, but we do know that it will dwarf the present system in its geographic coverage, and it will be far more sophisticated.

The new system will be designed to serve both existing customers and a new group of "globalites." This new and growing segment of the travel market is made up of a new breed of travelers who are comfortable with a 24-hour clock set to universal time; they can deal mentally with standard metric units of distance, volume and weight; they are at ease with currency conversions and international phone connections.

They are also comfortable with exotic menus; they can drive on the right side of the road or the left; they depend on the English language but try to enrich it with phrases from local languages wherever they are.

Most important, the new globalites are eager to apply new technologies. Today, they carry laptop computers that permit them to keep working on long flights and layovers. And, with a telephone modem, they can connect with the home office or information networks.

Soon, the globalites will carry in their briefcases a small satellite antenna that permits them to receive broadcasts direct to their portable units. This means that wherever they may be — even remote areas without telephone or radio — they can receive current news, weather and information.

And, they will soon use automated translation machines which, for example, can receive Swahili and transmit English. Speech-to-text converters will deliver a neat printed copy of an oral agreement or set of field notes.

These are the people who expect great airport cities to be built and who will appreciate them most.

At the core of this market are the top executives of huge global firms. They must fly and they demand superior service.

The new system will provide service to the parts of the world that on today's maps appear to be great blank spaces. These range from the polar regions across Oceania — the island world — to the Asian land mass, Siberia, Mongolia, mainland China, most of Africa and the Amazon Basin.

A Glimpse of Century 21

In planning the airport cities of tomorrow, it is necessary to think decades ahead. It may take one decade to plan and build the facility, and after it is built the facility should be expected to function for at least another two or three more decades. That is a span of 30 or 40 years.

This poses a real challenge in technology forecasting. We do well to predict the major developments of the next few years, but we have little confidence in forecasting the technology of, say, the year 2020 or 2030.

Yet we must.

It is already apparent that new airport cities will need to consider the requirements of a new family of SSTs (Super Sonic Transports). At about the turn of the century these new craft will begin to appear in passenger service. They will fly at about three times the speed of sound, and will have a range of close to 10,000 miles. Boeing sees a market for 400-500 SSTs early in the next century.

Soon after the new SSTs go into service, the first of the Trans-Atmospheric Vehicles (TAVs) will begin flight testing. The present proposal for a trans-atmospheric vehicle calls for an air-breathing engine for take-off from existing airports, plus a rocket booster to propel it into space. Commercial operations are forecast to begin in the 2005 to 2010 time frame.

In the meantime, the new global fleet may include super jumbo jets capable of carrying 1,000 passengers. The impact of such large groups on all kinds of airport facilities and services will require new thinking to avoid chaos.

An airplane carrying 100 passengers poses relatively few "people problems." As size increases, however, the likelihood grows that a passenger may have a heart attack, or give birth prematurely, or in some other way create an incident. Thus, aircraft carrying 1,000 passengers may need a small medical staff, a police force and other special services.

These are some of the questions for the designers of the new global super airport cities. For lesser airport cities there will be important roles to fill and they, too, will have new factors to consider.

Categories of Airport Cities and Communities

For this discussion of airport cities we have chosen not to use the standard terminology (hubs, etc.) used by airport planners. We want to make it clear that planned airport cities are not the same as airports.

•*Five-star global airport cities*. At the top of our list we have five-star airport cities, which will be in a class by themselves. They will be the key elements of the new global system.

These new airport cities will offer transoceanic service via 1,000-passenger jumbo jets, SSTs and TAVs. Mainly, they will serve to connect the three most important global regions — Pacific Rim, North America and Europe. This is where the global traffic is concentrated.

These sites will be close to the coast but with direct connections to major rapid rail and highway systems. The sites will be large — 10,000 hectares or more.

Economic analysis suggests that there may be two or three sites feasible in Europe, two or three in the Pacific Rim, two or three in the USA. The first 10 projects to be built may dominate the world air transport industry for decades.

Measured by present standards, these new airport cities will have virtually unlimited capacity. There will be few if any constraints on growth.

To begin with, the new cities will require sites several times as large as those that have been used for big airports. Further, they will require authority over surrounding land uses, which will raise big political questions.

A common denominator is that the new complexes will be very expensive. The risk to sponsors will be enormous. A few bold projects will gain new global roles, while those that come late or that compromise on criteria will be expensive failures.

The competition for world leadership has already begun. A number of groups are in various stages of planning and promoting new projects that could qualify as global airport cities.

Well before the year 2000 rolls around, some group somewhere will make the Big commitment — allocating funds to build the first true global airport city. The project may emerge from a group of proposals for "wayports" now being promoted in the USA.

•*Four-star international airport cities*. This category includes airport cities that are vital to a global region, such as the Pacific Rim, Europe or North America. This includes a number of existing airports as well as new projects.

These airport cities typically provide international service, as well as extensive service within the region. They play important roles in the economic life of their service areas.

These cities are mostly of the unplanned variety. They are hampered by limitations of airspace and site, as well as various noise, night operation and environmental restrictions.

Despite these obstacles, a number of these facilities, expanded and upgraded, will seek to compete for key roles in the new global system. In the near term, they may enjoy success, but their competitive position will deteriorate as new five-star facilities come into operation.

•*Three-star airport cities*. Our next category of airport cities includes scores of facilities that provide scheduled jet service within significant areas. They are oriented primarily to domestic origins and destinations but offer international service via transfer at a four- or five-star facility.

•*Two-star airport cities*. This category is involved primarily in providing commuter service to larger airport cities.

•*One-star airport cities*. These are the facilities that generally provide service via non-scheduled general aviation. They play a very important role in area development.

Within this category, there are several distinct groups. These include fly-in residential communities, fly-in resorts and fly-in frontier villages.

Residential Airport Communities

Quite a few observers are willing to accept the proposition that there are some transportation benefits in an airport community. They remain skeptical, nevertheless, regarding the total community concept, which includes residential uses. They ask, "Why would anyone want to live at an airport?"

The pilot-aircraft owner might well respond, "Why would an auto owner want to live on a street?" What strikes the non-pilot as peculiar is a perfectly natural reaction for those who depend primarily on a small airplane to achieve mobility.

There is already evidence that living in a fly-in residential subdivision is an accepted lifestyle. Once a project is opened and families start enjoying the new pattern, enthusiasm is contagious.

Example at Spruce Creek

During the 1960s and 1970s we had a hand in developing the first prototype fly-in community, called Spruce Creek, on a site near Daytona Beach, Florida. We selected the site, prepared an overall plan and launched development.

We chose a tract of some 1,100 acres that had been the site of an auxiliary landing field used by the Navy during WWII. There was a network of abandoned runways and taxiways and a drainage system of sorts. There were no buildings — making it unnecessary to tear down structures having some residual economic value or to keep units that would be eyesores.

The location was excellent, lying near an interchange on I-95 between Daytona Beach and New Smyrna Beach. Physically, the property was high enough to minimize hurricane risks, yet close enough to the ocean to offer small-boat access via Spruce Creek.

We laid out a plan for a community which would include a 3,000-foot runway, a golf course, tennis courts, residential areas, commercial areas, single-family homes, condos and a nature preserve. Also included were such infrastructure items as a water system, sewage treatment plant and a bridge to provide auto access to I-95.

Most important, we provided a system of taxiways serving most of the sites. There were many doubters, especially in the financial community.

Today Spruce Creek is a thriving community of several hundred homes and several hundred airplanes. It is a very attractive community, with distinctive homes and lush landscaping.

It is said that more airline pilots live in Spruce Creek than in any other community in the world. They commute via small aircraft to their jobs in major cities, where they step into the cockpits of big jets.

176

•*Space Ports*. Without doubt, the ultimate airport cities will be space ports, both those located on earth and those located on the moon or other planets.

There are numerous proposals and plans for new earth launching stations at such locations as Hawaii, Australia's York Peninsula and the island of Biak in Indonesia.

On the other hand, several groups are putting forward plans for "spaceport cities" on the moon. One Japanese firm has designed a hotel for tourists stopping over on the moon.

Some Noteworthy Airport City Projects

In our 1980 book we said, "There are no large jetports planned to make the main runway the center of a fly-in city. Funds have not even been provided to enable planners to begin the work." We were in a period of very limited airport development.

Today, the world has entered a new and exciting era of airport construction. In the next two decades the investment in new facilities will be greater than the combined total for all previous history.

It is estimated that some $300 billion in new construction will be required to meet needs for the year 2000. Some $20 billion will be spent on new automated airport systems and services.

There will be many new opportunities for innovative design and construction. We may well be entering the first phase of an era of large-scale airport city development.

Commitments and Compromises

By now it should be evident that almost all of the projects planned to date, no matter how bold, involve significant compromises of some kind. These include:
- Island sites with access limitations.
- Urban locations with restrictions on night operations.
- Sites not interfaced with main line surface transport.
- Sites with inadequate land for economic development.

The latter is the most common problem — and the easiest to understand. New airport projects are very expensive, and it is very difficult to find the resources needed to acquire land for which there is no immediate need.

The temptation is to acquire enough land for the airport and hope that in the future it will be possible to acquire more land as needed for related development. That is what has created the chaos we have today around large airports.

Of all of the airport projects underway today, it appears that only a very

177

few can hope to develop as our ultimate five-star global airport cities. With the creation of more development area near the runways, the new Hong Kong airport has a chance. With intensive planning and development of abutting properties, the new Denver and Munich airports have a chance.

Importance of Critical Mass

It is interesting to compare the present status of airport city development with the early stages of shopping center development. Highly successful enclosed-mall shopping centers with their acres of drive-in facilities did not spring suddenly on the scene.

There was a long period when advocates of shopping centers encountered disappointing results. A prime factor was the attempt to approach the new concept conservatively, minimizing front-end investment and planning to add amenities or expand in stages as the project developed.

This approach did not work. Components of the shopping center are interactive. The shoe shop attracts patrons for the dress shop, the luggage shop brings customers for the camera shop and each additional shop adds to the overall volume. For regional centers, it became obvious that a "lead" department store was essential.

Like the nuclear weapon, the shopping center had to reach critical mass in order to explode into success. The investors who eventually succeeded were those who built the entire complex and offered all amenities and services from the start.

So it will be for five-star global airport cities. Every venture to date has been a compromise. No one has yet made the total commitment necessary.

Airport City Planning

While there are common denominators, the task of planning airport cities is different for each type and size of city. Let's look first at some of the factors involved with large projects, possibly five-star global centers.

Those who develop plans for airport cities must think in terms of two distinct components — an area plan and an airport land plan. The area plan extends far beyond the boundaries of the airport property and calls for the skills of the urban planner.

The land plan covers only that acreage owned, controlled and developed by the airport. It must bring the expertise of the air carriers, fixed base operators and other airport users, as well as developers.

The two planning elements must, of course, be harmonized. That requires consideration of many diverse factors at the start of the planning process:

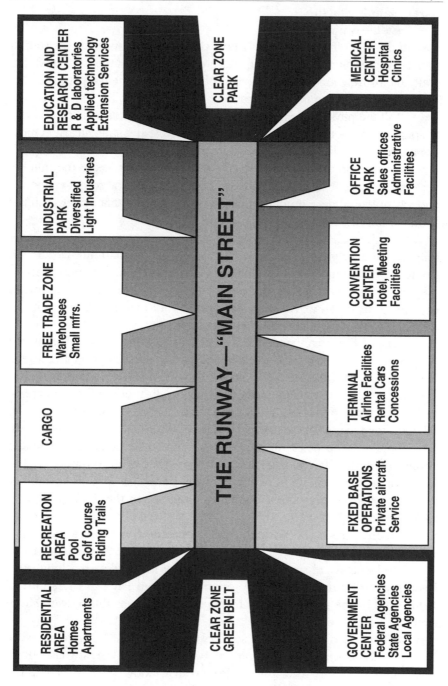

The runway is Main Street. For many new projects, the runway of the airport should be treated as the Main Street of a new city. All elements should relate to it.

•Area planning factors

First, the runway!

In the planning of the true airport city, the first considerations should be airspace for air traffic handling and ground space for the runway(s). Literally, the runway(s) should be the first physical element to be planned.

Why? The answer is fundamental.

Of all the physical elements in an urban area — roads, sewers, schools, hospitals, parks — the element that must be longest and straightest and most level is the airport runway. All other elements can be bent or built on slopes.

Moreover, in the true airport city, the runway belongs in the middle, with other elements arranged around it. There are several recent economic and technological developments that support the belief that a runway in the center of the city is not such a preposterous thought.

First, the assumption of the past that airport runways would always get longer as aircraft grew bigger and faster is no longer valid. Runway length for heavy jets has more or less stabilized because of economic constraints.

For both air carrier and business jets, the increased utility of aircraft capable of using short runways has spurred all manufacturers to make design changes. Newer aircraft can use shorter runways.

Second, the engineering profession, responding to environmental pressures, has reversed the trend toward ever-increasing decibel levels. Newer aircraft are quieter.

These trends give planners more latitude. A further significant decrease in jet noise levels promises to be a great aid to all concerned.

Another major site factor is the all-important interface with surface transportation. The objective must be to transfer the global air passenger within the airport terminal complex to high-speed surface transport. The latter connections will be of two types: local transit, or long-distance transfer to major population centers in the region served by the global port.

•High-speed rail

In many parts of the world the great opportunity is to link airport cities with new high-speed rail systems now under development. The importance of the high-speed rail systems and their appeal to travelers has long since been proven by the French TGV operations from Paris to the south of France and by the Japanese "bullet" trains running from Tokyo several hundred miles south to Osaka.

We have used both of these services and have found them to be excellent. The ride is smooth and comfortable. You don't realize how fast you're going until you try to make a photo from your window. Then you find it difficult to focus on a scene before it whizzes by.

Trains now in service can operate at 150-to-200 miles per hour. A new

French train has run at more than 300-miles per hour, and the Japanese have an even faster model on the drawing board.

High-speed rail development may not be a part of airport planning, but it is an essential part of airport city planning!

• **Highway access**

Coordinating airport city location and major highway construction is also essential. In the USA, this means connecting with the interstate highway system. In Europe and elsewhere, it means connection to the regional motorway system.

The best way to relate the airport city to the road system is via a loop that, ideally, encircles the airport city (*see sketch*). In existing metro areas where there is a circumferential route, the connection may best be achieved by locating the airport city adjacent to the loop or by building a loop next to the airport.

These connections are made feasible by the emergence of the loop city as a preferred urban form around the world. While circular city plans have been proposed for centuries, the new concept involves building a loop or loops around the city.

Originally planned by interstate highway engineers to serve as by-passes around cities, the perimeter routes quickly proved to be a solution to many urban needs. (*See next chapter, "loop cities."*)

Our point is that the loop city plan is here to stay, and airport city planners should be alert to capitalize on it. It offers many opportunities for integrating airport cities with urban areas and their hinterland.

Internal Corporate Airlines

It has been shown that a firm may enjoy increased convenience and efficiency by locating a new office or manufacturing facility within an airport city that affords taxiway access. However, the benefits are multiplied when the company has several such facilities in several such cities. The optimum system occurs when all major company units — headquarters office, manufacturing plants, warehouses and regional offices — are located in airport cities.

With such an arrangement, company aircraft can shuttle executive personnel from door-to-door at great savings of time and cost. Aircraft utilization is enhanced and operating costs are minimized. This is truly the corporate facility system of the future.

This new planning opportunity may be the only chance that facility executives have to propose company plans that 10 years from now will do a better and more economical job than can be done today.

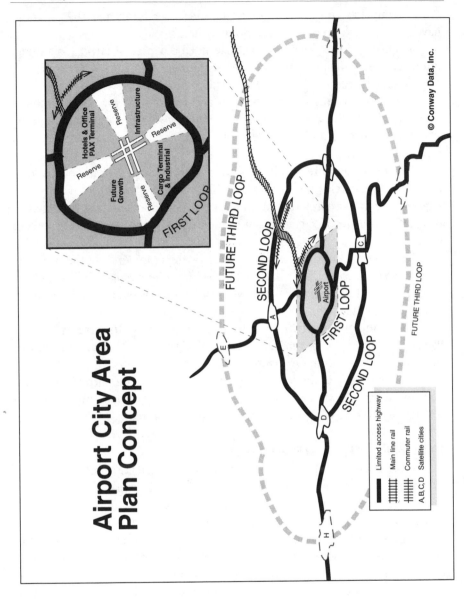

This is the conceptual arrangement for a future world-class airport city. It will involve a very large expenditure, a site of as much as 50,000 acres, and the collaboration of local, state, and national governments.

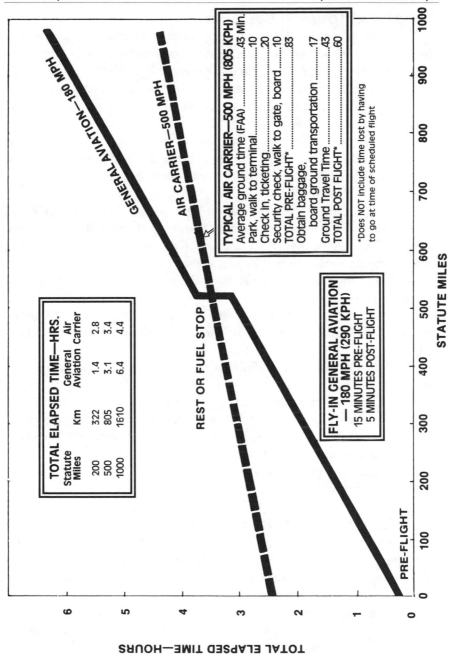

The short-haul picture. Business functions which are dependent on regional or short-haul executive transport (up to 500 miles) should study the advantages offered by fly-in airport sites utilizing small corporate aircraft.

Travel and Tourism Ventures

Nowhere does the airport city concept have more application than in the realm of tourism. No new hotel, destination resort, attraction or convention center should be planned without looking at fly-in possibilities.

Tourists are not under the same pressure to travel as are business travelers. They do not have to go. Thus, comfort and convenience are often the dominant market factors.

For example, in the past it has been customary to locate convention centers in the Central Business District, presumably because of proximity to most large hotels. This was a logical strategy when visitors arrived at the railroad station in the CBD.

However, the emergence of air transport as the dominant mode and the consequent development of airport hotels has changed the picture dramatically. Today, there may be cities in which the site selection study for the new convention center should include the airport. Here are a few reasons:

1. Why haul convention traffic through the city and back to the airport, adding greatly to congestion?

2. Perhaps the hotel rooms of the city are not really more accessible from the CBD location. Many newer hotels are in suburban and airport locations.

3. If the city also owns and operates the airport, there may be a combination of factors making it economically attractive to use a site already owned and, at the same time, to enhance the profitability of the airport.

4. Location of the center at the airport may give the city a competitive edge in attracting conventions and thus add to economic development potential. Before the year 2000, travel and tourism will be recognized as the world's largest and most dynamic industry. It is already growing 20 percent faster than the world economy.

The Coming Global Revolution in Personal Travel

The early years of the onrushing 21st Century will witness a global revolution in personal travel. We will enter the era of worldwide personal travel via private plane. This development will do for the world many of the things that the private automobile did for America in the 1920s.

The mystical appeal of flying will be discovered by the populations of the world. There will be a new sense of community, a new realization of vast opportunities yet to be explored.

There will be a new magnitude of freedom. Analogy: If you had ridden the bus all your life and then got an auto, you'd enjoy an exciting new perspective.

Until very recently iron curtains around the world restricted the flow of small aircraft, reducing or eliminating their usefulness. Now, the barriers are coming down and the skies are opening. A host of new opportunities is in sight.

The challenge now to the bureaucracies of the former communist nations is to complete the process of opening their skies to private global traffic. This means not only making open skies policy statements, but implementing via services and procedures to promote easy flow of aircraft.

The process has started. Nations that have long blocked out large areas of airspace and prohibited overflight for military or political reasons are now opening such areas. Those which have forbidden private planes to use key airports are relaxing restrictions.

It is now possible for small private aircraft to fly around the world, traversing the former USSR territories. That is progress!

New Travel Patterns

In the years just ahead new airport cities and communities will offer an exciting possibility for bringing the people of the world together and promoting overall quality of life.

Thus, we assert that in the world ahead there will be two great airplane-dominated travel markets — the big jet (air carrier) market and the small airplane (general aviation) market.

The big jet traffic is highly visible and well-known. Many are not even aware, however, of the small aircraft traffic, and that's why we will discuss it here in more detail.

Lack of awareness of the small aircraft activity is easy to understand. Among the first airport communities to emerge were those built around small resorts located in remote areas that lacked surface transportation. These emerging one-star airport resort communities are also sprinkled along the Baja California Peninsula of Mexico and throughout the Bahamas and along the islands of the Caribbean.

Utilization of small airplanes is greatest in nations that are large and have "open skies" policies. Thus, highest use is found in Canada, Alaska, Australia, Mexico and the USA.

Up to this point, the small airplane fly-in tourist traffic has been originating mostly in the United States. That's where the airplane owners are.

Vacationing aircraft owners in the Western states tend to go to Mexico, especially the Baja Peninsula. There are at least a dozen sites in Baja, some with a history of more than 20 years of operation.

Owners from the Eastern part of the U.S. typically fly to Florida, the Bahamas and to the islands of the Caribbean. It has been estimated that more than 500,000 tourists visit Florida by private aircraft each year. The traffic to the Bahamas or beyond has been estimated at 20,000 aircraft per year.

Fly-in resorts are found on almost every island and cay in the Bahamas. To the southeast, the Turks and Caicos Islands have several well-established fly-in resorts and a growing traffic volume.

The next phase of development of this pattern will be a push beyond to Central America, the north coast of South America, and onward to cover all of South America, even the Amazon Basin. (We made the first tourism survey flight across the Amazon Basin from the Pacific to the Atlantic in 1965.)

When we look at long-term trends, it seems inevitable that the fly-in trend launched in the U.S. will eventually cover the world. We are already beginning to see a number of aircraft make the trip to Europe via northern Canada, Greenland, Iceland and Scotland.

(Our first flight across the North Atlantic in a single-engine Mooney was an adventure. There were some very grim moments of truth. We encountered no traffic. In the future such flights will be relaxed and routine.)

Western Europe, technically, is open to traffic. However, development will accelerate as air traffic control is improved and airports are freed for private traffic. Eastern Europe is already moving to participate.

In the future, as their economies strengthen and private citizens can buy airplanes, we can look for explosive growth in Russia and the new nations of Southeast Asia. With development of a general aviation fleet, these areas will also spawn new travel patterns.

Look for European aircraft owners to flock to Africa. The beaches of Tunisia and the shopping attractions of Morocco are within easy reach. Exotic East Africa beckons!

A few isolated developments around the world indicate the enormous range of possibilities. We've enjoyed fly-in facilities at such diverse locations as Dunk Island, astride Australia's Great Barrier Reef, and at Lamu, in the Indian Ocean off the coast of Kenya.

The Magic of GPS

One of the factors that will greatly accelerate worldwide utilization of small aircraft is the new Global Positioning System (GPS). Under development by the military for many years, the system was put into application during Operation Desert Storm in the Middle East.

GPS is a very precise navigation system that uses satellites. Several thousand units were issued to U.S. forces, who used them to maneuver tanks and armored vehicles across desert areas lacking in landmarks.

Subsequently, GPS units have been made available for private airplanes, boats and other users. We quickly installed a unit in our airplane (a single-engine Mooney 201) and discovered a new world.

Sitting on the ramp at our home base, Atlanta's Peachtree-DeKalb airport, we can program the latitude/longitude for any spot on earth and the readout quickly tells us what heading to fly, the distance to destination and time en route. What we would have given for GPS while flying across the Amazon Basin or the Greenland icecap!

This new system will have an enormous impact on flying in Third World areas that have no ground-based navigation aids! This new instrument will enable some of the poor nations to jump ahead several decades.

Safe Skies Award Established

Finally, after reviewing various awards being given for contributions to society in general and aviation in particular, we decided to establish a new award. In early 1989 we posted a prize of $25,000 and an equal amount for administration of a new Safe Skies Award.

The immediate aim of the award is to provide global recognition for outstanding efforts to protect air travelers from acts of terrorism. The ultimate goal is to make more secure the air transport system that is vital to economic development and enhancement of quality of life around the world.

The award honoree may be any person (or group) from any nation. Possibilities include, but are not limited to, flight crews, passengers, ground crews, law enforcement officers, security personnel, aircraft designers, airport officials and scientists and technicians developing explosives detection devices and other security systems.

Recipients/honorees of the Safe Skies Award are selected without regard to race, creed, religion or ethnic background. They may come from any nation — north, south, east or west. All proceedings will be politically neutral.

The award consists of a cash prize plus recognition by news media around the world. After recipients have been selected, the presentation is made at the next global conference of the World Development Council.

The first award winner was Bert Ammerman, a New Jersey school principal whose brother was killed in the bombing of Pan Am 103. He formed a group called "Victims of Pan Am 103," which lobbied successfully for the passage of stronger air security regulations.

The second winner was Michael M. Charles, inspector of accidents for the Royal Aerospace Establishment in the UK. He was cited for his proposals for redesigning the aircraft baggage containers and cargo compartments so that they could withstand the explosion of a bomb planted inside.

The selections are made via a panel of distinguished people chosen to represent all regions of the globe, as well as diverse economic and social interests. Current chairman of the selection committee is Brigadier Malcolm

MacKenzie-Orr, of Melbourne, Australia, who is an authority on bombs and terrorism.

C. Bibliography

The following are citations of McKinley Conway's writings on this chapter's subject. As this book goes to press, work is underway to make many of these items available to researchers. To check status, look for a file on GeoTEAM/IDRCNET or telephone GeoTEAM/Fax at (404) 453-4200 for a free catalog.

207. Notes on Maximum Aircraft Angular Velocities. Washington, D.C. National Advisory Committee for Aeronautics (NACA, later NASA). 1943. 16 pp.

208. The Possible Use of Ceramic Materials in Aircraft Propulsion Systems. Washington, D.C. National Advisory Committee for Aeronautics (NACA, later NASA). 1944. 24 pp.

209. Tests of the Douglas BTD-1 Airplane in the 40x80-ft. Wind Tunnel — Estimates of Aileron Stick Force and Rolling Characteristics. Moffett Field, Calif. National Advisory Committee for Aeronautics (NACA, later NASA). 1944.

210. Tests of the Douglas BTD-1 Airplane in the 40x80-ft. Wind Tunnel — Aileron Characteristics. Moffett Field, Calif. National Advisory Committee for Aeronautics (NACA, later NASA). 1944. With Sam Davidson.

211. "Research Wins Wars," *Air Trails*. March 1944.

212. Tests of Ryan FR-1 in the 40x80-ft. Wind Tunnel — Critical Speeds for Several Cowling Configurations. Moffett Field, Calif., National Advisory Committee for Aeronautics (NACA, later NASA). 1945.

213. Tests of the Grumman F7F in the 40x80-ft. Wind Tunnel — cooling aerodynamic characteristics. Moffett Field, Calif., National Advisory Committee for Aeronautics, (NACA, later NASA) 1945.

214. Full Scale Wind Tunnel Investigation of a Wing Inlet Induction System for a Turbojet Engine. Ames Aero. Lab., Moffett Field, Calif. National Advisory Committee for Aeronautics (NACA, later NASA), 1945. 80 pp.

215. Investigation of the Engine Installation of the Ryan FR-1 airplane in the Ames 40x80-ft. Wind Tunnel — Cooling in Climb. Moffett Field, Calif., National Advisory Committee for Aeronautics (NACA, later NASA). 1945.

216. Investigation in the Ames 40x80-ft. Wind Tunnel of the Aerodynamic and Cooling Characteristics of the Grumman F7F-1 Power Plant Installation (MRA5N13). Moffett Field, Calif., National Advisory Committee for Aeronautics (NACA, later NASA) 1945.

217. Investigation of the Engine Installation of the FRI in the 40x80-ft. Wind Tunnel — Carburetor Air Induction System. Moffett Field, Calif., National Advisory Committee for Aeronautics (NACA, later NASA). 1945.

218. Investigation of the Engine Installation of the Ryan FR-1 in the 40x80-ft. Wind Tunnel — Cooling Correlation Analysis. Moffett Field, Calif., National Advisory Committee for Aeronautics (NACA, later NASA). 1945.

219. Tests of the Ryan FR-1 in the 40x80-ft. Wind Tunnel — Possible Improvements in the Forward Power Plant Installation. Moffett Field, Calif., National Advisory Committee for Aeronautics (NACA, later NASA), 1945.

220. Tests of Grumman F7F in the 40x80-ft. Wind Tunnel — Cooling Correlation Analysis. Moffett Field, Calif., National Advisory Committee for Aeronautics (NACA, later NASA). 1945.

221. Tests of the Grumman F7F Airplane in the 40x80-ft. Wind Tunnel — Cylinder Temperature Distribution. Moffett Field, Calif. National Advisory Committee for Aeronautics. (NACA, later NASA) 1945.

222. Investigation of Engine Installation of the Ryan FR-1 Airplane in the Ames 40x80-ft. Wind Tunnel — Summary of Results. Moffett Field, Calif., National Advisory Committee for

Aeronautics (NACA, later NASA). 1945.

223. Investigation in the Ames 40x80-ft. Wind Tunnel — Performance Characteristics of the Ryan FR-1 Airplane Drag Characteristics. Moffett Field, Calif., National Advisory Committee for Aeronautics (NACA, later NASA). 1946.

224. Investigation in Ames 40x80-ft. Wind Tunnel of Performance Characteristics of the Ryan FR-1 Airplane — Effect of Jet Engine Operation on Stability. Moffett Field, Calif. National Advisory Committee for Aeronautics (NACA, later NASA). 1946.

225. Investigation in Ames 40x80-ft. Wind Tunnel of Performance Characteristics of the Ryan FR-1 Airplane — Static Characteristics of the GE 1-16 Engine. Moffett Field, Calif., National Advisory Committee for Aeronautics. (NACA, later NASA) 1946.

226. Investigation in the Ames 40x80-ft. Wind Tunnel of Performance Characteristics of the Ryan FR-1 Airplane — Cooling of Fuselage Members around Jet Engine and Tailpipe. Moffett Field, Calif., National Advisory Committee for Aeronautics (NACA, later NASA). 1946.

227. Investigation in the Ames 40x80-ft. Wind Tunnel of a Wright R-1820 Engine Installed in a Ryan FR-1 Airplane. Moffett Field, Calif., National Advisory Committee for Aeronautics (NASA). 1946. (MRA6C28).

228. Full Scale Wind Tunnel Investigation of Some Turbojet Engine Installation Problems. Ames Aero. Lab., Moffett Field, Calif. National Advisory Committee for Aeronautics (NACA, later NASA). 1946.

229. Full Scale Wind Tunnel Tests of the Wake of a Turbojet Engine. Ames Aero. Lab., Moffett Field, Calif. National Advisory Committee for Aeronautics (NACA, later NASA). 1946. 32 pp.

230. *Principles of High Speed Flight.* Southeastern Research Institute. 1947. 142 pp.

231. *Control of Airplane Flight Path by Propulsive Jets.* Southeastern Research Institute. 1948. 22 pp.

232. Thrust Meter, U.S. Patent 2,516,855, issued Aug. 1, 1950.

233. Jet Direction Control (application for patent filed Jan. 26, 1951, serial no. 207,996).

234. "Roadblocks in the Sky," *Industrial Development.* Aug. 1958. pp. 6-10. (Military restricted areas hampering civilian air traffic.)

235. "Exploring Caribbean Potential by Light Plane," *Industrial Development.* Atlanta, Feb. 1961. pp. 6-12, 86-94.

236. "Airport Sites for Industry," *Industrial Development.* Nov., 1962 pp. 5-20.

237. "Air Transport Trends Affecting Industrial Development," Industrial Development Research Council, New York. May 14, 1963.

238. "The Airplane and Industrial Development," *AOPA Pilot,* Aircraft Owners and Pilots Assn., Washington, D.C. Oct. 1963.

239. "Air Transport" (remarks made at Industrial Development Research Council Area/Industry Conference), *Industrial Development.* Nov. 1963. pp. 14-16. Includes list of airport industrial sites.

240. *A Development Plan for John F. Kennedy Memorial Airport, Melbourne, Fla. Oct. 11, 1965. 43 pp.*

241. *"Airport Sites for Industry,"* Industrial Development. Nov. 1965. pp. 13-27. Includes index of projects in U.S.

242. "The Fly-in Concept." During the next few years this development will produce exciting changes in the design of industrial and commercial areas and even in the layout of cities and metropolitan areas. Here's a report reflecting ID's original research in the field. *Industrial Development.* Nov. 1965. pp. 13-28.

243. "Air Transportation and Your Company's Expansion Plans," Industrial Development Research Council, Atlanta, Nov. 17, 1965.

244. "Community Airports — How Important Are They in Industrial Development?" Society of Industrial Realtors. Point Clear, Ala., Feb. 18, 1966.

245. "Flying the Amazon" (expedition from the Andes to the Atlantic), *AOPA Pilot.* Washington, D.C. May 1966. pp. 64- 68.

246. *Charlotte County (Florida) Airport Development Plan.* June 1966. 94 pp. charts, maps.

247. "Airport Industrial Parks and the Fly-in Concept." Annual meeting, American Assn. of Airport Executives, Seattle, Wash., June 14, 1966.

248. *Meridian, Miss., Industrial Area Feasibility Study.* Aug. 1966, 36 pp. plus appendix.

249. *Key Field Industrial District, Three Site Plans.* Meridian, Miss., 32 pp., illus. 1967.

250. *Marianna (Fla.) Airport Industrial Park Development Plan.* 80 pp. charts, illus. 1967.

251. *Airport and Industrial Airpark Development Plan for DeQuincey, La. 116 pp., charts, illus. 1967.*

252. *"The Emerging Fly-in Concept," Wisconsin Airports Conference, Sheboygan, Wis. April 26, 1967. (Wisconsin Aero. Comm., Madison).*

253. *"Why an Airport: Economic Development Potential." Kentucky Airports Conference, Lexington. April 12, 1967.*

254. Sylvania Georgia Airport Development Plan. 49 pp. illus. June 1968.

255. *Airport Development Plan, Allen C. Thompson Field, Jackson, Miss.* 106 pp., illus. Sept. 1968.

256. *Planning Study of the Orange County, N.Y., Airport Area.* 32 pp. Oct. 1968.

257. "Crisis in Airport Planning," *Airport World.* Nov. 1968 pp. 50-52.

258. "Travel Investment and the Fly-in Resort," Western America Convention and Travel Institute. Portland, Ore. Dec. 4, 1968. Dept. of Commerce and Economic Development, State of Washington, Olympia.

259. "The Fly-in Concept of Development," League of Women Engineers, April 17, 1969. Atlanta.

260. *Airport Development Plan, Hawkins Field, Jackson, Miss.* July, 1969. 64 pp. illus.

261. "Today's Runway: Will It Be Tomorrow's Main Street?", *Flight Lines,* National Real Estate Fliers Assn., Washington, D.C. Sept. 1969. pp.4-6.

262. "The Fly-in Concept of Land Development", *Farm and Land,* National Assn. of Real Estate Boards, June 1970.

263. *An Airport Development Plan for Chester County, Pa.* Oct. 25, 1970. 110 pp., illus.

264. "The Airplane Is Here to Stay." Part 2. Man has failed miserably to coordinate ground facilities with the technological wizardry of the airplane. The potential for business purposes has hardly been realized. *Industrial Development,* May-June 1971. pp. 2-9.

265. "Using the Small Airplane: Exploring Areas." Risk and reward. *Airport City.*

266. "Spruce Creek: a fly-in community". *Site Selection,*1972. 16 pp.

267. *Wings Field, Montgomery County, Pa.: an Economic Feasibility Study and Conceptual Plan for a Fly-in Country Club Community.* March 1973. 100 pp., illus.

268. "Fly-in Business Centers Are Here." A topic of increasing discussion by flying business-men in the Sixties, fly-in business facilities are becoming a reality in the Seventies. Before the end of the decade, such projects may emerge as one of the major trends in urban plan-ning and economic development. *Industrial Development,* May-June, 1973, pp. 1-4.

269. *Airport Development Plan, Greene County, Pa.* Project for the Federal Aviation Agency. 240 pp. illus. April 1974.

270. "Opportunities in Intermodal Transportation." One of the few areas in which we can still improve overall operating efficiency by a whopping percentage. *Industrial Development,* March-April 1976. pp. 2-6.

271. "Are Intermodal Container Loop Sites an Endangered Species?" A recent issue of ID outlined the concept of "through" transport which is producing keen interest in sites from which manufacturers can receive and ship containerized cargo via all modes. A follow-up survey suggests that optimum sites are rare indeed. *Industrial Development,* May-June 1976.

272. "A Scan of Arctic Growth Potential." On the maps it is a great empty space. But for a development strategist privileged to gain a closer look, the Arctic is a region where interest-ing things are happening today and where men plan and dream of globally significant pro-jects tomorrow. *Industrial Development,* Sept.-Oct. 1981. pp. 10-15.

273. "From Kuujjuaq to Stornoway on One Engine." The North American mainland stops on a wind-swept airstrip at Kuujjuaq (formerly Fort Chimo) in northern Quebec. From there, pilots who wish to maximize the prospect for survival can navigate to Europe across Ungava Bay and the Hudson Strait to Baffin Island, over the Davis Strait to Greenland's west coast, across the Greenland ice cap, and then over the North Atlantic via Iceland. "Global Mini-Let-ter," Jan. 1982. pp. 1-2.

274. "Time to Reconsider Fly-In Sites?" Check your future corporate geography — what is the chance that you can move executives door-to-door between yours plants and offices as fast in 1995 as you can today? If you're faced with a deteriorating situation caused by urban congestion and slow ground travel, fly-in sites may offer a bright solution. *Site Selection,* Dec. 1985. pp. 1162-1165.

275. "What Happened to Fly-in Projects?" It has been a time of trial and tribulation for

almost all types of large-scale land development projects. In particular, the "fly-in" projects built on airports have ...suffered from ...factors peculiar to airport projects. *Site Selection,* Dec. 1985. p. 1140.

276. "New FAA Wayport Proposal Could Be Site Breakthrough Opening Opportunities for 21st Century Development," *Site Selection,* June 1989. p. 626.

277. "Air Terrorism Spawns New Award." Among corporate location and geo-political factors, none are more important that those which affect human lives. Near the top of the list is the security provided for international air travelers, for virtually every executive of every global business venture is at risk. *Site Selection,* Oct. 1989. p. 1180.

278. "Business Needs to Concern Itself with Air Terrorism." With peace breaking out all over the world, it appears that the likelihood of a major world war is smaller than it has been for decades. At the same time, terrorism looms as a continuing global risk for which the world does not yet have an answer. *Gwinnett Daily News,* Nov. 1989.

279. "'Wayport' System Deserves Consideration." The last major airport to be built in the United States was the Dallas-Fort Worth regional facility. That was in 1974. For two decades the nation's hub airports have been getting by with patchwork improvements and expansions, but that approach has reached its limits. *Gwinnett Daily News,* June 20, 1990.

280. "Will Man-powered Flight Be Next Transport Breakthrough?" For millions of people, the vehicle of the early 21st century may be something akin to a light-weight bicycle with wings. It will be pedaled at tree-top level across metro areas, avoiding the congestion on the streets below. *The Airport City, Development Concepts for the 21st Century,* 1980. 283 pp.

281. "Riding with the Airlines." Let's get this straight for the record! I have always preferred to fly myself from point A to point B. However, this does not reflect in any way on the airlines or, more particularly, on their crews. *Site World,* chapter 7. 1991.

282. *Airport Cities 21.* The new global transport centers of the 21st century. A study prepared for the World Development Council. 113 pp. 1993. *Airport City,* 1st ed., 1977. Comment received 1985 from Laurene Kliegl, executive secretary, British Columbia Aviation Council: "Our copy has been referred to so many times over the past eight years that it is now falling apart." *The Airport City, Development Concepts for the 21st Century,* 2nd ed. Introduction: unimodal to multimodal. Intermodal and transmodal systems. Market factors for airport projects. Design factors for airport projects. Office and industrial parks. Cargo and distribution facilities. Travel facilities, resorts, attractions. Planned airport communities. Jetport cities and metro complexes. A glimpse of century 21. 1980. 283 pp. World Future Society review: "timely, imaginative, and readable."

283. "Airport Cities: They Could Change Your Company's Future.," *Site Selection,* Feb., 1993. p. 6

4
Creating Projects as Elements of a New Megastructure

Chapter 4

A. Recent Comments
Planning Studies
The Project at Spruce Creek
Panic Warning!
Changing Urban Forms
The New Professional

B. Excerpts
Pitfalls in Development, 1978, Revised 1981
Will Two-loop Cities Dominate Site Selection?, *Site Selection*, June 1986
Super Metros, *Site Selection*, August 1987
R&D Clusters, Science Cities, 1987
Rethinking Urban Plans, *Gwinnett Daily News*, January 18, 1989
Tomorrow's Super Cities, *The Futurist*, May/June 1993

C. Bibliography

A. Recent Comments

"The feasibility looked good. The Pharaoh put up the front money, we bought a site near Giza for a song and built three pyramids and a Sphinx. Then the market collapsed..."

Some projects are bigger than others, but all share certain common denominators. In fact, all branches of development are inter-related. One cannot operate in a vacuum, thinking only of single-family housing, industrial plants, offices, hotels or infrastructure projects.

Every project undertaken today must be regarded as an element in a new global megastructure. There are no longer any stand-alone projects.

And, to a degree, every developer is an urban planner, an ecologist and a global strategist. Some projects bring out these relationships more than others.

During the 1960s and '70s we handled a wide variety of consulting and planning assignments which gave us a liberal education in many such matters. Our works ranged from high-level issues of national development strategies for several nations to such mundane things as the feasibility of a new slaughterhouse for a province in Nicaragua.

In the USA we prepared a management plan for the big Lake Lanier Islands recreation center in North Georgia. Another assignment was an analysis of the potential for barge traffic on the Chattahoochee River between Atlanta and the Gulf of Mexico.

All of these assignments involved getting out in the field, finding the old survey markers and planning from the ground up. They taught us that while you may learn a lot about development in the library, you will never really understand it until you get your shoes muddy.

I gained another viewpoint through serving in various public capacities, including chairman of the county planning commission, the airport board, the metro planning agency and the highway committee of the state Senate.

Most of our planning and consulting work at that time was for public agencies — FAA, HUD, state and others. After some years, we found there were just too many compromises involved. We cut off all work for federal agencies and concentrated on serving the private sector through our affiliation with the IDRC.

But the most vivid experience came from participation in a large-scale development project in which my ideas and money were at risk. Twenty years later I still have bruises and lacerations from that.

For some years, I had been consulting on airport-related office parks, industrial sites and travel facilities. My usual assignment was to evaluate a location, do a conceptual plan and suggest issues to be covered in subsequent feasibility studies.

During the early and mid-1960s I handled some 15 or 20 such projects from California to Florida and New York to Central America. Since there weren't many people in the field, I became known as the expert on what were called "fly-in" developments. There were mentions in *Time, Newsweek* and numerous other publications.

In all of these undertakings, I was a consultant. While I sometimes worked in association with developers, I did not occupy that role — that is, until Spruce Creek.

For years I had been flying across the country with a camera within reach. Every time I saw a promising site, I took a photo, and I built a file of thousands of them.

The Project at Spruce Creek

We sent one such photo of an abandoned military training field near Daytona Beach (Fla.) to the mayor's office and suggested that the site warranted study as a location for the world's first total fly-in community. A year or so later — after we'd forgotten about it — there was a phone call from the mayor.

It seems that the city had offered the site to the state for a new university but had lost the competition. Now, under fire from taxpayers, and with an election coming up, the city council wanted a new plan — quick!

The mayor's call was to set up a meeting in my office in Atlanta. He brought the entire city council and listened carefully to an outline of what we thought could be done with the site.

At the time, I thought we were making a pitch for a planning assignment. Thus, we were astounded when the mayor said that what he had in mind was selling the site to me.

I quickly explained that, first, I had no such money, and second, I was not a developer. He said, "No problem" — they would sell me the tract on terms I could not refuse, and then I could organize a company, find an appropriate developer and launch the project.

It was a prime 1,100-acre site just off I-95. Improvements included a drainage system and a usable runway. The offer was $500 an acre, with three years to pay.

I couldn't say no. I rounded up half a dozen pilot friends in Atlanta, we scraped up several hundred thousand dollars for a down payment and formed Fly-In Concept, Inc. (FIC). We began looking for a suitable developer.

This was in the early 1970s, and Florida was in the midst of a development frenzy. Every good developer had his pick of projects and had already made commitments up to or beyond capacity.

Some months later, with a payment on the tract coming due, the FIC board made a fateful decision. We would undertake just one stage of the project, put in utilities and offer one block of homesites for sale. That would provide enough cash flow to continue until a developer could be found to handle the long-term management.

I was asked to manage the process, relying on advice from some of the board members who were in the development business in Atlanta. Also, we would set up an office on the site and hire local engineers and other service providers.

It all sounded workable. I'm sure that's what the Pharaoh thought when the Egyptians started building the pyramids.

During the ensuing three years I became intimately familiar with the route from Peachtree-DeKalb Airport in Atlanta to Spruce Creek. I could recite the frequency of every navaid, every controller and every compass heading. I carried an instrument flight plan in my head.

First came the permits. Despite having the support of local officials, I had to collect a total of 42 local, state and federal permits. Some were easy and some were agonizing.

Then I enjoyed the thrills of construction management, supervising the building of roads, bridges, a sewage treatment plant, a water system, a hangar and other facilities.

As anyone with experience knows, there are many singular trials and tribulations that beset the builder. Here are a few we remember:

• We moved the golf course four times. First, we had an ecologist wade around in the swamp and tell us where the flood plain was. Then, we had an engineering firm survey it. We finally discovered that back at the state capital there was a kid looking at an 8x11 satellite photo taken from 200 miles out who said everybody was wrong.

After the flood plain was "redefined," I was advised to move one green on the golf course. That required moving three lot lines, which meant shifting street right-of-way, which involved utility lines, and overall, a change in land allocations under our PUD ordinance.

• I advised the Post Office I was building a new community and wanted to coordinate plans. They sent some idiot out to make a "survey." He couldn't find any houses and wrote a letter saying we should put a box on the road two miles away.

• About three months after we started construction a hearse and a string of cars showed up at the gate. They said they wanted to bury somebody on our land.

• The lender called the day before payday and said our draw was being held up because the monthly courthouse exam showed a lien on the property. We discovered it had been filed by a plumber who hadn't even asked us for payment — he said it was his standard collection procedure.

• I asked the new back-hoe man, tongue-in-cheek, how many survey markers he dug up his first week. He thought about it and said, very seriously, "Three, but I put them all back so nice you can hardly tell they were moved."

Despite such fun and games we got the construction done on schedule and within budget. And we made an impressive volume of sales.

But there were two factors we couldn't cope with — interest rates rose out of sight, and a recession set in. Even so, the lender's rep encouraged us to make plans for another stage of development. Since ours was a small project and we were making headway, he said more money would come.

However, our lender was taking a big beating on a large-scale land project in another state and abruptly decided to withdraw from all land projects, ours included. We were unceremoniously abandoned, and the project was sold to another entity.

When we launched the project they had spoken proudly of being the "financial partner" in the deal. When we asked for help they said, "We're not your partner, you know, we're just the people who hold the mortgage."

We had borrowed from an insurance company in the north through a mortgage broker down south, and all contacts had to be through the broker. It didn't take long to discover they used the broker as a legal defense mechanism — when they transmitted decisions through him to us, he was their agent, but when we responded to him, he was an independent.

At the bottom of one of the worst real estate recessions in recent history, it was impossible to refinance the project. The only people you heard saying good things about land projects were those who had one for sale.

What was the final result? We did succeed in launching the world's first complete fly-in community. Today, there are several hundred homes owned by happy people enjoying a truly unique life style. Taxiways lead to each home, most of which have both a garage and a hangar.

More airline pilots live at Spruce Creek than in any other subdivision anywhere. Some senior pilots commute via their own small aircraft to jet connections in Orlando or Jacksonville to jobs in New York or Chicago, where they fly global routes. Movie star John Travolta is one of the residents. He flies his own jet to film locations throughout the country.

Spruce Creek is indeed an element in the new global megastructure.

Looking back, one of the things I am proud of is that, despite all the trials and tribulations at Spruce Creek, we thought to save the best part of the natural environment — a corridor along the creek. It is a beautiful area of lush semi-tropical growth hanging over a sluggish stream that reminds one of movie versions of Suwanee River.

We got some good advice from friends in the environmental field, including Dr. Howard Odum, head of wetlands research at the University of Florida; Dr. Michael Duever, director of research for Audubon; Dr. I. Lehr Brisbin, specialist in impact studies; and the late Dr. Walter Boardman, former executive of the Nature Conservancy.

Today, residents of the community can visit the preserve via a boardwalk and scenic overlook. It is a great spot for meditating!

What happened to the original sponsors? Our project had two groups of investors: the first group, which had invested in shares in the development company, and a second group, which had bought sites in the community. Several of us were in both groups.

The investors in shares lost everything. Those who bought sites soon doubled or tripled their money. One taxiway site bought originally for $11,500 was recently on the market for $195,000.

We were disappointed that the original investors received no reward — not even thanks — for making the project possible. However, we firmly argue that you have to believe in the system enough to accept the harsh treatment it sometimes dishes out.

At least, the experience gave us a much better understanding and appreciation of developers. We had the learning experience of just one project. But for many developers every project is a new business at a new location in a new market with a new time frame.

Panic Warning!

After surveying the wreckage left by the great real estate recession of the mid-70s, we set out to warn the industry. While we knew that general business recessions were part of the inevitable business cycles, we did not think the great real estate disasters were necessary.

Thus, we covered many of the harsh lessons learned in the mid-1970s real estate crash in our book *Pitfalls in Development*, published in 1978. It was our hope that improved management strategies would avert similar real estate disasters during future business cycles.

Unfortunately, not enough people read our book! During the late 1980s there was another orgy of over-building, and by 1990 projects were crashing on all sides. The newer disaster was even greater than the one before — it happened on a global scale.

Again, we survey the damage and wonder if it could possibly happen again so soon. If so, the danger period would appear to be around year 2005. Don't say we didn't warn you!

Changing Urban Forms

City planning is an ancient art. Yet, within our lifetime we have seen many new urban forms and variations — so many, in fact, that providing terminology for all of them has been a problem. We attempted to define site, site complex, planned unit development, micropolis, mini-city, micro-city, satellite new town, frontier new town and rural growth center in *Industrial Development* (March-April, 1969, pp. 2-5).

A later report refers to large scale PUDs and new towns as Megapuds. Special complexes that harmonize economic development facilities with

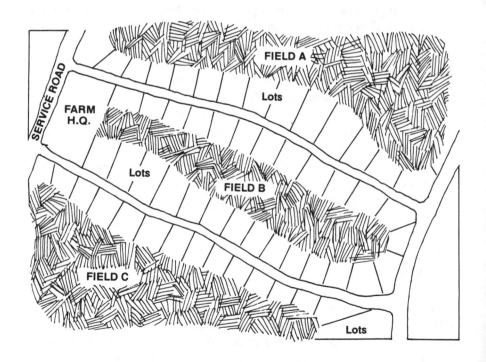

Agricultural PUD

This is the kind of innovative planning that can preserve agricultural and green space even in big metro areas. Of course, there are many such planned unit developments around golf courses, and there are some around equestrian areas. All provide permanent open space.

ecological needs — such as waste recovery, recycling and energy generation — have been designated as Decoplexes. An interesting variation is the "agricultural PUD."

More recently, we have discussed, at some length, "airport cities" (*see chapter 3*), "super metros,"[1] "loop cities,"[2] and "science cities."[3] A common denominator is that all involve a mixture of uses.

The ultimate sophistication might be found in a new airport city served by two circumferential highway loops as well as rapid rail. At one of the nodes where a radial crosses a circumferential route we might locate a science city or technopolis. Within the loops we would include decoplex installations and green infrastructure.

Obviously, our new city requires a lot of space. In fact, it is a means for integrating urban areas with large hinterlands. Clearly, we prefer a low-rise pattern of development in a garden setting.

Where space is very expensive and highly restricted, other plans must be followed. These include the ultra-high-rise and/or underground style of development, which has been given most serious attention in Japan. We covered such alternatives in a report on "super cities" for *T•e Futurist*.[4]

Development thus becomes more complicated every day. There are more challenges, and, yes, there is more excitement!

The New Professionals

Those who are just entering the field must deal not only with the rethinking of existing plans but also with new plans for projects unlike any we have seen before. These new professionals will combine the skills of the geo-economist, urban planner, architect, ecologist, engineer and ombudsman.

[1]Super Metros, *Site Selection*, August 1987
[2]Two Loop Cities, *Site Selection*, June 1986
[3]R&D Clusters, Science Cities, 1987
[4]Tomorrows Super Cities, *The Futurist*, May/June 1993

B. Excerpts

1978 Excerpt	*Pitfalls in Development.* The bureaucracy of development. Soft plans and feasibility studies. Hard plans and preconstruction activities. Construction and operation. Megapuds track record. Special pitfalls for special projects. Real estate panics. Pitfalls ahead. 1978 and 1981. 343 pp.

The great works of man exist today because someone had a dream and took a chance. Great plans were made, great efforts were expended in implementation, and, sometimes, great results were achieved. Sometimes there was disappointment.

There has never been a guarantee that any project would meet every expectation, nor will there ever be. Pitfalls of many types surround every development.

This study deals with the host of risks that surround those who undertake large and complex projects today. The objective is not to discourage new ventures, for they are urgently needed in all sectors, but to improve the odds for those that follow.

At the outset, it should be admitted that we have high regard for those who risk everything — money, reputation, even health and happiness — to build the communities and facilities that contemporary society enjoys. Often maligned, and seldom fully appreciated, developers have their successes taken for granted and their failures flaunted.

The nature of the business is such that the developer is personally and emotionally involved in the project. If he is a good developer, he regards the project as his. Success or failure of the project is tantamount to personal success or failure.

That very first and biggest "go, no-go" decision is thus a personal, emotional and philosophical decision as well as an economic rationalization. In many ways, the developer's choice is like the go, no-go decision the pilot of an aircraft must make before taking off in questionable weather.

Some pilots fly thousands of hours without accident or incident, while others kill themselves early in unnecessary and foolish accidents because of their cavalier approach to the go, no-go choice.

In aviation, beware of the pilot who regards a scheduled flight as a test of his courage. Equally dangerous is the pilot who jumps into the airplane and takes off without a pre-flight check of the airplane. Those who lack maturity and emotional stability should not fly, nor should they manage large projects!

The developer of large projects faces not only the big go, no-go decisions up front but also some key "stop-or-go" decisions at stages, plus many lesser choices throughout the planning and operation stages.

The Bureaucracy of Development

There was a time when the developer could examine the economic aspects of a proposed venture and, if the profitability was attractive, proceed without serious concern about governmental intervention. During the years following World War II, a gradual increase in bureaucracy of development occurred, however, and during the decades of the Sixties and Seventies, bureaucratic growth was explosive.

Like an enormous cancer, the stultifying bureaucracy has spread throughout the world, leaving scarcely any part of any country untouched. The investor or developer who has not been affected by this factor to date is as rare as a whooping crane. Those who venture without studying the bureaucratic environment for their project may expect a series of rude surprises.

Developers are by instinct and experience entrepreneurs who believe in the American system, with its profit motivation and its automatic supply-and-demand controls in the market-place. Many tend to assume that all Americans, including government officials, live by the same principles.

This is a big pitfall. It is a delusion to assume, for example, that the government attorney handling your permit application really believes in any of the following:

• The private enterprise system and the profit motive.
• Open competition as a governing mechanism.
• Fair play in a private/public sector confrontation.

Looking further for philosophical potholes, the developer finds another tier of potential frustration at the state and local levels, and, often, additional tiers embodied in multi-state, multi-county and multi-district commissions, boards and committees of various types.

These bodies often are conduits for federal funding or play a role in federal regulation; thus they suffer from many of the federal maladies as well as those peculiar to the local level.

A common problem among state and local groups is the tendency to conceive long-term plans but to implement them on a short-term basis, frequently failing to achieve major goals on any reasonable time schedule.

There are a number of reasons this failure occurs. The prime movers of implementation are elected officials who allocate funds. They think in terms of re-election in two to four years. Given a choice between spending for

203

item "A," which will be completed with appropriate ribbon-cutting ceremonies before the next election, and item "B," which will still be a hole in
the ground, item A often wins.

Also, it is difficult for public-sector entities to maintain the continuity of
programs and personnel over the span of a 10-year project. Many jurisdictions have legal limitations on the commitment of future revenues, requiring re-approval of every project in every budget.

Further, the opportunities for public projects to be delayed are endless.
Major street and highway projects frequently involve commitments from city
or county, state and federal entities. One entity may pay for preliminary planning, another may buy right-of-way, and a third may provide most of the construction funds. When a project is delayed, each entity points to another.

The developer who is dependent on a new publicly built access road
had better not depend on anybody's promise. The only safe approach is to
wait until he can touch the pavement.

Making capital budget decisions at the right time is another great problem for public entities. The Atlanta rapid transit system (MARTA) is a good
example.

MARTA went through the study commission and preliminary engineering stages in the early 1960s. It was concluded that a feasible system could
be built for $270 million. The legislature passed necessary enabling legisla-
tion, and detailed planning began.

Unhappily, the study and design process proved to be almost endless.
At last count, MARTA had been scrutinized by more than a dozen committees, boards and commissions. For about 10 years the design was revised
and revised again, the funding plan was kicked from one political arena to
another, and large new buildings grew up in the proposed right-of-way.
Finally, construction got underway in earnest in the mid-'70s. Cost of the
system is now estimated at more than $2 billion.

Here was a case of the real go-ahead decisions being made so late that
the taxpayer is going to be saddled with more than $1 billion in excess cost.
Further, scores of property owners and businesses located in the MARTA
corridor have been kept in suspense at great cost. Plans drawn by alert
developers to build complexes adjacent to MARTA stations have grown yellow with age.

Wherever the developer operates, he may have enough clout to get
small infrastructure projects in the public sector completed without great
risk of disappointment. But if the public project is large, complex and long-
term, beware! The Atlanta experience is the norm, not the exception.

Government Incentives

Before making a business decision based on a government incentive, you should check these possibilities:

1. Is the location wrong? Many tax incentives, loans and grants apply only to distressed areas, and there are usually some powerful reasons that the areas are depressed. You may get a good loan to launch your venture, but can you make a success of it in a ghetto area or on an Indian reservation?

2. Can you tolerate the bureaucracy? Despite all assurances from the top politicians, government funds come with strings attached. You may have to show outsiders your books; you may encounter so many delays you can't keep your schedule; you may have greatly increased administrative costs.

3. Examine the fine print! After you've gotten hooked, you may find some fine print that can be very expensive, very cumbersome, very frustrating, or all of the above. For example, you may have to meet a new wage level, accept a union or form a minority partnership.

4. Diversification or expansion may be stymied. The incentive you received at the outset may be limited by law to one activity or to a certain sized facility. You may not be able to sell if a good offer is made to you.

5. You may encounter public relations problems. Some citizen groups will accuse you of getting a free ride at taxpayers' expense. They may ask you to pay the local government a fee in lieu of taxes even though that wasn't in the deal. Whatever happens, you're in a fishbowl.

Soft Plans: 'Feasibility' Studies

There is a period when a project becomes a gleam in the eye of the developer and his interest grows serious, but he is still not committed to do it. This is the time to make "soft" plans that are tentative, exploratory and flexible. It is also the time to study the possibility of investing in the venture and achieving an attractive return on that investment.

At this stage, the developer can be rather deliberate. He hasn't borrowed any money and the interest meter is not running. He is spending his own money and does not have to account to someone else for what is going on.

The developer may take an option on a site during this soft planning process. Or, he may identify an opportunity that could be grasped by a competitor unless action is taken quickly. Only then does the pressure begin. But in no case can he afford to proceed with more than deliberate speed.

This is the time to do your best thinking about the conceptual plan, potential profits, future cash flow, how the venture should be structured and how it will be funded. Unsound thinking introduced here may carry through the entire project and doom it to failure, though no one may discover the error for years.

Enter the "feasibility" study. There is probably no more ill-defined or mis-used term in the developer's lexicon. For our purposes, let's say that a sound feasibility study should include: a conceptual plan, a profitability analysis, a cash flow projection, a corporate structure plan and a funding plan.

A. *Conceptual Plan*

Is it an apple or an orange? What does it look like? How big is it? Where will you put it? Who will buy it?

Let's stop talking in abstract terms and get down to "you." And let's not be ashamed to get down to elementary issues at this early stage. All of the basic questions are going to be answered by somebody. If you don't put a label on your product, lenders, regulatory officials or customers may give it one you don't like.

For internal analysis, you're probably going to look at a matrix of possi-bilities. You may consider, for example, a mixed-use community develop-ment project that ranges from two or three land uses to five or six, and size may vary by a factor of 10. You're going to explore scale effect in relation to potential environmental reactions and funding required.

This is the time to let yourself go. Far out ideas don't cost much, and sometimes unlikely combinations produce exciting possibilities. Possible mixes should be tested against potential situations. What is the possible impact of new technology, new life styles, international events?

In this early process of clarifying thinking and zeroing in on a specific objective, it is also important to distinguish between programs and projects. The private developer who gets carried away with a concept and starts thinking of a program for applying the concept is looking for trouble. Pro-grams are for the government. Programs may promote and encourage the launching of ventures and projects. They don't make money.

After reducing all of the ideas and concepts to an initial conceptual plan, variations are considered until one plan seems to have the most to offer. This is then matched with sample sites and further refinement occurs. The developer now begins to see the size and shape of the thing he may undertake.

This brainstorming may even lead to an artist's rendering at this early stage. This may serve to save some time in explaining the potential venture to those who are involved in soft planning, but it is vitally important to label all such material as "proposed" or "preliminary." More than one developer has been hung because his final product didn't include something shown on an early rendering.

B. *Profitability Analysis*

This section of the feasibility study dwells on estimates of project costs and potential revenues. The developer who has previously built small residential subdivisions or multi-purpose industrial buildings and warehouses cannot believe how complicated the analysis can be for a large mixed-use project. There are dozens of significant variables, and most are interactive.

Thus, the developer who selects one mix of uses, one estimate of costs, one prediction of sales and draws conclusions regarding project performance is truly playing Russian roulette. The recommended approach today is to buy a computer program that will project performance from starting date through completion (perhaps 10 years) in terms of costs, revenues, cash flow and profit.

With this tool available, the developer then plugs in a range of estimates for each variable. What happens when highest costs and lowest sales are assumed? What is the effect of density and price on revenues from the multi-family sites? What absorption rate for commercial sites is adequate? These and countless other questions will arise constantly, and the developer who can answer them quickly and reliably enjoys more favorable odds.

The capability of predicting project performance when key parameters are changed is particularly important when major surprises develop. For example, what would happen if another oil boycott reduced tourist traffic 50 percent? What would happen if the nearby military base was closed and the area payroll was cut 20 percent?

One of the biggest surprises, of course, would be the launching of new, directly competitive projects within the same time frame. That is what happened to hundreds of ventures that failed or suffered heavy losses during the 1974-76 real estate depression.

While the complete analysis may indicate the dire consequences of too many competitive projects, the computer will not tip the developer off regarding specific rival plans. The market research done as part of the feasibility study should seek to give some inkling as to the extent of this competitive project planning.

Hindsight is 20/20, and looking back, it is easy to see what some of the major mistakes of the early '70s were. In regard to feasibility analysis, it now appears that a common mistake was to analyze each project independently of others.

This resulted in studies that proved that a project was theoretically feasible at a certain location at a certain time. But as real feasibility guides the studies were dangerous instruments.

Some developers who were embarrassed during the depression put the blame entirely on the lending institutions, arguing that lenders, aware of a great many projects, should have seen the extent of proposed overbuilding and sounded warnings. It is true that large lenders did occupy a better vantage point from which to see the volume of activity, and they should have slowed the placement of funds before the overbuilding reached crisis proportions in certain areas.

But the developer still must bear the consequences of his decisions. He's like the pilot who takes off into a stormy night. He can't put all the blame on the National Weather Service.

The repercussions of 1974-76 have been so far-reaching that it is evident that the entire industry has learned a lesson. Among alert developers, the approach to every aspect of project planning will be more cautious. Those who fail to use this recent experience in new ventures will have no one but themselves to blame.

Enough regarding survival! The name of the game is to make a profit — in fact, to make a good profit. A prime purpose of a feasibility study is to determine whether a project will yield a good return on the funds invested. Each developer will have his own opinion as to what is a suitable return, but surely a development project, with all of its frustrations, will not be undertaken unless it offers substantially more return after taxes than a safe investment in government securities.

C. *Cash-flow Projection*

It is entirely possible for a development team to propose a beautiful and workable conceptual plan for a project that, on financial analysis, offers an excellent prospect for return on investment but which, if undertaken, would be a disaster. That old bugaboo, cash flow, is the demon that destroys many a project that is otherwise sound.

The most critical part of the financial analysis, then, is the projection of cash flow, month-by-month and year-by-year, for the term of the project. The computer program mentioned earlier is particularly helpful as costs vary, interest rates float and sales ebb and flow.

The cash flow projection can be full of surprises. At the point when the project is really moving with sales above estimates, a large cash deficit can occur, for example, if lot releases are not properly structured or if the developer has an unsatisfactory plan for financing the lots he sells. This produces a situation wherein the better the sales are, the more acute the cash crunch becomes.

The cash flow projection serves not only to spot flaws in the proposed plan but also to indicate how much money must be borrowed and for how long. It will also show when draws must be made.

Perhaps the biggest question today in the making of cash flow estimates is the time frame. The final result may be vastly different if a project does not move according to schedule. Consider Case A and Case B, which are identical except for schedule:

Case A: The developer arranges a $2 million, three-year loan to undertake Stage I of a community development project. Interest will float at four over prime. Within three months he has hard plans advanced enough to have final zoning approved and begin sales. At the end of the first year, sales are brisk, construction is going full-tilt on utilities, streets and golf course. During the second year, all construction is finished and sales continue. By the end of the third year, the developer has paid off the loan and has cash to begin opening Stage II.

Case B: The developer arranges a $2 million three-year loan to undertake Stage I, as in Case A. However, the zoning commission raises new issues and keeps the project in suspense for 14 months. During this time no sales program can be started. In the second year construction is well underway, but new federal regulations are holding up sales. Interest rates have gone to 13 percent, and the outstanding balance is over $1 million. Finally, in the third year, sales get underway in a down-turning economy but still go as well as forecast. However, the combination of interest rates, now 15 percent, and outstanding balance of $2 million, leave the project unable to meet the debt service. The lender forecloses.

This is the kind of squeeze many developers encountered in 1974-76 — an incredible combination of extreme interest rates, down-turning market and new regulations at local, state and federal levels.

Hence, the objective of the cash-flow prognostication is to identify deadly combinations and discover ways to avoid them. The good cash-flow plan seeks a fail-safe device. It also provides an early warning system. This is especially necessary in an economy wherein an official in Washington can make a decision overnight that may delay a project and place it in financial jeopardy.

D. *The Funding Plan*

The well-established developer with a string of successes in his immediate past found himself pursued by eager lenders in the early 1970s. The identical developer, with big projects in distress, encountered icy stares from the same people only a few short years later. How fickle lenders can be!

In setting out to arrange funding for a large new project, it is absolutely essential, therefore, to look at the long term. It is folly to launch a 10-year project with a 90-day construction loan, and it may be unwise to undertake the same project with a three-year commitment.

Many a developer learned in 1974-76 that a pledge of support made in good times, when expectations were high, evaporated when the going got rough.

This is one of the reasons that lenders for a major project should not be sought but selected. The mere fact that an institution has money to lend does not make it a satisfactory financial partner for a large, complex development. At the least, the lender must understand the difference between financing various kinds of projects.

While the lender is busy looking over your track record, check his experience in funding the kind of project you are about to launch. If all of his experience is with garden apartments and you're planning an office tower, beware! This caution is particularly well-noted if the project is a big, new PUD with potential environmental problems and consequent pre-development costs and delays.

How much expertise is really available in the lender organization to apply to your specific problems? Will you have to spend an inordinate amount of your time putting out fires because no one on the lender's staff understands your situation?

Once convinced that the lender is the kind of marriage partner with whom you can live through good times and bad, negotiate your deal, and get every significant item in writing.

Remind yourself that the closing of the loan will be the beginning of the "entrapment" process. A short-term loan may turn into a long-term financial plan.

At this point, you can withdraw with only minor damage. You may never be able to say that again!

Hard Plans: Pre-Construction Activities

A. *After the Loan Is Closed*

The fuse is lit! Now that the loan is closed you have moved overnight from the tentative stage to pre-construction hard planning. From concepts and pretty renderings you're moving to work schedules and budgets. Most important, the interest meter is running from now until the project is completed. You can hear it clicking away in the background.

Things are going to be different in a lot of ways. If you have managed to keep the project secret up to this point, you won't be able to enjoy your privacy much longer. That mortgage is going to be recorded, and an alert courthouse reporter will soon be telling the world about a huge, new multi-million-dollar project.

Rather than have information spread at random with rumors and distortions you'd better be ready with some kind of announcement and handout for the news media. Now is the time to establish a policy of dealing honestly with news outlets — try to help them do their jobs and they may reciprocate.

As you "go public," you begin your sales program, although it may be many months before you set up a sales office with staff and budget.

B. *Site Selection and Acquisition*

You may have already optioned a site, but no matter how you have sequenced events, it is crucial that a comprehensive study be made before your final commitment to a specific site.

Your objective is both positive and negative. You want to confirm the availability of certain things, such as services and institutions. Also, you want to prove that certain nuisances are not present. You hope to avoid surprises to the maximum extent possible.

For example, you may have optioned a site last spring in a bucolic rural setting. Unless you have examined the site in each season, you may be in for some rude surprises. The field that was just turning green last spring is now covered with rotting cabbage stalks that can be smelled two miles away. The farm outbuilding that looked picturesque a few months ago will be your nemesis in August when flies from the chicken houses and pig pens begin winging over your new subdivision.

Perhaps some of your adjacent land owners do not own the mineral rights on their farms. What happens if it becomes feasible to mine phosphate in the area? Your lots may not sell well alongside a strip mine.

Or, what will be the impact if commercial air service is suspended at the nearby airport? Many small cities are losing service as airlines consolidate operations and introduce larger jets for greater economy.

Site factors that may seem obscure to most observers can be critical to you. Shrewd investors may ignore what appears on the surface to be an excellent situation. Every component of every major project must be scrutinized to evaluate its site needs.

C. *Master Plan and Engineering*

This is the point at which you discover how complicated a new community or mixed-use development can be. As you undertake to finalize plans and go to work, you discover that just about everything affects everything else.

As you seek to harmonize conflicting space requirements, functional relationships and flow of work, you find yourself consulting your key planner, engineer, surveyor, contractors, land-use attorney and representatives of the power company, gas company and phone company with increasing frequency.

Why not bring some order out of this chaos? Organize these people on your team into a development committee structured to represent every vital interrelated activity. Then bring them together as often as necessary to maintain good communications.

At your first session you can set ground rules for the protection of the site. Establish responsibility for everyone who sets foot on the property, including those who come to plan and those who come to consult or make deliveries. Specify access routes, parking areas and rules respecting trash.

This is the time when you begin to incur damage to trees and foliage that will be noticeable for years to come and that will cost you money. First will come the surveyors. Not many years ago they used machetes to clear a line-of-sight. Now they have chain saws. If they slip up on a turn, they can cut through a quarter of a mile of trees before saying "oops" and starting back on a new angle.

Many developers set up a system of fines for trees cut unnecessarily, or for site damage. Others require a monitor to be present at any time equipment is brought on site. No matter what the method, watch anyone who shows up with more than a pocket knife!

All of these site visits serve the purpose, of course, of providing data essential to the completion of the working-drawing version of the master plan. Earlier estimates of land allocations and location of various elements can now be refined on the basis of hard facts: the street right-of-way that the survey shows going through a clump of beautiful trees will be shifted; a proposed bridge to cross a small stream will be moved to provide more scenic approaches; the sewage treatment last-stage lagoon will be shifted to an area having better percolation characteristics.

Such adjustments separate the good projects from the bad. Every failure to consider the facts is a pitfall. Before the plan hardens, every component must be checked out in detail.

For example, at this point you may have received your first layout from the golf course architect. He may be tops in his field, and he may have roughed in for you an outstanding course. But how does the golf layout harmonize with your other interests?

Check linear feet of fairway frontage available for single-family or multi-family use. Perhaps the architect planned the course with all golf holes abutting one another, and the only interface with the residential area is around the periphery of the course.

That may be less distracting for the golfers, but it minimizes fairway frontage and reduces your sales potential.

By extending streets into the golf area you can perhaps double your fairway frontage without creating an excessive number of street crossings for golf carts. You can, of course, carry this to the point that the crossings are a traffic problem and a safety hazard.

You are the one who must also worry about getting golf fairways so close to homes that there are future liability problems when a golfer drives a ball into someone's patio and causes damage or injury. You'll have to look at each hole, the protection afforded by trees and the building setback lines.

You'll also need to examine your staging plan. The golf course may be built early but may extend into a residential area not scheduled for development for several years. Where will you get water for irrigation? If from wells, where will you get power for pumping?

Each component brings its own set of planning questions. If you have frontage on a stream, what kind of marina or dock facility will you have? Will you separate power boats and canoes? Will you have "stream zoning," with areas of quiet water and speed limits? Where will home owners keep their boats?

Slowly, the whole plan moves from conceptual sketch to blueprints, although nothing is as easy as it would seem. Despite expensive photogrammetry producing two-foot contour data, the proposed drainage plan on the flat parcel looks unsatisfactory after a weekend when four inches of rain falls. The gas company advises it will be unable to provide service even though its main line right-of-way chews a hunk out of a prime parcel of your land.

Meanwhile, the power company says it will have to put in a temporary pole line to bring in service to your subdivision that is supposed to feature underground utilities. They promise to remove the pole line next year when they have equipment for the underground extension.

Get It in Writing!

By now, you are well aware that if anyone is going to coordinate plans for your project, it is you. And the time to do it is before any digging starts. Once the bulldozers and back hoes arrive, the workmen will remind you at inopportune times, by digging up new utility lines almost as fast as you can repair them.

Now is the time for your development team to agree on a typical street cross-section and typical utility corridor cross-section. This specifies where each line will be with respect to centerline, how deep it will be and in what sequence it will be installed. For example, the sewer line would go in first and deepest, then water, then power, then telephone and cable TV. Landscaping comes later!

D. *Initial Permits and Approvals*

As soon as you have some hard plans ready, you'll be anxious to get whatever permits and approvals are required before construction can start.

These may include hurdles that can make or break you and your project.

The required permits differ, of course, for each project, each location and, probably, for each instance. They involve local, state and federal agencies independently and, sometimes, in combination. A typical community development project may require several dozen permits to get started. The process is very expensive and time-consuming. Once started, the process never ends, since many approvals must be renewed periodically.

The first step might well be to get in the proper frame of mind. Now is the time to prepare for an experience that can be appreciated only by those who have been through it.

Right here in the good old USA you are about to be put on trial by a system that is basically un-American and often unconstitutional, as court cases are beginning to find.

As currently being operated, the system may subject you to a multiple veto process wherein you face double jeopardy at the least. You may be required to prove your innocence repeatedly, not before a jury of peers selected by lot, but before an appointed bureaucrat or a board of political appointees involved in numerous conflicts of interest. Often you cannot face your accusers, nor can you get change of venue. Your property may be taken from you without due process.

This is a responsibility you cannot delegate to a clerk. It is going to require the attention of top executives — perhaps a lot of their time for many months. If you try to economize by handing off the problem to less capable people, you may pay a high price in delays or unsatisfactory clearances. Look at your spread sheets and estimate how much a 10 percent reduction in overall density would cost!

Before the ink is dry on your expensive computerized schedules, you're going to start revising them. Even so, about all they're going to measure during the permit and approval stage is the degree of your frustration. They certainly will not tell you when you will receive your permits.

You are accustomed to making schedules wherein the amount of time allotted to an activity is related to the amount of work to be done. If there is one mile of chain-link security fence to install, you figure out how much can be done in one day and how many days the whole job will take. This won't work with the bureaucratic process, because the amount of time consumed often is unrelated to the amount of work to do.

You may submit a plan the professional staff can review in a week. The governing board meets once a month. You ought to be safe in predicting action in 60 days. Instead, someone at the commission meeting raises an objection, and your application is postponed for further study. This can go on for months or years.

You may have plans in hand and you may know the interest meter is running, but the local bureaucracy is feeling no pressure. The functionaries will not miss coffee breaks to speed you on your way. Neither will they hesitate to suggest "minor" changes in your plan, which will hold you up for weeks.

You will quickly discover that among the many civil servants you encounter in the regulatory agencies there are some general types:

• The experienced, competent specialist who is trying to do a good job in a common-sense way, carrying out the intent of the law but not overly zealous about jurisdictions, forms and procedures. He can give you some good advice. This public servant works quietly, usually has a heavy work load and often is underpaid. He is also a rare and endangered species.

• The incompetent appointee who is afraid to take a position or make a decision. His way of life is to keep his head down.

• The young-man-with-a-mission, who, fresh out of school and unencumbered with any practical experience, is going to fix everything, including your project. He will not hesitate to insist on absurd standards for even more absurd reasons.

• The opportunist who wants to make something out of the situation — either money or personal advantage. Trouble, trouble, trouble.

You're going to have to deal with them all, and while you will certainly respond to each in a different way, there's one common denominator. You'll be glad if you generate a written record of dealings with them all.

If you follow-up on permit actions entirely by telephone, your contacts are extremely easy to forget. Let's say you've been calling one minor official for weeks about a trivial matter. He keeps promising to do something, but nothing happens. You decide to go to his superior.

It's your word against his.

You'll be a lot better off to create a written record. Write a letter periodically. Every time you telephone, write a confirming note immediately afterward. Keep brief phone memos. Then, if you must complain, you can furnish a file that shows that you acted in good faith.

The file may also help communicate your problems to your investors, lenders or directors.

When action finally occurs, get some written confirmation of that approval. If necessary, write a letter to the official, get him to initial it and put the acknowledged copy in your file.

E. *Legal and Administrative Structure*

Those who have built large projects know that they are not erected on a foundation of clay and granite — it's paper, single-spaced and a copy for everybody.

The avalanche of paper starts with the first loan documents and carries through to the last sales contract. Since it can't be avoided, you will learn to do it right or pay a high price for your failure. And no matter how careful you are, you'll probably discover at least one crisis in every pound of paper.

Still another batch of pitfalls of the legal or administrative variety awaits you in the various filings or registrations you will be required to make with local, state or federal bodies. An example might be the handling of your utility system with your state public service commission. Does the law require privately owned systems to register at time of planning, construction or operation? At what point must you obtain approval of the rates you charge within your project? What justification or documentation is required?

Adding to the stack are affirmative action plans, emergency preparedness plans and others that arrive in large manila envelopes — all to be filled out in triplicate. Meanwhile, you try to squeeze in a little time for the prime purpose of all this — construction and sales.

F. *Scheduling*

You already have a cash-flow projection and loan repayment plan. That is your key schedule. Stay ahead of it or die!

Depending on the nature of your project, you'll need numerous other schedules, plus an overall schedule that relates all elements. Where virtually all functions are in the private sector and no major permits or approvals are involved after the start of the project, these methods enjoy optimum effectiveness.

In any case, you can't risk scheduling only the construction. You must include sales and administration in your overall plan. And, in the case of a land development or community development project, the permits and approvals become your biggest scheduling question.

One developer who was planning a project in a certain county went to the county manager and asked him, off the record, for his best guess as to how long it would take to get approvals for a small garden apartment project. The official said about six to eight months at the outside. Then the developer went to various county officials (engineer, planner, health) and asked each one to spell out exactly what they required, and in what sequence.

Putting it all together, our developer came up with a project lead time of 22 months. This checked roughly with the actual experience of several other developers in the county. In other words, you can't always base a realistic schedule on what the bureaucrats tell you in good faith.

Unhappily, you can't estimate your required lead time from national averages or general experience of others. It will depend on who you are, what your project is, where it is located, when it is undertaken and how you approach it.

Generally, project lead times have been increasing steadily during the past 10 years as government intervention has grown. One possible exception is small industrial and warehousing facilities. A decade ago, such a facility typically would have been located at the ring of the urban area on agricultural land and might have required an average of three years of lead time.

Today, the small industrial facility would very likely go onto a prepared site in an industrial park and might not require more than 18 months. Of course, the developer or the industrial park would have a different story to tell. Prepared sites are more popular now because the developer has born the brunt of the task of getting permits and working through the bureaucratic maze.

Other development projects are looking at gestation periods, which grow longer and longer. The pre-development lead time for a nuclear plant, for example, ranges from 10 years to infinity.

As these "planning" periods stretch out, a new phenomenon has emerged to plague developers. This is the problem-compounding effect: The longer a project is in the planning stage, the more questions are raised and the more planning is required. A project in planning for two years accumulates more than twice as many problems as a project in planning for one year.

This is especially true of projects that involve environmental questions. If project approval is postponed for any reason, large or small, this is seen by opponents as a sign of weakness, and their efforts are redoubled in the manner of a piranha attacking a wounded animal!

Also, the delayed project is exposed to new regulations, changes in procedures, personnel turnover and countless other excuses for subjecting it to multiple jeopardy. All such events have one thing in common: They cause delays and add to costs.

Most frustrating of all are the delays you suffer, not because of misunderstanding, apathy or inefficiency, but because someone in a government position attempts to sabotage your project. Almost every large project faces this risk.

If you're lucky, the saboteur will operate openly. Perhaps it will be a county commissioner who, in order to curry favor with a bloc of voters, will seek to get the county to ignore the rules or forget about a permit already issued. Worst is a minor official who thinks he alone knows what's best for the world and quietly loses your application or forgets to record it.

You may reach a point that reasonable professional relations with an official or an agency are impossible and, as a last resort, you must take legal action. Knowing that this may mean the doom of the project, few developers are willing to take this step. But you could find yourself in the shoes of one developer whose project was stalled for seven years by a county board. His patience ran out, he went to court, and the court required the county to approve the project.

Construction and Operation

A. *Coping with Calls and Visitors*

From the first day when you unload a construction-office trailer and portable toilet on the site, you are in business and, whether you like it or not, you are going to receive phone calls and visitors. These early contacts will range from curiosity-seekers to solid prospects to buy whatever you will later have to sell.

You don't want these early visitors consuming the time of construction supervisors, getting in the way of contractors or falling in ditches and suing. As soon as practical, you will need a visitor center, even though you may begin with a mobile office.

The key point is to have the visitor facility conveniently located and well marked in order to keep stray vehicles from wandering around the site.

The same facility may serve as the focal point for your early security system. Are you going to allow motor bikes or four-wheel drive vehicles to roam through the tract? How about campers? Horses? What about picnics, fires and guns? Now's the time to post the rules and begin controlling the situation.

Don't be surprised to discover that the vacant land you bought is regarded by everyone in the county as a public facility for whatever use serves their interest. Your property may be the place they have always come to chop down a Christmas tree or dump their garbage. It will take time, tact and vigilance to correct the situation.

B. *Beginning Site Work*

Speaking of vigilance, that beautiful forest you bought may soon begin to resemble a strip mine unless you defend it against every work crew of any type. Your problem begins the first day the first work crew arrives.

A disaster waiting to happen to the unsuspecting property owner is the first round of deliveries of heavy equipment and construction pipe and supplies. Unless a loading and turning area is designated, the big trucks will smash vegetation and leave ruts that become permanent scars.

Many pitfalls of this type can be avoided by having a form letter ready to hand to each contractor and supplier, advising him that he is responsible for having his drivers report to your foreman the first time they come to the site. On that first trip your foreman can give them the rules and show them the areas designated. Be sure to get them to initial a copy of the form letter for your records.

Megapuds: The Track Record

Types of Projects

Almost everyone who has bought a piece of property, held it a few years and sold at a profit is an expert on real estate. Similarly, because you have a good track record in one specific type of development, you tend to think you can handle any type of project. The temptation to think this way is reinforced by watching some people who are not as well-qualified as you get rich within a few years.

It is true, of course, that many fundamentals apply to management of any type of project. But it is equally true that new projects can be apples, oranges or bananas, and if you are an apple man, you'd better leave the bananas alone. At least, you ought to be able to tell the difference.

While large-scale, long-term projects have many characteristics in common, they may differ widely in ownership, management, land-use and market served. It may help to think in terms of a matrix that offers, for example, a vertical assortment of ownership-management plans and a horizontal distribution of land-use and market possibilities.

We are indebted to an anonymous contributor for this capsule of the stages in a typical unsuccessful project:

A. Enthusiasm

B. Disenchantment

C. Panic!

D. Search for the guilty

E. Punishment of the innocent

F. Reward for those who took no par

1986
Excerpt

Will Two-loop Cities Dominate Future Site Selection? During the past decade hundreds of site decisions have left no doubt that circumferential freeways are a powerful magnet in drawing new business facilities to certain metro areas. Now, it is argued that proposed new outer loops may become an even more important development attraction in those areas where government entities can get together and build them. "Will Two-Loop Cities Dominate Future Site Selection?" *Site Selection*, June 1986, pp. 582-588.

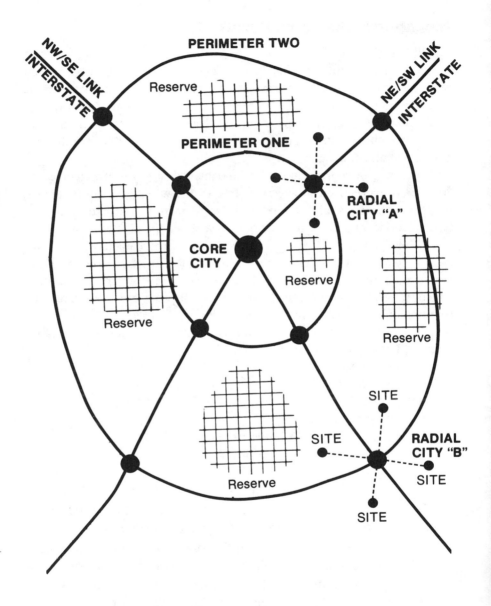

PERIMETER TWO

NW/SE LINK INTERSTATE

NE/SW LINK INTERSTATE

Reserve

PERIMETER ONE

RADIAL CITY "A"

CORE CITY

Reserve

Reserve

Reserve

Reserve

SITE

SITE

RADIAL CITY "B"

SITE

SITE

Reserve

Two-loop city planning concept.

A two-loop city and metro region. This is the concept we began promoting in the 1960s and that is beginning to take shape at Atlanta and other locations.

The first perimeter freeway to be credited with luring highly desirable industrial development was Boston's much publicized Route 128. While not a complete perimeter, that route attracted an impressive number of new facilities that could be seen by any passing motorist.

These new facilities drew particular attention because they were of the type that corporate facility planners consider to be trend-setters and that area developers consider most desirable. A healthy proportion were high-technology enterprises employing top-flight engineers and scientists.

As new perimeter freeways opened in Atlanta, Washington, Indianapolis and elsewhere, it soon became apparent that loop locations were in demand. They offered the advantages of suburban sites, while retaining the urban benefits of proximity (in terms of minutes) to important support services and institutions.

Originally conceived by highway engineers as by-passes around congested areas for through traffic, the perimeters quickly became the axis for new urban growth. Today, they serve as the new main streets of many metro areas, linking multi-county areas and combining markets hitherto separate and distinct.

This new pattern can be seen in some two dozen U.S. metro areas. To a degree, it can be noted in other situations where partial perimeter routes have been built. (A number of cities built on the shore or against a mountain range cannot complete perimeters because of natural barriers.)

A quick scan of an atlas reveals that larger cities having circumferential freeways include Baltimore/Washington, Dallas/Fort Worth, Atlanta, Indianapolis, Minneapolis/Saint Paul, Saint Louis, San Antonio and Houston. Also included are Columbus, Ohio; Raleigh, North Carolina; and Lexington, Kentucky.

A number of other cities have begun construction of loops, but at this point there are one or more missing links. Boston, backed up against the Atlantic, has, nevertheless, built two loops on the western side of the metro area — I-95 (replacing the old Route 128) as an inner loop, and I-495 as an outer loop.

While the loop city concept is further advanced in the U.S. than in other countries, it is by no means an exclusively American idea. Moscow, Rome, Cologne, Brussels, Paris and London have perimeter routes. These vary substantially in their geometry, however.

Paris has a loop route built relatively close to the city center, making it more of an urban artery and less of a development axis. Moscow, by contrast, has a large loop, which cuts through forests and undeveloped areas.

We have seen all of the loop routes mentioned above, except for the one at Bonn-Cologne. Also, we recently observed construction underway for a perimeter route at Guadalajara in Mexico. While they differ in some respects, we can safely say that all of these routes are producing a substantial impact on development patterns in the areas they serve.

Interestingly, we have not recorded any loop cities in Asia, Africa or South America.

Lessons Learned

Some of the U.S. circumferential routes have now been in use for two decades. The first visible impacts were the location, at interchanges, of motels, fast food facilities and other service establishments. Then, we began to see office and industrial facilities locating on the frontage roads — They wanted not only the easy freeway access but also the advertising value of Interstate exposure.

Not much later we began to observe the influence of the perimeter routes extending well beyond the frontage roads. Wherever the loop crossed a radial artery that extended from the urban center into the hinterland, a new development node was created.

These nodes quickly attracted development and emerged as new towns, overshadowing established towns not so strategically located. Industry site seekers began locating new facilities around these clusters rather than strip-fashion along the radials as was the practice earlier.

Once the pattern was clearly established, there was no contest between the cluster and the strip concept — the clusters served everyone better.

Now, there is reason to believe that a two-loop plan may be many times more effective than a single-loop plan. As suggested in the accompanying illustration, a well-planned two-loop metro area design may well accomplish these important results:

• Ease the pressure on the urban center.
• Generate economic development in rural areas.
• Facilitate the flow of through traffic.
• Add environmental and aesthetic values.

For the business community, prospects are exciting: Opportunities are provided for both local and outside investors. There are immediate and obvious plus factors for the corporate facility planner.

For once, we may have a development plan that offers substantial benefits for both rural and urban interests! This is not to suggest, however, that such a grand plan does not entail many conflicts — so many, in fact, that they can only be managed by a statewide or super-metro entity.

Of course, such an ambitious plan demands the close scrutiny of local, regional and state planning bodies. Implementation will be expensive and will require the cooperation of many jurisdictions. Such a project cannot be

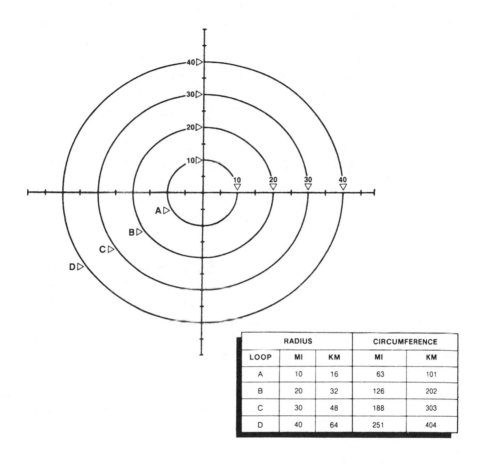

RADIUS			CIRCUMFERENCE	
LOOP	MI	KM	MI	KM
A	10	16	63	101
B	20	32	126	202
C	30	48	188	303
D	40	64	251	404

Geometric advantage of loop cities. Given a certain length of highway mileage that a region can afford, what layout plan will yield the most opportunities for economic development? The loop plan offers a clear advantage over the radial or linear strip plan.

223

regarded as a highway project or a building proposal. It is a total strategy for all concerned.

Much remains to be learned regarding loop city planning. What is the optimum loop radius? What is the cost of asymmetry? What is a good range of aspect ratios? What is optimum spacing between loops?

It is already evident that much skill is involved in designing a system that will balance the various components of the traffic flow. Ideally, office commuters moving from the hinterland into the urban center should balance the flow of inner city dwellers going to jobs in the suburban plants. Local urban movements should mesh with through Interstate traffic.

And, we suspect, all of these criteria vary according to the size of the metro area. Other parameters may include such factors as growth rate, land values and terrain.

For almost all areas, the biggest obstacle is money. With federal funding reduced, a greater share of costs must be borne by state and local governments.

The Atlanta Experience

Many years ago, as chairman of our (DeKalb) county planning commission, we watched the construction of I-285, which now circles metro Atlanta. As the freeway was completed the impact was swift and dramatic. It required no crystal ball to see that one day the route would be congested.

A few years later we had an opportunity, we thought, to do something about the situation. As a member of the State Senate and member of the Highway Committee, we proposed in 1967 that the state begin planning an outer loop. We were challenged immediately by members who pointed out that traffic on the inner loop (I-285) was nowhere near capacity.

We argued that if the state would only select the right-of-way and prevent construction in the path of our proposed outer loop, much time and money could be saved. We failed to make the case, and never got the proposal out of committee.

Twenty years later, Georgia is at long last giving serious consideration to the construction of our outer loop. Even if the project is approved immediately, however, there will be long delays for planning, costs of right-of-way through new developments will be astronomical, and construction will take years. We may not live to see completion.

Even so, the outer perimeter for the Atlanta metro area is, in our view, the very best project our leaders could undertake in order to promote the economic development of the metro area and state. No similar expenditure on "development roads" in South Georgia will bring as much new investment, as many jobs, or as many other benefits to the state.

The Atlanta outer loop is a sure-fire winner. Other proposals have a much lower probability of success. Ask any corporate facility planner!

One of the axioms in area development is to lead from strength. The Atlanta metro complex is Georgia's most powerful magnet. In seeking to improve Georgia's fortunes, those plans that capitalize on Atlanta's strength have the best chance to succeed in this highly competitive world.

In much of Georgia, this is not a popular political idea. Those who live in rural areas find it very difficult to vote for plans to spend more money around rich Atlanta and wait for future success to spill over. Not surprisingly, gubernatorial candidates prefer to propose piecemeal expenditures in the rural areas, even though they know the strategy may not produce as good a long-term return for the state.

Georgia's dilemma is not at all unusual. It is, in fact, the classic urban-rural conflict found in most state legislative halls and in government centers around the world.

Hence, completed perimeter routes are a measure not only of advanced highway planning concepts but also of maturity in political thinking and strategic planning. In the next century, we may well judge the world's great cities by the number of their loops.

1987
Excerpt

Enter The Super Metros!!! The preferred life style of most Americans involves a homesite in a quiet suburb, small town or rural area with a job just a few minutes away, plus easy access — in less than an hour — to all of the sophisticated services of a large metro complex. The area planning teams that provide for this style will be the big winners in the site competitions of the next decade. "Enter the super metros!" *Site Selection*. Aug. 1987. p. 756.

We Americans, in pursuit of the optimum quality of life, want to have our cake and eat it too. We want to live the simple, bucolic life, but we want all of the conveniences and pleasures of the space age at our fingertips.

We assert that firms that can find such optimum sites will be most competitive for the brainpower that will be the business currency of the future. Those that settle for less will have increasing difficulty in attracting talent and may begin a slide from which they cannot recover.

For the firm selecting a site for a new facility, we have thus complicated the task enormously. It is no longer enough to choose a good site for the plant. Now, we must, for our personnel, find:

• A metro center with excellent urban services: international airport, great universities, research and medical centers, major sports with a domed stadium, convention center, museums, a symphony and other cultural assets.

• A satellite area with high-performance business parks: office and/or industrial areas offering outstanding functional and aesthetic features, including water, waste and other environmental systems.

• A hinterland containing quiet, protected homesites: served by good schools, shopping, law enforcement and utility services.

Further, all of these sites must be linked by high-speed transport. And there must be a coherent overall plan for protecting values in the future.

This means that we must select a large area that contains all of the desired types of sites in the correct juxtaposition. Further, we'd like the whole area to be close to the shore, the lakes and the mountains and to have an ideal year-round climate.

These choice locations are the new "super metros." Few exist today if we insist on all elements. At least a dozen existing metro centers have the potential to become "supers" if they can muster the creativity and leadership to assemble all the components.

One such candidate is Atlanta, which already has many of the features needed. However, the state-city-county leadership is presently stumbling over several projects that may be the key to super status.

Such cases are to be found, we suspect in all parts of the country. It is extremely difficult to bring together all of the diverse interests in large metro areas to agree on a plan and harder still to find the funds and determination needed for implementation.

Yet that is what metro area economic competition is all about today — to be super or not to be.

Someone must lead. Why not area development organizations? For them, there has never been a bigger challenge or a greater opportunity.

1987
Excerpt

"R&D Clusters." Where do they occur? Why have they developed? What are new locations to watch? 1987. Monograph.

In 1962 we conducted a study in which we sought to identify existing clusters of R&D activity in the USA and to predict where new clusters might emerge. At that time, we found that the dominant centers of activity were in five locations: Boston, Baltimore-Washington, New York-New Jersey, San Francisco and Los Angeles.

We also described another 12 established clusters, situated mostly in the East and Midwest. We predicted that some 21 new clusters would

Science Centers Where R&D is Particularly Noteworthy - 1962

◇ **DOMINANT CENTERS**
1. Boston
2. Los Angeles
3. New York-New Jersey
4. San Francisco
5. Washington-Baltimore

○ **ESTABLISHED CENTERS**
6. Buffalo-Rochester
7. Chicago
8. Cleveland
9. Dayton-Cincinnati-Columbus
10. Detroit-Ann Arbor
11. Milwaukee-Madison
12. New Haven-Hartford
13. Philadelphia
14. Pittsburgh
15. St. Louis
16. Twin Cities
17. Tri Cities

☐ **EMERGING CENTERS**
18. Ames-Des Moines
19. Atlanta
20. Austin-San Antonio
21. Baton Rouge-New Orleans
22. Cape Canaveral-Orlando
23. Dallas-Ft. Worth
24. Denver-Boulder-Colorado Springs
25. Houston
26. Los Alamos-Santa Fe-Albuquerque
26. Miami-Palm Beach
26. Oak Ridge-Knoxville
27. Phoenix-Tucson
28. Raleigh
29. Redstone (Huntsville)
30. Richmond-Peninsula
31. St. Petersburg-Tampa
32. Salt Lake City
33. San Diego
34. Santa Barabara
35. Seattle
36. Tulsa-Oklahoma City-Norman

R&D cluster forecast. In 1962 we attempted to forecast where clusters of R&D activity would occur. We missed several but most of the development occurred very much as predicted.

emerge at sites from Cape Canaveral to San Diego.

From time to time thereafter, we reported on the development of new R&D centers and related facilities. However, our 1987 survey may be the most significant benchmark, since it occurred 25 years after the first study, affording an opportunity to measure the long-term validity of the early forecast.

During 1987-88 we examined the results and we believe they confirm the soundness of the original analysis. Most of the centers predicted to emerge have done so. Moreover, the centers we labeled as dominant have continued to be very strong.

What makes clusters happen?

Looking at the clusters that have emerged thus far, we conclude that the factors that appear most important are:

1. The existence of a very large R&D installation, such as a national government center, to serve as a nucleus

Certainly, the existence in an area of one large research facility goes a long way toward launching that area on the road to success provided the area has some other positive attributes.

What was the spark that set off the original Silicon Valley development? We believe it was the NASA Ames lab. During the last stages of WWII, Ames was developing a strong instrumentation program and venturing into computers. Of course, the facilities at Stanford and Berkeley were vitally important.

There's no doubt that the Redstone Arsenal rocket program built a fire in Huntsville, and the Johnson Space Center boosted Houston. Sometimes one such facility can make the difference.

However, we also observe that having a big facility does not guarantee spin-off successes. The hundreds of millions spent at Oak Ridge and at the Savannah River Plant have not spilled much across the fences, nor did the nuclear accelerator do that much for Chicago's technological development.

Government labs are not the only possibility. The Bell Labs have done much for the New York/New Jersey area. Austin and most of Texas have high hopes for benefits from the location of the microcomputer center there several years ago.

Of similar importance are research centers operated by universities — if they are in the MIT and Cal Tech class. These are built with funds from a variety of sources, including federal agencies, state governments, private firms and philanthropic groups.

2. Venture Capital

The best financial asset is wealth in the hands of individuals who accumulated their investment funds from successful business enterprises. Such entrepreneurs in the past were found in New York, Boston and Philadelphia. More recently, they have been conspicuous in Dallas, Houston, San Francisco and elsewhere.

Also helpful are formal venture capital funds and groups that organize to screen technological proposals and fund those that appear promising. Some areas, like Boston, have had them for 50 years. Others, like Atlanta, have developed such activities in the 1980s.

About half of the state governments have also set up venture capital funds to promote development. Examples range from the Massachusetts Technology Development Corp. to the New Mexico Energy Research and Development Institute and to the Utah Technology Corp. To date, the state units have achieved some successes, but they have not yet been the key factor.

3. Facilities built to breed or attract R&D facilities

The evidence also confirms that such facilities as research parks can make a difference. (We hasten to say that the mere existence of a vacant or partially developed piece of land heralded as a research park does not make any difference whatsoever.)

In our 1962 survey, we identified more than 100 projects around the country. About a dozen have flourished as R&D centers, and a number of others have successfully attracted technical industries. Many are still standing vacant.

Obviously, something more than the prepared site is needed. In many cases, the successful parks have been closely associated with university and/or industrial programs to spark interest. North Carolina's Research Triangle is a good example.

In other cases, "incubator" facilities for small, new, high-tech enterprises have produced results. Good examples are found in Atlanta at Georgia Tech's Advanced Technology Development Center and in Salt Lake City at the University of Utah Research Park.

Another key to park success is the availability of a special service tailored to the needs of R&D or high-tech units. For example, Technology Park/Atlanta boasts a "high-reliability" power circuit installed by Georgia Power to minimize the risk of power failures in large computer installations.

Perhaps the most unusual special service we have seen is the cold-water pipe in the new Hawaii Ocean Science and Technology Park adjacent to Keahole Airport. This conduit will deliver very pure water from ocean depths to park occupants engaged in aquaculture, pharmaceutical and related research. It provides an R&D opportunity not found elsewhere.

4. Highly Educated People

This is the intellectual base we described in our 1962 study. It refers both to the existing supply of educated people, as measured in such terms as scientists per 1,000 population, and to the mechanisms for enhancing the quality of this intellectual resource.

We have learned to look not just for college towns but also for metro areas with groups of institutions turning out numbers of technical people in the right disciplines.

Further, we are interested in graduate education programs, support for research, automated library services, arrangements whereby corporate personnel may work toward advanced degrees and vocational training for lab technicians.

5. Quality of Life

This is assumed by some to mean a resort environment. The presumption is that an area with other plus factors, which could also offer a year-round balmy climate with palm trees and beaches, would win hands down. The history of locations during the past two decades suggests, however, that inland areas having four distinct seasons are competing very successfully.

Obviously, there is more to quality of life than the outside air temperature and the smell of salt air. We know that most scientists are attracted by a combination of assets, tangible and intangible, which range from climate and scenic beauty, to quality of schools, to residential areas and recreational facilities, to open political and social structures.

Perhaps after several more decades of study we will understand better what counts most!

6. Services

As small R&D ventures begin to grow, they discover needs for special services, and the bigger they get, the more important this factor becomes. It can be the prime factor in the location of a large facility.

Most important is transportation. For short-distance travel, the key is proximity to expressway and Interstate highway links. For longer distances, the key is scheduled air service. General aviation airports are becoming more important.

Other important services include computer and instrument repair, reproduction, machine shop and compressed gases. Even among the more common professional services — attorneys, accountants, financial advisors — there is a wide difference in the technical expertise of those in one location as compared with another.

7. Politics

To be realistic, we must add politics to our list of prime factors. Observing events of the past several decades, we cannot overlook the fact that political decisions have determined the location of a number of governmental centers, some of which in turn have been very influential in the development of clusters.

Our first such political experience was with the Aircraft Propulsion

Research Center that NACA/NASA proposed to build after WWII in the state of Washington, near Grand Coulee Dam because of a large electric power requirement. When the project reached Congress, the late Sen. McKellar of Tennessee, then chairman of the Appropriations Committee, became interested. Soon, the facility became an Air Force project, was located at Tullahoma, Tennessee, and was served by TVA.

Some years later, President Lyndon Johnson located the NASA Manned Space Flight Center in Houston. Then, the Army, encouraged by Sen. Saltonstall, decided to put its Quartermaster Research Center in Natick, Massachusetts.

(We have suggested for 25 years that there be a National Site Selection Board made up of professionals who could be called upon to advise on the location of such projects. So far, Congress has shown no interest.)

For most local high-technology activities, however, the state political climate is more important than Washington politics. There are 50 legislative climates that differ significantly in the levying of taxes, the offering of incentives and the regulation of operations.

Moreover, there are many new areas of legislative interest to high-technology operations. These include such issues as state laws to control computer crime, restrictions on the use of CRTs, taxes on software and taxes on the interstate flow of data.

Some states have recognized that dealing with high-technology industries and R&D activities requires a new approach and have created new mechanisms to support and encourage development. If the author can be excused for lack of modesty, we will report that Georgia took the lead in this regard by creating a State Science and Technology Commission in the early 1960s. As a member of the Georgia Senate, I authored that program.

Unfortunately, the program encountered a man running for president of the United States, Jimmy Carter. In his state government reorganization program, he sought to make a spectacular reduction in the number of state programs and agencies — a commendable objective. Unhappily, he cut the R&D unit, thus wiping out the lead we had.

8. Exotic Factors of the Future

It is a certainty that when someone revises this list a decade or so hence, important new factors will be added. What will they be?

Will the clusters of tomorrow be situated at the intersections of our new fiber-optic highways? Will they require teleports? Will they coincide with a concentration of nodes on packet-switching networks?

Most difficult to predict is the future location pattern for the software industry. This is the most mobile industry of its size and importance that we have yet seen.

Literally, a new software unit can be located just about anywhere a programmer chooses to work. A scan of the listings in a software directory will reveal quite a number of small new ventures in remote locations from northern New England to the desert Southwest and throughout Oregon, Washington and British Columbia.

Most start-up ventures today need only a 110v electric power line and a telephone. Even these bare requirements may soon be reduced with the increased use of more sophisticated battery-powered computers.

Further, the introduction during the next few years of direct broadcast satellites and portable suitcase-size satellite uplinks and antennas will further distribute the industry. This will make it possible to set up shop on that legendary isle in the South Pacific and yet remain in instant contact with the corporate world.

That will add another set of factors. Productivity may get to be an even bigger issue!

Weighing these and other factors, what is the outlook for various locations? Here is a summary of opinions:

State-by-state summary

Alabama: In our 1962 forecast we predicted that the Huntsville area would emerge. It has come forth on schedule!

Alaska: No cluster forecast, nor is one yet in sight. Perhaps Anchorage will come forth later.

Arizona: We named Phoenix as a comer in 1962, and the area has exceeded all expectations. It appears that the Tucson area will emerge in the 1990s.

Arkansas: The winning combination of factors has not yet been assembled. The state does, however, have a strong industrial development program.

California: The state had two dominant centers in 1962: the Los Angeles/Orange County area and the San Francisco peninsula/Santa Clara Valley (now Silicon Valley!). We said San Diego and Santa Barbara would emerge. San Diego has come through magnificently, Santa Barbara less impressively. Now we've added Sacramento for the 1990s.

Colorado: We picked Colorado Springs to emerge in our 1962 study, and the area obliged. In the next growth phase, the Denver/Boulder area should develop strongly.

Connecticut: Lying between the big New York/New Jersey and Boston clusters, Connecticut growth will probably continue to be oriented toward those centers.

Delaware: With the big DuPont facilities in Wilmington as a nucleus, Delaware will attempt to develop an identity alongside the established

Philadelphia complex. There is also keen competition in the adjacent Baltimore-Washington cluster.

Florida: In 1962 we saw the beginning of a cluster in the Tampa/St. Petersburg and Orlando/Cape Canaveral areas. That cluster will eventually take in the entire I-4 corridor through Daytona Beach. We also saw Miami/Southeast Florida as an emerging center. In the 1990s we believe Gainesville has a good chance to emerge, and, as a long shot, we have cited the Fort Myers/Southwest Florida area.

Georgia: In 1962 we named Atlanta as a potential cluster center. For a decade not much happened, but in the past 10 years results have been impressive. The specific center has been Gwinnett County in the northeast quadrant of the Atlanta metro area, and we look for rapid growth in that direction extending as far as Athens in the 1990s.

Hawaii: While we have predicted no specific cluster center for the 1990s, we believe Hawaii will achieve significant progress in building R&D centers. A center could emerge near university facilities on Oahu, on Maui around the telescope sites or in the Hawaii/Kona OTEC (ocean thermal energy conversion) lab area.

Idaho: It will take a big effort to develop clusters, despite the existence of some key facilities such as the national reactor lab.

Illinois: The 1962 survey identified Chicago as one of the established centers in the nation. That big center will continue to grow.

Indiana: There was no obvious cluster in 1962, nor is there today. However, we believe there is potential in the Lafayette area, with its impressive Purdue facilities.

Iowa: In 1962 we picked the Ames/Des Moines area to emerge, but we were wrong. Too many of their good homegrown scientists chose to work in California!

Kansas: Perhaps the growing activities on the Missouri side of the river will link up with activities in the Lawrence and Manhattan areas.

Kentucky: We see some interesting things happening in the Lexington area. It could be a pleasant surprise in the 1990s.

Louisiana: We picked New Orleans as a comer in 1962, but the area has made slow progress. It has been difficult to convert the extensive resources of chemical process technology in the Baton Rouge and Lafayette areas into diversified R&D ventures.

Maine: Unless there is a major breakthrough, it does not appear that a cluster development will be evident until the late 1990s.

Maryland: In 1962 we said that the Baltimore/Washington area was one of the top five centers in the nation. That cluster has spread to the south, and the fastest growth is in northern Virginia.

Massachusetts: When we picked the Boston area as one of the top five in 1962, we were looking at Boston and Cambridge. Now it is evident that this key R&D cluster is going to sprawl over half of Massachusetts, southern New Hampshire and down into Rhode Island.

Michigan: We felt that Detroit was already an established center by 1962. It has continued to grow and will gain strength as it encompasses the Ann Arbor area.

Minnesota: The 1962 study tagged the Twin Cities as an existing center. It is still developing.

Mississippi: While the state has done an outstanding job of attracting manufacturing facilities, it has not yet lured a large number of R&D units. The NASA facility in Hancock County was a breakthrough and may serve as a nucleus for a future complex.

Missouri: The St. Louis area is a long-established center. The recent study suggested Kansas City will emerge as another cluster focus.

Montana: The state will have to muster a stronger development effort if it is to compete.

Nebraska: The best hope is to develop something based on the university programs at Lincoln.

Nevada: Many important military testing activities are conducted in the state. If they were declassified, we might be able to list Las Vegas as a cluster.

New Hampshire: This is developing as part of the Boston complex.

New Jersey: This is combined with the New York cluster. The Bell labs are a very important component. On our list of new clusters to emerge in the years just ahead, we have the Princeton/Trenton area.

New Mexico: In 1962 we predicted that the Albuquerque/Santa Fe area would emerge as a center. It has done well, with the Sandia labs, Los Alamos and other units.

New York: One of the top R&D centers.

North Carolina: In 1962 we hoped that the new Research Triangle project would lead to an emerging cluster. Did it ever!

North Dakota: Not yet.

Ohio: Twenty-five years ago there were already two established centers: at Cleveland and in the Dayton-Columbus-Cincinnati area. There are strong elements, such as the NASA Lewis Lab, Wright Field, Battelle, Ohio State University and numerous corporate facilities.

Oklahoma: Programs have suffered from the ups and downs of the petroleum industry.

Oregon: We overlooked Portland in our first study. The area has definitely emerged, and we look for strong growth ahead.

Pennsylvania: The Philadelphia and Pittsburgh areas were already established as R&D centers in 1962.

Rhode Island: Count this as part of the Boston complex.

South Carolina: With large nuclear facilities and growing industrial operations, the state may be able to put together a cluster in the Columbia area. The university is a key factor.

South Dakota: Much of the upper Midwest has had tough sledding in attracting R&D units. That can change, but it will take time and effort.

Tennessee: In our 1962 survey we said that the Knoxville/Oak Ridge area would emerge as a center, building around the nuclear facilities and the university. Development has occurred but not as fast as we expected. Meanwhile, the state has been eminently successful in attracting large manufacturing plants.

Texas: Our 1962 forecast listed three areas to emerge: Dallas/Forth Worth, Houston and the Austin/San Antonio corridor. They have all come through, with Austin setting the pace. Today, we see El Paso and the Bryan/College Station areas as potential cluster locations.

Utah: Salt Lake City was tagged as a potential cluster center in 1962, and the area succeeded handsomely.

Vermont: The state seems content to remain out of the competition.

Virginia: Northern Virginia is sparking the growth of the Baltimore/Washington cluster. In 1962 we also picked the Norfolk/Newport News area, recognizing the key role of the NASA Langley Lab.

Washington: Seattle was named in 1962 as having the potential to emerge, and it did. We were not farsighted enough, however, to guess that it might be a center for the development of microcomputer software.

West Virginia: This is a state surrounded by tough competition. It will take a big effort to succeed.

Wisconsin: The Milwaukee/Madison area was named in 1962 as an existing center.

Wyoming: A beautiful state with a bright future, but no R&D clusters.

Areas Outside the USA: We did not include non-U.S. areas in our 1962 survey. We know that there were some concentrations of scientific activity in Europe, but few clusters existed around the world. Today, we see a far different picture, with many areas becoming competitive. Here is a broad-brush scan:

Canada: In recent years we have been impressed with the programs being carried out by the national and provincial governments to spur R&D projects and promote centers.

At the federal level, there was the NAPLPS program for encouraging the formation of ventures to develop systems for transmitting images via digital communications links. Several dozen firms responded.

Today, there are existing clusters of R&D units in the Toronto, Ottawa, Vancouver and Montreal areas. Growth has been particularly strong in the engineering sciences related to the automobile industry.

Europe: In the UK we have the long-established London/Cambridge complex, plus the fast-growing "Silicon Glen" in Scotland. In France there are clusters appearing around Paris in the new towns such as Marne-la-Vallee and at Nice/Sophia Antipolis. There are several promising locations in Germany. Other areas to watch include Stockholm, Rome, Barcelona and Oslo.

Pacific Rim: Japan is developing a "science city" as well as several clusters. Taiwan has a successful research park at Hsinchu. A new research park is being developed in Singapore. There are several projects in Australia, including a technology park in Adelaide. Locations with strong potential include Hong Kong, Seoul and Kuala Lumpur.

Elsewhere: We may see future clusters emerge at Tel Aviv, Johannesburg, Sao Paulo, Bangkok and at several locations in India.

A New Phase Ahead

When it was suggested in 1947 that there was a direct relationship between investment in research centers and payoff in area economic development, only a few accepted the concept. It took decades to fund programs and launch activities.

Today, it is obvious that leaders around the world are now well aware that R&D centers can spawn economic development. Consequently, investment in these programs is flowing more freely, and new ventures are being launched much more swiftly. It is clear that the pace will increase and global competition will become even more intensive.

1989
Excerpt

"Rethinking Urban Plan." Is it time to divorce high-rise offices and regional shopping centers? A substantial segment of the population of Gwinnett County encounters major traffic congestion every working day. One change in strategy that might be considered ... pertains to the location of regional shopping centers, office parks, and other major complexes in relation to key transportation routes. *Gwinnett Daily News*, January 18, 1989.

A substantial segment of the population of Gwinnett County encounters major traffic congestion every working day. It is small comfort to

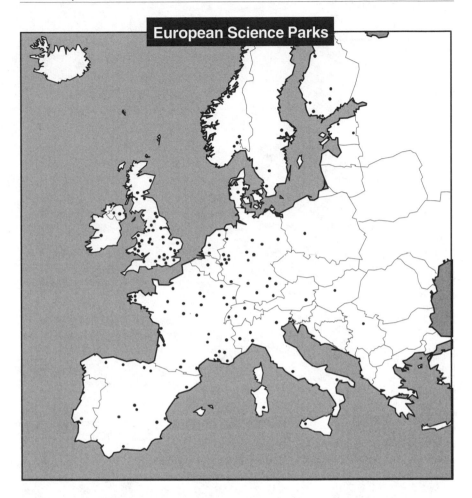

European Science Parks

After science parks began to succeed in the USA, the movement spread to Europe and the Pacific Rim. Today, it is a global phenomenon, providing concrete evidence that science does breed technology which breeds development. (Also see next page.)

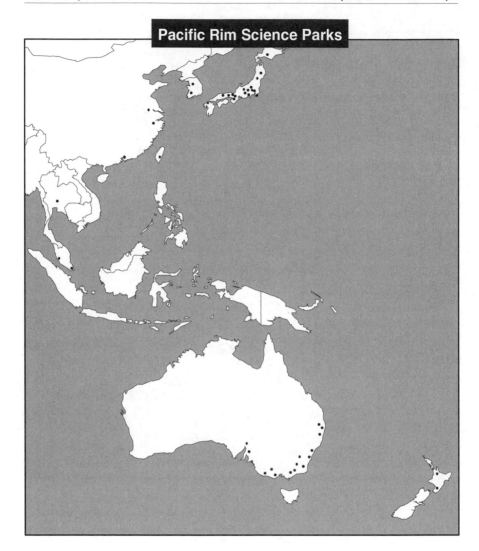

Pacific Rim Science Parks

think that the situation may be worse in DeKalb or Fulton.

The reality is that some traffic bottlenecks are going to occur in fast-growing Gwinnett despite the best efforts of the government units involved. We are paying today for the inability of our leaders a decade ago to forecast our growth rate.

What we must ask ourselves today is, "Is there a change in urban planning and development strategy we could implement now that could substantially reduce the magnitude of our future problems?"

Happily, Gwinnett is not too far gone for new strategies to make a big difference. Most of the county is still undeveloped.

One change in strategy that might be considered is already being seen around the country in a number of metro areas. It pertains to the location of regional shopping centers, office parks, and other major complexes in relation to key transportation routes.

The new thinking comes as a result of bad experience with development patterns of the past 20 years. All too often, the sequence of events follows a familiar pattern:

First, a new regional shopping center is located in a growing market area. Next, high-rise offices are located next to the shopping center. They are followed by hotels and other facilities. Then, many smaller retail and service facilities locate nearby, seeking to cash in on the customers attracted by the big facilities.

The result is an unplanned new city that is afflicted with the same congestion problems that are typical of older cities. Thoroughfares, access roads and parking areas are an uncoordinated mess. Everybody suffers.

What has happened is that most of the major traffic generators — the regional shopping center, the office towers and the visitor facilities — have been clustered. When the traffic generated by these activities is added to the traffic on an adjacent interstate highway, we have created the worst possible traffic situation.

Sound familiar? That is precisely what has been allowed to happen throughout the Atlanta metro area. The Gwinnett Mall area is the latest example.

Twenty years ago it was believed that there were significant economic advantages in locating office centers next to the big shopping centers. Executives locating new offices thought it would be nice if workers could dash over to the nearby mall at lunchtime. They also thought it would be nice if visiting businessmen could stay in a hotel just down the street.

What the corporate site planners did not think about was the future problems their workers would have in getting to and from the office every day. Now, that inconvenience far offsets any convenience achieved.

Today, corporate site selection specialists are alerted to the traffic gridlock around shopping centers, and many are already avoiding them. That resistance is expected to grow.

Many planners now believe that regional shopping centers should stand alone. Prohibiting high-density, traffic-generating activities in the immediate area then assures that shoppers will have ready access to the center in the future.

Similarly, if high-density office complexes are limited to specified areas free of other uses, workers have fewer problems getting to work.

There are, of course, exceptions to this thinking. There is a place for large-scale mixed-use developments where an overall traffic flow system is included from the start. This is best achieved when the entire project is launched under one ownership and management.

What about small projects developed by small firms? In order to compete, they may need to get together with others to formulate a cohesive plan for any cluster they might create. Where only piecemeal plans are put forward, local governments may have to deny permits.

There is no function of local government any more difficult than that of controlling growth without stifling it. Perhaps Gwinnett can earn distinction in meeting this challenge.

1993 Excerpt   "Tomorrow's Super Cities." *The Futurist.* World Future Society. May-June 1993.

With the world population constantly growing and putting ever more pressures on urban areas, the creativity of city planners will become extremely important during the next several decades.

Many city design and renewal efforts around the world can be classified as super projects — macroengineering efforts seeking new, multidisciplinary approaches for transportation, commercial, residential, and industrial site planning and development. Some cities have already begun such efforts, and many of the ideas on the drawing boards for the city of the future may put past feats of construction and planning to shame.

By Land and By Sea

A solution to the problem of high urban land costs is to build below ground. Planners argue that it makes more sense to develop downward than to go up.

Taisei, a Japanese engineering firm, has proposed to build an underground complex called Alice City, named for Alice in Wonderland. Another engineering firm, Shimizu, has proposed an underground development called Urban Geo Grid. [See "Underground Cities: Japan's Answer to Overcrowding," July-August 1990.]

Still another approach is to build over water. Tokyo already has a seaworthy office-building development, and other floating cities are being discussed.

The U.S.-based World City Corporation has a project called The Phoenix World City under development. A cruise ship capable of carrying more than 5,000 passengers, it would truly be a floating city, with several medium-rise apartment units, marina, conference center and many other amenities. Construction is scheduled to begin in early 1994 and be completed by either 1997 or 1998.

The 500-Story Skyscraper

Is the sky no longer the limit for skyscrapers? Proposed new high-rise structures boggle the mind. We will soon add a new term to our development vocabulary. In addition to low-rise, mid-rise and high-rise, we may begin talking about "super-rise" or "ultra-rise" projects.

Ohbayashi, a major Japanese engineering firm, proposes to build a 500-story high-rise building that would be a city within itself. The proposed tower, which would include offices and apartments, as well as shopping and service facilities, would cost an estimated $326 billion. Called Aeropolis 2001, the mammoth structure would be approximately five times higher than the World Trade Center in New York. It would take 15 minutes in a high-speed elevator to reach the top floor.

Incredible? Impossible? That's what people have been saying about tall structures since the trend began with the construction of the Eiffel Tower in Paris in 1889. Standing more than 900 feet (274 meters) high, the Eiffel awed visitors for decades.

Then came the Empire State Building in New York in 1931. It measures some 1,250 feet (381 m), with 102 floors. That was topped by the New York World Trade Center in 1972, with a height of 1,350 feet (411 m) and 110 floors. The Sears Tower, in Chicago, then took over the lead in 1974, with a height of 1,450 feet (442 m) and 110 floors. In 1975, the CN Tower, in Toronto, became the world's tallest structure at 1,820 feet (555 m).

Today, the Miglin Beitler Company of Chicago is planning to claim the lead with a proposed 125-story office tower. Their immediate competition is a project in Taipei, Taiwan, proposed to be 126 floors high.

But all of these towers may become pygmies if plans proceed with several projects in Japan such as the Aeropolis. Kajima, an engineering firm, proposes to build DIB-200, a 200-story tower in Tokyo that makes use of seismic-reactive technology. And Takenaka, a construction firm, has proposed to build Sky City 1000, also in Tokyo. This super building will be a city in itself, towering 3,300 feet (1,000 m), or about 300 floors high.

While some of the high-rise projects have been propelled by civic pride or the ego of developers, the key factor in the proposed new Japanese projects is economics. Land prices in Tokyo have skyrocketed to as high as $400,000 per square foot.

While few cities around the world have the same land cost pressures as Tokyo, there are many locations where planners argue in favor of increased high-rise development. There is a strong argument that more open space can be preserved in the central city if building capacity is achieved via tall structures rather than with sprawling low-rise projects.

Australia's Proposed Supercity

Without doubt, the proposed Australian-Japanese joint venture for building Multifunctionpolis (MFP) ranks among the world's most significant supercity proposals.

More than a new town or science city, MFP is planned as a prototype urban development to set new standards for quality of life in the 21st century. With a combination of elaborate resort facilities, telecommunications services, and high-technology programs, it will seek to attract firms from around the world.

Teams of planners have already devoted several years to defining the scope and character of a new globally significant MFP and its components. The planners believe they are designing something more advanced than any urban complex developed to date.

The MFP emerged in 1987 as the germ of an idea discussed briefly by Japanese and Australian trade representatives. After a heated competition among Queensland, New South Wales, Victoria and South Australia, planners selected a site near Adelaide, South Australia.

Investment in the new project will be massive. No precise figure is available yet, but planners are talking tens of billions of U.S. dollars. Needless to say, this project will be followed closely by investors and developers around the world.

New and Improved Cities

Since the beginning of recorded history, successive civilizations have built cities on the same sites, often building a new city on the ruins of the old. This process is occurring today in a more orderly fashion. Urban renewal projects loom large on the list of super projects.

For example, the city of Shanghai and the Chinese government are planning a massive redevelopment of the Pudong district. This venture will include an airport, container docks, bridges and tunnels, will cost $10 billion and will require the relocation of more than a million people.

The Docklands redevelopment effort in London is one of the most significant in the world. Within a few short years, many new job-creating activities have been attracted to new facilities in an area once considered dead. A new downtown commuter airport has been placed in operation — something no other major city has been able to do in decades.

The Mitsubishi Estate Company has proposed a gigantic redevelopment of the Marunouchi business district in Tokyo. The project would involve some 60 high-rise office towers, providing working space for approximately 200,000 workers.

The city of Yokohama is building Minato Mirai 21, a new waterfront/port development on the site of the 1989 exposition there. The new Osaka Business Park, a project of Matsushita Development, has given Japan's second-largest city a bright new center. This development is to Osaka what Rockefeller Center was to New York.

Another significant Japanese venture is Makuhari, in the Chiba prefecture. This new mini-city is located on the east side of Tokyo Bay, about halfway between Narita airport and downtown Tokyo. Within a few years, it has attracted blue-chip, multinational industrial firms, plus major new hotels and a great new convention center.

Other recent super projects creating "mini-cities" include Euro Disneyland, situated east of Paris near the new town of Marne-la-Vallee. In Myanmar (Burma), the Myanmar Concord Development venture, supported partly by the Japanese, has been awarded a contract to build a new city near Yangon (Rangoon). The complex will include an airport, a power plant and an industrial park. Before the Iraq invasion, Kuwait was building or planning new cities near Subiyah and Ras Az Zour. And Nigeria is still working on its new capital, Abuja, a project begun in 1976.

Olympic Trials and Tribulations

One of the more interesting phenomena in development is the impact of site competitions on infrastructure planning. The rule seems to be that the more media attention given to the competition, the more ambitious the plans become.

Since the competition among cities waiting to host the Olympic Games is the most publicized of global site searches, it is of particular interest. Every four years, several world-class cities compete to build new facilities of all types: hotels, airports, access routes, housing and a wide range of rather exotic sports facilities.

Typically, cities vying for the Games commit themselves to do things within a few years that they have been unable or unwilling to do in the past several decades and that, under other circumstances, they would not do for several decades.

Critics charge that the winning cities actually lose by flirting with bankruptcy; for instance, Montreal is still heavily in debt after hosting the Summer Olympics in 1976.

Other observers cite positive aspects — the motivation of local government and business leaders to undertake projects at the limit of their abilities. Barcelona, the host city for the 1992 Summer Games, added a perimeter freeway, new rail access, an expanded airport and a new city drainage system. Private investors built hotels and other facilities. And Atlanta, selected as the site for the 1996 Summer Games, is now drawing up plans for a $3 billion program, the greatest in the city's history.

Cities under Domes or Tents

Fly over many cities today and the most conspicuous thing you'll see is a shining dome covering a sports stadium. Fly over cities of the future and you may see only one huge dome.

There's definitely a fast-moving trend toward widespread and innovative use of huge, tentlike dome structures. Made of fabric or plastic and supported by cables, light frames or compressed air, domes are already being used to cover a variety of facilities, including sports arenas, airport terminals and industrial projects.

New technology is providing stronger, lighter fabrics for domes at lower cost. Many projects that were not considered feasible only a few years ago are beginning to look economically attractive now.

Perhaps the best-known dome today is the "big egg" in Tokyo, which covers a baseball stadium. The firm that built it, Taiyo Kogyo Corporation, made a name for itself when it built the U.S. pavilion for the Osaka Exposition of 1970.

More recently, the tent concept has been applied to such structures as the Pontiac Silverdome near Detroit, the new St. Petersburg, Florida, stadium, and a similar facility in Riyadh, Saudi Arabia.

Today, business is booming for Taiyo Kogyo, which has bought a half interest in O.C. Birdair, the largest U.S. tent maker, in Buffalo, New York. The firm is currently in the design stage for Twin Dome City, near Fukuoka, Japan, which will enclose a baseball stadium, plus other sports facilities and hospitality units.

Among the projects in various stages of planning are shopping centers, schools and mixed-use urban mini-cities. An enclosed ski slope is already under way, and golf courses are sure to follow. In fact, Mitsui Real Estate

Development has already announced an indoor ski slope at a site near Tokyo.

Agribusiness firms see potential for new "bubble farms," in which thousands of acres are covered by domed units to protect tender young seedlings, as well as to control the growth of new, genetically engineered crops.

In the future, dome enclosures may be especially useful for new towns in the Arctic region, where solar heat could be trapped and mosquitoes controlled.

Taiyo Kogyo also proposes to use huge tent structures to alter the climates of low-lying islands. Many such islands are arid and uninhabitable because there is no water to drink. However, a tent structure 2,000 feet (1,610 m) high and 10 miles (16 km) long would lift the prevailing wind, cause precipitation and make an island inhabitable.

Japanese planners also see the possibility of using such tent structures on the floor of the ocean to redirect currents and create new fishing zones.

Whether the super macroengineering projects of the future tower past the clouds or brave the ocean depths, neither the sky nor the deep may limit the potential of tomorrow's supercities.

C. Bibliography

The following are citations of McKinley Conway's writings on this chapter's subject. As this book goes to press, work is underway to make many of these items available to researchers. To check status, look for a file on GeoTEAM/IDRCNET or telephone GeoTEAM/Fax at (404) 453-4200.

284. "Austin: Coming Fast as R&D Center." *Industrial Development*, Aug. 1962. pp. 45-60.
285. "Sites for Science, Research Facility Planning," *Industrial Development*, Aug. 1962. pp. 5-43. Includes index of research parks.
286. "The Agricultural PUD: a New Concept to Preserve Croplands." The encroachment of urban growth on productive agricultural areas is a matter of national concern. A possible approach may lie in the design and development of a new type of planned unit development which includes selected agricultural areas in the same fashion that golf courses and recreational areas are included in typical PUDs. *Industrial Development*, Sept.-Oct. 1973. p. 3.
287. *Pitfalls in Development*. The bureaucracy of development. Soft plans and feasibility studies. Hard plans and preconstruction activities. Construction and operation. Megapuds track record. Special pitfalls for special projects. Real estate panics. Pitfalls ahead. 1978, 1981. 343 pp.
288. "Will Two-loop Cities Dominate Future Site Selection?" During the past decade hundreds of site decisions have left no doubt that circumferential freeways are a powerful magnet in drawing new business facilities to certain metro areas. Now, it is argued that proposed new outer loops may become an even more important development attraction in those areas where government entities can get together and build them. *Site Selection*, June 1986. pp. 582-588.
289. "Enter the Super Metros!!!" The preferred life style of most Americans involves a homesite in a quiet suburb, small town or rural area with a job just a few minutes away, plus easy access — in less than an hour — to all of the sophisticated services of a large metro complex. The area planning teams which provide for this style will be the big winners in the

site competitions of the next decade. Enter the super metros! *Site Selection,* Aug. 1987. p. 756.

290. "R&D Clusters." Where do they occur? Why have they developed? What are new locations to watch? 1987. Monograph.

291. "Atlanta as a World Class City." What is a world class city? The city/hinterland link. Building blocks for the future. Monograph. Based on presentation at the 12th annual Gwinnett Developers Conference, Gwinnett Chamber of Commerce, Gwinnett County, Ga. Sept. 24, 1987.

292. "The Super Collider Show — Who Will Make the Cut?" It's bigger than the District of Columbia, will cost $6 billion and has 25 states spending millions to promote sites. The DOE's search for a supercollider site is stirring what may be the biggest location battle ever. *Site Selection,* Dec. 1987. pp. 1234-1235.

293. "R&D Clusters." In 1962 Conway Data conducted a study in which we sought to identify existing clusters of R&D activity and to predict where new clusters might emerge. During 1987-88 we examined results and found that most of the centers predicted to emerge have done so. *Gwinnett Daily News,* Nov. 16, 1988.

294. "Outer Loop Could Focus World Attention on Metro Area." Some of the keenest observers of trends in urban planning believe that the "two loop" cities of the world will dominate future development patterns. *Site Selection,* October 1988.

295. "State's Best Minds Needed to Plan Outer Loop." In the legislative session just ended, the Georgia General Assembly authorized the beginning of work on the most important highway project in the state's history. That is the long-heralded outer perimeter. *Gwinnett Daily News,* April 19, 1989.

296. "Rethinking Urban Plan." Is it time to divorce high-rise offices and regional shopping centers? A substantial segment of the population of Gwinnett County encounters major traffic congestion every working day. One change in strategy which might be considered ...pertains to the location of regional shopping centers, office parks and other major complexes in relation to key transportation routes. *Gwinnett Daily News,* Jan. 18, 1989.

297. "Super Metro Areas." Americans want to have best of both worlds ...a homesite in a quiet suburb, small town, or rural area with a job just a few minutes away, plus easy access — in less than an hour — to all of the sophisticated services of a large metro complex. *Gwinnett Daily News,* Feb. 15, 1989.

298. "Outer Loop Highway Would Link Cities, Hinterland." We have often said that the proposed outer perimeter could do more for Georgia's economic development than any other project. *Gwinnett Daily News,* March 17, 1991. p. 3E.

299. "Tomorrow's Super Cities," *The Futurist.* World Future Society. May-June 1993.

5
Global Relationships

Chapter 5

A. Recent Comments

Adventures and Misadventures
New Patterns of Development
The High Tropics

B. Excerpts

The Global 2000

C. Bibliography

Global Reports, Comments
•Africa and the Indian Ocean
•Antarctica
•Asia and the Middle East
•Atlantic and Caribbean
•Central and South America
•Europe and the Mediterranean
•North America: Canada, Mexico, USA
•Pacific Oceania, Australia, Japan

A. Recent Comments

Adventures and Misadventures

You can learn a lot about the world by sitting at home and watching CNN or reading *National Geographic*. But you can't really prepare yourself for global operations without getting out there to the other side of the world and mixing with the people.

We have always been fascinated with maps and globes and have spent a lot of time just looking at them and trying to imagine what the world is like in places we have not visited. A long time ago we became curious about the great blank areas where there was very little printing on the map — such as the Arctic and Antarctic regions, Siberia, the Amazon Basin and Mongolia.

We made up our minds to try to go to all of these great blank areas and see what they were like. If you will read our reports, you will see that we found every one of these blanks to be filled with interesting real estate. They are all important in the world's future.

Since we set out to cover the world more than 30 years ago, we have spent a lot of time and money to gather information for field reports for our readers. Many of these reports are listed later in this chapter.

We now realize that in many cases the most interesting information we gathered was about our experiences in gathering the material for field reports, rather than the reports themselves. Thus, we offer some personal notes to help put you into the picture before you peruse the field studies.

Camels, Canoes, and Snowmobiles

We can now fly almost anywhere in the world at Mach .85 — jet speeds. On arrival, however, we are still looking for better ways to get around on the surface.

In the Far East we have seen some particularly interesting modes. On our first visit we tried a ricksha at Kowloon. We felt bad about having another human being serve as our beast of burden.

For some reason we found the pedicabs a bit more acceptable, even though they are simply rickshas married to a bicycle. They're also human-powered.

We were introduced to the tricab in Rangoon. That was a more acceptable marriage of the ricksha and a motorbike. Recently, in Bangkok we saw a modern version manufactured by Daihatsu, the Japanese firm. It looks like a practical, economical answer to many urban transport needs.

These ultralites of ground transportation are yet to find acceptance in the USA because they can't pass safety standards. In a collision with a heavy automobile they would be a total loss.

Small Boat Hails

Like many who were in naval aviation, I served a total of about 10 years of active and reserve duty without ever setting foot on a naval vessel. Yet, I remember that in boot camp we were thoroughly drilled in small boat hails — the communication used between small boats in a busy harbor.

Over the years I have used many small boats for urban taxi service, for boarding larger vessels and for other purposes. Yet I must report that I am still waiting for an opportunity to use one of the Navy's boat hails. Boats, however, have provided many wonderful opportunities.

I have used a rubber dinghy (Zodiac) to go ashore at remote locations in Antarctica; a small boat took us to the outer fringe of the Great Barrier Reef in Australia; a speedboat took us to examine the rock islands of Palau in the Carolines. And at Leticia in the Amazon Basin we used an airboat to travel shallow tributaries of the great river.

We were introduced to the basic Polynesian outrigger canoe at Bora Bora, where the canoe came as part of the standard equipment of our *fare* — a thatch-roofed cottage built on stilts over the lagoon. Having had some experience propelling ordinary canoes, we boldly climbed aboard our outrigger and set out across the nearby inlet.

We spent the first half-hour going around in circles and discovering that we were not making as much speed at those lithe brown athletes shown in Hollywood island scenes. Therefore, on another day we arranged for a local Polynesian lad to go with us to explore a *motu* (small island) along the barrier reef several miles away.

By the time we reached the motu the skies had darkened and my aide, who spoke no English, was signaling that we should return to the safety of our base. About half way across the lagoon the storm hit us. The gusts drove rain into our faces and whipped up whitecaps on the now-gray water.

Within a few minutes the storm was gone. I had gotten the merest inkling of what it must have been like for centuries as the Polynesians left their safe lagoons and ventured across the open seas. They not only had great navigating skills — they had guts.

Expedition to Sand Cay

Many times while flying along the Exumas — a line of cays in the central Bahamas — we have noted small, uninhabited islands with little crescent-shaped beaches. White sand, turquoise water and waving palms complete the fantasy-like scene.

Often we have wanted to land at some nearby airstrip, get a small boat and go for a close look at one of these idyllic spots. So one day we did.

Landing at Staniel Cay, we rented a boat and set out with grandson Adam, then 13, to find Sand Cay, a small island just a faint smudge on the horizon. After half an hour we could see the beach sparkling in the sun, and we navigated easily to the beach and dragged our anchor high up on the sand.

The cay was everything we had expected. There was a wonderful beach that was totally devoid of footprints. There was a small hillock dense with tropical growth inhabited by a colony of raucous sea birds. Adam alternated between exploring and splashing in the pristine water.

But we had brought only a couple of soft drinks for a short stay and soon it was time to return to base. That's when the trouble began. The motor would not start despite dozens of attempts. We were marooned.

We went to the top of the hillock and waved our shirts to boats that passed at some distance, but none paid any attention. Late in the day, someone from the marina — alerted by a worried wife/grandmother — came looking, found us and towed us back.

I was embarrassed that I had set out on even the tamest exploration without adequate emergency supplies. We could have been marooned on the island overnight or longer. Adam would have liked that!

Running the Reef at Haiti

Many of the most attractive locations in the world are surrounded by coral reefs — barriers of irregular and unpredictable size and shape made up of razor-sharp surfaces that can cut and maim any who fall into them. Pounded by the surf, they harbor forces that can wreck large ships or drown strong swimmers.

Today, the big ships with their sophisticated radar and navaids can easily avoid the reefs (if, unlike the crew of a certain tanker, their crew is alert). For small boats, however, the crossing of the reef has changed little for centuries.

On the north coast of Haiti we watched two expert boatsmen perform the reef-crossing maneuver flawlessly day after day. One stood up in the bow, looking into the water to gauge the location and depth of the coral. The other, a muscular giant, manned big oars.

The procedure was to launch through the surf and paddle out slowly to the opening (low spot) in the reef. The bow lookout then watched the incoming waves and picked one whose size and shape he liked. Then he gave the signal and both men rowed furiously to get the boat into open water before the wave subsided.

An error in timing or in wave appraisal would mean dropping the boat onto the coral where the next wave would find it helpless. The boat would be capsized, spilling its occupants onto the reef. On every trip the boatsmen bet their lives and those of their passengers that they could do it right.

We decided it was a good bet and hired the boat crew to take us to a site down the coast that could not be reached by other means. I can still remember coming back, when the tide had receded some. As we crossed the reef, I looked straight down and saw that we had almost zero clearance. Life is a game of inches!

Language Problem

It was in Puerto Rico in the early stage of their tourism program. From a small hotel at Parguera, on the southwest coast, a group of visitors from the USA was taken one night in a small boat to see Phosphorescent Bay.

The bay is famed for the lights that can be seen in the water at night. Small light-emitting organisms flit about, creating an eerie effect. The boatsman spoke no English, and some of the visitors spoke no Spanish, but the strange lights in the water required no description.

All of us were properly awed, except for one tourist, a rabid fisherman, who was trolling the light-streaked waters. Suddenly, there was a splashing commotion in the water and the fisherman started yelling at the boatsman, who understood not a word. Finally, the angler in desperation screamed, "*Señor, el line broke.*" The lack of language capabilities can be frustrating.

Miscellaneous Beasts

At various times we have also used animals for transportation. At Giza, we rented camels for a swing around the pyramids. In Southeast Asia we climbed aboard an elephant, and in Greece we rode a horse-drawn cart up to the Acropolis.

However, most of our confrontations with the animal kingdom have involved horses. One such meeting occurred at a dude ranch in Wyoming, where I stopped one weekend with grandson Adam when he was about 10.

We arrived late in the day at an impressive spread high up in the mountains west of Cody near the entrance to Yellowstone Park. While I took a nap, Adam learned the names of every dog and cat around the ranchhouse and went to see the head wrangler to sign us up for a trail ride the following day.

When we reported to the corral the next morning, I was alarmed to find that the wildest horse had been earmarked for me. I quickly reminded the wrangler that I was strictly a tenderfoot. He gave me a long look, then smiled, and explained, "Adam told me yesterday you were a great rider, that you were once in rodeos."

Never try to live up to the billing of an imaginative 10-year old!

Rails Come in All Sizes

Riding the Trans-Siberian Express eastward out of Irkutsk we were awakened one night by a terrible clatter. The car shook, and it sounded like people were hammering on the outside. Later we found that was precisely what was happening.

It seems that when the train crosses the Mongolia-China border it pulls into a shed where the cars are jacked up and the wheels are changed. This is necessary because of a difference in track gauge.

This is but one of the reasons the Trans-Siberian is noteworthy. It traverses the expanse of Siberia, swings around scenic Lake Baikal, winds through beautiful terrain in Northern Mongolia and then cuts straight across the Gobi Desert. Miles of monotony are broken by herds of wild camels or lonely outposts manned by sentinels whose faces reflect their boredom.

By contrast, we've ridden the TGV (high-speed train) from Paris to Lyons and Marseilles, continuing to Nice. Our only complaint is that the train is so fast (nearly 200 miles per hour) that it is difficult to make pictures of the passing scenes. Before you can aim and shoot the camera, the scene is gone.

We had the same problem riding the bullet train from Tokyo to Osaka.

One of the better train rides from the photo viewpoint is the leg through the Alps from Vienna to Rome. Another that we remember is the ride from Beijing to the Great Wall. The Chinese never stop offering tea, confections, souvenirs and handicrafts.

We've also checked out some rapid transit systems. We've ridden the subways in Moscow, Paris, Washington and New York. Also, we've looked at rapid transit facilities, especially the city-airport links, at Geneva, London, Montreal and elsewhere. (Of course, we've ridden MARTA in Atlanta — while a member of the State Senate in the 1960s we co-authored the bill to create MARTA.)

Ships, Plain and Fancy

On a mission in Burma we traveled across the Irrawaddy Delta one night on a rickety riverboat from Bassein to Rangoon. We shared a phone-booth-sized cabin on the upper deck and ate in a space loosely defined as the "salon." Most of the local passengers (economy-class, we assume) slept on the deck and built fires on the wooden deck to do their own cooking.

But cooking fires were not the main concern. It seems that guerrillas had been taking pot shots at the boat along the route, so the captain elected to navigate the narrow waterway late that night without lights.

By contrast, we traveled to Antarctica aboard a modern vessel equipped with the latest satellite navigation system and boasting a gourmet chef. We left Puerto William, in southern Chile, and steered across the famed Drake Passage to Antarctica. Using Zodiacs, we went ashore to visit research stations that could not be reached by air.

As the ship moved farther south toward the Antarctic circle, there was an increasing amount of ice in the water. Our German captain steered cautiously to avoid the big bergs and the broadening areas of pack ice.

We had been assured that the steel hull of our sturdy vessel had been reinforced for ice duty. Even so, it was disquieting at night as we lay in our berth with our head just a few inches from the steel plate separating us from the frozen world outside. Every time the ship scraped noisily through an area of ice we thought about the Titanic.

Private Yacht in the Aegean

Several years ago terrorist actions in Greece brought much of the tourist activity there to a screeching halt. As if someone turned a valve somewhere, the flow of American tourists was cut off, with a devastating impact on the Greek economy.

We wanted to see the situation first hand, so we booked a tour of the Greek islands on one of the more popular cruise lines. On boarding at Piraeus, we found a ship with a capacity of about 300 and a crew of some 100 ready to sail with 52 passengers. We were the only Americans.

The weather was idyllic, the Greek islands were wonderful, and we had as nearly a perfect cruise as you can have. It was like having a private yacht, with attendants quick to cater to every whim.

Because the terrorist acts had been directed at Americans, we were careful at each stop to blend into the group of passengers from Europe and other parts of the world. All went well until we stopped in Istanbul. The astute driver of our sightseeing bus spotted us, stopped the bus, stood up and said, "Let's give a cheer for the brave Americans who have come in spite of the danger." We tried the shrink under our seats.

The compensation for the risk was the view of Istanbul and its minarets rising out of the water as we came into port. Boats provide some of the best views to be found in travel.

In that connection, the Kowloon/Hong Kong ferry gives the greatest show for the money to be found anywhere. For a few cents you can cross one of the world's most interesting harbors — where picturesque junks mingle with ships from all over the world — and view the spectacle against a panorama of striking high-rise structures.

A View from the Water

Wherever we are working, we try to look at the area from the water-side. Within a few minutes one can learn much about the commerce of an area by looking at the working side of the harbor. Among the spots we have found this particularly useful are Stockholm, Seattle, London and New York.

Without doubt, the most fascinating areas are in Southeast Asia. We've used water taxi service in such locations as Brunei, Rangoon and, best of all, Bangkok. A morning spent in a water taxi prowling the canals (*klongs*) of Bangkok provides a wonderful profile. As the other water taxis and boats whiz by, you see businessmen in their three-piece suits, briefcases in hand, mingling with farmers bringing fruit, vegetables, chickens and other produce to market.

Along the canals people are seen washing clothes, dishes and children in the turgid waters. Floating markets display a dazzling array of wares, ranging from essentials to high-value handicrafts and works of art. It's better than a Hollywood show because you are part of it.

Perhaps the most unusual ride we've had was at Inle Lake, in northern Burma. There, we traveled in a long dugout canoe propelled by one of the rare leg rowers. That's right, they row with their legs. The rower stands in the bow on one foot, wraps his other leg around a long oar and uses his leg muscles to move the boat.

Awkward as it appeared, the system worked, and we were taken to a very unusual site. In the middle of the lake was a cluster of buildings resting on stilts. As we neared, we heard a clatter which turned out to be hand looms being used by the women of the water-based community to make exquisite silk fabrics.

As we were leg-rowed around the community we found that there were floating islands of sod on reed mats where the men farmed. There, in that remote location, we saw a form of aquaculture that, we suspect, has been practiced for centuries.

Alternate Modes Abound

By now, it should be clear that we like to try any and all alternate modes of transport in order to better understand the areas we study. Among those we recall are:

- Funiculars have been helpful at Athens, Rio de Janeiro and Hong Kong.
- We've used ski lifts — even in summer — in Colorado and California.
- We once rode a jeep across the Baja desert. On arrival, we were caked with dust, and our hair was so matted some of it had to be cut to untangle it. Never again!
- At Aspen, we scheduled a snowmobile ride to look at a large real estate development. We happened to be there on a February morning in the midst of a heavy snowfall. We were not worried because we were to be led by a veteran local guide.

It was a memorable morning. The guide gave me some basic instruction in snowmobile technology, which was all new to me, and we took off. In the blowing snow I needed only to follow him. Simple.

Soon my goggles were covered, and when I dared take a hand off the handlebars to have a swipe at them, the visibility was still poor to nil. We whizzed through groves of fir trees, skirted boulders, struggled up some slopes and dove down others. I was so busy trying to follow the guide, I saw nothing of the area.

It did not take long for me to lose interest. Blaming the 9,000-foot elevation for my lack of energy, we returned to base.

The next day, with the sun shining, I went back over part of the trail. To my amazement, I found that we had traveled across narrow bridges and clung to ledges where a skid would send us to the valley below. It was a trail I would not think of trying to negotiate. Ignorance is, indeed, bliss.

Solid Wall Ahead

As you grow older, you learn to be wary when someone offers you a ride in a strange conveyance. I had not yet learned this when I was offered a ride in the seaplane-testing-tank at the NACA/NASA laboratory at Langley, Virginia.

The facility is somewhat like a swimming pool, about 30 feet wide and 2,000 feet long. It is housed in a metal building. There is a vehicle that straddles the pool, running on tracks on either side. The operator sits in a cage, below which is suspended the test model — such as a seaplane hull or pontoon.

An electric drive system accelerates the test cage along the pool to a speed simulating the take-off of the seaplane, and then the test cage is braked to a stop just before it reaches the far end.

That sounds very routine until you ride in the cage. You are in a machine controlled by an external system. It starts smoothly and gets up to speed quickly. Suddenly you are hurtling through a tunnel which has a solid wall at the far end. The wall is now rushing toward you. It gets a lot closer in a hurry. You begin to wonder about the automatic brakes. After you have given up and braced for the fatal impact the brakes grab and you slam to a stop a few feet from the wall.

Why hasn't Disney thought of that?

To the Salt Mine!

All well-managed companies have disaster plans that include provisions for saving copies of key records in a secure place. Around the United States there are several underground depositories — located in such spots as an abandoned railroad tunnel in the East, a salt mine in the Midwest and an old gold mine in the West.

One day I decided to take a look at the place where we keep our back-up files. I landed at the small airport, rented a car and drove out of town along a local highway until I saw the reference point I had been given. I was not impressed.

The pot-holed entrance road wound past the rusting remains of some kind of processing plant to a small concrete block building. I was saying to myself, "This can't be the facility where some of the nation's largest firms keep their vital records."

Inside, the lady checked my credentials and said she would be glad to show me where the Conway Data files were kept. She motioned to a door, which I assumed was the elevator, and told me someone would be waiting for me downstairs.

It was not like any elevator I had seen before. It was a large metal bucket that once brought salt up from the mine below. I got in, a bell rang, and the bucket started dropping. Soon the light got dim. I realized there was no light in the bucket. As we rattled and scraped downward it got to be pitch black.

As I asked myself, "Do they have a lot of mechanical problems with mine buckets?", there was a faint glow below. It grew into a light, and we clanked to a stop. We stepped out into bright lights of a busy community operating 600 feet below ground. There were streets, marked by signs, and along them the names of storage areas.

I was pleased to find my small cache of computer disks resting along-side great stacks from the Federal Reserve Bank, *Encyclopedia Britannica* and many others. My only regret was that it would take another bucket ride to get me out of there.

Taxi — the Universal Word?

We have been told that the one word understood in all countries of the world is "taxi." We don't know if that is correct, but we do know that around the world one of the most abused phrases is "English speaking driver." We have hired quite a few drivers thus advertised who could not utter 10 words of English that we could comprehend.

We had one such driver in the Middle East who was to take us to a business appointment in a large bank in the middle of the city. By the time we drove from my suburban hotel into town it was obvious that verbal communication would be impossible.

I could only show him an address written in English, which he could not read. And all of the street signs were in Arabic, which I could not read.

I guessed that the bank would be in a prominent location, so with hand motions I directed him along what seemed to be the principal streets and was lucky enough to find the building in a few minutes.

I was not so lucky once when going to see a banker in a large city in Latin America. I gave the driver the name of the bank and he took me to that bank. Unfortunately, it was only one of six locations the bank had in that city, and it took several more tries before I got the right one.

Tokyo: A Challenge

In Tokyo, it is a good idea to show the taxi driver both a Japanese address and a location map. And, a picture of the building would help.

The situation is chaotic: In some sections the buildings are not numbered in sequence as you go along the streets. Instead, they have been given numbers chronologically as they were built, meaning that in the same block the numbers can vary wildly. Only foreign visitors seem to be perturbed by this system.

During a stop in Rio one night recently we got into a taxi at the airport to go into the city and found that the driver could understand neither my English nor my primitive Portuguese. That was disturbing because he soon turned off the main highway and took us via a winding route that seemed miles out of the way. The back road was full of pot holes and at places was partially under water.

Was he taking us to a remote site where his confederates were waiting to rob us? No, he finally delivered us to the hotel. And, the next day we learned that a storm had hit Rio just before our arrival, flooding the main airport road.

Bedrolls, Club Med and Bora Bora — Stopovers and Attractions

If your purpose in traveling around the world is simply to luxuriate in posh surroundings, there are a great many facilities from which to choose. However, if you have specific objectives in remote areas or must keep a tight schedule, you will need to be a bit more flexible — that is, take what you can get.

Further, you will find that a happy combination of a good hotel/resort where you want it when you want it is a rare stroke of good luck. Even without budget constraints, it is not easy to find that right combo.

It was probably Confucious who remarked that there is very little correlation between what you pay for accommodations and what you get. Some expensive hotels treat you shabbily, and some humble establishments are a delight.

•*Bring Your Own Bed*

During the heydey of their empire in India and Southeast Asia the British developed "guest houses" in outlying communities that were too small to rate a hotel. We've stayed in a few of those that still exist, and we can certify that they vary greatly in quality and comfort.

Typically, travelers bring their own bedrolls, consisting of a pad, pillow, sheets and blanket. At one guest house one might get a room with a bed; at another, one might wind up in a shed fitted with a wooden shelf on which to unfurl the bedroll.

A busy guest house might keep a regular staff, but in other locations it might be necessary to go down to the village square and employ a cook/attendant on the spot. Needless to say, this impromptu staffing plan does not always result in gourmet meals.

I recall one facility that was simply a large covered platform surrounded by a chicken-wire fence. We slept there secure in the knowledge that nothing larger than a medium-sized snake could come in during the night.

As a matter of fact, we learned to relax and watch the small lizards crawl around on the ceiling. They were hunting insects, which we were glad to concede to them.

Not so welcome was the bat, which flew into our room through an unscreened window one night where we stopped in East Africa. It proved to be a difficult quarry. When we turned the light on, it hid. When we turned the light off, it whizzed around looking for who knows what. We solved the problem by leaving the light on.

•*Community Rest Room*

The Morton Salt Company operates a salt pond facility on Great Inagua Island in the Bahamas. For the convenience of company personnel they also run a small boarding house in the village. On several occasions they have been kind enough to let us stay there.

Let's face it, the facility is plain. Morton is not trying to compete with Hilton. The first time we stayed there, my wife discovered that the other door in the bathroom opened to the outside. It was used by villagers who happened to be in the vicinity.

However, we met some interesting people around the community dinner table. Just one night the cast of characters included, besides my family, a cropduster ferrying a new airplane to South America; a pilot and girl friend (exotic type) taking a small amphibian to St. Thomas; and the Haitian manager.

As we were finishing dinner, we heard the drone of an airplane engine coming from the north. The assembled pilots agreed it was a single-engine craft, probably equipped with an old but larger-than-average engine. More important, it began circling, obviously wishing to land.

At that time, the Inagua airstrip had no lights. The strange airplane had homed in on a marine beacon on the island. Emergency!

Within minutes, several vehicles were rounded up, and they raced to the airstrip where they were positioned at each end of the runway. After a bumpy landing it was discovered that the visitors were three college students traveling in a pre-WWII Stinson.

The "senior pilot" had a grand total of 75 hours, none of it over water or at night. They had left Florida late in the afternoon, unconcerned about impending sundown, because their chart listed Great Inagua as an "international airport." They assumed it would have lights, radio, customs and other facilities.

Back at the boarding house, we learned about their venture, which seemed to be planned just as meticulously as their afternoon flight. They were headed for Guyana where they were going to dive for gold in a river located far back into the jungle. They had read about the riches awaiting there, and having had some scuba experience, thought it was just the project for them.

We never heard the outcome of the mission. Probably just as well.

•*Tribulations of an Inn-keeper*

One of the delightful people we've met at remote waypoints is Liam McGuire, a Scotsman and member of the Royal Surveying Society, London. We found Liam on South Caicos Island in the Turks and Caicos group just north of the Dominican Republic.

Liam had been sent down to survey the island and lay out some streets. And he had done a splendid job. Between the airstrip and the village there is a roundabout just like the ones used in the UK to handle busy intersections. At the time we saw it, traffic was flowing freely. Never mind that there was only one vehicle on the island.

Liam liked the island so much he stayed on and assumed a variety of responsibilities. When we met him he was running the airport, the marina (one pump, one dock), the bar, the boarding house (The Admiral's Arms) and sundry other institutions.

Life was just one long series of challenges and frustrations, which Liam took in stride. His special nemesis, however, was the ground transport situation.

As I said, there was only one vehicle. It had been assembled from the rusted-out parts of several others and could best be described as a Model A Ford pickup on a Chevrolet chassis with a flat deck replacing the cabin.

Liam met us at the airstrip, leaving the engine of his machine running. We learned that the battery had failed, and he was waiting for a new one to arrive.

Liam had ordered the new battery from Sears Roebuck in Miami. Every week he went to the Inagua airstrip to meet the weekly DC-3 from Nassau. He was getting tired of leaving his engine running or parking on a hill.

Finally, the big day came. He received a box from Sears in Miami and tore it open — to find they had gotten his order mixed and had sent him a Yogi Bear cookie jar. To add insult, the jar was broken.

•*Water Almost Everywhere*

The upper Amazon Basin is one of the world's wet places. The little town of Leticia sits there between the river and the rainforest, soaked almost every day by towering thunderstorms.

We arrived late in the day and were escorted to the small guest house. One of the children took a shower, then the other. As my wife followed, the pipe ran dry. There beside the world's greatest river, we were out of water.

Not defeated, we waited for the regular evening thunderstorm, and as soon as it got dark, Becky went outside behind the house — there was nothing but jungle beyond — with a bar of soap and finished her shower. Ditto for me.

All was well until the next morning when we went with Mike Tsilickis to visit his animal compound. Mike supplies zoos all over the world with snakes and animals collected in the Amazon jungles and waterways around Leticia. His compound was filled with sloths, jaguars, monkeys and snakes, ranging from small but deadly coral snakes to huge 25-foot anacondas capable of choking a man to death.

Becky took one look at the snakes and decided against going out into the Leticia night again, no matter how badly a shower was needed.

•*Before and After*

FONATUR, the Mexican tourism agency, has attracted global attention with its bold planning and development of destination resorts complexes. These facilities have been so successful in attracting tourists from other nations that tourism ranks as one of Mexico's three top income producers.

Beginning in the 1970s Fonatur earmarked sites at such locations as Cancun, on the Gulf of Mexico; Zihuatanejo and Puerto Escondido on the Pacific; and Loreto and Cabo San Luca on the Baja peninsula.

Because of the significance of the projects, we set out to look at the raw sites before construction began. This is definitely not good timing if your purpose is to enjoy a vacation.

Visiting resorts before they are built means no problems, with reservations and you have the beach all to yourself. However, there are a number of minor problems such as where to sleep, where to eat and where to find ground transportation.

Somehow these challenges were met, we saw the sites, and Fonatur got all of the huge complexes built — complete with utility systems, roads, airports and strings of resort hotels.

In later years we have visited the sites and luxuriated in the new hotels. At Ixtapa we saw evidence of a new standard: Our hotel had a waiter, decked out in a bright red jacket, going around the patio with a silver tray, picking up bougainvillea blossoms that had fallen on the grass during the night.

But the biggest improvement has been in places to land our airplane. To get to the early construction sites we had to use short, rough dirt strips with no facilities of any kind. Some were dangerous. I remember arriving at one site, circling to land, and noting two wrecked airplanes at the end of the strip.

•*On the Beach in Haiti*

Looking at the locale for a proposed major resort development in Haiti, we found ourselves staying in a thatched hut elevated about a foot above the high tide line at a point on the northwest coast. During the night every wave sounded like it was coming right over us. That would have kept us awake, except for the fact that the mosquitoes got there first.

•*No Bed of Roses in USA*

Not all hardships have come in remote parts of developing countries. In the early days before motels proliferated across the West, I recall spending a night in the car alongside a Nevada highway with a pack of coyotes howling outside.

Other memorable stopovers included a hot summer night at the old Lexington Hotel in New York when the power failed, and the air-conditioning went out. The temperature in the room rose steadily to about 100 and stayed there.

Sometimes, a bad experience is just bad luck. For example: We know the Swiss are among the world's best hotel keepers, but we happened to arrive in Zurich on a particularly hot summer day and were astonished to find that a widely advertised hotel had no air-conditioning.

The majestic old hotel in Glasgow (whose name we have forgotten) was equally lacking in heat when we arrived on a decidedly brisk day — true, it was summer, but everyone we saw was wearing a sweater.

And, we know that Club Med has some fantastic resorts. But we stopped at their unit in New Caledonia and were not thrilled by doors that could not be locked and a front desk that closed for hours at a time.

•*Some Bright Spots*

Hotel facilities can be categorized into three groups — places where the experience was very bad, places so ordinary they can't be remembered at all, and those very special places that make all of the rigors of travel worth while.

The Las Brisas in Acapulco consists of individual units clinging to a steep hillside overlooking the harbor. Each unit has a private pool and terrace surrounded by tropical plants. Each suite also has a little window where you find a pot of hot coffee, fruit and croissants every morning. It is very easy to relax.

Once when we arrived to a full house, the Las Brisas put us up in the home nearby of a movie star. It was a truly fabulous layout, with a huge pool deck overlooking the city and harbor.

Just as enjoyable is the Puente Romano at Marbella on Spain's Mediterranean coast. Units are clustered around an oasis filled with magnificent vegetation. There are many views across red tile roofs, whitewashed buildings, against a background of white sand and blue water or towering mountains.

Speaking of oases, one of the more unusual resorts we've found is at Djerba, Tunisia, on the edge of the Sahara. The gleaming white, windowless buildings feature parapets and domed roofs. It is easy to imagine that the clock has been rolled back, and you are approaching a French Foreign Legion post. (In fact, the site of one of the old posts is nearby.)

The buildings actually reflect the talent of Arab architects to build structures that provide comfort despite the heat of African summers. Each cluster of units is built around a small oasis which uses a fountain and garden to create a microclimate. When you walk from the desert into the garden through staggered openings you notice a temperature drop of at least 10 degrees.

Another winner of our architectural commendation is the Hotel Presidente at Oaxaca in the south of Mexico. A colonial monastery has been artfully converted into a very special hotel. There are rugged stone walls, massive wooden doors, and delightful little courtyards filled with flowers.

A hotel we once enjoyed was the Phoenicia in Beirut. From our window we had a commanding view of the city, the waterfront and the Mediterranean beyond. Soon after we left it was heavily damaged in the fighting. We understand they started to rebuild, but more fighting resulted in complete destruction.

Another hotel that we regret losing was the Astor at Times Square. Our children were amused for hours just watching the theatre marquees and street scenes from the windows. It fell victim to economic war and was razed.

Certainly one of the best hotels in the world is the Regent in Hong Kong. Located on the Kowloon side near the Star Ferry terminal, it features huge marble baths and superior service.

But the biggest attraction is a grandstand view of the world-famous harbor. I have spent hours watching the fantastic traffic — sampans, barges, freighters, cruise liners, water taxis, junks, ferries, lighters — all moving in different directions in close quarters, whistles and horns blowing, but somehow avoiding disaster.

As the sun goes down, the excitement builds. Lights go on and the neon signs blink into operation across the harbor. You can sit there and note the corporate logos of dozens of the world's largest firms. Meanwhile, a stream of jets, landing lights blazing, swing around for the tight approach into Kai Tak airport right in the middle of the complex.

In the same world class, but lacking the view, is the Shangri-La in Singapore. From your bed you can press a button to control the curtains shading your private bougainvillea-covered balcony. Every afternoon you receive a basket containing a pot of hot tea and cups.

Indicative of attention to detail, the elevator floor mats have "good morning" messages for each day of the week. The coffee shop is situated in a small botanical garden complete with waterfall.

Well, there are many more interesting hotels than we could mention. We've stopped at the Meridien in Nice, the Peninsula in Hong Kong, and most of the big ones along the strip in Vegas. We were at the St. Francis in San Francisco when the U.N. charter session was held there.

We're not going to evaluate hotel bars, although we did make the compulsory visit to Raffles in Singapore. We once bought a publishing company during a session at the Algonquin bar in New York.

On a scale of one to 10, one of the resorts we'd rank a 10 is the Hotel Bora Bora in French Polynesia. We had a small thatched cottage *(fare)* over the lagoon, with a private deck from which we had a panoramic view of lagoon, palm-fringed shore and startling volcanic mountains.

•*Rigged for Tourists*

Sometimes, the hotel and attraction people, in their eagerness to impress visitors, shoot themselves in the foot. In Mongolia, we were shown a typical *yurt* (a sort of tent made of skins) occupied by the nomads along the edge of the Gobi Desert. Despite the fact that there was no electric power, the furnishings included fluorescent light fixtures and a TV set.

At the Mandarin Hotel in Jakarta, an excellent hotel, the musical ensemble in the dining room sang a series of tunes which had a special quality. I remarked to my wife that I had never noticed before how some features of Oriental and American music are surprisingly similar.

Her ear was better than mine. She gleefully pointed out, "They're singing the latest American hits."

On another trip we spent a weekend at the fabulous new Meridien Phuket Island resort in Thailand. While we were there, they had a "Western Night" for the benefit of tourists from the USA.

There were cowboy hats and a stagecoach which carried a large ice sculpture. I couldn't help noticing it was the same wagon used for a farm scene for the Chinese night we had enjoyed the day before.

The music was particularly interesting. My favorite, in a collection of "popular western songs" was, "Yanki do do went to tay-on."

Plague Shots, Manioc and Cumis (Food, Drink, and Germs)

When flying my own airplane, I subsist on a diet of peanut butter crackers and canned soft drinks. Sometimes, for variety, I eat cheese crackers.

Many a hungry staff member, after a trip with me, will confirm that my tastes are repulsively simple. However, I do appreciate the better things when there is time.

Memorable meals involve the food, the environment and the circumstances. Thus, I remember, after decades, a luncheon at the Chateau Lake Louise at Banff. The entree was roast duckling a` l'orange. Our table in the huge paneled dining room was next to a window which commanded a view of the lake, the glacier beyond, magnificent mountains of the Canadian Rockies and azure blue sky.

We were young and it was an exotic new experience. No wonder the duck was good!

• *Fish Head Soup*

It was our first night in Rangoon. We had arrived from a cool climate to a suffocating 100-degree day, and our sluggishness was further aggravated by jet lag accumulated during a flight half way around the world.

We accepted the invitation of an official familiar with the city to leave the hotel and go to a restaurant nearby. We walked alongside open sewers, which stank to high heaven, and turned into a street which could only be described as an alley.

When we entered a small building, I couldn't believe we intended to eat there. Everything — the walls, tables and waiters — looked grimy. Next, we were introduced to a smudged menu which listed nothing recognizable.

Our friend ordered for us. The very first course was fishhead soup. I had heard of such a dish, usually mentioned jokingly, but I had never before been stared at by one. The fish heads looked old, the eyes sunken, and they floated in a thick, murky liquid that looked somewhat like used engine oil.

Finally, I thought to say that I had eaten so much on the plane that I was not hungry. And the latter part was true.

• *Crabs to Steaks*

I like shellfish. The lobster at Bangor or Bar Harbor is special. And the best crab is Dungeness, which we have enjoyed several times at Port Angeles, on Puget Sound.

Our vote for the best steak goes to a patio restaurant in Asuncion, Paraguay. We had been working for some time to assist a development group called "El Comite de Viente" (The Committee of Twenty), and they were nice enough to give a dinner party on the eve of my departure.

Paraguay and Argentina share the great pampas region, where much of the world's beef is produced. There is a lively debate as to which country produces the best steaks.

When we arrived, the restaurant already had a fire going in a large iron pot in the center of the patio. After several rounds of drinks (a local rum on which I commented very favorably), the steaks arrived.

Each steak was large enough to cover a dinner plate and, without exaggeration, was two inches thick. These were thrown casually into the fire which was by now a mass of red hot coals. Soon the charred steaks, covered in ashes but with red streaks showing, were retrieved.

More than 20 years later, I can still taste that steak. It was tender, juicy and had a distinctive flavor. I tried diligently but could not eat all of it.

But I was forgiven. The next day the committee, seeing me off at the airport, presented me with a cask of the rum we had enjoyed. Fortunately, Pan Am had an empty seat into which they strapped the cask for the return home.

• *Problems of Protocol*

The westerner, when off the beaten track in the Orient, is challenged to make unexpected adjustments. Call it the minor protocol of international dining.

For example, a group of several of us, representing the USA on an official mission, were seated for dinner with several cabinet ministers of the host country. They were anxious to make us feel at home, and we were anxious to have them know of our appreciation.

The custom was to serve the main dishes in bowls which were passed around to each diner. Chopsticks were the only devices furnished.

It was my bad luck to be served first. A bowl of shrimp was handed to me, and I was expected to select a choice bite, retrieve it with my chopsticks, and put it on my plate.

Every pair of eyes around the table was on me. Our delegation held its collective breath. They knew this was my first serious introduction to chopsticks. I broke out in perspiration. Pressure!

Somehow I managed to get a timid grip on a piece of shrimp and get it over my plate before it fell free. I generously gave myself a passing grade for the performance.

On another such occasion, we were invited to the home of a local official. All sat cross-legged on the floor and ate from a mat. As course after course was brought in, paralysis of our legs set in. Our host assumed the pained expression on our faces was a reaction to the cuisine. We worried that we would never walk again.

Then, there was a polite reception at the turf club where we were served drinks and saucers of toasted watermelon seed. One of our colleagues, treating the seed as he would a dish of peanuts, tossed a few in his mouth and crunched away, to the consternation of our hosts.

The locals, we learned, approach the seed in an entirely different manner. They turn each seed on its side, bring their teeth together just enough to crack the seed open, then flick the kernel aside with their tongues and eat it. The hard shell is rejected.

After returning home, we toasted some watermelon seed and tried without success to master the technique. After further thought, we realize that the orientals don't crack the seed for the small amount of meat inside — it is something to do while engaging in polite conversation.

When traveling in strange places, one is served many things which are unfamiliar or unidentifiable, or both. Sometimes it is best not to know.

However, with hot peppers, knowing is everything. One who roams at random across a buffet table covered, let's say, with Indian dishes, may pay a high price for his recklessness. An innocent-looking sauce or dip may lead to a paroxysm of coughing and strangling, followed by weeping and sniffling for the remainder of the dinner — plus open blisters in the mouth the next morning.

Where possible, we try to find a westerner familiar with local dishes to follow down the buffet line. By whispering, "Go easy on the red balls," or "Don't touch the green stuff," he can save your life.

• *Small is Beautiful*

Some of the very best restaurants in the world are small, remote and unknown. If we had another lifetime, maybe we'd go back around the world and write a book about them. We are utterly frustrated that we cannot remember the names of the ones that most deserve a mention.

In Kowloon, there is a wonderful little Cantonese restaurant with outstanding food, reasonable prices, excellent service and a spic-and-span environment. Try the bottom level of the New World center.

In Rome, we found, unheralded and unadvertised, one of the best restaurants in the world. The hole-in-the-wall establishment measures about 15 feet across the front, and, inside, there are about eight tables.

One of the tables is used to display a sample of the dishes being prepared that day. You may taste if you wish. Having made your choice, you may watch the cooking process in the open kitchen in the rear.

From the Piazza Barberini walk down past the fountain, turn right into the next street and go half a block. At noon, you'll probably see a line of people waiting for a table.

In New York, there was once a little restaurant in the Village that was situated below the sidewalk in a space not much bigger than a phone booth. There were four small tables. There was no menu. You sat down and the lady, of Middle European persuasion, brought you the dish she had chosen to prepare that day. It was always good.

Unhappily, the building has been razed.

• Traditions of a Sort

Around Washington you are not ranked very high unless you can comment from personal experience on the flavor of the bean soup in the Senate restaurant. You are a notch further along in one-upsmanship if you can refer casually to having had a steak on the presidential yacht while cruising down the Potomac.

Yes, we can report that both the bean soup and the steak were good. No, we've not been invited for dinner at Westminster, but we're told that the fare is almost equal to that at Dromolland Castle, near Shannon. And we rank Dromolland high on atmosphere, service and cuisine.

Speaking of tradition, the Chinese have a wonderful practice of putting a hot water thermos in your room so that you can have tea whenever the mood strikes you.

• Breakfast at the Oriental

Tired, disheveled and willing to settle for a hot shower and bed, we checked into the Oriental Hotel in Bangkok one night. With an early business appointment set for the next day, we picked up the card on which one can order room service breakfast by hanging the card on the doorknob.

The Oriental card routinely offered a breakfast of "champagne and/or orange juice; creamed quail eggs with caviar, or fresh gooseberries and truffles with scrambled eggs, or creamed pigeon eggs with smoked salmon and caviar." Also included was a plate of exotic fruits: "mala kaw papaya, lamyai longan, kluay banana, sap pa pineapple, som-oh pomelo, and ngaw rambutan." This offering was topped off with croissants and a pot of tea or coffee.

We knew then that we were not at the Holiday Inn in Peoria. The Oriental, one of the great hotels in the world, is a tradition in its own right. If you are ever privileged to stop there, be sure to order the seafood on Thai noodles in the coffee shop.

• Not on the Menu

A group of us on a development mission had stayed for six weeks at the old Strand Hotel in Rangoon. About the only recommendation we can give the Strand is that the other hotels are worse. Burma, despite great potential, has not made the investments necessary to promote tourism.

We ate dinner almost every night at the Strand — there were few alternatives — and the menu never varied. The staff had been trained years before in the British style, and every night we got what they deemed to be a proper meal for westerners: a fish course, a meat course and potatoes.

On the day before we were to leave, the cook said he would like to fix us a dish of his own for our last dinner there. Feeling that any change would be for the better, we quickly agreed.

That last evening, the old snaggle-toothed Chinese cook laid some tiles on the table, brought in a pot and poured in some water. Then he added some tidbits of chicken and shrimp and a sprinkling of spices. Soon, he served the first course, a light broth.

Then, the cook began adding chunks of meat and various types of vegetables to the pot. He varied the content as well as the consistency of the mix, giving us seven or eight courses ranging from stews to loaves — and all delicious.

It was one of the best dinners we'd ever had. What the veteran cook had given us was his own version of the famed Mongolian hot pot. When we realized what we had been missing for weeks, we could have cried.

• *Better in a Dim Light*

The famed Trans-Siberian Express offers an interesting means for seeing some of the more remote parts of the world. It did not gain its fame, however, from its food service.

Perhaps one reason is that there are no competing restaurants on the route across Mongolia and the Gobi Desert. We learned quickly that one has two choices: eat what is served or don't eat. At each mealtime it was a tough decision.

The standard fare was a dish of rice which had been colored gray by the addition of something. There were also dark-colored bits and pieces of something else mixed in, leading to considerable speculation among our fellow passengers as to the identity and origin of the materials involved.

By the second day a dark rumor had spread among the travelers — that what was not eaten of the gray rice concoction at one meal was being recycled for the next. Attempts to elicit information from the crew were futile. Was it a language barrier or something more sinister?

From the viewpoint of curbing one's appetite and aiding dieters, the gray rice does not, however, hold a candle to betel juice. Throughout Southeast Asia the nuts of the betel palm, wrapped in betel leaves and flavored with lime, is a favorite chew.

We recall a quick fuel stop at the airstrip on Yap island in the Carolines when most of the passengers jumped off and raced to a small shack near the ramp. We found that the shop's only product was betel kits — nuts, leaves, lime — and that Yap betel is considered by many to be superior.

To non-chewers, betel chewing is just as distasteful as tobacco chewing in the western world. The main difference is that the juice expelled after chewing betel is blood red.

We have visited many a public building in which the spatter of betel juice colors the walls of corridors and public areas from floor to almost waist high. We have never seen a cuspidor.

Someone told us not to worry about the spittle, because betel juice is a good insecticide. Maybe the bugs are just nauseated.

• *Catering to Western Tastes*

Once we went with several associates to meet with a district official at a small town toward the northern end of the Malay Peninsula. We were rare guests from the other side of the world, and they spared no effort to make us welcome and adapt to our strange ways.

They had somehow learned that fried chicken was popular where we came from, so they chose that for the main dish. When they proudly brought the bowl to the table, there was an awkward pause. The hosts thought we were surprised and somewhat overwhelmed by the sight of our favorite dish in such a far away place. We were without words because we didn't know what it was in the bowl.

Evidently, the chicken had been semi-plucked and then cooked until black. The pieces were brittle, and it was difficult to tell which part of the chicken they were. Our hosts ate lustily, chewing bones and all.

My own relish for the dish was dampened by a glimpse into the cooking area. When one of the waiters parted the curtains I saw another fellow wiping out the bowls we had used in our soup course with the dirtiest rag I had ever seen. I knew we would see those bowls again before the meal ended.

• *Surprises, Some Pleasant, Some ...*

Problems of usage bring culinary surprises. In Moscow we discovered one morning that "breakfast" that day was a bowl of sliced cucumbers. In Santo Domingo we learned to be more careful in ordering an enchilada so that we wouldn't get another *ensalada* (salad).

During a stay at the Sheraton in Seattle, the phone rang and hotel staff said "an amenity is coming up." We were totally surprised to receive a large brandy snifter filled with plump strawberries, sour cream and brown sugar.

And at the Shangri-La in Singapore my wife Becky finished a box of chocolates and was preparing to discard the box when, to her delight, she found that the box itself was chocolate.

• *To Drink or Not to Drink*

When you arrive tired, hot and thirsty at a strange destination, one of the immediate problems is something to drink. Our bodies can go a long way without food, but they do not function well without liquids.

Just about anywhere we go outside the USA we assume that the tap water is not potable. In developed countries we look for bottled mineral water or bottled soft drinks. In Latin America the local beers are good.

In remote areas of Third World nations, we don't trust the bottled drinks. As soon as we check into our room we fill a flask — which we carry — with water and treat it with Halazone tablets or one of the newer substitutes. We drink that and use it for brushing our teeth.

In these areas, when we are being hosted, we ask for hot tea, even if the room temperature is 110. We've survived in a lot of grim situations by drinking only hot tea and eating only bananas.

Despite all precautions, germs will find you. I learned that during a period of years when my company handled a large-scale development program in Central and South America for the Agency for International Development.

As project manager, I had employed a fellow who was a top Peace Corps official in South America. Between the two of us, we had a considerable amount of experience in traveling around the region. We never got sick and we preached to other staff members about the precautions to take — treat the water, never eat the lettuce, etc.

Then we went to Rio for a meeting with State Department officials at a top hotel on Copacabana. And both of us got sick as dogs.

On another project, I got very sick in Southeast Asia as a result of taking plague shots in the U.S. Embassy clinic. It's hard to believe the plague itself would have been any worse.

• *One Mosquito Bite*

While in Dakar, my wife and I had dinner on the hotel terrace. Evidently, she was bitten by a mosquito. By the time we got to Nairobi, she was feeling sick, and in Johannesburg her temperature rose to 104. We called in the best doctor we could find.

He was able to reduce her fever enough that we could fly her home, where the CDC determined that she had Dengue fever. It was the only case they reported in Africa that year.

• *When a Martini Is Not*

Americans whose drink is a martini must be on guard constantly when traveling around the world. In most places, if you order a martini, you will get a glass of Martini wine.

Becky has suffered this frustration from Nice to Buenos Aires and on air carriers from Qantas to Air Afrique. At worst, my Scotch and soda arrives with plain water.

There are other problems in Kuwait. Drinks are not served. However, don't give up. Sit down in the coffee shop of a certain internationally known hotel and explain your problem discreetly to the waiter.

If you are patient, some 30 minutes later you will be served a scotch in a coffee cup. The drinks come from a building next door.

And in Mongolia you need to be even more forgiving. The national drink, which we had just once, is fermented mare's milk.

Urdu, Nudity and Wong Fat (People, Customs, Languages)

Among the adverse trends in the world, we have such things as the destruction of rain forests and the depletion of the ozone layer. But none of these movements are taking place at anything like the speed of another threat — the homogenization of the world's cultures.

Before the jet airplane went into service, a miniscule portion of the world's population traveled around the world. Most remote areas never saw visitors from other continents. And those who were privileged to travel came home to relate their experience to rapt audiences.

In my lifetime, I have seen a lot of homogenization. Just about every main street has the same film and soft drink signs today. The items sold in airport shops look like they all came from the same wholesaler. You can walk through most airport terminals and you could be in Salt Lake City or Santiago.

In another generation, with every kid in the world watching the same global TV shows, the homogenization process will accelerate. It will require a dedicated global effort to preserve the rich local distinctions in traditions, customs, costumes, languages and lore which are so fascinating. I consider myself extremely fortunate to have lived in a time of worldwide variety.

• *Markets, Souks, and Malls*

One of the best ways to get to know about a strange city is to visit the local market. Very quickly, you can find out what the area produces, what the people eat, how much things cost, how safe it is, how visitors are treated and how well the marketing system works.

In some countries listed among the most underdeveloped we have found local markets laden with lush displays of fruit and vegetables and seafoods that are readily available at reasonable prices. In some more developed nations we've seen dirty, stinking displays of fly-covered meats.

In some of the more civilized areas, we've been persuaded to have an escort to protect against beggars, pickpockets and muggers. And in many markets at the ends of the earth we've been greeted with smiles, offered free samples and treated with great patience as we ask dumb questions.

Becky's hobby is making necklaces out of materials she collects on our travels. She has a collection of thousands of beads and pendants from all over the world. Her favorite spot is the flea market in Paris, but there are many other places where bargains are to be found.

Speaking of bargaining, techniques vary greatly in different areas. There are countries in which the accepted approach is to be belligerent, to make uncomplimentary remarks about the items offered, the store and the service. The deal is typically closed by stalking out, with the salesperson following at your footsteps, shouting and cajoling.

There are other areas in which both bargaining parties try to outdo each other with politeness. The customer compliments the shopkeeper on his establishment and on his scholarly and gentlemanly attributes. Much praise is heaped on the item under discussion, with the customer saying, "What a tragedy that I am too poor to consider it."

The shopkeeper's response is that he is so honored to have a person of such noble heritage in his humble place of business that he will make a once-in-a-lifetime sacrifice and offer the merchandise at an absurdly low price. After several such gushy exchanges, the wife — at the urging of a husband whose feet are hurting — makes her purchase.

• *Barefoot Billionaires*

We were honored to be invited to dinner at the home of a prominent Kuwaiti family. Our host, whom I had seen only in business suits at the office, greeted us in a traditional flowing robe which hung to the floor.

The mansion was impressive. Everything was new. The furnishings might have been found in a Manhattan penthouse suite. Throughout the house, floors were marble. There were tropical plants obviously not native to the surrounding desert.

We had cocktails and a lively discussion with other dinner guests from the Sudan and the Far East. Dinner was excellent, served in a relaxed but stylish manner.

As we were leaving, someone commented on the interesting patterns in the expensive marble floor. Our host quickly explained that the reason he had the marble floor was not so much for appearances but because he liked its feel. Lifting his robe, he displayed his bare feet.

• *Sunday at the Pagoda*

Some of the most fascinating hours I have spent were at the Schwedagon pagoda in Rangoon. It can best be described as a sort of oriental religious Disneyland.

Built on a hill, the Schwedagon towers over the city. Its golden spires can be seen for miles, beckoning faithful Buddhists to worship.

Buddhists are very tolerant and those of other faiths are free to visit the pagoda as long as they observe the customs and decorum. As you enter the gate, this means removing your shoes and socks. If you wish, you can buy candles and beads from stalls along the entranceway.

There is a long climb, up many flights of stairs. While climbing, we learned that it is also wise to watch where you put your feet. Those ahead may have been chewing betel, and it is disconcerting to step into a wet puddle of spittle.

(This probably explains why in Burma it is considered very bad manners when seated to cross one's legs and show the bottom of one's foot to someone.)

Once at the upper level, you discover that the Schwedagon offers something for everyone. If you are in a thoughtful mood, there are quiet chapels for meditation. Others are for chanting. There are booths where you may have someone dash you with a bucket of water. Another booth offers you the opportunity to hammer on a great log with a heavy hammer.

The passing parade of humanity is equally varied. There are laughing, playful children tugging at parents; unsmiling monks in their saffron gowns; and families decked out in their Sunday best — the ladies in brightly-colored silk blouses and the men wearing longhis, a sort of wrap-around skirt.

We attempted to learn some of the basic tenets of the religion. If we understood correctly, Buddhists believe one can amass "merit points" for doing good things, such as building pagodas. These can be used, like money in the bank, when one errs. Sounds like private enterprise!

• *Harvard Men Everywhere*

There was a time when one wore a T shirt with an insignia of one's school or home town. It was visible proof of one's heritage.

Our daughter Laura bought a Frobisher Bay shirt when we flew the Arctic route to Europe. Several years later she was accosted by a wildly enthusiastic young man in Auckland who had one just like it. He too had braved the Arctic.

Nowadays it appears that surplus T shirts are dumped on the world's markets at random. A kid who has never left Brooklyn may sport a University of Singapore shirt; a young lady in Caracas may wear a Pittsburgh Steelers decal; and Harvard men may be seen collecting the garbage in Karachi.

Somehow, we have achieved anonymity via excessive labeling.

• *Awkward Moment*

On a warm Sunday the line of people waiting to visit Lenin's tomb started on a side street, wound through a park and then stretched across Red Square. They had come from all over the Soviet Union, their features and costumes revealing their diverse origins.

Our group of 10 Britons and two Americans, plus our Intourist escort, had started at the tail-end of the queue and, after a hour or so, was approaching the tomb. The atmosphere was solemn, except for the giggling and loud talk of one of our colleagues.

Just as we were considering shushing her, a burly Russian soldier, weapon at the ready, bore in. While neither could understand the words of the other, it was obvious he was furious and she was scared to death. All of us were embarrassed.

• *Only a Smile*

Our DC-3 landed at the remote strip in the foothills of the Himalayas and taxied to the ramp where a local group was waiting. It turned out to be a welcoming delegation from the ruling tribe. There were several swarthy men in flowing robes and five or six little girls holding bunches of flowers.

As we stepped off the plane each little girl — about 10 years old, I'd guess — walked forward and presented one of us with a flower. The one who greeted me was a cute little lady with bright eyes and a timid smile.

I'm sure she had no idea who we were or where we had come from. How had she been chosen for the ceremonial duty? Was it an honor or a chore? Had she ever done that before? Was it a very special occasion? I couldn't ask because she spoke no English and I didn't know a single word of Urdu.

• *Starring as Guest Enemy*

We were at Koror, Palau, one of the Pacific islands administered by the U.S. since WWII under a mandate from the United Nations. Situated several hundred miles south of Guam and another several hundred miles east of the Philippines, Palau was one of the many islands taken by Japan and retaken by the U.S. during WWII.

During our visit long after the war we stayed at a small hotel run by Nikko, the Japanese hotel group. Many Japanese now live on the island — in fact, you could say the Japanese have taken it again.

At any rate, we went into the small hotel dining room one night for dinner. It was early and we were the first to arrive. We took a table and began our meal.

Soon, several Japanese arrived, looked at us strangely, held a whispered discussion, then proceeded to rearrange the chairs and tables. When they had finished, the seating was in a large "U," with us at the open end.

Other Japanese began to arrive. One carried what appeared to be a small shrine, another a jar of ashes. There were pendants, ribbons, swords, mats and paper cuttings — all arranged on their tables.

We asked the waiter what was happening and he said it was a reunion party for Japanese soldiers who had survived the bloody battle fought on the island. It seems that the Japanese, rather than offend us, had made us their guest enemy. It was a dinner we won't forget.

• *Pray, what to do?*

It was a bright, warm winter day on the Arabian Gulf. I had just finished a conference with a group of bankers and walked out on the busy street. Suddenly, everybody around me knelt on the sidewalk, heads touching the concrete. From a nearby minaret I could hear the call of the muezzin.

There I was, an infidel, in the midst of a host of devout Moslems, sticking out like a sore thumb. Panic!

What to do? To get down on the sidewalk would appear to be deceptive; to stand there staring at them was unthinkable. Slowly, I slunk into a doorway and remained absolutely quiet and motionless for what seemed like an eternity.

Suddenly, everyone got up and went on their way. No one gave me so much as a glance. If anyone had noticed me, they were kind enough not to let me know.

• *Poor Man's Guayabara*

During summers in Atlanta I can be seen at my office wearing a long sleeved sport shirt cut square across the bottom — and not tucked into my trousers. Most will regard this as yet another piece of evidence attesting to my general lack of good taste. For those who wish to hear my side, I will argue that my shirt selection is a practical solution to a global problem.

Try packing your needs for a two-or-three week swing through the Pacific Rim region into one suitcase and you quickly discover a problem. You need dress shirts for the meetings in Tokyo and sports shirts for the weekend in Thailand. And, for those later sessions in Manila, you need guayaberas — those light-weight combination dress-sports shirts worn in many tropical areas from Southeast Asia to Central America.

A long time ago in Hong Kong or Taiwan I found a workable compromise. It is a medium-weight, long-sleeved shirt styled like a guayabera but made from a cotton-synthetic blend rather than silk. When traveling, I wear them for all occasions, with or without a tie, with or without a jacket.

Using this "standard global shirt" greatly simplifies shopping, packing and laundry decisions. My wife, unimpressed by my shrewdness, says it also guarantees that I will never look quite right.

I retaliate by reminding her of the night we went to the Chinese National Opera in Beijing. She got her hair fixed, dressed up in a long gown with carefully matched necklace and otherwise prepared for a very special affair. When we walked into the theatre we discovered that the Chinese do not dress for their opera — many of the men were in their undershirts.

• *Torrent of Babel*

Without looking for the statistics, I would concede that we Americans rank near the bottom in language capabilities. When we travel, we envy Europeans and others who easily command several languages.

In any event, we often find it necessary to use interpreters for vital business sessions. One quickly learns those who offer their services as expert interpreters range from hopeless to wonderful.

For an inter-American seminar in Caracas we had brought in a crew from one of the top outfits in Washington. During one of the sessions, I happened to walk behind one of the booths in which a fellow of Colombian descent was working.

I knew his first language was Spanish, but at the moment he was doing a fast-paced simultaneous translation from Portuguese to English. He had the "feed" from the speaker's platform in one ear. In the other ear he had plugged in a small portable radio so he could listen to a soccer game. And I'm not even sure how parallel computers run two programs at the same time.

At the other end of the spectrum are the interpreters who require you to speak at a pace that would permit a sculptor to carve the words in granite. Also, there are those who insert their own opinions.

We had one of those once in the Kashin State. We would make a simple statement in a short sentence, and he would rattle along for several minutes. What really bothered us was that we were making a serious speech and he was getting laughs.

• *Check the Calendar*

When planning a trip you learn to check your itinerary against a list of holidays in the various locations to be visited. In every country there are holidays just as significant to the people there as our Fourth of July and Thanksgiving are to us. For those trying to arrange business appointments, these strange holidays are placed like booby traps all over the calendar.

On a trip to Australia, I planned to visit areas from Sydney on the east coast to Perth on the west coast. My visit would extend over the period

Investissez dans les Etats-Unis.

Voi investite negli Estati Uniti.

Invest in the U. S. A.

Investieren Sie Ihr Geld in den U. S. A.

A STUDY PUBLISHED BY

THE INTERNATIONAL GUIDE TO INDUSTRIAL PLANNING AND EXPANSION
CONWAY RESEARCH INC 2600 APPLE VALLEY RD ATLANTA GA. 30319, U.S.A.

Invest in the USA brochure. This is the cover for a brochure we prepared in the 1960s for use by U.S. embassies to solicit foreign investment in the USA. The introduction was written by President Lyndon Johnson. The preparation of such documents has become a company specialty — we have handled more than a hundred projects for such clients as Malaysia, Germany, Costa Rica, and many state and local groups around the world.

when they celebrate "Australia Day," so I expected to lose a day.

By the time I had finished in Australia, I had learned that each of the seven states can set the date when it recognizes Australia Day. Everywhere I went, they seemed to be celebrating.

While flying my own airplane around Latin America, I discovered many holidays you will never see on their calendars. This came about when the various local officials who process arriving and departing airplanes learned that they could charge extra fees on holidays.

The fees were never large enough to warrant confrontations, but they were impressive in their demonstration of creative thinking. The people who levied them — including, in one country or another, customs, immigration, public health, air traffic control and sundry police and armed forces personnel — sometimes had trouble keeping a straight face as they solemnly charged us $5 for entering on the "day of the feast of Jose Gonzalez," or "on the anniversary of the organization of the avocado pickers."

• *Chinese New Year*

Without doubt, one of the most enthusiastic celebrations to be found anywhere marks the beginning of the Chinese New Year in February. At various times we have encountered the holiday in Taiwan, Singapore, Mandalay, Hong Kong and San Francisco.

We rate the Taipei celebration as the most rambunctious. From a high hotel window we looked across the city one night as the celebration reached a climax. We doubt that a German raid on London during the Battle of Britain used as much firepower.

From all over the metro area rockets streaked into the sky. Bursts of fireworks exploded in rosettes of every color. In the streets below merrymakers tossed strings of firecrackers and cherry bombs at passing cars, into doorways and in the paths of fast-moving pedestrians. Scarcely heard in the din were the wail of sirens responding to emergency calls.

In Singapore, the highlight of the holiday season is the "Changay" parade. It is a wonderful spectacle of marching bands, drill teams, floats, figures, balloons and dancing groups. The feature, of course, is an enormous dragon which snakes from curb to curb.

Whether Chinese or not, it's a great event. It's too bad that, despite some effort, we have never been able to learn the correct Chinese spelling or pronunciation. In Hong Kong we were told *kong hai fat choy*. In Brunei it was *gong xi fa cai*, and in Bangkok we were given *kong lee fat choi*. All of our tutors were Chinese. Inscrutable!

• *Polynesia Wins!*

We've enjoyed watching many performances of native dances. The most energetic were the members of the national dance company of Senegal, which we saw in Dakar. They were not just talented dancers but also great athletes. Their leaps would have scored in the Olympics.

Perhaps the most stately were the flamenco team in Seville. Most unusual was a Burmese group who performed for us on the lawn of the president's mansion one sultry night. Then, there was the lively Swiss canton group at Crans-Montana and a West Indian troupe we saw at Trinidad.

Once, at Myitkyina, in the foothills of the Himalayas, we were trapped into taking part in a traditional Kashin sword dance. After a festive dinner our hosts presented each of us with a sword and led us into a circle. There we followed tribal chieftans around, jumping from one foot to the other, waving the swords wildly and shouting to the nearby mountains.

If anyone had made a video of that spectacle, they could have lived comfortably off the revenue from blackmailing the dignified representatives of Uncle Sam.

Our vote for best native dances must go to the Polynesians, from Hawaii to Tahiti. The girls are beautiful, the men are handsome, and their movements are fluid. They look like they were born to dance. And who is to say they were not?

• *Poverty Close at Hand*

It is one thing to read UN reports citing hunger statistics in Ethiopia and another to see hungry people an arm's length away. It is a very uncomfortable feeling.

We have arrived at remote airstrips and carried trash from the airplane — wrappers, cans, bottles — to the nearest waste barrel, watched closely but quietly by children standing near. Then, as soon as we turned away, they would scramble for the trash, tearing it apart to find food or things of value. We've seen children fighting over an empty vienna sausage can.

In Haiti, I recall having breakfast on the terrace of a resort hotel. It was a beautiful spot, surrounded by lush tropical foliage. A cage of brightly colored birds chirped in the background as a white-jacketed waiter brought in a tray of exotic fruits.

At that moment, I happened to see some motion behind a fence that separated the hotel grounds from the city street. Closer examination revealed several children staring intently — and they were not admiring the people; they were looking at the food.

• *"Neither Sleet nor Snow..."*

If you think our postal service is bad, you should bring up the subject

281

just about anywhere in the world and hear the horror stories. There are nations in which virtually no mail is delivered consistently. There are nations in which there are warehouses full of mail waiting for delivery for months. In others, there is no point in subscribing to magazines — the postmen take them home or sell them.

Even in those areas where the postal services are trying, there can be big problems with foreign mail. Postal codes and street addresses need to be in the right format for that nation. You must know the differences between *boite postal* (post office box) in France, *kampong* (neighborhood) in Indonesia and DF (Federal District) in Mexico.

For these and other reasons it is best to have your addressee tell you how to address mail. Otherwise, get an international guide from the post office.

Names are another problem area. They vary widely around the world in form, length and manner of addressing. Even between two neighboring countries the differences can be dramatic. For example, Burma offers some of the world's shortest names — typically one syllable. Remember their diplomat, U Nu?

Next door in Thailand, they have some of the world's longest names. A small child may have a name of six or seven syllables.

Also, names that seem rare to us in one nation may be common in another. On a trip to Kowloon I had carried a note about a major development project being carried out by a Mr. Wong Fat. I planned to call him for more information.

The Hong Kong telephone directory turned out to have more than a page of Wong Fats. I never found the right one.

• *Small Views of Big Events*

We had a wonderful day attending a Kentucky Derby at Churchill Downs, sitting in a box with our favorite Kentuckian, Katie Peden. We can't remember the name of the horse that won, but we still have a vivid memory of that moment, just before the race, when the band played "My Old Kentucky Home." That is the biggest emotional moment of the year for true Kentucky horse people, and there was scarcely a dry eye in the place.

We had another great time at the Paris Air Show at Le Bourget. There were exciting aerial demonstrations and impressive low-level fly-bys. But what we remember was the warm hospitality of the Messerschmidt group which had a little tent pavilion on the ramp. It had not been too many years since WWII when we were trying to shoot down those pesky ME 109s.

• *Will Clothes Disappear?*

282

When we travel to warm climates and especially when we visit beaches, we find ourselves wondering if mankind, starting without clothing a few millenia ago, is destined to return to the original natural state.

The leaders of the current movement are the Europeans. Wherever they spend their beach vacations tops are off. We have noted the phenomenon from the Promenade d'Anglais in Nice to the Greek islands, the Costa Brava and as far South as Djerba in North Africa.

Moreover, wherever European hotel and resort operators have located their facilities, the topless tourists have followed. Thus, you will see a bit of Nice, St Tropez or Cannes in such diverse places as Dakar, Martinique and Thailand's Phuket Island.

At the same time, there appears to be some confusion in some of the islands of the South Pacific. Here, clothing has been unnecessary until very recent times when missionaries told the natives they should cover up.

Some of the local citizens have followed the teaching of the missionaries, while others have observed that visitors from Europe are obviously not wearing clothes. Whom to follow?

In such places as Tahiti this leads to a casual indifference about the whole thing. To illustrate, one sunny day I walked into the large reception area of the principal government building in Papeete for an appointment with a top official.

I was greeted by a pretty young Polynesian girl at the front desk who identified me and phoned upstairs to announce my arrival. While waiting for someone to come down and escort me, I chatted with the receptionist.

I said something about the weather and she remarked, "Yes, it is very hot today." At the same time she opened her blouse and flapped it about to fan her bare top — all as casually as answering the phone.

I have forgotten a thousand receptionists but I remember her.

• *Soccer Game Interruption*

Another incident in Tahiti reveals something of the way the islanders handle the intrusion of European and American visitors and their customs. It was Sunday and the beach was busy.

In one area a group of young Tahitian men were playing soccer. Nearby, several bare-top Air France flight attendants were spending their time between flights improving their tans and attracting stares of other tourists.

After a while, one of the French girls, a statuesque blonde wearing only a string around her bottom, decided to take a stroll along the beach. We will not be so uncharitable as to assign a motive, but we can report that she marched (undulated) resolutely straight through the soccer area, bringing the game to a complete halt.

It was then that I discovered the true strength of Tahitian men. They stopped their game, waited stoically while the blonde paraded by, and then resumed play as if absolutely nothing had happened. Score Tahiti 1, France 0.

• *Unheralded Local Skills*

If you travel to the ends of the earth, you will find people who live there who have developed incredible skills in coping with local conditions. One who comes to mind is a remarkable fellow named Christophe whom I met in a swamp in Haiti.

I had taken off on a walk along a trail in an uninhabited area along the North coast. I was trying to find the site of a proposed new resort and, spying a crescent beach far below the trail, attempted to cut through some heavy growth. That's when I encountered the swamp.

At the same time, I heard a thrashing sound which came closer and closer. It was obviously a large animal. Happily, it turned out to be a large black man carrying a machete and wearing shredded shorts and a broad smile.

After a few minutes of labored Creole, plus much hand waving, I knew his name was Christophe and he knew I wanted to go to the beach. This established, Christophe started hacking at the canes and bushes clearing a narrow trail ahead.

I tried to cross the swamp by stepping from one fresh stump to the next, but it was hard to balance on the stumps and they were uncomfortable through my sneakers. I wound up plodding through the ooze and muck while Christophe, barefoot, jumped nimbly, from one sharp stump to the next.

On another day, on the opposite side of the globe, I found a young Polynesian teenager whose skill and prowess would win him an athletic scholarship to any major university.

We had gone out in a small outrigger canoe to swing around the atoll reef and visit a small island (*motu*) across the lagoon. We landed on the lagoon side, and I walked across to the open water side to look along the beach for shells.

I was so occupied that I did not notice a line of thunderstorms approaching. My guide was more alert and soon he came running to get me.

As we swung around the reef and headed back across the lagoon, the winds struck and then came a deluge. My teen-age skipper handled the storm like a veteran, never seeming to be near panic as the smooth surface turned to white caps and our small craft was more under water than on top.

What was an exciting expedition for me was probably routine for him.

Similarly, we had a guide/skipper ferry us about in a small native boat off the east coast of Kenya in the old kingdom of Zanzibar. He handled shifting winds and currents with an easy grace.

I'm sorry not to be able to hand out the same accolades to water taxi operators we have used in such places as Borneo and Bangkok. They were just like taxi drivers everywhere.

• *The Great Haircut Spectacle*

There comes a time in every long trip when a haircut is needed. One such time came in the Burmese hill country at a place called Tanggyi.

I was directed to a stall on the main street where I encountered a toothless man in a *longyi* (a sort of skirt) who spoke no English. Clearly, I had come to him because he was the barber, so he dragged a chair out into the street, seated me, and proceeded to do his thing.

A small crowd of curious onlookers soon encircled us. Traffic, mostly villagers on foot, detoured around, and all seemed to enjoy the rarity of seeing a foreigner properly shorn.

I don't remember how much the operation cost, but the side show was a bargain.

• *Making Appointments*

We are accustomed to making appointments in the U.S. by picking up the phone and calling someone. We say who we are, what we are about and ask to set a date. Most of the time, that simple procedure works just fine.

In some parts of the world, however, that approach will get you nowhere. There are many areas in which a stranger would not be so bold as to make a direct approach. The customary procedure is to go through an intermediary — the embassy, an association or a local business firm. When time permits, that's what we do.

If, however, time is short or other approaches have failed, we do the unthinkable — we go ahead without an appointment.

For example, many years ago we had received no response to attempts to arrange an interview with an official of MITI (the Ministry of Industry and Trade) in Tokyo. We knew the agency had some information we needed, and there was a reasonable expectation that, properly contacted, they would share it with us.

Having been unable to make an appointment, we went to Tokyo, took a taxi to MITI Headquarters and presented ourselves to the main reception desk. It took the better part of a morning, but we finally found a nice English-speaking staff member in the right department. He supplied us with the data we wanted.

Recently, we were having difficulty making an appointment in Brunei, a small sultanate on the island of Borneo. They either did not understand my request or did not wish to be impolite and say no.

However, when it became obvious I was going to show up in Borneo, they referred me to an office in London. It seems that the oil-rich little nation employs a world-recognized public relations agency to screen contacts. Believe it or not, the account executive met me in Brunei and helped me get the information I wanted.

All good data does not come to those who sit and wait!

New Patterns of Development

We live in a world of constantly changing patterns of development. While large nations launch new super projects, such as global airport cities, small nations look to the formation of new federations that will give them more clout.

Meanwhile, industrial firms conduct their constant search for new labor resources. Today, many eyes are focused on the vast human resources of mainland China where there are millions of unemployed or underemployed. In another generation, that focus may shift to Africa.

Tourism is already the most global of all industries. Eco-tourism is growing so rapidly that it in itself is an environmental concern.

Underlying all development is the technology driver. Changes are constant and dramatic.

All of these factors are making their impact on the map. New cities are springing up, influencing new transport routes. Eventually it all comes down to quality of life, as we have set forth in Chapter 7. For example, there is the trend to what we term the "high tropics."

The High Tropics

Both the data and our insight are too limited to enable us to project a future world pattern and its impact on each region and nation. However, we might rather timidly suggest that certain trends will be important in the coming decade.

First, it appears that climatic factors, always important in location, will loom even larger in the future. In the past, lack of climate control systems (heating and air-conditioning) influenced most development to occur in temperate zones. Since most land area in this climatic zone lay north of the equator, growth occurred in Europe, Russia, China and North America.

If we check the location of major cities of the world with distances from the equator, we find a very clear pattern:

Degrees from Equator	City	Elevation (Feet)
60 to 69	Helsinki	30
	Oslo	308
50 to 59	Copenhagen	43
	Berlin	187
	Amsterdam	5
	London	149
	Moscow	505
40 to 49	Istanbul	59
	Geneva	1,329
	Madrid	2,188
	Rome	377
	Paris	164
	Montreal	187
	Toronto	379
	Vancouver	127
	Vienna	664
30 to 39	Algiers	194
	Cairo	381
	Buenos Aires	89
	Santiago	1,706
	Shanghai	16
	Athens	351
	Beirut	111
	Lisbon	313
	Capetown	56
	Sydney	62
20 to 29	Rio de Janeiro	201
	Canton (Guangzhou)	59
	Havana	80
	Calcutta	21
10 to 19	Lima	394
	Manila	49
	Bangkok	53
	Guatemala City	4,855
	Mexico City	7,340
0 to 9	Djakarta	26
	Singapore	33
	Bogota	8,355
	San Jose	3,760
	Quito	9,220
	Nairobi	5,971

This simple analysis reveals very strikingly the fact that older established cities were typically located 30 to 50 degrees from the equator. Also, it points up the fact that where major cities were built close to the equator they were situated several thousand feet above sea level to achieve a temperate climate in a tropical zone.

Today, with tropical diseases under control and air conditioning available, it seems logical to expect a great increase in development in the areas closer to the equator, especially those at higher elevations. To examine this more closely, let's look at major land masses which fall between 20 degrees north of the equator and 20 degrees south.

In the Western Hemisphere, we find the vast Amazon Basin, large parts of South America, Panama, Central America, much of Mexico and the islands of the Caribbean. This is indeed an exciting growth region.

In the Far East, we find parts of India, Southeast Asia, Thailand, Malaysia, Singapore, the Philippines, Indonesia, Oceania and the northern part of Australia. This too is generally recognized as a region of outstanding growth potential.

The third major area is a huge slice of Central Africa bounded by the desert on the north but including major watersheds, highlands and rich resources. Given some degree of political stability, this too is an extraordinary region.

Within these regions it is easy to identify many plateau areas 3,000 to 6,000 feet above sea level. Areas offering a combination of high terrain and tropical location can be found in Indonesia, the Philippines, Papua New Guinea, Queensland, Central Africa, Western and Eastern Malaysia, South India (Deccan Plateau), Madagascar, the Altiplano region of the Andes chain, Venezuela, Brazil, Central America, Hispaniola and the islands of the West Indies.

Just as we predict that more population will be located closer to the equator, we believe it is safe to forecast greater interest in areas offering potential for solar energy recovery. Also, vast ocean areas which have heretofore supported little population will attract more people. Rapid growth will occur on many small islands in remote locations.

Despite the growing influence of climatic factors, we believe that for many growth regions the biggest consideration for the coming decade will be political stability. In the absence of law and order, sound development does not occur. Conversely, many obstacles can be overcome if both the physical and political climate are salubrious.

B. Excerpts

1991 Excerpt	The Global 2000. The new global executive. Global strategies. *Site World, The Book of Corporate Global Strategies*. 1991.

Thirty years ago I made what for me at that time was a startling discovery. In scanning the statistics on U.S. manufacturing activity, I noted to my amazement the great degree of concentration.

In many sectors, fewer than five percent of the firms accounted for more than 90 percent of production. We built the circulation program for our magazine, *Site Selection*, on "the mighty four percent" which dominated American industrial activity.

Later, we found that a similar concentration was found in the other industrial nations. Further, in planning *Site World* we discovered that the percentage of firms leading the global movement was even smaller.

Our present estimate is that a "Global 2000" firms are the leading players in putting together global super projects and globally significant ventures. Of course, there are thousands of other firms engaged in international commerce, but they are the minor players.

Only a few — less than one percent — of the world's business firms can qualify for global leadership on the basis of size, strength, company geography, creative strategy and performance.

What are these firms like? During recent months we mailed a "Global Leadership Survey" to some 2,000 corporations we consider to be the largest and/or most active in international venture activities. These firms are about equally divided among the Pacific Rim, North America and European regions.

We believe these firms are the most powerful, most influential corporations in the world. A number have been represented at our seminars or have been in communication with us regarding projects.

We have had an excellent response. Tallies tell us that the typical firm has annual sales of about $3.1 billion and assets of about $2.6 billion. Of course, many of the companies are much larger.

The average growth rate is 11 percent per year. One firm reported a rate of 193 percent for the past year!

The typical firm has already deployed units in some 63 countries. If we look at the five major global regions other than Africa, we find that 90 percent of the firms already have sales offices, 67 percent have distribution facilities, 50 percent have manufacturing plants and approximately 25 percent have research laboratories in every region.

If we compare global regions, we find that the top global firms have, to date, placed more facilities of all types in North America. Next follows Europe, then the Pacific Rim, Central and South America, Asia and the Middle East and, last, Africa.

With regard to expansion during the rest of this decade, 43 percent of the firms said they plan to give top priority to Europe, 27 percent named North America, 26 percent to the Pacific Rim, 21 percent to Asia and the Middle East, two percent to Central and South America. None listed Africa as a top priority.

Looking at Specific Firms

Of course, each global 2000 company has its own unique geography. It will be very interesting to observe during the years just ahead how company geographies change in an era of open borders and open markets.

We know, for example, that in the past the pattern has been to start in a new nation with a sales representative, then a sales office, and, if volume is sufficient, a warehouse or distribution facility. Only in large nations could a firm afford to proceed to build a manufacturing plant or even a research center.

Now, with national boundaries being eliminated in regions such as Europe, the large regional market makes possible an entirely different strategy.

It would not be practical in a work such as this to attempt to list all of the significant global ventures which have already been structured. There are thousands of noteworthy undertakings.

How to Think Globally?

Everywhere we go we hear variations of the catch phrase "think global, act local."

Sony describes the company's strategy as "global localization." Company spokesmen insist that this policy is *not* decentralization, but rather developing local managers who can make decisions. Sony policy is to manufacture where markets are.

For others, "localizing" is a catch word that may mean simply having a local sales rep. For some, it may mean having local managers making decisions on the spot. For a few, it means having local R&D centers.

Not many firms, including the Japanese, have truly "localized."

To be truly global, one must achieve 100 percent reciprocity in "acting locally," and that is very difficult. For example, enterprising Japanese may work diligently to fit into American society when on overseas assignments;

while at home they may be unable to accept Americans in their own society. Such problems exist for all ethnic groups and cultures.

We have, in fact, begun to have our doubts about "think global, act local" as a long-term strategy. Could it be a passing thing?

With the advent of worldwide TV networks and free circulation of all types of media, brand names will quickly become known to global audiences. Things that were strange and alien will become familiar and acceptable with breathtaking speed.

Look at what happened in the United States. Japanese and German company names, which during WWII were symbols of the nation's mortal enemies, soon were accepted and today are in many cases preferred brands.

After another decade of intense global communication it may no longer be advantageous for companies to conceal their identities behind different "localized" corporate facades in various countries. On the contrary, the advantage may go to those who shout their identities from the housetops.

Perhaps the slogan of the future should be "think new world, act new world."

We have also discovered that some firms have "global strategies" which are largely cosmetic. They rush into joint ventures or investments in order to be able to say to the public or to their shareholders that they are "globalizing." Ill-considered ventures resulting from this global imaging and posturing are already beginning to take a toll.

How Private?

Despite great strides in privatization, many of the Global 2000 are still governmental or quasi-governmental entities.

Aside from structural, financial and organizational differences, there are important psychological distinctions. These are growing in importance.

American firms take pride in being private and independent. They advertise these facts and cite them as reasons to do business with them. Those who depend on the government are regarded as weak. They think that the best endorsement one can get is that of the marketplace.

By contrast, in many nations, private companies still find it is necessary or desirable to obtain governmental endorsement for their programs and activities. Even in Western Europe and Japan some companies would not dare launch a new venture without getting the nod from appropriate government agencies.

In some cases, these endorsements extend down to trivial things, such as participating in an international meeting or having a technical paper run in a certain journal. In a way, they provide a measure of the maturity of the nation's democratic political system — or lack of it.

This is an especially important factor in the information industry. Americans defend the independence of the press with great emotion. Those in publishing are offended at the mere suggestion that they first get a government approval to undertake a project.

Who Is Global?

What constitutes a truly global firm? One measure is the extent to which major assets are deployed around the world. Certainly, those companies which have more than half of their assets in lands others than their homeland, can lay a claim to global status.

Among these, Europeans seem to have the lead. The list would include such giants as Saint-Gobain, Air Liquide, Unilever, ICI, Electrolux, Smithkline Beecham, Philips, Nestlè, Hoffman La Roche, SKF and Sandoz.

U.S. firms in this true global mix would include IBM, Xerox, CPC, Gillette. Northern Telecom would be a Canadian entry.

Interestingly, Japanese firms, despite big global programs, are still heavily weighted toward Japan insofar as asset deployment is concerned.

Some 15 to 20 percent of the assets of American firms are now situated overseas — three times the level of overseas deployment of Japanese firms.

What this tells us is that while many aspire to true global status, few have yet achieved that goal.

Knowing the Rules

A successful foreign trader once told me he could do business anywhere, no matter how bad the business climate, if he knew what the rules were.

Today, knowing what the rules are is the prime question in such areas as China, the USSR and Eastern Europe. Nissan, Ford and VW are making big new investments in Mexico following a clarification of investment rules.

Even in the well-managed EEC there will continue to be big questions now and after 1992. Witness the EEC flap about the Toyota plant in the UK, and charges that excessive inducements were offered. Special offers are said to be barred under European legislation governing "free competition."

Another important lesson is that — now that we have open communications worldwide — it is impossible to keep secrets for very long. No one — governments or huge multi-national conglomerates — can stop the flow of information any longer.

The New Global Executive

For bold and visionary executives, the new world of geo-economics affords unprecedented new business opportunities. This means thinking *big*, planning *big*, taking *big* risks and implementing *big* projects.

Obviously, this is no time for the timid. World leadership will go to those who have the imagination and creative ability, the managerial genius and the courage to venture into unplotted areas.

What are the concerns of global CEO? Based on our surveys, here is the new agenda for the 90s:

• World geography and economics. Global needs and opportunities. Learning and applying the new science of geo-economics.

• The future, futurism. Meshing long-term thinking with time scale condensation. Scanning the sweep of history while concentrating on history in the making.

• Intense competition — like nothing ever seen before! Competing for everything — new markets, new labor forces, new resources, public opinion.

• Joining forces. Creating new combinations, new affiliations, joint ventures. Collaboration not confrontation.

• Security. Protecting company personnel and facilities. Start with the risk of terrorism on global flights.

• Super projects, big plans, big projects, big risks. Linking the world's geographic parts and uniting its people. Using resources wisely, guarding the environment.

• New communications. Telecommunications networks, satellite systems. Serving corporate needs 24 hours per day, seven days per week, cutting through time zones, crossing borders, solving language problems.

• Business climate evaluation. Monitoring political trends on a global, national and regional basis. Implementing projects in an atmosphere of bureaucracy, corruption incompetence.

• QOL (Quality of Life) sensitivity. Assigning top personnel worldwide in harmony with cultural, religious, ethnic differences. Must be at home anywhere — multinational thinking at the local level.

• Glasnost everywhere. Total exposure to public scrutiny. Dealing with news media. Setting ethical and moral standards

• Massive data bases, automated systems. A wealth of information. Analysis and interpretation make the difference.

• "Can do" philosophy. Talk not enough. Implementation plans, not essays. Curiosity about unknown. Eager to scale the next peak.

• Above all, time management has priority. None can succeed without careful control of the clock and calendar.

• Quick response. Reacting to world events, disasters, opportunities. This is the era of the survival of the fastest.

C. Bibliography

The following are citations of McKinley Conway's writings on this chapter's subject. As this book goes to press, work is underway to make many of these items available to researchers. To check status, look for a file on GeoTEAM/IDRCNET or telephone GeoTEAM/Fax at (404) 453-4200.

Global Books, Comments

300. First session of UN Committee for Industrial Development in New York, March 27, 1961. *Industrial Development*, May 1961. pp. 2-3.
301. "A Challenge We Must Accept," *Area Digest*, Conway Research, Atlanta, Summer, 1962.
302. "Their Own Worst Enemy" (six reasons undeveloped nations fail in economic development) *Area Digest*, Fall 1962.
303. "Underdeveloped Nations: Their Own Worst Enemy?" Man-made factors play a significant part in the equation for development success. Undeveloped nations recognize this but often place the blame for their economic problems on the wrong factors. *Industrial Development*, May/June 1981. Inside cover. Also appearing in the "Global Mini-Letter," Jan. 1981. pp. 3-4.
304. "Agenda for the Future: 'Project Easylog'." A program for spurring global data exchange. *Geo-Micro*, Nov./Dec. 1984. pp. 1-2.
305. "The New 'Ion-Curtain' Countries." Today the world is faced with a new group of nations which are barricading themselves in and restricting the free flow of ideas. These are countries which, through apathy, ignorance, or design, are preventing the effective use of international data networks. *Geo-Micro*, Jan./Feb. 1985.
306. "How About a USA/USSR Common Market?" Now that we have glasnost and Perestroika — and Gorbachev has taken part in a summit session in Washington — where do we go from here? Amid doubts and suspicions, is there basis for hope for a dramatic upturn in business relations which could open vast new development opportunities? *Site Selection*. Feb. 1988. p. 4.
307. "Welcome Aboard!" With this new edition, *Site Selection* brings to our audience the top executives of Europe — men and women who are leading a development program which has captured the imagination of the world. *Site Selection Europe*. Nov./Dec. 1990. p. 2.
308. *Site Net World Guide*. Beyond perestroika. Country profiles, nations A to Z. Field reports and photos. The Super Projects. The development world tomorrow. Global investment incentives. 1989. 530 pp. With Laura Jones-Kelley and Linda L. Liston.
309. *Site World: The Book of Corporate Global Strategies*. Global strategies, super projects, national profiles, air terrorism, futurism and corporate management, adventures and misadventures in covering the globe, the Global 2000. 1991. 597 pp. With Laura Jones-Kelley and Linda L. Liston.
310. "Great Days Ahead!" We must not let the daily news media reports of global business recessions and political turmoil in the East obscure the fact that this is a great year and the beginning of even greater things for Europe and the World. *Site Selection Europe,* March 1992.
311. "The Rationale for Global Super Projects." Keynote presentation for Honolulu conference of World Development Council. *Site World*. 1992. pp. 15-18.
312. "Honolulu Sessions Launch New Era of Super Project Coordination," "Super Project Newsletter," Oct. 1992.

Field Reports on Development Situations

Africa and Indian Ocean

313. "Cairo Seeks Lost Luster." Throughout most of recorded history, Cairo has occupied a key role as a trading center and government axis. That reputation has faded in recent years ...Today, however, enlightened leadership seeks to reassert Egypt's position and find new

opportunities for regional economic activities. *Industrial Development,* Sept./Oct. 1974. pp. 3-4.

314. "A Scan of Africa's Development Prospects." Can African nations, beset by political upheavals, attract significant outside investments? Here is an overview (by the publisher) which follows visits to the continent's major regions. *Industrial Development,* March/April 1983. pp. 4-9.

315. "Tunisia: A New Look for the Mahgreb." Alert corporate planners are beginning to take an interest in the Arab nations of North Africa. A burgeoning young labor force close to the emerging European common market may attract firms servings markets from the Middle East to America. Here's a report on a key nation under new leadership. *Site Selection,* Feb. 1989. pp. 258-260.

Antarctica

316. "Antarctica — Research Facility for the World." The global programs underway in Antarctica today constitute the most significant cooperative international research venture in the history of the world. (Report on field trip to visit research stations.) *Site Selection.* June 1988. pp. 618-628.

Asia and Middle East

317. "Development of New Weapons by Soviet Union Suggests Need for More Emphasis on Industrial Dispersal Effort." *Industrial Development,* Atlanta. Oct. 1957. pp. 5-11.

318. "Checkpoints." (textile industry of Inle Lake, Northern Burma). *Industrial Development,* May 1962. pp. 2-3.

319. "Hong Kong: Free Trade and 'Squatter Factories,'" *Area Digest,* Summer, 1962. pp. 31-35.

320. "Trade Missions: Selling American Enterprise around the World," (mission to Southeast Asia), *Industrial Development, June 1962. pp. 6-16.*

321. *"A Catalog from Peking" (relative to development mission in Southeast Asia),* Industrial Development, April 1962. pp. 2-3. See also *Area Digest,* Summer 1963, pp. 29-32.

322. *Arab Investment in the U.S.* (general outlook plus special report on Kuwait). 1974. 300 pp. illus "The Banks of Beirut." For its size, Beirut is one of the world's busiest money centers. Many major international corporations have chosen the Lebanese capital for their Middle East regional facilities. Now, busy Beirut is battling for a role in handling huge new Arab oil receipts. *Industrial Development,* July/Aug. 1974. pp. 2-4.

323. "Proud Arabs Accept Global Challenge." If you enjoy fantasy, put away your copy of *A Thousand and One Arabian Nights* and pick up the Kuwait newspaper. Read about exotic places where big U.S. cars are still in demand and high-test sells for 28 cents a gallon. But the stories are real and they're being lived here, next door in Saudi Arabia, and down the road at Abu Dhabi, Qatar and Dubai. *Industrial Development,* May/June 1974, pp. 2-6.

324. "A Scan of Development in the USSR." In order to extend our editorial horizons, ID's publisher recently trekked through Siberia, across Mongolia and the Gobi desert, and into Northern China. Here is a rare picture of major development projects in one of the world's most remote regions. *Industrial Development," Nov./Dec. 1983. pp. 4-38.*

325. "Will Mainland China Emerge as a New Hub of Private Enterprise?" Here is a quick scan of Chinese developments from the remote northern Shanzi province to the booming hinterland of Hong Kong. It concludes with a rather startling prediction by ID's publisher regarding the direction the world's most populous nation may take in the years just ahead. *Industrial Development,* March/April 1984. pp. 4-8.

326. "China: the Sleeping Giant." Enter Deng Xiaping who has shaken the giant ..."we cannot depend on the works of Marx and Lenin to solve all of today's problems... the economy is a vast sea and there are many questions that ...require us to investigate reality." *Site Selection,* April 1985. p. 294.

327. "Turkey Offers Strategic Location on Intercontinental Trade routes." Where once Byzantium flourished as the center of the civilized world, Istanbul now claims increasing importance as the crossroads of Europe, Asia and the Middle East. New political changes make a more open society and a better climate for new investment. *Site Selection,* April 1987. pp. 536-538.

328. "The New Singapore Hinterland." How does a small island nation which is running out of land provide for future growth? Singapore shows the way via creative joint ventures with neighboring Malaysia and Indonesia. *Site Selection,* Aug. 1991. pp. 772-773.

329. "The New Hong Kong Metroplex." While timid investors hesitate, many far-sighted PacRim corporate planners are already betting on Hong Kong's bold new strategy. Key elements include the integration of a vast hinterland, the making of a new metro regional development concept and construction of major infrastructure improvements. *Site Selection,* June 1991. pp. 618-622.

Atlantic and Caribbean

330. "Puerto Rico — a New Horizon for Industry," *Industrial Development,* March 1959. pp. 17-48.

331. "The Caribbean Community: Opportunities Overshadow Problems," *Industrial Development,* Dec. 1961. pp. 4-10.

332. "A New Look at Opportunities in Puerto Rico," *Industrial Development,* March 1962. pp. 17-48.

333. "South Caicos Island" (Turks and Caicos Islands Group), *Area Digest,* Winter 1964, pp. 14-17.

334. "Development Outlook for the Caribbean." Here ...is a fresh scan of an island empire which is politically strategic, touristically popular but economically a sea of confusion. Given new hope by the Reagan initiatives, what are prospects that the region — with its track record of small successes and big frustrations — can meet urgent economic growth needs? *Industrial Development,* May/June 1984, pp. 4-9.

335. "The Bahamas. When Will the Time Come?" Always a tourist magnet, noted as a convenient off-shore financial haven, the Bahamas have enjoyed only limited success in attracting large-scale diversified investment in manufacturing, processing and support industries. Is such development a realistic expectation? *Site Selection,* June 1986. pp. 752-756.

336. "EEC Outpost in the Caribbean." Without fanfare, the French are building a strong economic base in the West Indies. Unlike other Caribbean islands which have become struggling independents, Martinique and Guadaloupe have emerged as thriving, integral departments of France. *Site Selection,* Aug. 1990. pp. 862-63.

337. "Puerto Rico: Super SEZ." Among SEZs (Special Economic Zones) around the world, Puerto Rico is the pioneer and pacesetter. Under the program, more than 1,000 new plants have been attracted. Now, strategic decisions must be made about the future. *Site Selection,* Oct. 1990. pp. 1170-73.

338. "A New Look at the Turks And Caicos Islands." A resort development boom triggered by a Club Med project suggests that these strategically situated islands may at last be reaching a takeoff stage. *Site Selection,* Feb. 1991. pp. 88-89.

Central and South America

339. "El Salvador: a bright spot in Central America" (project sponsored by Agency for International Development), *Industrial Development,* June 1963, pp. 5-36.

340. "Costa Rica" (economic potential survey sponsored by the Agency for International Development), *Industrial Development,* Sept. 1963, pp. 17-48.

341. "Colombia: Fertile Field for Creating Joint Ventures" (project sponsored by Agency for International Development), *Industrial Development,* Nov. 1963. pp. 57-88.

342. "Recommendations for Nicaraguan Development Program." 1964. 40 pp. (project for Agency for International Development).

343. "A Development Organization Structure for Colombia." Jan. 1964. 48 pp. (project for Agency for International Development).

344. "Opening Statement of Objectives," Interamerican Seminar on Organizing and Promoting Private Enterprise and Local Initiative, Agency for International Development. Caracas, Venezuela, June 15, 1965.

345. "Development Potential of the Amazon Basin," Southeastern Conference on Latin American Studies. Atlanta, April 14, 1967.

346. "Is Chile Poised for Takeoff?" The economic well-being of this unusual nation for the rest of the century may well rest on the plebiscite to be held soon. If Chile comes through

with a broader constitutional base and stronger public approval, prospects for economic development will be bright. Favorable factors include a wealth of forest, ocean and mineral resources, a resort climate, and an alert population reflecting strong European influence. *Site Selection*, Aug. 1988. pp. 880-884.

347. "Argentina: Will a New Capital Help?" Raul Alfonsin, Argentina's precedent-shattering president, says the nation has been stagnating in a sea of confusion. He proposes to get things better organized by moving the capital out of sprawling Buenos Aires to Viedma, a small town several hundred miles south. *Site Selection*, Oct. 1988. pp. 1162-1164.

348. "Rio: the Capital Is Gone but Life Goes on." A quarter-century ago Brazil decided to move its seat of government from this world-famous city to Brasilia, a raw site in the hinterland. It was one of the boldest development decisions any government has made. Political experts predicted chaos and economists forecast ruin. Despite all the gloom and doom talk, the plan seems to be working and gaining strength every day. *Site Selection*, Dec. 1988. pp. 372-374.

349. "Acres of Diamonds In Our Front Yard?" The death of development pioneer Teodoro Moscoso reminds us of what can be achieved in Latin America. Now it's time for us to implement his vision throughout the region. *Site Selection*, Oct. 1992. pp. 854.

Europe and Mediterranean

350. "The British Isles — Economic Potential," *Industrial Development,* Nov. 1960. pp. 17-32.

351. "A Fresh Oooutlook for France?" Traditionalists say that France and the French never change. But, of course, they do. France may at the moment, in fact, be laying the groundwork for a significant new phase of development. New Disney site. *Site Selection*, Oct. 1985. pp. 1104-1114.

352. "Will Long-awaited EEC Status Bring New Industrial Opportunities for Spain?" For many types of industrial projects site seekers have skipped Spain in favor of other European areas. Now ...there may be significant opportunities for new service industries and diversified manufacturing to complement the already flourishing tourist industry. *Site Selection*, Dec. 1985. pp. 1422-1427.

353. "Greece: A New Climate for Investment?" For more than a decade, Greece has had a political climate which repelled many investors. Now, there are signs of change — the views of the private sector are being noted and positive steps are being taken. *Site Selection*, Dec. 1986. pp. 1552-1555.

354. "Switzerland Attracts Industry the Old-fashioned Way." How does a small, landlocked nation surrounded by competitors manage to survive and prosper in the race to attract new growth? Energetic Swiss cantons do it with a reliable work force and high productivity. *Site Selection*, Feb. 1987. pp. 234-235.

355. "Changes in Europe Overtake Business World." The dramatic collapse of the communist regimes of Eastern Europe has caught all of the experts flat-footed. *Gwinnett Daily News,* Dec. 20, 1989.

356. "Eurotunnel Spurs Development of New Sites." With the opening still three years ahead, government units and private firms on both sides of the channel are already investing tens of millions of dollars in projects designed to complement the tunnel and exploit new corporate location opportunities. *Site Selection,* Feb. 1990. pp. 89-92.

357. "How Will Europe Handle All-out Site Competition?" The more we listen to Europeans discuss 1992, the more convinced we are that this magic date will mark the beginning, rather than the end, of many interesting debates and confrontations. *Site Selection,* Feb. 1990. pp. 4.

358. "Welcome Aboard!" With this new edition, *Site Selection* brings to our audience the top executives of Europe — men and women who are leading a development program which has captured the imagination of the world. *Site Selection Europe,* Nov./Dec. 1990. pp. 2.

359. "The Spanish Riviera." From Barcelona to Gibraltar, the Mediterranean Coast of Spain is alive with development plans and projects. Many observers believe this will be Europe's fastest-growing region in the decade ahead. *Site Selection*, Dec. 1990. pp. 1378-1379.

360. Memo for staff regarding visit to Malta, 09-04-92. "There is an active and determined development effort being run by savvy people."

North America: Canada, Mexico, USA

361. "Invest in the U.S.A.," *Industrial Development*, Feb. 1965. pp. 57-84. Report prepared for U.S. Dept. Commerce for distribution via U.S. consulates and commercial officers. Foreword by Pres. Lyndon Johnson.

362. "A New California Emerges." Imagine a new state of California, with two coastlines, a balmy climate, clear skies and only a few people, most of whom are willing and anxious to work, at a low scale. That is Baja California, Mexico. *Industrial Development*, March-April 1974. pp. 2-3.

363. "Ground Rules for Gringo Investors." During the past couple of years a new program has emerged in Mexico to regulate foreign investment in the highly attractive and politically sensitive coastal zones. Here's a quick review. *Industrial Development,* March-April 1975. pp. 2-3.

364. Canada: There Is a Difference." Perhaps no two major nations are as close ideologically as the U.S. and Canada. Despite this happy concurrence, each country does have its own views. There are new and significant differences in such areas as development strategy and techniques. *Industrial Development,* Nov./Dec., 1976. pp. 2-3.

365. "Mexico's Bold New Towns." While big new-town projects are floundering in the U.S., the Mexican government moves strongly ahead with ambitious projects. New developments at Ixtapa and Cancun are centered on tourism, but the implications are broad. *Industrial Development,* July-Aug. 1977. pp. 16-17.

366. "Updating Mexico's New Town Program." During the past decade we have reported several times on Mexico's bold and impressive program for building new resort cities. The projects at Cancun and Ixtapa have been highly successful in attracting a large volume of tourist traffic. *Industrial Development,* Jan./Feb. 1981. pp. 1-40. Also in "Global Mini-Letter for Development Executives," Jan. 1981. p. 2.

367. "Canada's NAPLPS Program Spurs Growth of Important New Electronics Industry." Proving that a shrewdly placed pump-priming investment can pay handsome dividends in a new mega-technology area, Canada has established a leadership position in an important segment of the telecommunications industry. *Site Selection*, June 1985. pp. 652-654.

368. "The State of Jalisco Lures Investors." IBM's recent choice of a site at El Salto, near Guadalajara, for its big new computer plant is focusing fresh attention on this state situated in the heartland of Mexico. Long a favorite of U.S. tourists and retirees, Jalisco has quietly attracted more than $1 billion in U.S. industrial investments. *Site Selection,* April 1986. pp. 522-528.

369. "Baja California del Sur — Growing Too Fast or Too Slow?" Is Mexico's Baja del Sur a state destined for greatness or just a dead-end hideaway for a few tourists? While opportunity pounds on the door, is the area dozing? Here's a fresh look by a gringo engineer who has been scanning the area's growth potential for 25 years. *Site Selection*, Oct. 1986. pp. 1224-1226.

370. "Auto Axis for New Assembly Plants Emerges along Toronto/Detroit/Atlanta Corridor." Car makers display a remarkable degree of agreement regarding the geo-economics of site selection. *Site Selection*, Feb. 1987. pp. 236-237.

371. "Guerrero has Acapulco, Ixtapa and Taxco, but Can It Add Industrial Diversification?" One of the key states in Mexico, Guerrero boasts some world-famous tourist destinations, but little else. Now, development strategists ponder the prospect for bringing "maquiladoras," or twin plants, to the hinterland and, perhaps, new high-tech services. *Site Selection*, April 1987. pp. 540-542.

372. "Atulco — Fonatur's Latest." In global super projects of the tourism variety, Mexico's far-sighted development agency sets the pace. "Super Projects" (newsletter), Feb. 1993.

Pacific Oceania, Australia, Japan

373. "The Philippines: Pride and Opportunity," *Area Digest*, Summer 1962. pp. 12-14.

374. "A Scan of Pacific Potential." Where do the Pacific islands fit into the global development picture? During a 20,000-mile survey trip, ID's publisher found serious attention being given to substantial projects amid a Hollywood backdrop of swaying palm trees and turquoise-fringed beaches. *Industrial Development*, Nov./Dec. 1981. pp. 5-8.

375. "Nauru, Pacific Investment Source." This tiny island in the vastness of Oceania has

been called the world's richest nation, even wealthier than Kuwait. Whatever the correct ranking, Nauru's development status must be regarded as unique. Unlike most of the world's small nations, Nauru Is not looking for foreign aid. Instead, the remote atoll is a source of investment funds for projects from Australia to China and the USA. *Site Selection*, June 1985. pp. 820-825.

376. "The New States of Micronesia." With scant public attention, Congress is about to determine the permanent status of hundreds of Pacific island territories administered by the U.S. since World War II. The action could have the effect of adding several new states — perhaps opening new development opportunities and certainly adding new costs for the taxpayer. *Site Selection*, April 1985. pp. 554-561.

377. "Ocean Science Projects — Will They Emerge as Prime Global Investment Opportunities?" German scientists propose "energy" islands of floating platforms covered with photovoltaic cells. Japanese developers are planning an entire city built on the water. In North America there are significant projects from Canada's tidal energy recovery plant at the Bay of Fundy to Mexico's solar desalting facility on the Sea of Cortez. *Site Selection*, Aug. 1985. pp. 168-181.

378. "Taiwan Competes Boldly in High-tech World." Few small nations have made as much progress as the Republic of China in developing industries based on advanced technologies. True, many Taiwan products are clones of U.S. prototypes, but new programs will yield more Taiwan originals. The science-based industrial park at Hsinchu is a vital element. *Site Selection*, June 1987. pp. 742-744.

379. "Singapore — a World-class Development Model." Of all the 100-plus small nations around the world, none has done a better job of implementing development than this city-state. After a five-year interval, we returned to find a new global airport, beautiful new high-speed expressways, clusters of new industrial estates and housing, the world's tallest hotel, several dozen gleaming high-rise office centers and a bustling science park. *Site Selection*, June 1987. pp. 738-40.

380. "New Zealand: a State of Indecision." This beautiful land down under offers many desirable quality-of-life factors, yet it does not rank high in the eyes of global investors. One explanation is that the average New Zealander is so content with the present that he doesn't worry much about plans and projects for the future. *Site Selection*, Aug. 1987. pp. 804-808.

381. "Indonesia — the World's Least-known Development Giant?" The great archipelago once known as the Spice Islands is now the fifth largest nation in the world, with a population of more than 160 million spread across a Seattle/Miami distance. Almost unknown to many investors, this emerging nation presents huge opportunities with problems to match. *Site Selection*, Oct. 1987. pp. 1022-1026.

382. "New Caledonia and Fiji — Question Marks in the South Pacific." Will New Caledonia remain a French territory or, like so many Pacific island groups, become a small new independent nation? Can newly independent Fiji achieve political stability? In any event, what kinds of opportunities do they offer outside investors? *Site Selection*. Feb.1988. pp. 58-60.

383. "Unique Brunei!" Around the world there are many small nations. Some are in remote locations. Most are new at self government. A few are rich. Brunei is all of those things and more — a fascinating geo-political anomaly. *Site Selection*, Oct. 1989. pp. 1192-94.

384. "Yokohama Bets on 'Minato Mirai' Project." Building a world's fair or Olympic games complex and then converting it to everyday use is a formula used successfully by many cities. Now Yokohama seeks to replace its 1989 exposition park with a global business center. *Site Selection*, Dec. 1989. pp. 1478-79.

385. "Western Australia: Big, Remote, Challenging." For many of our readers, there is no place farther from home than Perth, in the state of Western Australia. It is on the exact opposite side of the world and situated so that you're not likely to stop here on the way to someplace else. These facts don't provide an excuse, however, for alert global investors to ignore the burgeoning opportunities here. *Site Selection*, June 1990. pp. 636-643.

386. "The Global 2000." This is a discussion of the new global executive and global strategies. *Site World, The Book of Corporate Global Strategies*. 1991.

387. "Chiba: Tokyo's New Front Door." Situated in a growth corridor and offering new sites, Chiba prefecture is emerging as one of the world's top development areas. The sector is already dotted with multi-billion dollar projects. *Site Selection*, Oct. 1991. pp. 1242.

388. "Do the Japanese Really Want You?" Amid the confusion of high-level political blasts and the continuous sniping of opposing business leaders, what is the hard evidence that

299

Japan sincerely wants your new plant? *Site Selection*, April, 1992. pp. 250.

389. "Japan Offers Help for Outside Investors." Until very recently, American firms located facilities in Japan not *because* of Japanese promotion but in spite of its absence. Now, the Japanese business agency, MITI, has set up a foreign investment promotion unit and published a very helpful guide. Here's an evaluation of the new situation by a veteran observer of international development programs.

390. "Queensland's Far North." If we were ranking global sites according to growth potential we'd put this one near the top. Where else can you find such a combination: great open spaces, a Florida/Caribbean climate, proximity to the booming Pacific Rim, and a stunning array of environmental assets? *Site Selection*, June, 1993. pp. 714-716.

6
Improving the Political Climate

Chapter 6
A. Recent Comments
Accepting the Challenge
Running for Office
Bureaucracy — the Common Enemy
Looking for Real Freedom
Wars, Coups and Other Minor Inconveniences
•Dinner with the Rebels in Burma
•The Beirut War Zone
•Bullet Holes in Central America
•Escape from Guatemala
•Coup Attempt at Nairobi
•Bits and Pieces
•What, Specifically, to Do about It?

B. Excerpts
"A Challenge We Must Accept," 1962
Legislative Climates for Economic Development, 1979
"The Problem Voter," 1976, 1986
"Let the People Speak," 1985, 1991

C. Bibliography

A. Recent Comments

Accepting the Challenge

How do we formulate our own personal political philosophies? Why do so many of us grow up in the same country, live under the same system, and yet have such different ideas?

For example, I know of two young men who were born in small southern towns not too far apart. Each rural community had a population of 1,000, plus or minus.

The two boys came from families that were in agriculture-based activities — farming and cotton ginning. They went on to Georgia Tech, where both received technical educations. Then both served in the Navy in high-tech assignments.

After WWII both came home and took an interest in civic affairs, heading up planning in their local areas. Then, in the same year, both were elected to the Georgia Senate. Both served two terms and had similar voting records in the legislature.

One might think that here were two people with almost identical backgrounds and thus very similar thoughts about how our nation should be run. Yet, this was not true. One of those young men was Jimmy Carter. The other was me.

While I admire and respect Jimmy, I could not vote for him for president. From my viewpoint, he was on the wrong side! Let me explain, using the analogy of the goose that lays golden eggs. The goose is the productive segment of our economy, including workers, managers, and investors. It creates wealth.

The golden eggs are the social benefits produced by the goose. These include schools, police protection, welfare and other government services. Thoughtful, objective people realize that without a healthy goose there are no golden eggs and, even with a healthy goose, there is a limited supply of golden eggs.

Responsible leaders seek to keep the goose healthy. Unhappily, there is an irresponsible political element which constantly advocates giving away more golden eggs no matter what the consequences.

This is the group which I term the "give away crowd." It includes the unemployed, those on welfare, most union leaders and politicians who depend on such patronage to stay in office. They always urge more government spending and more giveaways no matter what.

In recent times, every national election has brought a clash between the producers and the give-away crowd. As candidates enter the races and the sides shape up, I watch to see where the give-away people land.

When Jimmy Carter ran for president, most of the give-away people supported him. The producers were mostly on the Reagan side. I thought the first Reagan victory was a crucial win for the producers.

I regretted very much not being a part of the Carter team. Few have the opportunity to have someone they know in the White House.

This painful experience serves to remind that the nurturing of the goose that lays the golden eggs is a very complex and difficult task. Even though we encounter all manner of setbacks and disappointments we must never give up.

When we get discouraged about the domestic political scene, we need to remind ourselves that 30 years ago the spread of communism around the world seemed to many to be unstoppable. Yet, the free world rallied and won the cold war. ("A Challenge We Must Accept," 1962).

Today, the achievement of a balanced budget and the retirement of our national debt seem equally impossible. Yet, I have no doubt that these goals can be reached. Let the war begin!

Running for Office

If you want to understand our system and what is wrong with it, there is no better way to learn than to run for public office. This does not mean becoming a full-time professional politician. You can run for the school board, or the city council in your suburban village.

One of the things you discover is that the intellectual level of the average voter is a lot different from that of the people with whom you normally mix. Also, you quickly discover that very few people are paying attention to anything other than the one or two specific issues that affect them personally.

Unhappily, you also learn right away that when you become a candidate you immediately become a target. Some or most of your opponents will resort to libel or slander without a moment's hesitation. They will make outrageous charges that are completely unfounded.

If you consult your attorney he will quickly inform you that, as a candidate, you have little defense in court. You will have to ignore a lot, counter some and launch counter attacks on a higher plane.

In order to get elected to the Georgia Senate, I had to run in a number of different primaries and general elections, as well as one special election.

There was always at least one unscrupulous opponent.

For example, one year I had an opponent who spread the word that my family was in the liquor business, even though the county in which I lived at that time was a dry county. It seems he had learned that my Dad was in the gin business — cotton gins, that is.

Another opponent, in a key campaign debate, accused me of being a "purveyor." It was before a rural audience which he hoped would interpret this to mean I was a sex pervert. When an explanation was demanded, he said he was referring to the fact that I was a purveyor of books and magazines.

There was also the opponent who put out an underground newsletter pointing to some of my foreign travel and revealing that I was "an international planner" and, possibly, a CIA agent. Since most of the people in my district would have been proud of me for serving the CIA, I have often wondered about his strategy.

Also, there was the party question. I must admit that I have never been charmed by political parties. I believe the notion that a two-party system guarantees political responsibility is a myth.

I have read and re-read the U.S. Constitution, and I find no mention of political parties. I believe many of the roles they play today have no constitutional basis and are merely devices installed to aid office holders.

The first time I ran for the Georgia Senate there was no effective two-party system in the state. The pattern was for everyone, conservative or liberal, who hoped to be elected to enter the Democratic primary.

Later, the Republican party made rapid strides in parts of the state. When Goldwater ran for president, he carried my district by a three-to-one margin.

As yet, independents have little chance. I once tried to run as an independent, and the party people buried my name near the bottom of the ballot.

I firmly believe that we get the best government when we vote for the best qualified men and women, no matter what their party. I have always felt that the election code should be changed to prohibit straight-ticket voting.

For these and other reasons, I never enjoyed campaigning. However, I thoroughly enjoyed my experience as a law-maker. Some of the legislative acts I authored during my two terms in the Georgia Senate are listed in the bibliography.

For example, I authored the bill creating the ocean science center at Skidaway Island and was co-author of the bill creating MARTA, the Metropolitan Atlanta Rapid Transit Authority. Also, I authored the first "sunshine" bill, which requires open meetings of governing bodies.

Bureaucracy — the Common Enemy

It becomes clearer every day that the common enemy of the people of the world is bureaucracy. It is a burden carried on the back of every productive worker. It afflicts nations of all sizes.

By far the most impressive example of global bureaucracy is the United Nations organization. Bloated and inefficient, it stands as a monument to poor administration.

It is pitiful to observe many of the small new nations — often no more populous than a small town elsewhere — carrying the burden of trying to act like big established nations. This means a cabinet of speech-making, do-nothing ministers, each with a chauffeured limousine; with foreign embassies which serve only to provide cushy assignments for relatives and political allies; and with more government employees than the combined private work force.

The fact that a nation is large and well-established does not mean that it performs any better. Witness the huge and non-productive bureaucracies built up in the communist nations during recent decades.

Which reminds me of an incident reported during the early days of the cold war. The USA and the USSR were both trying to curry favor among neutrals in Southeast Asia. The Soviets scored a coup, making one of their famous barter deals with a small nation which shall remain nameless. It was to be a boatload of cement for a boatload or so of rice.

The Soviet ship arrived at the designated port only to find that there were no warehouse facilities. The host nation apparently expected the Russians to sit there in the harbor while they used the cement a bag at a time.

The Russians had no such plan. The ship was needed elsewhere, so they just dumped the bags of cement on the dock and left. As might be expected in that part of the world, the rains came and the cement hardened.

Quickly, the pile of useless cement became "the monument to Soviet solidarity."

Let's not laugh too hard at the Russians. We Americans can develop bumbling, apathetic, public-be-damned bureaus as well as anyone. The recent mess with our savings and loan institutions was a world-class bureaucratic blunder.

We have problems in every agency — the only variation is in scope and degree. And sometimes it is the little things that irritate the most.

For example, we have for more than 30 years flown our private airplane into foreign countries — several dozen of them. The standard practice is to file an international flight plan. That lets the destination country know we are coming, and, when we land at one of their international airports, they are ready with customs, immigration and whatever else is required to process us.

The United States system is unique in that it is not enough, even for a U.S. citizen flying an airplane of U.S. registry, to file an international flight plan. The U.S. Customs Service, for reasons known only to them, insists that the pilot must telephone them and make an appointment.

Since the prime mission of the customs people is to catch smugglers, this leads us to wonder how many drug traffickers call up customs and arrange for the customs people to meet them at the airport. Incredible!

One of the greatest irritations we have is in dealing with development representatives who don't do their jobs. These are people appointed and paid to represent a nation or area seeking outside investment. They exist, presumably, to provide information for potential investors.

Over the years we have encountered scores of such people who do not return phone calls or respond to letters. And, when we are able to corner them at a meeting somewhere, they promise to send data but never do.

Usually, the representative has been sent by some Third World country to occupy an office in a large city, such as New York. The appointment, a political plum, goes not to someone qualified for that type of work but to a relative or political crony.

The small new nation would be much better off not to have any office or representative. Having an incompetent on hand reveals to the would-be investor just what kind of treatment the company could expect in that nation.

Looking for Real Freedom

The news media bombard us with reports on political situations around the world. Do not think for a moment, however, that these reports provide a sound analysis of investment climates.

For the investor, it is hazardous to depend too much on the popular news media. They tend to overplay surface situations and ignore basic performance.

Typically, a regime which is accused of discrimination or civil rights violations will be pilloried no matter how good a program it has for meeting the needs of the people for food, shelter, clothing and other necessities.

At the same time, a regime which has replaced a dictator with a supposedly democratic administration will get sympathetic coverage even though its performance in serving the people is disgraceful.

In other words, some elements of the media seem to be much more interested in theory than in practice.

We see this in reporting from South Africa, for example. We have seen countless hours of TV coverage and volumes of print material on the evils of apartheid — a system we do not endorse — but never a report on the outstanding job-creation program of the South African government.

In our observation, the South African government has established the finest economic development program in all of the 50-plus nations of Africa. This has yielded enormous benefits for all Africans, black and white. But try to find a line about that in your local newspaper.

Similarly, there were strong economic development efforts under the Somoza regime in Nicaragua, under Stroessner in Paraguay and under Pinochet in Chile. They set up business-like institutions, invested in projects, and made real efforts to improve quality of life through economic development.

Please don't interpret this to mean that we favor dictatorships. We do not. However, we want it understood that there is a huge difference between political freedom and total freedom.

Having the right to vote but having no food, shelter or clothing is not real freedom. No nation can claim to be free unless it has an economic base capable of sustaining it.

In evaluating developing nations, look for those wherein proper attention is being given to providing jobs and real opportunities for a better quality of life. Skip those in which the leaders are busy making speeches, waving flags and posing.

Wars, Coups and Other Minor Inconveniences

Most of the legislative climate problems we encounter are related to policies and procedures. They affect the pocket book of the investor.

Sometimes, however, political conflicts reach critical mass and an explosion follows. These are the rebellions, coups, and, sometimes, wars which can relate to life and death.

Get a group of old State Department hands together and they can give you a connoisseur's appraisal of coups. Those who have served in volatile areas can list governmental overthrows and attempts that were boring, or funny or frightening or all of the above.

When the rebel group takes over the government radio and starts bombarding the public with confusing announcements, the veteran diplomat knows whether to simply cancel his afternoon appointments or to start piling furniture up against the doors and windows.

If you explore opportunities in a true cross-section of the world's nations you will inevitably get involved in a few major or minor coups, revolutions, riots or miscellaneous acts of terrorism. For example:

Dinner with the Rebels

There were five of us constituting a U.S. development mission to Burma in the early 1960s. After some five or six weeks of meetings with officials at all levels in Rangoon and in the provinces, we were invited to have dinner with some top army officers.

We didn't regard the invitation as unusual. The army was active in a number of industrial activities.

On a sultry night we were driven by Jeep to a camp some distance outside Rangoon and plied with course after course of a traditional Burmese dinner. Late in the evening a messenger came with a note for one of the officers who then stood up and made an announcement.

The army had taken over the government, he said, and the prime minister and other officials with whom we had been negotiating were all in jail. We would be escorted back to our hotel where the army would like to have us remain until further notice.

The trip back into the city confirmed what we had been told. The army had indeed taken over and our hotel was surrounded. Apparently it was a quiet takeover — we heard only a scattering of small arms fire in the distance.

A couple of days later, we were allowed to leave. It was 25 years before the prime minister was released. Our mission was a failure.

The Beirut War Zone

For the past 20 years Beirut has endured long periods of active fighting, separated by short periods of relative quiet. Our last visit was during one of the quiet times before most of the city was reduced to rubble.

We were there to interview some bankers regarding the flow of Arab investment to the USA. Each bank was a little fortress, with concertina wire at the entrance and armed guards on each floor.

The offices had strange furniture layouts. Desks were in dark corners. File cabinets and bookshelves covered windows. Everything was laid out not for office efficiency, but to protect workers from sniper fire or stray bullets.

The protection for one key building struck us as being particularly odd. A 75-mm artillery piece was set up across the street and aimed directly at the front entrance. Maybe that discouraged anyone considering assaulting the building, but it didn't help my peace of mind while visiting there.

Most of the landmarks we knew are now gone. What was once the "oasis city" of the Middle East is now a place to avoid.

The rivalries and hatreds of the region are too old and complex for us to fathom. Will the combatants never learn to forgive, even if they cannot forget?

Bullet Holes in Central America

It was some years ago in one of the nations of Central America. We were meeting with an official in charge of siting some power projects. As he pointed out some locations on a big wall map, he paused to apologize for some rips in the map, explaining, "Several months ago a fellow came to the door over there and sprayed the room with automatic weapons fire — fortunately he didn't hit anybody."

We have not been back to that office.

Escape from Guatemala

When you fly your own airplane into some countries you tend to attract attention and sometimes to arouse suspicion. You get more scrutiny that the average visitor.

At various times we have been met by armed military personnel at airports in such locations as the Dominican Republic, Haiti, Venezuela and elsewhere in the region.

Once we filed a flight plan from El Salvador to Guatemala and were told our clearance would be delayed indefinitely. Having no explanation and needing to get back to the U.S., we filed a new plan to Mexico on an overwater route that skirted Guatemala completely.

Later we learned that a coup was underway in Guatemala and the deposed president was attempting to escape in an airplane similar to ours. Had we known that, we would have given Guatemala an even wider berth.

Coup Attempt at Nairobi

We went to Kenya for an interview with the minister of commerce and the head of the development bank. The next day we got on a southbound Swissair flight at the Nairobi airport about noon and departed for Johannesburg.

During the afternoon there was a bloody attempted coup in which several hundred people were killed. The shooting occurred in the office building we had visited, in the hotel where we had stayed and in the airport lounge where we had waited.

Most incidents are not so deadly. They simply remind that the business climate in some areas may be injurious to your health.

Bits and Pieces

If you travel around the world investigating investment opportunities and evaluating business climates, you meet an interesting variety of bureaucrats and politicians. We've met a few dozen heads of state, several hundred governors and legislators and countless officials at intermediate levels.

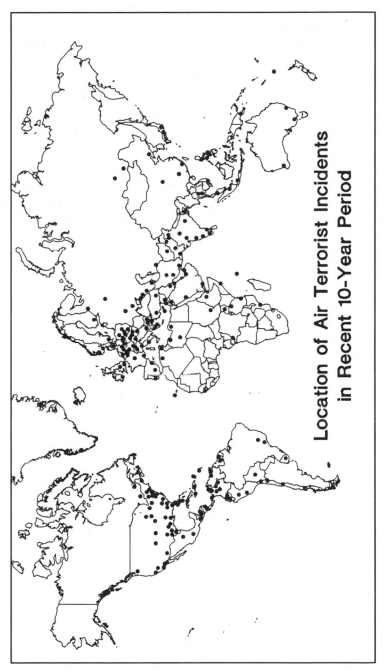

*Air terrorism incidents. Here is grim proof that air terrorism is a global problem.
These are locations of incidents during a recent 10-year period. This is why we
established the Safe Skies Award.*

We won't attempt to catalog contacts and issues. However, a few random experiences may be of interest.

• We served as a very minor aide at the UN charter session in San Francisco in the late 1940s. We remember that expectations were great but unrealistic. Today, the UN is the world's most embarrassing bureaucracy.

• During the height of the cold war we received better cooperation from Soviet officials in Irkutsk, Siberia, than we did from U.S. officials handling Antarctica.

• We had an interesting session with the president of Senegal and toured his free port zone. This is a small ray of hope in West Africa.

• We had a finger in the first technical services act passed by the U.S. Congress. Somewhere in a safe deposit box we have the pen President Johnson gave us after the signing ceremony in the East Room at the White House.

What, Specifically, to Do about It?

We have been studying and reporting legislative climates for several decades. We did a book (*Legislative Climates for Economic Development*) in 1979 and since then have continued to conduct and publish an annual survey.

These surveys reflect the status of legislating for the purpose of generating economic development. Inevitably, they raise such questions as, "How can government be made better?"

The basic problem lies not with elected officials but with the people who elect them — the voters. We pointed this out in 1976 ("The Problem Voter") and in subsequent follow-ups.

It is axiomatic that the quality of government is related to the quality of the electorate. Improvement can come only by enhancing the thinking of those who vote.

Getting more people to vote is not the answer. In fact, herding unthinking people to the polls is self-defeating.

How can the electorate be encouraged to think? We believe a national referendum which we proposed in 1985 would be of tremendous help.

Let's start there!

B. Excerpts

1962	"A Challenge We Must Accept," *Area Digest*,
Excerpt	Summer 1962.

The world today is a battleground of ideas. One great group of nations believes that a capitalistic enterprise system can produce the greatest benefits for the greatest number of people. The opposing Communist nations advocate a basically different approach to satisfying the needs and aspirations of the people of the world.

In the middle, still another group of nations wavers between the opposing ideologies. During the next decade, millions of people may shift their allegiance to one system or the other. The course of world history hangs in the balance.

How best can the free nations advocate their principles throughout the world? Realistic men believe that the capitalistic system must be *successfully demonstrated*. Talk is not enough! In specific situations, and on a wide scale, the enterprise system must be proven to be an effective approach to the problems of *today* and *tomorrow*.

In the period since World War II we have seen the rapid emergence of a new professional art or science: organized industrial and area development. This concept has spread rapidly into many other nations and today is truly international in scope. In effect, this is the science of building a strong base under a democratic society.

We can think of no higher calling than a career devoted to this new science. It is worthy of the best of all of us.

1979
Excerpt

Legislative Climates for Economic Development. Climates around the world. The 50 legislative climates of the U.S. The political process. Jimmy Carter as an architect of legislative climate. Future trends in legislating for development. Appendix covering incentives at national, state, local levels. 391 pp. 1979.

Most often, we use legislative climate to refer to legislative programs aimed specifically at encouraging and/or regulating economic development. Most important of these are special incentives, such as tax exemptions, financing and technical services designed to attract investment to a specific jurisdiction. In using these terms, we have not always been consistent!

It is important to recognize from the outset that at any given geographic location there may be several legislative climates, each a product of a tier of government. There are national programs in most countries — these are the prime shapers of the legislative climates that dominate international competition.

Within many nations, there are legislative programs that vary from province to province or state to state, setting up the ground rules for com-

FINANCIAL ASSISTANCE FOR INDUSTRY

	State Sponsored Industrial Development Authority	Privately Sponsored Development Credit Corporation	State Authority or Agency Revenue Bond Financing	State Authority or Agency General Obligation Bond Financing	City and/or County Revenue Bond Financing	City and/or County General Obligation Bond Financing	State Loans for Building Construction	State Loans for Equipment, Machinery	City and/or County Loans For Building Construction	City and/or County Loans For Equipment, Machinery	State Loan Guarantees For Building Construction	State Loan Guarantees For Equipment, Machinery	City and/or County Loan Guarantees for Building Construction	City and/or County Loan Guarantees for Equipment, Machinery	State Financing Aid for Existing Plant Expansions	State Matching Funds For City and/or County Industrial Financing Programs	State Funds for City and/or County Development-Related Public Works	State Authorized to Issue Industrial Revenue Bonds Under IRS 63-20
Alabama	●				●	● 1									7		● †	
Alaska	● *	● *	●	●	● 2	● 2	●	●							●		●	
Arizona		●																
Arkansas	● †	● †	● *		●	●												
California																	● †	
Colorado		●			● *													
Connecticut	●	●					●	●			●	●			●	●		
Delaware	●		●	●			● †	● †			● †	● †			●		● †	● †
Florida	●	●			3													
Georgia					●													
Hawaii	●	●			●	●	●	●			●	●			●	●	●	
Idaho		●																
Illinois		●			4 ● *												●	●
Indiana	●	●	● 5	●	●	●					●	●					●	●
Iowa		● †			● 6													
Kansas		●			●										7			
Kentucky	●	●			●	●	●	●							●			
Louisiana					●	●									7		●	●
Maine	●	● †	● †		● †						● †	● †			● †			
Maryland	●	●			●	●					●	●			●	● 8	●	
Massachusetts		●	9		● 1											● †	●	
Michigan					●													●
Minnesota	●	●			10 ● *		● 11	● 11							●		● †	
Mississippi	●	●			●	●									7			
Missouri		● 12			●	●												
Montana	● †				●													
Nebraska	●	●			●										7			● †
Nevada					● *													
New Hampshire	●	●	●				●				●	●			●		●	●
New Jersey		●															●	
New Mexico	● *		●		●		● *	● *	●	●							●	●
New York	●	●	13	13			●								●		● †	
North Carolina	●	●	● *		13												● *	●
North Dakota		●		●	●	●		●	●	●	●	●	●	●		●	●	●
Ohio	●	● †	●		● *	● †	● †	● †	● †	● †	●	●			●		●	● *
Oklahoma**	● †		● †	● †	● †	● †	● †		● †	● †					● †	● †	● †	
Oregon		●	15 ● *														●	●
Pennsylvania	●	●			● *		●		●						●	●	●	
Rhode Island	● †	●	●		● *						●	●			●			
South Carolina	● †				● *			● †	● †	● †							●	● †
South Dakota	● †	●			●													
Tennessee		●			● 14	● 14									7			
Texas					● *										● *			● †
Utah	●	●	●	●	● *	●												● *
Vermont	● *	● †			●		●	● †			●	●			● †			
Virginia	● †	●			●						● 10						●	●
Washington	●	●			15 ● †	15 ● †									7		●	
West Virginia	●				●		●	●							●			
Wisconsin		●			● 16	● 17			● 16	● 16					7		● 16	
Wyoming	● †	●			●												●	
STATE TOTALS	31	37	13	6	39	17	14	12	7	6	12	11	1	1	17	7	26	16

*Indicates incentive or assistance legislation was enacted in 1967 session.

**Indicates state did not respond to request for information. Data taken from a previous issue of Industrial Development.

†Indicates legislation previously reported but not submitted in the state's current report to Industrial Development.

1—Permitted only in specified municipalities.
2—Permitted by the Anchorage Port Authority.
3—A Constitutional amendment has been proposed to allow revenue bond financing.
4—Amendment to make enabling legislation effective is pending.
5—Indiana courts ruled revenue bond financing legal in 1967.
6—The 1967 Iowa Legislature authorized municipalities to pass revenue bond proposals without a local election and eliminated the dollar limits formerly placed on bond issues.
7—State allows city or county to offer financial aid for existing plant expansions.
8—In EDA designated areas State may match local government participation.
9—Legislature currently considering revenue bond financing.
10—Statute enacted but has yet to be tested in court.
11—Applicable in EDA-ARA-designated areas.
12—Legislation permits activity, but law not currently in operation.
13—Applicable only to public improvement projects; excludes private industrial projects.
14—Also accomplished through local industrial development corporations.
15—Responsibility is vested in Public Port Authorities rather than in cities and counties.
16—County Industrial Development Corporations inactive in bond financing, pending favorable IRS ruling.
17—Authorized for purchase of industrial land.

A "dot" chart. This is one of our infamous dot charts from the 1960s. Some 30 years ago we began making an annual survey of incentives offered by states in the USA. During the past decade we have also made similar surveys of incentives offered by nations around the world.

petition among the states or provinces. And, there are, of course, still other legislative programs put forward by local jurisdictions, such as cities and counties.

Wherever these multiple tiers of activity exist, they tend to become interactive. In fact, many national programs are planned to relate to state and/or local programs. This leads to a complex web of legislative climates in some areas.

It should also be stressed that legislative climates change constantly. Positive changes — that is, improvements in the climate — tend to occur slowly. Large negative changes, conversely, can occur with one hasty, impulsive act of a legislative body.

A good legislative climate for development is indeed a very fragile thing. It takes years to build but can be destroyed overnight. Rebuilding after a destructive action can take even longer than the original building effort.

For this reason, it is necessary in evaluating the legislative climate of an area to examine it over a span of years.

Legislative Incentives around the World

Even the most casual scan of the world's family of nations reveals striking variations in level of development. At any point in time, outside investment or some other index of success may be zooming to a new high in one nation, while stagnation or decline occurs in a neighboring state.

There are many explanations: some nations have great natural resources, a location near large markets or a strategic situation which minimizes threats to national security. Others are scraps of arid land sandwiched between belligerent neighbors in remote regions.

But no matter what competitive situation a country may have inherited, there are man-made factors which play a significant part in the equation for development success. We referred to this earlier in a study of developing areas.

Their Own Worst Enemy

In our visits to underdeveloped nations we have consistently asked local officials to tell us what, in their opinion, constituted the greatest obstacle to economic growth. Invariably, we have been told that the country we were visiting had failed to develop because of three main factors: the evils of outside economic domination, a lack of capital and a shortage of trained manpower.

It is increasingly obvious that this is a dangerous fallacy. In recent years a number of countries have been freed from outside economic influences, have been given large amounts of capital, have been provided with an impressive variety of technical personnel and still have failed miserably to show satisfactory progress.

From first-hand observation we can quickly list many other factors — all within the control of the emerging nation — which are often permitted to stifle development:

1. Personal ambition — leaders put their egos ahead of economics;

2. Blind nationalism — officials insist on such extravagances as their own flag airlines, shipping lines, etc.;

3. Corruption — selling of import/export licenses, trading in exchange allocations, plain bribery;

4. Lack of law and order — failure to guarantee safety of travel and to control banditry in rural areas where mining, forestry and other activities must be conducted;

5. Unsound politico-economic concepts — excessive regulation, fear of outside investment and general lack of appreciation of the private business sector;

6. Lack of government stability — one coup follows another.

Until the new nations learn to cope with these situations, they are going to continue to waste most of the capital and technical information supplied to them. For many, the greatest lesson they can learn from us is not the technique for investing capital and applying technology but the self-discipline which produces a stable government and a sound community structure.

Some small nations in remote areas lack the leadership in their early days to cope with such problems. Most, however, come soon to the realization that broad business climate issues must be confronted.

This confrontation often follows a familiar three-stage pattern. In the first stage, the unsophisticated leaders of the new nation, often a product of socialist or communist political conditioning, look upon business and industry with great distrust. They have been taught to think that private enterprise is evil, that all corporations are corrupt and that there are a host of huge multi-national firms waiting to pounce on their new nation with economic rape and plunder in mind.

Thus, the attitude in Stage I is defensive. The new nation hastens to enact laws to defend itself against the straw men its leaders have heard about from their socialist mentors. This continues for several years during which the defensive mechanism works perfectly — few significant investors show any interest in the new nation with its negative business climate.

During this time, consternation grows among the leaders of the new country. Where are all the greedy corrupt capitalists who were sure to come? Suspicion begins to grow that the minister of development, who has been attending seminars elsewhere, might be correct in advising a more moderate policy.

A decision is made. Enter Stage II! The new nation will, indeed, change its policy. It will announce that certain very carefully selected new industries will be accepted if they meet all conditions of a new investment law. The announcement is made with considerable fanfare, and the government sits back to interview the applicants who will now rush forward.

Nothing much happens. There are a few casual inquiries, but there is still no real interest from substantial investors. Several more years pass, while the leaders gain more knowledge and experience and the development department observes the activities of their opposite numbers in successful nations.

Finally, the realization comes that being willing to accept new economic development is by no means good enough. Scores of nations are not only willing to accept but they are also exerting every conceivable effort to promote investment.

At last committed to a realistic development policy (Stage III), the new nation finds itself a rookie playing in the major leagues. Competition is unbelievably tough. Many other nations have years of experience and skilled professionals.

The Political Process: An Insider's View

While the primary purpose of this study is to look at legislative climate-making from the viewpoint of the corporate facility planner and area development strategist, it may also be helpful to look briefly at the inner workings of a legislative body and the reactions of an individual legislator. After all, it is individual legislators, working within the legislative system, who enact the laws which condition the climate.

Atlanta: Ideological Epicenter?

For one who wished to observe changes in economic development and political thinking, there has been no better vantage point than Atlanta during the years since World War II. For reasons we will not attempt to fathom here, the area has been the launching pad for programs, personalities and philosophies that have captured the attention of the nation.

Many Americans may not yet be aware of the extent to which widely recognized leaders of differing philosophies grew up and worked in the same orbit. There may well have been a crowd at a ball game in Atlanta that included as spectators Martin Luther King, Lester Maddox and another dozen men destined to become nationally known political figures.

At one time, for example, Jimmy Carter, George Wallace and John

Birch lived within a 100-mile circle. Somehow, during this generation the Southeastern "epicenter" seems to have been involved in an inordinate proportion of key situations.

I grew up in this environment, and, while we usually minimize first-person material in research studies, the temptation to include some personal experiences here has been too much to resist.

When I was about 10 years old my family was living in Montgomery, Alabama, and my Aunt Mary Conway's brother, I.J. Browder, was a member of the Alabama Senate. I recall his asking me if I would like to serve as a page. I agreed, and he took me to the Capitol one day to do some campaigning. At the time, pages were chosen on a roll call vote from a list of those nominated by various Senators.

After a busy day, it seemed to me I had been introduced to every Senator and, without exception, each one assured me of his support. The next day I sat in the gallery, waiting for the roll call vote to confirm my election. I was absolutely unprepared for the shock that came when one Senator after another failed to vote for me. When the tally was complete, I had fallen several votes short of election and had learned my first political lesson.

Soon after, my family moved to Atlanta, and I forgot about the incident. It was many years later that I learned that one of the pages elected in Montgomery was a lad named George Corley Wallace who subsequently became a State Senator with an interest in industrial development, then became Governor and later ran for President.

During the 1950s I found myself serving as director of a regional research organization called the Southern Association of Science and Industry (SASI). This afforded me an opportunity for some years to work with the governors of the 16 states extending from Maryland through Texas and to gain some insight into the relationship between legislative programs and industrial development.

I remember well one year when Governor Faubus of Arkansas was serving as chairman of the Industrial Development Committee. At breakfast one morning he and I were going over a committee report when news came of the dispatch of federal troops to Central High in Little Rock. He left to cope with the crisis and to become a national figure.

The regional development program was overshadowed; I went back to research.

It was in this tumultuous era that I launched the journal *Industrial Development* and the reference book *Site Selection Handbook*. There appeared to be a real need for documentation of facts relative to economic development in an objective, non-political way, on a nationwide basis. As the years unfolded, these publications devoted increasing space to legislative climates.

Reapportionment: One Man, One Vote

By the time the 1960s dawned, a key issue in many parts of the nation was the steady disenfranchisement of voters in metro areas, as population moved in but legislative seats remained in the rural areas. The Georgia system, involving a "county unit" system, was notoriously inequitable — one voter in a small South Georgia county might have as much voice as 1,500 voters in Atlanta.

These conditions led to a series of historic court cases. The first pivotal ruling came in the now famous *Baker vs. Carr* decision of the Supreme Court in early 1962. There followed a battle in federal district court in Atlanta to require the reapportionment of the Georgia General Assembly.

In order to support this effort, I decided to be a political guinea pig and became a candidate for the State Senate. The newspapers said I was running for a seat that did not exist, and I suppose they were right at the time.

Here are the facts: Georgia then allocated Senate seats to groups of three counties and the counties took turns electing a Senator. My county, DeKalb, was in a three-county district with Gwinnett and Rockdale. According to the rotation plan, DeKalb would not elect a Senator in 1962.

It was my argument that the citizens of DeKalb County were thus disenfranchised — they had no voice in selecting a Senator. Therefore, I challenged the rotation plan, paid the entrance fee and became a candidate in the race for the Senate. My attorney, Ross Arnold, filed an intervention in the federal court case.

Judge Griffin Bell, later to become Attorney General in the Carter Administration, referring to me, said, "He was a sort of seer." The court ruling on the case was favorable, reapportionment was ordered, and the Georgia Senate became the nation's testing ground for the new political order.

When the Georgia Senate convened in January 1963, the national media representatives were here in force to record the historic event. Of the 54 members, 32 were new. Greatest attention was centered on Senator-elect Leroy Johnson, first black to be elected to the Georgia General Assembly since Reconstruction days.

As was customary, new Senators were sworn in in small groups. The first group included Senator-elect Johnson, several others and myself. We stepped forward, placed our hands on the Bible and took the oath of office. All cameras zoomed in on Senator Johnson.

Several groups later, the Senator-elect from the 14th district moved forward to take the oath, but the news photographers showed no interest. He was a peanut farmer and warehouseman from Plains named Jimmy Carter.

The Senate of '63

The swearing-in ceremonies that cold January day in 1963 marked the beginning of guaranteed one-man, one-vote legislative bodies throughout the nation. Subsequent reapportionments were destined to shake up a majority of the city councils, county commissions, state legislatures and the national Congress in the years just ahead.

In fact, it was Jim Wesberry, taking his seat that day in the Georgia Senate, who brought the next landmark case, *Wesberry vs. Sanders* before the U.S. Supreme Court, producing the decision in February 1964, which required one-man, one-vote reapportionment of the U.S. House of Representatives. The "Sanders" in this case was Carl Sanders, who moved from president pro tem of the 1962 Georgia Senate to the governor's office in 1963.

It would be a mistake to suggest that the members of the Senate of '63 were obsessed with the reapportionment issue. It would continue to arise in legislative debates for years — some members were, of course, bitterly opposed. But other issues would receive the bulk of the attention of the new Senate.

For one thing, the new body included a number of outstanding men who were there to get things done. For another, they assumed their responsibilities in a time of national tumult and change.

Some were businessmen: among them J.B. Fuqua who now heads the conglomerate, Fuqua Industries, and Brooks Pennington, who heads an international agri-business ("Pennington Green" seed, etc). Others were outstanding attorneys such as Robert Smalley, the parliamentary expert, and Ben Johnson, then Dean of the Emory University Law School; Senator Leroy Johnson, who was the promoter of Muhammed Ali's first comeback fight in Atlanta, and now is Ali's partner in an import-export business. Another was a research scientist from NACA/NASA (me).

Many moved on to key government posts. These included Zell Miller, who became Lt. Governor (and later Governor), several judges, a public service commissioner and a regent of the university system. A few still serve in the Senate, where they chair key committees and, of course, there was the member who later lived on Pennsylvania Avenue.

Of the 54 members, some 44 had college training and nearly a dozen had more than one degree. Most had attended the University of Georgia, but there were several Georgia Tech graduates, as well as alumni of Princeton, Harvard, Emory, Duke, Baylor and Mercer. There was one from the U.S. Military Academy and another from the U.S. Naval Academy.

When we took office, the Georgia House across the corridor had not yet been reapportioned. Thus, we had one "new" legislative body and one traditional house. Members of the Senate were definitely on trial and we knew it. There was a strong feeling that we would try to set standards not only in our decorum in the Senate Chamber (remove the spittoons, ban booze, discourage newspaper reading and other distractions during speeches. etc.) but also in the level of legislative responsibility.

Whatever the motivation, the Senate of '63 showed no hesitation in tackling new and difficult issues.

First issue was a "minimum foundation plan" for education, which set a base for financing public education in the state. It required local jurisdictions which had been lax in tax collections to adopt reforms so that taxpayers throughout the state would pay their fair share — one of those tough but necessary fights. We voted for education!

With a Senate rule book in one hand and a calendar in the other, the new Senate tackled a variety of other pieces of legislation. Much of it was routine, as is unavoidable, but there were such noteworthy items as authorization of punch-card, computer-counted voting procedures, launching of a new science and technology program, authorization of a constitutional referendum on the creation of an Atlanta metro rapid transit system and passage of the first open meetings, or "sunshine," bill.

Even so, the forward thrust provided by the new Senate of '63 could be seen for some years. I saw this in the 1967-68 Senate, when I served a second term. This was the legislature that had as its first duty the election of a governor, because the election of November 1966 had failed to give a clear majority to either candidate (a write-in campaign for former Governor Arnall diverted just enough votes to prevent a decisive vote).

The Republican candidate was Howard "Bo" Callaway, later to be Secretary of the Army, and the Democrat (victor over Jimmy Carter in the primary) was Lester Maddox, the Atlantan who had fought desegregation of his restaurant. Most of the members of both the House and Senate were Democrats.

This was one crucial vote from which there would be no escape. Cameras of the major networks focused on the proceedings as the roll call vote took place. History records that Lester Maddox won by a comfortable margin. Often overlooked, however, is the fact that members of the Senate gave a majority to Callaway.

(I have wondered how Jimmy Carter would have voted had he been a member of the Senate that day. Both Callaway and Maddox were his bitter rivals. As a strong party man, would Jimmy have been able to vote for Maddox? Or, would he have found it easier to support West Point graduate Callaway, whom he almost challenged for a Congressional seat?)

It is also of interest to note that most of the members of the Senate kept hands off when the controversy erupted in the House of Representatives over the seating of Julian Bond. (He had made some inflammatory remarks about the war in Viet Nam which many members considered to be treasonable, and he was not seated until a court order was issued.)

I recall that in the year after being seated, Representative Bond had one of the worst attendance records in the General Assembly. (He was much in demand for speaking engagements throughout the nation.) During the time our legislative service overlapped, I never got to know him.

In fairness, it must be said that as governor, Lester Maddox made a special effort to promote economc development. He listened to professional advisors, and his administration had a good record in this regard.

Adventures of an R&D Man in the Legislative Lab

I recall being told by an official of the Council of State Governments that I was the first state legislator to come from a scientific research laboratory background. Whether that was correct I don't know, but I did get a number of questions regarding my combination of interests, and on one occasion a delegation came down from Washington to interview me for a study being done by the Commerce Department.

It took only one session in the Senate for me to discover that there was a basic difference in the way scientists and politicians approach problems. The scientist attempts to go from point A to point B via the direct, airline route. The politician goes by way of point C and perhaps arrives at an alternate destination, point D. This is evidenced in every facet of law-making.

From an administrative viewpoint, therefore, legislative bodies are very cumbersome and inefficient organizations. I soon discovered that there were few Senate rules for expediting the movement of legislation and many for slowing it up. Moreover, the rules were contrived to give several key members, plus the presiding officer, great influence, while making it more difficult for the average member to be effective.

A case in point is the committee structure which, by permitting appointment of each Senator to several committees, promotes chaos when committees meet simultaneously or attempt to prepare bills for the same calendar. In a scientific organization, the manager would take one look at the situation, assign each senator to one committee, allocate proposed legislation to the committees to achieve a balanced workload, put everybody to work on a schedule, and produce better legislation at less cost.

A similar frustration was readily apparent in the scheduling of floor action on bills and resolutions. During the first few weeks of the session, we had a very light agenda. Many days we convened at 10 a.m. and finished at noon, with only an occasional committee session in the afternoon.

Toward the end of the session there was an incredible logjam of legislation — perhaps 1,000 bills waiting for action as we sat through long days and many evenings, while frantically calling quickie committee meetings in the hallway, the snack bar or even in the men's room.

A group of us, all new Senators in our first session, were appalled by the system we saw and began asking about making improvements. These ideas were given lip-service approval by some of the old hands, but specific resolutions proposing rule changes somehow got bogged down in the Rules Committee.

Later, we discovered what the real problem was. The confusion in the committees and the crush of legislative backlog at the end of each session provided a cover for pushing pet bills through the legislative mill and for side-tracking bills considered undesirable. During the last few days of each session, the discretion of the Rules Committee or presiding officer in putting a bill on the calendar for consideration by the Senate became a life-or-death decision for a bill.

These are just a few of the reasons that it is impossible for an unskilled observer to evaluate prospects for passage of a piece of controversial raw legislation by a legislative body. It is necessary to know the people involved, their positions and the rules of procedure.

1986
Excerpt

"The Problem Voter." *Site Selection.*
Oct. 1986. p. 980.

To many analysts, the biggest threat to our nation is not international communism. Neither is it the monstrous federal bureaucracy or the budget deficit. The most dangerous plague — which afflicts every jurisdiction — is the cadre of problem voters who make up a large percentage of the electorate.

Who are these people who are undermining our society?

They are businessmen, environmentalists, farmers, workers and little old ladies in tennis shoes — and sometimes you and me. How can they be identified? Here are some types frequently observed:

• *Ethnic Voters*. These are citizens who cast their ballots on the basis of race, creed or color in direct defiance of the tenets of the U.S. Constitution. In effect, they say they would prefer an incompetent office holder of their own kind to an able public servant of another kind.

What better way to guarantee bad government!

• *Straight-Ticket Voters*. This is another large group which clings to the unrealistic notion that all Democrats are better than all Republicans, or vice versa. By failing to select the best candidates of each party, they assure that some outstanding public servants will be thrown out and be replaced by less able party hacks.

• *Label Voters*. This group finds it necessary to tag each candidate with a "liberal," "conservative" or some other brand which they think permits instantaneous identification of friend or foe. They often accept second-hand labels from partisan groups. These voters apparently are too lazy to gather enough specific data about candidates to make a sound evaluation of their own.

• *Image Voters*. This group evidently believes that all office holders should be well-educated young professional men, clean-shaven, standing at least six feet, weighing a trim but muscular 180 pounds, displaying two perfect rows of teeth and exuding a charming TV personality somewhere between Johnny Carson and Marcus Welby. These voters seemingly will vote for the village idiot if he meets their superficial criteria.

• *Male (and Female) Chauvinist Voters*. This bloc includes women libbers who will vote only for a female candidate and male chauvinists who will never vote for a female candidate no matter how capable she may be.

• *Special-Interest Voters*. No group of problem voters does more damage to the public interest than these selfish citizens who vote for a candidate simply because he has done them a favor or promises to do so. Where is the integrity of those who will send a wastrel to Washington to promote a federal spending program for their special benefit, even though they know that the program is an unnecessary burden on the taxpayers? Where is the honesty of the voter who will elect an incompetent to the state assembly in return for his promise to vote for a special bill, or a scoundrel to the county government in trade for a zoning decision?

• *Identity Voters*. There are a surprising number of voters who must, above all else, identify personally with the candidate of their choice. A candidate having the same family name is an instant choice. Next best are candidates from the same geographic area, graduates of the same kind of school, members of the same fraternity, followers of the same sports or keepers of the same kind of pets. What a strange and narrow view!

• *Superstition Voters*. These voters may immediately be attracted, for example, to the lucky candidate who happens to be number seven on the ballot. Others attach significance to where the candidates name falls in the alphabet or how many syllables there are in the last name. Others will not vote for a man who is left-handed. Signs of the zodiac are probably the biggest influence with this group, with much significance being given to time of birth, time of the election and time of crucial campaign events.

• *Anti-Incumbent Voters*. There are surprising numbers of voters who vote against all incumbents. This cynical voter actually believes that all politicians are crooks, and the longer they stay in office the worse they get. At every election he wants to throw out all experienced people and bring in fresh material. In effect, this voter favors on-the-job training for governor, senator and other high officials.

• *Winning-Side Voters*. A number of voters somehow believe that it is humiliating to vote for a loser. They go to great lengths to be on the winning side, no matter who the candidates are or what the issues are. These are the voters who can be stampeded by a well-orchestrated political bandwagon. They apparently are content to have someone do their thinking for them. When a poll shows a particular candidate is ahead, they may swing abruptly. Sheep!

• *Ego Voters*. All voters are human, and candidates know it. They know that a poor record in office or lack of qualifications may be ignored by voters distracted by personal contacts. Such voters cite as reasons they cast their ballots for a particular man "because he asked me," or "because he shook my hand," or "because he wrote me a letter." Conversely, these voters may vote against a man they know is better qualified because he didn't do any of these things. They, not the candidates, are the ones to blame for many of the absurd campaign tactics we see!

Voting is not an exact science. It is not intended to suggest here that if all voters did sufficient research and voted with total objectivity all would vote alike. There will always be differences of opinion between honest, well-informed people.

What is needed is a heroic citizen's movement for improving the performance of the electorate. When we minimize the number of problem voters, we'll enjoy the best and most efficient government.

1991 "Let The People Speak!"
Excerpt   Monograph. 1991.

There's an important flaw in our great American political system. Today, despite our elaborate communications systems, there is no effective way for the people to express their collective opinion clearly and emphatically on any specific political issue.

Neither our political campaigns nor our elections produce a clear expression of voter opinion on specific issues. Instead, they reflect the personalities of the candidates or the composite positions of the candidates on multiple issues. They do little to reveal how the majority of voters feels about any certain question.

Further, there is good reason to believe that Congress often acts contrary to the wishes of the majority.

For these reasons, many elections serve only to confuse issues, leaving voters filled with frustration.

While there are numerous private polls conducted to sample public opinion on various issues, they don't help to ease voter frustration. Such polls are usually sponsored by groups having an ax to grind and thus may lack credibility. In any event, they are unofficial and can be disregarded by those who choose to do so.

Also, there are referenda conducted from time to time in various states, counties and municipalities. These usually deal with local issues and, taken together, give only spotty coverage of public opinion across the country.

National Referendum

What we need — urgently — is an official nationwide referendum that places on record how the American people feel about a list of key issues.

We propose that such a referendum be held every four years at the same time as the presidential election. It would be an extension of our usual general election ballot.

The list of issues would be selected by a three-member committee of private citizens — one member selected by the President, one chosen by the Speaker of the House and the third picked by the Chief Justice of the U.S. Supreme Court. The panel would not include political officeholders, lobbyists or government employees.

(This kind of referendum is not to be confused with the initiative referenda held in California and other jurisdictions. Those are processes for enacting laws directly by the people without legislative committee study and floor debate.)

Our proposed advisory referendum would be non-binding. It would not change existing laws nor enact new ones.

With the cooperation of Congress, we could schedule a referendum as part of the next general election. However, that cooperation will be difficult to obtain.

Our proposal will meet with a storm of opposition from special-interest groups, which do not want the great silent majority to have a voice. Their interests would be threatened.

Many of these groups can bring enough pressure to bear on Congress to protect their special interests even though they cannot control the way the masses vote. The last thing they want is a national referendum.

Special-interest groups are so numerous and so powerful that they may keep Congress from scheduling a referendum.

As an alternate approach, we can go to state legislatures and seek a constitutional amendment providing for a referendum. That would take longer but might have a better chance. We would need a resolution approved by two-thirds of the state assemblies.

We'd like to see both approaches undertaken, starting immediately!

Would a referendum be worth the effort? We believe the answer is an emphatic yes!

A national referendum could give us, for the first time since the signing of the Declaration of Independence, a national agenda on which the majority agrees. It could be a powerful force for good.

We believe that results would be dramatic. In every Congressional district, we would have official, undisputed guidelines for what the people want.

A carefully prepared list of issues could constitute a national reform program aimed at correcting abuses of our system. It could be a virtual hit list for special-interest provisions that have been systematically embedded in our system over a period of several decades.

The referendum could raise highly controversial issues that elected politicians avoid like the plague. It might end some of the long-standing arguments that have divided the nation.

Exactly what kinds of questions? For the sake of discussion, we have made up a list of issues that would deal with a wide range of special interests. While controversial, these are precisely the kinds of bold propositions in which large numbers of frustrated Americans are interested.

These Americans observe that we have a government going deeper and deeper into debt, and they fear that some of our key agencies are bankrupt. They are convinced that our Congress no longer represents them, that our legal system has broken down, that our schools are turning out incompetents and, not surprisingly, that we as a nation are losing our position of world leadership.

Most distressing, many of our young people, who have never seen our system when it was running smoothly, are accepting the decline of performance as inevitable. Something must be done and quickly.

We believe the answer is the national referendum. Let the people speak!

Sample Issues

Here is a list of some 70 issues. A national referendum should probably not include more than 20 issues, possibly as few as 10. Which ones would you select? What other issues would you add?

Congressional Issues

• Require every vote in Congress to be a roll call vote with results immediately available to the public. (This is easy to do with electronic systems already available.)

• Eliminate the franking privilege. (Congressional newsletters tell only what Congressmen want their constituents to know.)

• Instead of pay increases for Congressmen, provide a substantial bonus in each year that the national budget is balanced.

• Eliminate the role of Congressmen as "ombudsmen" handling executive department details and close the offices in their districts. (Congressmen got along without local offices for nearly two centuries. The offices are even less needed in this era of cheap and easy travel and communications.)

• Make it illegal for unopposed candidates to receive campaign contributions.

• Set a limit on the amount that candidates can spend for their campaigns. For Congressmen, set a cap of $1 for each registered voter in their districts (not to exceed $200,000). For Senators, set a cap of 10 cents for each registered voter in their states (not to exceed $500,000). This would give us a Congress far less committed to special interests.

Fiscal Policy Issues

As a general principle, cut government programs back to those absolutely essential for public health and safety. (Leave to the private sector the responsibility for supporting, on a voluntary basis, such matters as poetry, sculpture, painting, other arts and social programs — generally those things that are nice to have but are not essential.)

• Give the President the authority to veto specific line items in the budget. (This is a practical way to control pork-barrel projects. Further, it may be the only way to achieve a balanced budget.)

• Privatize! Wherever possible, allow private firms to take over government services on a competitive basis. (Let private firms bid for the opportunity to deliver the mail, operate schools and airports and run jails, for example.)

• To the maximum extent possible, let individual citizens decide religious issues — such as abortion and gambling — for themselves. (Get the government out of our private lives and maximize individual freedom.)

• Set up a government-wide accounting system! Consolidate all giveaway, benefit, rent-subsidy, entitlement and welfare programs so we can determine how much each recipient gets and how much each costs the taxpayers.

• Require competitive bidding on all significant government contracts, especially those for military equipment, and award contracts to low bidders. (Eliminate expensive special provisions relative to whom contractors may hire or which subcontractors they must use.)

• Set up a business-like personnel administration program for all federal employees. (Reject the idea that federal jobs are a form of welfare. Select and hire employees solely on the basis of the government's need and the qualifications of applicants. Eliminate automatic annual salary increases.)

• Get rid of incompetent public servants. (Require each of the major government agencies at the cabinet level to terminate the five percent of their employees with the poorest performance ratings each year.)

• Standardize all government retirement plans. (Require the government pension plan to be actuarially sound in relation to what employees pay in. Eliminate automatic annual increases.)

• Phase out public housing. (In situations where groups of tenants have proven themselves to be responsible, permit them to buy the properties they occupy on liberal terms.)

• Turn over to private enterprise the disposal of surplus government property, with a percentage of the proceeds going to sales agents.

• Focus on the future and stop trying to correct wrongs of the distant past. (Terminate Native American programs, payments for Japanese-Americans put in camps during WWII, proposed "reparations" for former slaves, etc.)

Legal System Issues

• Stop insisting on perfection in the judicial process. (It is absurd to insist that every trial process be perfect and, if it is not, to set criminals free. Apply common sense in permitting appeals and new trials. Also, set a time limit.)

• Disqualify practicing attorneys from holding legislative offices. Enforce the constitutional delineation of the three branches of government — executive, judicial, legislative — which was conceived as a system of checks and balances. (At present, lawyers, who are a part of the judicial system, dominate our legislative bodies, making it difficult or impossible to enact legal reforms. Drop the notion that the legal profession, the medical profession or any other professional group is capable of policing itself.)

• Eliminate life terms and other forms of tenure for judges.

• Abolish plea bargaining. Stop trading with criminals and letting the guilty go free.

• Before every trial, require the court to inform the jury of its right to judge both the facts and the law.

Business and Farm Policy Issues

• In general, promote competition to achieve efficiency! (This means allowing states to compete with each other, allowing cities and counties to compete with each other, and, of course, allowing private firms and individuals to compete with each other.)

• Eliminate the Small Business Administration. (The success of small businesses is inversely proportional to the amount of advice and support received from the government. The only real help government can give is to get out of the way and leave small businesses alone — for example, by exempting them from filling out forms.)

• Eliminate the Economic Development Administration. (This agency has a dismal record, proving once again that private investors can make better investment decisions than Washington bureaucrats.)

• Eliminate government-run job training programs and turn the responsibility over to private enterprise. (Offer incentives to employers who will accept the responsibility for training and who are willing to share costs.)

• Recognize that farming is a business and treat it as such. (From the standpoint of taxes, subsidies, market guarantees and other regulations or benefits, treat all types of businesses alike.)

• Phase out farm subsidies starting now and achieve complete elimination by the year 2000. (Start with the commodity programs, which promote bad conservation and agricultural practices. Stop paying people not to produce.)

• Stop telling firms whom they can hire. (All efforts to do so defeat the private enterprise system.)

• Enact a law that causes labor unions to lose their charters unless they devote most of their resources to such positive programs as increasing productivity, enhancing the environment, conserving resources and otherwise improving the global competitive position of the USA.

• Revamp the tax laws to support and reward those working to achieve such national goals as improving global competitiveness. (The present system is filled with disincentives, which inhibit our ablest producers and entrepreneurs — for example, the way we handle depreciation.)

Education Issues

• Install uniform progress tests throughout all public school systems from bottom grade to top. (Prepared and monitored by independent outside experts, these tests will serve as a first measure of the performance of the schools. Eliminate such ego programs as a state "achievement test," in which 35 percent of students are ranked in the upper 10 percent.)

• Give all high school seniors a special test to determine whether they have the basic reading, writing and arithmetic skills necessary to enter the work force — as determined by a panel of employers. Do not award a diploma to anyone not certified as ready.

• Measure the performance of teachers against the progress of their students and demote or terminate teachers with poor records.

• Eliminate "union" requirements for teachers. (Remove the need for teachers of math and other technical subjects to obtain certificates based on college courses in education theory.)

• Encourage public and private schools to compete! (Give tuition credits and permit students to go to the schools of their choice.)

• Eliminate busing of schoolchildren to other than the nearest schools to achieve social balance. (This failed social experiment is expensive, contributes to traffic problems, disrupts families, and, worst of all, inflicts hardships on children unable to defend themselves.)

• Eliminate tenure in government-aided university systems. (As in private industry, require all staff members to meet performance standards every year in order to keep their jobs. Demote or terminate those who fail.)

• Abolish the college loan program now costing $2 billion per year in defaults — cumulative losses $8 billion — and install a new plan wherein students go to school one term and work the next — like the very successful coop plans available at many schools already. (The free-loaders and incompetents would be dropped the first year. Those who stayed would be encouraged to focus on subject areas in which there are realistic job opportunities.)

• National service. Require all able-bodied men and women between the ages of 18 and 25 to contribute a year of national service. (This would be in the form of military training, except for conscientious objectors, who would receive training in health care or serve in such programs as the Peace Corps or Vista.)

• Require all school systems to teach basic principles of the American enterprise system beginning in the first grade.

Crime and Punishment Issues

• In those states where the death penalty is authorized, make it mandatory to carry out executions within a year of convictions. (It is absurd to permit our worst criminals to delay their punishment from five to 10 years through frivolous or technical appeals.)

• Have every criminal trial serve also as a civil trial. (Thus, when a criminal is convicted, require the court to award realistic damages to the victim.)

• Stop releasing criminals from prison because a judge somewhere decides that if a felon does not have a cell measuring a certain number of square feet his punishment is "cruel and unusual." (Go back to the origin of that constitutional provision, which was intended to ban beatings and torture. At the time the phrase was written, it was not considered cruel and unusual to lock criminals up in crowded, unsanitary facilities lacking such comforts as central heat, air-conditioning, radio, telephone and TV. In fact, it was not unusual to cut off the ears, slit the nose or brand the cheek of a criminal. Public flogging was common, and even minor miscreants were put in stocks.)

• Separate our prisons into categories based on how dangerous various prisoners are to society. Assign the worst prisoners to the crudest facilities built at minimum cost in remote locations.

• Require all law-enforcement agencies and courts to belong to a nationwide electronic database and communications network. (Require all convictions to be entered promptly and according to a uniform format so that those who commit crimes in more than one jurisdiction are easily identified. Make all conviction records open to the public.)

• Get habitual drunk drivers off the roads. After three convictions for drunk driving, make the next offense a federal crime with a mandatory jail sentence. Also, make it a felony for any official to thwart application of this punishment by manipulation of records or other action.)

• In all cases, make juries aware of previous convictions and jail records of those on trial.

• When felons are scheduled to be released, notify their victims 30 days in advance.

• When felons are released after serving their terms, set up schedules requiring them to repay the government for the cost of their trials and imprisonment. Until that debt is repaid, keep them on probation and deny them full civil rights. (When criminals serve out their terms, they have not "paid their debt to society." The taxpayers have paid!)

• In all cases, give the benefit of the doubt to law-abiding citizens when they act to protect their homes, families and businesses. (Shooting an intruder should not be considered a crime.)

• Abolish the notion that convicted felons should enjoy full civil rights. (These are people who have shown their contempt for law and order.)

• Hold officials of savings and loans, banks and other institutions that administer government-guaranteed investment programs personally responsible for failures, with criminal punishment mandatory where there is the slightest impropriety in the handling of money.

Population Policy Issues

• Enact a national population policy. (Recognize that many national problems, such as environmental protection, land-use and zoning, housing, traffic control and waste disposal are directly related to a population policy or lack of it.)

• Restrict immigration to those who can contribute substantially to the U.S. economy as investors or technical specialists. (Stop importing welfare cases, some with welfare application forms already filled out.)

• Cut the total annual immigration quota from the present level of more than 500,000 to less than 50,000. (We no longer need immigrants to

332

populate the states west of the Alleghenies.)

• Confirm English as the official U.S. language. (Require competency in English for entry into the U.S.)

• Recognize illegal aliens as criminals not entitled to civil rights.

• Provide adequate funding and support for birth control programs, especially among those on welfare. (On a voluntary basis, provide them with free operations to prevent further pregnancies.)

Environmental Issues

• Provide substantial financial incentives for those who enhance or provide special protection for the natural environment. (Make it financially attractive to landowners to reserve greenbelts in and around cities, protect native plant colonies and wetlands and restore habitats.)

Prosecute those who press the panic button for personal gain or notoriety and cause major disruptions without real cause. (An example is the "Alar" false alarm, which was amplified by publicity-seeking Hollywood stars and cost apple growers millions of dollars.)

• Require recycling of such major trash components as glass, aluminum cans and paper. (Stockpile those items for which there is currently no adequate processing capacity.)

• Require a cost-benefit analysis before any air and/or water pollution control legislation is enacted. (Eliminate unrealistic standards that require purity of the air or water far beyond what is found in nature.)

World Affairs Issues

• Insist that the United Nations be reorganized or scrapped in favor of a new world organization. (Eliminate voting memberships for nations unable to sustain themselves or govern themselves democratically. Require small nations to form blocs having a population comparable to large nations, with the bloc having one vote.)

• Separate foreign aid programs into three types: military, economic and emergency disaster relief. Confine military aid to improving our national security and use economic aid only to improve our global business competitiveness. Give disaster aid solely on a humanitarian basis for immediate assistance following such disasters as earthquakes and volcanic eruptions.

• Eliminate all foreign aid programs intended to buy friends — always an exercise in futility.

• Eliminate aid to Israel, Egypt and other Middle East nations until they arrive at a peace treaty and demonstrate that they can abide by it. Specify that the treaty must recognize a homeland for the Palestinians.

Conclusion

Looking over this list, most experienced politicians will quickly say that arranging such a referendum is impossible. Special interest groups will rise up to fight it with every ounce of strength they can muster. They do not want the majority to be heard.

In response, we must find some leaders who really mean it when they ask not what our country can do for them but what they can do for our country.

We need to recruit some one-term "kamikaze Congressmen" who are willing to sacrifice their political ambitions for their country. (For example, find a courageous Jewish member to lead the fight for a vote on suspending Middle East aid, a black member to propose a vote on eliminating minority contract subsidies and an Asian or Hispanic member to handle the vote on reducing immigration quotas.)

In short, we need a tidal wave of pure, unadulterated patriotism!

Maybe this is just a dream. Yet, some dreams come true. In recent months, public opinion has worked miracles behind the Iron Curtain. It could work another here!

Given a fresh agenda via a referendum, we can restore vitality to the American system. Then, as we move into the 21st century, we can look forward to our country's most glorious years.

C. Bibliography

The following are citations of McKinley Conway's writings on this chapter's subject. As this book goes to press, work is underway to make many of these items available to researchers. To check status, look for a file on GeoTEAM/IDRCNET or telephone GeoTEAM/Fax at (404) 453-4200 for a free catalog.

391. "Dispersal Efforts Have Been Inadequate — American Industry Is Still in Danger." *Industrial Development,* Jan./Feb. 1954, pp. 5-7.
392. A Report to the Southern Governors Conference, from the Subcommittee on Science and Industry, presented at White Sulphur Springs, West Va., Sept. 10, 1956. 15 pp. plus appendix.
393. "The Threat of Closing Public Schools Is Like the Sword of Damocles," Georgia Industrial Seminar, May 31, 1960, Georgia Dept. of Commerce, Atlanta. Reported in *The Atlanta Journal,* June 1, 1960.
394. "Public Schools and Community Development," DeKalb County School System annual meeting, Decatur, Ga., Oct. 22, 1960.
395. "Communism versus ...", (brief collection of opinions on a key word, including ideas of Henry Cabot Lodge, Sherman Adams, Henry Wallace, Richard Nixon and others). *Industrial Development*, Oct. 1960, pp. 2-3 and April 1961, p.2.
396. "We're Socializing the World," (comment on foreign aid economic program). *Industrial Development*, Feb. 1961, pp. 2-3.

397. "State Government Attitudes and Performance as These Relate to Developing New Industry," proceedings of the 1961 annual regional conference of the Council of State Governments. June 29-30, 1961, Mobile, Ala.

398. "Checkpoints," (editorial on the American example not being followed in overseas aid program). *Industrial Development*, Atlanta, Aug. 1961, pp. 2-3.

399. "A Challenge We Must Accept." *Area Digest,* Summer 1962.

400. A Bill Requiring All Meetings of the Governing Bodies to Be Public Meetings ("Sunshine Law"), Senate Bill No. 181, Georgia Senate, 1963-64.

401. A Bill to Provide for the Wearing of (Identification) Badges by Poll Workers, Senate Bill No. 40, Georgia Senate. 1963-64.

402. A Bill to Create the Georgia Science and Technology Commission, Senate Bill No. 283, Georgia Senate, 1963-64.

403. A Bill to Provide for the Use of Machines for Recording and Computing Votes at All Elections (punch cards and electronic computers), Senate Bill No. 340, Georgia Senate, 1964 (with Senator Leroy Johnson and others).

404. A Bill Proposing an Amendment to the Georgia Constitution to Make State Income Tax a Percentage of Taxpayer's Federal Income Tax. Senate Resolution No. 148, Georgia Senate, 1964 (with Senators Johnson and McWhorter).

405. A Resolution Proposing an Honesty Code for Public Officials, Senate Resolution 179, Georgia Senate, 1964 (with Senator Wesberry).

406. A Resolution to Create a Permanent Atlanta Metropolitan Council (MACLOG), Senate Resolution 213, Georgia Senate, 1964. (now the Atlanta Regional Commission — ARC).

407. A Resolution Proposing Establishment of the Atlanta Rapid Transit System (now MARTA), Senate Resolution 158, Georgia Senate, 1964 (with Senators Johnson and McWhorter).

408. "State Development Programs," *The Book of the States,* 1964-65. The Council of State Governments, Chicago.

409. "The Fifty Legislative Climates," *Industrial Development,* Dec. 1966, pp. 17-27. (Survey of financial and tax incentives in each state).

410. "How Should Sites for Federal Facilities Be Selected?" A question of growing national concern is the manner of choosing locations for new federal government installations. The much-publicized site for the nuclear accelerator has brought the issue forward. *Industrial Development*, Jan. 1967. p. 2.

411. "A Higher Premium on Education" (commencement address), Marist College, Atlanta, May 28, 1967.

412. An Act to Create the Ocean Science Center of the Atlantic Authority (Skidaway institute), Senate Bill 75, Georgia Senate, 1967.

413. A Bill to Require Open Meetings ("Sunshine Law"), Senate Bill 143. Georgia Senate, 1967.

414. A Bill to Regulate and Control "Fire Bombs" or "Molotov Cocktails," Senate Bill 45, Georgia Senate, 1967.

415. A Resolution Requiring the State Highway Department to Set Criteria for Allocating Funds, Senate Resolution 39, Georgia Senate. 1967.

416. A Bill to Establish a Program of Awards for Cutting the Cost of Government, Senate Bill 187, Georgia Senate, 1967.

417. A Bill to Establish a Code of Honesty for All State Employees, Senate Bill 74, Georgia Senate, 1967 (with Senators Wesberry and Bateman).

418. A Bill to Create the Georgia College Council (student government liaison), Senate Bill 5, Georgia Senate, 1967.

419. "In Search for a National Development Strategy." Introduction to working paper on new town strategy by Vice President Spiro Agnew. *Industrial Development,* May-June, 1969, pp. 2-3.

420. "The Bureaucracy of Development." In your plans for your new building, you'd better take a close look at the specifications for ladders. Make sure that wooden ladders have rungs at least one and one-eighth inch in diameter. The federal government, in all its bureaucratic majesty (OSHA), has risen up and delivered ...a new set of regulations running 248 pages. *Industrial Development*, March/April 1972. pp. 1-3.

421. "Why Not a Bill of Rights for Developers?" Never before have those who serve the public interest by building homes and places of business found themselves so harassed and

impeded by government policies and regulations. On all sides and at every level new bureaucracy is mushrooming. *Site Selection*, 1973. pp. 250-253.

422. "Can a Nationwide Planning Problem Be Solved without Help from Washington?" Industrial park developers have long since discovered that the shabby, sub-par project won't sell. That American system again! Introduction to guide to office and industrial park development. *Site Selection*, Nov. 1975. p. 376.

423. "Are You a Problem Voter?" Are you playing Russian roulette with your vote? If so, why not salute the bicentennial by checking your voting habits and pledging to make your 1976 vote your best ever? *Industrial Development*, July/Aug. 1976. pp. 19-20.

424. Improving the business climate means waging war on bureaucracy. *Site Selection and Industrial Development*. May 1977. p. 92.

425. *Legislative Climates for Economic Development*. Climates around the world. The 50 legislative climates of the U.S. The political process. Jimmy Carter as an architect of legislative climate. Future trends in legislating for development. Appendix covering incentives at national, state, local levels. 391 pp. 1979.

426. "The Free World's Secret Weapon Is Revealed." For a long time it appeared to be an extremely well-kept secret. Prominent politicians around the world didn't know it existed or couldn't recognize it. We refer to that economic super bomb called Private Enterprise — a weapon capable of reducing to shambles the defenses of nations which depend on state control of enterprises. *Site Selection*, Aug. 1985.

427. "We Need a National Referendum!" A national referendum would permit every voter to express his or her views on a list of, say, 10 key issues...The results would be tallied and published in the *Congressional Record* for all to see. *Site Selection*, Oct. 1985. p. 868.

428. "Launch! Launch! Launch!" We can't afford more delays with the space shuttle program. It's time to put the astronauts in charge, accept the risks, and get on with vital projects while support groups develop better systems for deployment later. *Site Selection*, April 1986. p. 260.

429. "Planning Vacuum at DOT?" Is it possible that DOT cannot assist facility planners in identifying present and future points of congestion on the interstate system? If true, within the next decade highway traffic gridlock is going to produce economic disasters from coast to coast. *Site Selection*, June 1986. p. 548.

430. "The Problem Voter," *Site Selection*, Oct. 1986, and monograph.

431. "To Compete Globally, Business Must Choose Optimum Sites." Some of the most dangerous ideas to be debated by the new Congress deal with restrictions on the right of industrial firms to select economically attractive sites or to close plants which have become uneconomic. Such proposals ignore the reality of world competition. *Site Selection*, Feb. 1987. p. 4.

432. "What's the Biggest Obstacle to Progress from (Name Withheld USA) to Naushki, Siberia, USSR?" An international traveler finds that petty bureaucracy can rear its ugly head in a small airport in the USA as easily as it can aboard the Trans-Siberian Express. *Site Selection*, April 1988. p. 544.

433. "Private Investment Instead of Government Aid: Can the New MIGA Plan Speed Global Shift?" Only a few developing nations have discovered that the world's private business community is a much better source of economic aid than all of the governments around the globe. *Site Selection*, Aug. 1988. p. 828.

434. "Education Key to America's Future." If we are to compete with the Japanese and Western Europe we must do a much better job of educating our young people and retraining our older workers. *Gwinnett Daily News*. Aug. 17, 1988.

435. "Skyrocketing Business Risks Hurt Consumer and Taxpayer." In this season of hyperbole and demagoguery, It's not likely that political leaders will come up with creative new policies for handling such hot potatoes as asbestos removal. Hopefully, however, the next administration will develop a rational policy for mitigating extraordinary business risks. *Site Selection*, Oct. 1988. p. 1068.

436. "It's Time to Redirect the Economic Development Elements of U.S. International Aid Programs!" Massive changes are needed in the way the U.S. handles its international development aid program. Here are some guidelines for establishing a new program that will help make sure U.S. assistance does what it's designed to do. *Site Selection*. June 1990. p. 608.

437. "Let The People Speak!" There's an important flaw in our great American political system. Today, despite our elaborate communication systems, there is no effective way for the

people to express their collective opinion clearly and emphatically on any specific political issue. Monograph. 1991.

438. "Would You Take This Job?" Here's a tip on an upcoming job opening which carries prestige beyond your fondest dreams. *Site Selection*, Feb. 1991. pp. 4.

439. "CEO Confidential." Here's how you can exert a powerful influence in the congressional election next November. You can help keep the good guys in while throwing the rascals out. *Site Selection*, Feb. 1992. p. 6.

440. "Where Do You Fit in the Washington Mess?" The truth is revealed: Congress doesn't really care what the people think. Special interests are running the system. Are you a part of the problem? *Site Selection,* Aug. 1992. pp. 622.

441. "A Special Message for the CEO Who Now Lives at 1600 Pennsylvania Avenue," *Site Selection*, April 1993. pp. 242.

7
Environment

Chapter 7

A. Recent Comments

The Importance of Walking
A Family Commitment
Mixing Personal and Professional Interests
Business Parks and Private Enterprise
Recognizing the Real Performers
Population — the Paramount Global Issue
Our Own Preserve

B. Excerpts

Disaster Survival, 1981
Industrial Park Growth — an Environmental Success Story, 1981
Good Life Index, 1982
"The Role of Private Enterprise," *Site Selection*, December 1987
"Future Political Battles," *Gwinnett Daily News*, May 1990
Weather Handbook, 3rd edition, 1990

C. Bibliography

A. Recent Comments

The Importance of Walking

When I was a small boy, we lived at the edge of a small town in a sparsely populated area in Alabama. From my back door I could tramp for miles through wooded areas, tracking rabbits, finding bird nests, eating wild muscadines, gathering maypops and discovering all of the other wonders of nature.

I have never lost that lust for walking. In fact, I have come to believe that walking is good for just about everything — your health, your peace of mind, and, not the least, the environment. I suppose my favorite walks are along deserted beaches. There is something very therapeutic about walking alone past the dunes and rocks and watching the surf roll in.

During those strolls I am reminded that we human beings are less permanent on this earth than the smallest grain of sand. Those waves have been crashing on those boulders for centuries past, and they will keep hammering away long after we're gone.

Yet, there is something inspiring about this concept of endless time. We finish our walk with the thought that while we are privileged to be here we will try to do our best.

We seldom set out on a walk with any real objective. That would spoil it. But we welcome the bonus of getting a glimpse of nature at work — the flash of a school of fish, a formation of geese or a small animal scurrying for cover.

I have worn out quite a few pair of sneakers during beachcombing strolls along the shores of countless islands and maritime provinces. We have walked beaches on every continent and on islands from the Indian Ocean to the South Pacific.

We never collect live shells, but we have picked up many a handful of those abandoned in the debris lines left by high tide. In our living room we have shell tables presenting modest collections from various parts of the world.

Some locations, like Sanibel Island in Florida, are so well known for good shell collecting that they are overrun. Yet, the best spot we have ever found — Punta Chivato, on Mexico's Sea of Cortez — is virtually unknown and typically is deserted.

Memories that pop to the surface include an early morning walk along a beach in Tunisia where an Arab woman, her robe dragging in the water, deftly speared a squid for the family table. There was another walk along an icy shore in Antarctica where we finally found a few shells to confirm that even there life goes on. And, we treasure the memory of a picture-perfect beach on an atoll in the South Pacific where there was not the slightest trace of mankind.

All too often, however, the beach walks remind us of the global pollution problem. We remember the garbage-strewn beach at Beirut, a boat harbor covered with debris in Hawaii and a community of stilt houses built over a stinking inlet in Brazil.

Almost every walk is a learning experience. One of the favorite stories in our family has to do with a beachcombing expedition in the Turks and Caicos Islands. One hot day, when we had reached a point several miles from our base, our daughter Laura found a large blob`of waxy gray material about the size of a football.

Daughter Linda, who had studied some marine biology, offered the possibility that the material might be ambergris. That is a substance regurgitated from the stomach of whales and highly prized as a material used in the perfume industry. To add credence, the shoreline we were walking was near the Ambergris Keys, so named because of passing whales.

Putting all of these ideas together, Laura was convinced that she had made a big discovery — she would be rich enough to buy the horse she wanted. Thus, we carried the weighty mass back to Atlanta, sent a slice to an assay house in New York and waited impatiently for the report.

Soon the news came. Laura had found a blob of grease used in the packing around ship propeller shafts.

A Family Commitment

Linda's interest in nature studies led to a career. As a student at the University of Georgia, she did part-time field work under noted ecologist Dr. Eugene Odum. Later she married Dr. Mike Duever, Audubon's director of research, and they manned a field station in the Corkscrew Swamp Sanctuary in Florida.

Linda later worked for The Nature Conservancy, identifying environmentally sensitive areas in Florida. Then, she joined an environmental planning firm for several years before becoming an independent consultant.

In one way or another, our whole family is involved in hands-on environmental work. When we built a new home several years ago on the Chattahoochee River near Atlanta we developed a site plan which included a native plants area, a small orchard, a raised bed area for vegetable gardening and two greenhouses.

Becky's greenhouse is for flowers and showy things like some of the cacti. Mine is more utilitarian, used mainly for experimenting with tropical fruits — trying to grow some of the exciting produce I've seen around the world.

I can still remember the first time — some 30 years ago — I encountered a display of tropical fruits and vegetables in a local market in Southeast Asia. There were stalls piled high with pink bananas, lichis, custard apples and many other exotic edibles which I had never seen before.

Importing plants and seeds from Asia, Latin America and elsewhere, we have experimented with several dozen species. Here is a quick scan revealing our trials and tribulations as a gardener:

Atemoya, a custard apple from Central America. One plant which has produced three apples in two years.

Avocado, dwarf variety. Two plants via the University of California at Davis experiment station. So far lots of blooms but no avocados.

Bananas. I have dwarf Cavendish, Jamaica Red and Lacatan Chiquita kept in the greenhouse, then outside. Nipped by frost last two years.

Calamondin. Dwarf orange. Produces some fruit every year.

Carambola. Star fruit. Several healthy plants. No fruit after three years.

Barbados cherry, the vitamin C bush or Acerola. So far lots of flowers, no fruit.

Fig, Brown Turkey and Celeste varieties. Both produce lots of good figs.

Guava, three types. My strawberry guava has been fruiting for two years. The Hawaiian variety started fruiting this year. The pineapple variety (Feijoa) has bloomed, but no fruit yet.

Jaboticaba. Healthy plant, but slow grower.

Jujube, or Chinese date. I have two plants not yet big enough for fruit.

Kiwi, one Japanese Issai, another from New Zealand. Big vines but no fruit after three years.

Kumquat, Chinese Meiwa and Japanese Nagami. Both produce well.

Lemon, dwarf Meyers. A bumper crop last winter.

Lime, Key lime variety. Last year small plant produced five or six limes.

Loquat. Plant is about three feet high. No bloom yet.

Miracle fruit. Small plant, first bloom this year.

Passion fruit or flower. I have several varieties grown from seed from Brazil, Australia, Hawaii. Beautiful flowers.

Papaya, babaco dwarf from Ecuador. Produced a good crop last winter in greenhouse.

Pepino dulce, Andes melonfruit. Started plants in greenhouse, put outside for summer. Bloomed, fruited, then killed by early frost.

Persimmon, oriental Fuyu. One small tree produced about a dozen nice fruits this year.

Sapote, white custard apple. Two plants, healthy, but no blooms yet.

Tangerine, Dancy. Our best citrus producer! We can count on fresh tangerines every winter.

The fauna. While we collect exotic plants physically, we have preferred to collect wild animals primarily via photos.

There was one exception, however. As mentioned later in this chapter, Laura brought back a pygmy marmoset from our Amazon expedition and it lived in our house for several years. Since it was the first small monkey of this type known to survive in captivity, it attracted the interest of the Yerkes primate center. Reluctantly, Laura gave it to them for safekeeping and scientific study.

Almost everywhere, there are wild things of interest. The highlight of our trip to Antarctica was going ashore on Anvers Island and walking amid a colony of penguins whose population was estimated at 30,000. Elsewhere in that frigid realm we saw creatures ranging from krill to seals and whales. Offshore there were cormorants and auks.

Do Pelicans Always Turn Left?

Perhaps our only contribution to the scientific knowledge of wild things has to do with brown pelicans. This vital bit of knowledge was garnered over a period of many years, during which we spent many vacations at a small hotel at Punta Pescadero in Baja. From our terrace we could watch pelicans diving for fish in a scenic cove.

After some years of dedicated pelican watching, we made an interesting discovery. Each time a low-flying pelican spotted a fish below, he would make a left-hand, counter-clockwise spiral dive for his prey. We have never seen a pelican make a right-hand, clockwise spiral dive.

Intrigued, we began speculating about the possibility that below the equator the pelicans might turn right. After all, water runs down the drain counter-clockwise here and the opposite way down under.

We tried to check this out personally during trips to Australia, New Zealand, South Africa, Chile and other places south of the equator but, unfortunately, could find no pelicans to cooperate.

For help, we then turned to the National Geographic Society, and received this reply from researcher Richard J. Arnold, dated April 12, 1988: "The Geographic has not published significant information on the motions of diving pelicans on both sides of the equator, nor do we have an expert on our staff who would be qualified to say if they differ or not."

Perhaps one of our readers can help. In any event, we promise that the hours spent watching the pelicans will be well invested.

Leticia: the Snake Capital

We've dug up some really big rattlers while building a golf course in Florida. We've encountered cobras while inspecting a rubber plantation on the Malay peninsula. And we've seen a community of water snakes in a lagoon near Fiji.

But our vote for the snake center of the universe is Leticia, Colombia, a small trading post in the upper Amazon Basin. Leticia has an extraordinary snake habitat in the surrounding rain forest, but also the collection system of Mike Tsilickis.

Mike is a fellow who began collecting snakes in the Florida Everglades, discovered they could be sold to zoos, and went looking for greener pastures. He discovered the Amazon where boas and anacondas of gigantic sizes were reported.

Mike built a compound at Leticia and let the Indians know he would pay for snakes. They started pouring in, and soon Mike could publish a catalog listing a great variety of snakes available at so much per foot. His list included some prize specimens more than 30 feet long.

By the time we visited Mike he was the leading supplier of zoos around the world. We spent several days around Leticia with Mike, walking jungle trails, whizzing into backwater areas in his airboat and examining the specimens.

Our family will not forget the morning we went to the airstrip to leave. After we had loaded and preflighted our airplane, Mike had some men bring forth two bundles. For my daughter Laura there was a pygmy marmoset — a monkey standing about six inches tall, in a neat little bamboo cage.

From the other bundle, a large burlap bag, they unfurled a 16-foot anaconda — a present for my snake-appreciating daughter Linda. It took me at least two seconds to formulate a new family policy — we do not carry large snakes in our airplane. The writhing anaconda went back to the compound.

Mixing Personal and Professional Interests

We mention these family experiences to underscore the fact that we have never attempted to draw a very fine line of distinction between our family interests and our business and professional interests. They are all mingled, almost every day.

Because we fly, we have always had a special interest in the weather. That led to our first *Weather Handbook*, which we published in 1962. The interest continued and we issued new editions in 1974 and again in 1990.

These editions provide concrete evidence that we have studied climatic data for locations around the world seriously for more than 30 years. We started looking for trends — or the lack of them — long before there was speculation about such matters as global warming or ozone depletion.

Our conclusion is that for any reporting station anywhere in the world, a new temperature or precipitation record may be set any day. But for the entire globe, the climate is extremely stable, suggesting that there may be an internal regulating system we do not yet understand.

Business Parks and Private Enterprise

One of the greatest myths extant today is that government regulatory agencies and community action groups prevent the destruction of our environment by greedy corrupt corporations. The fact is that responsible private interests do most of the significant conservation work, despite obstacles placed in their way by petty bureaucrats and self-appointed experts.

We reiterated this fact in an editorial in *Site Selection* in 1987. And, as we look back, we realize that nowhere is this better demonstrated than in the development of business parks.

Concurrent with our interest in physical climates has been our interest in the built environment. We have had the privilege of witnessing, almost from the start, an extraordinary environmental success story — the emergence of planned industrial and office parks.

Before business parks were introduced, industrial facilities were scattered throughout urban areas, with each plant having its own system (or lack thereof) for handling wastes. The new business parks brought central planning for such facilities. Many environmental problems were solved in advance by the developers of the parks.

In the early stages of this movement there was established a National Industrial Zoning Committee made up of one representative each from the IDRC and other key development groups. Some nine or 10 of us sat down in a room and drafted the first standards.

This highly significant environmental effort is covered in our book (*Industrial Park Growth, An Environmental Success Story*, 1981), excerpted later in this chapter.

Having long been concerned with global climate and environmental factors, it was inevitable that we would study the risks of major disasters that might affect us and/or our habitat.

We have encountered a few of the world's natural risks in bouncing around the globe. While snorkling in the Caribbean we have looked a big barracuda in the teeth; we've had an angry octopus squirt ink in our face off the Florida keys; we've waded among the poison cones, sea urchins, and stingrays of the Pacific, and we've somehow survived clouds of mosquitoes in the Canadian Arctic.

But these are the small environmental risks. The big ones are the earthquakes and volcanos. Happily, we have not yet been caught precisely in the middle of a really devastating phenomenon.

Sure, we've flown up the spine of Central America, steering from one smoking crater to the next, taking photos and smelling the sulfurous fumes. And we've been in earthquake zones when tremors cracked the walls of our hotel.

Our closest call was at Mount Saint Helens. On the afternoon before the earth-shattering blast we flew over the summit and made photos of the big bulge on the north slope.

They proved to be the last photos of that terrain. The next morning the old volcano blew its top, spreading fiery destruction in the immediate vicinity and sending ash hundreds of miles to the east. We saw it from our hotel balcony in Portland.

We put our analysis of various disaster risks and ways to minimize them into book form with *Disaster Survival* in 1981. (*See Excerpts*)

Recognizing the Real Performers

Those who pilot small airplanes for many years maintain a sort of constant environmental watch. From low altitude we can see where filth is being emptied into streams, where smokestacks are belching, where oil has been spilled at sea and where the forests have been cut. We don't try to act as police, but we do like to try to influence the course of events by reporting and saluting positive efforts. That is what led us, in 1972, to establish an annual award for those doing an extraordinary job of harmonizing new facilities with the natural environment.

At that time, the conflict between business firms and the new environmentalists was bitter. Self-appointed environmental experts sought to impose sweeping new regulatory programs on companies, without regard to cost or practicality. Companies became very defensive.

In that atmosphere, many companies simply did not want to talk about their environmental plans. The Industrial Development Research Council permitted me to present the award at their annual meeting, but they did not endorse it.

Some years later, the benefit of recognizing good work overcame the reluctance to talk and IDRC added its endorsement to the award. Today, it is the IDRC Award for Distinguished Service in Environmental Planning and is presented each fall at a luncheon attended by more than 1,000 corporate executives and geo-economists.

Nominations come from environmentalists, engineers, planners,

347

designers, managers, investors and many such interests. Each project is evaluated on the degree to which it achieves one or more of the following criteria: 1) ecological harmony of the project with the surrounding physical environment; 2) design and management factors that reduce energy resource
use and the magnitude or environmental harmfulness of waste output from
the facility; 3) visual harmony of the project with the surrounding physical
environment; and 4) innovations in achieving the criteria above, particularly
in overcoming existing or potential site problems.

For example, three projects were honored in the 1992 awards program. Here are the citations:

• "J.P. Berger, plant manager of The Clorox Co.'s Northeast Manufacturing Project, receives the IDRC 1992 Award for Distinguished Service in
Environmental Planning for his diligence in leading the combined efforts of
many people to build an environmentally safe and technologically advanced
manufacturing plant in Aberdeen, Md., for the company's internationally
known liquid bleach products.

"The 380,000-sq.-ft. (342,000-sq.-m.) facility is designed to promote
visual harmony, as well as provide cost and lighting efficiency. A centrally
located atrium and interior glass block walls create enhanced natural lighting. Local technical high school students landscaped grounds around the
building, which sits on a 150-acre (60-hectare) site that includes heavily
wooded wetland areas preserved by the company. The storm water deten-
tion system was designed to assure that the flow of storm water from the
site does not change from pre-development conditions.

"Initial public concern about storage of chlorine, which is used to
make liquid bleach, prompted a decision to eliminate it from the manufacturing process. High-strength bleach will be used instead. Clorox will also
mold its own bottles at the plant and will include post-consumer recycled
(PCR) plastic in the bottles. The improved job and tax bases generated by
the Northeast Manufacturing Process and the concerted effort by Clorox
project employees in maintaining open communication with their new
neighbors have helped make The Clorox Co. an asset to the community of
Aberdeen."

• "Gordon Gayda, director, design and construction management, for
GTE Realty Corp., receives IDRC's 1992 award for Distinguished Service in
Environmental Planning for his leadership in the development, design and
construction of GTE's Telephone Operations Headquarters in Irving, Texas.
Constructed on a 50-acre (20-hectare) site, the 1.3 million-sq.ft. (117,000-
sq.-m.) facility serves as a new world headquarters for 3,000 employees.

"To preserve the natural beauty of the North Texas prairie setting, all
employee parking and service vehicle areas are below grade. As a result, the

two office structures, though large, blend subtly with the site and create an elegant, unobtrusive presence on the horizon. The deliberate effect achieved by the design team is that of a horizontal skyscraper in which employees are afforded maximum exposure to natural light and vistas of the surrounding terrain. A curving red sandstone wall, which winds through the landscape and enters the structures to define primary elements of the interior spaces, provides a visual link throughout the external and interior environments of the development.

"As the focal point of the campus, a two-tiered pond was engineered from an existing body of water. All building and site drainage surrounding the upper and lower ponds was captured in storm sewers to preserve future water quality. The ponds are constantly aerated by a 20-foot waterfall and a fountain system. This enlarged water feature effectively increases the site's available wetland area and its botanical diversity. Tertiary treated effluent is used for all site irrigation to minimize the burden on the municipal water supply.

• "Patrick J. Martin, Xerox Corp. vice president and president of its Americas Operations, receives the IDRC 1992 Award for Distinguished Service in Environmental Planning for his leadership in successfully establishing a joint venture operation with registered capital of $30 million. The project consists of approximately eight buildings that house copier, toner and photoreceptor manufacturing plants, administrative offices and other support facilities.

"Located on 7.5 acres (three hectares) in the Minhang Economic and Technological Development Zone in the southwest area of Shanghai, the facilities are in compliance with Xerox's worldwide environmental policy and Chinese policy. The site is aesthetically designed with pools, fountains, trees, shrubs and other landscaping features. Development of this project involved many challenges — including language barriers, transforming U.S. drawings into Chinese specifications and obtaining approval from layers of bureaucracy (approximately 65 representatives from 29 governmental agencies).

"Basic design work for the production facilities was done by Xerox and consulting firms in the United States and transformed by the Shanghai Institute of Mechanical and Electrical Engineering."

Certainly, the good life to which everyone aspires requires a good environment. It is interesting, therefore, to compare conservation goals with criteria for the good life. In our book (*The Good Life Index*, 1981) we analyzed global, metro, city and local areas.

Population — the Paramount Global Issue

I defy anyone to travel the world and not become an ardent conservationist! We inhabit a sphere which offers an incredible variety of resources, plant and animal life, and natural systems.

In our case, we have been most intrigued with the possibilities of achieving conservation and development goals simultaneously. Thus, we have written reports on mariculture projects, such as the growing of giant clams at Palau, the green turtle farm on Grand Cayman, shrimp culture in Hawaii, eel farming on Guam and catfish farming in the Georgia.

Also, we have a great interest in the possibilities for desalting seawater using solar energy. We have no doubt that the centuries-old evaporation pond system used to obtain salt will give way to a highly sophisticated new system which can produce huge quantities of fresh water in an economically feasible way.

Further, we know that there is a bright future ahead for what we term "Decoplexes" and for the new "green infrastructure." These are the plans for new entities which satisfy both development and conservation needs at the same time.

Finally, we recognize that unmanaged population growth, not money, is the root of all environmental evil. That is the key issue of the years ahead.

Our Own Preserve

Talk, talk, talk!

Everybody talks about the environment, but not enough of us do anything about it. The time has come to change this, and for everyone to do whatever he can within his own sphere.

Recognizing this, our family and our company have committed ourselves to a challenging project. We have made a site search like none other in our history, looking for a spot that is not in the path of immediate economic development.

We have bought a tract in central Florida away from the interstates and tourism development to establish a preserve. We intend to study it, plan it and "develop" it to its fullest potential as a prime example of native Florida habitat.

B. Excerpts

1981 Excerpt	*Disaster Survival.* How to choose secure sites and make practical escape plans. Natural disasters. Manmade disasters. Evaluation of risk potential. Survival planning: site hardening. Public policies. International disaster risk data. 290 pp. Hard cover. 1981. The American Library Association review: "A frightening, valuable guide."

Much has been written recently about the disasters which threaten us. A quick scan of bookstore racks, TV programs or motion picture listings will reveal a bumper crop of such eye-stoppers as *The Late Great Planet Earth, The Towering Inferno, Earthquake, The Last Wave, Meteor, The Day The World Ended, Soylent Green, Dr. Strangelove, On the Beach, Fail Safe, The Omega Man, The Swarm, The Hellstrom Chronicle,* or *The Day the Earth Stood Still.* This out-pouring has been described by *Time* as "disastermania."

The present study should not be included among those volumes which scare, titillate or entertain the reader. A spin-off from a long career in planning, this is an attempt to assist thoughtful corporate executives and private citizens in preparing for future disaster risks. What follows is intended to be a factual briefing and basic survival manual for those concerned about their families, homes and businesses.

Attitudes toward disasters vary greatly among various segments of the population. It is probably safe to say that the majority give little thought to such risks until a disaster with which they can identify occurs. This apathetic group may always be a majority, meaning that broad public programs of disaster preparation will have low priorities.

At the other end of the spectrum is a small segment of the population which is almost hysterical about impending disaster and doom. This segment includes certain religious groups which, from time to time, predict that the world will come to an end on a specific date. Many such groups have made elaborate, even absurd, plans for an anticipated doomsday which, happily, has not yet arrived.

Herein, we will seek to deal with the calamities that come so swiftly that, if we are to have a maximum opportunity to survive, our preparations must have been made in advance. We have chosen to divide disasters into two main categories:

    • Natural disasters: earthquakes, volcanos, floods, hurricanes and tornados.

• Man-made or man-related physical disasters: nuclear risks, structural failures, fires and explosions, travel accidents, terrorism, wars and economic calamities.

There is an abundance of evidence to demonstrate that preparedness pays off. In every major disaster there are survivors, and survival is not entirely a matter of chance. The facts prove again and again that, while there are no guarantees, it is definitely possible, through preparation, to improve the odds on survival and reduce the chance of loss.

This is not a new idea. Noah was ready with his ark, and his party survived the flood. Throughout history the record suggests survival of the fittest, with fitness often being equated to preparedness.

Natural Disasters

The word "disaster" has its origin in "astrum" or "astron," the Greek word for "star." Hence, the first definition of disaster was, literally, an unfortunate aspect of the stars. While astrology or mythology may have introduced questionable explanations for many events in general, there is growing evidence that many mythical tales had their origin in natural events for which scientifically acceptable rationales are now possible.

Certainly, the earth has been bombarded by asteroids, meteorites, cosmic radiation and, no doubt, other forces yet to be identified. We know that the earth wobbles in its orbit enough today to require corrections to the sundial readings in our garden. In times past, we suspect much greater deviations have occurred, with dramatic effects. Science also reveals today that on a number of occasions in the past the earth's magnetic poles have reversed.

True, some of the dramatic events occurred hundreds or millions of years ago. There is a dangerous tendency to regard these facts merely as interesting bits of history. This complacency is reinforced by the assumption among most of the populace that all astronomical phenomena are predictable for years in advance.

Despite a wealth of information about the earth and its neighbors, there is still much we do not know. Only a few years ago a German astronomer found a new comet large enough to create a crater 50 miles in diameter if it should hit the earth. Happily, the new comet, Kohoutek, named for its discoverer, grazed the sun and missed the earth by a comfortable margin.

But what of deeper space, an awesome void about which we know very little? If we are on a collision course with something big, it could be the ultimate disaster. We must include that as a possibility, although the odds appear slim. More real is the possibility of a lesser collision which could cause large loss of life and damage. There appears good reason to believe that the earth has already suffered such disasters.

In his book *Worlds In Collision*, Velikovsky in 1950 offered a scientific explanation for catastrophic events reported in the Bible and elsewhere from China to the Mayan Empire. He postulated that the planet Jupiter spun off a large piece which became the new planet Venus. When Earth passed behind the new planet it encountered a trail of dust and gases, and Earth's rotational orbit was disturbed, causing, among other things, the shifting of the waters of the Red Sea (thus permitting Moses to lead his people across before the waters returned).

This same hypothesis may offer a satisfactory explanation for the legendary continent (or island) of Atlantis and what happened to it. According to the legend, which many serious scientists now believe to be based on fact, there existed, until some 12,000 years ago, a major civilization on a land mass situated in the Atlantic off the western entrance to the Mediterranean.

The civilization on Atlantis was believed to represent the highest degree of sophistication in the world at that time, and the influence was strong from the Americas to the Middle East. The central leadership on Atlantis may explain such common denominators as the pyramid designs of Egypt, Mesopotamia, Peru and Mexico.

The astronomical disaster described by Velikovsky may have caused the destruction of Atlantis (as reported by Plato) in a day and a night. The combination of earthquakes, eruptions and floods was swift and climactic. Atlantis tumbled into the ocean, new coastlines were formed, great mudslides obliterated features, and, in effect, a new world community was left to face the future without the enlightened leadership on which it had depended.

However accurate this hypothesis, it appears certain that this event, to which many historians refer as "the great deluge," was the greatest disaster of which we have any reports. Certainly, there were survivors. And, if our reports are correct, one of them was a man named Noah.

Earthquakes and Volcanic Eruptions

The typical U.S. resident thinks of the earthquake disaster risk in terms of San Francisco. He doesn't worry very much because the last really big quake occurred in 1906, and it is common knowledge that most of the damage resulted from fires that followed the tremor.

This bit of vaguely recalled history is accompanied by an assumption that the fires which destroyed San Francisco in 1906, when wooden structures prevailed, could not occur today in a city of brick and masonry structures. Right?

Wrong! Expert observers believe San Francisco may be more vulnerable today than in 1906. True, there are proportionally more brick buildings downtown, but there are also more flammable materials and a more complex system to protect — for example, fires in high-rise towers.

Also San Francisco today has a large network of natural gas lines which, ruptured, could feed fires. A major quake could also spill oil and gas from tank storage farms onto the waters of San Francisco Bay, spreading an inferno wherever the winds and tides might determine.

As to fire-fighting capability, San Francisco still must depend on its water system, which would surely be broken up and rendered useless by a large quake. Just as surely, bridges and freeways would be rendered useless, leaving the city almost inaccessible except by boat or helicopter.

The cold harsh facts are that a major quake in San Francisco would not be a surprise to seismologists. And, the result could be thousands of deaths and hundreds of thousands of injuries. It could be the greatest disaster in U.S. history.

This dire outlook stems from knowledge that earthquakes constitute one of the deadliest hazards of all the disaster risks. We live in a geologically unsettled world wherein new quakes and tremors appear inevitable.

While most of the more recent earthquake disasters have occurred outside the U.S., there is absolutely no reason for U.S. residents to be complacent. Almost every state has had at least one significant quake. And, contrary to popular opinion, the higher activity areas are not limited to California.

Fresh studies have alerted residents to potentials disasters in areas where earthquakes risks were largely forgotten along the New Madrid fault in Missouri and adjoining states, in New England, and in the South, particularly coastal South Carolina.

While earthquakes are sporadic, volcanic activity never stops. One can fly on a clear day from South America almost to the U.S., steering on the cones of volcanoes along the mountainous spine of Central America and Mexico. Not all are active at any given time, but the pilot usually sees wisps of smoke at several points.

There are five volcanoes on the U.S. mainland which are classified as active. These include Mt. Shasta and Mt. Lassen, in California; and Mts. Baker, Rainier, and St. Helens, in Washington. All had been relatively quiet during recent years until March 1980 when Mt. St. Helens came to life and provided an occasional display of smoke and light ash.

On the afternoon of May 17 we flew over the summit of St. Helens and made a series of photos. We circled, looking down into the crater, noting steam spurting from cracks and giving special attention to an ominous bulge on the north slope.

Evidently, our photos were the last record of these features, for on the next morning an explosive eruption occurred — the most devastating geological event in the U.S. during this century. The top 1,500 feet of the mountain disappeared in a huge cloud of ash and debris, a wave of fire and hot gases blasted the mountain area, while rocks, mud and debris flowed down the slopes. The noise of the blast was heard at Astoria, more than 50 miles away. We saw the puffs of smoke from downtown Portland.

The disaster was so large it concealed its own destructive effect in smoke, ash and clouds. It was literally several days before a tentative evaluation could be made. We know because we were there, trying to get a reading on the magnitude of damage.

Ecological Phenomena

If one considers the Earth as man's ecosystem range, all disasters are ecological. For this section, however, we will choose to discuss briefly a few situations in which some observers see disaster risks relative to certain ecological clashes within the large system.

First, there is man's continuing battle with the insect population. This battle is bigger, more expensive and deadlier than many realize. Scientists estimate that the weight of insects on the Earth is 10 times greater than that of the human population, the insect population is growing faster and, at this point, we are by no means sure man is winning.

Meanwhile, insect-oriented disasters do occur. In parts of the world swarming locusts can, within a few days, destroy an agricultural area and leave the human population hungry. In the U.S., for more than 100 years population of necessity avoided the lowlands, except for a fringe along the coast, until mosquitoes were controlled.

Floods

In the earliest days of man, camp sites were located near streams which provided drinking water. As man developed, his first mode of transportation was a dugout canoe, and for a long while thereafter, boat transportation was dominant. Thus, early communities sprang up where rivers met or where natural harbors occurred.

A great many of these communities, which later became cities, were built on lowlands that we now know to be flood plains. (British flood control engineers currently have underway a $1.5 billion construction program to control the Thames in London.) Risks are particularly prevalent in the United States where new areas were opened for commerce and development first by riverboats plying the Ohio, Mississippi and other rivers.

Despite great investment in flood control measures, many parts of many cities and towns still are exposed to the hazards of a flood disaster. But these are not the only exposed areas. Today we know that virtually everyone lives in or close to an area that is vulnerable to some type of flood risk.

Flash flooding is common even in arid lands. High risks occur where there is little vegetation to slow run-off. The same is true in urban areas where unplanned development has brought large paved areas without attention to drainage requirements. Terrain features are also highly significant. A dry canyon can become a raging torrent where heavy rains fall along the slopes above.

A state-by-state analysis of the percentage of population living in flood-prone areas shows the range is from 4.4 percent in Tennessee to 14.8 percent in Massachusetts. These percentages may seem small but when applied to the total population, the data reveal an enormous risk.

Wind Storms: Hurricanes, Typhoons and Cyclones

No other disaster risk so well dramatizes the issues of survival planning as does that of hurricanes. They are not an unknown quantity — millions of people have been threatened and thousands have seen the death and damage they can leave behind. Many have seen several hurricanes.

Hurricanes and, as they are known in the western Pacific, typhoons, clearly are important risks in many parts of the world wherever tropical cyclones (masses of warm, moist air rotating around a low pressure area) develop.

Three regions of the globe spawn most of the hurricane activity: the Atlantic and Caribbean, the eastern Pacific off Mexico and the western Pacific. Substantial cyclonic activity is also found in the Indian Ocean, but few typhoons are reported.

The area of greatest risk is the western Pacific where huge typhoons develop over great expanses of open water and spend themselves against the coast lines of Southeast Asia, China, Japan, the Philippines, Okinawa and lesser islands. The fury of these storms was confirmed during World War II when large "unsinkable" warships were capsized by monster waves.

Cyclonic activity in the Indian Ocean is heaviest in the Bay of Bengal. That a storm does not need to reach hurricane strength to be deadly has been proven many times in this area when cyclones have pushed water onto the lowlands of the Ganges Delta. One such storm a decade ago killed 300,000 people, making it one of the greatest disasters in recorded history.

Much has been learned about the relative strength and damage potential of hurricanes. First, it is well-established by now that nearly one-half of the deaths and destruction caused by hurricanes results not from the wind but from the surge of water driven ashore ahead of the storm, causing extreme tides. Second, it is impossible to predict the level of the surge at a specific location simply from knowledge of the velocity of the winds. The slope of the continental shelf and the shape of the shoreline must be considered.

Additional analysis of hurricane data reveals that most of those residents of coastal areas who have "experienced" hurricanes have not actually experienced the full fury of an intense storm (scale 4 or 5). This produces a false sense of security in many areas.

At the least, officials at some agencies believe more stringent standards must be adopted for new construction at coastal locations. For example, requiring buildings to be at least eight feet above sea level, a typical Florida requirement is not enough. It provides no security against storm surges of 10 to 20 feet. To qualify for federal programs, owners may be required to elevate structures to, say, 15 feet.

This type of situation caused public officials in several areas to ask, "Why continue to rebuild facilities on coastal barrier islands and exposed dunes?" Of course, environmentalists have long argued that these areas should have little development. The occasional sweep of a hurricane across such areas is, in fact, beneficial to the environment, they say.

The confrontation can only increase in intensity. Population growth in hurricane-prone areas is increasing at twice the national average. Continued high-density construction on some barrier islands may well be creating death traps for the future.

Many such resort and retirement communities rest on sand three to eight feet above sea level. In an emergency evacuation, thousands of residents would rely on one two-lane road connected to the mainland by a bridge or causeway subject to blockage by a single mishap.

Perhaps the greatest area of risk to lives and property is in the Florida Keys. Throughout the string of islands connected by bridge and causeway for nearly 100 miles, the only lifeline is the Overseas Highway, which ranges in elevation from three to 10 feet above sea level. Given 24 hours warning of a direct hit, it is very doubtful that the populace could be evacuated.

Thunderstorms and Tornados

Thunderstorms are fascinating. Lie on the beach at Daytona almost any summer day and watch them grow. At mid-morning, the sky is clear. An hour later, wispy scattered clouds appear. By noon they are puffy cumulus, the cotton-ball variety. Some, but not all, now begin to grow vertically. By mid-afternoon, there are great towering columns of heavy cumulus, dark at the bottom.

Then comes the first crack of lightning, the rumble of thunder, and spatters of big drops of rain. A few of the cumulus giants grow fat and black and dump deluges below. At the center of these cells is a fury of turbulence, including powerful down drafts which bring cool air from high altitude. The area beneath the cell is cooled, soaked and blasted by gusts.

An hour later, the cell is dissipating, and by late in the day, most are gone. The show is over until the next day.

The same performance can be witnessed around the world, wherever warm, moist air and conditions for convection development occur. We have watched the cells grow with equal fascination in Honolulu, Bangkok and Manaus.

Pilots soon become connoisseurs of thunderstorms. They learn that thunderstorms can be beautiful, majestic and inspiring, and they can be ominous, intimidating and awesome. The same storm can be safe and brilliantly white on top and black and deadly underneath.

Your author may someday attempt to write something called, "Dodging Thunderstorms For Fun and Profit." We have spent a large part of our life flying in warm climates where coping with thunderstorms is a way of life. Once we flew a small single-engine Cessna during the summer rainy season from Miami along the islands to Puerto Rico and Trinidad; then along the coast of South America to Venezuela, Colombia and Panama; and then back through Central America and Mexico to Texas, Mobile and Atlanta.

The flight covered more than 5,000 miles, and we were seldom out of sight of a towering cumulus build-up marking a cell. Off Trinidad we encountered an intertropical front studded with massive storms. Between Cartagena and Panama we crossed the Gulf of Turbo and Darien Peninsula, one of the wettest spots in the hemisphere. Arriving at Panama's Tocumen International Airport, we dodged thunderstorm cells as we have had to do every time we have visited the airport over a period of 25 years.

Clearly, the inhabitants of this large area learn to live with thunderstorms, as they do in Southeast Asia and India. One of the greatest displays of lightning we have ever seen occurred one night between Calcutta and Karachi as the monsoon season was beginning.

For sheer quantity of thunderstorms we'll nominate the upper Amazon Basin east of the Andes. We once flew that route from Peru to Manaus, crossing a sea of green jungle for more than 2,000 miles, every foot of the way plagued with cumulonimbus.

Most of our thunderstorm-dodging has been done, not in exotic foreign lands, but in routine travel around the U.S. The storms found in this country include not only those that start from tropical conditions but also those of other origins.

Thunderstorms develop along mountain ranges where prevailing winds drive warm moist surface air up the slopes to a point that condensation occurs. Downwind, the storms build regularly. Find a lounge chair and sit on a Colorado Springs patio on just about any late-summer afternoon and you can see them grow along the east front of the Rockies.

Still other thunderstorms result from air mass movements, typically the collision of a fast-moving cold front with warm moist air. While this can occur almost anywhere, certain parts of the country offer prime conditions more frequently.

Areas of greatest thunderstorm activity include Florida, the Gulf Coast and the east slopes of the Rockies. Some areas are almost immune. For example, we lived in the San Francisco Bay area for several years and seldom saw anything resembling a thunderstorm. (On a recent trip, however, we had to circumnavigate numerous cells between Oakland and Santa Monica.)

One of the biggest isolated thunderstorms we've ever seen was sitting right over Dodge City, Kansas. We detoured another monster half way across South Dakota and once pushed the airplane into a hangar in Austin just as golf-ball-sized hail started putting dents in everything around. And one of our worst experiences occurred over West Virginia when the controller stopped giving radar information suddenly, leaving us boxed in between several big ones. The airplane stood on end and blue flame skipped along the wings.

Once, over Kansas, we saw a small tornado develop. Flying alongside we watched the funnel drop down, slurp a large farm pond dry, then lift up in a cloud of dust and move on.

Man-Made Disasters

The preceding dealt with natural disasters — those visited upon mankind by the forces of nature and over which man has little or no control. By contrast, the physical disasters covered here have as a common denominator the fact that all stem from errors of commission or omission by man.

These man-made disasters cover a spectrum ranging from accidents to technical misunderstandings to ignorance. They include such newly recognized hazards as Thalidomide, DES, asbestos, PCBs, nuclear wastes, battery additives and swine flu vaccines, as well as such old, established risks as fire, pestilence, famine and war. All can be lethal.

Unlike most of the natural disasters described earlier, some of the disasters covered here do not give any warning. In fact, the victim may not realize he has been exposed to the risk until long after receiving a potentially fatal dosage. This peril is particularly pertinent to such risks as nuclear radiation and toxic materials. Others, such as fire, famine and revolution, provide varying degrees of advance notice.

359

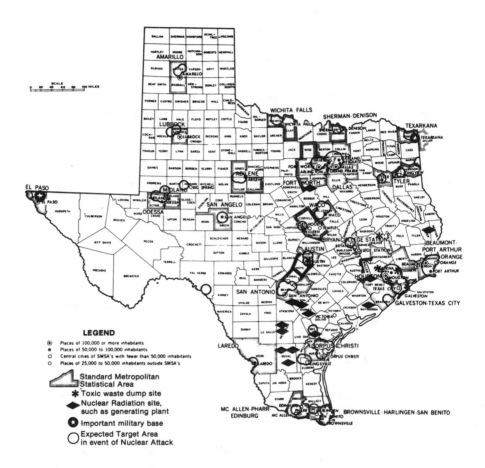

Texas

Disaster risks for a state. This is a typical state map from our book on disaster risks.

Ecosystem Mismanagement: 'Ecodoom'

Man's life support systems depend on air, water and food of reasonable purity. In a highly complex society, maintenance of a safe supply of these basic support elements is often difficult. Current life styles invite disaster hazards.

The Food Chain. Whether we examine the natural food chain of animals or today's mechanized food chain for people, we find many examples of hazards. A century ago, people grew their own food without chemicals and ate it at home, making it very unlikely that a toxic material could be spread throughout the food chain to large numbers of people. Today, however, millions of people shop at stores or eat in restaurants that are supplied by central food distributors who, in turn, buy from sources making wide use of pesticides, fungicides, fertilizers, preservatives, coloring agents and other materials.

In the present system, the possibilities for accidents, technical errors, blunders and mischief are almost endless. A sobering example is the 1973 Michigan disaster involving polybrominated biphenyls (PBBs). A mix-up occurred at a warehouse, and PBBs intended for use as a fire retardant were sent to a processing plant where the toxic material was put into cattle feed and distributed to local mills, and then to farmers throughout Michigan.

Before the problem was identified nearly a year later a large proportion of the residents of Michigan had ingested PBBs. The poisons have lodged in their body fat, perhaps for their lifetime. The ultimate effect on victims is not yet known.

However, the devastating effect of large doses received by animals in Michigan is all too clear — a total of more than 30,000 cattle died or had to be destroyed. Also, millions of chickens, birds and other small animals died. The economic cost continues, with the governor of Michigan in 1980 requesting federal disaster funds to clean up a PBB dump in Gratiot County.

International risks are greater because of communications problems, especially language barriers. This disaster risk was tragically confirmed in 1971 when inedible wheat intended for planting was shipped from Mexico to Iraq. Treated with a mercury compound to prevent fungus, the planting wheat was died pink, and each bag carried a notation that the wheat was not to be used as food for animals or people. The warning, unfortunately, was in Spanish.

It has been estimated that within two years several thousand Iraqi peasants died and thousands more were seriously poisoned. There is evidence also that the absorbed mercury is being passed on to the next generation in new-born babies.

About the time of the disaster in Iraq, a mercury scare hit the U.S. Surprisingly high mercury concentrations were found in tuna and swordfish. Mercury wastes being dumped into lakes and rivers were suspected, and an aggressive regulatory program resulted. Mercury pollution today seems to be under control, but past events reveal a fragile balance that requires close monitoring.

The decades of the Seventies also brought high-pitched battles over food additives. Many people in the early Seventies became paranoid about the great variety of additives put in almost all widely marketed foods — additives to add flavor, to preserve, to color or to tenderize.

The government overreacted, banning any product which could be proven to cause cancer in mice. Research methods and interpretations were, to say the least, questionable. The result was decisions reflecting a lack of common sense — an additive that might have saved lives by better preserving a food might, for example, be prohibited because it might cause cancer if the user every day drank 500 cans of a beverage containing the additive.

There were celebrated debates over Saccharin and artificial sweeteners; cyclamates in diet soda; BHA in peanut butter; and nitrites in cured ham. Research was expanded. Generally, the findings suggest that, taken in moderate amount, such materials are, at best, lesser risks.

This conclusion is reinforced by better understanding of the food chain. We now know that many of the foods that have sustained man throughout history — potatoes and even spinach — contain materials that may cause cancer in mice.

There also appears to be a more mature understanding of the role of pesticides and similar materials. We now know enough about them to recognize that they can do many good things for mankind, while at the same time posing great risks. The first big experience was with DDT during WWII, when the new insecticide was credited with preventing a typhus epidemic in Europe.

After WWII, DDT was introduced all over the world for pest control. Malaria deaths were reduced spectacularly in tropical regions, and agricultural production was boosted in the U.S. Subsequently, it became apparent that DDT, like many other materials to follow, had a darker side. It killed beneficial insects and the pests often developed an immunity.

More important, DDT got into the food chain. It was washed from fields into streams and impacted on aquatic life. Use was prohibited.

War: The Ultimate Man-Made Disaster

All wars are disasters, but some are worse than others. For this discussion we will classify them crudely as: Underground wars; Local or regional wars; Global wars using conventional weapons; and Global wars using NBC weapons.

1. *Underground Wars.* This type of conflict is most difficult to define and describe. It is just surfacing on the world scene. We are speaking of an undeclared or surrogate assault on another nation via propaganda and subversive activities, supported by terrorist actions, designed to weaken or overthrow the government of the enemy nation.

2. *Local Wars.* What is the real reason for the U.S. citizen to risk bloody battles in local wars in far-away places? The important consideration is that in today's shrunken world we cannot stand alone. With less than five percent of the world's population and lacking many critical materials, we must not permit any enemy power to pick off friendly or neutral nations one by one and eventually leave us isolated.

This is the reason we got involved in Viet Nam originally. The USSR and China were part of what appeared to be a strong communist global bloc which could move through Southeast Asia, take over vast resources, cut global sealanes at Singapore, outflank Australia and drastically alter the balance of world strength.

We tried to support the free nations of Southeast Asia, for which we should not apologize. We made the mistake, however, of committing ground forces to fight on enemy terms rather than utilizing our air and naval superiority promptly and fully.

Today, there are somewhat similar situations in the Middle East and elsewhere.

If we resist aggression in the local and regional situations — effectively — we may avoid a global war later. However, if we intervene clumsily or without effectiveness, we may hasten the advent of a larger war. It is the most difficult decision the White House faces.

3. *Global Wars Using Conventional Weapons.* (Not involving nuclear, bacteriological or chemical warfare.) When we view the threat of large-scale global warfare, we narrow the number of possible conflicts. Only a few powers have the forces to mount such a struggle, which would involve millions of men and great fleets of ships, aircraft and missiles.

To see what a third World War of this type would be like, we need only add to the WWII script some new technology and a revised list of combatants.

The war itself would involve attacks against U.S. cities and other targets via missiles launched from submarines, polar aircraft sorties and aircraft and missiles. At the same time, U.S. missiles and bombs would be launched from land bases, submarines and aircraft carriers. Both sides would absorb heavy damage, even though nuclear weapons were not used.

The losses to air and surface forces would also be heavy on both sides. Shipping would come to a virtual halt as a result of submarine action. It could be a long war, determined by the capability of the combatants to produce new armaments while under attack.

This could well result in mass movement of industrial operations to safer areas away from the big cities. Underground sites would be much in demand.

Destruction by bomb blast and fire in major cities would create housing shortages and generate a refugee problem. The WWII Battle of London gives some notion of what conventional weapons, even the "primitive" missiles of that era, can do to a city.

Such a war might be decisive, or it might end in a truce somewhat like the Korean War. If there were a winner, it would be a costly and hollow victory.

The least that the surviving U.S. citizen could expect from such a conflict would be disappearance of consumer goods from stores, rationing of all key commodities, wage and price control, and a lively black market. It might also include forced labor battalions and forced sharing of housing, something that was not required in the U.S. in WWII.

4. *Global Wars Using NBC Weapons.* This is the ultimate man-made disaster. It is a dirty-tricks war using megatons of nuclear bombs, germ warfare, nerve gas and any other evil scheme to kill the enemy. It would be fought with intercontinental missiles, and so much destruction might occur in the first day that the war would, for practical purposes, be over.

Some experts believe such a war would result in total destruction of the earth or of all life on it. It may be more accurate to forecast great ecological damage, plus a billion or more casualties.

At stake would be the survival of entire populations and the habitability of entire nations. Medical services for treatment of survivors would be totally and hopelessly inadequate.

We believe, however, that many would survive, and, the over-population problem having been solved, the survivors would find space to rebuild their lives. History tells us, however, that after such great shocks civilization has sometimes been set back for centuries.

Evaluation of Risk Potential

At first glance, the potential disasters may seem to be so many and so all-pervasive that the survival planner may feel that the task is hopeless. There are a lot of real risks, and there is no place on earth that is completely safe.

Closer examination of the risks, real or potential, reveals, however, that opportunities to reduce or avoid risk are abundant. First, look at the scope of disasters of various types. It is evident that only a few disasters have the capability of bringing destruction to the entire world.

Astronomical phenomena, such as an asteroid collision with the earth, or a rearrangement, even minor, in the solar system would probably constitute the greatest possible disaster threat. However, our present knowledge also suggests that this is a very low risk.

Only a few types of disasters pose an immediate threat to the globe. A very large volcanic eruption could send enough ash into the air to cause climatic changes for several years and, hence, create great problems. A bigger risk is an all-out global war wherein nuclear, bacteriological or chemical weapons are widely used. Even a limited or accidental use of such weapons could have global impact.

However, most disasters would have direct impact on a much smaller geographic area. Floods, blizzards and hurricanes while serious, are limited in scope. Even smaller is the scope of such hazards as tornadoes, oil spills and landslides.

In addition to the scope of the potential disaster, it is also necessary to consider:
- The probability that the disaster will occur;
- The potential damage to life and property if the disaster should occur;
- The opportunity which a private citizen might have to minimize the risk through sound planning and preparation.

Most of these considerations relate directly to location. Hence, the most important item on the planner's agenda must be a scrutiny of risk potential for each location in which he is interested. This must include the location of one's home, one's job location, locations where investments are made and locations which may be visited during travel.

Regardless of the location of the nation, state or city, many risk factors are related specifically to the site of one's home, business or other facility. Here are some questions:

Terrain
- Is the site in a flood plain?
- Is the site on a shore exposed to tidal wave or hurricane surge?
- Is the site in a canyon or narrow valley where flash flood waters would rise?
- Does the site lie between hills that might give blast protection?

Geological conditions
- Is the site subject to subsidence?
- Is the soil of the expansive type?

• Is the site subject to avalanches or landslides?

Atmospheric risks
• After checking prevailing wind, is there a nuclear facility upwind?
• Are there large smokestacks of any kind upwind?
• Is there a volcano upwind?

Drainage risks
• If using a well or stream, is there a toxic dump upstream?
• Is there a municipal treatment plant upstream?
• Is there an industrial treatment plant upstream?

Transportation risks
• Is access to the site dependent on a large bridge?
• Is the site dependent on a canal or narrow channel?
• Is the site exposed to toxic spills from abutting rail or highway?

Survival Planning: Site Hardening and Escape Contingencies

Having listed and evaluated disaster risks and having selected suitable geographic locations, we still enjoy numerous opportunities to further reduce our risk. By development of prudent survival plans for our households, our businesses and other interests, we can mitigate many disaster hazards or facilitate escape if our site becomes untenable.

We think current events suggest strongly that the facility planners re-examine the checklist in light of needs for providing greater corporate survival capability.

For most facility planners and developers this approach may require some fundamental adjustment in thinking. The typical pattern in real estate development is to go with the crowd, to build in clusters, to seek maximum visibility and proudly to display the facility to the public. Bring in a military tactician and he will argue that such factors make defense of the facility difficult, if not impossible.

More defensible is a secluded site, structures screened from view, with tightly controlled access. Windows on an inner courtyard pose fewer risks than those exposed to a busy thoroughfare.

Dispersal. Should your company pursue a deliberate plan of placing new units well apart and, perhaps, in areas of low population density?

Isolation. Should you select new locations not near or adjacent to other developments — military, governmental or industrial?

Seclusion. Should you plan for low visibility and limited access, sacrificing advertising or public relations values?

Perimeter protection. Should you require solid exterior walls, beams and similar defenses around buildings?

Self-contained services. Should you consider on-site utility back-up, such as an elevated water tank, auxiliary power generator, fuel storage?

Access. Should you have your own airstrip or heliport? Should you maintain ATVs (all-terrain vehicles)?

Building specification. Should you require earthquake-proof, blast-resistant, sprinklered construction? Should you consider building underground?

Without doubt, our greatest failure in setting national policy and establishing government programs is our neglect of the basic principle of self-help. We are being told, in effect, by some federal planners that if Congress will just appropriate enough money for their agency, we will be safe. In reality, the increased budgets appear to go into building larger staffs, setting up more offices and doling out more aid funds after the disasters occur.

Instead, we ought to be teaching that no individual or household survival plan is sound if it is based on the assumption that when panic occurs someone in Washington will fix it.

Will Civilization Survive?

Looking at the page count on our manuscript draft, we find that we have now devoted well over 400 pages to discussion of potential disaster, death and doom. It is not an exercise that lifts the spirits!

However, as we close, we want it clearly understood that we are optimistic about the future. We believe a large number of intelligent people are going to overcome whatever pitfalls the future holds. Our children and our grandchildren are going to find ways to cope with both old and new hazards.

Civilization will not only survive, it will flourish!

1981
Excerpt

Industrial Park Growth. Introduction — the dream of a good place to work. Emergence of the park concept and proliferation of units. Performance standards and design criteria. Types of parks. Park site supply and demand. Industrial Parks for the future. 1981. Second edition. Hard cover. 546 pp. With Linda L. Liston.

We live in an era in which much is said about "the good life." While there are no precise definitions, the phrase seems to conjure a vision of physical comfort, mental ease and a degree of affluence. "Quality of life" analyses bring in many factors in more detail. Aesthetic and environmental considerations loom ever larger.

For most citizens, the good life requires work at a regular job. Many workers, even in a modern society geared to the 35- to 40-hour week, spend a substantial proportion of their waking hours at or near their places of employment. When this necessity is combined with the aesthetic goals of the good life, a pleasing work place becomes an integral part of the revolution of rising expectations.

This dream of a good place to work is being delivered today in thousands of planned industrial parks. This is a success story that provides graphic testimony to confirm several important facts: The American enterprise system works!

Private sector organizations have developed the park idea and marketed the concept as well as the land. Corporate planners have designed facilities to increasingly high performance standards, not because of government prodding but because it was good business.

As in other fields of business, products of better quality sold better. Local governments in many cases have taken the initiative and provided infrastructure support, thus gaining an important competitive edge for their communities. This has been beneficial to taxpayers and park occupants as well.

Because of these and other aspects, we believe the flowering of the industrial park movement in our lifetime is highly significant, not only to the business community but also to society as a whole.

Emergence of the Park Concept

Organized in 1896, Trafford Park Estates in Manchester, England, claims the distinction of being the first planned district. A high-density project of 1,200 acres, Trafford eventually attracted more than 200 manufacturers having at one time a total of 50,000 workers.

In the U.S., the Central Manufacturing District, in Chicago, claims the distinction of being first. It was launched on a 220-acre site in 1903. A rival claim comes from a North Kansas City project incorporated in 1903 by Armour and Swift.

Despite these early starts, however, only a few dozen projects had been built prior to World War II. Undoubtedly, the stultifying depression of the 1930s was a factor. But the war brought a drastic increase in the mobility of the American people and their awareness of regions other than the one in which they lived.

In the postwar period, there was a fresh outlook toward geography and marketing. Firms once looking only at their own metro areas began thinking of regional opportunities; regional firms began seeking national distribution. New manufacturing and distribution facilities were an essential part of this expansion outlook. Simultaneously, corporations felt the psychological impact of well-traveled returning veterans who were willing and anxious to try new ideas.

Into this receptive business environment came the emerging concept of planned industrial districts which met such functional site needs as protected space, access to transportation routes, utilities and drainage. The approach made sense to the new executives.

Decade of the Take-Off

As the decade of the 1950s began there were, perhaps, 100 industrial districts underway. Growth appears to have been rather slow in the early Fifties and then to have exploded at mid-decade.

Reports in *Manufacturers Record*, the predecessor of *Industrial Development*, were spotty, but when *Industrial Development* began in 1954 a substantial amount of space was devoted to the launching of new districts.

In 1955, *Industrial Development* reported that Massachusetts was

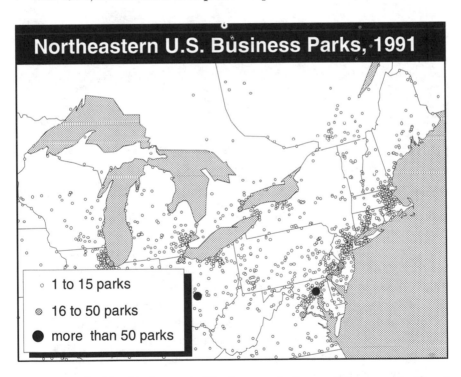

Northeastern U.S. Business Parks, 1991

○ 1 to 15 parks

⊛ 16 to 50 parks

● more than 50 parks

Business parks. The development of business parks is one of the more significant environmental movements of the 20th century. Our annual survey determines occupancy as well as geographic distribution.

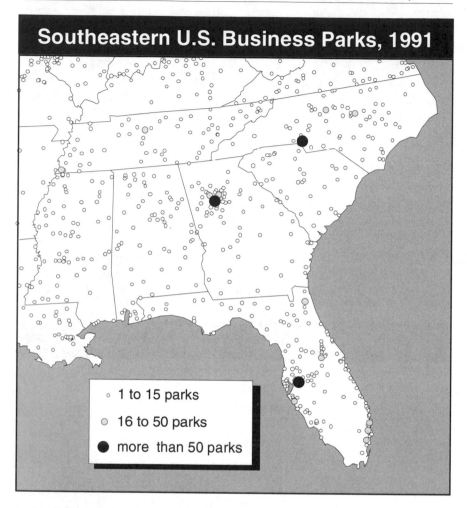

Southeastern U.S. Business Parks, 1991

○ 1 to 15 parks

◎ 16 to 50 parks

● more than 50 parks

going "all-out" to organize new districts and was a leader in the movement. The report included a map showing 16 projects.

Toward the end of the decade, the spread of industrial districts had reached all parts of the nation, and the total number of projects was nearing 1,000. Trends were also giving hints of changes to come.

In the beginning, railroads were a dominant factor in industrial district development. Most projects were either launched by railroads on railroad-owned sites or involved railroads heavily in their plans.

By the end of the decade, however, non-rail projects were appearing in increasing numbers. The rails were still dominant, but competition was on the way.

The Fifties also saw the beginning of a concern that was later to grow into a major confrontation — the relation of industrial districts to urban plans. Questions regarding jurisdictions, rights and principles were heard increasingly as new projects were undertaken and developers encountered newly enacted zoning ordinances in areas where no such standards had existed previously.

Terminology had become a problem. The early projects were called industrial districts, and they typically stressed the functional needs of industry — roads, rails and utility services — to the exclusion of other considerations. Projects which came later and which provided for aesthetic standards — landscaping, sign control, architectural compatibility — were typically called parks. In the United Kingdom and elsewhere the term "industrial estate" was used for either type of development.

This confusion was compounded by those who optioned a cow pasture and put up a sign proclaiming it to be the Podunk Industrial Park. (This was a major problem for the staff of *Industrial Development* at the time. We received many listings for "cow pasture parks," and while we weeded many of them out, enough slipped by and were reported to embarrass us.) As the industrial park movement grew, so did its credibility problem.

While the Interstate Highway system was launched following passage of the Federal Highway Act in 1956, only a limited amount of progress was visible until the 1960s. Then, as right-of-way swaths were cut across the country and concrete was poured, a revolution took place.

It is probably safe to say that thus far into the 20th century no government program has had such a profound physical impact on national growth and development. Hundreds of towns were reoriented; the center of gravity of scores of metro areas was moved; and thousands of prime new sites were created.

In terms of industrial location practices, the new highway system was truly a bombshell. Within the span of a decade the Interstate ramps became the magnets which attracted a high percentage of new industrial parks, most new office parks and many new shopping centers.

For many, this dramatic change in location patterns went almost unnoticed. The new Interstate system was not built overnight. The new routes were not contracted contiguously — even when half of the total mileage was paved, not one complete route was open to traffic!

Thus, the impact was felt one small segment at a time, and site opportunities were spotty. In some locations, where the radials and circumferential routes serving metro areas were the first segments built, there was immediate development. In other locations where this construction was delayed, developers suffered acute frustration.

Still another major development of the 1960s was the mushrooming expansion of corporate aviation. Literally thousands of firms, among them the cream of the new facility location market, began operating their own aircraft and discovered a new viewpoint toward site selection. Locations on or near airports rapidly gained favor.

This was also the period during which the industrial park movement spread around the world. Through U.S. programs, such as AID/PEP (Agency for International Development/Private Enterprise Promotion), groups in many countries were brought to the U.S. to see industrial parks and were briefed on planning, development and promotion strategies. Then they were supported in launching ventures in their own nations.

Concurrently, the United Nations issued publications and gave program support to many such projects. Some ambitious industrial estates were launched in remote areas where chances of success were very slim. Others, adapted to the scale and sophistication level of local situations, fared well.

The creeping bureaucracy of development was a matter of concern in the Sixties. But in the early Seventies bureaucracy exploded to unprecedented proportions. Vast new regulatory programs cascaded from Washington — the Clean Air Act, the water quality program, the Environmental Protection Agency, the HUD controls on interstate land sales and many others.

Industrial park developers, already committed to high performance standards for their projects, were, nonetheless, caught in a web of new procedures that soaked up managerial time, added to planning costs, and worse, delayed projects unreasonably.

Embattled developers circled the wagons and formed the National Association of Office and Industrial Parks. NAIOP soon proved its worth by assisting in the struggle to have industrial site sales excluded from the more onerous HUD regulatory procedures for interstate land sales.

As if the bureaucratic assault of the early Seventies were not enough, park developers was hit in 1974-76 with the worst real estate depression since the 1930s. One analysis termed this "the Panic of '75," reporting that few large projects in any part of the country escaped economic damage. Certainly, it was a monumental shake-out.

Surviving projects and ventures in the late Seventies are now involved in the fiercest competition ever seen in the industrial location profession. Where once a developer might have had the only planned park in town, today he may have 10 direct competitors.

One result of this competition is that newer parks are being planned as specialized projects with a specific appeal, such as airport location, Interstate access, R&D theme or distribution center. Some even feature golf courses and saunas. In general, metro area projects are more complex and more expensive.

It is a testimony to the determination of American developers that, despite all obstacles, the number of significant parks doubled again during 1970-78, giving a total of 4,300.

It must be noted, however, that it was possible to achieve this new total at least in part by virtue of a deliberate program of creating new parks in small towns and rural areas. Where parks had at one time been considered as an urban planning tool, they became a development mechanism wherever job-creating industries were sought.

Performance Standards and Design Criteria

The campus-like industrial parks of today compare with the switch-yard-like districts of yesterday as a corporate jet does with a Model T. This advance has come about through an evolutionary process of planning refinement which extends to every facet of park design, construction and operation.

Basically, park planning has moved through three phases — the early phase of emphasis on functional considerations; a second phase in which aesthetic factors became important; and, now, a third phase of refinement and specialization.

If the first phase of park development was aimed at meeting basic functional needs of industry — satisfying the symbolic stomach — the second phase responded to the needs of the mind and spirit, as aesthetic factors became more than a tangential concern.

It is likely that one reason for the rapid rise of aesthetics as a location factor was the change in the type of people employed in industrial plants. The aesthetic emphasis coincided with the emergence of large numbers of high-technology industries. This meant a work force of high-income graduate scientists and technicians who attached more importance to their personal environment.

Whether it was employee morale, company pride, advertising objectives, community relations, or, more likely, a combination of all, site-seeking firms increasingly looked for parks where they saw good landscaping, coordinated graphics, lower density, underground utilities and other evidence of good design and management. In any event, thousands of firms discovered that sites in such projects constituted a good corporate investment.

Much of this change occurred without any coercion from any governmental entity, long before EPA surfaced. In fact, a number of parks with very high standards were developed in the unincorporated areas of counties having no zoning programs. In many other cases, parks within jurisdictions having planning programs set higher standards than required by law.

Our point is that industrial parks of high standards were first developed by private sector developers to meet the demands of private sector tenants and buyers. This is not to discredit any efforts of public bodies seeking to promote industrial parks but to counter the current thinking that the private sector takes an interest in good environmental planning only when forced to do so.

Nonetheless, the industrial park movement soon encountered the parallel spread of local planning and zoning programs throughout the country. The same fast-growing suburban areas in which industrial firms were looking for new sites were turning to comprehensive planning to find approaches to growth management.

At first, the encounters between industrial park developers and local planners were peaceful enough. Each saw the other in a complementary role, often striving to resolve common problems. As the suburban population moved toward anti-growth and no-growth thinking, however, clashes came with increasing frequency.

While park development moved from the purely functional stage to the aesthetically pleasing stage, public-sector planning and zoning moved concurrently from zero planning to inadequate to comprehensive. For a time, there was rather general agreement on the elements of a comprehensive plan for an industrial area.

As sophistication grew, dissatisfaction with the old "classification" system of industrial zoning grew. This was the traditional designation of areas for "light industry" and "heavy industry," plus a listing of the types of activities permissible in each area.

Typically, chemical process, electrometallurgical, slaughtering and rendering, steel, cement and petroleum refining were assumed to be most undesirable and were placed in heavy industry areas. Printing, electronics, precision machining, service and distribution were allowed in the light industry areas.

Time proved the fallacy of this "label" approach. Once-small electronics operations in some cases grew to be very large operations with heavy traffic and difficult-to-treat wastes. New technology brought forth small electrometallurgical operations which were housed in attractive small buildings and created no effluent problems.

Clearly, a new system was needed which depended not on labels but on the reality of a plant's impact on its neighbors. This was the new system of performance standards. Originally, performance standards were put forward to cover such factors as:

- Noise
- Smoke

- Odor
- Dust and dirt
- Noxious gases
- Glare and heat
- Fire hazards
- Industrial wastes
- Transportation and traffic
- Aesthetics

This is not to report that performance standards provided an immediate solution to all industrial zoning questions in these areas. Some performance standards were easily defined, enacted and enforced. Others, especially in the realm of air emissions, proved to be extremely difficult to set and monitor, as witnessed by the 1979 debates over EPA's Clean Air Act amendments.

Among the various planning standards adopted for whatever reason the most significant probably was the space requirement. Usually specified in permissible site-to-building ratio (S/B), this standard has a major effect on the external appearance of a park and may have a large impact on such factors as environmental harmony and site economics.

The progression of events led to the situation today wherein many industrial parks are controlled by two sets of restrictions — the park deed covenants and the local zoning law. It is essential to know the difference between the two and understand their application.

Deed covenants are contractual agreements between private parties — the developer and the occupants of the park. Generally, they are recorded at the County Courthouse. All property owners agree to the covenants and any one of them can sue any other to seek to enforce them or to require adherence. Covenants are valid for a specified period of time, typically 20 years. They may apply not only to planning standards but also to future operations and maintenance.

It is usually difficult and often impossible to change deed covenants. In some cases, all of those who signed the original covenants must agree to any change.

Zoning laws, by contrast, are the creation of the local governing body and are susceptible to frequent change, for better or worse. Typically, zoning power is held by municipalities, counties and, in some states, townships, by virtue of home rule provisions of the state constitution or specific enabling laws enacted by the state legislature.

With the proliferation of planning standards, there has come a realization that not all industrial parks can or should meet the same criteria. What makes sense in a 3,000-acre waterfront tract laid out for large processing

375

plants may not be rational in a 25-acre, freeway-fronting, high-rise office park.

1982
Excerpt

The Good Life Index. Recognizing that "the good life" is a highly subjective concept, varying widely from person to person and corporation to corporation, this new approach provides the reader with a method for systematically seeking out the places which offer desired attributes. The quest for a QOL measure. Criteria for the good life. Analyzing states. Examining metro, city and local areas. Making global analyses. Making your own good life evaluation. 1981. 416 pp. Hard cover. With Linda L. Liston. Reviewed in *The Futurist*, World Future Society, June 1982. pp 75-77.

There is abundant evidence that freedom to move is considered priceless around the world.

Cubans and Haitians embark on treacherous voyages across a shark-infested sea in makeshift rafts and flimsy boats to move their place of residence to Florida. Eastern Europeans venture across fields of land mines, scale electric fences and risk automatic weapons fire to find new homes in the West. Vietnamese and Cambodians jump from overloaded ships and swim ashore on remote islands en route to new places to live.

In the United States, the right to move is one of the freedoms Americans treasure most highly. As a result, Americans have the greatest degree of mobility in the world.

A U.S. family can decide to move from Maine to Oregon or Montana to Texas and, without approval of any government entity, implement that decision whenever it pleases. The only constraints are economic, and they are not great.

Americans enjoy not only mobility, but also a great range of selections in terms of local government, climate and many other factors. This wonderful freedom of choice applies not only to individuals and families, but also to business ventures and investments, and site selection for offices, warehouses and manufacturing plants.

In the early days of development in the U.S., dire economic necessity was the dominant consideration in determining where people moved. Settlers went west to homestead on new land. Increasingly, the wealth of the nation permitted people to consider other factors to choose places where they wanted to live. The same thing happened for many business firms.

Today, there is such a rich variety of choices that both individuals and companies can make comprehensive studies to decide which of many opportunities offers the greatest prospect for the good life.

We have been engaged in gathering data and devising techniques for selecting industrial sites for more than 25 years. This work has yielded many studies which are listed in a cumulative index recently published. Also, we have recently published a book on disaster risks and their geographic aspects. *The Good Life Index*, therefore, is a companion to others in a series and, in fact, an answer to those who, after reading the disaster book, asked, "Now that you've told us where not to locate, why don't you tell us how to find the good places?"

We have sought to include in this study information that will be helpful both to business executives examining Quality of Life (QOL) factors as part of a broad site analysis, and to individuals planning to relocate or set up a new home. It should be useful both to those making a casual comparison of a few nearby areas, as well as to those who must study many far-flung locales.

The geographic scope of location studies is established by the nature of the entity involved and its policies. A multinational corporation may recognize no geographic constraints — it may extract minerals on one continent, process them on another and sell the products in a third. A couple from New York may choose, however, to limit its search for a retirement home to the Florida East Coast.

Whatever the scope of the search, it is generally best to start with comparisons of large geographic entities and proceed to increasingly smaller units. The multinational corporation may first compare nations, then states or provinces, then cities or counties, then sites. The retirement home seeker may start with states, then proceed to counties or cities.

Consideration of specific sites should be done last. If sites are compared first, the time and money spent to gather data on those in states, counties or other jurisdictions that fail to pass screening tests will be wasted.

The depth and, hence, the cost of a location analysis is almost infinitely variable. It is easily possible to spend millions on analysis of factors related to a large new industrial facility. Those who wish to spend less must, therefore, restrict the depth of their location research.

Data may be available to make hundreds of comparisons. To control the budget, however, it is necessary to select a limited number of factors for study. In this book, we have also limited our analyses to a fraction of those factors on which data is readily available.

Altogether, we have included data suitable for comparing states on the basis of 30 key factors. For metro areas, there are 13 points of comparison;

for counties, seven statistical keys; and for cities, another seven indices.

Recognizing that there can be a "best list" of factors for only one user, we have attempted to select those factors which are both universal in interest and pertinent to the needs of the people involved in making site selection decisions. Besides wanting a mixture of factors for broad usage, we felt the need for including factors for which data is readily accessible, frequently updated and generated by accepted reliable sources.

The Quest for a Quality of Life Measure

While there has always been interest in quality-of-life considerations, they did not loom as major economic factors for new plant location and professional planning until the 1960s. Interest grew concurrently with the emergence of high-technology industries which require locations attractive to highly mobile scientists and engineers.

During the past decade, federal agencies, leading research institutes, universities, non-profit professional organizations and countless private firms have invested large amounts of money, manpower and time in searching for a practical nationwide measure of quality of life.

A series of important studies was launched by Midwest Research Institute, based in Kansas City, resulting in a widely discussed report issued in 1973. MRI selected as prime factors the status of individuals, equality, living conditions, agriculture, technology, economic status, education, health and welfare and state and local government. In each of these categories, there were several sub-categories, and for each of them several more detailed facets. States were ranked for each of the major factors, and for an overall or composite measure.

Of course, the MRI study provoked an immediate reaction. Favored states in the Northwest hailed the study as gospel. Low-ranked states in the Southeast suggested flawed logic. Neutral observers pointed out that quality of life varies so much within individual states that state rankings by themselves were inherently inadequate.

MRI responded with a new and broader study which gave comparative quality of life ratings for metro areas. Made possible by a grant from the Environmental Protection Agency, the new study sought to compare the then 243 Standard Metropolitan Statistical Areas (SMSAs) on the basis of five main factors: economic, political, environmental, health and education and social. From these, more than 100 sub-factors were derived.

While this study again gave high ratings to West Coast and Mountain areas, MRI pointed out that the regional differential in QOL evaluation was much less significant in this metropolitan study than in the earlier state study. The implication of this, in MRI's words, was that "for urban policy to be efficient and effective, each SMSA must be examined independently and its priorities set individually."

Concurrent with the MRI work, other groups were probing QOL factors, seeking common threads and methods for quantitative analysis. One of the more significant efforts was reported by researchers at the Battelle Columbus Laboratories in a paper that appeared in *Industrial Development* (Sept/Oct 1975, pp. 9-15).

Utilizing an innovative procedure, researchers John M. Griffin and Norbert Dee compared QOL factors and physical characteristics to obtain an index based on three key factors: economic, environmental and social. Each of these subject areas was covered via a group of factors to yield a comparison of cities.

Once more, publication of the research findings appeared to raise as many questions as were answered. Of the cities examined by Battelle, highest ranking went to Allentown, Pennsylvania, while a very low rating went to Jacksonville, Florida. Even among those whose civic pride was not involved, it was difficult to correlate these findings with actual migration and growth experience.

Still another interesting study was conducted at the University of Nebraska. This study compared 100 major U.S. cities on the basis of 80 factors and gave them numerical rankings.

The Nebraska study showed Lincoln to be number one and Omaha to be number four in the nation. Some critics suggested criteria may have been selected, perhaps inadvertently, to reflect favorably on Nebraska cities.

All of these studies are useful. They serve to reveal the complexity of developing valid ranking systems. However, they have yet to provide numerical ratings suitable for use by both individuals and business firms making location decisions. After a decade of extensive research we are still a very long way from having a commonly accepted index similar to GNP, CPI or Dow Jones.

Let's look at some of the problems:

First, many studies were planned and funded by sponsors seeking to serve a federal agency or other public sector interest. Whether by design or inadvertence, they set out to support certain public policies.

For example, a study might be set up to measure quality of education, using as an index public expenditure on education per pupil. Thus, the greater the budget, the higher the ranking would be. This served the bureaucracy, providing ammunition for proponents of higher taxes and bigger budgets.

Another study might be planned to measure the welfare of individuals, using as an index the per capita public expenditure for welfare payments. A high level of payments would thus earn a high ranking. Again, the results would serve to support bureaucrats at local, state and federal levels.

Examination of the criteria selected and the way rankings were conferred suggests that many of the early studies gave high rankings where government expenditures were high. Inasmuch as site seeking individuals and business firms often prefer areas where government expenditures and, thus, taxes are lower, it is obvious that the QOL reports failed to serve. (In fact, exhaustive site studies conducted by private firms often reached conclusions directly opposite to those reported by public bodies.)

Another problem is that most of the studies reported to date are entirely theoretical in nature. They begin with a set of statistics and seek to predict which areas have the greatest degree of attractiveness. They rank areas by the appeal they are assumed to have, rather than by appeal actually demonstrated.

Criteria for the Good Life

James Hilton's *Lost Horizon*, written in the 1930s, described the adventures of our mythical kinsman Hugh Conway when he was kidnapped and taken to now-fabled Shangri-La. Of special interest was the reaction of Conway, a sophisticated product of English schools and diplomatic service, to confinement in a hidden valley set apart from the world he knew by forbidding Asian mountain ranges.

As seen half a century ago, Shangri-La offered most of the elements of the good life — a pleasant climate, ample food, wealth, opportunities for study, security, privacy and an orderly but not oppressive administration. Winter snows blocked the passes, and the Conway party was forced to live for a year in this environment, which they found increasingly satisfying.

Finally, with the coming of spring, a passing caravan offered a chance for the members of the group to return to homes, families and jobs in Europe and America. Each then faced a location decision not unlike that which confronts millions today.

Wherever populations enjoy the freedom to move, there is a difficult, often agonizing, weighing of good life factors which precedes a final compromise. Each member of the Conway party reacted differently, basing his or her ultimate decision on a different set of factors. Most chose to live in Shangri-La, yet one member risked his life in a hazardous attempt to "escape." Conway left, but as the book ends, he disappears into the Asian mountains, apparently seeking to return to Shangri-La.

Today, it is even clearer that the good life means different things to different people. If we look closely at the good life we also must recognize that specific events contribute much to an individual's "happiness index." Surveys have identified major plus factors, such as, getting married, getting a good job, buying a new home, having a baby and taking a trip abroad. Negative events include a death in the family, a divorce, losing a job or becoming the victim of a crime.

Such special events, mingled with the everyday routine, are part of a total experience which may thus be evaluated by an individual as a bad life or a good life. We note this only to stress that one must not expect absolute precision in making good life evaluations for individuals. One may anticipate better results when studying groups.

A. Life-style Groups and Criteria

For our purposes here, we are most interested in those groups which, for a variety of reasons, are mobile. We will now attempt to identify several such groups and suggest their thinking regarding good life criteria:

1. *Career Starters*. Likely to be young, future-oriented, often making site choice to launch career. Important criteria: Job opportunities, area economic trends, growth outlook, learning situations, facilities for advanced education, less-constrained life style, area image, "in" places.

2. *Family and Community Builders*. Moving into middle age group, "upwardly mobile" in socio-economic strata, planning for medium term, may conduct location analysis related to company transfer or new job offer. Important criteria: Schools, housing, services, access, transportation, shopping, churches, local government, civic institutions, "status," national and regional headquarters, air service.

3. *Retiring or Retired*. Planning for today or near term, often looking for "ideal" site. Important criteria: Climate; medical services, cost of living; community environment; maximal recreation opportunities, minimal stress; social contacts programs; low-cost public transportation; security.

4. *Sophisticates*. Intellectuals who may change location to find a more satisfying atmosphere, or to pursue a specific interest. Important criteria: Cultural and artistic activities and resources; big-city institutions (theatre, libraries, museums, symphony, ballet); international attractions (crafts, languages, cultures); fashion; new-town-in-town, restored areas.

5. *Frontier People*. Self-sufficient, naturalists, conservationists, escapists, survivalists, may relocate to gain greater privacy, space or security. Important criteria: Sites in the country, forests, mountains; perhaps acreage for animals, crops; or remote sites for hideaways, survival retreats; often willing to forego many conveniences, services; solar; "Mother Earth," scenic beauty.

6. *Blue Collar Workers*. Production-line, construction and service per-

sonnel who may relocate as result of local and regional economic trends or personal situations. Important criteria: Directly motivated by current job opportunities and wage scales. Labor legislation such as union activity, unemployment benefits; opportunity for spouse to work; vocational training; interest in professional sports, outdoor recreation; influence of ethnic factors.

7. *All-Americans.* A combination or composite of other types. Important criteria: Will consider a wide variety of sites, can adapt easily to different styles. May relocate simply to enjoy a new and different situation.

If one has the task of selecting a location for a facility that must accommodate a number of people — for example, a new corporate office — it may be helpful to classify the work force crudely into groups such as these. If most of the staff happens to fit one specific lifestyle group, the job will be easy.

It is more likely, however, that the staff will be made up of groups having many different life styles. In this case, it may be of some benefit to examine the potential for combinations of interests.

The criteria for individuals, of course, are far more diversified. Some individuals have only one dominant factor. For example, an immigrant may locate where there is a minority population group speaking his language. Clustering of ethnic groups is very evident in many areas. Another individual, a young woman, may establish as a major factor the ratio of unmarried men to unmarried women. The mix is endless.

So much for theory!

Given the discretion to select an ideal location for the good life, where do people go and what are the characteristics of the areas they choose?

B. Resort Areas: The Ideal?

Perhaps we can find some answers by examining the features of the most popular resort areas. True, many individuals, given the opportunity, would not want to work and live in a resort area. Yet, a great many do so at considerable sacrifice. Further, a large segment of the retired population has opted for resort areas for permanent locations. There must be something there beyond fun for a weekend.

Scanning the leading resort areas of the U.S. and around the world, we find that almost all have three attributes:

1. *A Physical or Natural Resource.* Such as a year-round mild climate or balmy winter; scenic mountains; or shoreline, beach or lakefront.

2. *Appropriate Facilities.* Including hotels, lodges, campgrounds, homes, golf courses, marinas or ski lifts suited to the location.

3. *A Reputation.* Gained through years of affording a good life experience for those who visit or live there.

These qualities, we conclude, would enhance the good life index of any area. Also, we should observe that islands appear to possess a mystique that gives them a special rating among good life locations.

Hollywood has long portrayed paradise as a South Pacific island with blue water, white sand and coconut palms waving in a gentle breeze. Is the attraction of islands mostly Hollywood hype or is the appeal based on something more substantial?

Returning recently from a business trip to Australia, we had an interesting experience in French Polynesia which bears on this issue. After spending a weekend at Bora Bora, we went to Papeete, Tahiti, to connect with Air New Zealand for the flight to Los Angeles, only to discover that ANZ was shut down by a strike.

A group of U.S. tourists was "stranded" at the same hotel at which we were staying and they took the strike as a lark — they were getting an extra vacation in a tropical paradise, with the airline paying the bills.

Spirits were high the first day but moderated somewhat on the second day when the airline announced it would not cover all costs. Some of the tourists were short of cash. They had been traveling for a month and were within one day of home when they were caught by the strike. The only news from the airline was that strike issues were being negotiated in Auckland.

During the next several days the news was the same, and isolated muttering about hotel service, the food and high costs grew to loud complaints from many of the stranded guests. Then came a couple of rainy days, and the tour director handed out yellow ribbons to the "hostages." Desperate passengers competed for a handful of seats on a Chilean airline that could take them to Santiago and then to the U.S. via a 5,000-mile detour. Others threatened to sue or to call their Congressmen. One tourist began referring to Tahiti as "Devil's Island."

For one thing, this experience taught us that without freedom of movement, a tropical paradise can quickly become Devil's Island for certain individuals. Further, the good life, like beauty, is to some extent in the eye of the beholder.

Despite all such complications, we are convinced, however, that for most people it is possible to select a reasonably valid set of good life criteria. These criteria can then be used as a basis for comparing areas and, finally, in selecting a location which will be much more suitable than a random choice.

Analyzing States

States are convenient units for screening and comparison of good life factors because much information is available from federal, state and other research centers. First, let us look at the kind of material that permits quick scanning of all 50 states.

A. An Overview of the 50 States

From the many statistical series available, we have selected 30 factors we believe will be useful to many readers with a variety of interests. For indication of economic well-being, we have included per capita income, a long-time indicator, as well as unemployment rate for a recent year. Another factor, new plant investment, may help describe the competitive position of the states; and still another factor, R&D laboratories, may suggest future potential. Number of millionaires per 1,000 population is also interesting.

Some evaluation of government may be offered by another group of factors, which include state bond ratings, self-sufficiency (as opposed to dependency on federal funding) and number of citizens on welfare.

Crime rates constitute another important group. We have included comparisons for manslaughter, rape, robbery, aggravated assault, burglary, larceny and motor vehicle theft. Health factors include the overall death rate, suicide rate, accidental death rate, heart disease rate and birth rate.

Education factors include the median school years completed, plus enrollment in institutions of higher learning. The energy cost is indicated by prices for gas for residential, commercial and industrial use. Other facets of life are indicated by boating and camping activity, home ownership and availability of eating and drinking establishments.

These factors were selected from a long list. Without doubt, every research team making such a selection would come up with a different group.

Examining Metro, City and Local Areas

Many years ago, the U.S. Dept. of Commerce designated Standard Metropolitan Statistical Areas (SMSAs) for purposes of convenience in collecting and presenting demographic information. While metro area boundaries may be adjusted from time to time, the basic plan for providing data for highly populated areas that spill over the limits of one city or county remain highly useful today.

Thirteen factors have been selected for quick-scan SMSA comparisons. When combined with city data, they provide a picture of the almost endless variations among the jurisdictions.

Enough! What we have proven is that QOL factors vary widely for different SMSAs, and the areas that rank high in a particular category may be scattered over the nation's map. Whatever one's interest, it is usually possible to identify a number of areas in which a satisfactory site might be found.

B. City and Local Comparisons

Certain types of data are available only for selected cities or for specific points. For example, weather observations are taken at specified reporting

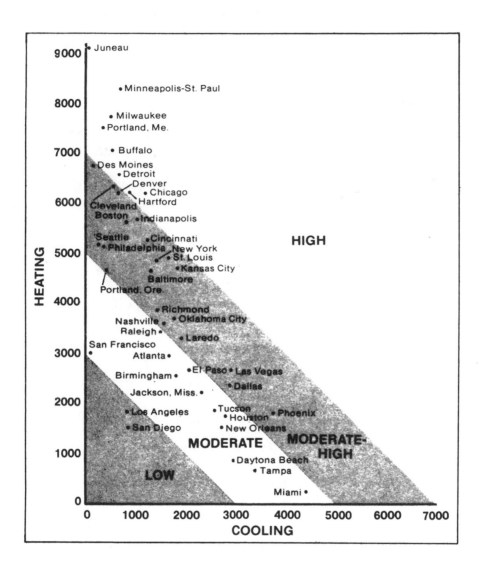

Gross energy requirements. When the cooling and heating requirements of a site are totalled, some rather surprising results are obtained. As shown in our Weather Handbook, *some sites in balmy climates have large needs.*

stations. Much economic and demographic information is limited in scope.

Many factors, such as cost-of-living, local taxes, local utility costs — all of which can vary significantly from SMSA, county or state averages — need to be studied at each location if these factors are important to the site seeker.

For this section we selected half a dozen local factors that affect the pocketbook. First, there are climatic factors which relate to energy costs and potential for solar recovery; and, second, there are cost-of-living factors.

Climate and Energy Analyses

There is no doubt that climatic factors play a significant role in evaluation of the good life, and there have always been geographic considerations. These factors continue to be important, but geographic bias is constantly changing because of technological and other developments.

For example, until recently, there were substantial health factors which kept many people from electing to live in tropical wetlands. As mosquitoes and malaria have been brought under control, however, many consider these areas particularly attractive.

Similarly, arid lands at high elevations have been shunned by some who disliked the harsh weather extremes and high fuel costs. Yet, such areas are receiving fresh attention today because of their potential for solar energy recovery. The weather remains the same, but man's growing capacity for adaptation brings new thinking about potential sites.

For each city, it is useful first to study the requirements for heating and air-conditioning expressed in "degree days." (Using a reference point, such as 65 degrees Fahrenheit, a 24-hour period with an average temperature of 64 degrees counts as one degree day, etc.)

For each location, we compiled data on annual heating degree days and annual cooling degree days. When these data are examined, it becomes apparent that the total energy requirements for cities in areas of climate extremes, either hot or cold, are comparable.

Of course, a precise comparison of annual cost of fuel or energy is much more complex. For each location, one must know what kind of equipment is to be used for heating or cooling and its efficiency. Further, one must know what kind of fuel (coal, oil, gas, wood) is to be used, its heating valuc and how much it costs. For these reasons, one should regard comparisons based simply on heating plus cooling degree days as only a first approximation.

Making Global Analyses

We chose to include a separate section on global analyses in order to stress that covering foreign areas must not be approached as merely a geo-

Legend

- 🔴 Baseball
- 🏈 Football
- 🏀 Basketball
- ⚽ Soccer
- 🏒 Hockey
- National Forest
- National Park
- Coastal Areas

Resort, Recreation Features

Good life factors for a state. This is a typical section from our book on quality-of-life factors.

387

graphic extension of U.S. studies. Consideration of locations in other nations — even those nearby — is a new ball game and should be undertaken with a healthy regard for potential pitfalls.

A. Criteria for Global Comparisons

First, it is necessary to establish additional criteria appropriate to your task. A different list will be needed for industrial plants, offices, investments, second homes and permanent homes. Among the new items to consider are:

1. *The political stability of the nation or area.* What is the prospect of sudden overthrow of the government? Is there a strong trend toward the political left? Will you ever become a fully accepted first-class citizen?

2. *Problems of cultural adjustment.* Do you speak the language? Will you be a member of an ethnic minority? What is the dominant religion, and is it government-sanctioned? Where will your small children go to school? Who will your older children date and marry?

3. *Convenience in travel and communication.* How many hours by jet from your family in the U.S.? How many time zones to consider when phoning? Metric system? Currency restrictions? Visas?

4. *Medical facilities.* Where are the nearest clinics, hospitals, specialists? How adequate are they in number? Will you have access to them when it counts?

5. *Psychological problems.* Can you be happy where there is no celebration on the Fourth of July, no baseball or football, no library of English-language literature, and the government runs the TV stations, giving you only the news it wants you to have?

These questions are raised only to emphasize the need for caution. Too many Americans have been lured into hasty investments in new homes in areas "where the sun shines every day and living costs are one-third the U.S. level." Many of these Americans discovered, after much frustration and many dollars, that they could live a lot cheaper only if they chose to live like the natives, and that was not fun, even in a balmy climate.

Thus, we urge a closer look before leaping. Armed with facts, some will abandon their global search, while others may find Shangri-La.

B. A Global Scan of QOL Factors

Many agencies, including the United Nations, the World Bank and the Agency for International Development, have long been concerned with measuring, monitoring and improving QOL around the world. Recently, the Overseas Development Council (ODC) undertook to gather data from all sources and to establish a simple measure of QOL that could be widely used.

ODC elected to search for an index of physical QOL (PQOL) which would not be biased in terms of ethnic values or reflect western patterns. Nor would it be strictly monetary. ODC also avoided specific nutritional standards (calorie consumption, etc.). After some deliberation, ODC settled on three basic factors: infant mortality, life expectancy and literacy.

C. Some Favored Areas Around the World

There are many surface indications that the attractiveness of nations varies greatly. Refugees stream out of areas where large segments of the population perceive negative QOL factors. Immigrants stand in line to gain access to nations they believe to be blessed with positive QOL factors. These differences in QOL act as a pressure gradient to move the winds of change in all parts of the world.

There are highly publicized, uncontrolled migrations, such as those involving refugees escaping Eastern Europe, Cuba, China and Vietnam; and the inward flow from many nations to the U.S., Kuwait, Australia and Israel. Such global shifts have led to very rapid growth of strategically located cities, often bringing about substantial change in population mix.

In the Far East, Hong Kong and then Singapore emerged as world centers as a result of this kind of growth and diversification. In the Middle East, Beirut was such a center before the recent war. Miami and Honolulu are U.S. cities with rapidly changing character and new international roles.

Many other areas have been favored by investors and relocating citizens, not only by necessity but also by deliberate choice. Many Europeans have elected to move to Australia. Many U.S. and Canada citizens have chosen to live in Mexico, Costa Rica and in the Caribbean.

Business firms have been attracted to growth centers having good business climates and to some rather unlikely locations set up as tax havens. These latter sites range from the UK's Channel Islands and postage-stamp-sized European nations to the Bahamas and Caymans in the Atlantic and Caribbean, and to small new island nations in the South Pacific. In fact, some enterprising investors have attempted to "discover" small uninhabited atolls and set them up as new nations having optimum tax laws.

A broader picture of areas deemed by outsiders to have special appeal is afforded by tourism patterns. Assuming that the existence of substantial resort facilities patronized by an international clientele is an indicator of certain positive QOL factors — particularly climate and/or scenery — one can at least identify starting points for more comprehensive site searches.

In addition to this crude indication of QOL appeals of various sorts, what other real evidence do we have that certain kinds of locations please more people? We can look at population trends, urban growth patterns and the reasons we believed they occurred as they did. Then, we can relate these patterns to what we have seen in tourism, immigration and economic development, and we can speculate about what it all portends.

1987
Excerpt

The Role of Private Enterprise. One of the greatest myths extant today is that government regulatory agencies and community action groups prevent the destruction of our environment by greedy, corrupt corporations. The fact is that responsible private interests do most of the significant conservation work, despite obstacles placed in their way by petty bureaucrats and self-appointed experts. *Site Selection.* December 1987. p. 1220.

In the mid-1950s we participated in a Southern Industrial Wastes Conference in New Orleans which attracted some 200 executives from Maryland through Texas. The prime focus of the meeting was the growing pollution of the region's streams by industrial and municipal wastes.

In retrospect, what was most significant about that long-forgotten conference is that it was planned and implemented by private industry. There were no representatives of federal environmental control agencies or community activists — for the simple reason that they did not then exist.

Our point is that private firms have always been the backbone of the fight to protect the environment. They are today, and they will be tomorrow.

This fact is usually overlooked by news media which publicize the sins of the bad actors in the business community and the occasional mistakes of the good firms. Seldom do we hear a good word for the companies which do outstanding work in harmonizing facilities with their habitat.

We were reminded of this as we reviewed the latest batch of nominations for the annual environmental planning awards made at the IDRC Fall World Congress. We launched these awards more than 15 years ago and there has never been a year in which we have failed to document a number of outstanding achievements by private firms. The award archives at IDRC HQ provide hard evidence that industry has aggressively cleaned up its act.

Meanwhile, the failure of hundreds of municipalities, large and small, to install suitable treatment facilities has become our biggest and most persistent environmental problem. It is the bureaucrats who are failing!

It is also clear that most of the expertise in dealing with environmental problems and waste facilities in a practical way is found in the private sector. It makes sense, therefore, for local governments to turn to private industry to finance, build and operate the plants they need.

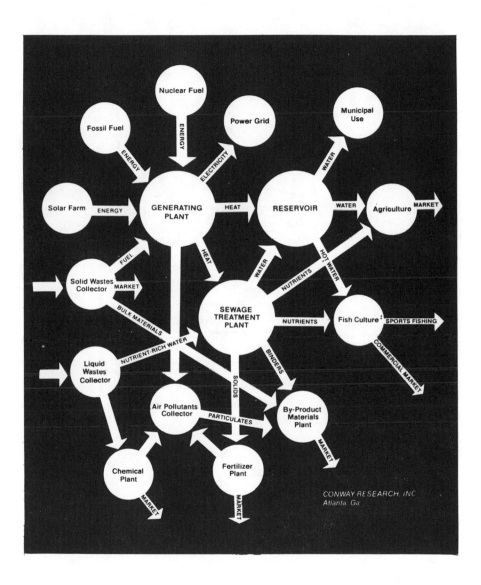

Nuclear Fuel

Fossil Fuel

Power Grid

Municipal
Use

Solar Farm — ENERGY → GENERATING PLANT — HEAT → RESERVOIR — WATER → Agriculture — MARKET

ENERGY

ELECTRICITY

ENERGY

WATER

HEAT

Solid Wastes Collector

FUEL

MARKET

BULK MATERIALS

WATER

NUTRIENTS

HOT WATER

SEWAGE
TREATMENT
PLANT

NUTRIENTS → Fish Culture — SPORTS FISHING

Liquid
Wastes
Collector

NUTRIENT-RICH WATER

BINDERS

COMMERCIAL MARKET

Air Pollutants
Collector — PARTICULATES

SOLIDS

By-Product
Materials
Plant

MARKET

Chemical
Plant

Fertilizer
Plant

MARKET

MARKET

CONWAY RESEARCH, INC
Atlanta, Ga

We began promoting the "decoplex" (development ecology complex) idea in the 1960s. It involves recycling urban wastes via industrial processes to obtain useful products.

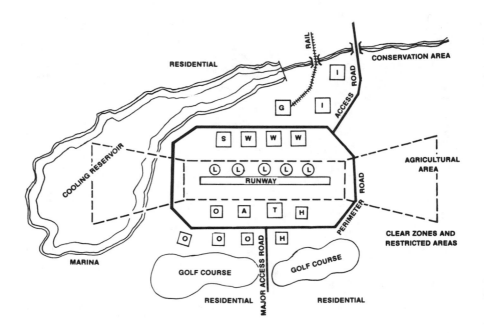

Decoplex locations.

Because there is always great citizen opposition to the siting of waste-handling facilities, we proposed that decoplex installations be planned as parts of other public works which require large land areas. One example is the use of airport approach clear zones.

Well-managed private firms long ago learned that good conservation was good business for them. Now, it appears that this is true not only for individual firms dealing with their own wastes but also for firms which can help solve the problems of towns and cities.

In most metro areas, we believe private enterprise must eventually take over the task of developing and operating the decoplex (development-ecology complex) installations needed for resource recovery and waste disposal. In the near future we must make it mandatory for metro agencies to phase out land fills and build such facilities.

Looking a little farther down the road, we believe environmental renewal — specifically habitat restoration — will become a very big business and a field of great opportunity for many companies. Already, there are a number of small firms engaged in fascinating projects aimed at reseeding, replanting, restocking and otherwise restoring damaged wetlands.

Long before the turn of the century we hope to see global groups letting contracts for the restoration of vast areas of tropical rain forests, denuded woodlands, desertized savannahs, and damaged coral reefs, barrier islands and seashores. These important programs will be carried out by private firms which merge the disciplines of developers and ecologists.

And that may be our finest hour!

1990
Excerpt

"The Future: Spectacular Political Fights Are Coming." If you think we are witnessing some all-out political campaign conflicts today, just wait. *Gwinnett Daily News*, May 1990.

In evaluating long-term global development trends and opportunities, it is clear that some monumental political debates are coming. They will deal with topics of intense interest to voters, and they will spill across national boundaries around the world.

For example, science will eventually provide some degree of control over weather, such as when and where to make it rain. How would you like to be a legislator dealing with that hot potato?

Or, if you think the abortion issue is a big one today, how about dealing with the future question of limiting each family to one or two children?

Such questions may be cocktail time discussion topics today, but in our future they are going to become very real. For example, let's look more closely at the population problem:

If present trends continue, mushrooming population growth will exceed the sustaining capacity of the earth long before the end of the next century. Within the lifetimes of younger members of our current society the time will come when it is obvious to all that drastic action must be taken.

The general public will finally become aware that many of the world's most pressing problems — waste disposal, traffic, urban sprawl and environmental degradation — are directly connected to population growth.

The question will not be whether governments should move to control population growth, but how soon.

Of course, China has already taken drastic action, seeking to limit new families to one child. Also, there are birth control programs in many Third World nations sponsored by international agencies. But, overall, the world is still losing the population growth battle.

Here in the United States, we see gridlock on our expressways, our garbage landfills are full, and we have acute shortages of low-income housing. Yet we are so far unable to face up to the population problem and enact effective control measures.

Meanwhile, it is interesting that a large segment of the American public blames these problems on developers. Developers are blamed for the inevitable conflicts involved in finding sites and building facilities to meet the basic needs of the growing population.

So far, those who complain about growth, such as the NIMBY (not in my back yard) groups, have not attacked the root cause of their problem — government policies with respect to population control. At zoning meetings one does not hear complaints about anti-abortion legislation or lenient immigration policies. Paradoxically, it is not unusual to find people active in the pro-life movement also active in opposing development!

Further, we still provide government incentives for having more children — income tax deductions for wage earners and welfare support for non-earners.

Clearly, there is little prospect for population control in the USA in the near term. It is apparent that the growth control situation will get a lot worse before action is taken. This must be our realistic forecast for the remainder of this century.

In some Third World areas, rapid growth may force earlier action. A dozen cities are virtually unmanageable today because of population growth, and they will each have populations of more than 20 million early in the next century.

Among these are Bombay, Cairo, Calcutta, Dhaka, Jakarta, Karachi, Lagos, Mexico City, New Delhi, Sao Paulo and Shanghai. Mexico City is probably the worst case, with a projected population of more than 30 million.

Why is the world facing such a dilemma? In earlier centuries a high death rate balanced birth rates. Average life span was less than 30 years. Waves of plagues and pestilences decimated entire populations.

Today, with improved health services, there are no known threats — other than nuclear war — to global population growth. Considering the political firestorms which will erupt when government population controls must be imposed, some politicians may favor the nuclear solution.

1990
Excerpt

The Weather Handbook. A summary of climatic conditions and weather phenomena for selected cities in the United States and around the world. 3rd edition, 1990. 548 pp. Hard cover. With Linda L. Liston. *The Weather Handbook.* A summary of weather statistics for selected cities around the world. 2nd edition, 1974. 255 pp. illus. *The Weather Handbook.* 1st edition, 1962. 256 pp. Statistical summaries of climatic factors for major cities in U.S. and around world.

For outdoor people the weather defines recreational opportunities. For farmers it determines good or bad times. And for those of us who fly small airplanes it is even more — it is truly a matter of life and death.

Pilots who survive to a ripe old age have learned to have a very healthy respect for a variety of weather phenomena. Probably the biggest concern is thunderstorms because they are so common and so lethal if ignored.

In many parts of the world thunderstorms can occur any day. In much of the United States they are a threat during about six warm months of the year. Usually the storms come on summer afternoons and they are scattered over wide areas.

Whether one flies a heavy jet or a light plane, the pilot's strategy is to avoid thunderstorm cells by zig-zagging around them. Life only gets grim when a line of heavy storms is encountered and the gaps between cells are narrow.

Sometimes a pilot gets boxed in and finds himself plowing through a cell. That is the source of the old saw that among pilots there are no atheists in thunderstorms.

At the least, going through an active cell is a nerve-wracking experience and a test of the ability of the pilot and the strength of the airframe. As thunderstorms grow in intensity, they spawn violent vertical gusts and hail. For the pilot, this means the possibility of loss of control, structural failure and a fatal accident.

Tornados are believed to develop from severe thunderstorms. Flying into such a cell is suicidal.

When the weather cools off and the thunderstorms wane, a new problem emerges — ice. While icing can be encountered at very high altitudes any time, anywhere, the biggest exposure for most pilots comes during the winter at lower altitudes.

The veteran pilot knows that there are different kinds of ice to be found in different weather systems and that there is a temperature range in which icing is most likely. He also knows that it can get too cold for icing to be a problem.

Another range of problems is associated with low ceilings and visibilities. Fog, which occurs when the temperature and dewpoint converge, is a major culprit.

There are many localities which have microclimates conducive to fog, smog, haze and other contributors to low ceilings and visibilities. The Los Angeles basin is a well-known example.

Around the world there are airports located many miles from the cities they serve because sites near the city are too often fog-bound. A good example is Halifax, Nova Scotia.

Elevations are also of critical importance to the pilot. Without consulting any reference book, an experienced pilot can tell you that Denver and Colorado Springs are more than 5,000 feet above sea level and Bogota and Quito are much higher.

Altitude also tells a lot about wind patterns. Below 12,000 feet in the Caribbean the trade winds blow steadily out of the east. Airports in the region have east/west runways wherever terrain permits.

At altitudes above 30,000 to 40,000 feet the winds always come from the west — because of the rotation of the earth. And, in the northern hemisphere the winds circulate counter-clockwise around a low pressure center, while they go clockwise south of the equator.

Similarly, in the Caribbean the hurricanes track from southeast toward the northwest, while in the South Pacific the typhoons may follow different routes.

Veteran pilots can also make easy estimates of latitude and longitude of key cities and suggest which ones may enjoy very long summer days or very short winter days.

With all of these and other variations, it is no wonder that weather is a universal topic of interest and conversation among those who fly.

The idea for this handbook emerged sometime in the years after WWII as the author was planning flights to remote parts of the U.S., Canada and Latin America. In those days it was difficult to get weather data quickly and conveniently for many locations.

Over a period of years we had managed to compile a considerable amount of data from various sources. In Central America, for example, we discovered military records of observations made at bases built by U.S. units during WWII and later abandoned. Also, we got access to records kept by other governments.

For some routes we collected enough data that other pilots began asking to borrow our files. Someone then suggested we put the data into a book. While that idea was germinating, better official sources at home and abroad became available, and so we launched the project.

We hasten to say that this new edition relies on data from current official records and not on our own spotty observations. Today, coverage is more complete and more reliable than ever.

This volume, however, was not compiled solely for the benefit of those who fly. We learned with earlier editions that the kind of data it contains is very useful for world travelers. Will a raincoat be needed in Bombay in February? How cold will it be in Rome in April?

Also, the previous editions found wide use among those involved in the planning of outdoor activities and those engaged in the design of facilities. Using the weather profiles for reporting stations, one can quickly get an idea of requirements for heating, air-conditioning and energy needs.

And now, we have a new and even wider audience — those who are interested in global weather patterns and threats to our environment. The news media give much space to alarmist predictions of global warming via the greenhouse effect. There are concerns regarding ozone depletion.

Just now, with satellite observations and other extensions of our observation capabilities, we are learning much about the intricate systems that affect the weather of the world. We now know, for example, that "El Nino" is a global phenomenon. Events which occur in one part of the world may be related to events in another hemisphere.

There are many rumors, myths and misconceptions in circulation. Extremists press the panic button, while apathetic segments of society ignore significant warnings.

We have reached the point, we believe, where every thoughtful citizen needs to have facts at hand.

C. Bibliography

The following are citations of McKinley Conway's writings on this chapter's subject. As this book goes to press, work is underway to make many of these items available to researchers. To check status, look for a file on GeoTEAM/IDRCNET or telephone GeoTEAM/Fax at (404) 453-4200 for a free catalog.

442. *Blueprint for progress* (documentary film script on planned industrial parks and performance standards, awarded 2nd prize, Congresso Mundial de Planificacion y Vivienda, Puerto Rico, 1960). Produced 1959 by Industrial Sound Films, Atlanta. Full Color. 16mm. 25 mins.

443. "Growth May Be Inevitable but Progress Is Not," Atlanta Real Estate Board, May 21, 1959.

444. "Opportunities in the Amazon Basin." It's been called the world's last great primeval wilderness. You can still meet a 16-foot anaconda at the airstrip. Here is a report by ID's publisher who made a pioneering flight (as pilot and navigator) from the Andes to the Atlantic to gather first-hand information. *Industrial Development,* Sept. 1965, pp. 15-20.

445. "Effect of Environmental Quality Factors on Investment Decisions, Improving the Physical Environment of the South," Agricultural Policy Institute, North Carolina State University, Feb. 1969.

446. "Blessed Are the Peacemakers" (role of professionals in resolving development/environmental conflicts). *Industrial Development,* annual "Environmental Planning Guide." Sept.-Oct. 1971. pp. 1.

447. "Georgia Environmental Standards" (special study). Nov. 1971. 150 pp. Foreword by Gov. Jimmy Carter. (Summary of regulations covering air quality, coastal marshlands, noise, radiation, scenic resources, solid wastes, surface mining, water quality.)

448. "Industry's Guide to Environmental Planning" (covering negative image, emotional pollution, myth of perfection, terminology and criteria, bureaucracy, solutions.) *Site Selection,* 1972. pp. 202-205.

449. "Is There a Decoplex in Your Future?" The strategy of Decoplex is to turn adversity to advantage. It involves taking some of the least attractive facilities and making them assets in the community. *Industrial Development,* May-June 1972. pp. 2-4.

450. "The Decoplex Concept Commands Attention." In implementing the Decoplex (Development/Ecology Complex) concept of harmonizing development with environmental requirements, there is a host of technical, economic and political problems. Despite these obstacles, the emergence of a Decoplex solution is inevitable! *Industrial Development,* Jan.-Feb. 1973. pp. 1-3.

451. "The Spruce Creek Research Center" (proposals for stream basin conservation plan and environmental field station, 1969-1974), for Fly-In Concept. June 1, 1974.

452. "Environmental and Land Use Controls," a survey for the Industrial Development Research Council. May 1975, 69 pp. plus appendix. IDRC Research Report #13.

453. "When Do You Chop That $12,000 Tree?" Amid increasing realization that trees, grass, and even swamps have significant economic value, the profit-oriented developer faces growing difficulty in making optimum economic decisions. *Site Selection,* "Environmental Planning Guide" edition, Sept. 1975. pp. 286-288.

454. "Industrial Site Performance Standards," a study for the Industrial Development Research Council, covering deed covenants and zoning regulations, space allocation and dimensional standards, architectural and aesthetic standards, performance and land-use criteria, implementation plans, construction and maintenance, proposed uniform outline. May, 1976. 307 pp. IDRC Research Report #15. With Linda L. Liston.

455. "Uniform Outline for Deed Covenants and Performance Standards." Covers land-use controls, performance standards, space allocations, architecture and aesthetics, implementation of plans, construction. *Industrial Development,* May-June, 1976. (by-line omitted).

456. *The Good Life Index.* Recognizing that "the good life" is a highly subjective concept, varying widely from person to person and corporation to corporation, this new approach provides the reader with a method for systematically seeking out the places which offer desired attributes. The quest for a QOL measure. Criteria for the good life. Analyzing states. Examining metro, city, and local areas. Making global analyses. Making your own good life evaluation. 1981. 416 pp. Hard cover. With Linda L. Liston. Reviewed in *The Futurist,* World Future Society, June 1982. pp. 75-77.

457. *Disaster Survival.* How to choose secure sites and make practical escape plans. Natural disasters. Man-made disasters. Evaluation of risk potential. Survival planning: site hardening. Public policies. International disaster risk data. 290 pp. Hard cover. 1981. The American Library Association review: "A frightening, valuable guide."

458. *Industrial Park Growth.* Introduction — the dream of a good place to work. Emergence of the park concept and proliferation of units. Performance standards and design criteria. Types of parks. Park site supply and demand. Industrial parks for the future. 1981. 2nd ed. Hard cover. 546 pp. With Linda L. Liston.

459. "Strategic Decisions for the Great Barrier Reef." Australian planners, determined to preserve the basic character of the reef region while permitting practical utilization, have undertaken what may be the world's most ambitious zoning plan. "Global Mini-Letter," July 1981. pp. 1-2.

460. "Pure Water from the Sun and Sea?" Pichilingue is a small Mexican town on the Baja peninsula some 800 miles south of Los Angeles. Recently we went to Pichilingue to look at what may be one of the most significant development projects to be found anywhere — an experimental processing plant to desalt seawater using solar energy. "Global Mini-Letter," July 1982. pp. 1-2.

461. "The Role of Private Enterprise." One of the greatest myths extant today is that government regulatory agencies and community action groups prevent the destruction of our environment by greedy corrupt corporations. The fact is that responsible private interests do most of the significant conservation work, despite obstacles placed in their way by petty bureaucrats and self- appointed experts. *Site Selection,* Dec. 1987. p. 1220.

462. One of the greatest myths extant today is that government regulatory agencies and community action groups prevent the destruction of our environment by greedy corrupt corporations. The fact is that responsible private interests do most of the significant conservation work, despite obstacles placed in their way by petty bureaucrats and self-appointed experts. *Gwinnett Daily News,* May 17, 1989.

463. *The Weather Handbook.* A summary of climatic conditions and weather phenomena for selected cities in the United States and around the world. 1st ed., 1962, 256 pp. 2nd ed. 1974, 255 pp. illus. 3rd ed. 1990. 548 pp. Hard cover. With Linda L. Liston.

464. "Business in for a Big Surprise from Greens." The Greens are coming and they're going to change your agenda! What was an obscure environmental movement in Europe a few years ago is mushrooming into an international effort with strong political clout. *Gwinnett Daily News,* Jan. 17, 1990.

465. "Damage from 'Panic Response' Can Be Great." Satellite communications systems have done wonderful things for the world. News can be flashed to almost every corner of the globe instantly. The bad news is that wonderful information systems can spread panic. *Gwinnett Daily News,* Feb. 14, 1990.

466. "Seawater Treatment the Wave of the Future." Quietly but surely scientists are moving toward a fantastic breakthrough which will literally reshape many regions of the world, bring great new economic development opportunities and provide a better quality of life for millions of people. *Gwinnett Daily News,* April 18, 1990.

467. "The Future: Spectacular Political Fights Are Coming." If you think we are witnessing some all-out political campaign conflicts today, just wait. *Gwinnett Daily News,* May, 1990.

8
Futurism, Faith in the Future

Chapter 8

A. Recent Comments
Futurism in Real Life
Global Super Projects
The Ultimate Questions

B. Excerpts
"The Geo-economic Explosion," *Site World*, 1991
"Rationale for Global Super Projects," Global Super Projects
    Conference, February 1992
 A Glimpse of the Future, 1992
"New Wonders of the World," *Leaders* Magazine, Summer 1993
"The Science and the Art of Futurism," *Georgia Tech Alumni*
    Magazine, September 1993

C. Bibliography

A. Recent Comments

Futurism in Real Life

Are different people born with different mental clocks? Do some just naturally look backward while others look ahead? Or, do some have a very narrow time scale focused on the present, while others have a very wide scale providing a panorama of the past, present and future?

Whatever genetic differences there may be, we believe that most people have a healthy interest in tomorrow. A few are fascinated with the future, and they become professional planners, forecasters and futurists.

In my case, it is easy to put my finger on the first case of serious futurism in which I was involved. It came while I was a member of the NACA/NASA staff at the beginning of WWII.

Those were the early days of budget planning in Washington. Typically, agencies were subjected to an annual review, and expenditure requests went to Congress every year. Then, a study group asked us for a five-year forecast of needed new research facilities.

I suspect this request was so unusual that it was not taken too seriously. Instead of convening a meeting of senior staff, the director called me into his office and asked me to prepare a preliminary draft.

That was my first assignment as a professional futurist. I consulted with our top engineers in Washington, checked with the laboratories and wrote up a composite picture. As I recall it, we simply asked for something of everything that was bigger or faster than what we had.

Futurism is involved, of course, in the launching of any new business. And futuristic thinking is enhanced by association with others of similar outlook.

For example, after WWII a small group of us who had been involved in various kinds of high-tech military assignments formed a Naval Research Reserve unit at Georgia Tech. We met at the Georgia Tech research institute and some of us spent our required two weeks of annual active duty at the Office of Naval Research in Washington.

I can't remember what the formal program was, but I know we met for several years and spent much time discussing possible research ventures. Looking back on it, I now realize we did some serious futures thinking.

403

In that group of 10 or 12 people we had several who launched highly successful new companies. There was Glenn Robinson, a founder of Scientific Atlanta; and Clyde Orr, who started Micromeritics, Inc.

That may well have been the genesis of an R&D cluster (*see chapter 4*) that eventually developed. A decade later, other Georgia Tech people helped implement a plan for a research park in suburban Gwinnett County. That became Technology Park/Atlanta, where our headquarters is located.

Today, in the area around this park there are more high-tech enterprises than there were in the entire South when we began talking. Futurism paid off!

Actually, life is full of situations in which we must practice futurism in some way. How about saving for a rainy day? How much insurance to buy? What kind of retirement plan?

Global Super Projects

In my years of work as a planning consultant, every project involved forecasts. We predicted growth of urban areas, growth of air traffic, expansion of the industrial base and many other such factors. We learned that when we predicted what the data said we should, most people thought we were much too optimistic. Almost always, a review 10 years later revealed that we had been too pessimistic.

To do a good job in forecasting you have to dare to be wrong, sometimes very wrong. This applies equally to planning personal affairs or to world-class projects.

A prerequisite is to understand the mechanism of change. We have written about that often, as, for example, in the *Site World* excerpt included later in this chapter.

In our 1992 study (*Glimpse of the Future*) we summarized our thinking relative to forecasting and futurism. It is a good starting point for those who want to develop their own future studies program.

We are not content, however, to dream about the future. We want to have something to do with the shape of things to come. Thus, we began more than a decade ago building a data base on what we termed "global super projects."

That research led to realization that there was no global team proposing, evaluating, planning and implementing those projects most important to the world. We set out to remedy that situation, as outlined in our presentation to the World Development Council in Honolulu.

Of course, the big, spectacular projects attract most interest. Every schoolchild learns of the pyramids, the hanging gardens and the other wonders of the ancient world. Now, a massive global construction program promises to yield a new list of wonders for today and tomorrow. (*Leaders* magazine, July 1993.)

Another statement of our outlook for the future appeared in the Georgia Tech magazine ("The Science and the Art of Futurism," Summer 1993).

The Ultimate Questions

Eventually, every futurist comes around to the fundamental questions of life and death. What are the biggest questions yet unanswered?

Certainly, one of the big ones relates to the possibility of life like ours being found on another planet. If some such life established communication with us, that would be the biggest news story of all time.

I don't think it will happen. If we ever find life on another planet, it will probably be of some entirely different form.

How about cryogenic burials — freezing people now and bringing them back to life later? I don't think any of those being preserved now have a chance. However, at some time in the distant future we may learn how to do that.

And, for the biggest question most of us face: What happens after death? I believe that will remain a mystery for a long, long time, perhaps forever.

Meanwhile, here is a closing message for my grandchildren, Adam and Piper:

I thought that when one got old and gray and full of wisdom your children and grandchildren were supposed to gather around in a circle, their eager faces upturned, and plead with you to tell them just one more tale about the fascinating events in your life.

I've been old and gray for some time now, and nothing like that has happened. In fact, when I volunteer to recount some really interesting incident from WWII, everybody seems to disappear.

We appear to have a communications problem.

Part of it may be that I am not too well informed about the latest rock videos or the social intrigues of teenagers. We're definitely dealing with a generation gap or two.

These things may make understanding a little bit difficult, but I'm not giving up. In fact I am even more determined since one of you, looking at some of my early photos recently, said, in apparent amazement, "You looked young.*"*

As a matter of fact, there was a time when I was not only young but also in good physical condition and mentally alert. *Furthermore, no one said I was not "with it" because I believed in such things as obeying my parents.*

So, I am going to publish this report on some of the things I have encountered. You don't have to read it now. However, I am hoping that when you get old you will take it from the shelf, dust it off and read for a while. I am assuming that someday you will have an attention span greater than that of a gnat.

This is in many ways a journal of the 20th century. You will spend most of your lives in the 21st century. Perhaps these notes will help you understand our world a little better.

Obviously, we have different time frames. My generation was one that believed in such things as "honor, duty, country." We paraded to Sousa marches, and when the band played "Stars and Stripes Forever" our hair stood on end.

Yes, we were obedient, dedicated, and we had a strong work ethic. For most of us, there were close family ties to rural backgrounds where agriculture was part of everybody's occupation.

We were taught to be self reliant — that it was a disgrace to be dependent on others or the government. Most of the time we were quiet, competent and responsible.

Because all of our old photos are black and white you may think we lived in a gray world. In fact, we lived in brilliant color — the sun was just as bright for us as it is for you!

And, you may think our lives have been dull and boring. But the truth is that our generation has stayed very busy doing things like developing air transportation, discovering antibiotics, inventing television and building communications systems that touch every corner of the world.

Furthermore, we don't think we're unsophisticated and naive because we treasure simple values like unqualified honesty and loyalty to family, team, company or country. Neither do we apologize. We like what we are.

So much for the sermon!

From your viewpoint, the most important thing we have done is open up some great new opportunities. Your generation is looking to a future that is truly fantastic.

Here's hoping you enjoy your century as much as we've enjoyed ours!

B. Excerpts

1991 Excerpt	"The Geo-economic Explosion. Understanding Change!" *Site World*, 1991.

From the boiling magma of the earth's inner core to the frigid vastness of outer space, the watchword today is change.

Change! Change! Change! More change than ever before. Cataclysmic changes. Megacosmic changes.

And every change brings new problems and new opportunities for someone. In the years just ahead we will have to absorb future shock and a never-ending series of after-shocks.

The next decade is going to be chaotic, frenzied and excruciatingly exciting. When it is over, the world will have an entirely new look.

No nation, no business sector nor any company will escape the impact of this global restructuring.

The evidence is all around us. Long-dormant political volcanos are erupting without warning. Within a matter of weeks the communist concept has been devastated. Democracy is replacing totalitarianism everywhere. Markets, travel and communication are suddenly open.

In the business world, every global executive needs a parimutuel board on his office wall to keep abreast of changes minute by minute. Mega-trends are multiplied. Around the world there are new super projects — colossal, stupendous projects. Scientific breakthroughs are spewing from countless R&D centers.

What it all means in that we are witnessing a global geo-economic explosion!!!

The business map of the world has been torn to shreds and is being redrawn. The new chart stresses markets, manpower, resources, science and technology. Political boundaries have become almost irrelevant.

The science of geo-economics that has been emerging quietly for several decades has suddenly been thrust to the forefront of modern business thinking. Corporate strategy, location analysis, site selection and allied area development topics are no longer obscure academic exercises. Geography has moved from the classroom to the board room.

Viewing the world scene, some scholars suggest that we are witnessing the end of history. We say it is just the beginning of a new business world!

What are the driving forces of change? Here are some primary factors:

• *Population growth*. Growth will continue and markets will expand in scope and depth.

• *Open societies*. Open systems will whet the appetites and inspire the productivity of groups that heretofore have not participated in the world economy.

• *Borderless nations*. Commerce will flow with increasing freedom.

• *Privatization*. Ownership will provide incentive and inspire management responsibility.

• *Stateless corporations*. Businesses will be at home anywhere.

• *Fear*. Globalize or paralyze!

• *Conversion of economies*. There will be reduced military spending, shifts in foreign aid, national debt.

• *The decline of unions*. Increased worker education.

• *Reduction of subsidies*. This will lead to the opening of competition in agriculture.

• *The rise of international standards of conduct*. These will range from genetic engineering to waste disposal.

• *Emergence of an international mechanism for controlling corporate tax evasion*. All global firms will compete on a level playing field.

• *The protection of intellectual property*. Creativity will be encouraged.

• *Effective international mechanisms will settle disputes*.

• *The new performance concept*. A post-free-market system.

• *Swords to plowshares*. Converting from military to civilian products and services.

1992
Excerpt

"The Rationale for Global Super Projects." Opening statement for the first annual Global Super Projects Conference, World Development Council, Honolulu, February 17, 1992.

This is a significant occasion.

If we do our work well, it is possible that in another decade or so this small beginning will be regarded as an historic occasion.

We have assembled here a select group representing a large constituency of experts and organizations responsible for the world's most important development plans and projects. We meet in a spirit of cooperation, with a sense of purpose and with considerable excitement about what the future may hold.

Let's begin with a quick scan of our global posture.

The World Scene
There are six major factors that have an impact on our strategy:

1. **The population situation**. The world has not yet implemented an

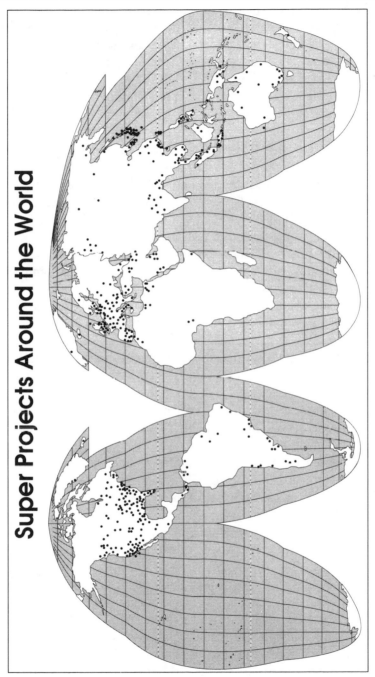

Our data base now lists more than 1,500 super projects around the world. These are projects which involve a cost of $1 billion or more or which involve a scientific breakthrough of global significance.

effective plan to manage population growth and migration.

That ticking in the background is the global population counter which is well past five billion and which will be beyond six billion by the year 2000. In the lifetimes of many members of this audience the count will be double what it is today.

The counter gives us some measure of the challenge faced by those who plan projects to meet global needs.

And, we must cope not only with population growth but also with sharply rising expectations. Thanks to global TV and other improvements in communications, those in the poorest nations can now see what they are missing.

This combination of increased population and increased desire grossly defines our world market. Those who seek to meet these needs are shooting at a fast-moving target!

Another factor we must deal with is:

2. **Leadership confusion**. We operate in a development world that has no governing authority. There is no world planning commission to review plans and issue permits for super projects.

Global needs are being met piecemeal via uncoordinated efforts. Much-needed projects which involve multiple jurisdictions often lie dormant for decades.

In this setting, communication among those sponsoring global projects is often poor or non-existent. The opportunity to benefit from exchange of ideas and experience is lost.

3. **We live in a time of great changes**. We must deal with swift and sometimes chaotic shifts in political institutions as well as economic systems and business practices.

There is a global rush to free market conversion and privatization. This is the magic year in which Europe will be unified and there will be new opportunities for taking advantage of the economy of scale. The new Soviet federation offers promise

Elsewhere, there are splintered markets and uncoordinated efforts. Latin America and Africa wait for global attention.

4. **We are faced with vital environmental imperatives**. Rainforests and other forests are still being destroyed faster than they can be replaced. There are pollution and waste disposal problems that threaten the air we breathe, the water we drink and the food we eat.

5. **Unsatisfactory QOL**. For much of the world, quality of life is not improving. That is true even in the wealthiest of nations.

Many small, new nations have discovered that the price of independence is steep — bringing corruption, incompetence and petty monopolies. Real freedom is only for a few.

Self-sustaining island paradises have been "civilized" and converted to grubby dependencies.

6. **The vulnerability of society to small wars and terrorist actions continues**. Our communications, power and transport systems are easy targets for fanatic groups. The world worries about disposition of the inventory of nuclear weapons of the former USSR. The threat that nuclear weapons will fall into the hands of fanatics hangs over us like the Sword of Damocles.

Everywhere there are great problems. Because we are positive thinkers, we must regard each of these as an opportunity to serve.

The New WDC Forum

Neither this new Council nor all of the super projects in our file will solve all of the world's problems. Yet, it is equally true that many of the problems will never be solved without investment in large-scale projects that are professionally planned and implemented. In some situations, we may be able to make a dramatic difference!

We will be unique — non-governmental, open, independent, objective, uncommitted to the past, not merely receptive to innovation but demanding it.

We will not be a parade of show horses. Instead, we will represent the work horses of global development — those who get the job done.

We do not seek to replace any organization nor to duplicate any program. We seek to fill a gap in the global network of development planning entities.

It appears that the backbone of our membership will consist of two primary groups: project sponsors (governments, private investors, consortia) and project implementors (planners, engineers, contractors).

We have some of the world's leaders in these fields here today. During the next several years we must mobilize many more.

In addition to these groups most directly affected, we must mobilize a much larger group of interested parties.

For example, there is a major role for area development executives operating at local, metro, state, regional and national levels. They can see the need for new infrastructure facilities, for example, create public awareness and serve as the catalyst in bringing together those who can make it happen.

Another group we must mobilize is the planning executives of global corporations.

Global super projects are already reshaping the world in which we do business. They are opening new sites, creating new access routes, stimulating new business climates and forever changing the pattern of world commerce.

Many firms have already set up global strategy units and hundreds of others will soon follow. We look forward to having the input of these uniquely qualified executives.

Our forum will thus serve to identify the leading thinkers and to help match expertise with projects. We need to bring together all types of global strategists — financial, technical, economic, political — and build winning teams.

Pursuing this goal, we expect to see the emergence of a new breed of global super strategists. In the 21st century these men and women will rank in importance with heads of state. These are grand objectives.

The World Need for Super Projects

Now, let's move from generalities to specifics.

There is already abundant evidence that the world sees a growing need for super projects. Here are some examples with which we are all familiar:

• *Global links*. We have the Eurotunnel and the Great Belt Crossing nearing completion. In the planning or discussion stage we have a Gibraltar crossing, the Thailand Kra Isthmus canal and a second Panama canal.

• *Communications projects*. We have just completed a major trans-Pacific fiber-optic cable that all of us use. Tomorrow Mr. Hatlelid will tell us about Motorola's new IRIDIUM satellite project.

• *Energy and power*. This is a particularly exciting area, with significant plans and projects ranging from the Iceland-to-Scotland underwater cable, to ongoing solar projects in the Mojave Desert, plus geothermal and pumped storage projects in numerous locations.

• *Water*. Global attention is focused on Turkey's Great Anatolia project and the proposed "Peace Pipeline" through the Middle East. We are eager to learn more about Libya's Great Man-made River, and the proposed Alaska-to-California water pipeline. Perhaps no topic is more vital than the development of large-scale desalting plants.

• *Urban redevelopment and new towns*. We have spokesmen here to describe the progress of the Australian-Japanese MFP or multifunctionpolis project and the impressive Saudi Arabian new towns at Jubail and Yanbu. We look forward to development of new cities in ultra high-rise and/or underground or domed structures.

• *Surface transport*. High-speed rail systems arc bcing built or planned throughout the world. Europe and Japan have pioneered. Now there are projects in Texas, Florida, Canada, Korea, Taiwan, Australia and elsewhere.

• *Airports and space ports*. Huge new airports are being built at Hong Kong and Osaka. The airport new town and wayport concepts are being actively explored. New spaceports are being considered at such locations as Australia's Cape York Peninsula and at Biak in Indonesia.

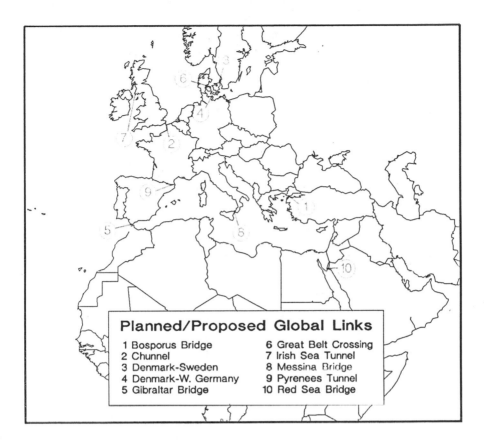

Proposed global links. In the Europe and Mediterranean area the tunnel between Calais and Folkstone is nearly complete, but there is not yet any work underway on the Gibraltar crossing or the Messina bridge.

> **Planned/Proposed Global Links**
> 1 Bosporus Bridge   6 Great Belt Crossing
> 2 Chunnel   7 Irish Sea Tunnel
> 3 Denmark-Sweden   8 Messina Bridge
> 4 Denmark-W. Germany   9 Pyrenees Tunnel
> 5 Gibraltar Bridge   10 Red Sea Bridge

    • *Environmental enhancement.* This may be our busiest field of activity. There are super projects in nuclear cleanup, waste processing, recycling and disposal. We have a great opportunity in restoration of wetlands and reclamation of desert areas. We also have a role in avoidance of disasters. Perhaps the ultimate project is to build a system for deflecting asteroids that threaten to strike the earth and destroy us.

    • *Economic development projects.* There are already many science cities and parks. There are special economic zones and free ports. We also have massive new industrial plants and destination resort complexes. All are indications of super projects yet to come — bigger, more complex, more expensive and more essential than ever before.

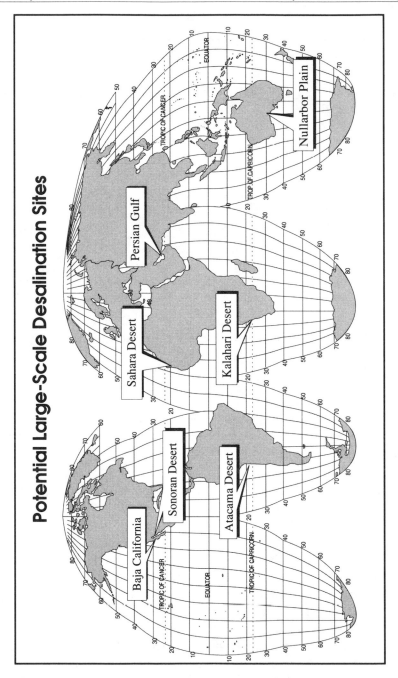

Potential Large-Scale Desalination Sites

Nullarbor Plain

Persian Gulf

Sahara Desert

Kalahari Desert

Sonoran Desert

Baja California

Atacama Desert

Proposed large desalting plants. Some of the most dramatic developments of the early 21st century will be the use of solar energy to desalt seawater and revive the major deserts of the world.

414

• *Social projects*. Needless to say, the world has great needs for new housing, medical centers, education facilities and other infrastructure elements.

• *New science and technology*. Finally, the world must provide for research and laboratory facilities to meet our new challenges. We are committed to building a space station and a human genome project. Perhaps the ultimate technical achievement will be the terraforming of other planets to make them habitable. I recently had a note from famed science writer Arthur Clarke reminding that this topic should be on our agenda.

Super Project Questions

Obviously, we need to know a great deal more about these projects. We have been building a data base for some years, but we have a lot more work to do.

There are now more than 1,300 projects in our file. Approximately one-third are under construction, one-third are being actively planned and the other one-third are still in the talk stage.

We need to know how to move new projects much faster through the planning stages into construction. We need much more information about the management of the projects under construction.

And, perhaps our weakest area is in the evaluation of new project proposals. Which make the best use of the world's limited resources? Which offer the best cost/benefit ratios? Which harmonize best with the environment? Which promise to solve long-standing political conflicts?

We are speaking about monumental decisions that will make an impact on the world for the next half century or longer.

Over the next few years it is possible that this forum can be a vehicle for establishing super project benchmarks in such areas as funding, scheduling and operation. Perhaps we can exert a positive influence in the setting of global priorities.

We may also make a contribution in identifying winning combinations. Through our sessions we may discover that a project planned in nation A and a project planned in nation B may each be made more feasible if joined in a global network or system.

Later this morning Dr. Mochida will offer a thought-provoking plan for a global transport network — not just a single tunnel or canal.

Perhaps our greatest opportunity is to build a body of information on how to make super projects pay for themselves — new ways to arrange funding and to build on time, on schedule; and how to privatize.

Finally, we will need to find ways to deal with opposition. Every super project — no matter how well-conceived and planned — will be faced with

415

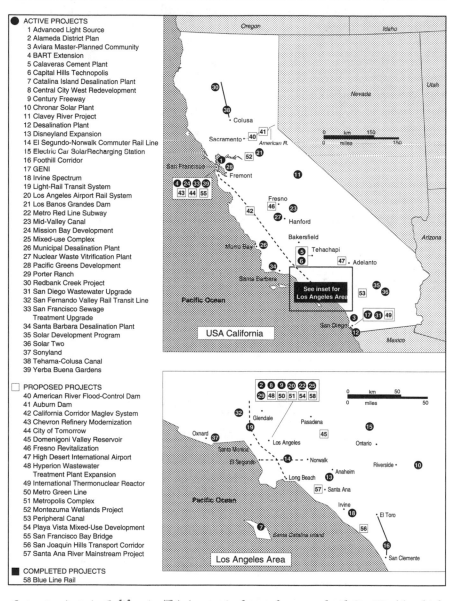

ACTIVE PROJECTS
1 Advanced Light Source
2 Alameda District Plan
3 Aviara Master-Planned Community
4 BART Extension
5 Calaveras Cement Plant
6 Capital Hills Technopolis
7 Catalina Island Desalination Plant
8 Central City West Redevelopment
9 Century Freeway
10 Chronar Solar Plant
11 Clavey River Project
12 Desalination Plant
13 Disneyland Expansion
14 El Segundo-Norwalk Commuter Rail Line
15 Electric Car SolarRecharging Station
16 Foothill Corridor
17 GENI
18 Irvine Spectrum
19 Light-Rail Transit System
20 Los Angeles Airport Rail System
21 Los Banos Grandes Dam
22 Metro Red Line Subway
23 Mid-Valley Canal
24 Mission Bay Development
25 Mixed-use Complex
26 Municipal Desalination Plant
27 Nuclear Waste Vitrification Plant
28 Pacific Greens Development
29 Porter Ranch
30 Redbank Creek Project
31 San Diego Wastewater Upgrade
32 San Fernando Valley Rail Transit Line
33 San Francisco Sewage
    Treatment Upgrade
34 Santa Barbara Desalination Plant
35 Solar Development Program
36 Solar Two
37 Sonyland
38 Tehama-Colusa Canal
39 Yerba Buena Gardens

PROPOSED PROJECTS
40 American River Flood-Control Dam
41 Auburn Dam
42 California Corridor Maglev System
43 Chevron Refinery Modernization
44 City of Tomorrow
45 Domenigoni Valley Reservoir
46 Fresno Revitalization
47 High Desert International Airport
48 Hyperion Wastewater
    Treatment Plant Expansion
49 International Thermonuclear Reactor
50 Metro Green Line
51 Metropolis Complex
52 Montezuma Wetlands Project
53 Peripheral Canal
54 Playa Vista Mixed-Use Development
55 San Francisco Bay Bridge
56 San Joaquin Hills Transport Corridor
57 Santa Ana River Mainstream Project

COMPLETED PROJECTS
58 Blue Line Rail

Super projects in California. This is a typical map from our book Site World, *which shows the locations of super projects around the world.*

416

criticism from self-appointed experts, special-interest groups and NIMBY spokespeople. They will contend that the new projects are too expensive, too complex and particularly vulnerable to failure.

Urgency — Why Now?

We are all familiar with the compression of the time scale. Management of time has become as important as management of money and other resources.

For example, we need to buy lead time for conversion to non-fossil energy sources. Lead time to meet global emergencies may prove to be the rarest of all commodities.

Despite the fact that a global recession has slowed economies and created havoc with budgets, this may be the optimum time to launch major infrastructure projects, such as high-speed rail systems, new super airports, urban redevelopments and environmental enhancement ventures.

• Investment in infrastructure is an excellent job creation strategy for governments seeking to hasten the end of the recession. Super projects help in two ways: They create jobs during construction and they generate new economic development upon completion.

• Planners, consultants, and contractors experienced in large-scale development are readily available today because of reduced levels of activity in real estate.

• Financing costs — interest rates — are probably lower today than they will be for years to come.

• Competition for projects in very keen today, a fact that works to the advantage of project sponsors.

• Total costs for projects launched today will be substantially less than those for projects postponed and made subject to future inflation.

Super projects can be the trigger that stimulates a global economic recovery!

Capture the Imagination of the World

There is a need and opportunity for all of those interested in super projects to join in a common promotion effort.

We need to capture the imagination of the public and spur leaders to act.

We need to encourage government and business leaders to think big, accept challenges, do great things.

We need spirited competition! The competition among cities that seek to host the Olympic Games offers an example of what can be accomplished under the spur of competition. Cities propose new facilities and infrastructure improvements which they would not otherwise build in several decades, if ever, and they do it.

Look at what Barcelona has done for the 1992 summer games and what Atlanta is planning for 1996.

Through competitive activities and other strategies we must move super projects to the top of the public agenda! We must make the public aware that we are about to enter the century of the super project! We must dedicate ourselves for the rest of this century to getting ready for this awesome responsibility.

Above all, we must challenge the imagination and creativity of the world's best thinkers. We must dream, but we must be more than dreamers. We must be dream implementors.

This morning, we begin.

1992 Excerpt	A *Glimpse of the Future*. Technology forecasts for global strategists. A study for the World Development Council. 103 pp. 1992.

Futurism serves the early warning needs of the world, its nations and its cities with regard to matters of security and quality of life. For companies and business ventures, futurism is a key factor in competitive survival and growth. And for the family and individual it provides psychological and emotional support during times of change.

Thinking years ahead gives us warnings about such possibilities as global warming, ozone depletion, over-population, species extinction and many other hazards. Via futurism we identify threats and gain lead time in which we can, it is hoped, take effective counter action.

It is no exaggeration to say that global lead time is a key to survival of our civilization!

An extreme example is the threat of a large asteroid appearing out of space on a collision course with the earth. At present we have no defense mechanism and, with only a few days warning, we could only watch helplessly as our destruction approached. However, with more time we might prepare a fleet of rockets armed with powerful missiles that could be fired at the asteroid to change its course enough to cause it to miss us.

A less dramatic example is the risk of losing our supply of petroleum. An embargo or war in the Middle East might leave much of the world without essential fuel. Yet, given decades of advance warning regarding depletion of fossil fuel reserves, we should have little difficulty in developing alternate fuels to meet our needs.

The accompanying table suggests that among those who devote themselves to future studies there are several more-or-less distinct groups working in different time frames.

Among those most concerned with the near term — less than 10 years — are economic forecasters and market researchers who use demographics, statistics and other data. They are typically trying to evaluate already-identified trends and answer questions regarding how big, or how much.

Another group, usually identified as futurists, is more concerned with events in the medium-range of 10 to 20 years. They are long-range planners, conceptual designers, researchers and scholars who seek to answer questions regarding the next technological breakthroughs and *when* they may come.

Finally, there is the "far-out" group looking beyond 20 years, perhaps to future centuries. They include science-fiction writers, philosophers, seers and others who speculate on what could happen, even though they do not know how it could. Some in this group are well-qualified scientists who have made important contributions to our technology.

Margin of safety

Where is the line between fiction and reality? None will suggest that Arthur Clarke and Isaac Asimov have not made substantial scientific contributions through their brilliant speculations.

Yet, there are charlatans who seek headlines by making pseudo-scientific predictions — for example, they do not hesitate to predict that the earth will come to an end on a specific date.

Also, there is abundant evidence that leading scholars can be far off in forecasts produced with great care. There is the classic case of Malthus in 1798.

In modern times, we have the Rand forecast made in 1965 and the Club of Rome "limits to growth" study of 1972. More recently, there is the Japanese "Plan for the Planet," issued in 1990. (To avoid embarrassment, we will not mention our own forecasts of recent decades.)

What we learn from all of these is that there is a substantial margin of error.

Moreover, we have the growing problem of faked research results. The lure of money and publicity has tempted scholars to create artificial findings — modern versions of the Piltdown Man.

Comparing Those Who Peer into the Future:

	0-10 Years	10-20 Years	20+ Years
Who	Market Researchers Business Forecasters	Futurists Planners Designers	Sci-Fi Writers Seers Philosophers
Level of Confidence	High degree that it will happen	Moderate Likely to happen	Queasy! Could happen
Prime Question	How much? How big?	How soon? How?	What?

Don't forget the unpredictable!

Many a forecaster from Malthus on down through the years has run aground because of failure to consider the unpredictable. This is akin to the mistake of a mechanical designer who fails to add a margin of safety, or the financial planner who leaves out the contingency fund.

At any point in time there are unseen forces at work which will yield surprises in the days ahead. No geo-economic scientist, research organization or combination of them can forecast all of the events that will occur.

During the 1930s the U.S. government made a study of coming technical developments. It failed to forecast such things as television, transoceanic jet service, lasers or microcomputers.

More recently, during the war in Kuwait, there was much gloom and doom forecasting by certain prominent scientists who predicted that the smoke from burning oil wells would cause global climate changes — a sort of "nuclear winter." They were badly wrong because they made a number of incorrect assumptions regarding the amount of smoke, its color and composition, and the altitude to which it would rise.

There are similar questions regarding forecasts of global warming, ozone depletion and other atmospheric changes. Scientists cannot agree on past events, let alone the future — witness the variety of explanations for the death of the dinosaurs or the decline of various civilizations.

Let's accept the fact that our error rate in forecasting may be large! We probably miss one-third to one-half of all the big developments that will occur in a forecast period of 10 years. Our 20-year forecasts are even less reliable, and our 30-year predictions are, for the most part, pure speculation.

Our task is made more difficult by the ever-increasing speed of development. The transoceanic jetliner that flew in the late 1950s took about 15 years from lab tests to commercial flight. The microcomputer exploded onto the scene during the 1970s in less than 10 years. With computerized design and automated manufacture today we have the prospect of important new products having a gestation period measured in months or days.

Knowing this, it is not intelligent to prepare a list such as that in this study and intimate that this is what is going to happen. At best, it *may* be a *part* of what will happen.

To be on the safe side, we suggest that the global planner assume that during the next 10 years there will be two to three times as many significant developments as we have listed. Now we have a fuzzy picture of the exciting things that are in store for us!

Looking Ahead by Looking Back

As we speculate on things to some, it is helpful to take a quick look backward. Where we have come in the past 30 years gives us a measure of how far we can go in the next few decades.

It seems safe to assume that the changes of the next 30 years will be at least as numerous and dramatic as those of the past three decades. We believe the time scale of development will continue to collapse, with changes occurring with ever-increasing frequency.

Futurism and Management

A generation ago, when things moved more slowly, the economic system was more tolerant of firms that failed to anticipate change. Today, failure to anticipate change can be abruptly fatal.

That's why large companies employ "technological forecasters" or "futurists." Many have large departments devoted to study of future trends and their implications for the company.

In the days ahead, the CEO himself must be a practicing futurist. In addition to staff input, he must develop an image of the future from such informal processes as reading newspapers, by observing business associates and by intuition.

Perhaps we can define the technological forecasting objective of most business managers very simply — the avoidance of surprises. Many will settle for that.

But the more astute managers want something more. They are not just trying to *defend* themselves against change — they are determined to *take advantage* of change and use it for their own benefit. They want to gain a competitive edge by outguessing the opposition.

It is a long-established axiom that without change there are no new opportunities. Almost every change brings with it exciting new opportunities for someone.

Further, we know that there are three essential factors in exploiting change: anticipating the change, being able to act quickly and willingness to bet on one's forecast.

Many people may anticipate change, but few are both willing and able to take advantage of it.

Where or when does this process start? The systems must be customized, of course, to fit the organization. However, we believe there are some common denominators.

We think the alert firm must have both a long-range *outlook* and a long range *plan*. The latter is a projected business activity and operations sequence. It is what the firm expects to do.

How far into the future should it go? There was a time when large corporations had formal plans for 10 years ahead and some prepared 20-year plans. Today, few firms attempt to develop operating plans covering more than five years and many consider a two-year plan to be long range.

This is all a result of the compression of the time scale. Events such as technological breakthroughs are happening faster and faster, and it becomes more and more difficult to predict future developments. Companies that ignore this change of pace will pay dearly.

A generation ago a typical product life cycle was 15 to 20 years. A firm that obtained a patent could hope to enjoy a strong market position for the life of the patent, 17 years. A product that held market position for 10 to 15 years was commonplace.

Under such conditions, decision-making was much easier. Managers could make commitments for new plants and equipment and feel confident that they would see a good return on investment over a period of years. Similarly, they could recruit, train and develop staff, looking toward years of service.

In today's volatile economy decision-making can be very difficult. Many product life cycles are measured in months, requiring great flexibility in the company's physical plan. Will the new plant being occupied this year be suitable for producing the new product — as yet unidentified — to be launched three years hence?

These are some of the reasons that many companies are depending heavily on detailed one-year plans, plus very sketchy five-year plans. Further, the one-year plans are monitored closely and updated during the year.

The long-range planning problem raises biggest questions in regard to fixed assets, such as real estate. Typically, corporations have invested in properties, expecting to use them for, say, 20 years and even then to enjoy substantial residual value.

In effect, such an investment today requires the manager to speculate on the value of his real estate investment well into the next century. Few managers claim any confidence in looking that far ahead.

The collapsing time scale also requires companies to prepare their long range plans more quickly. A plan developed slowly and deliberately over a year's time may be obsolete before it is promulgated. To develop valid plans quickly most companies need to maintain vital data bases constantly and employ automated systems for interpreting data and making instant extrapolations when needed.

Unlike the business plan, *outlook* is simply a vision of what may be coming. There are no constraints, economic or other, on the outlook. It can be "far out" and purely speculative.

The *outlook* should extend as far into the future as it is possible to foresee even a hint of change. It may include programs and projects which are but a gleam in someones eye.

Why Have a Plan?

Given the possibilities for error in predicting the future, why bother with a plan? Aside from the obvious fact that an imperfect plan is better than none, there is ample evidence that having a plan or a deadline spurs development dramatically.

There was the challenge by President Kennedy to put a man on the moon within a decade. Few believe it would have happened as quickly without that deadline.

More recently, there was the challenge to the world to put out the oil fires in Kuwait before they did great damage to global ecosystems. The job was done in six months — far sooner than even top experts thought possible.

Hence, global executives are urged to select objectives and challenge their corporate teams to achieve them!

1993 Excerpt	"New Wonders of The World." Every school child learns of the pyramids, the hanging gardens and the other wonders of the ancient world. Now, a massive global construction program promises to yield a new list of wonders for today and tomorrow. *Leaders* magazine. July/August/September 1993.

Some years ago we began keeping a file on "global super projects," which we defined as large-scale construction and development projects costing US $1 billion or more, or involving technological breakthroughs of global significance.

Today the file includes more than 1,500 projects around the world. About one-third are in planning stages and another one-third is under construction. The rest are still in the idea or "talk" stage.

It is apparent that in the years just ahead we will see many project completions and, thus, the realization of many dreams of mankind. A prime example, of course, is the EuroTunnel, which was proposed more than 200 years ago.

Sifting through the data base, we might list two new sets of "seven wonders" — one group which is underway now, and another which is projected to be developed in the early 21st century.

For our current list, we might cite:

• *EuroTunnel*. It has already had a substantial impact on economic activity in the Calais du Nord area of France and in Kent across the channel. When open, its effect will be felt throughout Europe.

• *The Rhine-Danube Canal*. It is said that the Emperor Charlemagne authorized the start of digging more than 12 centuries ago. The project was subsequently abandoned and restarted several times before the modern program completed the link last summer. At last, waterborne traffic can move from the Atlantic to the Black Sea!

• *The Great Belt*. Another important global link is the new system of bridges and tunnels that will provide a surface connection between Scandinavia and the Continent. The elements include the Oresund bridge between Malmo and Copenhagen; a northern bridge-tunnel link across Denmark to Jutland; and a southern route via bridges to Germany.

• *Libya's "Great Man-made River."* Another of mankind's dreams — to bring water to the Sahara — is being realized in North Africa. This $25 billion project involves pumping fresh water from southern Sahara aquifers to the Mediterranean coastal region, a distance of some 750 miles (1,200 km). Phase I, completed in 1991, delivers more than 70 million cubic feet (two million cubic meters) of water daily to areas between Benghazi and Sirt. Additional phases now underway will provide water to areas from Tripoli to Tobruk.

• *Kansai airport*. Japan has literally moved a mountain — one bargeload at a time — to create an artificial island in Osaka Bay for a new jetport. When completed in 1994, the multi-billion project will provide Japan with its first international jet port operating 24 hours per day.

• *Chek Lap Kok airport*. Another global airport project being built despite severe site limitations is Hong Kong's new $16 billion complex. A small island, Chek Lap Kok, is being leveled for runways and will be connected to the city via a new suspension bridge and causeway. The plan includes a new container port and a rapid rail line connecting the elements.

• *The Global Positioning System (GPS)*. Because the key elements are in space, the new GPS system is the least visible of the world's new wonders. Yet, it may be the most important of all. Conceived to use 24 satellites stationed at precise intervals around the earth, GPS provides precise location data via inexpensive instruments in airplanes, ships and other vehicles. Although all satellites are not yet in place, it is already revolutionizing surveying and navigation around the world.

What Will the Future Bring?

We have discussed projects now under construction or just completed. However, if we consider projects in the early "talk" or planning stages, we have an even more exciting list. Our projected new "wonders" for the early 21st century might include:

• *New Silk Road*. The great new economies of the Pacific Rim and unified Europe urgently need a good surface link. Already, site surveys are covering three possible routes: Berlin to Moscow to Japan; Mediterranean to India to Singapore; and a central route across China.

• *Gibraltar bridge-tunnel*. This long-discussed link between Europe and Africa is on the list of projects being studied by the Japan-based Global Infrastructure Fund (GIF).

• *Bering Strait crossing*. Several groups are planning and promoting a link between Asia and North America across the Bering Strait. It would include surface traffic as well as electric power transmission lines connecting the North American grid with the Siberian grid.

• *Desert reclamation*. Research now underway to develop economically feasible systems for desalting seawater using solar energy will lead to great new projects wherever deserts lie adjacent to the sea. Immediate sites include the Baja Peninsula of Mexico, the west coast of Peru and Chile; the Middle East, Namibia and many islands. These projects will create some of the world's most attractive new growth areas.

• *Multi-loop cities*. It is already apparent that a favored form of development in the years ahead will be the multi-loop cities which integrate urban and rural areas into a new metro complex. These new global centers will offer quiet suburban living within minutes of global jet service and regional rapid rail or freeways. Atlanta is an example of one such emerging complex.

• *Global cellular phone system*. This project will probably have a more profound impact on the people of the world than any of the construction projects listed above. It will mean that anyone anywhere in the world can talk to anyone else anywhere else in the world instantly. The leading proposal is the $3 billion Iridium Project, put forward by Motorola. It involves

77 satellites in low earth orbit. (The element Iridium has 77 electrons in the nucleus, hence the name.)

• *Space colony*. Most certainly the early 21st century will see the beginning of space colonization. Much planning and design is underway for the first moon base. And, the World Development Council recently held a seminar on "terraforming" Mars — that is, creating an atmosphere on Mars suitable for human habitation.

We have not listed as a prospective new wonder of the world the planned asteroid avoidance system, since we don't know that it will involve large new construction. Yet, it may turn out to be the most vital environmental project of all time. It involves planning to use a battery of missiles to deflect from its course any large asteroid that enters our solar system on a collision course with Earth.

There are so many new ideas and proposals being put forward today that we will need to revise our list of wonders almost every year. New needs will prompt new efforts. For example, we are now witnessing the emergence of a significant new emphasis on environmental projects.

Today we have the joint Russia-USA nuclear weapons decommissioning program, to cost some $100 billion. The largest continuing program is the modernization or decommissioning of nuclear power generating plants. During the coming decade more than 50 aging reactors will have to be phased out, at a cost of about $1 billion each.

There is also the program for clean-up of pollution sources in Eastern Europe. At just one site, a slurry pond near Oberrothenbach, clean-up will cost more than $10 billion.

Another multi-billion dollar environmental project is the Kuwait war follow-up. The oil fires have long been extinguished, but large crews are still busy removing mines and unexploded ammunition from the beaches and desert. And, there is a new problem in Yugoslavia.

Still another challenge is the shrinking Aral Sea in Kazakhkstan and Uzbekhistan. Global planners and strategists believe this area may become a model for decision-making with respect to river diversions, irrigation methods and advanced farming practices.

Other emerging environmental projects include such undertakings as Project Moses designed to protect Venice from flooding; a flood control plan for Bangladesh; and a wastewater system for Cairo.

As we may note, there is an interesting difference between these modern projects and those of the ancient world. Most of the ancient wonders were inspired by the desire to create a monument recognizing a ruler, a regime or a religious movement. An exception was the lighthouse of Pharaohs at Alexandria, which also filled an infrastructure need.

Today, however, almost all large-scale projects are designed to meet specific needs. They are being built more for function than for show. Perhaps none will rival the great pyramids in their awesome majesty, but they will do more to enhance the quality of life for the people of the world.

Viewed from that perspective, the new wonders may be even more wondrous than the famed projects of the ancient world.

| 1993 Excerpt | "The Science and the Art of Futurism." American technology — and the industries it supports — will survive in the competitive future in direct proportion to its ability to interpret the trends. *Georgia Tech Alumni Magazine*, September 1993, pp. 14-23. |

A generation ago, when things moved more slowly, the economic system was more tolerant of firms that failed to anticipate change. Today, failure to anticipate change can be abruptly fatal.

That's why many large companies employ technological forecasters or futurists devoted to the study of future trends and their implications for the company.

Few doubt that technology will be a dominant political and economic issue of the future. Many believe that scientific prowess will be the key to world leadership. Certainly the art of predicting upcoming events — futurism — will also play an important role.

Thinking years ahead gives us warnings about such possibilities as global warming, ozone depletion, over-population, species extinction and many other hazards. Via futurism we can identify threats and gain lead time in which we can, it is hoped, take effective counteraction.

Futurism thus serves the early warning needs of nations and cities with regard to matters of security and quality of life. For companies and business ventures, futurism is a key factor in competitive survival and growth.

Futurists are generally concerned with events that may happen in the next 10 to 20 years. They are particularly interested in new technological breakthroughs and the impact of those breakthroughs on society.

A distinction is thus drawn between futurists and, for example, market researchers, who are interested in a 0 to10-year time scale, and who typically evaluate already-identified trends. At the other end are science fiction writers and philosophers who look 30, or even hundreds of years ahead. They speculate on what could happen even if they do not know how it could happen.

Near-term Forecasts, 0-10 years

Super Metro Areas

The leading cities of the world will, in most cases, have two or more perimeter routes integrating the center city with the hinterland. The design concept of a loop highway encircling a city has moved rapidly from the status as a traffic by-pass, to an economic development tool, to the urban plan for the 21st century. Many central cities will become multi-level environments, with one level below ground, another at grade and a third built on air rights. There will be widespread construction over freeways and service corridors.

Genetic Science Revolution

Discoveries in genetic engineering will have a profound effect on politics, economics, homes and families. In 1990, Congress funded the Human Genome Project, a massive effort to map all the genes found in the human body. The result will be a guide to the 50,000 to 100,000 genes that control everything from vulnerability to disease to physical features. The use of DNA techniques for identification will be rapidly expanded. Beginning with infants and criminals, massive data banks will be created. The possibilities for social and political controversy are endless. People with "bad" genes may not be offered better jobs. Insurance firms may refuse to cover individuals likely to encounter specific health problems.

Anti-pollution Crusade

The coming decade will see an unprecedented global commitment to large-scale projects aimed at destroying nuclear weapons, cleaning up toxic wastes, conserving rain forests and repairing damaged environments.

Global Communications

The ultimate cellular telephone system will use satellites to cover every square foot of the Earth. It will be possible for someone in an isolated under-developed area to communicate with people in the world's cities. The refinement of systems for automatic translation of voice transmissions will minimize the language barriers among people. Global pacts will permit unfettered electronic transfer of data used for educational and scientific purposes. Facsimile and other electronic systems will replace manual mail delivery.

A Global Society

The next decade will see the emergence of a new global society made up largely of executives of global firms, government officials and others who have learned how to be at home wherever they are. These new "globalists" are comfortable with a 24-hour clock set to universal time. The metric system, currency conversions and international telephone connections. Most important, the globalists are eager to apply new technologies. Already, many of them carry in their briefcases a small satellite antenna which permits them to receive information wherever they may be.

Longer-term Forecasts, 10-20 years

Population Control

The nations of the world will finally implement a realistic program for controlling population as the general public becomes aware that many of the world's pressing problems — waste disposal, traffic, urban sprawl and environmental degredation — are directly connected to population growth.

Desalinated Seawater

Breakthroughs in a process to desalinate seawater using solar energy will foster tremendous development in some of the world's arid regions. Areas likely to benefit from the technology include Baja California, the Atacama Desert in South America and areas along the Arabian Gulf.

Smart Cars and Smart Roads

These are systems wherein vehicles are operated by automatic controls along specific routes. By the turn of the century, some municipalities will approve the operation of robot-run vehicles on designated routes. Use will increase rapidly, and by 2010, robot vehicles will become the feeder units for mass transit systems. Eventually, improved systems will serve high-speed traffic on the Interstates, improving traffic flow and safety.

Domed Cities and Bubble Farms

There's a fast-moving trend toward innovative use of huge tent-like dome structures. Agribusinesses see the prospect for new "bubble farms," in which thousands of acres are covered by dome units to protect tender seedlings as well as to control the growth of new genetically engineered crops. Dome enclosures may be particularly suitable for new towns in the Arctic and other cold regions. Planners also see the possibility of using such structures on the ocean floor to re-direct currents and create new fishing zones.

Faster Flight

The first decade of the 21st century will see the introduction of exciting new aircraft. A new generation of supersonic transport will fly at about three times the speed of sound and have a range of 10,000 miles. Trips to the opposite side of the world will take less than half of the present times. A new Trans-Atmospheric Vehicle will afford virtual space travel for global executives and will cut the time from the U.S. to Tokyo or Sydney to less than two hours. The effect on world business and government will be profound.

Alternative Energy

Solar power will become a significant economic factor in areas with abundant sunshine. The merit of hydrogen as a new fuel will also be realized.

Very Long-term Forecasts, 20 to 30 years

Brain-Computer Link

The most exciting prospect is linking the human brain to a computer, allowing people to download thoughts or upload information. The genius of great men and women could thus be saved, stored and used again. The uploading mode would revolutionize education.

Restoring Senses

New discoveries in biotechnology will give artificial eyesight to the blind, hearing to the deaf and voice to the mute. Millions of dysfunctional people will be elevated to new roles as more productive citizens.

Nuclear Waste

Effective means for neutralizing old nuclear wastes will be discovered. Already there is serious research into various transmutation schemes which use neutron bombardment to convert wastes into shorter-lived isotopes. Eventually, such a process could convert hot wastes into non-radioactive materials.

Space Tourism

Space travel will become commonplace, with rival companies offering inexpensive trips to the moon. Space colonies will be established to support mining and manufacturing operations as well as to handle tourists.

Human-powered Flight

Improvements in the strength/weight ratio in materials and in the efficiency of aerodynamic components will make human-powered flight possible for non-athletes. First applications will be in recreation, as pedaling around the neighborhood at treetop height will supplant jogging for many.

Asteroid Disaster Plan

The world will have in place a system to prevent disastrous collisions. It will consist of batteries of huge missiles which can be fired at incoming asteroids to alter their course.

C. Bibliography

The following are citations of McKinley Conway's writings on this chapter's subject. As this book goes to press, work is underway to make many of these items available to researchers. To check, look for a file on GeoTEAM/IDRCNET or telephone GeoTEAM/Fax at 404-453-4200 for a free catalog.

468. "The Next 10 Years of Southern Progress" (South to gain 3,000 major plants). Address at Chapel Hill. Excerpted in *Journal of Southern Research*, Atlanta. July-August. 1953. pp. 2-22.

469. "Biotechnology Atlanta" (a study for the Forward Atlanta program). Emory University, Atlanta. 1964. 44 pp. illus. With Dr. James Bain and others.

470. "Findings of the Governors Commission for Scientific Research and Development," State of Georgia, Jan. 1965. 12 pp. plus appendix.

471. "A proposal for the 200-Bev Proton Accelerator," Georgia Science and Technology Commission, submitted to the U.S. Atomic Energy Commission, Washington. June 15, 1965. 70 pp. With Dale Henson and others.

472. "Proposed Oceanographic Research Center" (Skidaway Institute). American Institute of Planners, Atlanta. March 27, 1967.

473. "Our Rate of Development Is Non-linear," (commencement address). West Georgia College, Carrollton, Ga., June 4, 1967.

474. Notes on future courses of action, Science for Society, National Science Conference, National Science Foundation, October. 12-14, 1970.

475. "Future Shock Arrived Yesterday!" We are reminded of an early reference to the so-called future shock phenomenon which we discussed in one of our publications some 20 years ago. We refer to Dr. Robert Wilson's suggestion that the pace of development can be better appreciated if we compress the entire span of man's evolution into a 50-year time scale. *Industrial Development,* Jan.-Feb. 1975. p. 2.

476. "The Future for North American Industrial Capitalism." The needs of the global population are so enormous that they will demand large-scale approaches. They will be the kinds of things that will attract newspaper headlines... and are regarded by many as frivolous. Proceedings of the 53rd annual conference, American Industrial Development Council, Albuquerque, N.M. May 21-23, 1978. pp. 24-27.

477. "A New Wave of Super Projects?" Is the world on the threshold of great new construction projects and creative ventures? Here is a survey by *Industrial Development's* publisher, who has visited more than 70 super project sites around the world. *Industrial Development,* May-June 1983. pp. 4-9.

478. "A Technology Review and Forecast for Development Strategists," 1986. Monograph.

479. "Super Projects 1986." With many of the world's nations suffering through economic slumps and debt crises, it might be assumed that the global agenda for huge, complex, multi-billion dollar ventures might have dried up. Yet the latest survey reveals a long list of new and exciting projects ranging from transatmospheric vehicles to Super Colliders. *Site Selection,* Feb. 1986. pp. 214-220.

480. "Looking into the Facility Planner's Fabulous Future." In celebration of *Site Selection's* first 30 years we have made a new technological forecast. Included is a summary of future events and discoveries considered most likely to impact corporate facility planning and area economic development. *Site Selection,* June 1986. pp. 566-580.

481. "True Professionals Don't Ignore Technology Forecasts!" There are some executives who ignore predictions of technical breakthroughs — allocating them to the status of cocktail conversation topics or themes for sci-fi movies. They treat the future as if it will never happen. Consequently, life is full of surprises, sometimes very rude ones. *Site Selection,* June 1987. p. 552.

482. In the years ahead it is a certainty that there will be revolutionary changes in the way we travel. Those who have any doubt that sweeping changes will affect the lives of most citizens living today need only glance backward at innovations that took place in the last 30

431

years. *Gwinnett Daily News,* July 20, 1988.

483. "Science May Solve Traffic Woes." Some expert observers say the auto traffic mess will get a lot worse before it starts getting better. Others believe high technology may come to our rescue. Among these developments are computer-controlled traffic lights, satellite positioning systems, navigation displays, radar controlled "car trains" and robot-driven vehicles. *Gwinnett Daily News,* March 15, 1989.

484. *The SiteNet World Guide.* Beyond perestroika. Country profiles, nations A to Z. Field reports and photos. The super projects. The development world tomorrow. Global investment incentives. 1989. 530 pp. With Laura Jones-Kelley and Linda L. Liston.

485. "Forecasting Change Can Mean Life or Death." A generation ago, when things moved more slowly, the economic system was more tolerant of companies that failed to anticipate change. Today, failure to anticipate change can be abruptly fatal. *Gwinnett Daily News,* June 21, 1989.

486. "Disaster Planning Vital for All Businesses." Planning for the future typically involves forecasting trends in technology, demographics and social patterns. However, futurists must never forget events which may not be positive. *Gwinnett Daily News,* July 12, 1989.

487. "Technology Makes Long-term Plans Obsolete." How far into the future does it make sense to project your company's plans? There was a time when large corporations had formal plans for 10 years ahead, and some prepared 20-year plans. Today few firms attempt to develop operating plans covering more than five years and many consider a two-year plan to be long range. *Gwinnett Daily News,* Aug. 9, 1989.

488. "Super Projects May Change the Future." Pause for a moment to ask what it would be like today without the interstate highway system. Or, ask where we would be without such products of the space program as microcomputers and communications satellites. Gwinnett Daily News, Sept. 13, 1989.

489. "The Sky's the Limit for Future 'Globalites'." Somewhere in your neighborhood there is someone — a business executive, or an avid traveler —who sees the world through a different set of lenses. He or she is part of the emerging new global society. *Gwinnett Daily News,* Oct. 18, 1989.

490. "A New Agenda for Site World." For global firms, strategic thinking is not just a business exercise — it is the difference between success and failure. Looking at the 1990s and beyond, global leaders are preparing a new agenda. *Site Selection,* April 1990. p. 268.

491. "Language Barriers Beginning to Fall." The language barrier which has separated nations and peoples for centuries is about to go the way of the Berlin Wall. *Gwinnett Daily News,* July 18, 1990.

492. "Super Projects, New Wonders of the World." Monograph based on opening statement made at the seminar on Corporate Global Strategy, arranged by the Institute of Social Engineering, Japan, held at the American Club, Tokyo, Aug. 27, 1990.

493. "Super Domes Will Cover New Cities." Fly over many U.S. cities today and the most conspicuous structure you see is a shining dome covering a football stadium. Fly over cities of the future and you may see only one huge dome. *Gwinnett Daily News.* Aug. 1990.

494. "Proposed High-rise City for Japan Boggles the Mind." While in Tokyo recently, we learned more about the proposal of a major engineering firm, Ohbayashi, to build a 500-story high-rise building that would be a city within itself. Called "Aeropolis 2001," the mammoth structure would be approximately five times as high as the World Trade Center in New York. *Gwinnett Daily News,* Sept. 19, 1990.

495. "Bullet Trains Put on Slow Track in U.S." How would you like to board a train in downtown Atlanta and step off in Savannah an hour later? Or, how about making a business appointment in Orlando and getting back to Atlanta the same day, rested and relaxed? *Gwinnett Daily News,* Oct. 17, 1990.

496. "Olympic Site Competitions Spur Top Officials to Set Unprecedented Goals for Themselves." One of the most interesting phenomena in urban development is the impact of site competitions on infrastructure planning. *Gwinnett Daily News.* Nov. 1990.

497. "Overlooking the Multiplier Effect of High Technology." A decade ago, when microcomputers began to appear in numbers in the workplace, there was great excitement. We would soon have "paperless" offices, the pundits said. *Gwinnett Daily News,* Dec. 19, 1990.

498. "The Geo-economic Explosion. Understanding change!" *Site World.* 1991.

499. "The Rationale for Global Super Projects." Opening statement for the first annual global super projects conference, World Development Council, Honolulu, February 17, 1992.

500. *A Glimpse of the Future — Technology Forecasts for Global Strategists.* A study for the World Development Council. 103 pp. 1992.

501. "Macro Engineering." As population pressures increase, it is logical to look for ways to use the vast ocean spaces to relieve congestion and to meet other global needs. Article for MacMillan *Encyclopedia of the Future.* 1992.

502. "Super Projects: New Wonders of the World." Bridges, tunnels, airports, high-speed rail systems, and telecommunications networks are among global super projects creating new links among the world's peoples. *The Futurist,* World Future Society, Washington. March-April 1993. pp. 25-28.

503. "Tomorrow's Supercities." In the next century we could be working in 500-story office buildings, living in cities afloat on the ocean, or going to domed enclosures to ski during summer months. *The Futurist,* May-June 1993, pp. 27-33. Cover story with illus.

504. *Airport Cities 21, the New Global Transport Centers of the 21st Century.* One in a series of studies prepared in support of the programs of the World Development Council. 1993. 113 pp. (Excerpt from review in "Future Survey" April 1993: "A lofty vision that is plausible, imaginative and important.")

505. "The Science and the Art of Futurism." American technology — and the industries it supports — will survive in the competitive future in direct proportion to its ability to interpret the trends. *Georgia Tech Alumni Magazine,* Sept. 1993, pp. 14- 23.

506. "New Wonders of the World." Every schoolchild learns of the pyramids, the hanging gardens and the other wonders of the ancient world. Now, a massive global construction program promises to yield a new list of wonders for today and tomorrow. *Leaders* magazine, July/Aug./Sept. 1993.

9
Appendix

Chapter 9

A. Explanatory Notes

B. Chronological Index of Published Works of McKinley Conway from 1943 to 1993

C. Print Status of more Significant Books

D. Automated Files and Information Services

A. Explanatory Notes

The following index has been prepared for the assistance of librarians and researchers. The typical entry includes:

* Title of the book, scientific paper, magazine report, newspaper article, speech, or presentation.
* Name of the publication or forum.
* Date.
* Length, number of pages.
* Format, maps, illustrations, cover.
* Associates (other authors or contributors).

Not repeated for each entry is the author's name which has appeared variously as:

* McKinley Conway (used in most computer files)
* H. McKinley Conway
* H. McKinley Conway, Jr.
* H.M. Conway
* Mac Conway

In various periodicals issued by the Conway companies, contributions may also be indicated by the initials "H.M.C.," or by such notations as "publisher," "editor," or "staff," where appropriate.

The publisher is not listed unless it is some entity other than one of the Conway group. The Conway group has included:

* Conway Data, Inc.
* Conway Research, Inc.
* Conway Publications, Inc.

The items published in *Industrial Development* and *Site Selection* can be found in larger public and business libraries. These may also be found via University Microfilms, Ann Arbor, Michigan, or in the H.W. Wilson *Business Periodicals Index*.

Studies conducted for the Industrial Development Research Council (IDRC) and the Industrial Development Research Foundation (IDRF) are identified in serial order. Example: IDRC #29.

Many of the NACA (NASA) reports written during the 1940s were classified at time of completion. Some were subsequently released in a different format, or simply declassified but not circulated.

Those items having file names beginning "GDAY" are part of a series of articles written for the *Gwinnett Daily News*, a *New York Times* affiliate in the Atlanta area.

Entries are in chronological order. As of May 15, 1993, there were more than 500 entries, including several dozen books and major studies.

This book refers only to the published works of McKinley Conway, author. It does not include several thousand items which he published but did not author.

B. Chronological Index of Published Works of McKinley Conway from 1943 to 1993

1943
1. Notes on Maximum Aircraft Angular Velocities. Washington, D.C. National Advisory Committee for Aeronautics (NACA, later NASA). 1943. 16 pp.

1944
2. The Possible Use of Ceramic Materials in Aircraft Propulsion Systems. Washington, D.C. National Advisory Committee for Aeronautics (NACA, later NASA).1944. 24 pp.
3. Tests of the Douglas BTD-1 Airplane in the 40x80-ft. Wind Tunnel — Estimates of Aileron Stick Force and Rolling Characteristics. Moffett Field, Calif. National Advisory Committee for Aeronautics (NACA, later NASA). 1944.
4. Tests of the Douglas BTD-1 Airplane in the 40x80-ft. Wind Tunnel — Aileron Characteristics. Moffett Field, Calif. National Advisory Committee for Aeronautics (NACA, later NASA). 1944. With Sam Davidson.
5. "Research Wins Wars," *Air Trails.* March 1944.

1945
6. Tests of Ryan FR-1 in the 40x80-ft. Wind Tunnel — Critical Speeds for Several Cowling Configurations. Moffett Field, Calif., National Advisory Committee for Aeronautics (NACA, later NASA). 1945.
7. Tests of the Grumman F7F in the 40x80-ft. Wind Tunnel — cooling aerodynamic characteristics. Moffett Field, Calif., National Advisory Committee for Aeronautics, (NACA, later NASA) 1945.
8. Full Scale Wind Tunnel Investigation of a Wing Inlet Induction System for a Turbojet Engine. Ames Aero. Lab., Moffett Field, Calif. National Advisory Committee for Aeronautics (NACA, later NASA), 1945. 80 pp.
9. Investigation of the Engine Installation of the Ryan FR-1 airplane in the Ames 40x80-ft. Wind Tunnel — Cooling in Climb. Moffett Field, Calif., National Advisory Committee for Aeronautics (NACA, later NASA). 1945.
10. Investigation in the Ames 40x80-ft. Wind Tunnel of the Aerodynamic and Cooling Characteristics of the Grumman F7F-1 Power Plant Installation. Moffett Field, Calif., National Advisory Committee for Aeronautics (NACA, later NASA) 1945.
11. Investigation of the Engine Installation of the FRI in the 40x80-ft. Wind Tunnel — Carburetor Air Induction System. Moffett Field, Calif., National Advisory Committee for Aeronautics (NACA, later NASA). 1945.
12. Investigation of the Engine Installation of the Ryan FR-1 in the 40x80-ft. Wind Tunnel — Cooling Correlation Analysis. Moffett Field, Calif., National Advisory Committee for Aeronautics (NACA, later NASA). 1945.
13. Tests of the Ryan FR-1 in the 40x80-ft. Wind Tunnel — Possible Improvements in the Forward Power Plant Installation. Moffett Field, Calif., National Advisory Committee for Aeronautics (NACA, later NASA), 1945.
14. Tests of Grumman F7F in the 40x80-ft. Wind Tunnel — Cooling Correlation Analysis. Moffett Field, Calif., National Advisory Committee for Aeronautics (NACA, later NASA). 1945.

15. Tests of the Grumman F7F Airplane in the 40x80-ft. Wind Tunnel — Cylinder Temperature Distribution. Moffett Field, Calif. National Advisory Committee for Aeronautics. (NACA, later NASA) 1945.
16. Investigation of Engine Installation of the Ryan FR-1 Airplane in the Ames 40x80-ft. Wind Tunnel — Summary of Results. Moffett Field, Calif., National Advisory Committee for Aeronautics (NACA, later NASA). 1945.

1946
17. Investigation in the Ames 40x80-ft. Wind Tunnel — Performance Characteristics of the Ryan FR-1 Airplane Drag Characteristics. Moffett Field, Calif., National Advisory Committee for Aeronautics (NACA, later NASA). 1946.
18. Investigation in Ames 40x80-ft. Wind Tunnel of Performance Characteristics of the Ryan FR-1 Airplane — Effect of Jet Engine Operation on Stability. Moffett Field, Calif. National Advisory Committee for Aeronautics (NACA, later NASA). 1946.
19. Investigation in Ames 40x80-ft. Wind Tunnel of Performance Characteristics of the Ryan FR-1 Airplane — Static Characteristics of the GE 1-16 Engine. Moffett Field, Calif., National Advisory Committee for Aeronautics. (NACA, later NASA) 1946.
20. Investigation in the Ames 40x80-ft. Wind Tunnel of Performance Characteristics of the Ryan FR-1 Airplane — Cooling of Fuselage Members around Jet Engine and Tailpipe. Moffett Field, Calif., National Advisory Committee for Aeronautics (NACA, later NASA). 1946.
21. Investigation in the Ames 40x80-ft. Wind Tunnel of a Wright R-1820 Engine Installed in a Ryan FR-1 Airplane. Moffett Field, Calif., National Advisory Committee for Aeronautics (NASA). 1946.
22. Full Scale Wind Tunnel Investigation of Some Turbojet Engine Installation Problems. Ames Aero. Lab., Moffett Field, Calif. National Advisory Committee for Aeronautics (NACA, later NASA). 1946.
23. Full Scale Wind Tunnel Tests of the Wake of a Turbojet Engine. Ames Aero. Lab., Moffett Field, Calif. National Advisory Committee for Aeronautics (NACA, later NASA). 1946. 32 pp.

1947
24. *Principles of High Speed Flight.* Southeastern Research Institute. 1947. 142 pp.

1948
25. *Control of Airplane Flight Path by Propulsive Jets.* Southeastern Research Institute. 1948. 22 pp.
26. "Geographical Distribution of Engineering Research and Related Industries in the United States." Southeastern Research Institute. 1948. 74 pp. Reprinted 1987 as IDRC research study number 37.
27. "Directory of Engineering Data Sources." Southeastern Research Institute, 1948, 64 pp. 22 cm. A guide to American literature in engineering and related sciences.

1949
28. "Industrial Research in Georgia." Southern Assn. of Science and Industry, Atlanta, Sept. 15, 1949. 9 pp.

1950
29. Thrust Meter, U.S. Patent 2,516,855, issued Aug. 1, 1950.
4. "Survey of Southern Organizations." Southern Assn. of Science and Industry, Atlanta, April 24, 1950, 13 pp.

1951
30. Jet Direction Control (application for patent filed Jan. 26, 1951, serial no. 207,996).
31. "Science and Insurance," *The Insurance Index*, Dunne Publications, Louisville, Ky., 1951.
32. "Research, The South's New Resource." Georgia Engineering Society. Atlanta, Jan. 29, 1951.
33. "Directory of Southern Research Services and Facilities," *Journal of Southern Research*,

Atlanta. Jan.-Feb., 1951. pp. 7-14.

34. "The Banker and the Scientist," *Southern Banker*, McFadden Publications, Atlanta, Aug. 1951, pp. 22-23.

35. "The Secret of Southern Progress," *Journal of Southern Research*, Sept.-Oct., 1951, pp. 11-16.

36. "Super Weapons in the Land of Cotton," *Think*, International Business Machines, New York, Oct. 1951.

37. "Are Science and Socialism Inseparable?" *Journal of Southern Research*, Atlanta. Nov.-Dec., 1951, pp. 11-12.

1952

38. "Dynamic New Forces Mold South's Future," *Southern Industrial Directory*, 1952. 60 pp.

39. "Automatic Processes for Southern Industry," *Journal of Southern Research*, Atlanta. Sept.-Oct. 1952. pp. 22-24.

40. "The Use of Research in Industrial Development," annual Southern Industrial Development Conference. Charlotte, N.C., Oct. 27, 1952.

41. "The Value of Research in Industrial Development," *Journal of Southern Research*, Atlanta. Nov.-Dec. 1952, pp. 29-31.

1953

42. "Ten Point Program for South," *Southern Industrial Directory*, Atlanta. 1953. 80 pp.

43. "Modern Research Progress in the South." (Presented before Food and Drug Law Forum, Emory University, in cooperation with the Food Law Institute, Atlanta, May 7, 1953) *The Food, Drug, Cosmetic Law Journal*, Commerce Clearing House, Chicago, July 1953. pp. 445-451.

44. "The Next 10 Years of Southern Progress" (South to gain 3,000 major plants). Address at Chapel Hill. Excerpted in *Journal of Southern Research*, Atlanta. July-August. 1953. pp. 2-22.

45. "Amazing Expansion of Industry," *Editor and Publisher*, Oct. 31, 1953. pp. 174-176, 188.

1954

46. "Dispersal Efforts Have Been Inadequate — American Industry Is Still in Danger." *Industrial Development,* Jan./Feb. 1954, pp. 5-7.

47. "To Grow or Not to Grow." Industrial Development Symposium. Indiana State Commercial Executives Assn., Michigan City, Ind. May 24, 1954.

48. "Regionalism and Regional Development," *Southern Chemical Industry*, Atlanta. May-June 1954. p. 6.

49. "Paint Industry Survey," (index of manufacturers of paint and allied products), *Southern Chemical Industry*, Sept.-Oct 1954. pp. 7-21.

50. "Opportunities for Small Manufacturers," Southern Farm Equipment Manufacturers Assn., Atlanta. Oct. 1, 1954.

51. "The Value of Libraries in Industrial Research," Southeastern Library Assn. 16th biennial conference. Atlanta, Oct. 1, 1954.

52. "Area Development Activities Across the U.S.," Western Area Development Conference, San Francisco, Stanford Research Institute. Nov. 17, 1954.

53. "Area Development Activities Across the U.S.," Long Beach Chamber of Commerce, Long Beach, Calif., Nov. 22, 1954.

54. "Chemical Industry Survey Soap and Allied Products," *Southern Chemical Industry*, Nov.-Dec. 1954. pp. 7-16.

1955

55. "Glass-making Industry in the South," *Southern Chemical Industry*, March-April, 1955. pp. 7-10.

56. "Industrial Progress Creates New Opportunities for the Legal Profession," Southeastern Law Review Conference, Emory University, Atlanta. April 29, 1955.

57. "Nationwide Competition in *Industrial Development.*" Proceedings of Western Area Development Conference, Sept. 8-9, 1955, Portland, Ore., conducted by Stanford Research Institute, Menlo Park, Calif. pp. 19-27.

58. "Public Relations Program for the South," (remarks on receiving Advertising Federation of America award for regional program) Birmingham, Ala., Sept. 13, 1955.

59. "How to Pick Growth Firms," *Industrial Development.* Sept.-Oct., 1955. pp. 7-10.
60. "The Research Approach to Promotion and Advertising." Southern Industrial Development Council, Jacksonville, Fla., Oct. 31, 1955.

1956
61. "Ten Reasons for Southern Economic Progress," *Manufacturers Record.* (Blue Book Supplement). Atlanta, 1956. pp. 9-14.
62. "The Atom - Multi-billion Southern Industry," *Manufacturers Record,* Jan. 1956. pp. 11-18.
63. "Building Blocks for Better Community Development," Great Lakes States Industrial Development Council, Madison, Wis., Jan. 6, 1956.
64. "Solar Energy Research Opens New Opportunities for South," *Manufacturers Record,* Atlanta. Feb. 1956. pp. 20-22.
65. "Agriculture and Industry: Partners in Southern progress," 53rd annual meeting, Assn. of Southern Agricultural Workers, Atlanta, Feb. 6, 1956.
66. "South Gains in Electronics," *Manufacturers Record,* April, 1956. pp. 9-13.
67. "Aircraft and Missile Industry (in South)," *Manufacturers Record,* July, 1956. pp. 8-17.
68. "Selecting, Contacting and Selling Industrial Prospects," Conference on Industrial Development, Midwest Research Institute, Kansas City, Mo., Sept. 7, 1956.
69. A Report to the Southern Governors Conference, from the Subcommittee on Science and Industry, presented at White Sulphur Springs, West Va., Sept. 10, 1956. 15 pp. plus appendix.
70. "Optimism is Essential," Oklahoma Development Council, Tulsa, Nov. 14, 1956.
71. "Advertising and Direct Mail in Industrial Development," Southern Assn. of State Planning and Development Agencies. Oklahoma City, Okla., Nov. 15, 1956.

1957
72. "Selecting, Contacting and Selling Industrial Prospects," Iowa Industrial Development Clinic, Iowa Development Commission. Des Moines, Iowa. Jan. 24, 1957.
73. "Increased Responsibility of the Chamber of Commerce in Industrial Development," American Chamber of Commerce Executives, annual conference, Boston, Oct. 23, 1956. *Journal of American Chamber of Commerce Executives,* Washington, D.C., Jan. 1957, pp. 23-24.
74. "Selecting, Contacting and Selling Industrial Prospects," Louisiana Industrial Development Conference, Shreveport, La., Feb. 7, 1957.
75. "The Phenomenon of Growth", Southern Industrial Editors Assn., Atlanta, Mar. 26, 1957.
76. "New Horizons for the Industrial Development Profession," American Industrial Development Council, 32nd annual meeting, Chicago, April 1, 1957.
77. "Nationwide Competition between Communities," How to Get Ready for Industry Conference, General Extension Division of Florida, Avon Park. April 24, 1957.
78. "The Intense Competition in Industrial Development," First Pennsylvania Industrial Development Clinic, Harrisburg, Pa., May 16, 1957.
79. "Competition in Industrial Development," South Texas Industrial Development Conference, San Antonio, Texas, June 17, 1957.
80. "Competition in Industrial Development," Arizona Development Luncheon, Phoenix, June 18, 1957.
81. "Cooperation between Public and Private Development Agencies," Proceedings of the Southern Assn. of State Planning and Development Agencies Point Clear Conference, Oct. 10, 1957.
82. "Development of New Weapons by Soviet Union Suggests Need for More Emphasis on Industrial Dispersal Effort." *Industrial Development,* Atlanta. Oct. 1957. pp. 5-11.

1958
83. *Gold Mine on Main Street,* documentary film script. 16mm, full-color, 25-min. Industrial Sound Films, Atlanta, 1958.
84. "What Specific Characteristics Industry Looks for in a Community: A Guide for Industrial Development," Chicago and Northwestern Railway, Chicago, 1958. (Proceedings of Conference on Industrial Development for Wisconsin). Milwaukee, Wis., March 20, 1958.
85. "What Industry Seeks When Locating Plants," Georgia State Chamber of Commerce, Atlanta, April 11, 1958.

86. "Optimism Can Be Justified," *Southern Advertising and Publishing*, Atlanta, April, 1958.

87. Introduction and premiere of film, *Gold Mine on Main Street*, American Industrial Development Council, April 14, 1958, Atlanta.

88. "Improving the Effectiveness of Development Programs," Annual Meeting of American Railway Development Assn., Cincinnati, Ohio. April 28, 1958.

89. "On the Brighter Side," (economic outlook), *The Editors Forum*, Georgia Press Assn., May, 1958, pp. 4-S.

90. "Roadblocks in the Sky," *Industrial Development*. Aug. 1958. pp. 6-10. (Military restricted areas hampering civilian air traffic.)

91. "Seven Hundred Plant Location Factors," *Industrial Development, Site Selection Handbook* Supplement. Oct. 1958. pp. 17-24.

92. "The 'Forward Look' in Industrial Development," address before the New England Council annual industrial development dinner, Springfield, Mass., May 21, 1958.

93. "Increasing the Effectiveness of Industrial Development Activities," American Management Assn. Seminar, Colgate University, Hamilton, N.Y., Aug. 4-8, 1958.

94. "Industrial Progress in the South," a report to the Southern Governors Conference, from the Committee on *Industrial Development*. Lexington, Ky., Sept. 24, 1958. 16 pp.

1959

95. "Plant Location Guide," *Industrial Development, Site Selection Handbook* supplement). 1959. pp. 16-32.

96. *Blueprint for Progress* (documentary film script on planned industrial parks and performance standards, awarded 2nd prize, Congresso Mundial de Planificacion y Vivienda, Puerto Rico, 1960). Produced 1959 by Industrial Sound Films, Atlanta. Full color. 16mm. 25 mins.

97. "The South Reports to the Nation," *Industrial Development*, (Blue Book edition) 1959. pp. 6-9.

98. "Industrial Land Prices" (a national survey), *Industrial Development*, Atlanta, Jan. 1959. pp. 11-14.

99. "Key Location Factors for Washington," Washington D.C. Board of Trade. Feb. 9, 1959.

100. "Realistic Criteria for Plant and Facilities Location Seminar," American Management Assn., New York, Feb. 18, 1959.

101. "Puerto Rico — a New Horizon for Industry," *Industrial Development*, March 1959. pp. 17-48.

102. "The Registered Community Audit," *Industrial Development*, April 1959. pp. 6-9. (A proposed uniform format for analyzing community economic potential.)

103. "Company Organization for Expansion Planning," *Industrial Development,* May 1959, pp. 6-9.

104. "Growth May Be Inevitable but Progress Is Not," Atlanta Real Estate Board, May 21, 1959.

105. "Ideal location, U.S.A." (criteria for a hypothetical community most appealing to industry site seekers), Annual Conference, Mississippi Assn. of Chamber of Commerce Executives, Natchez, Aug. 21, 1959.

106. "The South's Competitive Position," report to the Southern Governors Conference, presented by the Committee on Industrial Development, Asheville, N.C. Oct. 13, 1959. 16 pp.

107. "Prospects, Advertising" (marketing electric utility services), Edison Electric Institute, Sixth Annual Area Development Workshop, Phoenix, Ariz. Oct. 21, 1959.

108. "The State of Hawaii" (economic potential of statehood), *Industrial Development*, Dec. 1959. pp. 17-32.

1960

109. Area Development: A Guide For Community Leaders. 1960. 2 vols. With Frank Stedman. Vol. I. Understanding the Growth Process, Organizing for Area Development, Area and Community Analysis, Planning and Zoning, Financing, Buildings, Selling, Future Trends. 278 pp. Vol. II. Bibliography. 142 pp.

110. "Washington's Future in Industrial Development," The Governor's Industrial Development Banquet. Seattle. Mar. 9, 1960.

111. "National Roundup of Industrial Development Activity," American Industrial Development Council, 35th annual conference, Atlantic City, N.J. March 29, 1960.

112. "The Threat of Closing Public Schools Is Like the Sword of Damocles," Georgia Indus-

trial Seminar, May 31, 1960, Georgia Dept. of Commerce, Atlanta. Reported in *The Atlanta Journal*, June 1, 1960.

113. "Communism versus ...", (brief collection of opinions on a key word, including ideas of Henry Cabot Lodge, Sherman Adams, Henry Wallace, Richard Nixon and others). *Industrial Development*, Oct. 1960, pp. 2-3 and April 1961, p.2.

114. "The Factors for Expansion Planning," *Industrial Development, Site Selection Handbook* supplement. Oct. 1960. pp. 64-76.

115. "Public Schools and Community Development," DeKalb County School System annual meeting, Decatur, Ga., Oct. 22, 1960.

116. "What's Wrong with Industrial Development in the South?" Southern Industrial Development Council, Little Rock, Ark., Oct. 24, 1960.

117. "Development Trends Here and Abroad," Missouri Industrial Development Conference, Missouri Resources and Development Commission, Jefferson City. Oct. 31, 1960.

118. "The British Isles — Economic Potential," *Industrial Development,* Nov. 1960. pp. 17-32.

1961

119. "Exploring Caribbean Potential by Light Plane," *Industrial Development.* Atlanta, Feb. 1961. pp. 6-12, 86-94.

120. "We're Socializing the World," (comment on foreign aid economic program). *Industrial Development*, Feb. 1961, pp. 2-3.

121. First session of UN Committee for Industrial Development in New York March 27, 1961. *Industrial Development*, May 1961. pp. 2-3.

122. "Reference Value Success Factor in Development Advertising," *Industrial Development*, Atlanta. May, 1961. pp. 63-79. Includes bibliography.

123. "Success Factors in Industrial Development Advertising," Assn. of Railroad Advertising Managers, New Orleans, May 9, 1961.

124. "State Government Attitudes and Performance as These Relate to Developing New Industry," proceedings of the 1961 annual regional conference of the Council of State Governments. June 29-30, 1961, Mobile, Ala.

125. "Checkpoints," (editorial on the American example not being followed in overseas aid program). *Industrial Development*, Atlanta, Aug. 1961, pp. 2-3.

126. "North Dakota: Surprising Growth and Potential," *Industrial Development.* Atlanta. Sept. 1961. pp. 17-48.

127. "New Techniques of Regional Industrial Advertising," Southern Assn. of State Planning and Development Agencies annual meeting, Oct. 11, 1961, Atlanta.

128. "Site Selection: (10 Key Steps)," *Industrial Development Site Selection Handbook* supplement, Oct. 1961, pp.4-5.

129. "The Caribbean Community: Opportunities Overshadow Problems," *Industrial Development,* Dec. 1961. pp. 4-10.

130. "The Pressure Is on (competition for new industry)," Georgia State Chamber of Commerce, luncheon address. Atlanta, Dec. 13, 1961.

1962

131. "The Industrial Development Research Council Is Launched," *Industrial Development,* Jan. 1962. pp. 4-11. Outline of objectives of the Industrial Development Research Council, First Annual Conference, New York, Oct. 24, 1961.

132. "A New Look at Opportunities in Puerto Rico," *Industrial Development,* March 1962. pp. 17-48.

133. "Checkpoints." (textile industry of Inle Lake, Northern Burma). *Industrial Development,* May 1962. pp. 2-3.

134. "Air Transport Trends Affecting Industrial Development," Industrial Development Research Council, New York. May 14, 1963.

135. "A Challenge We Must Accept," *Area Digest*, Conway Research, Atlanta, Summer, 1962.

136. "The Philippines: Pride and Opportunity," *Area Digest*, Summer, 1962. pp. 12-14.

137. "A Challenge We Must Accept." *Area Digest,* Summer 1962.

138. "A Catalog from Peking (relative to development mission in Southeast Asia), *Industrial Development,* April 1962. pp. 2-3. See also *Area Digest*, Summer, 1963, pp. 29-32.

139. "Hong Kong: Free Trade and 'Squatter Factories,'" *Area Digest*, Summer, 1962. pp. 31-35.

140. Trade Missions: Selling American Enterprise around the World, " (mission to Southeast Asia), *Industrial Development," June 1962. pp. 6-16.*

141. *"Austin: Coming Fast as R&D Center."*Industrial Development, Aug. 1962. pp. 45-60.

142. "Sites for Science, Research Facility Planning," *Industrial Development*, Aug. 1962. pp. 5-43. Includes index of research parks.

143. "Their Own Worst Enemy" (six reasons undeveloped nations fail in economic development) *Area Digest*, Fall 1962.

144. "Getting the Most from Your Promotion Budget," ("Advertising Research Newsletter," 1956) *Area Digest.* Fall 1962. pp. 40-43.

145. "R&D Expansion Creates New Image for Long Island," *Industrial Development.* Nov. 1962. pp. 57-72.

146. "The Development Decade," Business Lecture Series, Georgia State College, Atlanta, Nov. 29, 1962.

147. "Airport Sites for Industry," *Industrial Development.* Nov., 1962 pp. 5-20.

148. "The Space Age Moves South," *Industrial Development* (54th annual "Blue Book of Southern Progress" edition). 1962. pp. 4-13.

149. *Code of Ethics for the Industrial Development Research Council.* Basic premise: to justify their status as professionals, members must seek to establish and maintain standards of conduct above that required by law. Covers honesty in dealing, integrity of information, confidentiality, environmental sensitivity, social and civic responsibility, freedom of information, support for common programs, avoidance of libel or slander, gifts or bribes, conflict of interest, and personal conduct. Pamphlet.

1963

150. "State and Provincial Development Agencies" (2nd annual study), *Industrial Development.* Feb. 1963. pp 6-16. Includes directory. See also Aug. 1961.

151. "El Salvador: a bright spot in Central America" (project sponsored by Agency for International Development), *Industrial Development*, June 1963, pp. 5-36.

152. "Costa Rica" (economic potential survey sponsored by the Agency for International Development), *Industrial Development,* Sept. 1963, pp. 17-48.

153. "The Airplane and Industrial Development," *AOPA Pilot,* Aircraft Owners and Pilots Assn., Washington, D.C. Oct. 1963.

154. "What Research Can Do for Overall Community Development," annual management conference, American Chamber of Commerce Executives, Atlanta, Oct. 29, 1963.

155. "Air Transport" (remarks made at Industrial Development Research Council Area/Industry Conference), *Industrial Development.* Nov. 1963. pp. 14-16. Includes list of airport industrial sites.

156. "Colombia: Fertile Field for Creating Joint Ventures" (project sponsored by Agency for International Development), *Industrial Development,* Nov. 1963. pp. 57-88.

157. A Bill Requiring All Meetings of the Governing Bodies to Be Public Meetings ("Sunshine Law"), Senate Bill No. 181, Georgia Senate, 1963-64.

158. A Bill to Provide for the Wearing of (Identification) Badges by Poll Workers, Senate Bill No. 40, Georgia Senate. 1963-64.

159. A Bill to Create the Georgia Science and Technology Commission, Senate Bill No. 283, Georgia Senate, 1963-64.

1964

160. "Recommendations for Nicaraguan Development Program." 1964. 40 pp. (project for Agency for International Development).

161. A Bill to Provide for the Use of Machines for Recording and Computing Votes at All Elections (punch cards and electronic computers), Senate Bill No. 340, Georgia Senate, 1964 (with Senator Leroy Johnson and others).

162. A Bill Proposing an Amendment to the Georgia Constitution to Make State Income Tax a Percentage of Taxpayer's Federal Income Tax. Senate Resolution No. 148, Georgia Senate, 1964 (with Senators Johnson and McWhorter).

163. A Resolution Proposing an Honesty Code for Public Officials, Senate Resolution 179, Georgia Senate, 1964 (with Senator Wesberry).

164. A Resolution to Create a Permanent Atlanta Metropolitan Council (MACLOG), Senate Resolution 213, Georgia Senate, 1964. (now the Atlanta Regional Commission — ARC).

165. A Resolution Proposing Establishment of the Atlanta Rapid Transit System (now MARTA), Senate Resolution 158, Georgia Senate, 1964 (with Senators Johnson and McWhorter).
166. "State Development Programs," *The Book of the States,* 1964-65. The Council of State Governments, Chicago.
167. "Biotechnology Atlanta" (a study for the Forward Atlanta program). Emory University, Atlanta. 1964. 44 pp. illus. With Dr. James Bain and others.
168. "A Development Organization Structure for Colombia." Jan. 1964. 48 pp. (project for Agency for International Development).
169. "South Caicos Island" (Turks and Caicos Islands Group), *Area Digest,* Winter 1964, pp. 14-17.
170. "Preparing Your Community for Industrial Development, 1964-68. (Series of monographs prepared for Agency for International Development). In Spanish and Portuguese.
    1. "What Development Means to Your Community." 16 pp.
    2. Sites and Buildings." 16 pp.
    3. Local Industrial Development Corporations." 16 pp.
    4. The War against Time." 16 pp.
    5. Filling the Prospect Gap." 16 pp.
    6. Improving the Business Climate." 16 pp.

1965

171. "Findings of the Governors Commission for Scientific Research and Development," State of Georgia, Jan. 1965. 12 pp. plus appendix.
172. "Project LAND: Locations in Appalachia for New Development." Feb. 1965. 30 pp.
173. "Invest in the U.S.A.," *Industrial Development,* Feb. 1965. pp. 57-84. Report prepared for U.S. Dept. Commerce for distribution via U.S. consulates and commercial officers. Foreword by Pres. Lyndon Johnson.
174. "Opening Statement of Objectives," Interamerican Seminar on Organizing and Promoting Private Enterprise and Local Initiative, Agency for International Development. Caracas, Venezuela, June 15, 1965.
175. "A proposal for the 200-Bev Proton Accelerator," Georgia Science and Technology Commission, submitted to the U.S. Atomic Energy Commission, Washington. June 15, 1965. 70 pp. With Dale Henson and others.
176. "Area and Industrial Development (El Desarrollo Regional e Industrial)," Proceedings of the First Interamerican Seminar on the Organization and Promotion of Private Enterprise, June 15-18, 1965. Caracas, Venezuela. Published in Spanish. 124 pp. Project for Agency for International Development.
177. "Opportunities in the Amazon Basin." It's been called the world's last great primeval wilderness. You can still meet a 16-foot anaconda at the airstrip. Here is a report by ID's publisher who made a pioneering flight (as pilot and navigator) from the Andes to the Atlantic to gather first-hand information. *Industrial Development,* Sept. 1965, pp. 15-20.
178. "A Development Plan for John F. Kennedy Memorial Airport," Melbourne, Fla. Oct. 11, 1965. 43 pp.
179. "Airport Sites for Industry," *Industrial Development.* Nov. 1965. pp. 13-27. Includes index of projects in U.S.
180. "The Fly-in Concept." During the next few years this development will produce exciting changes in the design of industrial and commercial areas and even in the layout of cities and metropolitan areas. Here's a report reflecting ID's original research in the field. *Industrial Development.* Nov. 1965. pp. 13-28.
181. "Air Transportation and Your Company's Expansion Plans," Industrial Development Research Council, Atlanta, Nov. 17, 1965.
182. "Progress Report on the AID/PEP Program." (Private enterprise promotion in Latin America). 1965. 68 pp. (Project for Agency for International Development).
183. *Fomento! Organizing for Progress,* Film script for 16mm full color and sound. 28 mins. English, Spanish, Portuguese. 1965. (Sponsored by Agency for International Development).

1966

184. "Community Airports — How Important Are They in Industrial Development?" Society of Industrial Realtors. Point Clear, Ala., Feb. 18, 1966.

185. "Flying the Amazon" (expedition from the Andes to the Atlantic), *AOPA Pilot.* Washington, D.C. May 1966. pp. 64- 68.

186. *Charlotte County (Florida) Airport Development Plan.* June 1966. 94 pp. charts, maps.

187. "Airport Industrial Parks and the Fly-in Concept." Annual meeting, American Assn. of Airport Executives, Seattle, Wash., June 14, 1966.

188. *Meridian, Miss., Industrial Area Feasibility Study.* Aug. 1966, 36 pp. plus appendix.

189. "What the Manufacturer Expects of theIndustrial Development Man," Northeastern Industrial Development Assn., New York. Oct. 4, 1966.

190. "The Fifty Legislative Climates," *Industrial Development,* Dec. 1966, pp. 17-27. (Survey of financial and tax incentives in each state).

191. *Area Development Organizations.* Principles of organizing for development. The pyramid concept. Secret of U.S. progress. Organizations above the state level. State development organizations. Local development organizations. Rural community improvement organizations. Supporting organizations. 1966. 331 pp. includes geographical index of several thousand U.S. organizations.

1967

192. *Key Field Industrial District, Three Site Plans.* Meridian, Miss., 32 pp., illus. 1967.

193. *Marianna (Fla.) Airport Industrial Park Development Plan.* 80 pp. charts, illus. 1967.

194. *Airport and Industrial Airpark Development Plan for DeQuincey, La.* 116 pp., charts, illus. 1967.

195. "How Should Sites for Federal Facilities Be Selected?" A question of growing national concern is the manner of choosing locations for new federal government installations. The much- publicized site for the nuclear accelerator has brought the issue forward. *Industrial Development,* Jan. 1967. p. 2.

196. "Is Your Company Flying Blind?" It is truly astonishing that only a handful of manufacturing firms have put their growth planning on a professional basis. It is probably safe to say that more than 90 percent of U.S. companies have no professional or systematic approach to planning their future growth. *Industrial Development,* Feb. 1967. p 4.

197. "Proposed Oceanographic Research Center" (Skidaway Institute). American Institute of Planners, Atlanta. March 27, 1967.

198. "Does Development Effort Pay?" Report shows $65 to $1 return. One of the things we like best about the Puerto Rican program is that officials have been alert enough to keep a running tally on the amount of money invested in the development effort and the benefits enjoyed. *Industrial Development.* March-April 1967. p. 1.

199. "State Science Programs," Joint Army-Navy Research Reserve Seminar, Lockheed-Georgia Research Laboratory, April 15, 1967.

200. "Role of Science in the Economic Development of Georgia," annual banquet, Georgia Academy of Science. Stone Mountain, Ga., April 28, 1967.

201. "The Emerging Fly-in Concept," Wisconsin Airports Conference, Sheboygan, Wis. April 26, 1967. (Wisconsin Aero. Comm., Madison).

202. "Why an Airport: Economic Development Potential." Kentucky Airports Conference, Lexington. April 12, 1967.

203. "Development Potential of the Amazon Basin," Southeastern Conference on Latin American Studies. Atlanta, April 14, 1967.

204. "A Research Program for Industry," Industrial Development Research Council. Washington, D.C., May 19, 1967.

205. "A Higher Premium on Education" (commencement address), Marist College, Atlanta, May 28, 1967.

206. "The Management of and Response to Urbanization in the South: Industrial Viewpoint," Southern Regional Conference on Urbanization, University of Georgia and North Carolina State University, Atlanta, May 31, 1967.

207. "The Most Underrated Generation in American History," (commencement address) DeKalb College, Decatur, Ga., June 3, 1967.

208. "Our Rate of Development Is Non-linear," (commencement address). West Georgia College, Carrollton, Georgia, June 4, 1967.

209. "The War against Time: Improving the Time Cycle in Development," Interamerican development seminar, Arequipa, Peru, July 12, 1967. Agency for International Development.

210. *Study of the Potential Traffic for the Proposed Chattahoochee River Navigation Chan-*

nel to Atlanta, Sept. 1967. 140 pp. plus appendix.

211. An Act to Create the Ocean Science Center of the Atlantic Authority (Skidaway institute), Senate Bill 75, Georgia Senate, 1967.

212. A Bill to Require Open Meetings ("Sunshine Law"), Senate Bill 143. Georgia Senate, 1967.

213. A Bill to Regulate and Control "Fire Bombs" or "Molotov Cocktails," Senate Bill 45, Georgia Senate, 1967.

214. A Resolution Requiring the State Highway Department to Set Criteria for Allocating Funds, Senate Resolution 39, Georgia Senate. 1967.

215. A Bill to Establish a Program of Awards for Cutting the Cost of Government, Senate Bill 187, Georgia Senate, 1967.

216. A Bill to Establish a Code of Honesty for All State Employees, Senate Bill 74, Georgia Senate, 1967 (with Senators Wesberry and Bateman).

217. A Bill to Create the Georgia College Council (student government liaison), Senate Bill 5, Georgia Senate, 1967.

218. "Organizing for Development: the Pyramid Concept." 1967. 24 pp. illus. (Issued also in Spanish and Portuguese). Sponsored by Agency for International Development.

219. "Community Audit and Area Data Outline, 1967. 32 pp. (Issued in English and Spanish.) Sponsored by Agency for International Development.

1968

220. "A Feasibility Study for a Regional Slaughterhouse in Carazo, Nicaragua." For Agency for International Development. Feb. 1968. 53 pp. illus.

221. "AID at the Crossroads!" June 1968. 56 pp. illus.

222. *Sylvania Georgia Airport Development Plan.* 49 pp. illus. June 1968.

223. *Airport Development Plan, Allen C. Thompson Field, Jackson, Miss.* 106 pp., illus. Sept. 1968.

224. *Planning Study of the Orange County, N.Y., Airport Area.* 32 pp. Oct. 1968.

225. "Crisis in Airport Planning," *Airport World.* Nov. 1968 pp. 50-52.

226. "Travel Investment, a New Guide to Investment Opportunities in Resort, Recreation and Hospitality Facilities," Nov. 1968, pp. 2-3 (foreword to new reference publication), 128 pp.

227. "Travel Investment Study for the Economic Development Council of Northeast Pennsylvania," Dec. 1968. 30 pp.

228. "The AID/PEP Program for Mobilizing Private Enterprise and Local Initiative in Latin America." A. Short-term orientation tours. B. Interamerican development seminars. C. Working materials. D. Investment promotion reports. E. U.S. development specialists. F. Interns. (Summary Report). Dec. 1968.138 pp. illus. Appendix. Sponsored by the Agency for International Development.

229. "Mobilizing Private Enterprise and Local Initiative in Latin America: the AID/PEP Program," Dec. 1968. 22 pp.

230. "Travel Investment and the Fly-in Resort," Western America Convention and Travel Institute. Portland, Ore. Dec. 4, 1968. Dept. of Commerce and Economic Development, State of Washington, Olympia.

1969

231. "Effect of Environmental Quality Factors on Investment Decisions, Improving the Physical Environment of the South," Agricultural Policy Institute, North Carolina State University, Feb. 1969.

232. *Travel Investment Opportunity: "Otocsin" Proposed Resort Complex*, Clearfield County, Pa. For Commonwealth of Pennsylvania. March 1969, 91 pp. illus.

233. *Travel Investment Study: Moraine Reservoir, Butler County, Pa., and Shenango Reservoir, Mercer County, Pa.* For Commonwealth of Pennsylvania. April 1969, 73 pp. illus.

234. *Travel Investment Opportunity: Prince Gallitzen State Park, Cambria County, Pa.* For Commonwealth of Pennsylvania. April 1969. 83 pp. illus.

235. "The Fly-in Concept of Development," League of Women Engineers, April 17, 1969. Atlanta.

236. "In Search for a National Development Strategy." Introduction to working paper on new town strategy by Vice President Spiro Agnew. *Industrial Development,* May-June, 1969, pp. 2-3.

237. *Travel Investment Study: Black Moshannon State Park and Blanchard Reservoir, Centre County, Pa.* For Commonwealth of Pennsylvania. May 1969. 51 pp. illus.
238. *Travel Investment Study: Kinzua Dam - Allegheny National Forest, Warren and Forest Counties, Pa.* For Commonwealth of Pennsylvania. June 1969. 51 pp.
239. *Travel Investment Study: Ohiopyle-Great Meadows, Fayette County, Pa.* For Commonwealth of Pennsylvania. June 1969. 40 pp.
240. *Airport Development Plan, Hawkins Field, Jackson, Miss.* July, 1969. 64 pp. illus.
241. "Today's Runway: Will It Be Tomorrow's Main Street?", *Flight Lines,* National Real Estate Fliers Assn., Washington, D.C. Sept. 1969. pp.4-6.
242. *Summary of Investor Reaction to Pennsylvania's Travel Investment Opportunities.* For Commonwealth of Pennsylvania. Oct. 15, 1969. 153 pp.

1970
243. *Corporate Facility Planning Survey.* A study for the Industrial Development Research Council. 36 pp. April 1970. IDRC #5.
244. "New Trends in Travel Investment," *Texas Realtor,* June 1970. Ten reasons large diversified firms go into real estate investments.
245. "The Fly-in Concept of Land Development," *Farm and Land,* National Assn. of Real Estate Boards, June 1970.
246. Notes on future courses of action, Science for Society, National Science Conference, National Science Foundation, October. 12-14, 1970.
247. *An Airport Development Plan for Chester County, Pa.* Oct. 25, 1970. 110 pp., illus.
248. *IDRC Skill Inventory.* A survey for the Industrial Development Research Council. A compilation of member skills. Types of projects handled, geographic areas covered. 81 pp. Nov. 1970. IDRC #6.
249. *A Management Concept for the Lake Lanier Islands.* A guide to investor/concessionaire arrangements and operating policies. 1970. 100 pp.

1971
250. *Survey of Community Audit Programs.* A study for the Industrial Development Research Council. May 1971. IDRC #7.
251. "The Airplane Is Here to Stay." Part 2. Man has failed miserably to coordinate ground facilities with the technological wizardry of the airplane. The potential for business purposes has hardly been realized. *Industrial Development,* May-June 1971. pp. 2-9.
252. "Blessed Are the Peacemakers" (role of professionals in resolving development/environmental conflicts). *Industrial Development,* annual "Environmental Planning Guide." Sept.-Oct. 1971. pp. 1.
253. *Surplus Property Index.* A study for the Industrial Development Research Council. Nov. 1971. IDRC #8.
254. "Georgia Environmental Standards" (special study). Nov. 1971. 150 pp. Foreword by Gov. Jimmy Carter. (Summary of regulations covering air quality, coastal marshlands, noise, radiation, scenic resources, solid wastes, surface mining, water quality.)

1972
255. Spruce Creek: a fly-in community. *Site Selection,*1972. 16 pp.
256. "Industry's Guide to Environmental Planning" (covering negative image, emotional pollution, myth of perfection, terminology and criteria, bureaucracy, solutions.) *Site Selection,* 1972. pp. 202-205.
257. "The Bureaucracy of Development." In your plans for your new building, you'd better take a close look at the specifications for ladders. Make sure that wooden ladders have rungs at least one and one-eighth inch in diameter. The federal government, in all its bureaucratic majesty (OSHA), has risen up and delivered ...a new set of regulations running 248 pages. *Industrial Development,* March/April 1972. pp. 1-3.
258. "Is There a Decoplex in Your Future?" The strategy of Decoplex is to turn adversity to advantage. It involves taking some of the least attractive facilities and making them assets in the community. *Industrial Development,* May-June 1972. pp. 2-4.
259. *Survey of the Availability of Electric and Gas Service for New Development Projects.* Response to concerns about an energy shortage. A study for the Industrial Development Research Council. Nov. 1972. IDRC #9.

1973

260. "The Decoplex Concept Commands Attention." In implementing the Decoplex (Development/Ecology Complex) concept of harmonizing development with environmental requirements, there is a host of technical, economic and political problems. Despite these obstacles, the emergence of a Decoplex solution is inevitable! *Industrial Development,* Jan.-Feb. 1973. pp. 1-3.

261. *Wings Field, Montgomery County, Pa.: an Economic Feasibility Study and Conceptual Plan for a Fly-in Country Club Community.* March 1973. 100 pp., illus.

262. "Fly-in Business Centers Are Here." A topic of increasing discussion by flying business-men in the Sixties, fly-in business facilities are becoming a reality in the Seventies. Before the end of the decade, such projects may emerge as one of the major trends in urban planning and economic development. *Industrial Development,* May-June, 1973, pp. 1-4.

263. "The Agricultural PUD: a New Concept to Preserve Croplands." The encroachment of urban growth on productive agricultural areas is a matter of national concern. A possible approach may lie in the design and development of a new type of planned unit development which includes selected agricultural areas in the same fashion that golf courses and recreational areas are included in typical PUDs. *Industrial Development,* Sept.- Oct. 1973. p. 3.

264. *Survey of Sales and Lease Prices for Industrial Land, Buildings and Office Buildings.* Sept. 1973. IDRC #10.

265. "Why Not a Bill of Rights for Developers?" Never before have those who serve the public interest by building homes and places of business found themselves so harassed and impeded by government policies and regulations. On all sides and at every level new bureaucracy is mushrooming. *Site Selection,* 1973. pp. 250-253.

1974

266. *Survey of Salaries and Job Responsibilities.* A study for the Industrial Development Research Council. 1974. IDRC #12.

267. *IDRC Skill Inventory.* Study for the Industrial Development Research Council. Jan. 1974. IDRC #11.

268. *Arab Investment in the U.S.* (general outlook plus special report on Kuwait). 1974. 268. *Airport Development Plan, Greene County, Pa.* Project for the Federal Aviation Agency. 240 pp. illus. April 1974.

269. "A New California Emerges." Imagine a new state of California, with two coastlines, a balmy climate, clear skies and only a few people, most of whom are willing and anxious to work, at a low scale. That is Baja California, Mexico. *Industrial Development,* March-April 1974. pp. 2-3.

270. "Proud Arabs Accept Global Challenge." If you enjoy fantasy, put away your copy of *A Thousand and One Arabian Nights* and pick up the Kuwait newspaper. Read about exotic places where big U.S. cars are still in demand and high-test sells for 28 cents a gallon. But the stories are real and they're being lived here, next door in Saudi Arabia, and down the road at Abu Dhabi, Qatar and Dubai. *Industrial Development,* May/June 1974, pp. 2-6.

271. "The Spruce Creek Research Center" (proposals for stream basin conservation plan and environmental field station, 1969-1974), for Fly-In Concept. June 1, 1974.

272. "The Banks of Beirut." For its size, Beirut is one of the world's busiest money centers. Many major international corporations have chosen the Lebanese capital for their Middle East regional facilities. Now, busy Beirut is battling for a role in handling huge new Arab oil receipts. *Industrial Development,* July/Aug. 1974. pp. 2-4.

273. "Cairo Seeks Lost Luster." Throughout most of recorded history, Cairo has occupied a key role as a trading center and government axis. That reputation has faded in recent years...Today, however, enlightened leadership seeks to reassert Egypt's position and find new opportunities for regional economic activities. *Industrial Development,* Sept./Oct. 1974. pp. 3-4.

274. "The War against the Clock." Everyone in the development field today is engaged in an uphill struggle against the most relentless enemy of all time. Never in the history of the profession have there been so many time-consuming pre-development activities. And never has the monetary cost of time been so great. *Site Selection.* 1974. p. 242.

1975

275. "True Professionals Give Due Credit." The magazine (not named) would have its read-

ers believe that it was the pioneer in development of a comprehensive plant location checklist or community audit. The comprehensive checklist was published here in ID in our October 1957 issue nearly 10 years before our rival. *Industrial Development.* Jan 1975. p 2.

276. "Future Shock Arrived Yesterday!" We are reminded of an early reference to the so-called future shock phenomenon which we discussed in one of our publications some 20 years ago. We refer to Dr. Robert Wilson's suggestion that the pace of development can be better appreciated if we compress the entire span of man's evolution into a 50-year time scale. *Industrial Development,* Jan.-Feb. 1975. p. 2.

277. "Ground Rules for Gringo Investors." During the past couple of years a new program has emerged in Mexico to regulate foreign investment in the highly attractive and politically sensitive coastal zones. Here's a quick review. *Industrial Development,* March-April 1975. pp. 2-3.

278. "Environmental and Land Use Controls," a survey for the Industrial Development Research Council. May 1975, 69 pp. plus appendix. IDRC Research Report #13.

279. "When Do You Chop That $12,000 Tree?" Amid increasing realization that trees, grass, and even swamps have significant economic value, the profit-oriented developer faces growing difficulty in making optimum economic decisions. *Site Selection,* "Environmental Planning Guide" edition, Sept. 1975. pp. 286-288.

280. "Can a Nationwide Planning Problem Be Solved without Help from Washington?" Industrial park developers have long since discovered that the shabby, sub-par project won't sell. That American system again! Introduction to guide to office and industrial park development. *Site Selection,* Nov. 1975. p. 376.

1976

281. *IDRC Skill Inventory.* A study for the Industrial Development Research Council. Jan. 1976. IDRC #14.

282. "Opportunities in Intermodal Transportation." One of the few areas in which we can still improve overall operating efficiency by a whopping percentage. *Industrial Development,* March-April 1976. pp. 2-6.

283. "Industrial Site Performance Standards," a study for the Industrial Development Research Council, covering deed covenants and zoning regulations, space allocation and dimensional standards, architectural and aesthetic standards, performance and land-use criteria, implementation plans, construction and maintenance, proposed uniform outline. May, 1976. 307 pp. IDRC Research Report #15. With Linda L. Liston.

284. "Are Intermodal Container Loop Sites an Endangered Species?" A recent issue of ID outlined the concept of "through" transport which is producing keen interest in sites from which manufacturers can receive and ship containerized cargo via all modes. A follow-up survey suggests that optimum sites are rare indeed. *Industrial Development,* May-June 1976.

285. "Uniform Outline for Deed Covenants and Performance Standards." Covers land-use controls, performance standards, space allocations, architecture and aesthetics, implementation of plans, construction. *Industrial Development,* May-June, 1976. (by-line omitted).

286. "Are You a Problem Voter?" Are you playing Russian roulette with your vote? If so, why not salute the bicentennial by checking your voting habits and pledging to make your 1976 vote your best ever? *Industrial Development,* July/Aug. 1976. pp. 19-20.

287. "Canada: There Is a Difference." Perhaps no two major nations are as close ideologically as the U.S. and Canada. Despite this happy concurrence, each country does have its own views. There are new and significant differences in such areas as development strategy and techniques. *Industrial Development,* Nov./Dec., 1976. pp. 2-3.

1977

288. *The IDRC Seminar Series.* Establishing a professional Forum for industrial planning objectives. A study for the Industrial Development Research Council. Not many years ago industry planners worked in secrecy. There was no systematic sharing of information. This report describes the progress which has been made in creating a much-needed forum. Includes program for IDRC's first annual meeting in 1961. May 1977. 151 pp. IDRC #16.

289. *The Industrial Facility Planner's View of Special Incentives.* A study for the Industrial Development Research Council. Conducted at a time when there was considerable debate about the propriety of incentives, this survey reveals diversity of thinking among IDRC members. 36 pp. plus Appendix. May 1977. IDRC #17.

290. Improving the business climate means waging war on bureaucracy. *Site Selection and*

Industrial Development. May 1977. p. 92.

291. "Mexico's Bold New Towns." While big new-town projects are floundering in the U.S., the Mexican government moves strongly ahead with ambitious projects. New developments at Ixtapa and Cancun are centered on tourism, but the implications are broad. *Industrial Development,* July-Aug. 1977. pp. 16-17.

292. "Using the Small Airplane: Exploring Areas." Risk and reward. *The Airport City, Development Concepts for the 21st Century.* 1977. 283 pp.

1978

293. *New Industries of the Seventies.* Federal statistics. State summaries. *Industrial Development* magazine reports. Trends in HQ relocations. Geographic index of new plants. 302 pp. 1978.

294. *New Industries of the Seventies.* 1978. 302 pp. With Linda L. Liston.

295. *Pitfalls in Development.* The bureaucracy of development. Soft plans and feasibility studies. Hard plans and preconstruction activities. Construction and operation. Megapuds track record. Special pitfalls for special projects. Real estate panics. Pitfalls ahead. 1978, 1981. 343 pp.

296. "The Future for North American Industrial Capitalism." The needs of the global population are so enormous that they will demand large-scale approaches. They will be the kinds of things that will attract newspaper headlines... and are regarded by many as frivolous. Proceedings of the 53rd annual conference, American Industrial Development Council, Albuquerque, N.M. May 21-23, 1978. pp. 24-27.

297. *A Composite Case History of New Facility Location.* A study for the Industrial Development Research Council. Project profile. Financing. Site characteristics. Utility services. Environmental planning. Personnel requirements. Strategies considered. International projects. Techniques used in site decision. Final cost analysis. Lessons applicable to future projects. May 1978. IDRC #19. With Linda L. Liston.

1979

298. *New Project File and Site Selection Checklist.* Corporate strategy. Company organization for expansion planning. Criteria for site and facility. An index of hundreds of location factors from which the user can prepare a custom checklist for a particular project. 1979. Binder.

299. *Legislative Climates for Economic Development.* Climates around the world. The 50 legislative climates of the U.S. The political process. Jimmy Carter as an architect of legislative climate. Future trends in legislating for development. Appendix covering incentives at national, state, local levels. 391 pp. 1979.

300. *Corporate Record Systems For Facility Planning and Management.* A study for the Industrial Development Research Council. Includes 160 forms used By companies to assist them in maintaining property records. These include forms related to property acquisition, construction and start-up, inventory, operating expenses, maintenance and surplus property. Jan. 1979. 429 pp. IDRC #20. With Linda L. Liston.

301. *Improving Career Skills: Professional Training Programs in the Field of Facility Planning and Real Estate Management.* Rankings of subjects of interest. Programs members have attended. Justifying education and training programs. Future personnel requirements. A study for the Industrial Development Research Council. Nov. 1979. 350 pp. IDRC #21. With Linda L. Liston.

1980

302. *Career Paths.* A study for the Industrial Development Research Council. This is undoubtedly the most detailed study of member interests, expertise and aspirations ever conducted by the Council. It reflects the "state-of-the-art" of corporate growth planning. Sept 1980. 140 pp. IDRC #23.

303. "Will Man-powered Flight Be Next Transport Breakthrough?" For millions of people, the vehicle of the early 21st century may be something akin to a light-weight bicycle with wings. It will be pedaled at tree-top level across metro areas, avoiding the congestion on the streets below. *The Airport City, Development Concepts for the 21st Century,* 1980, 283 pp.

304. *Marketing Industrial Buildings and Sites.* Introduction: promotion is not a dirty word! The sellers: promotion and marketing organizations. The customers: target industry groups, companies, executives. Elements of a marketing plan. Media advertising. Special publica-

tions. Selling a specific building or site. Marketing professional services. Outlook for the future. 1980. 358 pp. Hard cover.

1981

305. *IDRC Code of Ethics.* 1981.

306. *Corporate Facility Planning.* A compilation of more than 100 papers of interest to those involved in corporate real estate. Asset management and strategy. Property administration. Location analysis and site selection. Design and construction. 1981. 442 pp. Hard cover. With Linda L. Liston.

307. "Updating Mexico's New Town Program." During the past decade we have reported several times on Mexico's bold and impressive program for building new resort cities. The projects at Cancun and Ixtapa have been highly successful in attracting a large volume of tourist traffic. *Industrial Development,* Jan./Feb. 1981. pp. 1-40. Also in "Global Mini-Letter for Development Executives," Jan. 1981. p. 2.

308. *Real Estate Profit Centers.* A study for the Industrial Development Research Council. Some manufacturing companies have had real estate profit centers for decades. While the idea, thus, is not new, there has been in recent years a fresh and growing interest in such profit centers, their purpose, their operating principles and their performance. March 1981. 23 pp. plus appendix. With Linda L. Liston and James D. Mathis. IDRC #24.

309. "Underdeveloped Nations: Their Own Worst Enemy?" Man-made factors play a significant part in the equation for development success. Undeveloped nations recognize this but often place the blame for their economic problems on the wrong factors. *Industrial Development,* May/June 1981. Inside cover. Also appearing in the "Global Mini-Letter," Jan. 1981. pp. 3-4.

310. *The Good Life Index.* Recognizing that "the good life" is a highly subjective concept, varying widely from person to person and corporation to corporation, this new approach provides the reader with a method for systematically seeking out the places which offer desired attributes. The quest for a QOL measure. Criteria for the good life. Analyzing states. Examining metro, city, and local areas. Making global analyses. Making your own good life evaluation. 1981. 416 pp. Hard cover. With Linda L. Liston. Reviewed in *The Futurist,* World Future Society, June 1982. pp. 75-77.

311. "Strategic Decisions for the Great Barrier Reef." Australian planners, determined to preserve the basic character of the reef region while permitting practical utilization, have undertaken what may be the world's most ambitious zoning plan. "Global Mini-Letter," July 1981. pp. 1-2.

312. "A Scan of Arctic Growth Potential." On the maps it is a great empty space. But for a development strategist privileged to gain a closer look, the Arctic is a region where interesting things are happening today and where men plan and dream of globally-significant projects tomorrow. *Industrial Development,* Sept.-Oct. 1981. pp. 10-15.

313. *Survey of Consultants.* A study for the Industrial Development Research Council. Experience of IDRC members in using consultants. Types of consultants used. Evaluation of consultant performance. Roster of consultants. Oct. 1981. 188 pp. IDRC #26.

314. "A Scan of Pacific Potential." Where do the Pacific islands fit into the global development picture? During a 20,000-mile survey trip, ID's publisher found serious attention being given to substantial projects amid a Hollywood backdrop of swaying palm trees and turquoise-fringed beaches. *Industrial Development,* Nov./Dec. 1981. pp. 5-8.

315. *Disaster Survival.* How to choose secure sites and make practical escape plans. Natural disasters. Man-made disasters. Evaluation of risk potential. Survival planning: site hardening. Public policies. International disaster risk data. 290 pp. Hard cover. 1981. The American Library Association review: "A frightening, valuable guide."

316. *Industrial Park Growth.* Introduction — the dream of a good place to work. Emergence of the park concept and proliferation of units. Performance standards and design criteria. Types of parks. Park site supply and demand. Industrial parks for the future. 1981. 2nd ed. Hard cover. 546 pp. With Linda L. Liston.

1982

317. "From Kuujjuaq to Stornoway on One Engine." The North American mainland stops on a wind-swept airstrip at Kuujjuaq (formerly Fort Chimo) in northern Quebec. From there, pilots who wish to maximize the prospect for survival can navigate to Europe across Ungava Bay and the Hudson Strait to Baffin Island, over the Davis Strait to Greenland's west coast,

across the Greenland ice cap, and then over the North Atlantic via Iceland. "Global Mini-Letter," Jan. 1982. pp. 1-2.

318. *Developing the IDRC Computer Network.* New revolution in computer applications. Computer utilization by IDRC members. Launching network services for members. Implications of emerging network system. Index of on-line information sources. Glossary of EDP terminology. May 1982. 90 pp. IDRC #29.

319. "Pure Water from the Sun and Sea?" Pichilingue is a small Mexican town on the Baja peninsula some 800 miles south of Los Angeles. Recently we went to Pichilingue to look at what may be one of the most significant development projects to be found anywhere — an experimental processing plant to desalt seawater using solar energy. "Global Mini-Letter," July 1982. pp. 1-2.

1983

320. *Survey of Compensation and Career Paths.* A study for the Industrial Development Research Council. It is intended that this report assist members in achieving their own personal goals... and that the report will be useful to companies in making their real estate and facility planning functions more effective. 1983. 76 pp. IDRC #30.

321. "A Scan of Africa's Development Prospects." Can African nations, beset by political upheavals, attract significant outside investments? Here is an overview (by the publisher) which follows visits to the continent's major regions. *Industrial Development,* March/April 1983. pp. 4-9.

322. *Geo-Economics: A New Science in the Service of Mankind.* A study for the Industrial Development Research Council. The new geo-economic discipline is directly responsible for significant achievements in the planning and implementation of a large number of projects which have created jobs and other benefits for societies around the world. Yet the new technical capability is little known or appreciated outside the circle of those who practice it. May 1983. 45 pp. IDRC #31.

323. "Geo-Economics: A New Science in the Service of Mankind." Monograph. 5pp. Excerpted from IDRC Research Report No. 31.

324. "A New Wave of Super Projects?" Is the world on the threshold of great new construction projects and creative ventures? Here is a survey by *Industrial Development's* publisher, who has visited more than 70 super project sites around the world. *Industrial Development,* May-June 1983. pp. 4-9.

325. "A Scan of Development in the USSR." In order to extend our editorial horizons, ID's publisher recently trekked through Siberia, across Mongolia and the Gobi desert, and into Northern China. Here is a rare picture of major development projects in one of the world's most remote regions. *Industrial Development,"* Nov./Dec. 1983. pp. 4-38.

1984

326. *Survey of the Industrial Facility Planner's View of Special Incentives: an Update.* Study for the Industrial Development Research Council. March 1984. IDRC #32.

327. "Will Mainland China Emerge as a New Hub of Private Enterprise?" Here is a quick scan of Chinese developments from the remote northern Shanzi province to the booming hinterland of Hong Kong. It concludes with a rather startling prediction by ID's publisher regarding the direction the world's most populous nation may take in the years just ahead. *Industrial Development,* March/April 1984. pp. 4-8.

328. "The Geo-Economists: A New Profession for the Market of Jobs," *The Futurist.* World Future Society. April 1984. pp. 58-59.

329. "Development Outlook for the Caribbean." Here ...is a fresh scan of an island empire which is politically strategic, touristically popular but economically a sea of confusion. Given new hope by the Reagan initiatives, what are prospects that the region — with its track record of small successes and big frustrations — can meet urgent economic growth needs? *Industrial Development,* May/June 1984, pp. 4-9.

330. "Geo-Economics: The Emerging Science." The first of a series which outlines the origin, present scope, and future of a new science which is significant for all professionals involved in the facility planning profession. *Industrial Development.* Sept.-Oct. 1984. pp. 4-7.

331. "Agenda for the Future: 'Project Easylog'." A program for spurring global data exchange. *Geo-Micro,* Nov./Dec. 1984. pp. 1-2.

332. "Geo-Economics and Corporate Asset Management." A summary of the early efforts to

develop the subscience of corporate growth planning and real property management. *Industrial Development.* Nov.-Dec. 1984. pp. 14-19.

1985
333. "IDRC Set to Assume Greater Role in Geo-Economic Research." The executive director of IDRC explores the potential for a massive new geo-economic research program. *Industrial Development,* Jan.-Feb. 1985. pp. 74-75.
334. "The New 'Ion-Curtain' Countries." Today the world is faced with a new group of nations which are barricading themselves in and restricting the free flow of ideas. These are countries which, through apathy, ignorance, or design, are preventing the effective use of international data networks. *Geo-Micro,* Jan./Feb. 1985.
335. "China: the Sleeping Giant." Enter Deng Xiaping who has shaken the giant ..."we cannot depend on the works of Marx and Lenin to solve all of today's problems... the economy is a vast sea and there are many questions that ...require us to investigate reality." *Site Selection*, April 1985. p. 294.
336. "The New States of Micronesia." With scant public attention, Congress is about to determine the permanent status of hundreds of Pacific island territories administered by the U.S. since World War II. The action could have the effect of adding several new states — perhaps opening new development opportunities and certainly adding new costs for the taxpayer. *Site Selection*, April 1985. pp. 554-561.
337. "The Megatech Industries: What Determines Their Location?" What are the essential components of a Silicon Valley or a Route 128 complex? Do the location factors for R&D activities cover the production of CPUs, peripherals and software? Is the mix changing? *Site Selection,* June 1985. pp. 626-635.
338. "Canada's NAPLPS Program Spurs Growth of Important New Electronics Industry." Proving that a shrewdly placed pump-priming investment can pay handsome dividends in a new mega-technology area, Canada has established a leadership position in an important segment of the telecommunications industry. *Site Selection,* June 1985. pp. 652-654.
339. "Nauru, Pacific Investment Source." This tiny island in the vastness of Oceania has been called the world's richest nation, even wealthier than Kuwait. Whatever the correct ranking, Nauru's development status must be regarded as unique. Unlike most of the world's small nations, Nauru is not looking for foreign aid. Instead, the remote atoll is a source of investment funds for projects from Australia to China and the USA. *Site Selection*, June 1985. pp. 820-825.
340. "Ocean Science Projects — Will They Emerge as Prime Global Investment Opportunities?" German scientists propose "energy" islands of floating platforms covered with photovoltaic cells. Japanese developers are planning an entire city built on the water. In North America there are significant projects from Canada's tidal energy recovery plant at the Bay of Fundy to Mexico's solar desalting facility on the Sea of Cortez. *Site Selection*, Aug. 1985. pp. 168-181.
341. "The Free World's Secret Weapon Is Revealed." For a long time it appeared to be an extremely well-kept secret. Prominent politicians around the world didn't know it existed or couldn't recognize it. We refer to that economic super bomb called Private Enterprise — a weapon capable of reducing to shambles the defenses of nations which depend on state control of enterprises. *Site Selection*, Aug. 1985.
342. "We Need a National Referendum!" A national referendum would permit every voter to express his or her views on a list of, say, 10 key issues...The results would be tallied and published in the *Congressional Record* for all to see. *Site Selection*, Oct. 1985. p. 868.
343. "A Fresh Outlook for France?" Traditionalists say that France and the French never change. But, of course, they do. France may at the moment, in fact, be laying the groundwork for a significant new phase of development. New Disney site. *Site Selection*, Oct. 1985. pp. 1104-1114.
344. "Time to Reconsider Fly-In Sites?" Check your future corporate geography — what is the chance that you can move executives door-to-door between yours plants and offices as fast in 1995 as you can today? If you're faced with a deteriorating situation caused by urban congestion and slow ground travel, fly-in sites may offer a bright solution. *Site Selection*, Dec. 1985. pp. 1162-1165.
345. "What Happened to Fly-in Projects?" It has been a time of trial and tribulation for almost all types of large-scale land development projects. In particular, the "fly-in" projects

built on airports have ...suffered from ...factors peculiar to airport projects. *Site Selection,* Dec. 1985. p. 1140.

346. "Will Long-awaited EEC Status Bring New Industrial Opportunities for Spain?" For many types of industrial projects site seekers have skipped Spain in favor of other European areas. Now ...there may be significant opportunities for new service industries and diversified manufacturing to complement the already flourishing tourist industry. *Site Selection,* Dec. 1985. pp. 1422-1427.

1986

347. "Super Projects 1986." With many of the world's nations suffering through economic slumps and debt crises, it might be assumed that the global agenda for huge, complex, multi-billion dollar ventures might have dried up. Yet the latest survey reveals a long list of new and exciting projects ranging from transatmospheric vehicles to Super Colliders. *Site Selection,* Feb. 1986. pp. 214-220.

348. "Thanks for Helping Us Pick the Superlatives!" *Site Selection* begins its 31st year. During this action-packed 30-year period corporate executives have planned and built more than 100,000 new plants. Area developers have launched several thousand office and industrial parks. *Site Selection,* Feb. 1986. p. 4.

349. "Weighing Development Factors for the High-Tech Age." If you are responsible for plotting the development strategy for a major corporation or organization, you will want to study this review of factors which have played a dominant role during the past 30 years. The compilation is based on a scan of our bound volumes, staff research and opinions of several hundred readers working in a wide variety of development positions. *Site Selection,* April 1986. pp. 280-288. (Summarized in the monograph, "A Technology Review and Forecast for Development Strategists".)

350. "The State of Jalisco Lures Investors." IBM's recent choice of a site at El Salto, near Guadalajara, for its big new computer plant is focusing fresh attention on this state situated in the heartland of Mexico. Long a favorite of U.S. tourists and retirees, Jalisco has quietly attracted more than $1 billion in U.S. industrial investments. *Site Selection,* April 1986. pp. 522-528.

351. "Launch! Launch! Launch!" We can't afford more delays with the space shuttle program. It's time to put the astronauts in charge, accept the risks, and get on with vital projects while support groups develop better systems for deployment later. *Site Selection,* April 1986. p. 260.

352. "Planning Vacuum at DOT?" Is it possible that DOT cannot assist facility planners in identifying present and future points of congestion on the interstate system? If true, within the next decade highway traffic gridlock is going to produce economic disasters from coast to coast. *Site Selection,* June 1986. p. 548.

353. "Looking into the Facility Planner's Fabulous Future." In celebration of *Site Selection's* first 30 years we have made a new technological forecast. Included is a summary of future events and discoveries considered most likely to impact corporate facility planning and area economic development. *Site Selection,* June 1986. pp. 566-580.

354. "Will Two-loop Cities Dominate Future Site Selection?" During the past decade hundreds of site decisions have left no doubt that circumferential freeways are a powerful magnet in drawing new business facilities to certain metro areas. Now, it is argued that proposed new outer loops may become an even more important development attraction in those areas where government entities can get together and build them. *Site Selection,* June 1986. pp. 582-588.

355. "The Bahamas. When Will the Time Come?" Always a tourist magnet, noted as a convenient off-shore financial haven, the Bahamas have enjoyed only limited success in attracting large-scale diversified investment in manufacturing, processing and support industries. Is such development a realistic expectation? *Site Selection,* June 1986. pp. 752-756.

356. "Good Life Index — Now It's Here to Stay!" Early checklists of facility location factors listed quality of life items at the bottom, among incidentals. Today, for many facilities, QOL evaluations determine location decisions. *Site Selection,* Aug. 1986. p. 772.

357. "Terrorism: Growing Factor in Location Decisions." Recent events reveal all too starkly the clouds which hang over development programs in many parts of the world. Business travelers, investors and facility planners must be concerned not only with traditional war risk and political risk, but also with the added risk of bombings, assassinations, hijackings and

455

taking of hostages carried out by international terrorist groups. *Site Selection,* Aug. 1986. pp.952-956.

358. "The Problem Voter," *Site Selection,* Oct. 1986, and monograph.

359. "Baja California del Sur — Growing Too Fast or Too Slow?" Is Mexico's Baja del Sur a state destined for greatness or just a dead-end hideaway for a few tourists? While opportunity pounds on the door, is the area dozing? Here's a fresh look by a gringo engineer who has been scanning the area's growth potential for 25 years. *Site Selection,* Oct. 1986. pp. 1224-1226.

360. "Crisis in Corporate Facility Planning!" One of the most critical issues facing corporate management today is the necessity for providing flexibility in future facility plans. Firms which ignore this warning may find themselves unable to compete and survive in the years just ahead. *Site Selection,* Dec. 1986. p. 1256.

361. "Greece: A New Climate for Investment?" For more than a decade, Greece has had a political climate which repelled many investors. Now, there are signs of change — the views of the private sector are being noted and positive steps are being taken. *Site Selection,* Dec. 1986. pp. 1552-1555.

362. "A Technology Review and Forecast for Development Strategists," 1986. Monograph.

1987

363. "Switzerland Attracts Industry the Old-fashioned Way." How does a small, landlocked nation surrounded by competitors manage to survive and prosper in the race to attract new growth? Energetic Swiss cantons do it with a reliable work force and high productivity. *Site Selection,* Feb. 1987. pp. 234-235.

364. "Auto Axis for New Assembly Plants Emerges along Toronto/Detroit/Atlanta Corridor." Car makers display a remarkable degree of agreement regarding the geo-economics of site selection. *Site Selection,* Feb. 1987. pp. 236-237.

365. "To Compete Globally, Business Must Choose Optimum Sites." Some of the most dangerous ideas to be debated by the new Congress deal with restrictions on the right of industrial firms to select economically attractive sites or to close plants which have become uneconomic. Such proposals ignore the reality of world competition. *Site Selection,* Feb. 1987. p. 4.

366. *Status of the Corporate Facility Planner: a Progress Report.* Research study for the Industrial Development Research Council. March 1987. IDRC #36.

367. "Geo-economics Today and Tomorrow." Quantification of the key variables in the science of geo-economics is of paramount importance to efficient industrial development. A great deal of work remains. Building data bases and improving our research methods are high priorities. Paper for IDRC Orlando conference. *Industrial Development.* March-April 1987. pp. 304-306.

368. "The New Basic Industries Have You Revised Your Strategy?" A recent IDRC seminar discussed the concept that knowledge is now the world currency, and the top facility location factor is where the brains are. To this we add that factories that produce ideas and data are the new basic industries. *Site Selection.* April 1987. p. 252.

369. "Guerrero has Acapulco, Ixtapa and Taxco, but Can It Add Industrial Diversification?" One of the key states in Mexico, Guerrero boasts some world-famous tourist destinations, but little else. Now, development strategists ponder the prospect for bringing "maquiladoras," or twin plants, to the hinterland and, perhaps, new high-tech services. *Site Selection,* April 1987. pp. 540-542.

370. "Turkey Offers Strategic Location on Intercontinental Trade routes." Where once Byzantium flourished as the center of the civilized world, Istanbul now claims increasing importance as the crossroads of Europe, Asia and the Middle East. New political changes make a more open society and a better climate for new investment. *Site Selection,* April 1987. pp. 536-538.

371. "Taiwan Competes Boldly in High-tech World." Few small nations have made as much progress as the Republic of China in developing industries based on advanced technologies. True, many Taiwan products are clones of U.S. prototypes, but new programs will yield more Taiwan originals. The science-based industrial park at Hsinchu is a vital element. *Site Selection,* June 1987. pp. 742-744.

372. "Singapore — a World-class Development Model." Of all the 100-plus small nations around the world, none has done a better job of implementing development than this city-

state. After a five-year interval, we returned to find a new global airport, beautiful new high-speed expressways, clusters of new industrial estates and housing, the world's tallest hotel, several dozen gleaming high-rise office centers and a bustling science park. *Site Selection*, June 1987. pp. 738-40.

373. "True Professionals Don't Ignore Technology Forecasts!" There are some executives who ignore predictions of technical breakthroughs — allocating them to the status of cocktail conversation topics or themes for sci-fi movies. They treat the future as if it will never happen. Consequently, life is full of surprises, sometimes very rude ones. *Site Selection,* June 1987. p. 552.

374. "New Zealand: a State of Indecision." This beautiful land down under offers many desirable quality-of-life factors, yet it does not rank high in the eyes of global investors. One explanation is that the average New Zealander is so content with the present that he doesn't worry much about plans and projects for the future. *Site Selection*, Aug. 1987. pp. 804-808.

375. "Enter the Super Metros!!!" The preferred life style of most Americans involves a home-site in a quiet suburb, small town or rural area with a job just a few minutes away, plus easy access — in less than an hour — to all of the sophisticated services of a large metro complex. The area planning teams which provide for this style will be the big winners in the site competitions of the next decade. Enter the super metros! *Site Selection*, Aug. 1987. p. 756.

376. "Atlanta as a World Class City." What is a world class city? The city/hinterland link. Building blocks for the future. Monograph. Based on presentation at the 12th annual Gwinnett Developers Conference, Gwinnett Chamber of Commerce, Gwinnett County Ga. Sept. 24, 1987.

377. "Indonesia — the World's Least-known Development Giant?" The great archipelago once known as the Spice Islands is now the fifth largest nation in the world, with a population of more than 160 million spread across a Seattle/Miami distance. Almost unknown to many investors, this emerging nation presents huge opportunities with problems to match. *Site Selection*, Oct. 1987. pp. 1022-1026.

378. "Privatization Be Sure to Read the Instructions!" The tried and true American private enterprise system that we couldn't give away 25 years ago has a new name: "privatization." And, it's suddenly the straw at which many a floundering socialist bureaucrat from darkest Africa to main street USA is grasping. Even Soviet planners are succumbing to the charm of the "new" concept. *Site Selection*. Oct.1987. p. 956.

379. "The Super Collider Show — Who Will Make the Cut?" It's bigger than the District of Columbia, will cost $6 billion and has 25 states spending millions to promote sites. The DOE's search for a supercollider site is stirring what may be the biggest location battle ever. *Site Selection*, Dec. 1987. pp. 1234-1235.

380. "The Role of Private Enterprise." One of the greatest myths extant today is that government regulatory agencies and community action groups prevent the destruction of our environment by greedy corrupt corporations. The fact is that responsible private interests do most of the significant conservation work, despite obstacles placed in their way by petty bureaucrats and self-appointed experts. *Site Selection*, Dec. 1987. p. 1220.

381. *Facility Planning Technology*. A selection of over 200 articles contributed by what resembles a "who's who" of the corporate real estate and industrial development profession. Corporate asset management and strategy. Property administration. Location analysis and site selection. Design and construction. The automated office. 935 pp. Hard cover. With Linda L. Liston. 1987.

382. "R&D Clusters." Where do they occur? Why have they developed? What are new locations to watch? 1987. Monograph.

383. "New Plant Locations." A review and forecast. Monograph. 1987. 10 pp.

384. Paper for Maryland Industrial Development Association special publication. 1987.

1988

385. "Club Med Shifts Strategy." While continuing to develop new sites around the world, the French-based resort chain seeks to broaden its market appeal to "every interest and every age group". *Site Selection*, Feb. 1988. pp. 18-19.

386. "How About a USA/USSR Common Market?" Now that we have glasnost and Perestroika — and Gorbachev has taken part in a summit session in Washington — where do we go from here? Amid doubts and suspicions, is there basis for hope for a dramatic upturn in business relations which could open vast new development opportunities? *Site Selection*.

Feb. 1988. p. 4.

387. "New Caledonia and Fiji — Question Marks in the South Pacific." Will New Caledonia remain a French territory or, like so many Pacific island groups, become a small new independent nation? Can newly independent Fiji achieve political stability? In any event, what kinds of opportunities do they offer outside investors? *Site Selection*. Feb. 1988. pp. 58-60.

388. "Why Joe Lost His Job." It's a jungle out there. We all know that. Nothing is absolutely guaranteed. Even the biggest companies fall flat. And a great many are trimming management costs, especially in staff areas. Even so, Joe might have survived the cuts. *Site Selection,* April 1988. p. 276.

389. "What's the Biggest Obstacle to Progress from (Name Withheld USA) to Naushki, Siberia, USSR?" An international traveler finds that petty bureaucracy can rear its ugly head in a small airport in the USA as easily as it can aboard the Trans-Siberian Express. *Site Selection*, April 1988. p. 544.

390. "Changes in the South." When I was a student at Georgia Tech during the late 1930s Gwinnett County was a place out in the country where people grew cotton. Now my neighbors create satellite equipment and other sophisticated systems for customers around the world. *Gwinnett Daily News*. June 15, 1988.

391. "Antarctica — Research Facility for the World." The global programs underway in Antarctica today constitute the most significant cooperative international research venture in the history of the world. (Report on field trip to visit research stations.) *Site Selection*. June 1988. pp. 618-628.

392. In the years ahead it is a certainty that there will be revolutionary changes in the way we travel. Those who have any doubt that sweeping changes will affect the lives of most citizens living today need only glance backward at innovations that took place in the last 30 years. *Gwinnett Daily News,* July 20, 1988.

393. "Private Investment Instead of Government Aid: Can the New MIGA Plan Speed Global Shift?" Only a few developing nations have discovered that the world's private business community is a much better source of economic aid than all of the governments around the globe. *Site Selection*, Aug. 1988. p. 828.

394. "Education Key to America's Future." If we are to compete with the Japanese and Western Europe we must do a much better job of educating our young people and retraining our older workers. *Gwinnett Daily News*. Aug. 17, 1988.

395. "Is Chile Poised for Takeoff?" The economic well-being of this unusual nation for the rest of the century may well rest on the plebiscite to be held soon. If Chile comes through with a broader constitutional base and stronger public approval, prospects for economic development will be bright. Favorable factors include a wealth of forest, ocean and mineral resources, a resort climate, and an alert population reflecting strong European influence. *Site Selection*, Aug. 1988. pp. 880-884.

396. "Argentina: Will a New Capital Help?" Raul Alfonsin, Argentina's precedent-shattering president, says the nation has been stagnating in a sea of confusion. He proposes to get things better organized by moving the capital out of sprawling Buenos Aires to Viedma, a small town several hundred miles south. *Site Selection*, Oct. 1988. pp. 1162-1164.

397. "Skyrocketing Business Risks Hurt Consumer and Taxpayer." In this season of hyperbole and demagoguery, it's not likely that political leaders will come up with creative new policies for handling such hot potatoes as asbestos removal. Hopefully, however, the next administration will develop a rational policy for mitigating extraordinary business risks. *Site Selection*, Oct. 1988. p. 1068.

398. "Outer Loop Could Focus World Attention on Metro Area." Some of the keenest observers of trends in urban planning believe that the "two loop" cities of the world will dominate future development patterns. *Site Selection,* October 1988.

399. "R&D Clusters." In 1962 Conway Data conducted a study in which we sought to identify existing clusters of R&D activity and to predict where new clusters might emerge. During 1987-88 we examined results and found that most of the centers predicted to emerge have done so. *Gwinnett Daily News*, Nov. 16, 1988.

400. "Are You Building Your Own Personal Data Base?" The most important data base you will ever have to consult is the one between your ears. Just about everything to which you aspire depends on it. Are you giving it the attention it deserves? *Gwinnett Daily News,* Dec. 21, 1988.

401. "Where Will You Land after the Merger?" The time to make your job secure is before

the blood-letting starts. And one of the very best strategies is to develop an automated property inventory with which you are thoroughly familiar. Learn from the sad experience of the veteran real estate manager who was not prepared. *Site Selection,* Dec. 1988.

402. "Rio: the Capital Is Gone but Life Goes on." A quarter-century ago Brazil decided to move its seat of government from this world-famous city to Brasilia, a raw site in the hinterland. It was one of the boldest development decisions any government has made. Political experts predicted chaos and economists forecast ruin. Despite all the gloom and doom talk, the plan seems to be working and gaining strength every day. *Site Selection,* Dec. 1988. pp. 372-374.

403. "Geo-Economics: A New Science in the Service of Mankind." Definition: geo-economics is the science of integrating investment strategies with the resources and objectives of specific geographic entities to achieve appropriate economic development and, thus, a better quality of life. Pamphlet. 1988.

404. "Three Strong Forces Allied for the Advancement of the Vital New Science of Geo-economics". Pamphlet. 1988.

405. "New Plant Locations — a Review and Forecast." New corporate facilities bring to the chosen area new investment, new jobs and new economic opportunities. While some residents may perceive negative aspects, the area usually enjoys improved community services and other significant benefits. A summary of new plant announcements by state. Monograph. 1988.

1989

406. "Rethinking Urban Plan." Is it time to divorce high-rise offices and regional shopping centers? A substantial segment of the population of Gwinnett County encounters major traffic congestion every working day. One change in strategy which might be considered ...pertains to the location of regional shopping centers, office parks and other major complexes in relation to key transportation routes. *Gwinnett Daily News,* Jan. 18, 1989.

407. "Does Your Real Estate Setup Make Your Company a Takeover Target?" Experts in the takeover game have discovered that the real estate department is the Achilles heel of many large corporations. Unmanaged or under-managed properties have become a major lure. It proves once more that what you don't know can hurt you in a big way. *Site Selection,* Feb. 1989. p. 4.

408. "Super Metro Areas." Americans want to have best of both worlds...a homesite in a quiet suburb, small town, or rural area with a job just a few minutes away, plus easy access — in less than an hour — to all of the sophisticated services of a large metro complex. *Gwinnett Daily News,* Feb. 15, 1989.

409. "Tunisia: A New Look for the Mahgreb." Alert corporate planners are beginning to take an interest in the Arab nations of North Africa. A burgeoning young labor force close to the emerging European common market may attract firms servings markets from the Middle East to America. Here's a report on a key nation under new leadership. *Site Selection,* Feb. 1989. pp. 258-260.

410. "Science May Solve Traffic Woes." Some expert observers say the auto traffic mess will get a lot worse before it starts getting better. Others believe high technology may come to our rescue. Among these developments are computer-controlled traffic lights, satellite positioning systems, navigation displays, radar controlled "car trains" and robot-driven vehicles. *Gwinnett Daily News,* March 15, 1989.

411. "Site Planners Take Note!" With the highways and major airports facing gridlock, why not locate your corporate facilities at an uncongested airport with your company plane parked at your door? *Site Selection,* April 1989. p. 276.

412. "State's Best Minds Needed to Plan Outer Loop." In the legislative session just ended, the Georgia General Assembly authorized the beginning of work on the most important highway project in the state's history. That is the long-heralded outer perimeter. *Gwinnett Daily News,* April 19, 1989.

413. One of the greatest myths extant today is that government regulatory agencies and community action groups prevent the destruction of our environment by greedy corrupt corporations. The fact is that responsible private interests do most of the significant conservation work, despite obstacles placed in their way by petty bureaucrats and self-appointed experts. *Gwinnett Daily News,* May 17, 1989.

414. "New FAA Wayport Proposal Could Be Site Breakthrough Opening Opportunities for 21st Century Development," *Site Selection,* June 1989. p. 626.

415. "Forecasting Change Can Mean Life or Death." A generation ago, when things moved more slowly, the economic system was more tolerant of companies that failed to anticipate change. Today, failure to anticipate change can be abruptly fatal. *Gwinnett Daily News,* June 21, 1989.

416. "Disaster Planning Vital for All Businesses." Planning for the future typically involves forecasting trends in technology, demographics and social patterns. However, futurists must never forget events which may not be positive. *Gwinnett Daily News,* July 12, 1989.

417. "Technology Makes Long-term Plans Obsolete." How far into the future does it make sense to project your company's plans? There was a time when large corporations had formal plans for 10 years ahead, and some prepared 20-year plans. Today few firms attempt to develop operating plans covering more than five years and many consider a two-year plan to be long range. *Gwinnett Daily News,* Aug. 9, 1989.

418. "Super Projects May Change the Future." Pause for a moment to ask what it would be like today without the interstate highway system. Or, ask where we would be without such products of the space program as microcomputers and communications satellites. Gwinnett Daily News, Sept. 13, 1989.

419. "The Sky's the Limit for Future 'Globalites'." Somewhere in your neighborhood there is someone — a business executive, or an avid traveler —who sees the world through a different set of lenses. He or she is part of the emerging new global society. *Gwinnett Daily News,* Oct. 18, 1989.

420. "Air Terrorism Spawns New Award." Among corporate location and geo-political factors, none are more important that those which affect human lives. Near the top of the list is the security provided for international air travelers, for virtually every executive of every global business venture is at risk. *Site Selection,* Oct. 1989. p. 1180.

421. "Unique Brunei!" Around the world there are many small nations. Some are in remote locations. Most are new at self government. A few are rich. Brunei is all of those things and more — a fascinating geo-political anomaly. *Site Selection,* Oct. 1989. pp. 1192-94.

422. "Business Needs to Concern Itself with Air Terrorism." With peace breaking out all over the world, it appears that the likelihood of a major world war is smaller than it has been for decades. At the same time, terrorism looms as a continuing global risk for which the world does not yet have an answer. *Gwinnett Daily News,* Nov. 1989.

423. "Are Latin American Investment Programs Forever Comatose?" During the past 20 years, while many nations sharpened their skills at attracting outside investment, the nations of Latin America have become less effective. Many have virtually dropped out of competition abandoning programs that were once very promising. *Site Selection.* Dec. 1989. p. 1464.

424. "Yokohama Bets on 'Minato Mirai' Project." Building a world's fair or Olympic games complex and then converting it to everyday use is a formula used successfully by many cities. Now Yokohama seeks to replace its 1989 exposition park with a global business center. *Site Selection,* Dec. 1989. pp. 1478-79.

425. "Changes in Europe Overtake Business World." The dramatic collapse of the communist regimes of Eastern Europe has caught all of the experts flat-footed. *Gwinnett Daily News,* Dec. 20, 1989.

426. *Site Net World Guide.* Beyond perestroika. Country profiles, nations A to Z. Field reports and photos. The Super Projects. The development world tomorrow. Global investment incentives. 1989. 530 pp. With Laura Jones-Kelley and Linda L. Liston.

1990

427. "Business in for a Big Surprise from Greens." The Greens are coming and they're going to change your agenda! What was an obscure environmental movement in Europe a few years ago is mushrooming into an international effort with strong political clout. *Gwinnett Daily News,* Jan. 17, 1990.

428. "Damage from 'Panic Response' Can Be Great." Satellite communications systems have done wonderful things for the world. News can be flashed to almost every corner of the globe instantly. The bad news is that wonderful information systems can spread panic. *Gwinnett Daily News,* Feb. 14, 1990.

429. "Eurotunnel Spurs Development of New Sites." With the opening still three years ahead, government units and private firms on both sides of the channel are already investing tens of millions of dollars in projects designed to complement the tunnel and exploit new

corporate location opportunities. *Site Selection,* Feb. 1990. pp. 89-92.

430. "How Will Europe Handle All-out Site Competition?" The more we listen to Europeans discuss 1992, the more convinced we are that this magic date will mark the beginning, rather than the end, of many interesting debates and confrontations. *Site Selection,* Feb. 1990. pp. 4.

431. "A New Agenda for Site World." For global firms, strategic thinking is not just a business exercise — it is the difference between success and failure. Looking at the 1990s and beyond, global leaders are preparing a new agenda. *Site Selection,* April 1990. p. 268.

432. "Seawater Treatment the Wave of the Future." Quietly but surely scientists are moving toward a fantastic breakthrough which will literally reshape many regions of the world, bring great new economic development opportunities and provide a better quality of life for millions of people. *Gwinnett Daily News,* April 18, 1990.

433. "The Future: Spectacular Political Fights Are Coming." If you think we are witnessing some all-out political campaign conflicts today, just wait. *Gwinnett Daily News*, May, 1990.

434. "Western Australia: Big, Remote, Challenging." For many of our readers, there is no place farther from home than Perth, in the state of Western Australia. It is on the exact opposite side of the world and situated so that you're not likely to stop here on the way to someplace else. These facts don't provide an excuse, however, for alert global investors to ignore the burgeoning opportunities here. *Site Selection*, June 1990. pp. 636-643.

435. "It's Time to Redirect the Economic Development Elements of U.S. International Aid Programs!" Massive changes are needed in the way the U.S. handles its international development aid program. Here are some guidelines for establishing a new program that will help make sure U.S. assistance does what it's designed to do. *Site Selection.* June 1990. p. 608.

436. "'Wayport' System Deserves Consideration." The last major airport to be built in the United States was the Dallas-Fort Worth regional facility. That was in 1974. For two decades the nation's hub airports have been getting by with patchwork improvements and expansions, but that approach has reached its limits. *Gwinnett Daily News,* June 20, 1990.

437. "Language Barriers Beginning to Fall." The language barrier which has separated nations and peoples for centuries is about to go the way of the Berlin Wall. *Gwinnett Daily News,* July 18, 1990.

438. "Super Projects, New Wonders of the World." Monograph based on opening statement made at the seminar on Corporate Global Strategy, arranged by the Institute of Social Engineering, Japan, held at the American Club, Tokyo, Aug. 27, 1990.

439. "Super Domes Will Cover New Cities." Fly over many U.S. cities today and the most conspicuous structure you see is a shining dome covering a football stadium. Fly over cities of the future and you may see only one huge dome. *Gwinnett Daily News.* Aug. 1990.

440. There's a siren song being wafted on the breezes out there. It is beguiling, and some CEOs are intrigued. The alluring refrain suggests that you can farm out your corporate real estate function to a consultant, eliminate the real estate staff, save a lot of and perform just as well. *Site Selection* Aug. 1990. p. 800.

441. "EEC Outpost in the Caribbean." Without fanfare, the French are building a strong economic base in the West Indies. Unlike other Caribbean islands which have become struggling independents, Martinique and Guadaloupe have emerged as thriving, integral departments of France. *Site Selection,* Aug. 1990. pp. 862-63.

442. "Proposed High-rise City for Japan Boggles the Mind." While in Tokyo recently, we learned more about the proposal of a major engineering firm, Ohbayashi, to build a 500-story high-rise building that would be a city within itself. Called "Aeropolis 2001," the mammoth structure would be approximately five times as high as the World Trade Center in New York. *Gwinnett Daily News,* Sept. 19, 1990.

443. "Bullet Trains Put on Slow Track in U.S." How would you like to board a train in downtown Atlanta and step off in Savannah an hour later? Or, how about making a business appointment in Orlando and getting back to Atlanta the same day, rested and relaxed? *Gwinnett Daily News,* Oct. 17, 1990.

444. "This Is a Test!" Show us a copy of your company map! We're not looking for anything in particular - we just want to know if you have one. Here's why. *Site Selection,* Oct. 1990. p. 1040.

445. "Puerto Rico: Super SEZ." Among SEZs (Special Economic Zones) around the world, Puerto Rico is the pioneer and pacesetter. Under the program, more than 1,000 new plants have been attracted. Now, strategic decisions must be made about the future. *Site Selec-*

tion, Oct. 1990. pp. 1170-73.

446. "Olympic Site Competitions Spur Top Officials to Set Unprecedented Goals for Themselves." One of the most interesting phenomena in urban development is the impact of site competitions on infrastructure planning. *Gwinnett Daily News.* Nov. 1990.

447. "Welcome Aboard!" With this new edition, *Site Selection* brings to our audience the top executives of Europe — men and women who are leading a development program which has captured the imagination of the world. *Site Selection Europe,* Nov./Dec. 1990. pp. 2.

448. "Had Your Annual Checkup?" No, not the one at the Mayo Clinic. We're talking about the in-house review of your company's real property assets. *Site Selection,* Dec. 1990. p. 1288.

449. "Overlooking the Multiplier Effect of High Technology." A decade ago, when microcomputers began to appear in numbers in the workplace, there was great excitement. We would soon have "paperless" offices, the pundits said. *Gwinnett Daily News,* Dec. 19, 1990.

450. "The Spanish Riviera." From Barcelona to Gibraltar, the Mediterranean Coast of Spain is alive with development plans and projects. Many observers believe this will be Europe's fastest-growing region in the decade ahead. *Site Selection,* Dec. 1990. pp. 1378-1379.

451. *The Weather Handbook.* A summary of climatic conditions and weather phenomena for selected cities in the United States and around the world. 1st ed., 1962, 256 pp. 2nd ed. 1974, 255 pp. illus. 3rd ed. 1990. 548 pp. Hard cover. With Linda L. Liston.

452. "Global Competition for Jobs." Let it be known that your company plans to make an investment in a new manufacturing plant and the world will beat a path to your door. Article for *Atlanta Journal.* 1990.

1991

453. "Would You Take This Job?" Here's a tip on an upcoming job opening which carries prestige beyond your fondest dreams. *Site Selection,* Feb. 1991. pp. 4.

454. "A New Look at the Turks And Caicos Islands." A resort development boom triggered by a Club Med project suggests that these strategically situated islands may at last be reaching a takeoff stage. *Site Selection,* Feb. 1991. pp. 88-89.

455. "Outer Loop Highway Would Link Cities, Hinterland." We have often said that the proposed outer perimeter could do more for Georgia's economic development than any other project. *Gwinnett Daily News,* March 17, 1991. p. 3E.

456. "Are You Preparing Your Asset Managers for Global Operations?" A memo from your real estate department. *Site Selection,* April 1991. pp. 248.

457. In the process of gathering information for you, we deal with a lot of corporate PR executives. Some of them are great, but some, we regret to say, look like bums to us. *Site Selection,* June 1991. pp. 564.

458. "The New Hong Kong Metroplex." While timid investors hesitate, many far-sighted PacRim corporate planners are already betting on Hong Kong's bold new strategy. Key elements include the integration of a vast hinterland, the making of a new metro regional development concept and construction of major infrastructure improvements. *Site Selection,* June 1991. pp. 618-622.

459. "The New Singapore Hinterland." How does a small island nation which is running out of land provide for future growth? Singapore shows the way via creative joint ventures with neighboring Malaysia and Indonesia. *Site Selection,* Aug. 1991. pp. 772-773.

460. "Don't Be Misled!" One of the alleged experts in the development field recently made a speech about "the end of the golden age of real estate". The implication was that all of the really exciting projects are behind us and we can look forward only to years of stultifying no-growth. *Site Selection,* Aug. 1991. pp. 708.

461. "Are You Waging Guerrilla Warfare against the Problems of Planning, Locating and Building a New Plant?" Does each new project provide a lesson in crisis management? Are your staff departments and operating units stepping on each others toes? Have you considered setting up a new project team? *Site Selection,* Oct. 1991. pp. 924.

462. "Chiba: Tokyo's New Front Door." Situated in a growth corridor and offering new sites, Chiba prefecture is emerging as one of the world's top development areas. The sector is already dotted with multi-billion dollar projects. *Site Selection,* Oct. 1991. pp. 1242.

463. "Let The People Speak!" There's an important flaw in our great American political system. Today, despite our elaborate communication systems, there is no effective way for the people to express their collective opinion clearly and emphatically on any specific political issue. Monograph. 1991.

464. *Site World: The Book of Corporate Global Strategies.* Global strategies, super projects, national profiles, air terrorism, futurism and corporate management, adventures and misadventures in covering the globe, the Global 2000. 1991. 597 pp. With Laura Jones-Kelley and Linda L. Liston.

465. "The Global 2000." This is a discussion of the new global executive and global strategies. *Site World, The Book of Corporate Global Strategies.* 1991.

466. "The Geo-economic Explosion. Understanding change!" *Site World.* 1991.

467. "Area Development Executives and Global Super Projects." Those who provide the leadership for economic development programs around the world are very special. They are creative people who necessarily and routinely make bold development plans. They are not afraid to dream. Pamphlet for World Development Council. 1991.

468. "Engineers, Builders and Global Super Projects." A conservative estimate indicates that the world will add one billion more people by the year 2000. What a monumental challenge for the construction industry! The world must have new productive facilities built on a scale to match its needs. Pamphlet for the World Development Council. 1991.

469. "Global Corporations and Global Super Projects." Never before have the productive forces of the world faced such great opportunities and enormous responsibilities. We have the awesome task of meeting global needs for food, shelter, clothing and essential services in a time of mushrooming population growth and explosive pressures of rising expectations. Pamphlet for World Development Council. 1991.

470. "Riding with the Airlines." Let's get this straight for the record! I have always preferred to fly myself from point A to point B. However, this does not reflect in any way on the airlines or, more particularly, on their crews. *Site World*, chapter 7. 1991.

1992

471. Here's how you can exert a powerful influence in the congressional Election next November. You can help keep the good guys in while throwing the rascals out! *Site Selection,* Feb. 1992, pp. 6.

472. "CEO Confidential." Here's how you can exert a powerful influence in the congressional election next November. You can help keep the good guys in while throwing the rascals out. *Site Selection*, Feb. 1992. p. 6.

473. "Great Days Ahead!" We must not let the daily news media reports of global business recessions and political turmoil in the East obscure the fact that this is a great year and the beginning of even greater things for Europe and the World. *Site Selection Europe*, March 1992.

474. "Do the Japanese Really Want You?" Amid the confusion of high-level political blasts and the continuous sniping of opposing business leaders, what is the hard evidence that Japan sincerely wants your new plant? *Site Selection*, April 1992. pp. 250.

475. If your company is typical, more than one-fourth of your assets are represented by your real estate. Do you have a strategic plan for these important assets? Do you have a career plan for the executives responsible? *Site Selection*, June 1992. pp. 510.

476. "Where Do You Fit in the Washington Mess?" The truth is revealed: Congress doesn't really care what the people think. Special interests are running the system. Are you a part of the problem? *Site Selection,* Aug. 1992. pp. 622.

477. "There is an active and determined development effort being run by savvy people." Memo for staff regarding visit to Malta, 09-04-92.

478. "Acres of Diamonds in Our Front Yard?" The death of development pioneer Ted Moscoso reminds us of what can be achieved in Latin America. Now it's time for us to implement his vision through the region. *Site Selection*, Oct. 1992. pp. 854.

479. "Honolulu Sessions Launch New Era of Super Project Coordination," "Super Project Newsletter," Oct. 1992.

480. "It's Eleven A.M. Do You Know How Safe Your Facilities Are?" When was the last time you sat down with your facilities managers and reviewed company thinking regarding disaster risk and recovery? *Site Selection*, Dec. 1992. pp. 1090.

481. "The Rationale for Global Super Projects." Keynote presentation for Honolulu conference of World Development Council. *Site World.* 1992. pp. 15-18.

482. *A Glimpse of the Future — Technology Forecasts for Global Strategists.* A study for the World Development Council. 103 pp. 1992.

483. "Macro Engineering." As population pressures increase, it is logical to look for ways to use the vast ocean spaces to relieve congestion and to meet other global needs. Article for

MacMillan *Encyclopedia of the Future.* 1992.

484. "Japan Offers Help for Outside Investors." Until very recently, American firms located facilities in Japan not because of Japanese promotion but in spite of its absence. Now, the Japanese business agency, MITI, has set up a foreign investment promotion unit and published a very helpful guide. Here's an evaluation of the new situation by a veteran observer of international development programs. 1992.

1993

485. "Airport Cities: They Could Change Your Company's Future." Can you walk out of your office door, jump into the company airplane, and fly direct to any of your plant sites — all located on airports with taxiways leading to their main entrances — thus completely avoiding the time, expense and frustration of ground transportation? *Site Selection,* Feb. 1993, pp. 6.

486. A special message for the CEO who now lives at 1600 Pennsylvania Avenue. *Site Selection,* April 1993. pp. 242.

487. "Super Projects: New Wonders of the World." Bridges, tunnels, airports, high-speed rail systems, and telecommunications networks are among global super projects creating new links among the world's peoples. *The Futurist,* World Future Society, Washington. March-April 1993. pp. 25-28.

488. "Tomorrow's Supercities." In the next century we could be working in 500-story office buildings, living in cities afloat on the ocean, or going to domed enclosures to ski during summer months. *The Futurist,* May-June 1993, pp. 27-33. Cover story with illus.

489. "CEOs Come in All Shapes, Sizes and Persuasions." Some were born with the proverbial silver spoon, but most come from more humble beginnings — they earn their way to the top. Perhaps the common denominator is ability to recognize an opportunity and make the most of it. *Site Selection,* June 1993

490. "Queensland's Far North." If we were ranking global sites according to growth potential we'd put this one near the top. Where else can you find such a combination: great open spaces, a Florida/Caribbean climate, proximity to the booming Pacific Rim, and a stunning array of environmental assets? *Site Selection,* June, 1993. pp. 714-716.

491. "New Wonders of the World." Every schoolchild learns of the pyramids, the hanging gardens and the other wonders of the ancient world. Now, a massive global construction program promises to yield a new list of wonders for today and tomorrow. *Leaders* magazine, July/Aug./Sept. 1993.

492. "This Is a Test!" What is the name of your company's top expert in managing real property assets? When is the last time you talked to him? Do you know his needs and support him? More important, does he know your needs and support you? *Site Selection,* Aug. 1993. (Based on presentation made to first IDRC Management Team Seminar, Aug. 16, 1988).

493. "The Science and the Art of Futurism." American technology — and the industries it supports — will survive in the competitive future in direct proportion to its ability to interpret the trends. *Georgia Tech Alumni Magazine,* Sept. 1993, pp. 14-23.

494. *Airport Cities 21.* The new global transport centers of the 21st century. A study prepared for the World Development Council. 113 pp. 1993. *Airport City,* 1st ed., 1977. Comment received 1985 from Laurene Kliegl, executive secretary, British Columbia Aviation Council: "Our copy has been referred to so many times over the past eight years that it is now falling apart." *The Airport City, Development Concepts for the 21st Century,* 2nd ed. Introduction: unimodal to multimodal. Intermodal and transmodal systems. Market factors for airport projects. Design factors for airport projects. Office and industrial parks. Cargo and distribution facilities. Travel facilities, resorts, attractions. Planned airport communities. Jetport cities and metro complexes. A glimpse of century 21. 1980. 283 pp. World Future Society review: "timely, imaginative, and readable."

495. "Atulco — Fonatur's Latest." In global super projects of the tourism variety, Mexico's far-sighted development agency sets the pace. "Super Projects Newsletter," February 1993.

(Editors' note: The reference numbers in this chapter do not correspond with those in earlier chapters. The editors have attempted to mention a reference only once here. The same reference may be noted at the conclusion of more than one chapter.)

Summary of Books and Major Studies

1947. Principles of High Speed Flight. 142 pp. Paper. Also in French.

1960. Area Development Guide. 278 pp. Binder.

1962. The Weather Handbook. 256 pp. Hard cover.

1966. Area Development Organizations. 331 pp. Hard cover.

1967. Chattahoochee River Navigation Study. 140 pp. Paper.

1968. Airport Plan, Thompson Field, Miss. 106 pp. Paper.

1968. The AID/PEP Program Summary. 138 pp. Paper.

1969. Penn. Travel Investment Opportunities. 153 pp. Paper.

1970. Airport Development Plan, Chester Co., Pa. 110 pp. Paper.

1970. Management Concept for Lake Lanier. 100 pp. Paper.

1971. Georgia Environmental Standards. 150 pp. Binder.

1974. The Weather Handbook. 255 pp. 2nd edit. Hard cover.

1974. Arab Investment in the U.S. 300 pp. Paper.

1977. The Airport City. 333 pp. Paper.

1978. New Industries of the Seventies. 302 pp. Paper.

1979. Legislative Climates for Economic Development. 450 pp. Paper.

1979. New Project File & Checklist. Binder.

1980. The Airport City. 283 pp. 2nd edit. Hard cover.

1980. Marketing Industrial Buildings and Sites. 359 pp. 2nd edit. Hardcover.

1981. Pitfalls in Development. 343 pp. 2nd edit. Hard cover.

1981. Industrial Park Growth. 546 pp. 2nd edit. Hard cover.

1981. Corporate Facility Planning. 442 pp. Hard cover.

1981. The Good Life Index. 416 pp. Hard cover.

1981. Disaster Survival. 290 pp. Hard cover.

1987. Facility Planning Technology. 935 pp. Hard cover.

1989. The SiteNet World Guide. 530 pp. Hard Cover.

1990. The Weather Handbook. 548 pp. 3rd edit. Hard cover.

1991. Site World. 597 pp. Hard cover.

1992. A Glimpse of the Future. 103 pp. Paper.

1993. Airport Cities 21. 113 pp. Paper.

C. Print Status of More Significant Books.

(Unless otherwise stated, items are available from Conway Data)

1993. Airport Cities 21. 113 pp. Paper. $75.

1992. Site World. Profiles of global super projects. 277 pp. $75.

1992. A Glimpse of the Future. 103 pp. Paper. $75.

1991. Site World. 597 pp. The book of corporate global strategy, with country summaries. Hard cover. $75.

1990. The Weather Handbook. 548 pp. 3rd edit. Hard cover. $45.

1989. *The SiteNet World Guide.* 530 pp. Hard cover. $45.

1987. *Facility Planning Technology.* 935 pp. Hard cover. $35.

1981. *Disaster Survival.* 290 pp. Hard cover. $15.

1981. *The Good Life Index.* 416 pp. Hard cover. $15.

1981. *Corporate Facility Planning.* 442 pp. Hard cover.$15.

1981. *Industrial Park Growth.* 546 pp. 2nd edit. Hard cover. $15.

1981. *Pitfalls in Development.* 343 pp. 2nd edit. Hard cover. $15.

1980. *Marketing Industrial Buildings and Sites.* 359 pp. 2nd edit. Hard cover. Out of print.

1980. *The Airport City.* 283 pp. 2nd edit. Hard cover. Out of print.

1979. *New Project File & Checklist.* Binder. Out of print.

1979. *Industrial Park Growth. Paper.* Out of print.

1979. *Legislative Climates for Economic Development.* 450 pp. Paper. Out of print.

1978. *New Industries of the Seventies.* 302 pp. Paper. Out of print.

1977. *The Airport City.* 333 pp. Paper. Out of print.

1974. *Arab Investment in the U.S.* 300 pp. Paper. Out of print.

1974. *The Weather Handbook.* 255 pp. 2nd edit. Hard cover. Out of print.

1966. *Area Development Organizations.* 331 pp. Hard cover. Out of print.

1962. *The Weather Handbook.* 256 pp. Hard cover. Out of print.

1960. *Area Development Guide.* 278 pp. Binder. Out of print.

1947. *Principles of High Speed Flight.* 142 pp. Paper. Also in French. Out of print.

D. Automated Files and Information Services

The quickest and easiest way to obtain copies of many of the Conway papers is to utilize GeoTEAM/Fax, the fax-on-demand service acessible via telephone. Papers are delivered within minutes. For information, telephone (404) 453-4200.

Information is also available via the digital on-line service, GeoTEAM, using a personal computer. This on-line service provides a complete index to documents available via fax.

Certain older papers are available only by searching archives for hard copy or microfiche records. Researchers who needs such documents should contact Conway Data for an estimate of search time, which is billed at an hourly rate.

10
Index